# ESSENTIALS *of* MARKETING RESEARCH

# ESSENTIALS *of* MARKETING RESEARCH

## WILLIAM G. ZIKMUND

*Oklahoma State University*

### THE DRYDEN PRESS

### HARCOURT BRACE COLLEGE PUBLISHERS

FORT WORTH  PHILADELPHIA  SAN DIEGO  NEW YORK  ORLANDO  AUSTIN  SAN ANTONIO

TORONTO  MONTREAL  LONDON  SYDNEY  TOKYO

| | |
|---:|:---|
| **Publisher** | George Provol |
| **Acquisitions Editor** | Bill Schoof |
| **Senior Product Manager** | Lisé Johnson |
| **Product Manager** | Debbie Anderson |
| **Developmental Editor** | Jennifer Sheetz Langer |
| **Project Editor** | Sandy Walton Mann |
| **Art Director** | Burl Sloan |
| **Production Manager** | Eddie Dawson |

*Address for Orders*
The Dryden Press, 6277 Sea Harbor Drive, Orlando, FL 32887-6777
1-800-782-4479

*Address for Editorial Correspondence*
The Dryden Press, 301 Commerce Street, Suite 3700, Fort Worth, TX 76102

*Web Site Address*
http://www.hbcollege.com

ISBN: 0-03-024356-4
Library of Congress Catalog Card Number: 98-71173

THE DRYDEN PRESS, DRYDEN, and the DP LOGO are registered trademarks of Harcourt Brace & Company.

Printed in the United States of America

9 0 1 2 3 4 5 6 7   048   9 8 7 6 5 4 3 2

The Dryden Press
Harcourt Brace College Publishers

*To Sybil*

# THE DRYDEN PRESS SERIES IN MARKETING

Assael
*Marketing*

Avila, Williams, Ingram, and LaForge
*The Professional Selling Skills Workbook*

Bateson
*Managing Services Marketing: Text and Readings*
Third Edition

Blackwell, Blackwell, and Talarzyk
*Contemporary Cases in Consumer Behavior*
Fourth Edition

Boone and Kurtz
*Contemporary Marketing WIRED*
Ninth Edition

Boone and Kurtz
*Contemporary Marketing 1999*

Churchill
*Basic Marketing Research*
Third Edition

Churchill
*Marketing Research: Methodological Foundations*
Seventh Edition

Czinkota and Ronkainen
*Global Marketing*

Czinkota and Ronkainen
*International Marketing*
Fifth Edition

Czinkota and Ronkainen
*International Marketing Strategy: Environmental Assessment and Entry Strategies*

Dickson
*Marketing Management*
Second Edition

Dunne and Lusch
*Retailing*
Third Edition

Engel, Blackwell, and Miniard
*Consumer Behavior*
Eighth Edition

Ferrell, Hartline, Lucas, and Luck
*Marketing Strategy*

Futrell
*Sales Management: Teamwork, Leadership, and Technology*
Fifth Edition

Grover
*Theory & Simulation of Market-Focused Management*

Ghosh
*Retail Management*
Second Edition

Hoffman and Bateson
*Essentials of Services Marketing*

Hutt and Speh
*Business Marketing Management: A Strategic View of Industrial and Organizational Markets*
Sixth Edition

Ingram, LaForge, and Schwepker
*Sales Management: Analysis and Decision Making*
Third Edition

Lindgren and Shimp
*Marketing: An Interactive Learning System*

Krugman, Reid, Dunn, and Barban
*Advertising: Its Role in Modern Marketing*
Eighth Edition

Oberhaus, Ratliffe, and Stauble
*Professional Selling: A Relationship Process*
Second Edition

Parente, Vanden Bergh, Barban, and Marra
*Advertising Campaign Strategy: A Guide to Marketing Communication Plans*

Rosenbloom
*Marketing Channels: A Management View*
Sixth Edition

Sandburg
*Discovering Your Marketing Career CD-ROM*

Schaffer
*Applying Marketing Principles Software*

Schaffer
*The Marketing Game*

Schellinck and Maddox
*Marketing Research: A Computer-Assisted Approach*

Schnaars
*MICROSIM*

Schuster and Copeland
*Global Business: Planning for Sales and Negotiations*

Sheth, Mittal, and Newman
*Customer Behavior: Consumer Behavior and Beyond*

Shimp
*Advertising, Promotion, and Supplemental Aspects of Integrated Marketing Communications*
Fourth Edition

Talarzyk
*Cases and Exercises in Marketing*

Terpstra and Sarathy
*International Marketing*
Seventh Edition

Weitz and Wensley
*Readings in Strategic Marketing Analysis, Planning, and Implementation*

Zikmund
*Exploring Marketing Research*
Sixth Edition

Zikmund
*Essentials of Marketing Research*

## Harcourt Brace College Outline Series

Peterson
*Principles of Marketing*

# PREFACE

This first edition of *Essentials of Marketing Research* is the direct result of listening to the collective voice of professors. The Dryden Press' marketing research indicated a segment of marketing professors wanted a shorter book.

*Essentials of Marketing Research*, which consists of 16 chapters, is shorter than my other book, *Exploring Marketing Research*, sixth edition, but it shares many of the same attributes. *Essentials of Marketing Research* presents a lively picture of marketing research. It emphasizes an applied approach with practical applications that gives students a basic understanding of the scope of marketing research. *Essentials of Marketing Research* is also contemporary, reflecting the emergence of our digital age. For example, the Internet's World Wide Web with its ability for instantaneous and interactive access to information from around the globe has a prominent place in this book.

I believe a student's first exposure to the subject of marketing research should create an appreciation of the full range of activities involved in marketing research in businesses and other organizations. This textbook was written under the assumption that few individuals will truly appreciate the marketing research process if their first exposure to the material requires them to study an exhaustive technical handbook filled with advanced statistical techniques and abstract research designs.

During my student years, my professors presented marketing research as a dynamic, creative, and enjoyable pursuit. This approach turned out to be more accurate than the dry, analytical image of marketing research presented in most marketing research textbooks.

My own experience in the marketing research industry and in teaching marketing research for many years at the university level has convinced me that a topically relevant and exciting textbook is necessary for students enrolled in their first course in marketing research. I have put forth my best effort to communicate the energy and creativity of marketing research without compromising integrity or accuracy.

In writing a shorter book, I have not simply pared down our coverage to the essentials of marketing research but have organized many topics in a unique way. For example, the material on data analysis is organized to show the "big picture" of data analysis rather than to focus on advanced techniques that undergraduate students have difficulty understanding.

## ■ ORGANIZATION OF THE BOOK

The organization of *Essentials of Marketing Research* follows the logic of the marketing research process. The book begins by discussing the scope of marketing research. It provides an overview of problem definition and the entire marketing research process. A discussion of global information systems and the Internet follows. The many new information technologies and new methodologies for collecting data are covered at this point in the textbook. Next, the need for exploratory research and secondary data collection are explained. Research designs for primary data collection, surveys, observation research, and experiments are discussed next. A practical explanation of measurement and questionnaire design follows. Sampling designs and sample size are examined. Finally, basic data analysis is explained and a conceptual overview of advanced data analysis is presented.

## ■ FEATURES STUDENTS WILL LIKE

*Essentials of Marketing Research* addresses students' need to comprehend the field literally. To achieve these objectives, the text emphasizes the following elements:

- *Numerous real, easy-to-understand examples* help students gain insight and perspective concerning marketing research. They are designed to stimulate students to search for additional information about marketing research. The "What Went Wrong?" and "What Went Right?" boxes portray failures and successes in specific marketing research situations.

- A *straightforward prose style* portrays marketing research as it is actually practiced. There is a balanced coverage of conceptual and managerial issues. Considerable effort has been directed toward explaining topics with examples that clarify rather than mystify.

- *The text explains statistical concepts* in a simple, straightforward manner. This is a managerially oriented marketing research textbook, not a statistics monograph. The statistical and quantitative aspects of the text were written for those who need a book that provides an understanding of basic concepts. Too many students, approach the prospect of statistical material with a great deal of unnecessary trepidation. The text devotes an entire section to a review of statistics. Even students with rusty statistical skills will benefit from a quick review of the basic statistical concepts.

- *Each chapter begins with a clear statement of learning objectives* to provide students with an expectation of what is to come. Students can also use the objectives to determine whether they understand the major points of the chapter.

- *An opening vignette* describing an actual situation relevant to the chapter focuses students' attention on the pragmatic aspects of each chapter.

- To enhance students' understanding of conceptual materials, *Essentials of Marketing Research* includes many exhibits that indicate relationships among variables and that *visually highlight ideas.* A full-color format enhances the imagery and appeal of the artwork and photographs.

- *Learning the vocabulary* of marketing research is essential to understanding the topic. *Essentials of Marketing Research* facilitates this in three ways. First, key concepts are boldfaced and completely defined when they first appear in the textbook. Second, all key terms and concepts are listed at the end of each chapter, and many terms are highlighted in a marginal glossary. Third, a glossary summarizing all key terms and definitions appears at the end of the book for handy reference. A glossary of frequently used symbols is also included.

- *End-of-chapter materials* were carefully designed to promote student involvement in the classroom. The end-of-chapter questions stimulate thinking about topics beyond the text's coverage. Review materials enhance students' understanding of key concepts.

- *The end-of-chapter cases present interesting, real-life research situations* that require students to make thoughtful decisions. These real-world cases offer the opportunity for active participation in a decision-making process, one of the most effective forms of learning. The cases portray actual research activities and companies such as Walker Marketing Research and Upjohn that conduct marketing research around the world.

- "Exploring the Internet" exercises appear at the end of every chapter. This feature helps students navigate the Internet. These activities range from going to the Census Bureau's Pop Clock to being participants in Internet surveys.

- A new feature *Exploring the Internet* provides links to other relevant Web sites helpful for both students and professors.

# ■ FEATURES THE PROFESSOR WILL LIKE

*Essentials of Marketing Research* is for the undergraduate student who must meet the future challenge of marketing management. The professor should find this book and its supplements an extremely useful aid in facilitating student achievement.

Materials to supplement the content of the textbook are available to help instructors perform their vital teaching function. The extensive learning package provided with *Essentials of Marketing Research* includes a test bank, a computerized test bank, an instructor's manual, PowerPoint presentation software, transparency masters, videocassettes containing case materials, a floppy disk containing databases for several cases, a Web site on the Internet (http://www.dryden.com), and other ancillary materials.

- All chapters that follow Chapter 4, "The Human Side of Marketing Research: Organizational and Ethical Issues," include end-of-chapter questions dealing with ethical issues.

- *Cases with questions for homework assignments or classroom discussions* are included in the text. These cases allow classroom discussions of the case solutions to be integrated with video materials. Teaching notes are provided for these video cases as well as for all other cases in the *Instructor's Manual.*

- *PowerPoint Presentation Software* is a state-of-the-art presentation graphics program for IBM compatible computers. This integrated program allows instructors to retrieve and edit any of the preloaded transparency slides that accompany the book. Images can easily be edited, added, or deleted. The instructor can present the transparency slides electronically in the classroom.

- A new *Web site on the Internet* for this textbook enhances the way marketing research can be taught. The Web site will provide the latest information about "what's new" and "what's cool" in marketing research. Links to other research-related sites, tips about using the supplemental video library, and much more are planned for the site.

The Dryden Press will provide complimentary supplements or supplement packages to those adopters qualified under its adoption policy. Please contact your local sales representative to learn how you may qualify. If as an adopter or potential user you receive supplements you do not need, please return them to your sales representative or send them to:

Attn: Returns Deparment
Troy Warehouse
465 South Lincoln Drive
Troy, MO 63379

# ■ OUR REVIEWERS ARE APPRECIATED

Several of our colleagues reviewed various drafts of the manuscript to evaluate scholarly accuracy, writing style, and pedagogy. Many aspects of this book are based on their suggestions. We greatly acknowledge their help. They are:

Leopoldo G. Arias-Bolzmann, *Palm Beach Atlantic College & Universidad Adolfo Ibanez, Chile*

Neeraj Arora, *Virginia Polytechnic Institute and State University*

Paul Christ, *West Chester University*

David Crocker, *Brandenberg Consulting*

Stacey Menzel Baker, *Texas A&M University*

Kumar C. Rallapalli, *Troy State University*

Jackie Snell, *San Jose State University*

Tom Steele, *University of Montana*

Rajneesh Suri, *Northern State University*

Also, thanks to my colleagues who reviewed *Exploring Marketing Research* in its many editions. From their suggestions we have created *Essentials of Marketing Research.*

Gerald Albaum, *University of Oregon*

William Bearden, *University of South Carolina*

Joseph A. Bellizzi, *Arizona State University–West*

James A. Brunner, *University of Toledo*

F. Anthony Bushman, *San Francisco State University*

Thomas Buzas, *Eastern Michigan University*

Roy F. Cabaniss, *Western Kentucky University*

Michael d'Amico, *University of Akron*

Ron Eggers, *Barton College*

H. Harry Friedman, *City University of New York–Brooklyn*

Ron Goldsmith, *Florida State University*

Larry Goldstein, *Iona College*

David Gourley, *Arizona State University*

Jim Grimm, *Illinois State University*

Al Gross, *Robert Morris College*

Don Heinz, *University of Wisconsin*

Craig Hollingshead, *Marshall University*

Victor Howe, *University of Kentucky*

Roy Howell, *Texas Tech University*

DeAnna Kempf, *Indiana University*

Susan Kleine, *Arizona State University*

C. S. Kohli, *California State University–Fullerton*

Jerome L. Langer, *Assumption College*

James H. Leigh, *Texas A&M University*

Larry Lowe, *Bryant College*

Karl Mann, *Tennessee Technological University*

Charles L. Martin, *Wichita State University*

Tom K. Massey, *University of Missouri–Kansas City*

Sanjay Mishra, *University of Kansas*

G. M. Naidu, *University of Wisconsin–Whitewater*

Charles Prohaska, *Central Connecticut State University*

Alan Sawyer, *University of Florida*

Robert Schaffer, *California State University–Pomona*

Leon G. Schiffman, *Rutgers University*

Mark Speece, *Central Washington University*

Harlan Spotts, *Northeastern University*

Wilbur W. Stanton, *Old Dominion University*

Bruce L. Stern, *Portland State University*

James L. Taylor, *University of Alabama*

Gail Tom, *California State University–Sacramento*

David Wheeler, *Suffolk University*

Richard Wilcox, *Carthage College*

Margaret Wright, *University of Colorado*

William Lee Ziegler, *Seton Hall University*

---

## ■ ACKNOWLEDGMENTS

*Essentials of Marketing Research* was completed because of the hard work of a team of people at The Dryden Press company. My editor, Bill Schoof, was responsible for encouraging the initial project and the strategic focus for the book. He was sympathetic to my needs and always offered support and encouragement. He worked with me to make the important decisions that gave a clear focus to this book. I appreciate Lisé Johnson, executive marketing strategist, for her enthusiasm. For years she has been a friend and colleague. The efforts of Jennifer Langer, developmental editor, show in the close coordination between the book and the supplementary instructor's materials. She managed the details and eliminated many problems. Sandy Walton was always pleasant to talk to. Even her voice mail encouraged me to have a nice day. Her production skills were greatly appreciated. Eddie Dawson efficiently guided this book through production. Burl Sloan designed an attractive cover for this book. Humberto Calzada graciously allowed us to reproduce another one of his paintings for the cover. Many thanks to Adele Krause who oversaw the permissions process for this book. The excellence of Nancy Maybloom's copyediting will be apparent to all readers of this book.

. . . I appreciate working with such fine professionals.
For debts extending over a longer period and less directly, I wish to thank
Leo Aspinwall, Phillip Cateora, Charles Hinsderman, Jerome Scott,
and William Stanton.

William G. Zikmund

# ABOUT THE AUTHOR

A native of the Chicago area, William G. Zikmund now lives in Tulsa, Oklahoma. He is a professor of marketing at Oklahoma State University. He received a bachelor of science in marketing from the University of Colorado, a master of science in marketing from Southern Illinois University, and a Ph.D. in business administration with a concentration in marketing from the University of Colorado.

Before beginning his academic career, Professor Zikmund worked in marketing research for Conway/Millikin Company (a marketing research supplier) and Remington Arms Company (an extensive user of marketing research). Professor Zikmund also has served as a marketing research consultant to several business and nonprofit organizations. His applied marketing research experiences range from interviewing and coding to designing, supervising, and analyzing entire research programs.

During his academic career, Professor Zikmund has published dozens of articles and papers in a diverse group of scholarly journals ranging from the *Journal of Marketing* to the *Accounting Review* to the *Journal of Applied Psychology*. In addition to *Essentials of Marketing Research*, Professor Zikmund has written *Exploring Marketing Research, Business Research Methods, Marketing, Effective Marketing,* and a work of fiction, *A Corporate Bestiary.*

Professor Zikmund is a member of professional organizations such as the American Marketing Association, the Academy of Marketing Science, the Association for Consumer Research, the Southern Marketing Association, Western Marketing Educator's Association, and the Southwest Marketing Association. He has served on the editorial review boards of the *Journal of Marketing Education, Marketing Education Review, Journal of the Academy of Marketing Science,* and the *Journal of Business Research.*

# BRIEF CONTENTS

# CONTENTS

# PART II  Designing Research Studies 83

# PART III  Measurement  213

## PART IV    Sampling and Statistical Theory  273

# PART V  Analysis and Reporting 327

# PART

# *I* INTRODUCTION

*1*

# THE ROLE OF MARKETING RESEARCH

**WHAT YOU WILL LEARN IN THIS CHAPTER:**

To understand the importance of marketing research as a management decision-making tool.

To recognize that the essence of marketing research is to fulfill the marketing manager's need for knowledge of the market.

To define marketing research.

To explain the difference between basic and applied marketing research.

To understand that marketing research is a means for implementing the marketing concept.

To discuss the various categories of marketing research activities.

To describe the managerial value of marketing research and its role in the development and implementation of marketing strategy.

To understand when marketing research is needed and when it should not be conducted.

Chee-tos, the cheesy corn puffs made by Frito-Lay, were introduced in the United States almost 50 years ago. Recently Chee-tos became the first major brand of snack food to be made and marketed in China.[1] Frito-Lay's research established that per capita expenditures on snack food in China were small—in fact, nearly zero—compared to the Netherlands ($35 per person) and the United States ($52 per person). Yet the large number of people in China indicated a vast market potential if the company could successfully introduce its brand into that market. However, marketing research also discovered that cheese and other dairy products are not staples in the Chinese diet.

Product taste tests revealed that traditional cheese-flavored Chee-tos did not appeal to Chinese consumers. So the company conducted consumer research with 600 different flavors to learn which flavors would be most appealing. Among the flavors tested and disliked by Chinese consumers were ranch dressing, nacho, Italian pizza, Hawaiian barbecue, peanut satay, North Sea crab, chili prawn, coconut milk curry, smoked octopus, caramel, and cuttlefish. However, research did show that consumers liked some flavors. So when Chee-tos were introduced to China, they came in two flavors: savory American cream and zesty Japanese steak.

Although cheeseless Chee-tos may seem like a contradiction in terms, the name mattered little in the Chinese market. After six months, Chee-tos were such a big hit that processing plants had trouble keeping Chinese retailers' shelves stocked.

The brand name Chee-tos corresponds to the Chinese characters *qi duo,* translated as "new surprise." The name is fortunate for the marketers at Frito-Lay. However, Frito-Lay did not count on good fortune to achieve success in the Chinese market. The company spent considerable effort researching flavors and learning how the Chinese would react to Chester Cheetah as an advertising spokestoon (a cartoon spokesperson) to avoid surprises like the one it got in the United Kingdom.

In 1990 Chee-tos were introduced to the United Kingdom with little, if any, consumer research. The London managers boldly stormed ahead using the American flavors and positioning strategy. The product bombed. The company had not worked diligently to understand British consumers' snacking behaviors and adapt the product characteristics to local tastes.

Although many factors have contributed to Chee-tos' success in China, marketing research was a major influence. At Frito-Lay and thousands of other organizations in the United States and around the globe, marketing research is an important management tool.

## ■ THE NATURE OF MARKETING RESEARCH

Marketing research covers a wide range of phenomena. In essence, it fulfills the marketing manager's need for knowledge of the market. The manager of a food company may ask, "Will a package change improve my brand image?" The sales manager of a sporting goods firm may ask, "How can I monitor my sales and retail trade activities?" A marketing manager in the industrial tools market may ask, "To whom am I losing sales? From whom am I taking sales?" Marketing questions such as these require information about how customers, distributors, and competitors will respond to marketing decisions. Marketing research is one of the principal tools for answering such questions because it links the consumer, customer, and public to the marketer through information—information used to identify and define marketing opportunities and problems; to generate, refine, and evaluate marketing actions; to monitor marketing performance; and to improve the understanding of marketing as a process.[2]

The task of marketing research is to help specify and supply accurate information to reduce the uncertainty in decision making. Although marketing research provides information about consumers and the marketplace for developing and implementing marketing plans and strategies, it is not the only source of information. Every day marketing managers translate their experiences with marketing phenomena into marketing strategies. Information from a manager's experiences frequently is used in an intuitive manner because of the time pressures of business decisions or because the problem does not warrant more formal methods. However, the primary task of marketing management is effective decision making. Flying-by-the-seat-of-the-pants decision making—decision making without systematic inquiry—is like betting on a long shot at the racetrack because the horse's name is appealing. Occasionally successes occur, but in the long run intuition without research can lead to disappointing results. Marketing research helps decision makers shift from intuitive information gathering to systematic and objective investigating.

### ■ Marketing Research Defined

**Marketing research**
The systematic and objective process of generating information to aid in making marketing decisions.

**Marketing research** is defined as the systematic and objective process of generating information to aid in making marketing decisions. This process includes specifying what information is required, designing the method for collecting information, managing and implementing the collection of data, analyzing the results, and communicating the findings and their implications.[3]

This definition suggests first that research information is not intuitive or haphazardly gathered. Literally, *research* (re-search) means "to search again." The term connotes patient study and scientific investigation wherein the researcher takes another, more careful look at the data to discover all that is known about the subject.

Second, if the information generated, or the data collected and analyzed, is to be accurate, the marketing researcher must be objective. The need for objectivity was cleverly stated by the 19th-century American humorist Artemus Ward: "It ain't the things we don't know that gets us in trouble. It's the things we know that ain't so." The researcher should be detached and impersonal rather than biased, attempting to support his or her preconceived ideas. If the research process is contaminated by bias, its value is considerably reduced.

As an example, a developer owned a large area of land and wished to build a high-prestige shopping center. He wanted a research report to demonstrate to prospective retailers that there was a large market potential for such a center. He conducted his survey exclusively in an elite neighborhood. Not surprisingly, the findings showed that a large percentage of the respondents wanted a high-prestige shopping center. Results of this kind are misleading and should be disregarded. The importance of striving for objectivity cannot be overemphasized; without objectivity, research is valueless.

This definition of marketing research also points out an objective to facilitate the managerial decision-making process for all aspects of the firm's marketing mix: pricing, promotion, distribution, and product decisions. The definition is not restricted to any one aspect of the marketing mix. By providing the necessary information on which to base decisions, marketing research can reduce the uncertainty of a decision and thereby decrease the risk of making the wrong decision. However, research should be an aid to managerial judgment and not a substitute for it.

Finally, this definition of marketing research is limited by one's definition of marketing. Certainly research in the marketing area of a for-profit corporation is marketing research. A broader definition of marketing research, however, includes nonprofit organizations such as the American Heart Association, the San Diego Zoo, and the Boston Pops Orchestra. Each of these organizations exists to satisfy social needs, and each requires marketing skills to produce and distribute the products and services people want. Hence, marketing research may be conducted by organizations that are not business organizations.

## ■ Basic Research and Applied Research

**Basic (pure) research**
Research conducted to expand the boundaries of knowledge itself; undertaken to verify the acceptability of a given theory.

**Applied research**
Research undertaken to answer questions about specific problems or to make decisions about particular courses of action.

One purpose of conducting marketing research is to develop and evaluate concepts and theories. **Basic** or **pure research** attempts to expand the limits of knowledge. It does not directly involve the solution to a particular pragmatic problem. It has been said that there is nothing as practical as a good theory. Although this is true in the long run, basic marketing research findings generally cannot be immediately implemented by a marketing executive. Basic research is conducted to verify the acceptability of a given theory or to learn more about a certain concept. **Applied research** is conducted when a decision must be made about a specific real-life problem. Our focus is on applied research: those studies undertaken to answer questions about specific problems or to make decisions about particular courses of action or policies.

This discussion emphasizes applied research because most students will be oriented toward the day-to-day practice of marketing management. It is aimed at students and researchers who will be exposed to short-term, problem-solving research conducted for businesses or nonprofit organizations. However, the procedures and techniques used by applied and basic researchers do not differ substantially; both employ the scientific method

■ The Partnership for a Drug Free America is a nonprofit organization that conducts applied marketing research. In 1997, its research indicated that the Partnership should target younger children. As a result, it created a public service announcement called "Big 'ol Bug" to appeal to children ages 6 to 8. The rock music lyrics include the line, "I'd rather eat a big 'ol bug than ever take a stupid drug."

**Scientific method**
Systematic techniques or procedures used to analyze empirical evidence in an unbiased attempt to confirm or disprove prior conceptions.

to answer the question at hand. Broadly defined, the **scientific method** refers to the techniques and procedures used to recognize and understand marketing phenomena. In the scientific method, empirical evidence (facts derived from observation or experimentation) is analyzed and interpreted to confirm or disprove prior conceptions. In basic research, testing these prior conceptions or hypotheses and then making inferences and conclusions about the phenomena lead to the establishment of general laws about the phenomena. Use of the scientific method in applied research ensures objectivity in gathering facts and testing creative ideas for alternative marketing strategies. The essence of research, whether basic or applied, lies in the scientific method. Much of this book deals with scientific methodology. Thus, the techniques of basic and applied research differ largely in degree rather than substance.

# ■ THE MARKETING CONCEPT

**Marketing concept**
The marketing philosophy that stresses a consumer orientation, emphasizes long-range profitability, and suggests the integration and coordination of marketing and other organizational functions.

Although our discussion focuses on marketing research, marketing managers should understand how marketing research fits into the broader scope of marketing. Research is one of the primary tools that enables firms to implement the philosophical idea of the marketing concept. The **marketing concept** is the most central idea in marketing thinking. It has evolved over time as production- and engineering-oriented firms have responded to changes in the economic environment to become marketing-oriented firms. The marketing concept is a threefold conceptualization concerned with

1. Consumer orientation
2. Long-run profitability rather than sales volume
3. Cross-functional perspective

## ■ Consumer Orientation

According to the marketing concept, marketers must view the consumer as the pivotal point around which the business revolves. Simply put, the firm creates products, whether goods, services, or both, with consumers' needs in mind. Many marketing theorists and operating marketing managers believe that the satisfaction of consumers' wants is the justification for a firm's existence.

Crisco Savory Seasonings, a new line of flavored vegetable oils patterned after more expensive gourmet cooking oils, is a good example of a consumer orientation. The oils come in four all-natural flavors: Roasted Garlic, Hot & Spicy, Classic Herb, and Lemon

Butter.[4] The oils fill a consumer need for quick and easy preparation. The flavored oils can be used in a wide range of cooking methods—stir-frying, sautéing, pan frying, marinades, and dressings—as either an ingredient or a cooking medium. Savory Seasonings can be thought of as a "speed-scratch product" that helps consumers cut down on meal preparation time, yet satisfies their desire for giving meals a homemade touch. Procter & Gamble's research showed that 72 percent of households still prepare dinner at home nightly and 32 percent of households prepare the meal in less than 30 minutes. Armed with this information, Procter & Gamble leveraged the strong brand equity of Crisco to make an affordable, convenient product for everyday use. Procter & Gamble realized that knowledge of consumers' needs, coupled with product research and development, leads to successful marketing strategies and that industry leadership—indeed, corporate survival—depends on satisfying consumers.

### ■ Profit Orientation

Consumer orientation does not mean slavery to consumers' every fleeting whim. Implicit in the marketing concept is the assumption of the continuity of the firm *within a competitive environment.* The firm must make a profit to survive in the long run. Most consumers would prefer to have a Porsche priced under $15,000. However, the production costs of this car exceed that figure, and the firm surely would fail if it attempted to satisfy this desire.

The second aspect of the marketing concept argues against profitless volume, or sales volume for the sake of volume alone. Marketing cost analysis has taught numerous firms that 20 percent of their customers have been responsible for 80 percent of their profits and that salespeople have spent too much time on unprofitable accounts. The marketing concept suggests that these firms should reevaluate their efforts to sell to small, unprofitable accounts.

### ■ A Cross-Functional Perspective and Integrated Marketing Effort

Marketing personnel do not work in a vacuum, isolated from other company activities. The actions of people in areas such as production, credit, and research and development may affect an organization's marketing efforts. Similarly, the work of marketers will affect activities in other departments. Problems are almost certain to arise from a lack of an integrated, companywide effort. Marketers need to take a cross-functional perspective.

Problems occur when focusing on consumer needs is viewed as the sole responsibility of the marketing department. Indeed, other functional areas' goals may conflict with customer satisfaction or long-term profitability. For instance, the engineering department may want long lead times for product design, with simplicity and economy as major design goals. Marketing, however, may prefer short lead times and more complex designs with custom components and optional features for multiple models. The finance department may want fixed budgets, strict spending justifications, and prices that cover costs, whereas the marketing department may seek flexible budgets, liberal spending rationales, and below-cost prices to develop markets quickly.

Similar differences in outlook may occur among the other functional areas of the organization, and these may be sources of serious conflicts. When a firm lacks organizational procedures for communicating marketing information and coordinating marketing efforts, the effectiveness of its marketing programs will suffer.

### ■ Marketing Research: A Means for Implementing the Marketing Concept

Satisfying the consumer is a major goal of marketing. One purpose of marketing research is to obtain information that identifies consumers' problems and needs, bridging the information gap between marketing executives and consumers. Researching consumer needs in this way enables firms to fulfill the marketing concept.

Rubbermaid's new-product development process epitomizes this function.[5] Every new Rubbermaid product starts with research that asks one simple question: What's wrong with existing products? No consumer problem is considered too small, no concern too finicky. One marketing research study uncovered an inner secret of the bathroom: Women found it distasteful that family members' toothbrushes touched one another in the toothbrush holder. After finding what was wrong, Rubbermaid's new-product team went back to the lab and created a toothbrush holder that angled each brush outward to prevent the offending contact.

Consider another example from Rubbermaid of how marketing research found a natural answer to consumers' needs. The company now markets a shower caddy that has a dispenser that can hold a shampoo bottle upside down. Why? Research showed that many consumers wanted to make sure they could use the last drop of their shampoo, but they hated to stand in the shower waiting for those last drops.

In research about children's lunchboxes, parents indicated they often worried about where to put milk money, allergy medicines, keys, and other small items their kids needed to bring to school. When Rubbermaid came out with its backpack lunchbox, which was designed to slip easily into a backpack, it built in a change holder.

Measuring consumer satisfaction is another means of determining how well a company is fulfilling the marketing concept. Customer satisfaction research can ascertain whether an organization's total quality management program is meeting customer expectations and management objectives. General Electric's major-appliance division sent the questionnaire shown in Exhibit 1.1 to customers after repair calls to determine how well the company was accomplishing its objective of consumer satisfaction. The questionnaire asked whether the appointment was scheduled promptly, the repairperson showed up on time and was polite, and the customer was satisfied with the service. Customer satisfaction surveys such as this tend to be standardized and ongoing so that performance can be compared against previously established standards. These measures lead to the evaluation of managers according to consumers' perceptions of quality, in addition to the evaluation of actual operational quality.

Marketing research can also help eliminate commercialization of products that are not consumer oriented. Sometimes ideas that look like technological breakthroughs in the laboratory fall flat when presented to consumers. For example, a powdered pain reliever was supposed to be a soothing remedy because it was to be mixed with milk. It did not soothe customers, however. Research showed that the public thought this great step forward was a step backward in convenience of usage. The form was there, but someone forgot the consumer benefit.

By improving efficiency, research also facilitates profitability. For instance, during the introduction of a new product, accurate forecasting of the product's potential sales volume is an essential basis for estimating its profitability. A firm considering the introduction of a low-calorie candy bar might rely on a test-market experiment to determine the optimal price for this new concept. Extensive testing should be done to ensure that the marketing program is fine-tuned to maximize the firm's profitability while satisfying the consumer.

Analysis of data may also be a form of marketing research that can increase efficiency. Marketing representatives from Exxon Chemical Company used laptop computers to run a complex set of calculations to show sales prospects the advantage of Exxon products over competitors.' Such analysis of research data improves the salesperson's batting average and the firm's efficiency.

Because of the need to integrate company efforts, a marketing researcher must be knowledgeable not just about marketing research but about the entire spectrum of marketing activities as well.

**■ Exhibit 1.1**

**Marketing Research
May Measure
Consumer Satisfaction**

## QUALITY OF SERVICE SURVEY

Please rate the service you recently received from GE Factory Service (product and date shown on the reverse side). Consider all service calls required for this particular problem. Indicate your answers by checking the appropriate box for each question.

1. When you called for service were you able to get through on the first call without getting a busy signal? — YES / NO

2. When you called, were you placed on hold? — YES / NO

3. Did the person you talked with on the phone give you the feeling that he/she really cared about your problem? — YES / NO

4. What day was your appointment scheduled for? — SAME DAY / NEXT DAY / 3RD DAY / 4TH DAY / LATER

5. Was this the day you most preferred? — YES / NO

6. If not, what day would you have most preferred? — SAME DAY / NEXT DAY / 3RD DAY / 4TH DAY / LATER

7. When was the technician scheduled to arrive? — AM 8-12 / PM 12-5 / EVENING AFTER 5 / ALL DAY 8-5

8. Was this time of day you most preferred? — YES / NO

9. Did the technician come on the scheduled day? — YES / NO

10. Did the technician arrive during the scheduled time period? — YES / NO

11. Did the technician give you the feeling he/she really cared about your problem? — YES / NO

12. Did the technician seem to be knowledgeable and competent about your product? — YES / NO

13. Did the technician explain what was done to fix your problem? — YES / NO

14. Were the charges on the invoice explained to you? — YES / NO

15. Considering the service you received, how would you rate the charges for:

| | NO CHARGE INVOLVED | VERY REASONABLE | REASONABLE | UNREASONABLE | VERY UNREASONABLE |
|---|---|---|---|---|---|
| LABOR (incl. home call) | ☐ | ☐ | ☐ | ☐ | ☐ |
| PARTS | ☐ | ☐ | ☐ | ☐ | ☐ |
| TOTAL CHARGE | ☐ | ☐ | ☐ | ☐ | ☐ |

16. How many trips were required to complete the repair? — 1 / 2 / 3 / 4 / MORE THAN 4

17. Overall, how would you rate our technician? — EXCELLENT / GOOD / FAIR / POOR

18. If a part was needed to complete the repair, was the part: — AVAILABLE ON SERVICE TRUCK / MAILED TO YOU / BROUGHT BACK LATER BY A TECHNICIAN / NO PART NEEDED

19. If a part was ordered, how many days did it take for you to get the part? — NO PART ORDERED / SAME DAY / 1-4 DAYS / 5-9 DAYS / MORE THAN 9 DAYS

20. Considering all these questions, how satisfied are you with the overall service you received? — VERY SATISFIED / SATISFIED / NEITHER SATISFIED/DISSATISFIED / DISSATISFIED / VERY DISSATISFIED

21. If you needed to replace the product you had repaired, how likely would you be to buy the General Electric or Hotpoint brand? — DEFINITELY WOULD BUY GE/HOTPOINT / PROBABLY WOULD BUY GE/HOTPOINT / MIGHT OR MIGHT NOT BUY GE/HOTPOINT / PROBABLY WOULD NOT BUY GE/HOTPOINT / DEFINITELY WOULD NOT BUY GE/HOTPOINT

22. Please add any comments you have about the service you received.

## ■ THE MANAGERIAL VALUE OF MARKETING RESEARCH FOR STRATEGIC DECISION MAKING

The primary managerial value of marketing research comes from its ability to reduce uncertainty. It generates information that facilitates decision making about marketing strategies and tactics.

Developing and implementing a marketing strategy involves four stages:

1. Identifying and evaluating opportunities
2. Analyzing market segments and selecting target markets
3. Planning and implementing a marketing mix that will satisfy customers' needs and meet the objectives of the organization
4. Analyzing marketing performance[6]

## ■ Identifying and Evaluating Opportunities

Before developing a marketing strategy, an organization must determine where it wants to go and how to get there. Marketing research can help answer these questions by investigating potential opportunities to identify attractive areas for company action.

Marketing research may provide diagnostic information about what is occurring in the environment. A simple description of some social or economic activity, such as trends in consumer purchasing behavior, may help managers recognize problems and identify opportunities to enrich marketing efforts.

One reason for Mattel Toys' success in the rapidly changing toy market is the company's commitment to consumer research. Much of its success may be traced to the way it goes about identifying opportunities for its new products. For example, marketing research showed that instead of military, spy, or sports heroes, young boys preferred fantasy figures. Boys spend much time fantasizing about good versus evil. Research showed that timeless fantasy figures, both ancient and futuristic, were visually exciting, and because they were timeless, boys could do more with them. Action figures for boys were a result of this research. Video games by Nintendo and Sony Playstation also reflect an awareness of this research finding.

A research study on running shoes investigated the situations associated with product use, that is, when individuals wore their running shoes. The researchers found that most owners of running shoes wore the shoes while walking, not running. Also, most walked while performing a routine daily activity such as shopping or commuting to work rather than for exercise. Many of the people who wore running shoes for routine activities considered them an alternative to other casual shoes. This research ultimately led to the development of the walking shoe designed for comfortable, everyday walking.[7]

Market opportunities may be evaluated using several performance criteria. In many cases, marketing research supplies the information to determine which opportunities are best for the organization. For example, when market demand is the performance criterion, this information typically is estimated using marketing research techniques.

Estimates of market potential or predictions about future environmental conditions allow managers to evaluate the sizes of opportunities. Accurate sales forecasts are among the most useful pieces of planning information a marketing manager can have. Complete accuracy in forecasting the future is not possible because change is constantly occurring in the marketing environment. Nevertheless, objective forecasts of demand or changing environments may be the foundations on which marketing strategies are built.

## ■ Analyzing and Selecting Target Markets

The second stage of marketing strategy development is to analyze market segments and select target markets. The American Marketing Association found that more than 90 percent of the organizations it surveyed engaged in research to determine market characteristics and trends.[8] Marketing research is a major source of information for determining which market segments' characteristics distinguish them from the overall market.

Market segmentation studies at Harley-Davidson provide a good example of this essential activity. Marketing research depicts the Harley-Davidson motorcycle purchaser as a

38-year-old male (80 percent) with some college (44 percent). He is likely to be married (72 percent) and have no children (55 percent). The average Harley owner has a personal income of $34,300 and lives in a household with an income of $43,000.[9]

## ■ Planning and Implementing a Marketing Mix

Using the information obtained in the two previous stages, marketing managers plan and execute a marketing mix strategy. However, marketing research may be needed to support specific decisions about any aspect of the marketing mix. Often the research is conducted to evaluate an alternative course of action. For example, advertising research investigated whether an actress, one of Hollywood's most beautiful women, would make a good spokesperson for a specific brand of hair coloring. She was filmed in some test commercials to endorse the brand, but the commercials were never aired because, although viewers recognized her as an outstanding personality in the test commercials, they did not perceive her as a user of home hair-coloring kits or as an authority on such products.

Managers face many diverse decisions about marketing mixes. The following examples highlight selected types of research that might be conducted for each element of the marketing mix.

**Product Research**  Product research takes many forms and includes studies designed to evaluate and develop new products, measure perceptions of the quality of goods and services, and learn how to adapt existing product lines. Concept testing exposes potential customers to new product ideas to judge the concepts' acceptance and feasibility. Product testing determines a product prototype's strengths and weaknesses or whether a finished product performs better than competing brands or according to expectations. Brand name evaluation studies investigate whether a name is appropriate for a product. Package testing assesses size, color, shape, ease of use, and other attributes of a package. Total quality management studies involve routinely asking customers to rate a product against its competitors.

Product research encompasses all applications of marketing research that seek to develop product attributes that will add value for consumers. One reason Mazda has succeeded in the highly competitive automotive industry is the company's commitment to marketing research to develop products. For example, Mazda designed the Miata's exhaust system to match consumers' ideas of what a lightweight sports car should sound like. The company experimented with more than 150 variations of tunings for the Miata exhaust system before it was satisfied that the automobile's sound fit consumers' perceptions.

**Pricing Research**  Most organizations conduct pricing research. A competitive pricing study is a typical marketing research project in this area. However, research designed to discover the ideal price level or to determine if consumers will pay a price high enough to cover cost is not uncommon. Pricing research may also investigate when to offer discounts or coupons, explore whether certain critical product attributes determine how consumers perceive value, or determine if a product category, such as soft drinks, has price gaps among national brands, regional brands, and private labels.[10]

Research may answer many questions about price. Is there a need for seasonal or quantity discounts? Are coupons more effective than price reductions? Is a brand price elastic or price inelastic? How much of a price difference will best differentiate items in the product line?

**Distribution Research**  Manufacturers, wholesalers, and retailers often cooperate to conduct research about the distribution process. Frito-Lay, for example, has developed research expertise in supermarket space management. The snack food company conducts

■ British Airways' marketing research revealed that many travelers find air travel a frustrating experience—from the office to the airport to a hotel or meeting and back again. Air travelers want to know they're being cared for. With these findings in mind, executives at British Airways made a decision to alter its service. The airline relaunched its Club Europe business-class services to smooth business travelers' paths, providing them with more time and space and, above all, eliminating the hassles. The new Club Europe service, whose cost exceeded 70 million British pounds, includes new seats, more business lounges, telephone check-in, limousines at taxi rates, and speedier service through security and customs at Heathrow's Terminal One.[11]

research to help Pathmark, Safeway, and other supermarkets improve consumer traffic flows and increase snack food purchases.

A typical study in the distribution area may be conducted to select retail sites or warehouse locations. A survey of retailers or wholesalers may be conducted because the actions of one channel member can greatly affect the performances of other channel members. Distribution research often is needed to gain knowledge about retailers' and wholesalers' operations and/or learn their reactions to a manufacturer's marketing policies.

The 3M Corporation surveys its industrial distributors to determine, anonymously, how they feel about doing business with each of their suppliers, including 3M. The purpose of the research is to investigate distributors' attitudes about relationships with sales representatives, ordering procedures, on-time delivery, training of distributor personnel, product quality, and many other activities that help build long-term relationships.

**Promotion Research**   Research that investigates the effectiveness of premiums, coupons, sampling deals, and other sales promotions is classified as promotion research. So is advertising research, which includes buyer motivation studies to generate ideas for copy development, media research, and studies of advertising effectiveness.

The marketing research findings of Zale's, a large retailer of jewelry, helped create advertising with large, one-word headlines that simply asked, "Confused?" "Nervous?" or "Lost?" The advertisements overtly acknowledged the considerable emotional and financial risks consumers face in jewelry purchases. Research had shown that typical consumers felt unable to determine the relative quality of various jewelry items, believed jewelry purchases were expensive, and needed reassurance about their purchases, especially because they often purchased jewelry for someone else.

Media research helps advertisers decide whether television, newspapers, magazines, or other media alternatives are best suited to convey the advertiser's message. Choices among alternative magazines or television programs may be based on research that shows how many people in the target audience each advertising vehicle can reach.

**The Integrated Marketing Mix**   The individual elements of the marketing mix do not work independently of the other elements. Hence, many research studies investigate various combinations of marketing ingredients to gather information to suggest the best possible marketing program.

### ■ Analyzing Marketing Performance

After a marketing strategy has been implemented, marketing research may serve to inform managers whether planned activities were properly executed and are accomplishing what they were expected to achieve. In other words, marketing research may be conducted to obtain feedback for evaluation and control of marketing programs.

**Performance-monitoring research** Research that regularly, sometimes routinely, provides feedback for evaluation and control of marketing activity.

**Performance-monitoring research** refers to research that regularly, sometimes routinely, provides feedback for evaluation and control of marketing activity. For example, most firms continuously monitor wholesale and retail activity to ensure early detection of sales declines and other anomalies. In the grocery and drug industries, sales research may use Universal Product Codes on packages read by electronic scanners and computerized checkout counters to provide valuable information about each brand's retail sales volume and market share. Market share analysis and sales analysis are the most common forms of performance-monitoring research. Almost every organization compares its current sales with previous sales and competitors' sales. However, marketing performance analysis is not limited to the investigation of sales figures.

Performance-monitoring research is especially important for the continuous improvement of product and service quality necessary for a successful total quality management program.[12] Implementing a total quality management program requires considerable measurement. It involves routinely asking customers to rate a product against its competitors, measuring employee attitudes, and monitoring company performance against benchmark standards. Because these activities use marketing research extensively, marketing research with external customers and with employees in the organization (internal customers) contributes much to a total quality management program.

United Airlines' Omnibus in-flight surveys provide a good example of performance-monitoring research for quality management. United routinely selects sample flights and administers questionnaires concerning in-flight service, food, and so forth. The Omnibus survey is conducted quarterly to determine who is flying and for what reason. It enables United to track demographic changes and monitor customer ratings of its services on a continuing basis, allowing the company to gather vast amounts of information at low cost. The information regarding customer reaction to services can be compared over time. For example, suppose United decided to change its menu for in-flight meals. The results of the Omnibus survey might indicate that shortly after a menu change, customers' ratings of food and meals declined. Such information would be extremely valuable because it would allow management to quickly spot similar trends in passengers' attitudes toward other areas such as airport lobbies, gate-line waits, or cabin cleanliness. Thus, management could act rapidly to improve deficiencies.

When analysis of marketing performance indicates things are not going as planned, marketing research may be required to explain why something went wrong. Detailed information about specific mistakes or failures is frequently sought. If a general problem area is identified, breaking down industry sales volume and a firm's sales volume into different geographical areas may yield explanations for specific problems. Exploring problems in greater depth may indicate which managerial judgments were erroneous.

## ■ WHEN IS MARKETING RESEARCH NEEDED?

A marketing manager confronted with two or more alternative courses of action faces the initial decision of whether or not to conduct marketing research. The determination of the

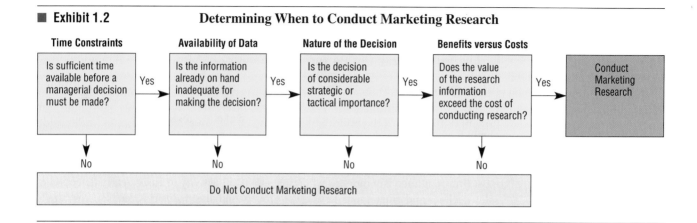

■ **Exhibit 1.2**    **Determining When to Conduct Marketing Research**

need for marketing research centers on (1) time constraints, (2) the availability of data, (3) the nature of the decision to be made, and (4) the value of the research information in relation to costs. Exhibit 1.2 outlines the criteria for determining when to conduct marketing research.

## ■ Time Constraints

Systematic research takes time. In many instances, management will believe that a decision must be made immediately, allowing no time for research. Decisions sometimes are made without adequate information or thorough understanding of market situations. Although not ideal, the urgency of a situation sometimes precludes the use of research.

## ■ Availability of Data

Often managers already possess enough information to make sound decisions with no marketing research. When they lack adequate information, however, they must consider research. Managers must ask themselves, "Will the research provide the information needed to answer the basic questions about this decision?" Further, if a potential source of data exists, managers will want to know how much it will cost to obtain those data.

If the data cannot be made available, research cannot be conducted. For example, prior to 1980 the People's Republic of China had never conducted a population census in mainland China. Organizations engaged in international business often find that data about business activity or population characteristics found in abundance when investigating the United States are sparse or nonexistent when the geographic area of interest is a developing country. Imagine the problems facing marketing researchers who wish to investigate market potential in places such as the Czech Republic, Yugoslavian Macedonia, and other emerging countries.

## ■ Nature of the Decision

The value of marketing research will depend on the nature of the managerial decision to be made. A routine tactical decision that does not require a substantial investment may not seem to warrant a substantial expenditure for marketing research. For example, a computer company must update its operator's instruction manual when it makes minor product modifications. The research cost of determining the proper wording for updating the manual is likely to be too high for such a minor decision. The nature of the decision is not totally independent of the next issue to be considered: the benefits from conducting the research versus the costs of the research. In general, however, the more strategically or tactically important the decision, the more likely research will be conducted.

## ■ Benefits versus Costs

Earlier we discussed some of the managerial benefits of marketing research. Of course, conducting research to obtain these benefits requires an expenditure. There are both costs and benefits to conducting marketing research. In any decision-making situation, managers must identify alternative courses of action, then weigh the value of each alternative against its costs. Marketing research can be thought of as an investment alternative. When deciding whether to make a decision without research or to postpone the decision in order to conduct research, managers should ask three questions:

1. Will the payoff or rate of return be worth the investment?
2. Will the information gained by marketing research improve the quality of the marketing decision enough to warrant the expenditure?
3. Is the proposed research expenditure the best use of the available funds?

For example, *TV-Cable Week* was not test marketed before its launch. Although the magazine had articles and stories about TV personalities and events, its main feature was program listings, channel by channel, showing the exact programs available to a particular subscriber. Producing a custom magazine for each individual cable TV system in the country required developing a costly computer system. Since the development necessitated a substantial expenditure, one that could not be scaled down for research, conducting research was judged to be an improper investment. The value of the research information was not positive, because the cost of the information exceeded its benefits. Unfortunately, pricing and distribution problems became so compelling after the magazine was launched that the product was a marketing failure. Nevertheless, managers, lacking the luxury of hindsight, made a reasonable decision not to conduct research. They analyzed the cost of the information (that is, the cost of test marketing) relative to the potential benefits of the information.

## ■ Marketing Research Is a Global Activity

Marketing research, like all business activity today, has become increasingly global. Some companies have extensive international marketing research operations. Upjohn conducts marketing research in 160 countries.

Companies that conduct business in foreign lands must understand the nature of those particular markets and judge whether those markets require customized marketing strategies. For example, although the 15 nations of the European Union now share a single formal market, marketing research shows they do not share identical tastes for many consumer products. Marketing researchers have found no such thing as a "typical" European consumer; the nations of the European Union are divided by language, religion, climate, and centuries of tradition. Scantel Research, a British firm that advises companies on color preferences, found inexplicable differences in the ways Europeans take their medicine. The French prefer to pop purple pills, but the English and Dutch favor white ones. Consumers in all three countries dislike bright red capsules, which are big sellers in the United States. This example illustrates that companies that do business in Europe must judge whether they need to adapt to local customs and buying habits.[13]

■ The world economy has become global, and corporations market products in many countries. People think of their home culture as the normal way of life, but consumers in other cultures may have different values, beliefs, and behaviors. Marketing research helps marketers understand cultural differences. Colgate-Palmolive is a progressive company that conducts marketing research around the world. Colgate-Palmolive used marketing research when introducing Axion dishwashing gel in Colombia, where it is sold in outdoor markets.

Nielsen/IMS International—which includes A. C. Nielsen, the television ratings firm—is the world's largest marketing research company. More than 60 percent of its business comes from outside the United States.[14] Although the nature of marketing research can change around the globe, the need for marketing research is universal.

Throughout this book, we will discuss the practical problems involved in conducting marketing research in Europe, Asia, Latin America, the Middle East, and elsewhere.

## ■ SUMMARY

Marketing research is a tool companies use to discover consumers' wants and needs so that they can satisfy those wants and needs with their product offerings. Marketing research is the marketing manager's source of information about market conditions. It covers topics ranging from long-range planning to near-term tactical decisions.

Marketing research is the systematic and objective process of generating information—gathering, recording, and analyzing data—to aid marketing decision making. The research must be systematic, not haphazard. It must be objective to avoid the distorting effects of personal bias. Basic or pure research aims to expand on knowledge of a concept or to verify the acceptability of a theory. Applied research seeks to address specific problems or aid in decisions about particular courses of action.

Marketing research is a means of implementing the marketing concept, the most central idea in marketing. The marketing concept says that a firm must be oriented toward both consumer satisfaction and long-run profitability (rather than short-run sales volume). Further, all aspects of the firm need to be integrated to achieve these goals.

Marketing research can help implement the marketing concept by identifying consumers' problems and needs, improving efficiency, and evaluating the effectiveness of marketing strategies and tactics.

The development and implementation of a marketing strategy involves four stages: (1) identifying and evaluating opportunities, (2) analyzing market segments and selecting

target markets, (3) planning and implementing a marketing mix that will
tomers' needs and meet the objectives of the organization, and (4) analyzin
performance. Marketing research helps in each stage by providing informatio
gic decision making.

Managers also use marketing research to determine what went wrong with past marketing efforts, describe current events in the marketplace, or forecast future conditions.

A marketing manager determines whether marketing research should be conducted
based on (1) time constraints, (2) availability of data, (3) the nature of the decision to be
made, or (4) the benefit versus the costs of the research information.

## ■ Key Terms and Concepts

| | |
|---|---|
| Marketing research | Scientific method |
| Basic (pure) research | Marketing concept |
| Applied research | Performance-monitoring research |

## ■ Questions

1. Is it possible to make sound marketing decisions without conducting marketing
research? What advantages does research offer to the decision maker over seat-of-the-
pants decision making?
2. An advertising agency's slogan is "People listen to us because we listen to them." Has
this firm integrated the marketing research function with the marketing concept?
3. Name some products that logically might have been developed with the help of marketing research.
4. In your own words, define *marketing research* and describe its task.
5. Which of the following organizations are likely to use marketing research? Why? How?
   (a) Manufacturer of breakfast cereals
   (b) Manufacturer of nuts, bolts, and other fasteners
   (c) Federal Trade Commission
   (d) Hospital
   (e) Computer software publisher
6. An automobile manufacturer is attempting to predict the type of car consumers will
desire in the year 2020. Is this effort basic or applied research? Explain.

7. The owner of 22 restaurants was asked how he does marketing research. He answered
that he does it after driving around in a pickup truck at midnight: "I stay up late. If it's
midnight and I don't have anything else to do, I drive around town and look at the
lines in front of places. I'll look at the trash and see if a guy's doing business. If he's
got a real clean bunch of trash cans and an empty dumpster, he's not doing any business. I find out a lot by talking to my vendors. I ask the bread guy how many boxes of
buns the drive-in down the street is buying. Very few restaurateurs do that. But that's
the way I research my market." Is this marketing research?
8. Comment on the following statements:
   (a) Marketing managers are paid to take chances with decisions. Marketing
       researchers are paid to reduce the risk of making those decisions.
   (b) A marketing strategy can be no better than the information on which it is formulated.
   (c) The purpose of research is to solve marketing problems.
9. In what specific ways can marketing research influence the development and implementation of marketing strategy?
10. What is the relationship between marketing research and customer satisfaction?

## EXPLORING THE INTERNET

The Internet is a worldwide network of computers that allows an individual access to information and documents from distant sources. In essence, the Internet is a combination of worldwide communication systems and the world's largest public library for a seemingly endless range of information. The Internet is discussed in depth in Chapter 2. The home page for this textbook is located at http://www.dryden.com/mktng/zikmund. The author's home page is located at http://www.bus.okstate.edu/zikmund. An "Exploring the Internet" exercise is included in each of the remaining chapters. This feature gives you an opportunity to use the Internet to gain additional insights about marketing research.

---

## CASE 1.1 Porsche

After selling a record 30,000 automobiles in the United States in 1986, Porsche saw its sales begin to decline, reaching a low of approximately 4,000 in 1993. During the 1980s, the price of a Porsche 911 Carrera coupe was less than the average U.S. household's annual income. But in 1993, the price was about 25 percent more because of the strength of the deutsche mark and a luxury tax passed by Congress.[15] However, after conducting marketing research to learn which market segments were prime customers, Porsche Cars North America found out that a higher price was not the only thing that had gone wrong.

The research showed that the demographics of Porsche owners were utterly predictable: a 40-year-old male college graduate with an income of over $200,000 a year.[16] The psychographics, however, were another aspect of the company's marketing problem. The categories of Porsche owners appear in Case Exhibit 1.1-1.

Porsche's vice president of sales and marketing found the results astonishing. He said, "We were selling to people whose profiles were diametrically opposed. You wouldn't want to tell an elitist how good he looks in the car or how fast he could go."

As a result of the new insights from its marketing research, Porsche cut its prices, launched a new advertising campaign, and introduced a redesign of its classic rear-engine car, the 911.

### Questions

1. What role should marketing research play in the marketing of a luxury sports car like Porsche?
2. What type of marketing research studies does this case indicate?
3. In your opinion, why didn't Porsche discover this problem earlier? Do you think Porsche's use of marketing research is typical of most major corporations?

---

### ■ Case Exhibit 1.1-1

**Psychographic Profile of Porsche Buyers**

| Type | Percent of All Owners | Description |
|------|------|-------------|
| Top Guns | 27% | Driven, ambitious types. Power and control matter. They expect to be noticed. |
| Elitists | 24% | Old-money blue bloods. A car is just a car, no matter how expensive. It is not an extension of personality. |
| Proud Patrons | 23% | Ownership is an end in itself. Their car is a trophy earned for hard work, and who cares if anyone sees them in it? |
| Bon Vivants | 17% | Worldly jet setters and thrill seekers. Their car heightens the excitement in their already passionate lives. |
| Fantasists | 9% | Walter Mitty types. Their car is an escape. Not only are they uninterested in impressing others with it, they also feel a little guilty about owning one. |

## ■ Endndotes

[1]Karen Benezra, "Fritos Around the World," *Brandweek,* March 27, 1995, p. 32; "Chinese Chee-tos," *New York Times,* November 27, 1994, p. 31; "Chee-tos Make Debut in China but Lose Cheese in Translation," *USA Today,* September 2, 1994, p. B-1.

[2]American Marketing Association, *Report of the Committee on Definitions of Marketing Research,* 1987.

[3]Adapted from the definition of research in American Marketing Association, Committee on Definitions, *Marketing Definitions: A Glossary of Marketing Terms* (Chicago: American Marketing Association, 1960), p. 17; American Marketing Association, *Report of the Committee on Definitions of Marketing Research,* 1987. The official AMA definition is as follows: "Marketing research is the function which links the consumer, customer, and public to the marketer through information—information used to identify and define marketing opportunities and problems; generate, refine, and evaluate marketing actions; monitor marketing performance; and improve understanding of marketing as a process. Marketing research specifies the information required to address these issues; designs the method for collecting the information; manages and implements the data collection process; analyzes the results; and communicates the findings and their implications."

[4]Mary Kuhn and Kitty Devin, "The 1995 New Product Hit Parade," *Food Processing,* November 1, 1995.

[5]Adapted from Jon Berry, "The Art of Rubbermaid," *Adweek,* March 16, 1992, p. 24.

[6]For a detailed discussion of marketing strategy and tactics, see William G. Zikmund and Michael d'Amico, *Marketing* (Cincinnati: Southwestern, 1999), Chapter 2.

[7]David Schwartz, *Concept Testing: How to Test Product Ideas Before You Go to Market* (New York: AMACOM, 1987), p. 91.

[8]Thomas C. Kinnear and Ann R. Root, eds., *1994 Survey of Marketing Research* (Chicago: American Marketing Association, 1995), p. 43.

[9]Aimee L. Stern, "Courting Consumer Loyalty With Feel-Good Bond," *New York Times,* January 17, 1993, p. F-10; see also Ian P. Murphy, "Aided by Research, Harley Goes Whole Hog," *Marketing News,* December 2, 1996, p. 16.

[10]N. Carroll Mohn, "Pricing Research for Decision Making," *Marketing Research,* Winter 1995, pp. 11–12.

[11]David Churchill, "Cabin Pressures," *Management Today,* October 1, 1994, p. 96.

[12]For a more extensive discussion of this issue, see Zikmund and d'Amico, *Marketing* (Cincinnati: Southwestern, 1999).

[13]"You Say Tomato, I Say Tomahto," *Express Magazine,* Spring 1992, p. 19.

[14]Kenneth Wylie, "100 Leading Research Companies," *Advertising Age,* May 20, 1996, p. 44.

[15]Wilton Woods, "Not Priced for the Nineties," *Fortune,* September 22, 1993, p. 87.

[16]Alex Taylor III, "Porsche Slices Up Its Buyers," *Fortune,* January 16, 1995, p. 24.

# 2

# GLOBAL INFORMATION SYSTEMS AND THE INTERNET

A customized communications network gives Texas Instruments the ability to communicate with and control all its branches around the world from its headquarters in Dallas, Texas.

Texas Instruments works constantly to maintain its competitive advantage in an ever-changing semiconductor market. Leadership in the marketplace is difficult in an industry which experiences such rapid change and incredible technological advances. Semiconductor manufacturers are constantly struggling to make a profit on products which have continually shortened life-cycles.

One of the ways Texas Instruments (TI) has been able to survive in such a volatile market is by networking its global operations. TI's decision over 20 years ago was to develop a new information system called the single-image network. With manufacturing and marketing facilities all over the world, accurate and fast communication between branches and the home office are vital to the development of new products.

With the help of the single-image network, TI's 76,000 employees are able to communicate with over 50,000 workstations to obtain information from other employees or to access any of TI's 20 data centers around the world. Electronic messages are no longer a novel idea to employees since they transmit over 250,000 messages and documents daily, such as information to match and schedule orders with production facilities on opposite sides of the globe. TI is also finding an increasing number of orders being placed electronically by their customers, distributors, and suppliers. The great advantage in networking, not only for employees but also customers and distributors, is all information is stored in the network. Analysis on inventory and future production can easily be run on this data to make forecasts for the future.

According to TI headquarters, this company still sees room for development within their network. However, they have a head start on competitors. The single-image network has created linkages across continents saving thousands of hours previously lost in data entry, inventory planning and delivery of products to customers. This incredible cost savings will strengthen TI's position in the semiconductor marketplace.

The network has streamlined communications from the production operation to the order processing department. The head office can easily print reports on operations and pinpoint order positions, identify when orders will be shipping, print order lists, and provide shipping instructions to remote plants so that those managers will know what they are able to ship to any other destination on any particular day. Functions between the branches are harmonious since they are coordinated by the central computer in Dallas. For example, a designer in Dallas or Japan could use the network to send a document electronically to a fabrication facility in Lubbock, Texas. That document could be printed to obtain the specifications within and used to alter the fabrication manufacturing at the Lubbock plant. Silicon slices could be shipped from Lubbock to an assembly and test facility in Malaysia. If the systems are timed accurately, the network would provide destination points for the end products coming out of Malaysia and ship directly to the customer instead of having to first route through a warehouse.

Texas Instruments' single-image network is a complex information system. It streamlines all of the company's manufacturing plants to harmonize product flow. In this chapter, we will discuss the nature of such global information networks and their decision support systems.

## ■ GLOBAL INFORMATION SYSTEMS

**Global information system**
An organized collection of computer hardware, software, data, and personnel designed to capture, store, update, manipulate, analyze, and immediately display information about worldwide business activity.

The well-being of a multinational corporation—indeed, the health of any business organization that plans to prosper in the twenty-first century—will depend on information about the world economy and global competition. Contemporary marketers require timely and accurate information from around the globe to maintain competitive advantages. Today's managers can access a wealth of information instantaneously, a phenomenon that has changed the way business is conducted.

Increased global competition and technological advances in interactive media have given rise to global information systems. A **global information system** is an organized collection of computer hardware, software, data, and personnel designed to capture, store, update, manipulate, analyze, and immediately display information about worldwide business activities.[2]

Consider a simple example. At any moment, United Parcel Service (UPS) can track the status of any shipment around the world. UPS drivers use hand-held electronic clipboards called *delivery information acquisition devices (DIADs)* to record appropriate data about each pickup or delivery. The data are then entered into the company's main computer for recordkeeping and analysis. A satellite telecommunications system allows UPS to track any shipment for a customer.

Using satellite communications, high-speed microcomputers, electronic data interchanges, fiber optics, CD-ROM data storage, fax machines, and other technological advances in interactive media, global information systems are changing the nature of business. If executives at Motorola must price their cellular phones for European markets, they can get immediate information about international exchange rates without leaving their desks. An advertising agency can find out the next day how many urban viewers remember its Nike commercial aired during the Super Bowl. A library researcher can generate a bibliography of hundreds of abstracts on a particular subject with a few simple keystrokes.

The information age has already begun, yet today's amazing technology will seem primitive in the 21st century. Of course, current information system technology provides many insights about the future of information retrieval and its impact on global business.

## ■ DATA VERSUS INFORMATION

**Data**
Facts or recorded measures of certain phenomena.

**Information**
Any body of facts in a format suitable for decision making or in a context that defines the relationship between two pieces of data.

Marketing managers must distinguish between data and information. **Data** are simply facts or recorded measures of certain phenomena; **information** is a body of facts in a format suitable to support decision making or define the relationship between two pieces of data. To see the difference between data and information, consider that Toys "Я" Us records thousands of unsummarized facts. A store clerk feeds data into the computer system each time he or she enters a transaction into a cash register. Simultaneously the data are also entered into a computerized inventory system. These data lack any meaning, however, until managers request the information system to translate the data into product sales totals by store, by country, or by state when they request forecasts for future time periods.

## ■ THE CHARACTERISTICS OF VALUABLE INFORMATION

Not all information is valuable to decision makers. Marketing information is useful if it helps a marketing manager make a decision. Information can be evaluated using four characteristics: relevance, quality, timeliness, and completeness.

### ■ Relevance

Information is relevant if it suits the needs of the marketer. The decision maker gets exactly what he or she wants from relevant information. Relevant information applies to the situation if it clarifies the questions the decision maker faces.

### ■ Quality

High-quality information is accurate, valid, and reliable. High-quality data present a good picture of reality. Information quality depends on the degree to which the information represents the true situation.

This author regularly receives two catalogs from Bloomingdale's, one addressed to Mr. Zikmund and one to Mr. Vikmund. Bloomie's mailing list has problems with its information quality.

■ Markets gather data from around the globe. Their goal is to convert it to the right quantity of relevant, accurate, and timely information.

Information quality is a critical issue in marketing research, and it will be discussed throughout this textbook.

## ■ Timeliness

Marketing is a dynamic field in which out-of-date information can lead to poor decisions. Marketing information must be timely, that is, provided at the right time.

Computerized information systems can record events and dispense relevant information soon after a transaction takes place. A great deal of marketing information becomes available almost at the moment a transaction occurs. As the earlier example of UPS illustrates, computer technology has redefined standards for timely information.

## ■ Completeness

Information completeness means having the right quantity of information. Marketing managers must have sufficient information about all aspects of their decisions. For example, a researcher investigating Eastern European markets may plan to analyze four former Soviet-bloc countries. Population information may be available for all four countries, along with each country's inflation rate. However, information about disposable personal income may be available only for three of the countries. If facts about disposable personal income or another economic characteristic cannot be obtained, the information is incomplete. Often incomplete information leads decision makers to conduct marketing research.

## ■ DECISION SUPPORT SYSTEMS

**Decision support system**
A computer-based system that helps decision makers confront problems through direct interaction with databases and analytical software programs.

A marketing **decision support system** is a computer-based system that helps decision makers confront problems through direct interaction with databases and analytical software programs. The purpose of a decision support system is to store data and transform them into organized information that is easily accessible to marketing managers.

Decision support systems serve specific business units within a company, operating within the context of the global information system. Exhibit 2.1 illustrates a decision support system.

Raw, unsummarized data are input to the decision support system. Data collected in marketing research projects are a major source of this input, but the data input may be purchased or collected by accountants, sales managers, production managers, or company

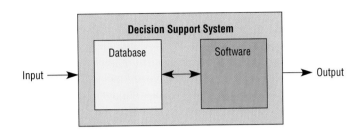

■ **Exhibit 2.1**
**Decision Support System**

employees other than marketing researchers. Effective marketers spend a great deal of time and effort collecting information for input into the decision support system. Useful information is the output of a decision support system.

A decision support system requires databases and software.

## ■ Databases and Data Warehousing

**Database**
A collection of raw data arranged logically and organized in a form that can be stored and processed by a computer.

A **database** is a collection of raw data arranged logically and organized in a form that can be stored and processed by a computer. A customer mailing list is one type of database. Population characteristics may be recorded by state, county, and city in another database. Databases often reside in computer storage devices such as hard-disk drives, but other types of databases may exist in a vendor company's computers.

Because most companies compile and store many different databases, they often develop data warehousing systems. *Data warehousing* is the term managers of information technology use to refer to the process that allows important data collected from day-to-day computer systems (often called operational systems) to be stored and organized into separate systems designed for simplified access.[3] More formally, data warehousing refers to the multitiered, computerized storage of current and historical data and the mechanics of selecting and using information that is relevant to decision-making tasks. Data warehouse management requires that the detailed data from operational systems be extracted and transformed so that layers of summarized data "tables" can be stored (warehoused) to make the various databases consistent. Organizations that use data warehousing may integrate databases from both inside and outside the company.[4]

The development of data warehouses requires database management software to provide easy access to the data.

## ■ Software

**Software**
Consists of various types of programs that tell computers, printers, and other hardware what to do.

The **software** portion of a decision support system consists of various types of programs that tell computers, printers, and other hardware what to do. Advances in spreadsheet and statistical software have revolutionized the analysis of marketing data. A decision support system's software allows managers to combine and restructure databases, diagnose relationships, build analytical models, estimate variables, and otherwise analyze the various databases.

Depending on the software, computer-based reporting systems provide a wealth of information related to costs, shipments, sales, and so on. The database of internal records can generate a number of periodic reports to help managers improve performance. Often accounting information can be transformed, using an electronic spreadsheet, to provide marketing information. A product manager might ask the computer for sales by product line, inventory reports, back-order reports, and so forth every month or every week (in some cases, every day).

■ ESRI's ArcView databases and computer software for colorful maps allow researchers to exhibit marketing data by geographical area such as zip code, census track, or sales territory. ArcView integrates visualization and data management tools, making customization of maps an easy point-and-click task.

Decision support systems have advanced internal reporting in many ways. Desktop computer terminals with graphics software now convert endless columns of numbers to color charts, graphs, and maps. For example, members of PepsiCo's business planning group can generate on demand hundreds of charts and graphs that compare sales and earnings for each division with past performance and corporate projections.

Most of today's software is so user friendly that nonexperts can easily maintain direct control over a computer's tasks and outcomes. A manager can sit at a computer terminal and instantaneously retrieve data files and request special, creative analyses to refine, modify, or generate information in a format tailor-made for evaluating particular consequences or alternatives.

## ■ Input Management

To this point, we have focused on the organization and accessibility of computerized information. Now let's look at the input function in detail.

Inputs include all the numerical, text, voice, and image data that enter the decision support system. Systematic accumulation of pertinent, timely, and accurate data is essential to the success of a decision support system. Clearly, the input function must be managed.

Decision support system managers, systems analysts, and programmers are responsible for the system as a whole, but many functions within an organization provide input data. Marketing researchers, accountants, corporate librarians, sales personnel, production managers, and many others within the organization help to collect data and provide input for the decision support system.

Input data can come from both internal and external sources. Exhibit 2.2 shows four major sources of input for marketing data: internal records, proprietary marketing research, marketing intelligence, and outside vendors/external distributors of data. Each source can provide valuable input.

Internal records, such as accounting reports of sales and inventory figures, provide considerable data that may become useful information for marketing managers. An effective data collection system establishes orderly procedures to ensure that data about costs, shipments, inventory, sales, and other aspects of regular operations are routinely collected and entered into the computer.

Marketing research has already been defined as a broad set of procedures and methods. To clarify the decision support system concept, let's consider a narrower view of marketing research. **Proprietary marketing research** emphasizes the company's gathering of new data. Few proprietary marketing research procedures and methods are conducted regularly or continuously. Instead, research projects conducted to study specific company problems generate data; this is proprietary marketing research. Most of this book deals with this kind of marketing research. Providing managers with nonroutine data that otherwise would not be available is a major function of proprietary marketing research.

The term *marketing intelligence* has been defined in a variety of ways. A restrictive and specialized definition works best: A marketing intelligence system consists of a network of sources and regular procedures by which marketing executives obtain everyday information about nonrecurrent developments in the external marketing environment.

For example, Procter & Gamble discovered a need to change its slogan for Puritan Oil, "Make it his oil for life," through marketing intelligence. Ongoing investigations of consumer complaints registered via the company's toll-free telephone number indicated that the slogan was considered sexist. Consumers didn't like the new theme, even though it was only slightly changed from the earlier "Make it your oil for life." Toll-free numbers and consumer correspondence are two of many sources of intelligence about external environments.

Sales forces work in firms' external environments and thus routinely provide essential marketing intelligence. Sales representatives' call reports frequently alert managers to changes in competitors' prices and new-product offerings.

Outside vendors and external distributors market information as their products. Many organizations specialize in the collection and publication of high-quality information. One outside vendor, the A. C. Nielsen Company, provides television program ratings, audience counts, and information about the demographic composition of television viewer groups. Other vendors specialize in the distribution of information. Public libraries have always purchased information, traditionally in the form of books, and they have served as distributors of this information.

**Proprietary marketing research**
A data collection system that gathers new data to investigate specific problems.

| ■ **Exhibit 2.2** | Source | Example |
|---|---|---|
| **Four Major Sources of Marketing Input for Decision Support Systems** | Internal records | Orders, goods-in-process inventory, product-line sales histories |
| | Proprietary marketing research | Survey findings, test-market results |
| | Marketing intelligence | Competition price changes, new industry technology |
| | Outside vendors and external distributors | Industry sales trends, competitors' market shares, demographic trends |

## WHAT WENT RIGHT?

### Insight from Microsoft

One of the first ways Microsoft began using information tools internally was by phasing out printed computer reports. In many companies, when you go into a top executive's office you see books of bound computer printouts with monthly financial numbers, dutifully filed away on a shelf. At Microsoft, those numbers are made available only on a computer screen. When someone wants more detail, he or she can examine it by time period, locale, or almost any other way. When we first put the financial reporting system on-line, people started looking at the numbers in new ways. For example, they began analyzing why our market share in one geographic area was different from our share somewhere else. As we all started working with the information, we discovered errors. Our data-processing group apologized. "We're very sorry about these mistakes," they said, "but we've been compiling and distributing these numbers once a month for five years and these same problems were there all along and no one mentioned them." People hadn't really been using the print information enough to discover the mistakes.

Media representatives often provide useful data about their audiences' characteristics and purchasing behavior. *Advertising Age, The Wall Street Journal, Sales and Marketing Management,* and other trade and business-oriented publications are important sources of information. These publications keep managers up to date regarding the economy, competitors' activities, and other aspects of the marketing environment.

Companies called *data specialists* record and store certain marketing information. Computer technology has changed the way many of these organizations supply data, favoring the development of computerized databases.

### ■ Computerized Data Archives

Historically, collections of organized and readily retrievable data were available in published form at libraries. The *Statistical Abstract of the United States,* which is filled with tables of statistical facts, provides a characteristic example. Printed copies of this book can be found in most public and corporate libraries. In recent years, the *Statistical Abstract* has also become available in a digital format on CD-ROM, and certain portions are available on the Internet. The entire 1990 census is also available in print and on CD-ROM, and certain databases can be accessed on the Internet. In the 21st century, even more data will be stored in digitized form in computerized data archives.

Today businesspeople can use personal computers and modems to access on-line information services, such as Nexis/Lexis or Dow Jones News Retrieval, without leaving their offices. The amount of data accessible by computer is extensive.

### ■ Commercial Database Search Systems

Numerous database search and retrieval systems are available as subscription services or in libraries. Computer-assisted literature searches have made the traditional method of searching for relevant publications—thumbing through a library card catalog—obsolete. Modern library patrons command a computer to search databases from a range of vendors. University students may find computer terminals in the main lobbies of libraries, in dormitories, and at many other campus locations. A researcher can query the library computer to learn whether the library owns a particular book and whether that book is on the shelf or checked out. This process obviously is much faster than using a card catalog.

Computerized database searches offer the most efficient and exhaustive way to find published information. Major wholesalers or on-line vendors of bibliographic databases include BRS (BRS Information Technologies), DIALOG (Dialog Information Services, Inc.), NEXIS (Mead Data Central, Inc.), ORBIT (ORBIT Search Services), and Dow Jones News/Retrieval Services. These services provide access to computer-readable databases for business executives and scholars.

DIALOG, for example, maintains more than 350 databases. A typical database may have a million or more records, each consisting of a one- or two-paragraph abstract that summarizes the major points of a published article along with bibliographic information. One of DIALOG's databases, ABI/INFORM, abstracts important articles in more than 800 current business and management journals.

Our discussion thus far has focused on bibliographic databases, but many computerized archives provide more than abstracts of published articles and journals. The *New York Times* database and the Dow Jones/Text-Search Services are full-text databases that allow the retrieval of an entire article or document. ABI/INFORM offers full-text versions of the articles on CD-ROM.

Several types of databases from outside vendors and external distributors are so fundamental to decision support systems that they deserve further explanation.

**Statistical Databases**  Statistical databases contain numerical data for market analysis and forecasting. Statistical databases are exemplified by geographical information systems and scanner databases.

*Geographic Databases*  A geographic information system is a decision support system that maps geographic areas by demographic, sales, and other relevant marketing variables. For various purposes and in various ways, these systems use powerful software to prepare computer maps using databases of relevant variables. Companies such as Claritas, Urban Decision Systems, and CACI all offer geographic/demographic databases that are widely used in industry.

*Scanner Databases*  As they total customers' purchases, optical character recognition systems read bar codes such as the Universal Product Code (UPC) and store valuable data about the marketing environment in computers. Optical scanners in supermarkets and other retail outlets provide a wealth of product and brand sales information collectively known as *scanner data* or *single-source data*. (The term *single-source data* refers to the ability of these systems to gather several types of interrelated data, such as purchase, sales promotion, or advertising frequency data, from a single source in a format that will facilitate integration, comparison, and analysis.) As the number of scanner-equipped stores continues to increase, scanner systems are replacing mechanical systems for in-store auditing. Substituting mechanized recordkeeping for human recordkeeping results in greater accuracy and rapid feedback about store activity.

One disadvantage of single-source scanner data is that the largest stores, such as supermarkets and warehouse retailers, are most likely to have scanner systems, causing the sample of stores to be less representative than in-store audits. Grocery and drug retailers are also more likely than other types of retailers to have scanner systems. However, things are changing. A. C. Nielsen and the National Housewares Manufacturers Association formed a partnership to provide data generated by the Universal Product Codes scanned at housewares retailers' checkouts. Nevertheless, if a large percentage of a product category's sales occur in small stores or in vending machines (for example, candy) that tend not to have scanners, the marketer should be aware that the scanner data may not be representative.

The UPC contains information about the category of goods (differentiating grocery and drug items, for example), the manufacturer, and product identification based on size, flavor, color, and so on. As the laser beam at the checkout counter reads the code, a computer-assisted sales receipt is printed with price and other descriptive information, and the computer records this information in its memory for inventory management and analytical purposes.

**Financial Databases**   Competitors' and customers' financial data, such as income statements and balance sheets, may interest marketing managers. These are easy to access in financial databases. CompuStat publishes a financial database of extensive financial data about thousands of companies broken down by industry and other criteria. To illustrate the depth of this pool of information, CompuStat's Global Advantage offers extensive data on 6,650 companies in 31 countries in Europe, the Pacific Basin, and North America.

**Image and Video Databases**   In the twenty-first century, image and video databases of digitally stored photographs and films will be commonplace. Today the University of Illinois offers up-to-the-minute weather forecasts and hourly updated satellite photographs of weather conditions in every city in the United States.

Video databases will have a major impact on the marketing of many goods and services. For example, marketing of health care will radically change, especially in rural areas, when computerized patient records, including X rays and other medical images, become instantly available to any hospital or faraway medical specialist.[5] Imagine the value of video databases to advertising agencies' decision support systems!

Exhibit 2.3 describes the most popular on-line information services. For a more extensive listing, see the *Gale Directory of Databases*.[6]

## ■ NETWORKS AND ELECTRONIC DATA INTERCHANGE

Although personal computers work independently, they can connect through networks to other computers. Networking involves linking two or more computers to share data and software.

**Electronic data interchange (EDI)** systems integrate one company's computer system directly with another company's system. Today much input to a company's decision support system comes through networks from other companies' computers. Companies such as Computer Technology Corporation and Microelectronics market data services that allow corporations to exchange business information with suppliers or customers.

**Electronic data interchange (EDI)**
The process of integrating one company's computer system with another company's system.

## ■ WHAT IS THE INTERNET?

**Internet**
A worldwide network of computers that allows users access to information and documents from distant sources.

The **Internet** is a worldwide network of computers that allows users access to information and documents from distant sources. It is a combination of a worldwide communication system and the world's largest public library for a seemingly endless range of information. It has changed the way millions of people think about getting and distributing information.

It is estimated that more than 10 million computers and 100 million users are linked across the Internet. The number of users doubles annually, making it the fastest-growing communications medium in history.[7] Many people believe the Internet is the prototype of a new communications infrastructure that will be as widespread and influential as the international telephone network, satellite television, and the postal system.[8]

Computer communication and resource discovery are two central functions of the Internet. For example, users send messages on the Internet via **e-mail** (electronic mail) to ask questions of experts or communicate in other ways with individuals who share similar interests. Just as a letter delivered by a postal worker requires an address, so does e-mail.

**e-mail**
Electronic mail that users send over the Internet to ask questions of experts or communicate in other ways with individuals who share similar interests.

■ **Exhibit 2.3**  **Selected On-line Information Services and Examples of Their Databases**

| Information On-line Service | Selected Sample Databases | Type of Data |
|---|---|---|
| BRS (BRS Information Technologies) | ABI/INFORM* | Abstracts of significant articles in over 800 business and management journals |
| | Disclosure Database | Financial data on over 12,500 publicly held companies that file reports with the Securities and Exchange Commission |
| | PTS PROMT | Abstracts of articles on industries, companies, products, markets, and similar topics in leading business/trade journals, with some full-text records |
| DIALOG (Dialog Information Services, Inc.) | ABI/INFORM* | See description under BRS |
| | ASI (American Statistics Index) | Abstracts and indexes of federal government statistical publications |
| | Business Dateline* | Full texts of articles in U.S. and Canadian regional business publications |
| | CENDATA | Current economic and demographic statistics and facts from U.S. Census data |
| | Disclosure Database | See description under BRS |
| | Investext* | Full texts of reports on companies and industries prepared by investment analysts in investment banks and other financial research organizations |
| | PTS Marketing & Advertising Reference Service (MARS) | Abstracts of articles on marketing and advertising for consumer goods and services, including advertising as a function and market strategies |
| | PTS PROMT | See description under BRS |
| | Trade and Industry Index | Index of over 300 trade, industry, and commercial journals, with selected coverage of many more, plus local and regional publications |
| NEXIS (Mead Data Central, Inc.) | ABI/INFORM* | See description under BRS |
| | Advertising Age | Full texts of articles in this basic advertising weekly |
| | Business Dateline | See description under DIALOG |
| | New York Times* | Full text for articles in this newspaper |
| | Value Line Datafile* | Financial facts about some 1,800 companies in over 80 industries |
| Dow Jones News/Retrieval (Dow Jones & Company) | Advertising Age | See description under NEXIS |
| | Business Dateline* | See description under NEXIS |
| | Disclosure Database | See description under BRS |
| | Dow Jones Enhanced Current Quotes | Current price quotations for stocks, bonds, options, mutual funds, Treasury issues. Related databases cover current and historical price quotations for stocks, bonds, futures, and indexes. |
| | Dow Jones Text-Search Services | Six files, which include full text in *The Wall Street Journal, Washington Post, Barron's, Business Week,* and other business periodicals |
| DRI/McGraw-Hill (DRI/McGraw-Hill Data Products Division) | DRI Japanese Forecast | Historical time-series and forecast data on the Japanese economy |

*These databases are also on CD-ROM.

An *e-mail address* consists of two parts, separated by the *at* symbol (@). The name of the user's mailbox is on the left-hand side. The name of the system on which the mailbox resides is on the right-hand side. System, or *domain,* names have two or more fields, separated by periods, and can follow many different naming schemes, such as by country (.us, .jp) or by type of activity (.com, .org).

The domain is typically a company name, an institutional name, or an organizational name associated with the host computer. For example, *Forbes'* Internet edition is located at forbes.com. The *com* indicates this domain is a commercial site. Educational sites end in *edu,* government sites end in *gov,* and other types of organizations end in *org.* (Some new host names, such as *info* and *store,* have been proposed and may be in effect by the time this book is published.)

The Internet allows users to instantaneously and effortlessly access a great deal of information. Noncommercial and commercial organizations make a wealth of data and other resources available on the Internet. For example, the U.S. Library of Congress provides full text of all versions of House and Senate legislation and full text of the *Congressional Record.* The Internal Revenue Service makes it possible to download an income tax form. Harcourt Brace College Publishers and The Dryden Press have an on-line directory (http://www.hbcollege.com) that allows college professors to access information about the company and its textbooks.

### ■ A Network of Connected Computers

The Internet began in 1969 as an experimental hookup among computers at Stanford University, the University of California at Santa Barbara, the University of California at Los Angeles, and the University of Utah in conjunction with the Department of Defense.[9] The Defense Department was involved because it wanted a research and development communications network that could survive infrastructure destruction resulting from severe battlefield conditions. The Internet gradually grew into a nationwide network of connected computers and today is a worldwide network often referred to as the "Information Superhighway." The Internet has no central computer; instead, each message sent bears an address code that lets the sender forward a message to a desired destination from any computer linked to the Net.[10] Many benefits of the Internet arise because the Internet is a collection of thousands of small networks, both domestic and overseas, rather than a single computer operation. These many small networks contain millions of databases that are accessible to Internet users, mostly without fees.

**Host**
A computer that one or more people can use directly by logging on to a personal computer connected to it to access network services.

**Server**
A computer that provides services on the Internet.

The Internet consists of host computers that access servers to reach data.[11] A **host** is a computer that performs user services, either client or server, such as e-mail and World Wide Web access. A host may be dedicated to one person or be shared among many. A client computer is the requester of an activity that mediates between the end-user and a remote server. Thus, the client computer asks for work, but the **server,** the computer that provides services on the Internet, does the actual work. The same computer can do double duty as client and server. A personal computer usually is only a client; however, a campus mainframe can be both a server for local users and a client allowing access to computers elsewhere on the Internet.

There are several types of servers. A *file server* contains documents and programs that can be accessed and downloaded via the host to a user's own personal computer. A *list server* permits subscribers to a mailing list to communicate with others around the globe. A *user discussion server* allows multiple users to communicate in real-time with others. Note that the same university mainframe that provides access for the faculty may also act as a server, providing the faculty and other Internet users with a collection of publicly accessible files.

In the following pages, we discuss the World Wide Web and how to use the Internet. However, bear in mind that the Internet is constantly changing. Many aspects of the Internet described here, especially home page addresses, may be out of date by the time this book is published. The Internet of today will not be the Internet of tomorrow.

### ■ Navigating the Internet

Anyone with a computer and a modem can access the Internet by subscribing to a gateway company, such as America Online or Southwestern Bell Internet Services, known as an *Internet Service Provider (ISP).* In addition, many college and university campus networks offer Internet access either in common user laboratories or through off-campus dial-up services.

One of the most important portions of the Internet is a retrieval system called the World Wide Web. The **World Wide Web (WWW),** a graphical interface system of thousands of interconnected pages (documents), allows access to all the resources of the Internet from one interface displayed on any computer screen. Over the past few years, academic associations, government agencies, universities, newspapers, TV networks, libraries, and corporations have set up documents consisting of graphical pages of information on servers connected to the Internet. The introductory page, or opening screen, is called the **home page** because it provides basic information about the purpose of the document along with a menu of selections, or **links,** that lead to other screens with more specific information. Thus, each page can have connections, or **hyperlinks,** to other pages, which may be on any computer connected to the Internet. World Wide Web users may view information on their host computers or on a computer halfway around the world. The World Wide Web allows users to point and click where they want to go and to call up video, sound bytes, and graphics from different participating computer networks around the world.

The World Wide Web is a do-it-yourself hypermedia publishing system.[12] A *hypermedia publishing system* is based on pages of text and images that are stored on thousands of computers around the world. If you look at a raw page, you will see normal paragraphs of information, along with a code known as *HTML* (Hypertext Markup Language) that provides references to other pages as well as graphics images, video clips, and sound clips stored on the host computer or on computers thousands of miles away. *HTTP* (Hypertext Transfer Protocol) is a method for transferring and displaying HTML information on the Internet. *JAVA* is programming language that also helps to display information on the Internet.

**World Wide Web**
A portion of the Internet that is a graphical interface system of thousands of interconnected pages, or documents.

**Home page**
A single Web page that serves as the "main entrance" to all of an organization's Internet documents.

**Link**
A connection to another screen or document.

**Hyperlink**
An element in an electronic document that, when a user clicks on it, changes the screen to another document.

■ It has been said that "Computing is not about computers anymore. It is about living."[13] Certainly this holds true for researchers investigating secondary data. Seemingly overnight, marketplace data have become digital. The PointCast Network is a personalized information service that allows the user to select what types of information will automatically be sent to his or her computer.

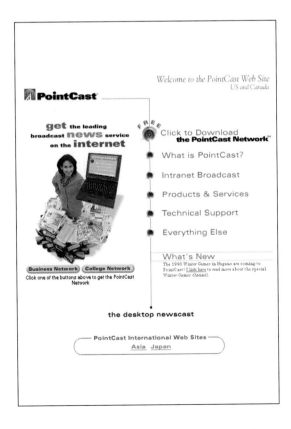

**Web browser**
A software program that allows a user to locate and display Web pages.

To access the World Wide Web, the typical home user needs a **Web browser.** A Web browser is a software program with a graphical user interface that allows a user to locate and display Web pages.[14]

Popular Web browsers, such as Netscape Navigator and Microsoft Explorer, are menu-based software systems that present the user with a menu of the files on a particular server and make it easy to move from server to server on the Internet (often called *navigating the Net, navigation,* or *surfing*). These Web browsers allow even an Internet novice to search for information by simply using point-and-click graphics that resemble the familiar Windows or Macintosh interface. The links to other documents are usually highlighted in another color, with underlining, or with a unique icon.

For example, Netscape may link the user to a series of expanded menus containing descriptions of the contents of various files and documents around the Internet. Using a mouse, the user points to highlighted words or colorful icons and then clicks the mouse button to immediately go to the file, regardless of what server it is stored on. At this point, the user can either read or download the material. By clicking on "US Government Information Servers" in one electronic document, for example, a Netscape user may connect to a computer with more information in Washington, D.C. With a few more clicks, the user can peruse files from the United States Census or the Small Business Administration.

**Uniform Resource Locater (URL)**
The global address of a Web site on the World Wide Web.

Most Web browsers also allow the user to directly enter a **Uniform Resource Locator,** or **URL,** into the Web program. The URL is really just a Web site address that Web browsers recognize. A *Web site* is any computer host that serves as a location that can be accessed with the browser software. Many Web sites allow any user or visitor to access their Web pages without previous approval. However, many commercial sites require that the user have a valid account and password before granting access.

**Search engine**
A computerized "search and retrieval" system that allows anyone to search the World Wide Web for information in a particular way.

A researcher who wants to find a particular site or document on the Internet or is just looking for a resource list on a particular subject can use one of the many Internet search engines.[15] A **search engine** is a computerized "search and retrieval" system that allows

■ Using a search engine such as Yahoo enables a user to search by selecting from menus of categories or by typing search strings. The page shows that as each menu comes up, the computer user makes a selection and the search engine progressively narrows it until, eventually, the user accesses a specific Web site.

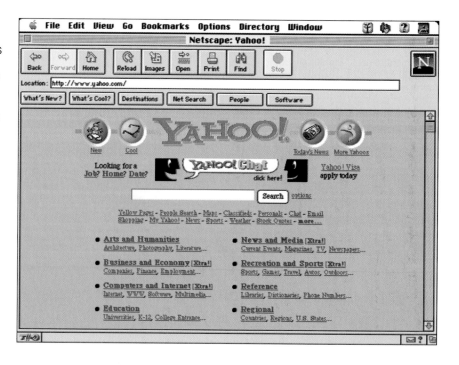

users to search the World Wide Web for information in a particular way. Some search titles or headers of documents, others search words in the documents themselves, and still others search other indexes or directories. Yahoo is one of the most popular search engines. A person using Yahoo (http://www.yahoo.com) will find lists of broad topics, such as Art, Business, Entertainment, and Government. Clicking on one of these topics leads to other subdirectories or home pages. An alternative way to use a search engine is to type key words and phrases associated with the search and wait for a list of Web sites to be displayed. InfoSeek (http://www.infoseek.com) is another of the Internet's most comprehensive and accurate WWW search engines.

Exhibit 2.4 describes some of the most popular search engines.

## ■ Push Technology

**Push technology**
An information technology that delivers personalized content to the viewer's desktop, using computer software known as smart agents.

**Smart agent**
Software that is capable of learning an Internet user's preferences and automatically searches out information in selected Web sites and then distributes the information.

**Push technology** delivers content to the viewer's desktop, using computer software known as smart agents or intelligent agents to find information without the user having to do the searching, or stores entire Web sites complete with images and links on a user's computer for later viewing.[16] **Smart agent** software is capable of learning an Internet user's preferences and automatically searches out information in selected Web sites and then distributes the information.

The PointCast Network provides an example. This company is a pioneer in the development of personalized Web pages through push technology. PointCast's software "surf the Web" automatically sends personalized information to an individual's computer. Users get stock quotes for their personal portfolio and information about selected sports teams, local weather, and designated news categories. Users customize the sections of the service they want delivered. Push technology continuously updates the information and displays it at the user's request. With PointCast, advertising messages for products that coincide with the computer user's interests appear in the upper right-hand corner of each screen.

Push technology may employ surveys of customer preferences or they may use cookies to learn users' interests. *Cookies* or "magic cookies" are small computer files that a content provider can save onto the computer of someone who visits a Web site. The cookies allow a computer connected to the Internet to track Web sites visited by the user and stores these Web sites into a file that uses the cookie in place of the user's name, which, in most cases, the user never knows. If a person looks up a weather report by keying in a zip code using Time-Warner's Pathfinder, the computer notes that. This is a clue to where the person lives or wishes he or she could live. The computer notes whether a user looks up stock quotes (though Time-Warner does not capture the symbols of the specific stocks the person follows). If the person visits the Netly News, Pathfinder will record the person's interest in technology. Then, the next time this person visits, Pathfinder might serve up an ad for a modem or an on-line brokerage firm or a restaurant in Mountain View, California, depending on what the computer managed to learn.[17]

| ■ Exhibit 2.4 | Search Engine | Address |
| --- | --- | --- |
| **Popular Search Engines** | Hotbot | http://www.hotbot.com |
| | Excite | http://www.excite.com |
| | Yahoo | http://www.yahoo.com |
| | Lycos | http://www.lycos.com |
| | Alta Vista | http://www.altavista.digital.com |
| | InfoSeek | http://www.infoseek.com |
| | WebCrawler | http://www.webcrawler.com |

## ◼ Intranets

**Intranet**

A company's private data network that uses Internet standards and technology.

An **intranet** is a company's private data network that uses Internet standards and technology.[18] The information on an intranet—data, graphics, even video and voice—is available only inside the organization. Thus, a key difference between the Internet and an intranet is that "firewalls," or security software programs, are installed to limit access to only those employees authorized to enter the system.[19]

A company's intranet uses Internet features, such as electronic mail, Web pages, and browsers, to build a communications and data resource at the company itself.[20] Company information is accessible using the same point-and-click technology found on the Internet. Managers and employees use links to get complete, up-to-date information. An intranet lets authorized personnel, some of whom previously were isolated on departmental local area networks, look at product drawings, employee newsletters, sales forecasts, and other sources of company information. Whether the information comes from a spreadsheet or a word processing document is not an issue for the user of an intranet. Managers and employees do not have to worry about the format of the information.

In short, setting up an intranet involves adding Web-like functionality to an organization's existing global information system.

## ◼ SUMMARY

Increased global competition and technological advances in interactive media have spurred development of global information systems. A global information system is an organized collection of computer hardware, software, data, and personnel designed to capture, store, update, manipulate, analyze, and immediately display information about worldwide business activity.

Marketing managers distinguish between data and information. Data are simply facts or recorded measures of certain phenomena; information refers to a body of facts in a format suitable for decision making or in a context that defines relationships between two pieces of data.

Information can be evaluated based on four characteristics: relevance, quality, timeliness, and completeness. Relevant information provides the information a marketer needs. High-quality information is accurate, valid, and reliable; it presents a good picture of reality. Timely information is obtained at the right time. Computerized information systems can record events and present information soon after a transaction takes place, thus improving timeliness. Complete information presents the right quantity of information. Marketing managers must have sufficient information to relate all aspects of their decisions together.

A computer-based marketing decision support system helps decision makers confront problems through direct interaction with databases and analytical software. A decision support system stores data and transforms them into organized information that it makes easily accessible to marketing managers.

A database is a collection of raw data arranged logically and organized in a form that can be stored and processed by a computer. Marketing data come from four major sources: internal records, proprietary marketing research, marketing intelligence, and outside vendors and external distributors. Each source can provide valuable input.

Numerous database search and retrieval systems are available by subscription or in libraries. Computer-assisted database searching has made the collection of external data faster and easier. Marketers refer to many different types of databases.

Although personal computers work independently, they can connect to other computers in networks to share data and software. Electronic data interchange (EDI) allows one company's computer system to join directly to another company's system.

The Internet is a worldwide network of computers that allows users access to information and documents from distant sources. It is a combination of a worldwide communication system and the world's largest public library. The World Wide Web (WWW), a system of thousands of interconnected pages, or documents, can be easily accessed with Web browsers and search engines.

## ■ Key Terms and Concepts

| | |
|---|---|
| Global information system | Server |
| Data | World Wide Web (WWW) |
| Information | Home page |
| Decision support system | Link |
| Database | Hyperlink |
| Software | Web Browser |
| Proprietary marketing research | Uniform Resource Locator (URL) |
| Electronic data interchange (EDI) | Search engine |
| Internet | Push technology |
| e-mail | Smart agent |
| Host | Intranet |

## ■ Questions

1. What is the difference between data and information? Provide examples of both.
2. What are the characteristics of useful information?
3. What are the key elements of a decision support system?
4. What types of databases might be found in the following organizations?
    (a) Holiday Inn
    (b) Las Vegas gambling casino
    (c) Anheuser-Busch
5. If a manufacturer sells directly to retailers, what type of marketing intelligence information would you expect to find in the company's sales force call reports?
6. What types of questions could a brand manager of a packaged goods firm expect to answer with the company's decision support system?
7. What makes a decision support system successful?
8. What are the four major sources of input for a decision support system?
9. Go to your college's or university's library. Provide three examples of computerized databases that are available.
10. In your own words, describe the Internet. What is its purpose?

## EXPLORING THE INTERNET

1. Go to your school's computer center to learn how to obtain an e-mail address and how to establish an account that allows you to access the Internet. Get instructions explaining how you can get on (and off) the Internet using your local computer system.

2. The Spider's Apprentice is a Web site that provides many useful tips about using search engines. To learn the ins and outs of search engines, go to:

    http://www.monash.com/spidap.html

3. Use a Web browser to visit Yahoo at:

   http://www.yahoo.com

   You will see a list of the major search categories. Click on Business and Economics. What additional search categories become available to you?

4. Use a Web browser to visit the Small Business Administration's home page at:

   http://www.sbaonline.sba.gov

   What type of information can be accessed?

---

 ## CASE 2.1   Barclays Bank Group PLC

Barclays Bank Group PLC has its headquarters in London and employs 105,000 people worldwide. Its assets exceed £127 billion ($197 billion). Barclays sees political boundaries blurring as it expands its business throughout Europe and around the globe.[21] Barclays' chief information officer, Trevor Nicholas, says the bank envisions becoming an "integrated worldwide entity that provides top-quality services to multinational customers."

The European Union, formerly known as the Common Market, is an economic community that consists of Austria, Belgium, Denmark, Finland, France, Germany, Greece, Ireland, Italy, Luxembourg, the Netherlands, Portugal, Spain, Sweden, and the United Kingdom of Great Britain and Northern Ireland. Although Europeans have been working to build a borderless economy composed of its member nations for more than 30 years, the end of 1992 marked the elimination of national trade barriers, differences in tax and banking laws, conflicting product standards, and other restrictions that separated the member nations.

Today the European Union is the largest single market in the world, with total spending of more than $44 trillion.[22] A single market with more than 325 million consumers offers an enormous opportunity for a European bank like Barclays. With the unification of Europe, the bank's plans for Europe are part of its overall strategy to position itself as one of the leading players in the world financial market.

Extending its global reach has required Barclays to restructure basic operations in Britain. Information systems are essential to that revamp. "We are in the process of building a $245 million global banking system and electronic mail network for 3,800 users," says Nicholas. This system will provide standard applications and electronic mail facilities to country branch offices.

To do this, Nicholas wants to establish standards for data that will enable information flows from all locations to be coherently managed and exploited. Such coherent management, he says, does not imply integration. "To give the semblance of integration, you must modularize systems, not integrate them."

The backbone of Barclays' global banking system will be its telecommunications network, which will span some 30 countries.

### Questions

1. What databases would you expect to find in Barclays' global information system?
2. How important is Barclays' global information system to its goal to achieve a competitive market position as one of the leading financial firms in the world market?
3. What does Barclays mean by "modularize systems"?

---

### ■ Endnotes

[1] Angeline Pantages, "TI's Global Window." DATAMATION, September 1989.

[2] See Thomas G. Exter, "The Next Step Is Called GIS," *American Demographics Desk Reference,* May 1992, p. 2.

[3] Steven Crofts, "Business Intelligence," special advertising section, *Fortune,* October 27, 1997, p. s4.

[4] The following is a more detailed explanation of data warehousing: "Bill Inmon is often quoted and referenced for his ideas on data warehouses. . . . In Inmon's eyes a warehouse has a multi-tiered structure of data/information . . . which includes examples from employee data. Snapshots of current, detailed data from operational systems are extracted, reformatted, and loaded to the warehouse tables. These detailed data form

the basis, the foundation for the other layers. Then, from the detailed data can be developed one or more layers of summarized data tables (which he would call 'lightly summarized' and 'highly summarized'). Also, as detailed data are historically accrued in the warehouse, the older snapshots can be archived to a historical layer. Inmon also adds a supporting element of metadata—descriptions of the data and of the data transformation rules—to the mix. This descriptive/help information enables much greater understanding of the data by all warehouse users." Source: Michael Bosworth, "Rolling out a Data Warehouse Quickly at Umass: A Simple Start to a Complex Task," *Cause/Effect,* Spring 1995. See also Bill Inmon, "The Structure of the Information Warehouse," *Data Management Review,* August 1993, pp. 5–8.

[5]John Markoff, "Building the Electronic Superhighway," *New York Times,* January 24, 1993, p. F-6.

[6]*Gale Directory of Databases* (Detroit: Gale Research, Inc., 2 volumes).

[7]Author's estimates based on calculations from data in Thomas A. Stewart, "The Netplex: It's a New Silicon Valley," *Fortune,* March 7, 1994, p. 98.

[8]Nicholas Negroponte, *Being Digital* (New York: Knopf, 1995), p. 6; Clive Sanford, *Exploring the Internet* (Burr Ridge, Ill.: Irwin, 1995), p. 3.

[9]Patrick A. Moore and Ronald E. Milliman, "Application of the Internet in Marketing Education" (Paper presented to the Southwest Marketing Association, Houston, Texas, 1995).

[10]Rick Tetzeli, "The Internet and Your Business," *Fortune,* March 7, 1994, p. 92.

[11]Moore and Milliman, "Application of the Internet."

[12]Michael Himowitz, "Prodigy Software Untangles Internet Web," *Tulsa World,* January 29, 1995, p. B-12.

[13]Negroponte, *Being Digital,* p. 6.

[14]SpectraCom's Web Site Services: http://www.spectracom.com/webbar.gif

[15]Adapted from Internet information published by the Netscape Communications Company (http://www.netscape.com).

[16]Lee Fleming, "Digital Delivery: Pushing Content to the Desktop," downloaded from the Digital Information Group, 1997.

[17]Joshua Quittner, "Invasion of Privacy," *Time,* August 25, 1997.

[18]"Three Visions of an Electronic Future," *New York Times,* March 24, 1996, p. F-22.

[19]Paul Schneider, "Behind Company Walls: It's the Intranet," *Arizona Business Gazette,* March 7, 1996.

[20]"Technology: Sun Microsystems Planning to Unveil 'Intranet' Products," *The Wall Street Journal,* March 26, 1996.

[21]Linda Runyan, "Borderless Banking Draws Its Interest," *DATAMATION,* April 1, 1990, pp. 98–99.

[22]Bryan Iwamoto, "1992: A Wake-up Call," *Express,* September 1989, p. 24.

# THE MARKETING RESEARCH PROCESS: AN OVERVIEW

**WHAT YOU WILL LEARN IN THIS CHAPTER:**

To classify marketing research as either exploratory research, descriptive research, or causal research.

To list the stages in the marketing research process.

To identify and briefly discuss the various decision alternatives available to the researcher during each stage of the research process.

To explain the difference between a research project and a research program.

Suppose you are assigned to take charge of the marketing research effort when R. J. Reynolds Tobacco Company is developing an almost smokeless cigarette. You are told that the smokeless cigarette does not burn tobacco and greatly reduces the production of harmful substances linked to health concerns. R. J. Reynolds' executives believe it will be the world's cleanest cigarette. The new cigarette is lit like a normal cigarette; then a carbon heat source at its tip generates warm air that passes through tobacco extract, flavorings, and glycerine to form smoke that tastes like cigarette smoke. The cigarette includes carbon monoxide and nicotine at levels similar to low-tar brands now on the market. However, because tobacco does not burn, most of the combustion products linked to cancer and other health risks are eliminated or greatly reduced. The new cigarette produces almost no sidestream smoke, and after the first few puffs there is no ash and no odor. Further, the exhaled smoke dissipates quickly. The cigarette does not burn down. It remains lit for as long as a king-size cigarette does and extinguishes itself.

Will a smokeless cigarette appeal to smokers? Will nonsmokers be more tolerant of a smokeless cigarette? In what situations will a smokeless cigarette be preferred to a regular cigarette? The research process can help answer questions such as these, but what form should the research take? Should a laboratory taste test be conducted? Should a survey of nonsmokers be part of the research strategy?

This chapter discusses how managers make decisions about research strategies and tactics. It overviews the types of research designs and briefly discusses the stages in the research process.

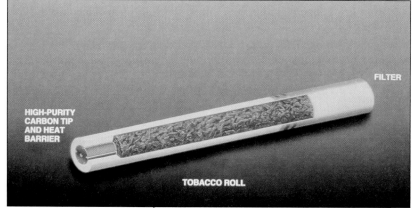

HIGH-PURITY CARBON TIP AND HEAT BARRIER

FILTER

TOBACCO ROLL

## ■ INFORMATION REDUCES UNCERTAINTY

Marketing research provides information to reduce uncertainty. It helps focus decision making. Sometimes marketing researchers know exactly what their marketing problems are and design careful studies to test specific hypotheses. For example, a soft-drink company introducing a new, clear citrus drink might want to know whether a gold or a silver label would make the packaging more effective. This problem is fully defined, and an experiment may be designed to answer the marketing question with little preliminary investigation.

In more ambiguous circumstances, management may be totally unaware that a marketing problem exists. For example, suppose McDonald's managers notice that Mo's Burgers, a competitor in the Japanese market, introduced Mo's Roast Katsu Burger, a roast pork cutlet drenched in traditional Japanese katsu sauce and topped with shredded cabbage. The managers may understand little about Japanese consumers' feelings about this menu item. In this case, some exploratory research will yield insights into the nature of this problem.

To understand the variety of research activity, it is beneficial to categorize the types of marketing research.

## ■ TYPES OF MARKETING RESEARCH

Marketing research can be classified on the basis of either technique or function. Experiments, surveys, and observational studies are just a few common research techniques. Classifying research by its purpose or function shows how the nature of the marketing problem influences the choice of methods. The nature of the problem will determine whether the research is (1) exploratory, (2) descriptive, or (3) causal.

### ■ The Nature of Exploratory Research

**Exploratory research**
Initial research conducted to clarify and define the nature of a problem.

**Exploratory research** is conducted to clarify the nature of ambiguous problems. Management may have discovered a general problem but may need research to gain a better understanding of the dimensions of the problem and to aid analysis. Exploratory research is not intended to provide conclusive evidence from which to determine a particular course of action. Usually exploratory research is conducted with the expectation that subsequent research will be required to provide such conclusive evidence. Rushing into detailed surveys before less expensive and more readily available sources of information have been exhausted can lead to serious mistakes.

For example, suppose a Chinese fast-food restaurant chain is considering expanding its hours and product line with a breakfast menu. Exploratory research with a small number of current customers might find a strong negative reaction to eating a spicy vegetable breakfast at a Chinese fast-food outlet. Thus, exploratory research might help crystallize a problem and identify information needed for future research.

### ■ Descriptive Research

**Descriptive research**
Research designed to describe characteristics of a population or phenomenon.

The major purpose of **descriptive research,** as the name implies, is to describe characteristics of a population or phenomenon. Marketing managers frequently need to determine who purchases a product, accurately portray the size of the market, identify competitors' actions, and so on. Descriptive research seeks to determine the answers to *who, what, when, where,* and *how* questions.

Infiniti learned from descriptive research that Americans generally start to shop for a car by considering six models. They then narrow the field and usually visit three show-rooms before they settle on a model. This process takes an average of two weeks. How-ever, buyers of luxury cars typically take twice as long to complete the decision and make a purchase. These descriptive findings, combined with knowledge that the company faced competition from dozens of luxury models on the market, influenced Infiniti to encourage dealers to enhance the quality of the consumer's shopping experience. The company made sizable investments in expanded showrooms with elegant furnishings where customers can contemplate car purchases without pressure from salespeople.[1]

Unlike exploratory research, descriptive studies are based on some previous under-standing of the nature of the research problem. Although the researcher may have a general understanding of the situation, the conclusive evidence that answers questions of fact nec-essary to determine a course of action has yet to be collected. Many circumstances require descriptive research to identify the reasons consumers give to explain the nature of things. In other words, a diagnostic analysis is performed when consumers answer questions such as "Why do you feel that way?" Although they may describe why consumers feel a certain way, the findings of a descriptive study such as this, sometimes called *diagnostics*, do not provide causal evidence. Frequently descriptive research attempts to determine the extent of differences in needs, attitudes, and opinions among subgroups.

**Causal research**
Research conducted to identify cause-and-effect relationships among variables.

### ■ Causal Research

The main goal of **causal research** is to identify cause-and-effect relationships among vari-ables. Exploratory and descriptive research normally precede cause-and-effect relationship

■ Magazines typically conduct descriptive surveys to identify the characteristics of their audience. For years *Teen* magazine managers sensed that 12- to 15-year-old girls cared a lot about fragrances, lipstick, and mascara, but they lacked any quantitative evidence. Their descriptive research found that 94.1 percent of 12- to 15-year-old girls use cream rinse/ conditioner, 86.4 percent use fragrance, and 84.9 percent use lip gloss. Of the girls using fragrance, 77 percent preferred using their own brand, 17 percent shared their brand, and 6 percent used someone else's brand. Results showed that most girls use cosmetics, brand loyalty begins early, and 12- to 15-year-olds prefer using and choosing their own brands.[2]

studies. In causal studies, researchers typically have an expectation about the relationship to be explained, such as predicting the influence of price, packaging, advertising, and the like on sales. Thus, researchers must be quite knowledgeable about the subject. Ideally the manager wants to establish that one event (say, a new package) is the means for producing another event (an increase in sales). Causal research attempts to establish that when we do one thing, another thing will follow. The word *cause* is common in everyday conversation, but from a scientific research perspective, a true causal relationship is impossible to prove. Nevertheless, researchers seek certain types of evidence to help them understand and predict relationships.

A typical causal study has management change one variable (for example, advertising) and then observe the effect on another variable (such as sales). Some evidence for causality comes from the fact that the cause precedes the effect. In other words, having an *appropriate causal order of events,* or temporal sequence, is one criterion for causality that must be met to be able to measure a relationship. If a consumer behavior theorist wishes to show that an attitude change causes a behavior change, one criterion that must be established is that attitude change must precede the behavior change in time.

**Concomitant variation**
The way in which two phenomena or events vary together.

In the preceding example, some evidence of **concomitant variation** exists because advertising and sales appear to be associated. Concomitant variation occurs when two phenomena or events vary together. When the criterion of concomitant variation is not met—that is, when no association exists among the variables—reasoning suggests that no causal relationship exists. If two events vary together, one event may be the cause; however, this by itself is not sufficient evidence for causality because the two events may have a common cause; that is, both may be influenced by a third variable. For instance, a large number of ice cream cones were sold one morning at Atlantic City's beach. That afternoon, a large number of drownings occurred. Most of us would not conclude that eating ice cream causes drownings; more likely, on that day the beach was crowded and the number of people probably influenced both ice cream sales and drownings. The effect could have been produced in other ways. Thus, causation requires more than concomitant variation and a proper time sequence between the occurrence of two events. There may be several plausible alternative explanations for the observed relationship.[3]

Consider a presidential candidate who reduces advertising expenditures near the end of the primary campaign race and wins many more delegates in the remaining primaries. To infer causality—that reducing advertising increased the number of delegates—may be inappropriate, because the presumed cause of the increase in delegates may not have been the real cause. It is more likely that near the end of the race, marginal candidates withdrew. The real cause probably was unrelated to advertising.

In these examples, the third variable that is the source of the spurious association is a very salient factor readily identifiable as the true influence of change. However, within the complex environment in which managers operate, identifying alternative or complex causal facts can be difficult. A researcher can never be completely certain that the causal explanation is adequate.

## ■ Uncertainty Influences the Type of Research

The uncertainty of the research problem is related to the type of research project. As Exhibit 3.1 illustrates, exploratory research is conducted during the early stages of decision making, when the decision-situation is ambiguous and management is very uncertain about the nature of the problem. When management is aware of the problem but lacks some knowledge, descriptive research usually results. Causal research requires sharply defined problems but uncertainty about future outcomes.

■ **Exhibit 3.1**    **Types of Marketing Research**

| | Complete Certainty | Uncertainty | Absolute Ambiguity |
|---|---|---|---|

| Degree of Problem Definition | Exploratory Research (Ambiguous Problem) | Descriptive Research (Aware of Problem) | Causal Research (Problem Clearly Defined) |
|---|---|---|---|
| Possible situation | "Our sales are declining and we don't know why." | "What kind of people are buying our product? Who buys our competitor's product?" | "Will buyers purchase more of our product in a new package?" |
| | "Would people be interested in our new-product idea?" | "What features do buyers prefer in our product?" | "Which of two advertising campaigns is more effective?" |

Note: The degree of uncertainty of the research problem determines the research methodology.

## ■ STAGES IN THE RESEARCH PROCESS

As previously noted, marketing research can take many forms, but systematic inquiry is a common thread. Systematic inquiry requires careful planning and an orderly investigation. Marketing research, like other forms of scientific inquiry, involves a sequence of highly interrelated activities. The stages of the research process overlap continuously, and it is somewhat of an oversimplification to state that every research project follows a neat, ordered sequence of activities. Nevertheless, marketing research often follows a generalized pattern. Exhibit 3.2 shows the stages: (1) problem discovery and definition, (2) planning a research design, (3) sampling, (4) gathering the data, (5) processing and analyzing the data, and (6) formulating the conclusions and preparing the report.

In practice, the stages overlap chronologically and are functionally interrelated; sometimes the later stages are completed before the earlier ones. Sometimes the earlier stages of research influence the design of the later stages.

### ■ Alternatives in the Research Process

The researcher must choose among a number of alternatives during each stage of the research process. The research process can be compared to a map.[4] On a map, some paths are better charted than others; some are difficult to travel, and some are more interesting and beautiful than others. Rewarding experiences may be gained during the journey. One must remember that there is no right or best path for all journeys. The road one takes depends on where one wants to go and the resources (money, time, labor, and so on) available for the trip. The map analogy is useful for the marketing researcher because each stage of the research process offers several paths to follow. In some instances, time constraints may dictate that the quickest path lead to appropriate research. In circumstances where money and human resources are plentiful, the appropriate path may be quite different. Exploration of the various paths of marketing research decisions is the primary purpose.

The following sections briefly describe the six stages of the research process.[5] Exhibit 3.2 shows the decisions researchers must make in each stage. Our discussion of the research process begins with problem discovery and definition, because most research projects are initiated to remedy managers' uncertainty about some aspect of the firm's marketing program.

As Exhibit 3.2 shows, the research process begins with problem discovery. Identifying the problem is the first step toward its solution. In general usage, the word *problem* suggests that something has gone wrong. Actually, the research task may be to clarify a problem, define an opportunity, or monitor and evaluate current operations. The concept of problem discovery and definition must encompass a broader context that includes analysis of opportunities. Note that the initial stage is problem *discovery* rather than *definition*. The researcher may not have a clear-cut statement of the problem at the outset of the research process; often only symptoms of the problem are apparent at that point. Sales may be declining, but management may not know the exact nature of the problem. Thus, the problem statement often is made only in general terms; what is to be investigated is not yet specifically identified.

Albert Einstein noted that "the formulation of a problem is often more essential than its solution."[6] This is good advice for marketing managers as well. Too often they concentrate on finding the right answer rather than asking the right question. Many managers do not

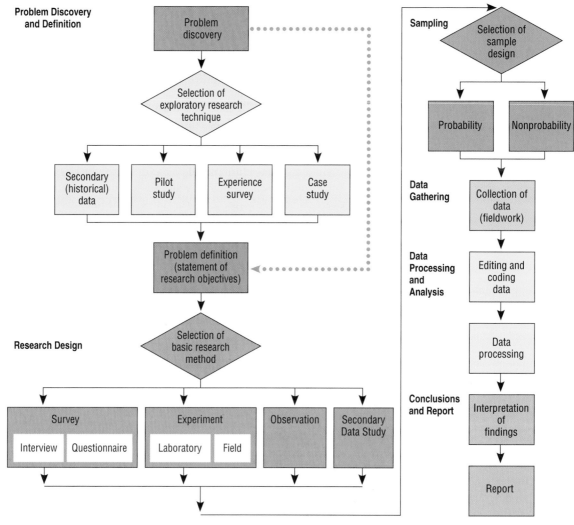

■ **Exhibit 3.2**                **Problem Discovery and Definition**

realize that defining a problem may be more difficult than solving it. In marketing research, data that are collected before the nature of the marketing problem is carefully thought out probably will not help solve the problem.

It should be emphasized that the word *problem* refers to the managerial problem (which may be a lack of knowledge about consumers or advertising effectiveness) and the information needed to help solve it. This must precede determination of the purpose of the research. Frequently the marketing researcher will not be involved until line management has discovered that some information about a particular aspect of the marketing mix is needed. Even at this point, the exact nature of the problem may be poorly defined. Once a problem area has been discovered, the marketing researcher can begin the process of precisely defining it.

**Defining the Problem**    In marketing research, the adage "a problem well defined is a problem half solved" is worth remembering. This emphasizes that an orderly definition of the research problem lends a sense of direction to the investigation. Careful attention to the **problem definition stage** allows the researcher to set the proper research objectives. If the purpose of the research is clear, the chances of collecting necessary and relevant information and omitting surplus information will be much greater.

**Ascertain the Decision Makers' Objectives**    As a staff person, the research investigator must attempt to satisfy the decision makers' objectives: those of the brand manager, sales manager, and others who requested the project. Management and organizational theorists suggest that the decision maker should express goals to the researcher in measurable terms. Unfortunately, this rarely occurs. Instead, the decision maker is likely to state his or her objectives in a vague, generalized form, leaving it up to the researcher to determine what those objectives really are. In so doing, the researcher may well be performing his or her most useful service to the decision maker.[7]

**Problem definition stage**
The stage in which management seeks to identify a clear-cut statement of the problem or opportunity.

---

## WHAT WENT WRONG?

### A Sea Horse's Tale

Once upon a time, a sea horse gathered up his seven pieces of eight and cantered out to find his fortune. Before he had traveled very far he met an Eel, who said,

"Psst. Hey, bud. Where ya goin'?"

"I'm going out to find my fortune," replied the Sea Horse, proudly.

"You're in luck," said the Eel. "For four pieces of eight you can have this speedy flipper, and then you'll be able to get there a lot faster."

"Gee, that's swell," said the sea horse, and paid the money and put on the flipper, and slithered off at twice the speed. Soon he came upon a Sponge, who said,

"Psst. Hey, bud. Where ya goin'?"

"I'm going out to find my fortune," replied the sea horse.

"You're in luck," said the Sponge. "For a small fee I will let you have this jet-propelled scooter so that you will be able to travel a lot faster."

So the Sea Horse bought the scooter with his remaining money and went zooming through the sea five times as fast. Soon he came upon a Shark, who said,

"Psst. Hey, bud. Where ya goin'?"

"I'm going out to find my fortune," replied the sea horse.

"You're in luck. If you'll take this shortcut," said the Shark, pointing to his open mouth, "you'll save yourself a lot of time."

"Gee, thanks," said the sea horse, and zoomed off into the interior of the Shark, there to be devoured.

The moral of this fable is that if You're not sure where You're going, You're liable to end up someplace else—and not even know it.

**Isolate and Identify the Problem, Not the Symptoms**    Anticipating the many influences and dimensions of a problem is impossible for any researcher or executive. For instance, a firm may have a problem with its advertising effectiveness. The possible causes of this problem may be low brand awareness, the wrong brand image, the wrong media, or perhaps too small a budget. Management's job is to isolate and identify the most likely causes. Certain occurrences that appear to be the problem may be only symptoms of a deeper problem.

### ■ The Iceberg Principle

**Iceberg principle**
The principle indicating that the dangerous part of many marketing problems is neither visible to nor understood by marketing managers.

The **iceberg principle** helps explain why so many marketing research projects begin without clear objectives or adequate problem definitions (see Exhibit 3.3). A sailor on the open sea notices only the 10 percent of an iceberg that extends above the surface of the water while 90 percent is submerged. The dangerous part of many marketing problems, like the submerged portion of the iceberg, is neither visible to nor understood by marketing managers. If the submerged portions of the problem are omitted from the problem definition (and subsequently from the research design), the decisions based on the research may be less than optimal. Omission of important information or faulty assumptions about the situation can be extremely costly. Exhibit 3.4 illustrates how symptoms may mask the nature of the true problem.

The objective of the problem definition stage is to prepare a written statement that clarifies any ambiguity about what the research is intended to accomplish. Formulating a series of research questions and hypotheses adds clarity to the statement of the marketing problem. A personal computer company made the following statement about an advertising problem:

- In the broadest sense, the marketing problem is to determine the best ways [name of the company] can communicate with potential purchasers of laptop computers.
- How familiar are consumers with the various brands of computers?
- What attitudes do consumers have toward these brands?
- How important are the various factors for evaluating the purchase of a laptop computer?
- How effective are the communications efforts of the various competitive marketers in terms of message recognition?

Research questions clarify what is perplexing managers and indicate what issues have to be resolved. A research question is the researcher's translation of the marketing problem into a specific inquiry.

---

### ■ Exhibit 3.3
**The Iceberg Principle**

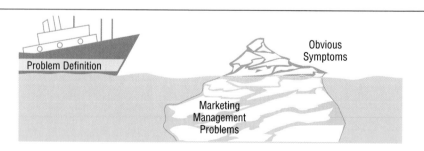

| ■ Exhibit 3.4 | **Symptoms Can Be Confusing** | | |
|---|---|---|---|
| Organization | Symptoms | Problem Definition Based on Symptom | True Problem |
| Twenty-year-old neighborhood swimming association in a major city | Membership has been declining for years. New water park with wave pool and water slides moved into town a few years ago. | Neighborhood residents prefer the expensive water park and have negative image of swimming pool. | Demographic changes: Children in this 20-year-old neighborhood have grown up. Older residents no longer swim. |
| Cellular phone manufacturer | Distributors complain prices are too high. | Investigate industrial user to learn how much prices need to be reduced. | Sales management: Distributors do not have adequate product knowledge to communicate product's value. |
| Microbrewery | Consumers prefer the taste of competitor's brand. | What type of reformulated taste is needed? | Package: Old-fashioned package influences taste perception. |

A research question can be too vague and general if stated in terms such as "Is advertising copy X better than advertising copy Y?" Advertising effectiveness can be variously measured by sales, recall of sales message, brand awareness, intention to buy, and so on. Asking a more specific research question (e.g., "Which advertisement has a higher day-after recall score?") helps the researcher design a study that will produce pertinent information.

The goal of defining the problem is to state the research questions clearly and to develop well-formulated hypotheses. A **hypothesis** is an unproven proposition or possible solution to a problem. Hypothetical statements assert probable answers to research questions. A hypothesis is a statement about the nature of the world; in its simplest form, it is a guess. A sales manager may hypothesize that salespeople who show the highest job satisfaction will be the most productive. An advertising manager may believe that if consumers' attitudes toward a product are changed in a positive direction, consumption of the product will increase. Problem statements and hypotheses are similar. Both state relationships, but problem statements are interrogative while hypotheses are declarative. Sometimes the two types of statements are almost identical in substance. An important

**Hypothesis**
An unproven proposition or supposition that tentatively explains certain facts or phenomena; a probable answer to a research question.

---

## WHAT WENT RIGHT?

### They May Want to Strangle You!

Hugh Dubberly, creative director of Netscape, advocates the following step-by-step process to help clearly define the problem to be solved:

"How do we define the problem? Begin by assembling all the relevant players in a room. Ask each player to describe the unmet need, or in other words, to suggest the cause of the problem. Write down each suggestion. Nothing you will do on the project will be more important. With each suggestion, ask in turn for its cause. And then the cause of the cause. And then the cause of the cause of the cause. Keep at it like a two-year-old. By the time everyone in the room wants to strangle you, you will very likely have found the root cause of the problem.

"After you've developed the problem statement, you need to be sure to gain consensus on it from all the relevant parties. Failure to get 'buy-in' from all the right people at this stage creates the potential for trouble later in the process. Someone who hasn't agreed on the definition up front is likely to want to change it later."

**Research objective**
The researcher's version of the marketing problem; it explains the purpose of the research in measurable terms and defines standards for what the research should accomplish.

difference, however, is that hypotheses usually are more specific than problem statements; typically they are closer to the actual research operations and empirical testing.

The **research objective** is the researcher's version of the marketing problem. After the research questions or hypotheses have been stated, the research project's objectives are derived from the problem definition. They explain the purpose of the research in measurable terms and define standards for what the research should accomplish. In addition to explaining the reasons for conducting the project, research objectives help ensure that the scope of the research project will be manageable.

In some instances, the marketing problem and the project's research objectives are identical. However, the objectives must specify the information needed to make a decision. Identifying the needed information may require that managers or researchers be extremely specific, perhaps even listing the exact wording of the question in a survey or explaining exactly what behavior might be observed or recorded in an experiment. The objective of obtaining X information about research questions from this unit should be specifically stated.

The research objectives should be limited to a manageable number. Fewer study objectives make it easier to ensure that each will be addressed fully.

**Managers Often Neglect the Problem Definition Stage**    Although problem definition probably is the most important stage of the research process, it frequently is a neglected area of marketing research. Too many researchers forget that the best place to begin a research project is at the end. Knowing what is to be accomplished determines the research process. A problem definition error or omission is likely to be a costly mistake that cannot be corrected in later stages of the process.

## ■ Exploratory Research Techniques

Exploratory research usually is conducted during the initial stage of the research process. The preliminary activities undertaken to refine the problem into researchable form need not be formal or precise. The purpose of the exploratory research process is to progressively narrow the scope of the research topic and transform ambiguous problems into well-defined ones that incorporate specific research objectives.

By investigating any existing studies on the subject, talking with knowledgeable individuals, and informally investigating the situation, the researcher can progressively

---

### WHAT WENT WRONG?

#### Ha-Psu-Shu-Tse

Consider the Ha-Psu-Shu-Tse brand of Native American fried bread mix (from the Pawnee Indian word for *red corn*). The owner of the company, Mr. Ha-Psu-Shu-Tse, thought that his product, one of the few Native American food products available in the United States, was not selling because it was not widely advertised. He wanted a management consulting group to conduct some research concerning advertising themes. However, the management consultants pointed out to the Ha-Psu-Shu-Tse family that using the family name on the bread mix might be a foremost source of concern. They suggested that consumer behavior research to investigate the brand image rather than advertising copy research might be a better initial starting point. Family management agreed.

To be efficient, marketing research must have clear objectives and definite designs. Unfortunately, little or no planning goes into the formulation of many research problems.

sharpen the concepts. After such exploration, the researcher should know data to collect during the formal phases of the project and how to conduct Exhibit 3.2 indicates that a decision must be made regarding the selection of one exploratory research techniques. The exhibit presents the exploratory research stage yellow to indicate that this stage is optional.

The marketing researcher can employ techniques from four basic categories to obtain insights and gain a clearer idea of the problem: secondary data analysis, pilot studies, case studies, and experience surveys. These are discussed in detail in Chapter 5. This section briefly discusses secondary data and focus group interviews, the most popular type of pilot study.

**Secondary Data**   *Secondary* or *historical data* are data previously collected and assembled for some project other than the one at hand. (*Primary data* are gathered and assembled specifically for the project at hand.) Secondary data often can be found inside the company, at a public or university library, or on the Internet. In addition, some firms specialize in providing information, such as economic forecasts, that is useful to many organizations. The researcher who gathers data from the *Census of Population* or *The Survey of Current Business* is using secondary sources.

A literature survey of published articles and books that discuss theories and past empirical studies about a topic is an almost universal first step in academic research projects. A literature survey also is common in many applied research studies. Students who have written term papers should be familiar with using computer search systems, indexes to published literature, and other library sources to compile bibliographies that portray past research.

Consider a bank that wishes to determine the best sites for additional automated teller machines. A logical first step would be to investigate the factors that bankers in other parts of the country consider important. By reading articles in banking journals, management might quickly discover that the best locations are inside supermarkets located in residential areas where people are young, highly educated, and earning higher-than-average incomes. These data might lead the bank to investigate census information to determine where in the city such people live. Reviewing and building on the work already compiled by others is an economical starting point for most research.

**Pilot study**
A collective term for any small-scale exploratory research technique that uses sampling but does not apply rigorous standards.

**Pilot Studies**   The term **pilot study** covers a number of diverse research techniques. Pilot studies collect data from the ultimate consumers or the actual subjects of the research project to serve as a guide for the larger study. When the term *pilot study* is used within the context of exploratory research, the data collection methods are informal and the findings may lack precision.[8] For instance, a downtown association concerned with revitalization of the central business district conducted a very flexible survey using open-ended questions. The interviewers were given considerable latitude to identify changes needed in the shopping area. The results of this survey suggested possible topics for formal investigation.

The focus group interview is a more elaborate kind of exploratory pilot study that has become increasingly popular in recent years. The focus group session brings together six to ten people in a loosely structured format based on the assumption that individuals are more willing to share their ideas as they share in the ideas of others. Information obtained in these studies is qualitative and may serve to guide a subsequent quantitative study.

For example, the Philadelphia Museum used focus groups to investigate how well its exhibits and shows were catering to the public. A local resident who had never visited the museum mentioned he was not aware of any important artwork at the museum. Another participant in the same focus group assumed the museum would be filled with "pictures I would not understand. . . . I've seen art where it looked like kids splashed paint." These findings (confirmed by other research) influenced the museum to reinstate an image of van Gogh's *Sunflowers* on the cover of its brochures.[9]

We have looked at two basic methods of exploratory research, but such research does not have to follow a standard design. Because the purpose of exploratory research is to gain insights and discover new ideas, researchers may use considerable creativity and flexibility. Data generally are collected using several exploratory techniques. Exhausting these sources usually is worth the effort because the expense is relatively low. Further, insights into how and how not to conduct research may be gained from activities during the problem definition stage. If the conclusions made during this stage suggest marketing opportunities, the researcher is in a position to begin planning a formal, quantitative research project.

**Statement of Research Objectives**  A researcher must initially decide precisely what to research. After identifying and clarifying the problem, with or without exploratory research, the researcher should make a formal statement of the problem and the research objectives. This delineates the type of information to be collected and provides a framework for the scope of the study.

A typical research objective might seek to answer a question such as "To what extent did the new pricing program achieve its objectives?" In this sense, the statement of the problem is a research question.

The best expression of a research objective is a well-formed, testable research hypothesis. A **hypothesis** is a statement that can be refuted or supported by empirical data. For example, an exploratory study might lead to the hypothesis that a market share decline recognized by management is occurring predominantly among households in which the head of the household is 45 to 65 years old with an income of $45,000 per year or less. Another hypothesis might be that concentrating advertising efforts in monthly waves (rather than conducting continuous advertising) will cause an increase in sales and profits. Once the hypothesis has been developed, the researcher is ready to select a research design.

## ■ Planning the Research Design

After the researcher has formulated the research problem, he or she must develop the research design as part of the **research design stage.** A **research design** is a master plan that specifies the methods and procedures for collecting and analyzing the needed information; it is a framework for the research plan of action. The objectives of the study determined during the early stages of the research are included in the design to ensure that the information collected is appropriate for solving the problem. The researcher also must determine the sources of information, the design technique (e.g., survey or experiment), the sampling methodology, and the schedule and cost of the research.

**Selection of the Basic Research Method**  Here again, the researcher must make a decision. Exhibit 3.2 shows the four basic design techniques for descriptive and causal research: surveys, experiments, secondary data, and observation. The objectives of the study, the available data sources, the urgency of the decision, and the cost of obtaining the data will determine which design technique to choose. We will consider the managerial aspects of selecting the research design later.

*Surveys*  The most common method of generating primary data is through surveys. Most people have seen the results of political surveys by Gallup or Harris, and some have been respondents (members of a sample who supply answers) to marketing research

**Research design stage**
The stage in which the researcher determines a framework for the research plan of action by selecting a basic research method.

**Research design**
A master plan that specifies the methods and procedures for collecting and analyzing needed information.

■ Design and style are important ways to differentiate a product from its competition. This Red Devil Ergo 2000 wall scraper is ergonomically designed with soft, oversized handles contoured to fit plam, thumb, and fingers. The design was based on research findings that people found conventional putty knives and scrapers too short, hard, and squared off, causing them to slam their thumbs against the side of the blade while scraping. Simplicity of the functional design is reinforced by the aesthetic design, which evokes comfort.

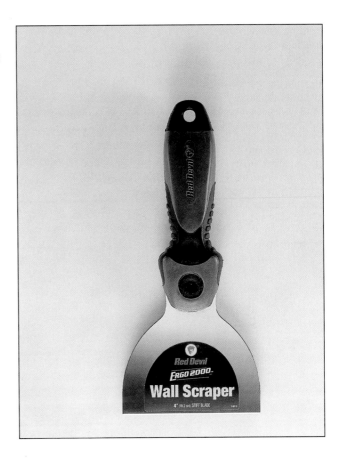

questionnaires. A *survey* is a research technique that gathers information from a sample of people through a questionnaire. The task of writing a questionnaire, determining the list of questions, and designing the format of the printed or electronic questionnaire is an essential aspect of the development of a survey research design. Research investigators may choose to contact respondents by telephone, by mail, in person, or through another communication medium. An advertiser spending $1,400,000 for 30 seconds of commercial time during the Super Bowl may telephone people to quickly gather information concerning their responses to the advertising. A forklift truck manufacturer trying to determine a cause for low sales in the wholesale grocery industry might choose a mail questionnaire because the appropriate executives are hard to reach by telephone. A manufacturer of a birth control device for men might determine the need for a versatile survey method wherein an interviewer can ask a variety of personal questions in a flexible format. Personal interviews are expensive, but they are valuable because investigators can use visual aids and supplement the interviews with personal observations. Each of these survey methods has advantages and disadvantages. The researcher's task is to find the most appropriate way to collect the needed information.

*Experiments* Marketing *experiments* hold the greatest potential for establishing cause-and-effect relationships. Experimentation allows investigation of changes in one variable, such as sales, while manipulating one or two other variables, perhaps price or advertising, under controlled conditions. Ideally experimental control provides a basis for isolating

■ Movie marketers try to select representative samples of moviegoers to gauge audiences' responses to trailers, movies, and television commercials. Audience previews have been responsible for the decisions about the final versions of many films. Survey respondents thought the use of musical numbers in *I'll Do Anything* was untimely. So when the feature film was released, the singing debuts of stars Nick Nolte and Julie Kavner ended up on the cutting-room floor.[10]

causal factors by eliminating outside, or exogenous, influences. Thus, an experiment controls conditions so that one or more variables can be manipulated to test a hypothesis.

Test marketing is a frequently used form of marketing experimentation. Chelsea, Anheuser-Busch's "not-so-soft soft drink," illustrates the usefulness of marketing experiments. Anheuser-Busch first introduced Chelsea as a drink with a slight alcoholic content—about 0.4 percent—that was a socially acceptable alternative to beer for adults who did not want to get intoxicated. During an experiment to test market the "not-so-soft soft drink" and the "not-so-sweet" concept, a Virginia nurses' association and some religious groups strongly criticized the company and the new product. These critics suggested that Anheuser-Busch had introduced a product that might encourage children to become beer drinkers. They contended that Chelsea was packaged like beer and looked, foamed, and poured like it. The criticism led the brewery to suspend production, advertising, and promotion of the drink. Later it reintroduced the product as a soft drink with only "a trace of alcohol" as a "natural alternative" to soft drinks with not-so-sweet and stylish attributes. Similar problems occurred in the second experiment. This experiment pointed out to Anheuser-Busch that the variable, alcohol level, caused an inadvertent miscommunication: Consumers confused the original Chelsea with beer.

*Secondary Data for Descriptive and Quantitative Analysis*   Like exploratory research studies, descriptive and causal studies use previously collected data. Although the terms *secondary* and *historical* are interchangeable, we will use the term *secondary data* here. An example of a secondary data study is the use of a mathematical model to predict sales on the basis of past sales or a correlation with related variables. Manufacturers of color printers for personal computers may find that sales are highly correlated with discretionary personal income. To predict future market potential, projections of disposable personal income from the government or a university may be acquired. This information can be used mathematically to forecast sales. Formal secondary data studies have benefits and

■ Direct marketers often conduct experiments to determine how to increase response to pamphlets, catalogs, or offerings. Experiments have shown that the wording of headline copy and prices can greatly influence the success of direct marketing.

limitations similar to those of exploratory studies that use secondary data, but generally the quantitative analysis of secondary data is more sophisticated.

*Observation*    The objective of many research projects is merely to record what can be observed, for example, the number of automobiles that pass by a proposed site for a gasoline station. This can be mechanically recorded or observed by humans. Research personnel known as *mystery shoppers* may act as customers to observe actions of sales personnel or do comparative shopping to learn prices at competing outlets.

The main advantage of the *observation* technique is that it records behavior without relying on reports from respondents. Observation methods often are nonreactive because data are collected unobtrusively and passively without a respondent's direct participation. For instance, A. C. Nielsen Company uses a "people meter" attached to television sets to record the programs each household member is watching. This eliminates the possible bias of respondents stating that they watched the president's State of the Union address rather than a situation comedy on another station.

Observation is more complex than mere "nose counting," and the task is more difficult than the inexperienced researcher would imagine. Several things of interest, such as attitudes, opinions, motivations, and other intangible states of mind, simply cannot be observed.

**The "Best" Research Design** It is argued that there is no one best research design and there are no hard-and-fast rules for good marketing research. This does not mean, however, that the researcher faces chaos and confusion. It means the researcher can choose among many alternative methods to solve a problem. An eminent behavioral researcher has stated this concept quite eloquently:

> There is never a single, standard, correct method of carrying out a piece of research. Do not wait to start your research until you find out the proper approach, because there are many ways to tackle a problem—some good, some bad, but probably several good ways. There is no single perfect design. A research method for a given problem is not like the solution to a problem in algebra. It is more like a recipe for beef Stroganoff; there is no one best recipe.[11]

Consider the researcher who must forecast sales for the upcoming year. Some commonly used forecasting methods are executive opinion, sales force composite opinions, user expectations, projection of trends, and analysis of market factors.

The ability to select the most appropriate research design develops with experience. Inexperienced researchers often jump to the conclusion that the survey method is the best design because they are most familiar with this method. When Chicago's Museum of Science and Industry wanted to determine the relative popularity of its exhibits, it could have conducted a survey. Instead, a creative researcher familiar with other research designs suggested a far less expensive alternative: an unobtrusive observation technique. The researcher suggested that the museum merely keep track of the frequency with which the floor tiles in front of the various exhibits had to be replaced, indicating where the heaviest traffic occurred. When this was done, the museum found that the chick-hatching exhibit was the most popular. This method provided the same results as a survey but at a much lower cost.

After determining the proper design, the researcher moves on to the next stage: planning the sample.

## ■ Sampling

**Sampling stage**
The stage in which the researcher determines who is to be sampled, how large a sample is needed, and how sampling units will be selected.

Although the sampling plan is included in the research design, the **sampling stage** is a distinct phase of the research process. For convenience, however, we will treat the sample planning and the actual sample generation processes together in this section.

If you take your first bite of steak and conclude that it needs salt, you have just conducted a sample. *Sampling* involves any procedure that uses a small number of items or parts of the population to make a conclusion regarding the whole population. In other words, a sample is a subset from a larger population. If certain statistical procedures are followed, a researcher need not select every item in a population because the results of a good sample should have the same characteristics as the population as a whole. Of course, when errors are made, samples do not give reliable estimates of the population. A famous example of error due to sampling is the 1936 *Literary Digest* fiasco. The magazine conducted a survey and predicted that Alf Landon would win over Franklin D. Roosevelt by a landslide. The magazine made an error in sample selection. The postmortems showed that *Literary Digest* had sampled telephone and magazine subscribers. In 1936 these people were not a representative cross section of voters because a disproportionate number of them were Republicans. This famous example suggests that the first sampling question to ask is "Who is to be sampled?" The answer to this primary question requires the identification of a *target population*. Defining this population and determining the sampling units may not be easy. If, for example, a savings and loan association surveys people who already have accounts for answers to image questions, the selected sampling units will not represent potential customers. Specifying the target population is a crucial aspect of the sampling plan.

The next sampling issue concerns sample size. How big should the sample be? Although management may wish to examine every potential buyer of a product or service, doing so may be unnecessary as well as unrealistic. Typically larger samples are more precise than smaller ones, but proper probability sampling can allow a small proportion of the total population to give a reliable measure of the whole. A later discussion will explain how large a sample must be to be truly representative of the universe, or population.

The final sampling decision concerns choosing how to select the sampling units. Students who have taken a statistics course generally understand simple random sampling in which every unit in the population has an equal and known chance of being selected. However, this is only one type of sampling. For example, a cluster sampling procedure may reduce costs and make data-gathering procedures more efficient. If members of the population are found in close geographical clusters, a sampling procedure that selects area clusters rather than individual units in the population will reduce costs. Rather than selecting 1,000 individuals throughout the United States, it may be more economical to first select 25 counties and then sample within those counties. This will substantially reduce travel, hiring, and training costs. In determining the appropriate sampling plan, the researcher will have to select the most appropriate sampling procedure for meeting the established study objectives.

There are two basic sampling techniques: probability and nonprobability sampling. In a *probability sample,* every member of the population has a known, nonzero probability of selection. If sample units are selected on the basis of personal judgment (for example, a test market city is selected because it appears to be typical), the sample method is a *nonprobability sample.* In reality, the sampling decision is not a simple choice between two methods. Simple random samples, stratified samples, quota samples, cluster samples, and judgmental samples are among the many methods for drawing a sample. A full discussion of these techniques must be postponed to a later chapter.

## ■ Data Gathering

**Data-gathering stage**
The stage in which the researcher collects the data.

Once the research design (including the sampling plan) has been formalized, the process of gathering or collecting information, the **data-gathering stage,** may begin. Data may be gathered by humans or recorded by machines. Scanner data illustrate electronic data collection by machine.

Obviously, the numerous research techniques involve many methods of data gathering. The survey method requires some form of direct participation by the respondent. The respondent may participate by filling out a questionnaire or interacting with an interviewer. If an unobtrusive method of data gathering is used, the subjects do not actively participate. For instance, a simple count of motorists driving past a proposed franchising location is one kind of data-gathering method. However the data are collected, it is important to minimize errors in the process. For example, the data gathering should be consistent in all geographical areas. If an interviewer phrases questions incorrectly or records a respondent's statements inaccurately (not verbatim), major data collection errors will result.

Often there are two phases to the process of gathering data: pretesting and the main study. A *pretesting phase* using a small subsample may determine whether the data-gathering plan for the *main study* is an appropriate procedure. Thus, a small-scale pretest study provides an advance opportunity for an investigator to check the data collection form to minimize errors due to improper design elements, such as poor question wording or sequence. A researcher may also benefit by discovering confusing interviewing instructions, learning that the questionnaire is too long or too short, and uncovering other such field errors. Tabulation of data from the pretests provides the researcher with a format of the knowledge that may be gained from the actual study. If the tabulation of the data and statistical results does not answer the researcher's questions, the investigator may need to redesign the study.

## ■ Data Processing and Analysis

**Data-processing and analysis stage**
The stage in which the researcher performs several interrelated procedures to convert the data into a format that will answer management's questions.

After the fieldwork has been completed, the data must be converted into a format that will answer the marketing manager's questions. This is part of the **data-processing and analysis stage.** Data processing generally begins with editing and coding the data. *Editing* involves checking the data collection forms for omissions, legibility, and consistency in classification. The editing process corrects problems such as interviewer errors (an answer recorded on the wrong portion of a questionnaire, for example) before transferring the data to the computer.

Before data can be tabulated, meaningful categories and character symbols must be established for groups of responses. The rules for interpreting, categorizing, recording, and transferring the data to the data storage media are called *codes.* This coding process facilitates computer or hand tabulation. If computer analysis is to be used, the data are entered into the computer and verified. Computer-assisted (on-line) interviewing is a recent development that illustrates the impact of technological change on the research process. Telephone interviewers, seated at a computer terminal, read survey questions displayed on the monitor. The interviewers ask the questions and then type the respondents' answers on the keyboard. Thus, answers are collected and processed into the computer at the same time, eliminating intermediate steps that could introduce errors.

**Analysis** *Analysis* is the application of logic to understand the data that have been gathered about a subject. In its simplest form, analysis may involve determining consistent patterns and summarizing the relevant details revealed in the investigation. The appropriate analytical technique for data analysis will be determined by management's information requirements, the characteristics of the research design, and the nature of the data gathered. Statistical analysis may range from portraying a simple frequency distribution to very complex multivariate analysis, such as multiple regression. Later chapters will discuss the most popular techniques for statistical analysis.

## ■ Conclusions and Report Preparation

**Conclusions and report preparation stage**
The stage in which the researcher interprets information and draws conclusions to be communicated to the decision makers.

As mentioned earlier, most marketing research is applied research with the purpose of making a marketing decision. An important but often overlooked aspect of the marketing researcher's job is to look at the analysis of the information collected and ask, "What does this mean to management?" The final stage in the research process, the **conclusions and report preparation stage,** consists of interpreting the information and making conclusions for managerial decisions.

The research report should effectively communicate the research findings. All too many reports are complicated statements of technical aspects and sophisticated research methods. Frequently management is not interested in detailed reporting of the research design and statistical findings but wishes only a summary of the findings. If the findings of the research remain unread on the marketing manager's desk, the study will have been useless. The importance of effective communication cannot be overemphasized. Research is only as good as its applications.

Marketing researchers must communicate their findings to a managerial audience. The written report serves another purpose as well: It is a means of providing historical documents that will be a source of record for later use, such as repeating the survey or providing a basis for building on the survey findings.

# ■ THE RESEARCH PROPOSAL

**Research proposal**

A written statement of the research design that includes a statement explaining the purpose of the study and a detailed, systematic outline of procedures associated with a particular research methodology.

Now that we have outlined the research process, a brief discussion of research proposals is in order. The **research proposal** is a written statement of the research design. It always includes a statement explaining the purpose of the study (research objectives) or a definition of the problem. It systematically outlines the particular research methodology and details the procedures that will be followed during each stage of the research process. Normally the research proposal includes a schedule of costs and deadlines. Exhibit 3.5 on pages 60 and 61 illustrates a short research proposal for the Internal Revenue Service that explored public attitudes toward a variety of tax-related issues.

# ■ THE RESEARCH PROGRAM STRATEGY

Our discussion of the marketing research process began with the assumption that the researcher wishes to gather information to achieve a specific marketing objective. We have emphasized the researcher's need to select specific techniques to solve one-dimensional problems such as identifying market segments, selecting the best packaging design, or test marketing a new product.

However, when we think about a firm's marketing mix activity over a given period of time (such as a year), we realize that marketing research is not a one-shot activity; it is a continuous process. An exploratory research study may be followed by a survey, or a researcher may conduct a specific research project for each aspect of the marketing mix. If a new product is being developed, the different types of research might include (1) market potential studies to identify the size and characteristics of the market, (2) product usage testing to record consumers' reactions to prototype products, (3) brand name and packaging research to determine the product's symbolic connotations, and (4) test marketing the new product. Because research is a continuous process, management should view marketing research at a strategic planning level. The **program strategy** refers to the firm's overall plan to use marketing research. It is a planning activity that places a series of marketing research projects in the context of the company's marketing plan.

**Program strategy**

The overall plan to conduct a series of marketing research projects; a planning activity that places each marketing project in the context of the company's marketing plan.

The marketing research program strategy can be likened to a term insurance policy. Conducting marketing research minimizes risk and increases certainty. Each research project can be seen as a series of term insurance policies that make the marketing manager's job a bit safer.

# ■ SUMMARY

Marketing research provides information to reduce uncertainty. The clarity with which the research problem is defined determines whether exploratory, descriptive, or causal research is appropriate. Exploratory research is appropriate when management knows only the general nature of a problem; it is used not to provide conclusive evidence but to clarify problems. Descriptive research is conducted when management has some understanding

■ **Exhibit 3.5**

**An Abbreviated Version of a Research Proposal for the IRS**

Purpose of the Research

The general purpose of the study is to determine the taxpaying public's perceptions of the IRS's role in administering the tax laws. In defining the limits of this study the IRS identified the study areas to be addressed. A careful review of those areas led to the identification of the following specific research objectives:

1. To identify the extent to which taxpayers cheat on their returns, their reasons for doing so, and approaches that can be taken to deter this kind of behavior
2. To determine taxpayers' experience and level of satisfaction with various IRS services
3. To determine what services taxpayers need
4. To develop an accurate profile of taxpayers' behavior relative to the preparation of their income tax returns
5. To assess taxpayers' knowledge and opinions about various tax laws and procedures

Research Design

The survey research method will be the basic research design. Each respondent will be interviewed in his or her home. The personal interviews are generally expected to last between 35 and 45 minutes, although the length will vary depending on the previous tax-related experiences of the respondent. For example, if a respondent has never been audited, questions on audit experience will not be addressed. Or, if a respondent has never contacted the IRS for assistance, certain questions concerning reactions to IRS services will be skipped.

Some sample questions that will be asked are:

**Did you (or your spouse) prepare your federal tax return for (year)?**
☐ **Self**

☐ **Spouse**

☐ **Someone else**

**Did the federal income tax package you received in the mail contain all the forms necessary for you to fill out your return?**
☐ **Yes**

☐ **No**

☐ **Didn't receive one in the mail**

☐ **Don't know**

---

of the nature of the problem; it provides an accurate description of the characteristics of a population. Causal research identifies cause-and-effect relationships when the research problem has been narrowly defined.

Research proceeds in a series of six interrelated phases. The first is problem definition, which may include exploratory research using secondary data, experience surveys, or pilot studies.

Once the problem is defined, the researcher selects a research design. The major designs are surveys, experiments, observation, and secondary data analysis. Creative research design can minimize the cost of obtaining reliable results. After the design has been selected, a sampling plan is chosen, using a probability sample, a nonprobability sample, or a combination of the two.

The design is put into action in the data-gathering phase. This phase may involve a small pretest before the main study is undertaken. In the analysis stage the data are edited and coded, then processed, usually by computer. The results are interpreted in light of the decisions management must make. Finally, the analysis is presented to decision makers in a written or oral report. This last step is crucial, because even an excellent project will not lead to proper action if the results are poorly communicated.

■ **Exhibit 3.5**
*continued*

**If you were calling the IRS for assistance and someone were not able to help you immediately, would you rather get a busy signal or be asked to wait on hold?**
☐ **Busy signal**
☐ **Wait on hold**
☐ **Neither**
☐ **Don't know**

During the interview a self-administered questionnaire will be given to the taxpayer to ask certain sensitive questions such as:

**Have you ever claimed a dependent on your tax return that you weren't really entitled to?**
☐ **Yes**
☐ **No**

### Sample Design

A survey of approximately 5,000 individuals located in 50 counties throughout the country will provide the database for this study. The sample will be selected on a probability basis from all households in the continental United States.

Eligible respondents will be adults, over the age of 18. Within each household an effort will be made to interview the individual who is most familiar with completing the federal tax forms. When there is more than one taxpayer in the household, a random process will be used to select the taxpayer to be interviewed.

### Data Gathering

The field-workers of a consulting organization will be utilized to conduct the interview.

### Data Processing and Analysis

Standard editing and coding procedures will be utilized. Simple tabulation and cross-tabulations will be utilized to analyze the data.

### Report Preparation

A written report will be prepared, and an oral presentation of the findings will be made by the research analyst at IRS convenience.

### Budget and Time Schedule

Any complete research proposal should include a schedule of how long it will take to conduct each stage of the research and a statement of itemized costs.

---

Quite often research projects are conducted together as parts of a research program. Such programs can involve successive projects that monitor an established product or a group of projects undertaken for a proposed new product to determine the optimal form of various parts of the marketing mix.

The research proposal is a written statement of the research design.

## ■ Key Terms and Concepts

Exploratory research
Descriptive research
Causal research
Concomitant variation
Problem definition stage
Iceberg principle
Hypothesis
Research objective
Pilot study

Research design stage
Research design
Sampling stage
Data-gathering stage
Data-processing and analysis stage
Conclusions and report preparation stage
Research proposal
Program strategy

## ■ Questions

1. For each of the following situations, decide whether the research should be exploratory, descriptive, or causal.
   (a) Establishing the functional relationship between advertising and sales
   (b) Investigating consumer reactions to the idea of a new laundry detergent that prevents shrinkage in hot water
   (c) Identifying target market demographics for a shopping center
   (d) Estimating sales potential for concrete vibrators in a northwestern sales territory
2. Describe a research situation that allows one to infer causality.
3. In the following nine-dot square, connect all nine dots using no more than four straight lines and without lifting the pencil from the paper. What does the solution of this problem suggest about the solutions of problem definition situations?

•    •    •
•    •    •
•    •    •

4. Why is the problem definition stage of the research process probably the most important stage?
5. What is the iceberg principle?
6. Do the stages in the research process follow the scientific method? Explain.
7. Which research design seems appropriate for the following situations?
   (a) The manufacturer and marketer of flight simulators and other pilot-training equipment wish to forecast sales volume for the next five years.
   (b) A local chapter of the American Lung Association wishes to identify the demographic characteristics of individuals who donate more than $500 per year.
   (c) A major petroleum company is concerned about the increasing costs of marketing regular leaded gasoline and is considering dropping this product.
   (d) A food company researcher wishes to know what types of food are carried in brown-bag lunches to learn if the company can capitalize on this phenomenon.
8. What purpose does the research proposal serve?
9. What role should managers play in the development of the research proposal?
10. Comment on the following statements:
    (a) "The best marketing researchers are prepared to rethink and rewrite their proposals."
    (b) "The client's signature is an essential element of the research proposal."
11. Should the marketing research program strategy be viewed as a strategic planning activity? Why or why not?

## EXPLORING THE INTERNET

1. Use a Web browser to go to the Gallup Organization's home page at:

   http://www.gallup.com

   The Gallup home page changes on a regular basis. However, it should provide an opportunity to read the results of a political poll. (a) Select the "Gallup poll" option; then view the results by selecting the "findings" option. (b) On a sheet of paper, list the various stages of the research process and how they were followed in Gallup's Internet poll.

2. Use Netscape or another Web browser to access Lycos at:

   (http://www.lycos.com).

What Web guide topics can be investigated? How might the information you find help you design a research project?

3. Use your Web browser to view the Advertising Media Internet Center's home page at:

   http://www.amic.com

   The Advertising Media Internet Center will show an icon for Research Monitor. Click on Research Monitor. What research information can be accessed?

---

 ## CASE 3.1  The S⊁ool

The S⊁ool was a singles bar in Chicago's Rush Street area. This area, located on Chicago's Near North Side by the Gold Coast, is approximately seven blocks long and three blocks wide and is popular for evening entertainment.

The S⊁ool once was one of the most popular spots on Rush Street. There had always been wall-to-wall people on Friday afternoons, but lately the crowds had begun to go elsewhere.

A marketing research consultant who patronized The S⊁ool because it was two blocks from his home knew the manager, Sandy Walton, well. After some discussions with her, the consultant sent a letter proposing that The S⊁ool conduct some marketing research. (See Case Exhibit 3.1-1.)

### Questions

1. Has the research problem been adequately defined?
2. Evaluate the research proposal.

---

### ■ Case Exhibit 3.1-1    The S⊁ool's Marketing Research Proposal

Dear Sandy:
Here is a brief outline of what I believe The S⊁ool must consider if it is to regain its popularity on Rush Street. As you know, The S⊁ool's management has changed the decor and exterior of The S⊁ool, hired exceptional bands, and used various other promotions to improve business. In spite of this, a decline in The S⊁ool's popularity has been evidenced. As these efforts have not brought back the crowd The S⊁ool once had, I suggest The S⊁ool undertake a marketing research investigation of consumer behavior and consumer opinions among Rush Street patrons.

I recommend this project because The S⊁ool once had what it takes to be a popular bar on Rush Street and should still have the potential to regain this status. Most likely, the lack of patronage at The S⊁ool is caused by one or both of the following factors:

1. A change in the people or type of people who patronize Rush Street bars
2. A change in the opinions of The S⊁ool held by people who patronize Rush Street bars

The problem for The S⊁ool's management is to determine the specifics of the change either in the people or in the opinions of the regular patrons of Rush Street and The S⊁ool.

Determining what type of information is desired by The S⊁ool's management depends on some underlying facts about the popularity of the bars on Rush Street. An assumption must be made concerning this question: Does the crowd (weekend and Wednesday patrons) go where the regulars go, or do the regulars go where the crowd goes? If you believe that the regulars follow the crowd, a general investigation should be conducted to test why the masses go to the popular bars. If the assumption is made that a bar is popular because there are always people (regulars) there, the best method to increase business is to get a regular following who will attract the crowd.

Of course, the optimal position is to appeal to both the regulars and the crowd. Thus, there are numerous areas for investigation:

- Who visits Rush Street bars? What are the group characteristics?
- What motivates these people to go to the various bars and thus makes them popular? For example, to what extent does the number of stag girls in the bars bring about more patrons? (Note: Remember that The S⊁ool, Rush-up, Filling Station, and Barnaby's had female servers at the start of their popularity. Could this have been a factor in their appeal?) How important is bartender rapport with the patrons?

*continued*

■ **Case Exhibit 3.1-1**    *continued*

- What do drinkers like and dislike about The Sxool?
- What is the awareness among beer drinkers of Pete's Wicked Ale quality? Do they like it? How does having several microbrewery beers on tap affect a bar's popularity?
- What image does The Sxool project? Is it favorable or unfavorable? Has it lost the image it once had because it is trying to be the Store Annex, Barnaby's, Rush-up, and The Sxool combined? Is the decor consistent? How can a favorable image be put back into Rush Street drinkers' minds? You might think The Sxool can appeal to all Rush Street people, but you can't be all things to all people. A specialization of image and customers may bring back the crowd for The Sxool.
- How important is it to be first with a new promotion? For example, did Barnaby's idea of starting a wine and chicken feast make it the place to go to, at least in the short run? If a food promotion would go over, what should The Sxool try?
- There are many ways in which The Sxool would benefit if it conducted a marketing research survey. Of course, the above suggestions for investigation are not all-inclusive, as I have not had a chance to talk with you to determine which areas are the most important. If you would like to have me submit a formal research proposal to determine how The Sxool can improve its business, I will be happy to talk with you any evening.

Sincerely yours,
Lisé Johnson

■ **Endnotes**

[1] Adam Bryant, "Zen and Art of Buying a Car," *New York Times,* September 8, 1992, p. F-10.

[2] "Those Precocious 13-Year-Old Girls," *Brandweek,* January 25, 1993, p. 13.

[3] Claire Selltiz, Lawrence S. Wrightsman, and Stuart W. Cook, *Research Methods in Social Relations* (New York: Holt, Rinehart and Winston, 1976), pp. 114–115.

[4] Phillip J. Runkel and Joseph E. McGrath, *Research on Human Behavior: A Systematic Guide to Method* (New York: Holt, Rinehart and Winston, 1972), p. 2.

[5] Each topic is discussed in greater depth in later chapters.

[6] A. Einstein and L. Infeld, *The Evolution of Physics* (New York: Simon and Schuster, 1942), p. 95.

[7] Russell L. Ackoff, *Scientific Method* (New York: John Wiley and Sons, 1962), p. 71.

[8] Pretests of full-blown surveys and experiments also are considered pilot studies. These smaller versions of the formal studies generally are used to refine techniques rather than for problem definition and hypothesis clarification.

[9] Carol Vogel, "Dear Museumgoer: What Do You Think?" *New York Times,* December 20, 1992, pp. H-1, H-32.

[10] Fred Pampel, Dan Fost, and Sharon O'Malley, "Marketing the Movies," *American Demographics,* March 1, 1994, p. 48.

[11] Julian Simon, *Basic Research Methods in Social Science: The Art of Empirical Investigation* (New York: Random House, 1969), p. 4.

# 4

# THE HUMAN SIDE OF MARKETING RESEARCH: ORGANIZATIONAL AND ETHICAL ISSUES

WHAT YOU WILL LEARN IN THIS CHAPTER:

To recognize the degree of marketing research sophistication in various organizations.

To discuss the organizational structure of marketing research in various organizations.

To identify the various individual job titles within the marketing research industry.

To understand the role research suppliers and research contractors play in the marketing research industry.

To explain why ethical questions are philosophical questions.

To describe the three parties involved in most research situations and discuss how the interaction among them may identify a series of ethical questions.

To discuss the rights and obligations of the respondent.

To discuss the rights and obligations of the researcher.

To discuss the rights and obligations of the client sponsor.

To take each of the three parties' perspectives and discuss selected issues such as deception, privacy, and advocacy research.

A research manager and a sales manager had to cross a swiftly flowing river. The sales manager immediately flung off his clothes, dove in, and, with many furious strokes and the help of a strong downstream current, finally managed to cross the river. With much loud huffing and puffing, he emerged, pounded his chest, and proudly told everyone of his exploit. The research manager, in the meantime, carefully calculated the speed of the current, observed the location of shoal water and sandy bottom, the height of the banks, and other factors, determined the best starting point, and quietly waded across. Upon arriving on the other side, he didn't say anything to anyone.[1]

While this story undoubtedly stereotypes sales managers and marketing researchers, it should be remembered that most jokes originate as some form of complaint. The story makes some salient points about the difference between line and staff marketing managers.

Most of this text deals with research methodology and the research process. However, several organizational, managerial, and ethical issues are important concerns. In this chapter, we investigate the human side of marketing research. First, we explore the role of research in the organization and the part researchers play. Then we discuss the roles of research suppliers and contractors. Finally, we look at a variety of ethical issues that confront managers and marketing researchers.

## ■ THE MISSION OF THE RESEARCH DEPARTMENT

A mission statement identifies the marketing research department's purpose within the organization. It explains what the department hopes to accomplish.

Exhibit 4.1 details the mission statement of General Foods' marketing research department. It shows the importance of a complete program of research that meets the needs of decision makers. It also suggests that the mission of the research department is a key factor in the success of a research function within an organization.

An executive at R. J. Reynolds has stressed that the research mission should be integrated with other units in the organization:

> The most successful research departments are those whose mission is directly linked to the decision makers' needs. In most cases this means the research department must be a valued, integrated, and active part of the company's marketing process.

Conversely those research departments that have not been successful seem to be independent of the decision makers' needs. Such departments tend to be isolated and operate within a vacuum. Their output may be technically precise but it is rarely put to use because research is independent of the decision makers.[2]

## ■ DEGREE OF MARKETING RESEARCH SOPHISTICATION

As businesspeople have come to recognize that marketing research is a useful decision-making tool, its use has become more widespread. An organization's willingness to use research generally parallels its acceptance of the marketing concept. Just as some firms

---

### ■ Exhibit 4.1

**General Foods' Research Department Mission/Roles**

The research mission is to:

Support General Foods' best food company strategy by providing the highest quality marketing intelligence upon which strategic and tactical decisions are based.

The Department will accomplish its mission by:

* Providing ad hoc marketing information which is relevant to the issues, appropriate (in terms of accuracy, timeliness, and risk), and commensurate with the true needs of the marketing decision maker.
* Integrating market/marketing information in a total intelligence to facilitate the identification, development, and execution of significant, long-term strategic planning.
* Exercising leadership in accumulating GF marketing experience and utilizing it to develop a knowledge base about marketing and the marketing process.
* Exercising leadership in the development of research methods which will significantly improve marketing decision making.
* Maintaining a high degree of consistency of methodology to facilitate decision making across GF's many businesses.
* Maintaining assurance of objectivity in the collection, analysis, interpretation, and use of marketing information.

**Research sophistication**
A stage in which managers have considerable experience in the proper use of research techniques.

remain in the production-oriented stage, some ignore or are ignorant of marketing research. The use of marketing research has evolved from a stage in which managers make decisions intuitively to a stage of **research sophistication** in which managers have considerable experience in the proper use of research techniques. Marketing management's attitudes toward research methodology can range along a continuum from ignorance of research and intuition-centered decision making to sophisticated, research-centered decision making (see Exhibit 4.2). For purposes of discussion, we can identify three levels of marketing research sophistication.

### ■ Stage of Intuitive Decision Making

Marketing managers in this stage may be ignorant about marketing research; or they may believe that research methodology is appropriately confined to the ivory tower of academia or, at best, to technical research conducted elsewhere in the organization. These managers depend heavily on intuition and experience, and obtain their information informally.

### ■ Stage of Sophistication

In this stage, marketing research has become a proactive force to identify decision makers' information needs. Marketing managers in this final stage recognize the potential of research to improve the decision-making process. They recognize that a fortune teller is probably a better bargain than poor research. They also recognize that while good research does not completely eliminate uncertainty, it can be an economically warranted means of at least reducing that uncertainty.[3]

### ■ Stage of Development

Most companies are neither completely ignorant nor completely informed about what marketing research can and cannot do. They have passed beyond intuitive decision making. They are in the process of developing research sophistication. Companies may use marketing research for the first few times on blind faith. Marketing managers in this stage naively believe that the result of the application of research methodology is the decision itself rather than the information on which to base a good decision. They fail to see that good research can only reduce uncertainty; it cannot eliminate it. Managers developing a knowledge of research seem most impressed with complex research they are not capable of evaluating. Some statistical analysis in a research report impresses these managers. Show them the same analysis on a computer graphic and they are awestruck.

Over time managers gain experience and become increasingly familiar with marketing research. They begin to use research more often and to recognize occasions when it should be applied.

■ **Exhibit 4.2**    **Continuum of Marketing Research Sophistication**

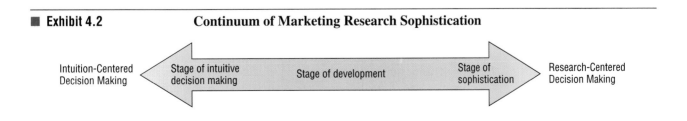

Sometimes marketing managers become disillusioned as they develop more research sophistication, perhaps even feeling betrayed by marketing research. These managers become very cynical because they have made costly mistakes in research-based decisions. This vulnerability arises from a failure to distinguish good from bad research or from an assumption that good research effectively makes a management decision.

This is a learning stage. Companies employ marketing research, but they do not exploit its full potential. Gradually, they increase their research sophistication.

## ◼ ORGANIZATIONAL STRUCTURE OF MARKETING RESEARCH

A survey of companies that belonged to the American Marketing Association found that 76 percent reported having formal marketing research departments. Formal research departments are most common among consumer goods firms, manufacturers, and retailers. Larger companies are more likely to have marketing research departments.[4]

The place of marketing research in an organization and the structure of the research department will vary substantially depending on the firm's acceptance of the marketing concept and its stage of marketing research sophistication. Given that research and the decision makers are linked together, the best organizational structure is to report as high up in the senior management ranks as possible—at least to the senior marketing vice president and preferably higher. The research department should also be able to have as broad a perspective across the company as possible. This is because of the information flow, which the research department manages, interprets, and communicates. Improper placement of the marketing research department can isolate it. Researchers may lack a voice in executive committees when they have no continuous relationship with marketing management. Sometimes the research department is positioned at an inappropriately low level.

### ◼ Marketing Research as a Staff Function

**Client**
Term often used by the research department to refer to line management for whom it performs services.

Research departments that perform a staff function must wait for management to request assistance. Often the research department uses the term **client** to refer to line management for whom it performs services.

The research department responds to clients' requests and is responsible for design and execution of all research. It should function as an internal consulting organization that develops action-oriented, data-based recommendations.

In a small firm, the vice president of marketing may be in charge of marketing research. This officer generally will have the sales manager collect and analyze sales histories, trade association statistics, and other internal data. If a survey needs to be conducted, an advertising agency or a firm that specializes in marketing research will be contracted to do the job. At the other extreme, a large company such as Procter & Gamble may staff its research departments with more than 100 people.

**Director of marketing research**
The person who provides leadership and integrates staff-level activities by planning, executing, and controlling the marketing research function; sometimes called **director of marketing information systems.**

In a medium-size firm, the research department might include a director of marketing research and individuals with titles such as *research analyst, research assistant,* and *manager of decision support systems.* The **director of marketing research** or **director of marketing information systems** provides leadership and integrates staff-level activities. The director of marketing research plans, executes, and controls the marketing research function. This person typically serves on executive committees that identify competitive opportunities and formulate marketing strategies for the organization. The director's responsibility is to provide the research point of view on these strategic issues. In many cases, the director serves as an internal consultant to the organization about consumer behavior and strategic business issues.[5]

**Research analyst**
The person responsible for client contact, project design, preparation of proposals, selection of research suppliers, and supervision of data collection, analysis, and reporting activities.

**Research assistant**
The person who provides technical assistance with questionnaire design, analysis of data, and so on.

**Manager of decision support systems**
The person who supervises the collection and analysis of sales data and other recurring data.

**Forecast analyst**
The person who provides technical assistance such as computer analysis to forecast sales.

**Manager of customer quality research**
The person who specializes in conducting surveys to measure consumers' satisfaction and perceptions of product quality.

The **research analyst** is responsible for client contact, project design, preparation of proposals, selection of research suppliers, and supervision of data collection, analysis, and reporting activities.[6] Normally the research analyst is responsible for projects for all or several of a medium-size firm's products. He or she works with product or division management and makes recommendations based on analysis of collected data. A junior analyst, or **research assistant** (associate), provides technical assistance with questionnaire design, analysis of data, and so on. The **manager of decision support systems** supervises the collection and analysis of sales, inventory, and other periodic data. Sales forecasts for product lines usually are developed using analytical and quantitative techniques. Sales information is provided to satisfy the planning, analysis, and control needs of decision makers. The manager of decision support systems may be assisted by a **forecast analyst,** who provides technical assistance such as running computer programs and manipulating data to forecast sales.

The marketing research function in a medium-size firm may be performed by personnel within a planning department. These individuals may plan or design research studies and then contract with outside firms that supply research services such as interviewing or data processing.

As marketing research departments grow, they tend to specialize by product or strategic business unit. For example, Marriott Corporation has a director of marketing research for lodging (e.g., Marriott Hotels and Resorts, Courtyard by Marriott, and Fairfield Inn) and a director of marketing research for contract services and restaurants (e.g., Roy Rogers, Big Boy, and Senior Living Services). Each business unit's research director reports to the vice president of corporate marketing services. Many large organizations have **managers of customer quality research** who specialize in conducting surveys to measure consumers' satisfaction with product quality.

Exhibit 4.3 on page 70 illustrates the organization of the marketing research department of a major firm. Within this organization, the centralized marketing research department conducts research for all of the division's product groups. This department is typical of a large research department that conducts much of its own research, including fieldwork. The director of marketing research reports to the vice president of marketing.

The department in Exhibit 4.3 does not use outside marketing research contractors. To some extent, this is rare; nevertheless, the full-service department example facilitates discussion of marketing research's interfaces with other departments.

## ■ Cross-Functional Teams

As more companies arise to the challenge of the global information age and the need to act quickly, old forms of organizational structures are fading fast. Today everyone in a progressive organization, from accountants to engineers, engages in a unified effort to consider all issues related to the development, production, or marketing of new products.

**Cross-functional teams**
Teams composed of individuals from various organizational departments, such as engineering, production, finance, and marketing, who share a common purpose.

**Cross-functional teams** are composed of individuals from various organizational departments, such as engineering, production, finance, and marketing, who share a common purpose. Current management thinking suggests that cross-functional teams help organizations focus on a core business process, such as customer service or new-product development. Working in teams reduces the tendency for employees to focus single-mindedly on an isolated functional activity. The use of cross-functional teams to help employees improve product quality and increase customer value is a major trend in business today.

At trend-setting organizations, many marketing research directors are members of cross-functional teams. New-product development, for example, may be done by a cross-functional team of engineers, finance executives, production personnel, marketing managers, and marketing researchers who take an integrated approach to solve problems or

■ **Exhibit 4.3**               **Organization of the Marketing Research Department in a Large Firm**

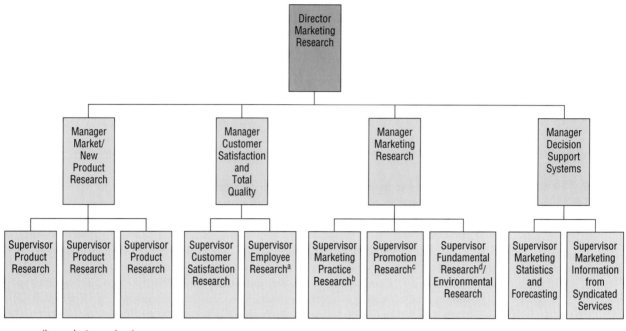

(by product groupings)

[a]Conducts research to improve total quality management in production.

[b]Conducts research which cuts across product lines or involves competitive marketing practices or characteristics of customer groups.

[c]Conducts research to measure the effectiveness of promotional activities that cut across product lines

[d]Conducts research aimed at gaining a basic understanding of various elements of the marketing process

exploit opportunities. In the old days, marketing research may not have been involved in developing new products until long after many key decisions about product specifications and manufacturing had been made. Today marketing researchers' input is part of an integrative team effort. Researchers act as both business consultants and providers of technical services. Researchers working in teams are more likely to understand the broad purpose of their research and less likely to focus exclusively on research methodology.

The effective cross-functional team is a good illustration of the marketing concept in action. It reflects an effort to satisfy customers by using all of the organization's resources. Cross-functional teams are having a dramatic impact on how the role of marketing research is viewed within the organization.

## ■ RESEARCH SUPPLIERS AND CONTRACTORS

**Research supplier**
A commercial marketing research service that conducts marketing research activity for clients.

The marketing research manager (in smaller firms, the marketing manager) must also interact with **research suppliers,** or commercial marketing research services. Although much marketing research activity is conducted in private companies' marketing research departments, much of it occurs in firms that may be variously classified as marketing research consulting companies (for example, Market Facts, Inc.), advertising agencies (such as J. Walter Thompson), suppliers of syndicated research services (such as Roper

■ At General Motors, the marketing research department's goal is to provide cost-effective market understanding that allows GM to beat competitors to opportunities for existing and new products. The marketing research department's primary mission is to provide relevant, accurate, usable, and timely market information. The director of research says, "Our added value is found when we participate as an active and equal member of the decision-making team. This active role must be accomplished by being perceived as coming to the team without a personal point of view as that perception could negatively affect the credibility of our primary mission."[7]

Starch), interviewing agencies, universities, and government agencies. The growth of global business and the trend toward being a "right-sized organization" focusing on core competencies has led to a greater emphasis on working with research suppliers as "partners."

No matter how large a firm's marketing research department, some projects are too expensive to perform in-house. A **syndicated service** is a marketing research supplier that provides standardized information for many clients. For example, J. D. Power and Associates sells research on customers' ratings of automobile quality and reasons for satisfaction. Most automobile manufacturers and their advertising agencies subscribe to this syndicated service because it provides important industrywide information gathered from a national sample of thousands of car buyers. By specializing in this type of customer satisfaction research, J. D. Power gains certain economies of scale.

**Syndicated service**
A marketing research supplier that provides standardized information for many clients.

Syndicated services can provide expensive information economically to numerous clients because its value is specific not to one client but to many. Such suppliers offer standardized information to measure media audiences, collect wholesale and retail distribution data, and conduct other forms of data gathering.

A number of organizations supply **standardized research services** at the request of individual clients. Typically the research organization has developed a unique methodology for investigating a specialty area, such as advertising effectiveness or brand name evaluation. These research suppliers will conduct studies for individual clients using the same methods they use for other clients. For example, BASES/Burke Institute's Day After Recall (DAR) is an organization that tests advertising recognition/recall and supplies data so a client can compare its scores with the average score for a product category.

**Standardized research service**
A research organization that has developed a unique methodology for investigating a specialty area, such as advertising effectiveness.

Even when a firm could perform the research task in-house, research suppliers may be able to conduct the project at a lower cost, faster, and from a completely objective perspective. A company that wishes to quickly evaluate a new advertising strategy may find the research department at an ad agency able to provide technical expertise on copy development research that is not available within the company itself.

Limited-service research suppliers specialize in particular research activities, such as syndicated service, field interviewing, or data processing. Full-service research suppliers contract for entire ad hoc marketing research projects. The client usually controls these marketing research agencies or management consulting firms, but the research supplier handles most of the operating details of these **custom research** projects, tailoring them to the client's unique needs. A custom research supplier may employ individuals with titles such as *account executive, account group manager,* and other titles that imply relationships with clients, as well as functional specialists such as *statistician, librarian, director of field services, director of data processing,* and *interviewer.*

**Custom research**
A marketing research study designed for an individual client and tailored to the client's unique needs.

A. C. Nielsen, IMS International, Information Resources, The Arbitron Company, Westat Inc., Maritz Marketing Research, and the NPD Group are among the top U.S. research suppliers. Most of these firms provide a variety of services ranging from design activities to fieldwork. Their services are not covered in detail here because they are discussed throughout the book.

In many cases, the marketing research manager's job is primarily administrative: hiring interviewing services, data-processing services, and so on. When it is necessary to hire outside research suppliers or contractors, the marketing researcher must be able to evaluate such specialized services. An analogy is the make-or-buy decision in the factory: The researcher can hire a research service to conduct the project or conduct the project with internal personnel.

Who you do
# BUSINESS with
makes
a world of
# DIFFERENCE.

Products and ideas are now flowing across international borders as quickly as they once moved across town. You need an information partner who is right there beside you. Region by region. Country by country.

You need ACNielsen.

Our information network extends across more than 90 countries and covers 4.7 billion people.

But just as important is the scope of our services. From tracking daily information at store 52 in Peoria, Illinois, to monitoring product introductions and expansions across four continents, ACNielsen gives you real solutions to your business needs.

When you want to identify emerging concepts from around the world, we can help. We know what new ideas are succeeding. Where they are succeeding. And why.

If you're penetrating new markets, our international household panels in fifteen countries give you the consumer insight you need to succeed. No other information company comes close to this capability.

Let ACNielsen make a world of difference to your business. **Call 1-800-988-4226.**

**ACNielsen**

ONLY
ACNielsen
has the
ANSWER.

ACNielsen is a copyright of A.C.Nielsen Company
©1996 ACNielsen. All rights reserved.

■ A. C. Nielsen is one of the world's largest research suppliers. This advertisment describes some of the services it supplies across four continents.

# ■ ETHICAL ISSUES IN MARKETING RESEARCH

As in all human interactions, ethical issues arise in marketing research. Throughout this book, we will encounter selected ethical issues concerning fair business dealings, proper research techniques, and appropriate use of research results. The remainder of this chapter addresses society's and managers' concerns about the ethical implications of marketing research.

## ■ Ethical Questions Are Philosophical Questions

**Societal norms**
Codes of behavior adopted by a group that suggest what a member of a group ought to do under given circumstances.

Ethical questions are philosophical questions. There is no general agreement among philosophers about the answers to such questions. However, the rights and obligations of individuals generally are dictated by the norms of society. **Societal norms** are codes of behavior adopted by a group; they suggest what a member of a group ought to do under given circumstances. This chapter reflects the author's perceptions of the norms of our society (and undoubtedly his own values to some extent).[8]

## ■ General Rights and Obligations of Concerned Parties

Most research situations involve three parties: the researcher, the sponsoring client (user), and the respondent (or subject). The interaction of each party with one or both of the other two parties identifies a series of ethical questions. Consciously or unconsciously, each party expects certain rights and feels certain obligations toward the other parties. Any society imposes a set of normatively prescribed expectations of behavior (including rights and obligations) associated with a social role, such as researcher, and another, reciprocal role, such as respondent. Certain ethical behaviors may be expected only in specific situations, while other expectations may be more generalized. Conflicting perspectives about behavioral expectations may create ethical problems. For instance, several ethical issues concern the researcher's expected rights versus those of the respondent/subject. A number of questions arise because researchers believe they have the right to seek information, but subjects believe they have a right to privacy. A respondent who says, "I don't care to answer your question about my income" believes he or she has the right to refuse to participate. Yet some researchers will persist in trying to get that information. In general, a fieldworker is expected not to overstep the boundary society places on consumer privacy.

For each of the subject's rights, the researcher has a corresponding obligation. For example, the individual's right to privacy dictates that the researcher has an obligation to protect the respondent's anonymity. When that respondent discloses information about personal matters, it is assumed that such information will be guarded from all people other than the researcher.

## ■ Rights and Obligations of the Respondent

The ethical issues vary somewhat depending on whether the participant has given willing and informed consent. In an unobtrusive observation study, the participant's rights differ from a survey respondent's rights because he or she has not willingly consented to be a subject of the research.

**The Obligation to Be Truthful**   When a subject provides willing consent to participate, he or she is generally expected to provide truthful answers. Honest cooperation is the main obligation of the respondent or subject.

**Privacy** Americans relish their privacy. A major polling organization has indicated that almost 80 percent of Americans believe the collecting and giving out of personal information without their knowledge is a serious violation of their privacy.[9] Hence, the right to privacy is an important issue in marketing research. This issue involves the subject's freedom to choose whether or not to comply with the investigator's request. Traditionally researchers have assumed that individuals make an informed choice. However, critics have argued that elderly, low-income, poorly educated, and other disadvantaged individuals may be unaware of their right to choose. They have further argued that the interview may begin with some vague explanation of its purpose, initially ask questions that are relatively innocuous, and then move to questions of a highly personal nature. It has been suggested that subjects be informed of their right to be left alone or to break off the interview at any time. Researchers should not follow the tendency to "hold on" to busy respondents. However, this view definitely is not universally accepted in the research community.

Another aspect of the privacy issue is illustrated by this question: Is a telephone call that interrupts someone's favorite television program an invasion of privacy? The answer to this issue, and to most privacy questions, lies in the dilemma of where the individual's rights end and society's need for better scientific information on consumer preferences takes over. Generally interviewing firms have set certain standards of common courtesy, for example, not to interview late in the evening and at other inconvenient times. However, several critics may never be appeased. The computerized interview (sometimes called a "junk phone call") has stimulated increased debate over this aspect of the privacy issue. As a practical matter, respondents may feel more relaxed about privacy issues if they know who is conducting the survey. Thus, it is generally recommended that field interviewers indicate they are legitimate researchers by passing out business cards, wearing name tags, or in other ways identifying the names of their companies.

In an observation study, the major ethical issues concern whether the observed behavior is public or private. Generally it is believed that unobtrusive observation of public behavior in places such as stores, airports, and museums is not a serious invasion of privacy. However, recording private behavior with hidden cameras and the like represents a violation of this right. For example, a survey showed that approximately 95 percent of research directors and line marketing executives disapproved of the practice of observing women putting on brassieres through a one-way mirror.[10]

**Deception** In a number of situations, the researcher creates a false impression by disguising the purpose of the research. At least at the outset of the research, the researcher is not open and honest. Bluntly stated, to avoid biased reactions, the researcher lies to the subject. Deception or concealment results from the researcher's failure to observe or straightforwardly ask about the phenomenon of interest, and hold all other factors constant, without partially deceiving the respondent. Generally, such deception is justified under two conditions: (1) The researcher assumes no physical danger or psychological harm will result from the deception, and (2) the researcher takes personal responsibility for informing the respondent of the concealment or deception after the research project ends. This issue is interrelated with the subject's right to be informed.

The issue of deception concerns the means-to-an-end philosophical issue. The primary question is: Does a minor deception substantially increase the value of the research? Suppose a survey research project involves contacting busy executives. Pretending to be calling long distance might improve the response rate, but is this a justifiable means to this end?

A distinction has been made between deception and discreet silence. The ethical question concerning the apparent content of a questionnaire versus the true purpose of the research has been cleverly stated as follows:

Must we really explain, when we ask the respondent to agree or disagree with the statement, "prison is too good for sex criminals; they should be publicly whipped or worse," it is really the authoritarianism of his personality we are investigating, and not the public opinion on crime and punishment?[11]

**The Right to Be Informed**   It has been argued that subjects have a right to be informed of all aspects of the research. This includes information about its purpose and sponsorship. The argument for the researcher's obligation to protect this right is based on the academic tradition of informing and enlightening the public.

A pragmatic argument for providing respondents with information about the nature of the study concerns the long-run ability of researchers to gain cooperation from respondents. If the public understands why survey or Internet information has been collected and that the researchers may be trusted with private information, it may be easier in the long run to conduct research. Several research suppliers have suggested that public relations work is needed to convince consumers of the integrity of the research industry.

## ■ Rights and Obligations of the Researcher

General business ethics should be a standard for marketing research firms and marketing research departments. Our concern is not with issues such as bribery or the welfare and safety of one's employees but with ethical issues that are specifically germane to marketing research practices.

More has been written about the ethics of researchers than about those of the other two parties because this group's purpose is clearly identifiable. Researchers have obligations to both subjects and clients as well as corresponding rights. A number of professional associations have developed standards and operating procedures for ethical practices by researchers. (Go to *http://www.dryden.com/mktng/zikmund* for links to the codes of ethics for two professional associations, the American Marketing Association and the Marketing Research Association.) These **codes of ethics** show that several opinions exist about the nature of ethical practices. Several major issues invite further exploration.

**Code of ethics**
A set of guidelines that states the standards and operating procedures for ethical practices by researchers.

**The Purpose of Research Is Research**   Businesspeople are expected not to misrepresent a sales tactic as marketing research. The Federal Trade Commission has indicated that it is illegal to use any plan, scheme, or ruse that misrepresents the true status of the person making the call as a door opener to gain admission to a prospect's home, office, or other establishment. This sales ploy is considered unethical as well as illegal. No research firm should engage in any practice other than scientific investigation.

**Objectivity**   Throughout this book, the text stresses the need for objective scientific investigation to ensure accuracy. Researchers should maintain high standards to ensure that their data are accurate. Further, they must not intentionally try to prove a particular point for political purposes.

**Avoid Misrepresenting Research**   Research companies (and clients) should not misrepresent the statistical accuracy of their data, nor should they overstate the significance of the results by altering the findings. Basically the researcher has the obligation to both client and subjects to honestly analyze the data and correctly report the actual data collection methods. For example, the failure to report a variation from a technically correct probability sampling procedure is ethically questionable. Likewise, any major error that has occurred during the course of the study should not be kept secret from management or the sponsor. Hiding errors or variations from the proper procedures tends to distort or shade the results. A more blatant breach of the researcher's responsibilities would be the outright distortion of data.

## WHAT WENT WRONG?

### Hertz Was Not Amused

A few years ago, a magazine called *Corporate Travel* published the results of a consumer survey of the travel industry. In the category of rental cars, the magazine declared Avis the winner of what was to be its first annual Alfred Award, named for Alfred Kahn, former chairman of the Civil Aviation Board. Avis, not surprisingly, quickly launched an advertising campaign touting its standing in the poll.

Joseph Russo, vice president for government and public affairs at Avis's archrival, Hertz, was not amused. He called the magazine's editor and asked if he could see a press release and any other material that might explain the survey's results and methodology. "We've won virtually every other poll that's ever been done," said Russo. (Indeed, surveys like these are popularity contests that tend to favor bigger competitors over smaller ones; and they are almost impossible to duplicate or verify.) "So we wanted to see if we were missing the beat." But Russo said he could not get much information about the survey. "I said, How many people voted in this, was it bigger than a bread basket?"

It turned out that the survey responses had disappeared under mysterious circumstances. The magazine's marketing manager, who had overseen the poll, had left the magazine. "A search of their files has also failed to turn up any statistical tabulation or record of the responses for any category," wrote the president of *Corporate Travel*'s parent to Hertz. Meanwhile, said Russo, "We had corporate accounts saying, I see you guys came in after Avis."

Eventually Hertz filed suit against the publisher of the magazine and Avis, charging false advertising. "We said if we allow this to go on, anyone will be able to do anything on the basis of a survey," Russo said. The parties settled, with Avis agreeing to stop calling itself the car rental company of choice among business travelers.

**Protect the Right to Confidentiality of Both Subjects and Clients**    A number of clients may desire a list of favorable industrial sales prospects generated from a research survey. It is the researcher's responsibility to ensure that the privacy and anonymity of the respondents are preserved. If the respondent's name and address are known, this information should not be forwarded to the sponsoring organization under any circumstances.

Information a research supplier obtains about a client's general business affairs should not be disseminated to other clients or third parties. The client or user of marketing research has a number of rights and obligations. The primary right is to expect objective and accurate data from the research supplier. This party should also expect respect for any instructions of confidentiality.

**Avoid Dissemination of Faulty Conclusions**    The American Marketing Association's marketing research code of ethics states that "a user of research shall not knowingly disseminate conclusions from a given research project or service that are inconsistent with or not warranted by the data." A dramatic example of a violation of this principle occurred in an advertisement of a cigarette smoker study. The advertisement compared two brands and stated that "of those expressing a preference, over 65 percent preferred" the advertised brand to a competing brand. The misleading portion of this reported result was that most respondents did not express a preference; they indicated that both brands tasted about the same. Thus, only a very small percentage of those studied actually revealed a preference, and the results were somewhat misleading. Such shading of results violates the obligation to report accurate findings.

**Competitive Research Proposals**    Consider a client who has solicited several bids for a marketing research project. The client requests the research supplier that wins the bid to appropriate ideas from the proposal of a competing research supplier and include them in the research study. This practice generally is regarded as unethical.

### ■ Rights and Obligations of the Client Sponsor (User)

**Ethical Behavior between Buyer and Seller**    The general business ethics expected between a purchasing agent and a sales representative should hold in the marketing research situation. For example, if the purchasing agent has already decided to purchase a product (or research proposal) from a friend, it would be unethical for that person to solicit competitive bids that have no chance of being accepted just to fulfill a corporate purchasing policy stating that a bid must be put out to some number of competitors. The typical business and other commitments unrelated to a specific marketing research situation are ethical questions with which we will not deal here.

**An Open Relationship with Research Suppliers**    The client sponsor has the obligation to encourage the research supplier to objectively seek out the truth. To encourage this objectivity, a full and open statement of the problem, an explication of constraints in time and money, and any other insights that may help the supplier anticipate costs and problems should be provided. In other words, the research sponsor should encourage efforts to reduce bias and to listen to the voice of the public.

**An Open Relationship with Interested Parties**    Conclusions should be based on the data. A user of research should not knowingly disseminate conclusions from a research project or service that are inconsistent with or not warranted by the data. Violation of this principle is perhaps the greatest transgression a client can commit. Justifying a political position that the data do not warrant poses serious ethical questions. Indicating that the data show something to make a sale is also an unethical practice.

**Advocacy research**
Research undertaken to support a specific claim in a legal action.

  **Advocacy research,** research undertaken to support a specific claim in a legal action, puts the client in a unique situation. Advocacy research, such as a survey conducted to show that a brand name is not a generic name, differs from research that traditionally has been intended for internal use only. The conventional factors, such as sample size, people to be interviewed, and questions to be asked, are weighted against cost when making an internal decision. In advocacy research, the court's opinion of the value of the research may be based exclusively on sampling design or some methodological issue. Thus, the slightest variation from technically correct sampling procedures may be magnified by an attorney until a standard marketing research project no longer appears adequate in the judge's eye. How open should the client be in the courtroom?

  The ethics of advocacy research present a number of serious questions. Consider the following quote:

> Almost never do you see a researcher who appears as an independent witness, quite unbiased. You almost always see a witness appearing either for the FTC or for the industry. You can almost predict what is going to be concluded by the witness for the FTC. And you can almost predict what will be concluded by the witness for industry. That says that research in this setting is not after full truth and it is not dispassionate in nature. And for those of us who consider ourselves to be researchers, that is a serious quandary.[12]

Advocacy researchers do not necessarily bias results intentionally. However, attorneys rarely submit advocacy research evidence that does not support their clients' positions.

  The question surrounding advocacy research is one of objectivity: Can the researcher seek out the truth when the legal client wishes to support its position at a trial? The ethical question stems from a conflict between legal ethics and research ethics. Although the courts have set judicial standards for marketing research methodology, perhaps only the client and the individual researcher can resolve this question.[13]

**Privacy**  Suppose a database company is offering a mailing list compiled by screening millions of households to obtain brand usage information. The information would be extremely valuable to your firm, but you suspect a fake survey was used to obtain the data. Would it be ethical to purchase the mailing list? If respondents have been deceived about the purpose of a survey and their names are subsequently sold as part of a user mailing list, this practice is certainly unethical. The client as well as the research supplier has the obligation to maintain respondents' privacy. Sales managers who know a marketing survey of their business-to-business customers has been keyed to increase the response rate must resist the temptation to seek those accounts that are the hottest prospects.

**Commitment to Research**  Some potential clients have been known to request research proposals from research suppliers when there is a low probability that the research will be conducted. For example, obtaining an outsider's opinion of a company problem via a research proposal provides an inexpensive consultation. If the information supports a given manager's position in an intracompany debate, it could be used politically rather than as a basis for research. A research consultant's opinion may be solicited even though management is not really planning research and funds have not been allocated for the project. Most research practitioners believe that because the research supplier must spend considerable effort planning a custom-designed study, the client has the obligation to solicit proposals only for seriously considered projects.

**Pseudo-Pilot Studies**  Clients should be open about the marketing problem to be investigated. However, there is a special case of this problem. Sometimes a client suggests that a more comprehensive study is in the planning stages, and the proposal on which the research supplier is bidding is a pilot study. This can be best phrased by the statement "I don't want to promise anything, but you should know that this is the first in a very ambitious series of studies we are planning to undertake, and if you sharpen your pencil in estimating cost. . . ."[14] The research consultant is told that if he or she does a good job during the pilot study stages, there will be an additional major contract down the line. Too often such pilot studies lead to nothing more; the comprehensive study never materializes, and the consultant must absorb a loss.

### ■ A Final Note on Ethics

Certainly unethical researchers exist in the world and a number of shady dealings occur. The marketing researcher's honesty is no different from any other aspect of business ethics—or of personal morality, for that matter. One may occasionally encounter a researcher who produces a report on fabricated findings. Likewise, interviewers occasionally cheat by filling out the questionnaires themselves. Under some circumstances even honest researchers take shortcuts, some of which may be ethically questionable. However, researchers, like most businesspeople, generally are ethical people. The answer to the question "What is ethical?" is not easy; only one's conscience can prevent any questionable practice.

### ■ SUMMARY

Different firms possess varying degrees of marketing research sophistication. In the first stage of such sophistication, firms ignore research and rely on intuition. In the second stage, they are naively impressed with marketing research and expect it to remove all risk from marketing decisions. During this development stage, managers may become disillusioned with research because they have made costly mistakes based on its findings (including poor research). In the last stage, the firm has a realistic appreciation for marketing research and uses it as a tool to reduce risk rather than to foretell the future.

A marketing research function may be organized in any number of ways depending on the firm's size, business, and stage of research sophistication. Marketing research managers must remember they are managers, not just researchers.

Various individual job titles exist in the marketing research industry. Some of the most common include director of marketing research, research analyst, research assistant, manager of decision support systems, forecast analyst, and manager of customer quality research.

Research suppliers and contractors can augment the research staff of a small firm, or they can provide services impossible for even large firms to handle internally.

The ethical questions that surround marketing research have no universal answers. However, societal norms suggest the codes of conduct that are appropriate in given circumstances. There are three concerned parties in marketing research situations: the researcher, the sponsoring client (user), and the respondent (subject). Each party has certain rights and obligations. The respondent's rights include privacy and being informed about all aspects of the research; the subject's main obligation is to give honest answers to research questions. The researcher is expected to adhere to the purpose of the research, maintain objectivity, avoid misrepresenting research findings, protect subjects' and clients' rights to confidentiality, and avoid shading research conclusions. The client is obligated to observe general business ethics when dealing with research suppliers, avoid misusing the research findings to support its aims, respect research respondents' privacy, and be open about its intentions to conduct research and the marketing problem at hand. A potential transgression occurs when advocacy research—research conducted to support a specific legal claim—is undertaken.

## ■ Key Terms and Concepts

Research sophistication

Client

Director of marketing research

Director of marketing information systems

Research analyst

Research assistant

Manager of decision support systems

Forecast analyst

Manager of customer quality research

Cross-functional teams

Research supplier

Syndicated service

Standardized research service

Custom research

Societal norms

Code of ethics

Advocacy research

## ■ Questions

1. What are the stages of marketing research sophistication? Name some companies that you think are in one of each of these stages.
2. What might the organizational structure of the research department be like for the following organizations?
   (a) A large advertising agency
   (b) A founder-owned company that operates a 20-unit restaurant chain
   (c) Your college or university
   (d) An industrial marketer with four product divisions
   (e) A large consumer products company
3. What problems do marketing research directors face in their roles as managers?
4. To whom should marketing research be accountable?
5. Identify a research supplier in your area, and determine what syndicated services and other functions are available to clients.

6. Go to your library to learn the job titles and responsibilities for the various types of marketing research jobs. (Hint: One of the best sources is Thomas Kinnear and Ann Root, eds., *1994 Survey of Marketing Research* [Chicago: American Marketing Association, 1995].)

7. What do you think would be the best way to find work in marketing research?

8. Name some marketing research practices that may be ethically questionable.

9. What actions might the marketing research industry take to convince the public that marketing research is a legitimate activity and firms that misrepresent their intentions and distort findings to achieve their aims are not "true" marketing research companies?

10. Page through your local newspaper to find some articles derived from survey research results. Was the study's methodology indicated for this news item? Could this research have been considered advocacy research?

11. Comment on the ethics of the following situations:

    (a) A food warehouse club advertises "savings up to 30 percent" after a survey showed a range of savings from 2 to 30 percent below average prices for selected items.

    (b) A radio station broadcasts the following message during a syndicated rating service's rating period: "Please fill out your diary."

    (c) A sewing machine retailer advertises a market test and indicates that the regular price will be cut to one-half for three days only.

    (d) A researcher tells a potential respondent that the interview will last 10 minutes rather than the 30 minutes he or she actually anticipates.

    (e) A respondent tells an interviewer that she wishes to cooperate with the survey, but her time is valuable and therefore she expects to be paid for the interview.

12. Comment on the following interview:

**Interviewer:** Good afternoon, sir. My name is Mrs. Johnson with Counseling Services. We are conducting a survey concerning Memorial Park. Do you own a funeral plot? Please answer yes or no.

**Respondent:** (pauses)

**Interviewer:** You do not own a funeral plot, do you?

**Respondent:** No.

**Interviewer:** Would you mind if I sent you a letter concerning Memorial Park? Please answer yes or no.

**Respondent:** No.

**Interviewer:** Would you please give me your address?

---

## EXPLORING THE INTERNET

1. Use a Web browser to go to the Gallup Organization's home page at:

   http://www.gallup.com

   Select the "Mission Statement" option. What are the key aspects of this research company's mission?

2. Use a Web browser to go to the NPD, Inc., home page at:

   http://www.npd.com

   Select the "Career Opportunities" option. Then select "Getting started at NPD" and "Building a Career" options. What would a career in marketing research be like at NPD?

3. Many Internet sites list job opportunities and information that is useful for job applicants. Use your Web browser to search for marketing management and marketing research jobs at the following URL addresses:

http://www.westga.edu/~coop/

http://www.careerpath.com

http://www.job-hunt.org

---

## CASE 4.1    Push-Polling

The question, in the midst of a telephone poll, was as shocking as it was designed to be: Would you still favor Rudy Silbaugh, a Republican candidate for the Wisconsin state assembly, if you knew he voted to give guns back to juveniles who had used them in crimes?

Mr. Silbaugh and other Wisconsin Republicans filed a lawsuit because of that damaging assertion, which the Republican Party said was made recently by a telemarketing firm calling on behalf of Democratic candidates. But they recognize the campaign tactic, having used it themselves.

It's known as "push-polling," and it has increasingly become implemented at the last minute of political campaigns when the airwaves have grown saturated with political messages.

For years, campaign pollsters have conducted surveys of a few hundred voters to test the potency of negative information for later use in broad attacks, such as television advertising. What's different about push-polling, though not easy to trace, is the use of phone calls as the means of disseminating attacks to thousands of voters at a time. But unlike the case with TV ads or direct-mail brochures, federal law doesn't require congressional campaigns to identify who's paying for the calls.

"If people want to lie, cheat, and steal, they should be held accountable," said Representative Tom Petri, Republican of Wisconsin, who complains that anonymous callers in 1992 told constituents that he was a tool of Japanese auto dealers and responsible for the savings and loan mess.

In Colorado, the campaign of Democratic Governor Roy Romer, who was reelected, complained to the state attorney general that opponent Bruce Benson's campaign used push-polling in violation of a Colorado statute forbidding anonymous campaigning.

The advocacy in question, according to a script obtained by the governor's aides, asked voters if they'd be more or less likely to support Mr. Romer if they knew that "there have been nearly 1,300 murders in Colorado since Romer was first elected and not one murderer has been put to death." Follow-up questions informed voters that the state parole board "has granted early release to an average of four convicted felons per day every day since Romer took office," that Mr. Romer spent "one out of every four days outside of Colorado" during his four-year term and "is being sued for mismanaging the state's foster-care system."

The attorney general declined to prosecute, but Romer campaign manager Alan Salazar complained the lack of accountability of push-polling, as well as the enhanced credibility of an attack delivered personally to voters, makes the practice worrisome.

### Questions
1. Why do political organizations conduct push polls? Is push-polling a legitimate form of marketing research?
2. Is push-polling ethical?

---

## ■ Endnotes

[1]Lee Adler and Charles S. Mayer, *Managing the Marketing Research Function* (Chicago: American Marketing Association, 1977), p. 18.

[2]James B. Stuart, R. J. Reynolds Tobacco Company, personal communication.

[3]Eli P. Cox III, *Marketing Research: Information for Decision Making* (Englewood Cliffs, N.J.: Prentice-Hall, 1979) pp. 54–55.

[4]Thomas C. Kinnear and Ann Root, eds., *1994 Survey of Marketing Research* (Chicago: American Marketing Association, 1995).

[5]Kathie Julian and Sarah Coffer, "Kaleidoscope of Change," *Marketing Research,* Fall 1996, pp. 8– 14.

[6]Job titles vary substantially in industry. This title could also be *supervisor of research, manager of research, project director,* or *senior research analyst* in a larger firm with several levels of management.

[7]Barabba, "Market Research Techniques."

[8]For an alternative perspective, see Kenneth C. Schneider's excellent article "Marketing Research Industry Isn't Moving toward Professionalism," *Marketing Educator,* Winter 1984, pp. 1, 6; Steven J. Skinner, O. C. Ferrell, and Alan J. Dubinsky, "Organizational Dimensions of Marketing-Research Ethics," *Journal of Business Research* 16 (1988), pp. 209–223; Patrick E. Murphy and Gene R. Laczniak, "Traditional Ethical Issues Facing Marketing Researchers," *Marketing Research,* March 1992, pp. 8–21.

[9]Lawrence D. Wiseman, "The Present Value of Future Studies," speech to the Advertising Research Foundation, March 1980.

[10]C. Merle Crawford, "Attitudes of Marketing Executives toward Ethics in Marketing Research," *Journal of Marketing,* April 1970, pp. 46–52; Ishmael P. Akaah and Edward A. Riordan, "Judgments of Marketing Professionals about Ethical Issues in Marketing Research: A Replication and Extension," *Journal of Marketing Research,* February 1989, pp. 112–120.

[11]Leo Bogart, "The Researcher's Dilemma," *Journal of Marketing,* January 1962, pp. 6–11.

[12]H. Keith Hunt, "The Ethics of Research in the Consumer Interests: Panel Summary," ed. Norleen M. Ackerman, *Proceedings of the American Council of Consumer Interests Conference,* 1979, p. 152.

[13]Fred W. Morgan Jr., "Judicial Standards for Survey Research: An Update and Guidelines," *Journal of Marketing,* January 1990, pp. 59–70.

[14]Robert Bezilla, Joel B. Haynes, and Clifford Elliot, "Ethics in Marketing Research," *Business Horizons,* April 1976, pp. 83–86.

# 5

# EXPLORATORY RESEARCH AND QUALITATIVE ANALYSIS

**WHAT YOU WILL LEARN IN THIS CHAPTER:**

To understand the differences between qualitative research and quantitative research.

To explain the purposes of exploratory research.

To identify the four general categories of exploratory research.

To explain the advantages and disadvantages of experience surveys, case study methods, focus group interviews, projective techniques, depth interviews, and other exploratory research techniques.

To identify when exploratory techniques are appropriate and to understand their limitations.

To understand how technology is changing the nature of exploratory research.

**O**n a gray and gusty day in June, 35 girls between the ages of 5 and 9 were gathered in a conference room near the San Francisco Airport, looking at prototypes of a toy they'd never seen before. Lewis Galoob Toys had convened a series of focus groups to watch real live kids interact with a doll being developed for 1995. The name of the doll was Sky Dancer.

Deborah Rivers, the research consultant who led the groups, would have preferred a

less sterile environment to put the girls at their ease, but this windowless room would have to do. On one wall were pictures of military airplanes. Directly across was a one-way mirror, so that the precise reactions of the participants could be videotaped and analyzed later.

The grainy tapes show bunches of girls—some scruffy, some bright-eyed, some with bows in their hair. Rivers begins by making a "pinkie promise" with each girl to ensure that everything said between these walls will be the truth. The children are happy to swear on their honor. They have a good idea that, just around the bend, there will be a reward for their consultations. So they like everything, agree to everything.

"You know," Rivers says dubiously to the kids, "some people say that flying toys are only for boys. Is that true?" The response is immediate: "No!" The notion that anything could be "only for boys" is summarily rejected. Then Rivers's tone changes. She has the girls close their eyes and then reads a brief set piece from her clipboard: "I'd like to welcome you to the enchanted world of Sky Dancers! Each beautiful Sky Dancer unfolds her elegant wings and flies with the wind. . . ." She goes on to evoke ocean waves and shimmering moons— cue words to let the Sky Dancer whammy take effect.

The girls open their eyes. By now Rivers has brought out a bevy of dolls—winged ballerinas, from the look of them. They are garish and plastic, with pink-and-lavender nylon hair. The girls blink a few times at the dolls. Many love them at first sight; others praise faintly, hoping they won't blow their chance to get the money they've been promised. Two of the 35 girls react to the doll with open disdain. "Well," says a girl named Kate, who's missing a front tooth, "she's not the best thing in the world."

But Rivers isn't discouraged; this doll's got a gimmick. She picks up her prototype by its flowery base—or, more accurately, its pistol-grip launcher—and tugs at a string. The doll starts to twirl; its wings lift, by virtue of aerodynamic design, until all at once the Sky Dancer has risen free of its base and whizzed straight up in the air, winged arms whirring like a helicopter blade. The girls respond in a hushed chorus: "Cooool!"

Postflight, Rivers elicits comments on the doll and asks the girls how they like it. One claims she wants a Sky Dancer "more than the whole universe." At a certain point, Rivers leaves the room. Behind the mirror are a few Galoob employees, including Scott Masline, the firm's vice president of marketing and a driving force in the doll's development. Rivers wants to check with Masline to see if he'd like any departures from the script. It's also an ideal chance to observe the girls at their most candid.

In one group, Rivers's exit is greeted with silence. Finally, Emily, a blond girl with a ponytail, speaks: "She's probably going to get the money," she says quietly.

"How much are you guys getting?" asks a waif from across the table.

"We're all getting $25," Emily replies.

Behind the glass, Scott Masline is ignoring the girls' discussion. He's pleased. It seems that girls don't need an elaborate story line to understand his product; "flying doll" is clear to them. Best of all, he has heard the elongated syllable "Cooool" uttered eight out of eight times.[1]

Focus group research serves as a source for developing new toys that are then subjected to further research investigation. At Galoob, research helps reduce some of the risks in the volatile toy industry. This chapter discusses the various exploratory research techniques used in marketing research.

## ■ EXPLORATORY RESEARCH: WHAT IT IS AND WHAT IT IS NOT

When a researcher has a limited amount of experience with or knowledge about a research issue, exploratory research is a useful preliminary step. It helps ensure that a more rigorous, conclusive future study will not begin with an inadequate understanding of the nature of the marketing problem. The findings of the Sky Dancer exploratory research, for instance, would lead the researchers to emphasize learning more about girls' preferences in subsequent, more generalizable studies.

Conclusive research answers questions of fact necessary to determine a course of action. Exploratory research, on the other hand, never has this purpose. Most, but certainly not all, exploratory research designs provide *qualitative* data. Usually exploratory research yields greater understanding of a concept or crystallizes a problem rather than providing precise measurement, or *quantification*. A researcher may search for numbers to indicate economic trends but does not perform a rigorous mathematical analysis. Any source of information may be informally investigated to clarify which qualities or characteristics are associated with a product, situation, or issue.

Alternatively, the purpose of quantitative research is to determine the quantity or extent of some phenomenon in the form of numbers. Most exploratory research is not quantitative. This chapter discusses exploratory research under the assumption that its purpose is qualitative.

**Exploratory research**
Initial research conducted to clarify and define the nature of a problem.

**Exploratory research** may be a single investigation or a series of informal studies to provide background information. Researchers must be creative in the choice of information sources to be investigated. They must be flexible enough to investigate all inexpensive sources that may possibly provide information to help managers understand a problem. This flexibility does not mean that researchers need not be careful and systematic when designing exploratory research studies. Most of the techniques discussed in this chapter have limitations. Researchers should be keenly aware of the proper and improper uses of the various techniques.

## ■ WHY CONDUCT EXPLORATORY RESEARCH?

The purpose of exploratory research is intertwined with the need for a clear and precise statement of the recognized problem. Researchers conduct exploratory research for three interrelated purposes: (1) to diagnose a situation, (2) to screen alternatives, and (3) to discover new ideas.

### ■ Diagnosing a Situation

We already have seen that situation analysis is necessary to clarify a problem's nature. Exploratory research helps diagnose the dimensions of problems so that successive research projects will be on target; it helps set priorities for research. In some cases, exploratory research helps orient management by gathering information on an unfamiliar topic. A research project may not yet be planned, but information about an issue will be needed before the marketing strategy can be developed.

For example, when an advertising agency got an account for a new coffee containing chicory, the firm began the research process with exploratory research to diagnose the situation. The researchers learned that almost nobody had heard of chicory. It wasn't being used, and nobody seemed to know how to use it. This led to the hypothesis that the advertising could portray the chicory ingredient any way the client wanted.

### ■ Screening Alternatives

When several opportunities arise, such as numerous new-product ideas, and budgets don't allow trying all possible options, exploratory research may be used to determine the best alternatives. Many good products are not on the market because a company chose to market something better. Some new-product ideas are found to be unworkable, or an exploratory look at market data (size, number, and so on) may depict a product alternative as not feasible because the market is too small. This aspect of exploratory research is not a substitute for conclusive research; however, such studies can yield certain evaluative information.

**Concept testing**
Any exploratory research procedure that tests some sort of stimulus as a proxy for an idea about a new, revised, or repositioned product, service, or strategy.

Concept testing is a frequent reason for conducting exploratory research. **Concept testing** is a general term for many different research procedures, all of which have the same purpose: to test some sort of stimulus as a proxy for a new, revised, or repositioned product or service. Concept testing portrays the functions, uses, and possible applications for the proposed good or service. Typically consumers are presented with a written statement or filmed representation of an idea and asked if they would use it, whether they like it, and so on. Concept testing is a means of evaluating ideas by providing a feel for their merits prior to the commitment of any research and development, manufacturing, or other company resources.

Keebler's Sweet Spots, a combination of shortbread cookie and chocolate drop, was more than a cookie; it was almost a candy.[2] When Keebler researched the positioning concept for Sweet Spots, it considered two alternative concepts: (1) an upscale product for the self-indulgent cookie eater and (2) a lunchbox filler for children.

Researchers look for trouble signals in consumer evaluations of concepts to reduce the number of concepts under consideration or improve them to avoid future problems. For example, marketers scrapped a concept for a men's shampoo that claimed to offer a special benefit to hair damaged by overexposure to the sun, heat from a hair dryer, or heavy perspiration after exploratory research showed that consumers thought the product was a good idea for someone with an outdoor lifestyle but not for themselves.[3] Early research indicated that although the product was seen as unique, the likelihood of persuading men that it matched their self-images was low.

### ■ Discovering New Ideas

Marketers often conduct exploratory research to generate ideas for new products, advertising copy, and so on. For example, automobile marketers have consumers design their dream cars on video screens using computerized design systems adapted from those used by automotive designers. This exploratory research generates ideas that would never have occurred to the firms' own designers.[4]

Uncovering consumer needs is a great potential source of product ideas. One goal for exploratory research is to first determine what problems consumers have with a product category. When research has to determine what kinds of products people will buy, there is a difference between asking people about what they want or need and asking them about their problems. When you ask a customer what he or she wants in a dog food, the reply likely will be "Something that is good for the dog." If you ask what the problems with dog food are, you may learn that "The dog food smells bad when it is put into the refrigerator."[5] Once research has identified problems, the marketing job is to find solutions.

## ■ CATEGORIES OF EXPLORATORY RESEARCH

There are many techniques for investigating undefined research problems. Several of the most popular qualitative techniques are discussed in the next section. However, the purpose, rather than the technique, determines whether a study is exploratory, descriptive, or causal. For example, telephone surveys (discussed in Chapter 7) are sometimes used for exploratory purposes, although they are used mainly for descriptive research. The versatile qualitative techniques discussed in this chapter tend to be used primarily, but not exclusively, for exploratory purposes.

A manager may choose from four general categories of exploratory research methods: (1) experience surveys, (2) secondary data analysis, (3) case studies, and (4) pilot studies. Each category provides various alternative ways to gather information.

## ■ EXPERIENCE SURVEYS

**Experience survey**
An exploratory research technique in which individuals who are knowledgeable about a particular research problem are questioned.

If management decides that an idea is worthwhile, the decision maker may personally spend some time analyzing the situation. In attempting to gain insight into the problems at hand, researchers may discuss the concepts with top executives and knowledgeable individuals, both inside and outside the company, who have had personal experience in the field. This process constitutes an informal **experience survey.**

■ A chain saw manufacturer received from its Japanese distributor a recommendation to modify its product with a drilling attachment on the sprocket (replacing the chain and guide bar) for use as a mushroom-planting device. The distributor indicated that many such units had been sold in Japan. However, an experience survey with only one individual, the president of the Mushroom Growers Association, indicated that the product was not feasible in the United States. Americans favor a white, cultured mushroom grown in enclosed areas or caves rather than the variety of mushrooms grown on wood in Japan. The mushroom expert indicated that Americans believe too many superstitious tales about poisonous mushrooms and would not change their eating habits to include large enough quantities of the Japanese variety.

People who are knowledgeable about the area to be investigated often are willing to share their experiences with others (competitors excluded, of course). For example, a firm that is ready to launch a new product may discuss the general nature of the product with some of its key retailers and wholesalers. Members of the company's sales force also may be a valuable source of information. The purpose of such discussions is to exhaust the information available from relatively inexpensive sources before gathering expensive primary data. While the interviews with knowledgeable individuals may reveal nothing conclusive, they may help define the problem more formally.

Exploratory research during situation analysis may be quite informal. Input from knowledgeable people both inside and outside the company may come merely from informal conversations. To simply get ideas about the problem, the marketing manager, rather than the research department, may conduct an experience survey. An experience survey may consist of a small number of interviews with some carefully selected people. Some formal questions may be asked, but the respondents generally will be allowed to discuss the questions with few constraints. Knowledgeable people who are articulate on a particular subject should be selected rather than taking a representative probability sample. The purpose is to help formulate the problem and clarify concepts rather than develop a conclusive evidence.

## ■ SECONDARY DATA ANALYSIS

Another economical and quick source of background information is trade literature in the public library. Searching through such material is exploratory research with secondary data. Basic theoretical research rarely is conducted without extensive reviews of the literature in the field or reviews of similar research reports. Using secondary data may be equally important in applied research.

Suppose the brand manager of a company that manufactures dental hygiene products is contacted by an inventor of a tongue cleaner. The inventor states that her stainless steel device cleans the tongue deposits that cause bad breath. Shortly thereafter, the brand manager finds information in the library that explains the practice of tongue cleaning: It began centuries ago and is common practice among certain Asian people. If the problem had concerned an existing product, the manager's situational analysis might have begun with an analysis of sales records by region, customer, or some other source of internal data.

Investigating data that have been compiled for some purpose other than the project at hand, such as accounting records or trade association data, is the most frequent form of exploratory research. Because this is also a technique for conclusive research (both descriptive and causal research), a separate chapter (Chapter 6) is devoted to the investigation of secondary sources.

## ■ CASE STUDIES

**Case study method**
An exploratory research technique that intensively investigates one or a few situations similar to the problem situation.

The purpose of the **case study method** is to obtain information from one or a few situations that are similar to the researcher's problem situation. For example, a bank in Montana may intensively investigate the marketing activities of an innovative bank in California. A shirt manufacturer interested in surveying retailers may first look at a few retail stores to identify the nature of any problems or topics that a larger study should investigate.

The primary advantage of the case study is that an entire organization or entity can be investigated in depth with meticulous attention to detail. This highly focused attention enables the researcher to carefully study the order of events as they occur or to concentrate on identifying the relationships among functions, individuals, or entities. A fast-food restaurant chain may test a new menu item or a new store design in a single location to learn about potential operating problems that could hinder service quality before launching the change throughout the chain.

Conducting a case study often requires the cooperation of the party whose history is being studied. A successful franchisee may be willing to allow the franchisor access to records and reports. Intensive interviews or detailed discussions with the franchisee and his or her employees may provide insights into the situation. The researcher has no standard procedures to follow; she or he must be flexible and attempt to glean information and insights wherever they appear. This freedom to search for whatever data an investigator deems important makes the success of any case study highly dependent on the

---

### WHAT WENT RIGHT?

#### TGI Friday's

Because TGI Friday's thought the Navy was an extremely efficient food handler, perhaps more efficient than for-profit companies, the restaurant wanted to understand the sources of that efficiency. Friday's executives concluded that successful imitation of the Navy's food-handling operations might help the firm gain some expertise and lead to increased proficiency in performing its service. This matter was of particular interest to Friday's because the firm's strategy calls for building smaller restaurants with almost the same number of seats as were included in the older designs (5,700 square feet with 210 seats compared to 9,200 square feet with 240 seats). These smaller designs place a premium on handling food product efficiently.

To study the Navy's food-based work processes, Friday's CEO spent a day aboard the nuclear submarine *USS West Virginia.* His visit occurred when a crew of 155 was engaged in a 70-day voyage. Because the submarine had a crew on duty 24 hours per day, the Navy served four meals daily in an extremely confined space. A quick calculation shows that 4 daily meals, for 70 days, for 155 people, is more than 43,000 meals.

The Navy was pleased to let Friday's use its operations as a case study. According to one Navy official, "These aren't things we want to keep secret. All of our food service research and development is funded by American tax dollars."

alertness, creativity, intelligence, and motivation of the individual performing the case analysis.

As with all exploratory research, the results from case analyses should be seen as tentative. Generalizing from a few cases can be dangerous, because most situations are atypical in some sense. The bank in Montana may not be in a market comparable to the one in California. Even if the situations are not directly comparable, however, a number of insights can be gained and hypotheses suggested for future research. Obtaining information about competitors may be very difficult because they generally like to keep the secrets of their success to themselves. Thus, the researchers may have limited access to information other firms consider confidential.

# ■ PILOT STUDIES

**Pilot study**
A collective term for any small-scale exploratory research technique that uses sampling but does not apply rigorous standards.

The term *pilot study* covers a number of diverse research techniques. Within the context of exploratory research, the term indicates that some aspect of the research (e.g., fieldwork) will be on a small scale. Thus, a **pilot study** is a research project that involves sampling but relaxes the rigorous standards used to obtain precise quantitative estimates from large representative samples.

In one kind of pilot study, researchers or managers try to experience what consumers experience to gain inexpensive and valuable insights. Without indicating their real positions with the company, researchers/managers may wait on customers, ride in repair trucks, and answer telephones. For example, the chairperson of Avis occasionally gets in line with airport customers waiting for cars or works behind the counter to get customer reactions. This form of pilot study may yield true comprehension of the situation to be investigated.

A pilot study generates primary data, but usually for qualitative analysis. This characteristic distinguishes pilot studies from research that gathers background information using secondary data. Some researchers refer to pilot studies that generate qualitative information as *qualitative research*. The primary data usually come from consumers or other subjects of ultimate concern rather than from knowledgeable experts or case situations. This distinguishes pilot studies from experience surveys and case studies. Major categories of pilot studies include focus group interviews, projective techniques, and depth interviews.

## ■ Focus Group Interviews

**Focus group interview**
An unstructured, free-flowing interview with a small group of people.

Focus group interviews, such as the one for Sky Dancer described at the beginning of this chapter, are so popular that many marketers consider them the only qualitative research tool. A **focus group interview** is an unstructured, free-flowing interview with a small group of people. It is not a rigidly constructed question-and-answer session but a flexible format discussion of a brand, advertisement, or new-product concept. The group meets at a central location at the predesignated time; typically it consists of an interviewer or a moderator and six to ten participants, although larger groups are sometimes used. The participants may range from consumers talking about hair coloring, petroleum engineers talking about problems in the oil patch, or children talking about toys. The moderator introduces the topic and encourages group members to discuss the subject among themselves. Ideally, the discussion topics emerge at the group's initiative. Focus groups allow people to discuss their true feelings, anxieties, and frustrations, as well as the depth of their convictions, in their own words. The primary advantages of focus group interviews are that they are relatively fast, easy to execute, and inexpensive compared to quantitative research. However, a small group of people will not be a representative sample no matter how carefully they are recruited. Focus group interviews cannot take the place of quantitative studies.

The flexibility of group interviews has some advantages, especially when compared with the rigid format of a survey. Numerous topics can be discussed and many insights gained, particularly with regard to the contingencies of consumer behavior. Responses that would be unlikely to emerge in a survey often come out in group interviews. For example, when an advertising agency conducted focus groups with serious tennis players, they learned that however pleasant these tennis players were off the court, those who played two or three times per week were concerned with only one thing when on the court: winning. These players were enthusiastic about any product that gave them a competitive edge. One focus group member said, "I want a weapon when I buy a tennis racquet. A menacing racquet with lots of power is very important."[6] A researcher who is investigating a target group to determine consumption behavior or why a consumer purchases a certain brand must take situational factors into account.

Carnation Company provides an interesting example of the type of information focus group interviews can provide.[7] Past research had revealed that many people did not drink powdered milk because of a perceived taste deficiency relative to fluid milk. Carnation decided to reposition the brand to make it more appealing. First, Carnation sought answers to the following questions:

Why do the majority of consumers who drink milk shun powdered milk?

What would get them to drink it?

In contrast, why do present powdered-milk drinkers find the product acceptable?

These research questions suggested the need to develop hypotheses through the focus group technique. Separate sessions with users and nonusers were conducted. Discussions with nonusers confirmed that taste was a major barrier to use. Sessions with users revealed that a large percentage solved the taste problem by mixing powdered milk half and half with fluid whole milk, producing a cheaper, better-tasting, low-fat milk. Carnation hypothesized that nonusers would be more likely to convert if the company repositioned its product as a milk extender. Quantitative research confirmed this hypothesis, and Carnation executed the strategy with an advertising and promotion campaign that told the milk extender story.

Focus groups often are used for concept screening and concept refinement. The concept may be continually modified, refined, and retested until management believes it is acceptable.

■ Synergy among focus group participants can trigger a chain of responses that help diagnose situations. During a focus group of people who had never visited the J. Paul Getty Museum, a middle-aged man said, "I've been told there's heavy, very classical type of art, somewhat stuffy and standoffish. It's the kind of place you wouldn't want to take your kids and let them run around." An older woman agreed: "I get the impression it's a little stuffy and has old art." A younger man put in his two cents: "I was driving up past Malibu and I saw the sign. I'd never heard of it before. I thought it was a place where they were going to show you how to refine oil or something."[8]

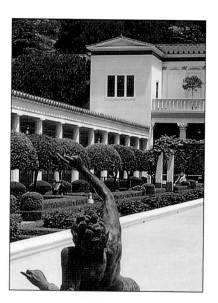

The advantages of focus group interviews stem from group *synergy* and the emphasis on the group rather than on the individual.[9] The combined effort of the group will produce a wider range of information, insights, and ideas than will the cumulation of separately secured responses from a number of individuals. A bandwagon effect often operates in a group interview situation. A comment by one individual often triggers a chain of responses, a brainstorming of ideas, from the other participants.

Because no individual is required to answer any given question in a group interview, a participant's responses can be more spontaneous and less conventional. Ideas often drop out of the blue. This often affords the moderator the opportunity to develop an idea to its full potential.

In a well-structured group, the individual usually finds some comfort in the fact that his or her feelings are similar to those of others in the group and that each participant can expose an idea without being obligated to defend it or follow through and elaborate on it. With the security the group provides, participants are more likely to be candid because the focus is on the group rather than on the individual.

Finally, the group interview allows several people to observe the session; this provides a check on the consistency of the interpretations. Further, the session can be tape recorded or even videotaped. Later, detailed examination of the recorded session can offer additional insight and help clear up disagreements about what happened.

**Group Composition**   The ideal size of the focus group is six to ten relatively homogeneous people. If the group is too small, one or two members may intimidate the others. Groups that are too large may not allow for adequate participation by each group member. Homogeneous groups seem to work best. Because group members share similar lifestyles, experiences, and communication skills, the session does not go off track with numerous arguments and different viewpoints stemming from diverse backgrounds.

When the Centers for Disease Control and Prevention tested public-service announcements about AIDS through focus groups, it discovered that single-race groups and multicultural groups reacted differently.[10] By conducting separate focus groups, the organization was able to gain important insights about which creative strategies were most appropriate for targeted versus broad audiences.

Typically, in a homogeneous group, married, full-time homemakers with children at home would be separated from unmarried, working women. Having first-time mothers in a group with women who have three or four children reduces the new mothers' participation; even if they differ in their opinions, they defer to the more experienced mothers for advice.

Researchers who wish to collect information from different types of people should conduct several focus groups; for example, one focus group might consist only of men and another only of women. Thus, a diverse sample may be obtained even though each group is homogeneous. Most focus group experts believe that four focus group sessions (often in different cities) can satisfy the needs of exploratory research.

**Environmental Conditions**   The group session may take place at the research agency, the advertising agency, a hotel, or one of the subjects' homes. Research suppliers that specialize in conducting focus groups operate from commercial facilities that have videotape cameras in observation rooms behind one-way mirrors and microphone systems connected to tape recorders and speakers to allow observation by others outside the room. Some researchers suggest that a "coffee klatch" or "bull session" atmosphere be established in the commercial research facility to ensure that the mood of the sessions will be as relaxed and natural as possible. More open and intimate reports of personal experiences and sentiments might be obtained under these conditions.

**Moderator**
The person who leads a focus group discussion.

**The Moderator**   The **moderator's** job is to develop a rapport with the group and promote interaction among its members. The moderator should be someone who is really interested in people, carefully listens to what others have to say, and can readily establish rapport and gain people's confidence and make them feel relaxed and eager to talk. Careful listening is especially important, because the group interview's purpose is to stimulate spontaneous responses. The moderator should ensure that everyone gets a chance to speak. The moderator also should focus the discussion on the areas of concern. When a topic is no longer generating fresh ideas, the effective moderator changes the flow of discussion. The moderator does not give the group total control of the discussion, but normally has prepared questions on topics that concern management. However, the timing of these questions in the discussion and the manner in which they are raised are left to the moderator's discretion. The term *focus group* thus stems from the moderator's task: He or she starts out by asking for a general discussion, but usually focuses in on specific topics during the session.

**Planning the Focus Group Outline**   Effective focus group moderators prepare discussion guides to help ensure that the groups cover all topics of interest. The **discussion guide** begins with a written statement of the prefatory remarks to inform the group about the nature of the focus group. Then it outlines topics or questions to be addressed in the group session.

**Discussion guide**
A document prepared by the focus group moderator that contains remarks about the nature of the group and outlines the topics or questions to be addressed.

**Focus Groups as Diagnostic Tools**   Researchers use focus groups predominantly as a means of conducting exploratory research. Focus groups can be helpful in later stages of a research project, but the findings from surveys or other quantitative techniques raise more questions than they answer. Managers who are puzzled about the meaning of survey research results may use focus groups to better understand what consumer surveys indicate. In such a situation, the focus group supplies diagnostic help after quantitative research has been conducted.

**Focus Groups That Use Videoconferencing**   The videoconferencing industry has improved in quality and grown dramatically in recent years. And, as the ability to communicate via telecommunications and videoconferencing links has improved, the number of companies using these systems to conduct focus groups has increased. With traditional focus groups, marketing managers and creative personnel often watch the moderator lead the group from behind one-way mirrors. If the focus group is being conducted out of town, the marketing personnel usually have to spend more time in airplanes, hotels, and taxis than they do watching the group session. With videoconferenced focus groups, the marketing personnel can stay home.

Focus Vision Network of New York is a marketing research company that provides videoconferencing equipment and services for clients. The Focus Vision system is modular, which allows it to be wheeled around to capture close-ups of each group member. The system operates via a remote keypad that allows observers in a far-off location to pan the focus group room or zoom in on a particular participant. The system allows marketing managers at remote locations to send messages to the moderator. For example, while testing new-product names in one focus group, an observing manager had an idea and contacted the moderator, who tested the new name on the spot.[11]

**Shortcomings of Focus Groups**   The shortcomings of focus groups are similar to those of most qualitative research techniques, as discussed in the section "A Warning about Exploratory Research" later in this chapter. However, two specific shortcomings of focus groups should be pointed out here. First, they require sensitive and effective moderators;

self-appointed participants may dominate these sessions, yielding somewhat misleading results. If participants react negatively toward the dominant member, a "halo effect" on attitudes toward the concept or topic of discussion may occur. This situation should be carefully avoided. Second, some unique sampling problems arise in focus groups. Researchers often select focus group participants because they have similar backgrounds and experiences or because screening indicates that the participants are more articulate or gregarious than the typical consumer. These participants may not be representative of the entire target market. (The Exploring Research Ethics box on this page also addresses this issue.)

## ■ Exploratory Research Using Interactive Media

When a person uses the Internet, he or she interacts with a computer. It is an interactive medium because the user clicks a command and the computer responds. Two or more individuals who communicate via e-mail or a service such as America Online are also using interactive media.

Research using interactive media is beginning to emerge. For example, Nickelodeon is now on-line with a group of young viewers via CompuServe.[12] These kids use personal computers and modems to talk with one another and with network researchers about pets, parents, peeves, and pleasures. They post notes on the computer bulletin board whenever they want to. Three times a week, they log on for scheduled electronic conferences in which Nickelodeon researchers lead discussions on topics such as "Is this a good scoring methodology for a game show?" or "Do kids understand if we show a sequence of program titles and air times?" On one occasion, the kids told researchers they were confused by the various locations shown in a segment of "The Tomorrow People," a five-part series with events occurring around the world. Realizing that the sight of a double-decker bus wasn't enough for a modern kid to identify London, the producers wrote the name of the city on the screen.

Using the Internet for focus groups or other exploratory research works best when the product is an Internet service, software, or another type of product targeted at Internet users. At this moment in time, Internet users are not represtative of all U.S. households.

## ■ Projective Techniques

There is an old story about asking a man why he purchased a Mercedes. When asked directly why he purchased a Mercedes, he responds that the car holds its value and does

**EXPLORING RESEARCH ETHICS**

### Typical Consumers or Professional Respondents?

Clients that lack physical facilities for conducting focus groups regularly hire research suppliers that specialize in focus group research. What is a research supplier's responsibility when recruiting individuals to participate in a focus group? Should respondents be recruited because they will make the session go well or because they are typical consumers?

A disturbing example of a lack of objectivity in research occurred when managers of a client organization observed a focus group interview being conducted by a research supplier that had previously worked for the client on other projects. They noticed that some of the respondents looked familiar. A review of the video recordings of the session found that, to make the session go smoothly, the focus group moderators had solicited subjects who in the past had been found to be very articulate and cooperative. It is questionable whether such "professional respondents" can avoid playing the role of expert.

not depreciate much, that it gets better gas mileage than you'd expect, or that it has a comfortable ride. If you ask the same person why a neighbor purchased a Mercedes, he may well answer, "Oh, that status seeker!" This story illustrates that individuals may be more likely to give true answers (consciously or unconsciously) to disguised questions. Projective techniques seek to discover an individual's true attitudes, motivations, defensive reactions, and characteristic ways of responding.

The underlying assumption behind these methods lies in Oscar Wilde's phrase "A man is least himself when he talks in his own person; when he is given a mask he will tell the truth." In other words, advocates of projective techniques assume that when directly questioned, respondents may not express their true feelings because they are embarrassed about answers that reflect negatively on their self-concepts; they wish to please the interviewer with the "right" answer, or they cannot reveal unconscious feelings of which they are unaware. However, if respondents are presented with unstructured, ambiguous stimuli, such as cartoons or inkblots, and are allowed considerable freedom to respond, they will express their true feelings.

**Projective technique**
An indirect means of questioning that enables a respondent to project beliefs and feelings onto a third party, onto an inanimate object, or into a task situation.

A **projective technique** is an indirect means of questioning that enables respondents to project beliefs and feelings onto a third party, onto an inanimate object, or into a task situation. Respondents are not required to provide answers in any structured format. They are encouraged to describe a situation in their own words with little prompting by the interviewer. Individuals are expected to interpret the situation within the context of their own experiences, attitudes, and personalities and to express opinions and emotions that may be hidden from others and possibly from themselves. The most common projective techniques in marketing research are word association tests, sentence completion methods, third-person techniques, and thematic apperception tests.

**Word association test**
A projective technique in which the subject is presented with a list of words, one at a time, and asked to respond with the first word that comes to mind.

**Word Association Tests**    During a **word association test,** the subject is presented with a list of words, one at a time, and asked to respond with the first word that comes to his or her mind. Both verbal and nonverbal responses (such as hesitation in responding) are recorded. For example, a researcher who reads a list of job tasks to sales employees expects that the word association technique will reveal each individual's true feelings about the job task. A sales representative's first thought presumably is a spontaneous answer because the subject does not have enough time to think about and avoid making admissions that reflect poorly on himself or herself.

Word association frequently is used to test potential brand names. For example, a liquor manufacturer attempting to market a clear-colored light whiskey tested the brand names Frost, Verve, Ultra, and Master's Choice. Frost was seen as upbeat, modern, clean, and psychologically right; Verve was too modern; Ultra was too common; and Master's Choice was not upbeat enough.[13]

Interpreting word association tests is difficult, and the marketing researcher should make sure to avoid subjective interpretations. When there is considerable agreement in the free-association process, the researcher assumes the test has revealed the consumer's inner feelings about the subject. Word association tests are also analyzed by the amount of elapsed time. For example, if the researcher is investigating alternative advertising appeals for a method of birth control, a hesitation in responding may indicate that the response was delayed because the subject is emotionally involved in the word (possibly seeking an acceptable response). The analysis of projective technique results takes into account not only what respondents say but also what they do not say.

Word association tests also can be used to pretest words or ideas for questionnaires. This enables the researcher to know beforehand whether and to what degree the meaning of a word is understood in the context of a survey.

**Sentence completion method**
A projective technique in which respondents are required to complete a number of partial sentences with the first word or phrase that comes to mind.

### Sentence Completion Method

The **sentence completion method** also is based on the principle of free association. Respondents are required to complete a number of partial sentences with the first word or phrase that comes to mind. For example:

**People who drink beer are** _____.

**A person who drinks a microbrewery's red ale is** _____.

**Imported beer is most liked by** _____.

Answers to sentence completion questions tend to be more extensive than responses to word association tests. The intent of sentence completion questions is more apparent, however.

**Third-person technique**
A projective technique in which the respondent is asked why a third person does what she or he does or thinks about a product. The respondent is expected to transfer his or her attitudes to the third person.

### Third-Person Technique and Role Playing

The Iowa Poll once asked, "Will you wind up in heaven or hell?" Nearly all Iowans believed they would be saved, but one-third described a neighbor as a "sure bet" for hell.[14]

Almost literally, providing a mask is the basic idea behind the **third-person technique.** Respondents are asked why a third person (for example, a neighbor) does what he or she does or what she or he thinks about a product. For example, male home owners might be told:

> We are talking to a number of home owners like yourself about this new type of lawn mower. Some men like it the way it is; others believe that it should be improved. Please think of some of your friends or neighbors, and tell us what it is they might find fault with on this new type of lawn mower.

Respondents can transfer their attitudes to neighbors, friends, or coworkers. They are free to agree or disagree with an unknown third party.

**Role-playing technique**
A projective technique that requires the subject to act out someone else's behavior in a particular setting.

Role playing is a dynamic reenactment of the third-person technique in a given situation. The **role-playing technique** requires the subject to act out someone else's behavior in a particular setting. The photo on page 98 shows a child in a role-playing situation. She projects herself into a mother role using a pretend telephone and describes the new cookie she has just seen advertised. Child Research Service believes this projective play technique can be used to determine a child's true feelings about a product, package, or commercial:

> When they [children] do speak, youngsters frequently have their own meaning for many words. A seemingly positive word such as "good," for example, can be a child's unflattering description of the teacher's pet in his class. In a role-playing game, the child can show exactly what "good" means to him.[15]

Role playing is particularly useful in investigating situations where interpersonal relationships are the subject of the research, for example, salesperson-customer, husband-wife, or wholesaler-retailer relationships.

**Thematic apperception test (TAT)**
A projective technique that presents a series of pictures to research subjects and asks them to provide a description of or a story about the pictures.

### Thematic Apperception Test (TAT)

A **thematic apperception test (TAT)** presents subjects with a series of pictures in which consumers and products are the center of attention. The investigator asks the subject to tell what is happening in the pictures and what the people might do next. Hence, themes (*thematic*) are elicited on the basis of the perceptual-interpretive (*apperception*) use of the pictures. The researcher then analyzes the contents of the stories the subjects relate.

The picture or cartoon stimulus must be sufficiently interesting to encourage discussion but ambiguous enough not to disclose the nature of the research project. Clues should not be given to the character's positive or negative predisposition. A pretest of a TAT

### Cigarette Smoking: Are Smokers Being Honest with Themselves?

Cigarette smoking in public spaces is an emotionally charged and hotly debated issue. Direct, undisguised questioning may not be the best alternative because cigarette smoking seems to trigger ego defense mechanisms. Marketing researchers directly questioned why 179 smokers who believed cigarettes to be a health hazard continued to smoke. The majority answered, "Pleasure is more important than health"; "Moderation is OK"; "I like to smoke." Such responses suggest that smokers are not dissatisfied with their habit. However, in another portion of the study, the researchers used the sentence completion method. Respondents were asked to respond with the first thing that came to mind after hearing the sentence "People who never smoke are _____." The answers were "better off," "happier," "smarter," "wiser," "more informed." To "Teenagers who smoke are _____," smokers responded with "foolish," "crazy," "uninformed," "stupid," "showing off," "immature," "wrong." The sentence completion test indicated that smokers are anxious, uncomfortable, dissonant, and dissatisfied with their habit. The sentence completion test elicited responses the subjects would not have given otherwise.

investigating why men might purchase chain saws used a picture of a man looking at a very large tree. The research subjects were home owners and weekend woodcutters. When confronted with the picture of the imposing tree, they almost unanimously said they would get professional help from a tree surgeon. Thus, early in the pretesting process, the researchers found out that the picture was not sufficiently ambiguous for the subjects to identify with the man in the picture. If subjects are to project their own views into the situation, the environmental setting should be a well-defined, familiar problem, but the solution should be ambiguous.

Frequently a series of pictures with some continuity is presented so that stories may be constructed in a variety of settings. The first picture might portray two women discussing a product in a supermarket; in the second picture, a person might be preparing the product in the kitchen; the final picture might show the product being served at the dinner table.

**Picture frustration**
A version of the TAT that uses a cartoon drawing in which the respondent suggests a possible dialogue between the characters.

**Cartoon Tests**   The **picture frustration** version of the TAT uses a cartoon drawing in which the respondent suggests a possible dialogue between the characters. Exhibit 5.1 is a purposely ambiguous illustration of an everyday occurrence. The two office workers are placed in a situation, and the respondent is asked what the woman might be talking about. This setting could be used for discussions about products, packaging, merchandise displays, store personnel, and so on.

■ A child placed in a role-playing situation may be better able to express her true feelings. A child may be told to pretend she is a parent talking to a friend about toys, food, or clothing. Thus, the child does not feel pressure to directly express her opinions and feelings.

■ **Exhibit 5.1**

**Picture Frustration
Version of TAT**

## ■ Depth Interviews

Motivational researchers who want to discover reasons for consumer behavior may use relatively unstructured, extensive interviews during the primary stages of the research process. The **depth interview** is similar to the client interview of a clinical psychologist or psychiatrist. The researcher asks many questions and probes for additional elaboration after the subject answers. Unlike with projective techniques, the subject matter is generally undisguised. The interviewer's role is extremely important in the depth interview. He or she must be a highly skilled individual who can encourage the respondent to talk freely without influencing the direction of the conversation. Probing statements such as "Can you give me an example of that?" and "Why do you say that?" stimulate the respondent to elaborate on the topic. The interviewer constantly strives to get the respondent to reveal and elaborate on his or her emotions and or motivations.

**Depth interview**
A relatively unstructured, extensive interview in which the interviewer asks many questions and probes for in-depth answers.

International marketing researchers find that in certain cultures, depth interviews work far better than focus groups. They provide a quick means to assess buyer behavior in foreign lands.

The depth interview may last more than an hour and requires an extremely skilled interviewer; hence, it is expensive. In addition, the area for discussion is largely at the discretion of the interviewer, so the success of the research depends on the interviewer's skill—and, as is so often the case, skilled people are hard to find. A third major problem stems from the need to record both surface reactions and subconscious motivations of the respondent. Analysis and interpretation of such data are highly subjective, and it is difficult to settle on a true interpretation.

An example of conflicting claims is illustrated by a study of prunes done by two organizations. One study used projective techniques to show that people considered prunes to be shriveled, tasteless, and unattractive; symbolic of old age and parental authority (thus disliked); and associated with hospitals, peculiar people, and the army. The other study stated that the principal reason people did not like prunes was the fruit's laxative property.

Finally, alternative techniques, such as focus groups, can provide much of the same information depth interviews do.

## A WARNING ABOUT EXPLORATORY RESEARCH

Exploratory research cannot take the place of conclusive, quantitative research. Nevertheless, a number of firms use what should be exploratory studies as the final, conclusive research project. This has led to incorrect decisions. The most important thing to remember about exploratory research techniques is that they have limitations. Most of them are qualitative, and interpretation of the findings typically is judgmental. For example, the findings from projective techniques can be vague. Projective techniques and depth interviews were frequently used in the 1950s by practitioners who categorized themselves as motivational researchers. They produced some interesting and occasionally bizarre hypotheses about what was inside the buyer's mind, such as "A woman is very serious when she bakes a cake because unconsciously she is going through the symbolic act of giving birth" and "A man buys a convertible as a substitute mistress."[16]

Unfortunately, bizarre hypotheses cannot be relegated to history. Not so long ago, researchers at the McCann-Erickson advertising agency interviewed low-income women about their attitudes toward insecticides. The women indicated that they strongly believed a new brand of roach killer sold in little plastic trays was far more effective and less messy than traditional bug sprays. Rather than purchase the new brand, however, they remained stubbornly loyal to their old bug sprays. Baffled by this finding, the researchers did extensive qualitative research with female consumers. They concluded from the women's drawings and in-depth descriptions of roaches that women subconsciously identified roaches with men who had abandoned them. Spraying the roaches and watching them squirm and die was enjoyable. The women thus gained control over the roaches and vented their hostility toward men.[17] Evidently, conclusions based on qualitative research may be subject to considerable interpreter bias.

Findings from focus group interviews likewise may be ambiguous. How is a facial expression or a nod of the head to be interpreted? Have subjects fully grasped the idea or concept behind a nonexistent product? Have respondents overstated their interest because they tend to like all new products? Because of such problems in interpretation, exploratory findings should be considered preliminary.

Another problem with exploratory studies deals with the ability to make projections from the findings. Most exploratory techniques use small samples, which may not be representative because they have been selected on a probability basis. Case studies, for example, may have been selected because they represent extremely good or extremely bad examples of a situation rather than the average situation.

Before making a scientific decision, the researcher should conduct a quantitative study with an adequate sample to ensure that measurement will be precise. This is not to say that exploratory research lacks value; it simply means that such research cannot deliver what it does not promise. The major benefit of exploratory research is that it generates insights and clarifies the marketing problems for hypothesis testing in future research. One cannot determine the most important attributes of a product until one has identified those attributes. Thus, exploratory research is extremely useful, but it should be used with caution.

However, occasions do arise when the research process should stop at the exploratory stage. If a cheese producer conducts a focus group interview to get a feel for consumers' reactions to a crispy snack food made from whey (the product left over from cheesemaking) and exploratory findings show an extremely negative reaction by almost all participants, the cheese manufacturer may no longer wish to continue the project.

One researcher suggests that the greatest danger in using exploratory research to evaluate alternative advertising copy, new-product concepts, and so on is not that a poor idea will be marketed, because successive steps of research will prevent that. The real danger is that a good idea with promise may be rejected because of findings at the exploratory stage. On the other hand, when everything looks positive in the exploratory stage, the temptation is to market the product without further research. Instead, after conducting exploratory research, marketing management should determine whether the benefits of the additional information would be worth the cost of further research. In most cases where a major commitment of resources is at stake, conducting the quantitative study is well worth the effort. Many times good marketing research only documents the obvious. However, the purpose of business is to make a profit, and decision makers want to be confident that they have made the correct choice.

## SUMMARY

Qualitative research is subjective in nature. Much of the measurement depends on evaluation by the researcher rather than rigorous mathematical analysis. Quantitative research determines the quantity or extent of an outcome in numbers. It provides an exact approach to measurement.

This chapter focused on qualitative exploratory research. Exploratory research may be conducted to diagnose a situation, screen alternatives, or discover new ideas. It may take the form of gathering background information by investigating secondary data, conducting experience surveys, scrutinizing case studies, or utilizing pilot studies. The purpose of the research, rather than the technique, determines whether a study is exploratory, descriptive, or causal. Thus, the techniques discussed in this chapter are primarily but not exclusively used for exploratory studies.

The case study method involves intensive investigation into one particular situation that is similar to the problem under investigation.

Focus group interviews are unstructured, free-flowing group dynamics sessions that allow individuals to initiate the topics of discussion. Interaction among respondents is synergistic and spontaneous, characteristics that have been found to be highly advantageous.

As the ability to communicate via the Internet, telecommunications, and videoconferencing links improves, a number of companies are beginning to use the new media to conduct focus group research and other forms of exploratory research.

Projective techniques are an indirect means of questioning respondents. Some examples are word association tests, sentence completion tests, the third-person technique and role playing, and thematic apperception tests.

Depth interviews are unstructured, extensive interviews that encourage a respondent to talk freely and in depth about an undisguised topic.

Although exploratory research has many advantages, it also has several shortcomings and should not take the place of conclusive, quantitative research. Knowing where and how to use exploratory research is important. Many firms make the mistake of using exploratory studies as final, conclusive research projects. This could lead to decisions based on incorrect assumptions. Exploratory research techniques have limitations: The interpretation of the findings is based on judgment, samples are not representative and rarely provide precise quantitative measurement, and the ability to generalize the quantitative results is limited.

## ■ Key Terms and Concepts

| | |
|---|---|
| Exploratory research | Projective technique |
| Concept testing | Word association test |
| Experience survey | Sentence completion method |
| Case study method | Third-person technique |
| Pilot study | Role-playing technique |
| Focus group interview | Thematic apperception test (TAT) |
| Moderator | Picture frustration |
| Discussion guide | Depth interview |

## ■ Questions

1. Comment on the following remark by a marketing consultant: "Qualitative exploration is a tool of marketing research and a stimulant to thinking. In and by itself, however, it does not constitute market research."
2. What type of exploratory research would you suggest in the following situations?
   (a) A product manager suggests development of a nontobacco cigarette blended from wheat, cocoa, and citrus.
   (b) A research project has the purpose of evaluating potential brand names for a new insecticide.
   (c) A manager must determine the best site for a convenience store in an urban area.
   (d) An advertiser wishes to identify the symbolism associated with cigar smoking.
3. Develop a concept statement for a diet chocolate candy bar that has 190 calories, 45 of them from fat.
4. What benefits can be gained from case studies? What dangers, if any, do they present? In what situations are they most useful?
5. What is the function of a focus group? What are its advantages and disadvantages?
6. If a researcher wanted to conduct a focus group with teenagers, what special considerations might be necessary?
7. A focus group moderator plans to administer a questionnaire before starting the group discussion about several new-product concepts. Is this a good idea? Explain.
8. Discuss the advantages and disadvantages of the following focus group techniques:
   (a) A videoconferencing system that allows marketers to conduct focus groups in two different locations with participants who interact with one another
   (b) A system that uses telephone conference calls to hold group sessions
9. A packaged goods manufacturer receives many thousands of customer letters a year. Some are complaints, some are compliments, and they cover a broad range of topics. Are these letters a possible source for exploratory research? Why or why not?
10. How might exploratory research be used to screen various ideas for advertising copy in television commercials?

11. Most projective techniques attempt to assess a respondent's true feelings by asking indirect questions rather than using direct questions that could give the respondent a good idea about the researcher's true motives. Is this a form of deception?

## EXPLORING THE INTERNET

1. How might the following organizations use a usernet bulletin board for exploratory research?
   (a) A zoo

      (b)  A computer software manufacturer

      (c)  A video game manufacturer

2.  Connect with a special-interest bulletin board such as one for college students. Conduct an electronic focus group exploring what factors are used as a criteria to choose destinations for spring break.

---

 **CASE 5.1**   Hamilton Power Tools Corporation (A)

On July 13, 1988, Mr. Campagna, the marketing manager for Hamilton Power Tools, was anxiously awaiting his meeting with the marketing research firm. He felt the findings from the marketing research would change Hamilton from a sales-oriented company to one that would adopt the consumer-oriented philosophy of the marketing concept.

For more than 35 years, Hamilton Power Tools had been marketing industrial products by catering to the construction and industrial tool markets. Its construction product lines included power trowels, concrete vibrators, generators, and power-actuated tools. Its industrial products were primarily pneumatic tools: drills, screwdrivers, and so on. One of its products, the gasoline-powered chain saw, differed somewhat from traditional construction and industrial tools. The chain saw line had been added in 1949 when John Hamilton, Sr., had the opportunity to acquire a small chain saw manufacturer. Hamilton believed construction workers would have a need for gasoline-powered chain saws. He acquired the business to diversify the company into other markets.

During the 1980s, the chain saw market was rapidly changing and Hamilton Power Tool executives began to realize they needed some expert marketing advice. Mr. Campagna believed a major change in the company's direction was on the horizon. Campagna had been in the chain saw business for 15 years. Reports from trade publications, statistics from the Chain Saw Manufacturers' Association, and personal experience had led him to believe the current chain saw industry was composed of roughly the following markets: professionals (lumberjacks), farmers, institutions, and casual users (home or estate owners with many trees on their lots). The casual-user segment was considered to be the future growth market. Campagna wished to ensure that Hamilton would not make any mistakes in marketing its product to this segment of weekend woodcutters who once or twice a year used a chain saw to cut firewood or prune trees in the backyard.

In March 1988, when chain saw sales began to slow down because of the seasonal nature of the business, Campagna and Ray Johnson, the chain saw sales manager, had

a meeting with John Hamilton, Sr. Although Hamilton believed they had been doing well enough in chain saw sales over the past decade, Campagna and Johnson were able to persuade the aging executive that some consumer research was necessary. After talking with several marketing research firms, Hamilton Power Tools hired Consumer Metrics of Chicago to perform two research projects. The first was a thematic apperception test (TAT).

The TAT research was completed the first week of July. Campagna arranged for a meeting with the marketing research firm the following week. As Dale Conway and Frank Baggins made their presentation of the results of the survey of chain saw users, Campagna thought back to the day Consumer Metrics had originally suggested the idea of a TAT to John Hamilton. Conway had sold him on the idea with his argument that motivational research was widely used in consumer studies to uncover people's buying motives. Conway had mentioned that Consumer Metrics had recently hired a young, bright M.B.A. This M.B.A.—Baggins, as it turned out—had specialized in consumer psychology and marketing research at a major state university. Conway thought Baggins was one of the best-qualified people to work on this type of project. Since Hamilton Power Tools had no experience in consumer research, Campagna was eager to proceed with the in-depth TAT.

Conway told Campagna, Hamilton, and Johnson that in the TAT, respondents are shown a series of photographs and asked to tell their feelings concerning the people depicted. He told Campagna that although the present study was exploratory, it could be used to gain insights into the reasons people make certain purchases. He also suggested that the test would be a way to get the flavor of the language people use in talking about chain saws, and it could be a source of new ideas for copywriting.

Campagna remembered that at one time he had thought this project wouldn't be very worthwhile; however, he also realized he knew little about the consumer market. During the initial meeting with the research firm, it was

■ **Case Exhibit 5.1-1**

**Hamilton TAT Study**

Exhibit A

Exhibit B

Exhibit C

Exhibit D

proposed that an exploratory research project be conducted within the states of Illinois and Wisconsin to obtain some indication of the attitudes of potential casual users toward chain saws. The researcher had suggested a TAT. Campagna knew little about this type of research and needed time to think. After a week's deliberation, he called Conway and told the researchers to go ahead with the project. Case Exhibit 5.1-1 shows the TAT the researchers used.

At the meeting, Conway and Baggins carefully presented the research results. They pointed out that in the TAT study, several screening questions were asked at the beginning of the interview. The findings of this study were based on those respondents who either planned to purchase a chain saw in the next 12 months, already owned a chain saw, or had used a chain saw in the past. The presentation closely followed the written report submitted to Campagna. The findings were as follows.

The first picture (Exhibit A of Case Exhibit 5.1-1) shown to the respondents pictured a man standing looking at a tree. The interviewer asked the respondent the following question:

I have a problem that you may find interesting. Here's a picture of a man who is thinking about the purchase of a chain saw. Suppose that such a man is your neighbor. What do you suppose he is thinking about?

After the respondent's initial answer, the following probing question was asked:

Now, if he came to you for advice and you really wanted to help him, what would you tell him to do? Why do you think this would be the best thing for him to do?

Initial responses centered around what the man would do with the tree. Many respondents expressed an interest in the tree and were concerned with preservation. It seemed that pride in having a tree that beautified the owner's property was important to some respondents. Some typical responses given are as follows:

He's thinking about cutting the tree down.

Why cut a whole tree when you can save part of it?

He could trim out part of those trees and save some of them.

We lose trees due to disease and storm damage.

Trees beautify property and make it more valuable.

I don't like to destroy trees.

Considering the alternatives to buying a chain saw was the next step many respondents took. Basically the ultimate consumer sees the alternatives to the purchase of a chain saw as

1. Using a hand saw
2. Hiring a tree surgeon
3. Renting or borrowing a chain saw

These alternatives were in the respondents' minds partly because they were concerned about the cost of doing the job. They seemed to be worried about the investment in a chain saw, about whether it paid to buy one for a small, single-application job. (Another reason for the alternatives came out in responses to a later picture.) Some responses illustrating these points are as follows:

He's thinking how to go about it. He will use his hand saw.

He doesn't have to invest in a chain saw for only one tree.

He's thinking about how to get the tree down—the cost of doing it himself versus having someone else do it.

Have him cut it down himself, it's not too big a tree. He'll save the cost.

He's thinking whether it pays for a couple of trees.

If it would be worth it. How much longer with an ax.

He's thinking whether he should do it himself or get someone else to do it for him. Get someone who knows what he is doing.

He's thinking he'll rent a chain saw for a small area and would buy one for a large area.

The best way to get a job done. Chain saw is faster, but a hand saw is cheaper. Depends on how much work he has to do.

An interesting comment made by two respondents was "He's thinking about Dutch elm disease." The area had recently been hit by that disease. The respondents were projecting their own situations into the TAT pictures.

Other statements were made concerning the ease and speed of using a chain saw. Some questions regarding the characteristic performance of a chain saw were raised in response to this question; however, Exhibit B covered this area more adequately. This picture showed two men standing in a chain saw store looking at a chain saw. The question asked went as follows:

Here is a picture of the same man in a chain saw store. Suppose he's a friend of yours—your next-door neighbor, perhaps. Tell me what you think he will talk about with the chain saw clerk.

The issue most frequently raised was how the chain saw worked. An equal number of respondents wanted to know first how much it cost. Weight (lightness) was the next most frequently raised issue. Horsepower was a concern among many respondents. Other subjects they thought the man would talk about with the clerk were maintenance and availability of repair, performance (what size tree the chain saw would cut), durability and expected life, safety (what safety features the chain saw had), and ease of starting the chain saw. In relation to price, comments included the following:

Well, price is the most important, of course.

He's wondering how he will pay for it.

One respondent said, "He's not considering price; price means nothing in regard to safety." One individual was concerned whether the chain would come off the "blade" (respondents referred to the guide bar as a "blade" rather than a "guide bar").

Respondents raised various other issues. These are as follows:

Ease of handling

Length of blade

Which was the best brand?

Whether it had direct drive

Whether it had a gas protector

Self-lubrication

The warranty (guarantee)

Ease of controls

Specifications

Availability of credit

Possibility of mixing oil and gas

The third picture (Exhibit C) showed a man cutting a felled tree with the chain saw. The question asked was as follows:

> The man in the picture is the same man as in the last picture. He purchased the chain saw he was looking at. Knowing that he purchased the chain saw, what can you tell me about him? Can you tell me anything about the character and personality of this man?

A follow-up question was:

> What do you suppose this man is thinking about while he's using his chain saw?

A common response was that the man was satisfied. Typical responses were "He's pleased"; "He's happy he bought the chain saw"; "Lots of time saved"; and "He's happy with the chain saw; he made the right decision." Many favorable overtones to using a chain saw were given, for example,

> Sure beats bucking with an ax.

> He's thinking about speed of getting through, time saved.

> How much easier it is to cut a tree down with a chain saw than a hand saw.

> He seems to be saying, "Why didn't I buy a chain saw sooner?"

Respondents in general seemed to think the man was using the chain saw for the first time.

Very prominent in many respondents' answers was the fear of using a chain saw; it seemed to be a major reason people would not purchase one. Some typical comments were

> He's a little frightened. He doesn't know how to go about it, but he's willing to learn.

> If he gets caught in that blade . . .

> He's watching what he's doing—he could lose a limb.

> He might be somewhat apprehensive about the use of it.

> He looks scared of it.

> He better think safety.

In general, the test, as it is designed to do, made the respondents project their own personalities and backgrounds onto the character of the man. They gave a wide variety of descriptions of the man. He was described as a blue-collar worker, an office worker laboring after hours and on weekends, a somewhat wealthy man able to afford a chain saw, and a home owner. A number of responses indicated he was a do-it-yourselfer, a man who liked to "do his own thing." "Farmer" was another more than scattered response. Associations with an "outdoor type," a person who liked to keep in shape, were also indicated. One quotation seems to sum it all up:

> This seems to be his first job. He seems to be happy about it. He seems to think the chain saw will lighten his workload. He looks like he has not owned many power tools. He looks excited. He seems like he will be able to do a lot of cleanup work that he would not have been able to do without the chain saw. The chain saw is sure an improvement over the hand saw. It's faster, easier to use.

The fourth picture (Exhibit D) showed a man and a woman seated before a fireplace. The question read,

> Here's a picture of the same man as in the previous pictures, sitting and talking with a woman; what do you suppose they're talking about?

An analysis of the fourth picture in the projection test showed that respondents felt the man and woman in the picture were happy, content, cozy, and enjoying the fireplace. The man was "enjoying the fruits of his labor." It came out very strongly that a man who uses a chain saw is proud of himself after he cuts the wood; he thinks his cutting of wood with a chain saw is a job well done. Some typical comments concerning this were

> He's very happy to cut his own wood for his fireplace— real proud of himself.

> He's telling her how much he saved by cutting it himself.

> They're talking about the logs, how pleased he is with himself.

He's thinking about the beauty of the fire, fire logs he himself sawed from their property.

The people projecting onto the picture seemed to think that because the job was well done, purchasing a chain saw was worthwhile:

The man in the picture is saying, "The chain saw pays for itself. There's a $300 job, and you will be able to use the chain saw afterwards."

Work's done, and there's enough for winter, and he has trees for winters to come.

What a good buy that chain saw was! Cut wood costs, save money.

The woman in the picture was also described as very happy; she was satisfied and probably thinking about the future. But most of all, she was very proud of her husband. This came out very strongly. For example,

The woman is looking to the enjoyment of the fireside and of the money saved because they cut their own wood. She might have questioned the investment before this, before sitting in front of the fireplace.

She is proud of her husband.

She is pleased the tree is down.

The woman is probably proud of the fireplace and starting the fire. He's probably thinking about the wood he sawed.

The man and woman are congratulating each other on finally getting around to buying a chain saw and cutting firewood.

She is complimenting him on his ability and on how handy it is to have a man around the house.

She is also thinking that possibly it was easier for her husband to use a chain saw.

The woman didn't care about the chain saw, but she was satisfied. The husband's concern over his wife's approval of this investment was also brought out by this picture; evidently men were worried that their wives would not see the value of a chain saw purchase. Also, there were implications that the man should be tired after using the chain saw, "and he had to work hard in the afternoon to get the logs for the fireplace."

After the presentation, Campagna was reasonably impressed. He asked Hamilton what his opinion was. Hamilton said, "This is all very interesting, but I don't see how it can lead to greater profits in our chain saw division."

**Questions**
1. How should Conway and Baggins respond to Hamilton's question?
2. Is Hamilton investigating the casual-user market segment correctly?
3. What conclusions would you draw from the thematic apperception test? Do you think this is a valid and reliable test?
4. What specific recommendations would you make to Campagna concerning the casual-user chain saw market?

---

 **VIDEO CASE 5.2**   Upjohn's Rogaine[18]

The Upjohn Company, based in Kalamazoo, Michigan, manufactures and markets pharmaceuticals and health-related products. With over 19,000 employees and distribution in over 30 countries, from Australia to Zaire, its annual sales top $1 billion. Upjohn is constantly developing and marketing new products. One recent example is Rogaine.

Originally developed as an antihypertension drug, Rogaine was shown in clinical tests to encourage moderate hair growth on some balding male volunteers. Thereafter,

Upjohn quickly applied to the U.S. Food and Drug Administration (FDA) for the right to market the drug as a hair-growth product in the United States.

**Questions**
1. Define Rogaine's marketing problem from a marketing research perspective.
2. What type of exploratory marketing research should Rogaine conduct?

■ **Endnotes**

[1]Marshall Sella, "Will a Flying Doll . . . FLY?" *New York Times,* December 25, 1994, pp. 20–25, 40–43.

[2]Dave Fusaro, "Food Products of the New Millennium," *Prepared Foods,* January 1, 1996.

[3]David Schwartz, *Concept Testing: How to Test New Product Ideas before You Go to Market* (New York: AMACOM, 1987), p. 57.

[4]Gary Hamel and C. K. Prahalad, "Corporate Imagination and Expeditionary Marketing," *Harvard Business Review,* July–August 1991, p. 85.

[5]"Light Says Problem Research Will Give More Benefits Than Benefit Research," *Marketing News,* September 20, 1975, p. 7.

[6]*1990 Winners: The Effie Gold Awards* (New York: American Marketing Association of New York/American Association of Advertising Agencies, 1990), pp. 47–48.

[7]Edward M. Tauber, "Research to Increase Sales of Existing Brands" *Business Horizons,* April 1977, p. 31.

[8]Carol Vogel, "Dear Museumgoer: What Do You Think?" *New York Times,* December 20, 1992, p. H-1.

[9]Based on the discussion in John M. Hess, "Group Interviewing," in *New Science of Planning,* ed. R. L. King (Chicago: American Marketing Association, 1968), p. 194.

[10]Steve Rabin, "How to Sell across Cultures," *American Demographics,* March 1, 1994, p. 56.

[11]Rebecca Piirto Heather, "Future Focus Groups," *American Demographics,* January 1, 1994, p. 6.

[12]Adapted from Tibbett Speer, "Nickelodeon Puts Kids Online," *American Demographics,* January 1, 1994, p. 16.

[13]Robert F. Hartley, *Marketing Mistakes* (Columbus, Oh.: Grid, 1976), p. 87.

[14]The Iowa Poll, August 1977.

[15]Liz Laurie, "Play Techniques Probe Kids' Real Feelings, Opinions of New Products," *Marketing News,* January 28, 1977, p. 2.

[16]Philip Kotler, "Behavioral Models for Analyzing Buyers," *Journal of Marketing,* October 1965, pp. 37–45.

[17]Ronald Alsop, "Advertisers Put Consumers on the Couch," *The Wall Street Journal,* May 13, 1988, p. 19.

[18]Louis E. Boone and David L. Kurtz, *Contemporary Marketing* (Fort Worth, Tex.: Dryden Press, 1995), p. 279.

# 6

# SECONDARY DATA RESEARCH IN A DIGITAL AGE

Published facts and statistics from secondary data sources can tell us a lot about markets. Consider these interesting findings about the market for sports.[1]

Football didn't start out as a southern sport. Today, however, the emotional attachment to football is much stronger in the Deep South than in any other area of the United States. Families and coaches groom and train ten times as many players per capita in Georgia and Alabama as in New York and Vermont. New Yorkers support pro football, but they lag far behind southerners in efforts to learn how to play football.

Football blocks women from involvement in sports in much of the Southeast. This region offers about one-quarter of the opportunity that women find in states like Wisconsin, Michigan, Iowa, and Illinois. Cultural and social traditions underpin these patterns.

Basketball, by all indicators, is now the universal American sport. Participation rates and attendance patterns have surpassed football and baseball in breadth as well as depth. For one reason, it's become a better sport. Today's basketball isn't the same game that was played 35 years ago. It's more exciting for both men and women.

Basketball is the only game that both men and women play from junior high through college and into recreational leagues. Title IX legislation has increased opportunities for women in American sports, particularly in schools, but we still have a long way to go. An article in *USA Today* showed that most major colleges devote only about 20 percent of their sports support to women's sports.

In the 1960s Illinois, Indiana, and Kentucky were the major per capita sources of basketball talent in America. The midsection of the United States, from Utah across to the District of Columbia, New Jersey, and New York City, also provided basketball talent.

Through the 1970s and 1980s Illinois, Indiana, and Kentucky held their positions, the District of Columbia area became a hotbed of basketball, and the Deep South began to emerge. Finally, in the 1980s and into the 1990s the South has emerged as the major per capita source of American basketball talent for both men and women.

Maryland is the leading sports state overall. Its per capita participation and production rate rose 1,000 percent between 1960 and 1990.

Why have these shifts in sports participation occurred? Two reasons: One, the South was just beginning to emerge in the 1960s as a sports region. Most major southern state institutions were totally segregated in the 1960s. In particular, the opportunity for African American athletes probably tripled between 1970 and 1980 as they realized that basketball was a way to get to college and make money as professionals. Another trend in southern sports was the diffusion of inner-city basketball from places like New York, Philadelphia, and Washington, D.C., to southern cities such as Atlanta, New Orleans, and Birmingham. From 1938 to 1960 the South was not represented among the top teams. In the 1990s involvement is much more universal, geographically speaking, in American basketball.

For golf, involvement is highest in the Midwest, lowest in the South. The U.S. Tennis Association says the Rocky Mountain region is its most popular per capita area and the South is above average.

Texas and Minnesota are examples of two extremes. Texas is a football area. Of all high school coaches in Texas, one-third are assigned to football. Few out-of-the-way sports are represented in Texas high schools. This is mainstream football, track, baseball, and basketball country. The Minnesota profile is very different. The Minnesota philosophy is participation; don't groom and breed superstar athletes, but provide fundamentals and get people involved for a lifetime of sport.

The center of the country is the sports-for-sports'–sake region. This area's patterns share an underlying philosophy with Minnesota—the idea is to participate, to get involved. Virtually any individual sport, from youth to adult, shows much higher participation rates here than in any other place in the United States. There is also a heavy emphasis on education in these states. They don't shortchange grade-school and high-school education as many states in the South do. Less emphasis is placed on big-time college or professional sports, while more emphasis is given to involvement in things like golf, tennis, softball, bowling, and so on. This is great country for companies like Reebok, Nike, Spalding, and Titleist.

The Pigskin Cult region is quite different. There, football reigns supreme. It is the tail that wags the entire sports dog. Because football is so important there, other sports are shortchanged. The typical high school in Mississippi, Alabama, or Georgia provides only four to six sports for its students. Things like gymnastics, swimming, and wrestling are not common in southern schools. They're simply not there except in the major cities and surrounding suburbs. They're not a part of the sports culture. Women are also badly shortchanged in this region—their role is not participation, but spectating, cheerleading, and the like.

Texas and the Southwest have much in common with the Pigskin Cult area, with the exception of women's involvement and the influence of the cowboy culture—things like rodeo, quarter-horse racing, and barrel-racing.

California and the Pacific Cornucopia lead the country in sports innovation, stressing new sports, changes in existing sports, and involvement as opposed to spectatorship. This region is also extremely strong in all of the mainstream sports—football, basketball, and baseball—but water polo, beach volleyball, polo, hang gliding, and air racing all reach their pinnacles here.

This rich analysis of the sports market in America was based on an extensive analysis of secondary data—data that have already been collected for other purposes. This chapter discusses the general nature of research designs that use secondary data. It also illustrates many diverse sources for secondary data.

# ■ SECONDARY DATA RESEARCH

**Secondary data**
Data that have been previously collected for a project other than the one at hand.

**Secondary data** are data gathered and recorded by someone else prior to and for purposes other than the current project. Secondary data usually are historical and already assembled. They require no access to respondents or subjects.

## ■ Advantages

The primary advantage of secondary data comes from availability. Obtaining them is almost always faster and less expensive than acquiring primary data. This is particularly true when electronic retrieval is used to access digitally stored data. In many situations, collection of secondary data is instantaneous.

Consider the money and time saved by researchers who obtained updated population estimates for a town during the interim between the 1990 and 2000 census. Instead of doing the fieldwork themselves, they could acquire estimates from a firm dealing in demographic information or from sources such as Sales and Marketing Management's *Survey of Buying Power* (www.salesandmarketing.com). Many of the activities normally associated with primary data collection (for example, sampling and data processing) are eliminated.

In some instances, data cannot be obtained using primary data collection procedures. For example, a manufacturer of farm implements could not duplicate the information in the *Census of Agriculture* because much of the information there (for example, taxes paid) might not be accessible to a private firm.

## ■ Disadvantages

An inherent disadvantage of secondary data is that they were not designed specifically to meet the researchers' needs. Thus, researchers must ask how pertinent the data are to a particular project. To evaluate secondary data, researchers should ask questions such as these:

- Is the subject matter consistent with our problem definition?
- Do the data apply to the population of interest?
- Do the data apply to the time period of interest?
- Do the data appear in the correct units of measurement?
- Do the data cover the subject of interest in adequate detail?

Consider the following typical situations:

- A researcher interested in forklift trucks finds that the secondary data on the subject are included in a broader, less pertinent category encompassing all industrial trucks and tractors. Further, the data were collected five years earlier.
- An investigator who wishes to study individuals earning more than $125,000 per year finds the top category in a secondary study reported at $100,000 or more per year.
- A brewery that wishes to compare its per-barrel advertising expenditures with those of competitors finds the units of measurement differ because some report point-of-purchase expenditures with advertising while others do not.
- Data from a previous warranty card study show where consumers prefer to purchase the product, but provide no reasons.

Each of these situations shows that even when secondary information is available, it can be inadequate. The most common reasons secondary data do not adequately satisfy research needs are (1) outdated information, (2) variation in definition of terms, (3) different units of measurement, and (4) lack of information to verify the data's accuracy.

Information quickly becomes outdated in our rapidly changing environment. Because the purpose of most studies is to predict the future, secondary data must be timely to be useful.

Every primary researcher has the right to define the terms or concepts under investigation to satisfy the purpose of his or her primary investigation. This is little solace, however, to the investigator of the African American market who finds secondary data reported as "_____ percent nonwhite." Variances in terms or variable classifications should be scrutinized to determine if differences are important. The populations of interest must be described in comparable terms. Researchers frequently encounter secondary data that report on a population of interest that is similar but not directly comparable to that population the researcher is investigating. For example, Arbitron (www.arbitron.com) reports its television audience estimates by geographical areas known as ADI (Areas of Dominant Influence). An ADI is a geographic area consisting of all counties in which the home market commercial television stations receive a preponderance of total viewing hours. This unique population of interest is used exclusively to report television audiences. The geographical areas used in the census of population, such as Metropolitan Statistical Areas, are not comparable to ADIs.

Units of measurement may cause problems if they do not conform exactly to a researcher's needs. For example, lumber shipments in millions of board feet is quite different from billions of ton-miles of lumber shipped on freight cars. Head-of-household income is not the same unit of measure as total family income. Often the objective of the original primary study may dictate that the data are summarized, rounded, or reported such that, although the original units of measurement were comparable, aggregated or adjusted units of measurement are not suitable in the secondary study.

When secondary data are reported in a format that does not exactly meet the researcher's needs, data conversion may be necessary. **Data conversion** (also called *data transformation*) is the process of changing the original form of the data to a format suitable to achieve the research objective. For example, sales for food products may be reported in pounds, cases, or dollars. An estimate of dollars per pound may be used to convert dollar volume data to pounds or another suitable format.

Another disadvantage of secondary data is that the user has no control over their accuracy. Although timely and pertinent secondary data may fit the researcher's requirements, the data could be inaccurate. Research conducted by other persons may be biased to support the vested interest of the source. For example, media often publish data from surveys to identify the characteristics of their subscribers or viewers, but they will most likely exclude derogatory data from their reports. If the possibility of bias exists, the secondary data should not be used.

Investigators are naturally more prone to accept data from reliable sources such as the U.S. government. Nevertheless, the researcher must assess the reputation of the organization that gathers the data and critically assess the research design to determine whether the research was correctly implemented. Unfortunately, such evaluation may not be possible if the manager lacks information explaining how the original research was conducted.

Researchers should verify the accuracy of the data whenever possible. **Cross-checks** of data from multiple sources—that is, comparison of the data from one source with data from another—should be made to determine the similarity of independent projects. When the data are not consistent, researchers should attempt to identify reasons for differences or determine which data are most likely to be correct. If the accuracy of the data cannot be established, the researcher must determine whether using the data is worth the risk. Exhibit 6.1 illustrates a series of questions one should ask to evaluate secondary data before use.[2]

**Data conversion**
The process of changing the original form of the data to a format suitable to achieve the research objective. Also called *data transformation*.

**Cross-check**
A comparison of data from one source with data from another source to determine the similarity of independent projects.

**■ Exhibit 6.1**

**Evaluating Secondary Data**

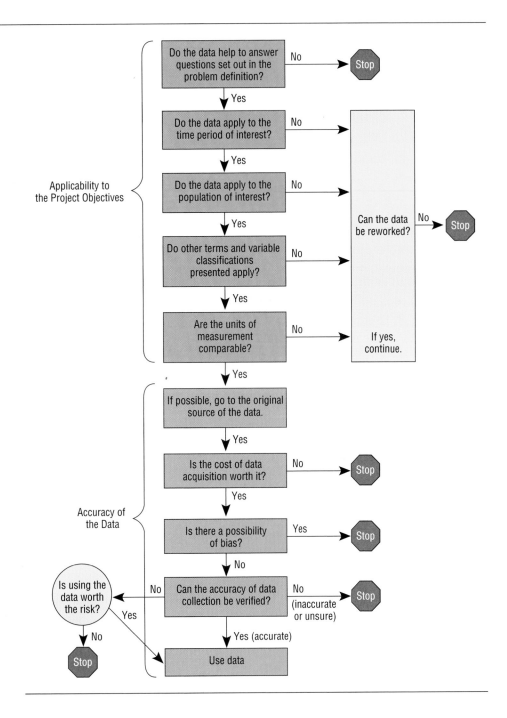

## ■ TYPICAL OBJECTIVES FOR SECONDARY DATA RESEARCH DESIGNS

It would be impossible to identify all possible purposes of marketing research using secondary data. However, it is useful to illustrate some common marketing problems that

| | Broad Objective | Specific Research Example |
|---|---|---|
| ■ **Exhibit 6.2** | Fact finding | Identifying consumption patterns |
| **Some Common Research** | | Tracking trends |
| **Objectives for Secondary** | Model building | Estimating market potential |
| **Data Studies** | | Forecasting sales |
| | | Selecting trade areas and sites |
| | Database marketing | Enhancement of customer databases |
| | | Development of prospect lists |

secondary research designs can address. Exhibit 6.2 shows three general categories of research objectives: fact finding, model building, and *database marketing.*

## ■ Fact Finding

The simplest form of secondary data research is fact finding. A marketer of frozen food might be interested in knowing how often frozen pizza is consumed in the United States. Secondary data available from National Eating Trends, a service of The NPD Group, Inc. (www.npd.com), show that U.S. households serve frozen pizza an average of 11 times per year, most often for dinner (59 percent), followed by lunch (32 percent). Nielsen Marketing Research data indicate that the deluxe/combination is the best-selling type of frozen pizza in the country, at 34 percent. Next is pepperoni, at 25 percent; then cheese, at 21 percent; followed by sausage, beef/hamburger, and Canadian bacon. According to the Nielsen data, frozen pizza preferences tend to be regional. More than half the frozen pizzas sold in the New York area are plain cheese. In Dallas, frozen pepperoni pizza outsells frozen sausage pizza three to one, whereas in Chicago, sausage is twice as popular as pepperoni. Canadian bacon has its largest share in Minneapolis.[3] These simple facts would interest a researcher who was investigating the frozen-foods market. Fact finding can serve more complex purposes as well.

**Identify Consumer Behavior for a Product Category**   A typical objective for a secondary research study might be to uncover all available information about consumption patterns for a particular product category or to identify demographic trends that affect an industry.

■ In 1960 only 6 percent of Americans regularly ate salsa. By 1990 38 percent said they regularly ate salsa, and since 1992 sales of salsa have exceeded sales of ketchup. In 1993 Heinz introduced its Salsa Style Ketchup, a ketchup with peppers, onions, and other salsa ingredients, blending two of Americans' favorite condiments, ketchup and salsa. Unfortunately, this tasty product failed. Ketchup and salsa generally sit in different supermarket aisles, and consumers were confused about the proper use for this product.

**■ Exhibit 6.3**

**Secondary Data to Show TV Rights Fees Paid to the NFL**

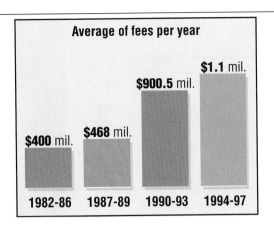

Average of fees per year

$400 mil.  1982-86
$468 mil.  1987-89
$900.5 mil.  1990-93
$1.1 mil.  1994-97

For example, this chapter began with a description of the sports market in the United States. This example illustrates the wealth of factual information about consumption and behavior patterns one can obtain by carefully collecting and analyzing secondary data.

**Market tracking**
The observation and analysis of trends in industry volume and brand share over time.

**Trend Analysis**   Marketers watch for trends in the market and the environment. **Market tracking** refers to the observation and analysis of trends in industry volume and brand share over time. Scanner research services and other organizations provide facts about sales volume to support this work.

Almost every large consumer goods company routinely investigates brand and product category sales volume using secondary data. This type of analysis typically involves comparisons with competitors or the company's own sales in comparable time periods. It also involves industry comparisons among different geographic areas. Exhibit 6.3 shows trends in NFL rights fees—the money television networks pay to the National Football League.

**Environmental Scanning**   In many instances, the purpose of the fact finding is vague. The purpose of much fact finding is simply to study the environment to identify trends. **Environmental scanning** entails all information gathering and fact finding that is designed to detect indications of environmental changes in their initial stages of development. For example, a few years ago, as a result of scanning the environment, marketers of lingerie and brassieres noticed that women found the new push-up Wonderbra very fashionable. Maidenform and other competitors, betting that curves and cleavage were coming back into fashion, introduced push-up and body enhancers with names such as It Really Works!, The Super Uplift, Bodysationals, Her Secrets, and It Must Be Magic! Because of its vastness, the Internet is an especially useful source for scanning many types of changes in the environment.

**Environmental scanning**
Information gathering and fact finding designed to detect indications of environmental changes in their initial stages of development.

A number of on-line information services, such as Dow Jones News Retrieval (www.dowjones.com), allow for routine collection of news stories about industries, product lines, and other topics of interest that have been specified by the researcher. As we mentioned in Chapter 2, push technology is an Internet information technology that automatically delivers content to the researcher's or manager's desktop.[4] Push technology uses an "electronic smart agent" to find information. "Smart agent" is a custom software program to filter, sort, prioritize, and store information for later viewing.[5] This frees the researcher from doing the searching. The true value of push technology is that a researcher who is scanning the environment can customize the nature of the news and information desired, have it quickly delivered via a PC, and view it at leisure.

■ The director of MIT's Media Lab, Nicholas Negroponte, thinks of a smart agent "as a computerized English butler. An agent builds a model of you, which can be likened to the process of human-to-human acquaintanceship. The longer you know somebody, the better you can guess what they mean (versus say), what they want (versus ask for) and what they do (versus say they do). So, too, with agents.

One type of agent looks at millions of bits go zooming past and tries to pick out the ones that are of interest to you. Like catching fly balls.

Another type of agent works in the network. They go searching and sifting through stacks of libraries, reading daily newspapers, and joining electronic chat groups, to find answers to specific questions or topics that may interest you."[6]

## ■ Model Building

**Model building**
Involves using secondary data to help specify relationships between two or more variables; can include the development of descriptive or predictive equations.

The other general objective for secondary research, model building, is more complicated than simple fact finding. **Model building** involves specifying relationships between two or more variables, perhaps extending to the development of descriptive or predictive equations. Models need not include complicated mathematics, though. In fact, decision makers often prefer simple models that everyone can readily understand over complex, less comprehensible models. For example, market share is company sales divided by industry sales. Although some may not think of this simple calculation as a model, it represents a mathematical model of a basic relationship.

We will illustrate model building by discussing three common objectives that secondary research can satisfy: estimating market potential, forecasting sales, and selecting sites.

**Estimating Market Potential for Geographic Areas** Marketers often estimate market potential using secondary data. In many cases, exact figures are published by a trade association or another source. However, when the desired information is unavailable, the researcher may estimate market potential by transforming secondary data from two or more sources. For example, managers may find secondary data about market potential for a country or other large geographic area, but this information may not be broken down by state, county, metropolitan area, sales territory, or zip code.

An example will help explain how secondary data can be used to calculate market potential. A marketer of crackers is contemplating building a processing plant in Europe. Managers wish to estimate potential for the United Kingdom, Germany, Spain, Italy, and France. Using secondary research, per capita cracker consumption and population projects for the year 2000 were obtained. The data for the United States and the five European countries appear in Exhibit 6.4.[7] The per capita cracker consumption was obtained from A. C. Nielsen Company. The population estimates were obtained from P. C. Globe, a software database.

To calculate market potential for Italy in the year 2000, multiply that country's population in the year 2000 by its per capita cracker consumption:

$$58,708 \times 4.33 = 254,205$$

In Italy the market potential for crackers is $254,205 in thousands, or $254,205,000. Note that Germany has a higher population but a much lower market potential.

Of course, the calculated market potential for each country in Exhibit 6.4 is a simple estimate. The marketer might recognize that dollar sales volume will be influenced by each country's inflation rate and other variables. Past inflation rates, also found in secondary data sources, could be added to the calculation to improve the estimate.

**Forecasting Sales**  Marketing managers need information about the future. They need to know what company sales will be next year and in future time periods. *Sales forecasting* is the process of predicting sales totals over a specific time period.

Accurate sales forecasts, especially for products in mature, stable markets, frequently come from secondary data research that identifies trends and extrapolates past performance into the future. Marketing researchers often use internal company sales records to project sales of mature products.

A rudimentary model would multiply past sales volume by an expected growth rate. A researcher might investigate a secondary source and find that industry sales are expected to grow by 10 percent; multiplying company sales volume by 10 percent would give a basic sales forecast.

Exhibit 6.5 illustrates trend projection using a moving average projection of growth rates. Average daily room rates for U.S. hotels are secondary data from Lodging Research Network (www.lodgingresearch.com).[8] The moving average sums growth rates for the latest three years and divides by 3 (number of years) to forecast the increase in ticket prices.

■ **Exhibit 6.4**

**Market Potential for Crackers in Europe**

| Country | (1) Population Projection for 2000 (thousands) | (2) Annual per Capita Cracker Consumption (U.S.$) | (3) Market Potential Estimate ($000) (1) × (2) |
|---|---|---|---|
| United Kingdom | 273,646 | $9.48 | $2,594,164 |
| Germany | 76,839 | 1.91 | 146,762 |
| Italy | 58,708 | 4.33 | 254,205 |
| France | 58,187 | 3.56 | 207,145 |
| Spain | 41,776 | 0.62 | 25,065 |

■ **Exhibit 6.5**

**Sales Forecast Using Secondary Data and the Moving-Average Method**

| Year | Average Daily Room Rate | Growth Rate from Previous Year | Three-Year Moving Average Growth |
|------|-------------------------|--------------------------------|----------------------------------|
| 1990 | $58.01 | – | – |
| 1991 | 58.14 | 0.2% | – |
| 1992 | 58.96 | 1.4% | – |
| 1993 | 60.59 | 2.8% | 1.5 |
| 1994 | 62.90 | 3.8% | 2.7 |
| 1995 | 65.89 | 4.7% | 3.8 |
| 1996 | 70.00 | 6.2% | 4.9 |
| 1997 | 74.29 | 6.1% | 5.7 |

Forecast for 1998 $74.29 + $74.29 × 5.7% = $78.52

Using the three-year average growth rate for 1995, 1996, and 1997, 5.7 percent, the forecast for the 1998 season is calculated as $74.29 + $74.29 × 0.057 = $78.52.

Moving-average forecasting best suits a static competitive environment. More dynamic situations make other sales forecasting techniques more appropriate.

Statistical trend analysis using secondary data can be much more advanced than in the preceding simple example. Many statistical techniques build forecasting models using secondary data. This chapter emphasizes secondary data research rather than statistical analysis. Chapter 15, "Relationships between Variables and Differences among Groups," explains more sophisticated statistical model-building techniques for forecasting sales.

**Site analysis techniques**
Involve use of secondary data to select the best locations for retail or wholesale operations.

**Analysis of Trade Areas and Sites**[9]    Marketing managers examine trade areas and use **site analysis techniques** to select the best locations for retail or wholesale operations. Secondary data research helps managers make this site selection decision. Some organizations, especially franchisers, have developed special computer software based on analytical models to select sites for retail outlets. The researcher must obtain the appropriate secondary data for analysis with the computer software.

**Index of retail saturation**
A calculation that describes the relationship between retail demand and supply.

The **index of retail saturation** offers one way to investigate retail sites and describe the relationship between retail demand and supply. It is easy to calculate once the appropriate secondary data are obtained:

$$\text{Index of retail saturation} = \frac{\text{Local market potential (demand)}}{\text{Square feet of retailing space}}$$

Exhibit 6.6 shows the relevant secondary data for shoe store sales in a five-mile ring surrounding a Florida shopping center. These kinds of data can be purchased from vendors of market information such as Urban Decision Systems.

First, local market potential (demand) is estimated by multiplying population by annual per capita shoe sales. The index of retail saturation is:

$$\text{Index of retail saturation} = \frac{\$14,249,000}{41}$$
$$= 152$$

This index figure can be compared with those of other areas to determine which sites have the greatest market potential with the least amount of retail competition. An index value above 200 is considered to indicate exceptional opportunities.

■ **Exhibit 6.6**

**Secondary Data for the Calculation of an Index of Retail Saturation**

| | |
|---|---:|
| 1. Population | 261,785 |
| 2. Annual per capita shoe sales | $54.43 |
| 3. Local market potential (line 1 × line 2) | $14,249,000 |
| 4. Square feet of retail space used to sell shoes | 94,000 sq. ft. |
| 5. Index of retail saturation (line 3/line 4) | 152 |

## ■ Database Marketing

**Database marketing**
The practice of maintaining customer databases with relevant data on individual customers as well as demographic and financial data.

As we have already mentioned, a database is a collection of data arranged in a logical manner and organized in a form that can be stored and processed by a computer. **Database marketing** is the practice of maintaining customer databases with customers' names, addresses, phone numbers, past purchases, responses to past promotional offers, and other relevant data such as demographic and financial data. It also means organizations use their databases to develop one-to-one relationships and highly targeted promotional efforts with their individual customers. For example, a fruit catalog company maintains a database of previous customers that includes the purchases they made during the Christmas holidays. The following year, it sends last year's gift list so that customers can send the same gifts to their friends and relatives.[10]

Because *database marketing* requires vast amounts of data compiled from often numerous sources, much secondary data are acquired exclusively to develop or enhance a customer database. The transaction record, which often provides the item purchased, its value, and the customer's name, address, and zip code, is the building block for many databases. This may be supplemented with data customers provide directly, such as data on a warranty card, and with secondary data purchased from third parties. For example, credit services may sell databases pertaining to applications for loans, credit card payment history, and other financial data. Several other companies, such as Donnelley (Cluster Plus) and Claritas (PRIZIM), collect primary data and then sell demographic data that can be related to small geographic areas such as zip code. (Remember that data collected by the vendor are primary data, whereas data incorporated by the database marketer into its database are secondary data.)

Now that we have looked at some of the purposes of secondary data analysis, let's consider sources of secondary data.

## ■ SOURCES OF SECONDARY DATA

**Internal and proprietary data**
Secondary data that originate inside the organization.

Secondary data can be classified as either internal to the organization or external. Modern information technology makes this definition somewhat simplistic, however. Some accounting documents are indisputably internal records of the organization; researchers in another organization cannot have access to them. Clearly, a book published by the federal government and located at the public library is external to the company. However, in today's world of electronic data dissemination, the data that appear in a book published by the federal government may also be purchased from an on-line information vendor for instantaneous access and subsequently stored in a company's decision support system.

*Internal data* should be defined as data that originated in the organization or data created, recorded, or generated by the organization. **Internal and proprietary data** is perhaps a more descriptive term.

## ■ Internal and Proprietary Data Sources

Most organizations routinely gather, record, and store internal data to help them solve future problems. The accounting system usually provides a wealth of information. Routine documents such as sales invoices allow external financial reporting, which in turn can be a source of data for further analysis. If the data are properly coded into a modular database in the accounting system, the researcher may be able to conduct more detailed analysis using the decision support system. Sales information can be broken down by account or by product and region; information related to orders received, back orders, and unfilled orders can be identified; sales can be forecast on the basis of past data.

Researchers frequently aggregate or disaggregate internal data. Other useful sources of internal data include salespeople's call reports, customer complaints, service records, warranty card returns, and other records. For example, a computer service firm used internal secondary data to analyze sales over the previous three years, categorizing business by industry, product, purchase level, and so on. The company discovered that 60 percent of its customers represented only 2 percent of its business and that nearly all of these customers came through telephone directory advertising. This simple investigation of internal records showed that, in effect, the firm was paying to attract customers it did not want.

## ■ Data Mining

Large corporations' decision support systems often contain millions or even hundreds of millions of records of data. These data volumes are too large and complex for most managers to understand. Consider a credit card company collecting data on customer purchases. Each customer might make, on average, 10 transactions in a month, 120 per year. With 3 million customers and five years of data, it's easy to see how record counts quickly grow beyond the comfort zone for most humans.[11]

Two points need to be made about data volume. First, relevant marketing data often reside in independent and unrelated files. Second, the number of distinct pieces of information each data record contains is often large. When the number of distinct pieces of information contained in each data record and data volume grows too big, end-users don't have the capacity to make sense of it all. Data mining helps unravel the underlying meaning of the data. **Data mining** refers to the use of powerful computers to dig through exceedingly large volumes of data to discover patterns about an organization's customers and products. It is a broad term that applies to many different forms of analysis. For example, neural networks are a form of artificial intelligence in which a computer is programmed to mimic the way human brains process information. One computer expert put it this way: "A *neural network* learns pretty much the way a human being does. Suppose you say 'big' and show a child an elephant. Then you say 'small' and show her a poodle. You repeat this process with a house and a giraffe as examples of 'big' and then a grain of sand and an ant as examples of 'small.' Pretty soon she will figure it out and tell you that a truck is 'big' and a needle is 'small.' Neural networks can similarly generalize by looking at examples.[12]

*Market basket analysis* is a form of data mining that analyzes anonymous point-of-sale transaction data to identify coinciding purchases or affinities between products purchased and other retail shopping information.[13] Consider this example. Grocery chains that have mined their databases provided by checkout scanners have found that when men go to a supermarket to buy diapers, they sometimes walk out with a six-pack of beer as well. Knowing this behavioral pattern, a supermarket chain could lay out its stores so that these items are closer together.[14]

The credit card company with large volumes of data illustrates a *customer discovery* data-mining application. The credit card company will probably track information about each customer: age, gender, number of children, job status, income level, past credit his-

**Data mining**
The use of powerful computers to dig through large volumes of data to discover patterns about an organization's customers and products.

tory, and so on. Often these data will be mined to find the patterns that make a particular individual a good or bad credit risk.[15]

When the identity of the customer who makes repeated purchases from the same organization is known, an analysis can be made of sequences of purchases. *Sequence discovery,* the use of data mining to detect sequence patterns, is a popular application among direct marketers such as catalog retailers. A catalog merchant has information for each customer regarding the sets of products the customer buys in every purchase order. A sequence discovery function can then be used to discover the set of purchases that frequently precedes the purchase of a microwave oven. As another example, sequence discovery used on a set of insurance claims could help identify frequently occurring medical procedures performed on patients, which in turn could be used to detect cases of medical fraud.

Data mining requires sophisticated computer resources, and it is expensive. For these reasons, companies such as DataMind, IBM, Oracle, Information Builders, and Acxiom Corporation offer data-mining services. The customer sends the databases its wants analyzed and lets the data-mining company do the "numbers crunching."

## ■ External Data: The Distribution System

**External data**
Data created, recorded, or generated by an entity other than the researcher's organization.

**External data** are created, recorded, or generated by an entity other than the researcher's organization. The government, newspapers and journals, trade associations, and other organizations create or produce information. Traditionally this information has been in published form, perhaps available from a public library, trade association, or government

IBM
Solutions for a small planet™

To our data mining system, they're twins. Because both order milk with their hamburgers. A subtle, if somewhat unusual, connection that ordinary data mining systems just don't dig deep enough to find. Which is why IBM developed Intelligent Miner.™ With patented algorithms that can unearth the most unexpected patterns and parallels in customer behavior. Because it's often the thing you weren't looking for that ends up being the thing you need to stay a step ahead. And since our data miners already have in-depth knowledge of your industry, they can start digging right away. For more information, or to find out about an upcoming data mining teleseminar, visit our Website at www.software.ibm.com/datamining.

■ This advertisment's copy says "To our data mining system, they're twins. Because both order milk with their hamburgers." It illustrates an example of market basket analysis.[16]

## WHAT WENT RIGHT?

### Marriott Vacation Club International

Over the past three years Marriott Vacation Club International, the nation's largest seller of vacation time-share condos, has slashed the amount of junk mail it has to send out to get a response. How? With a computer, a database and some help from Acxiom Corporation, which specializes in data processing of secondary data for marketers.

What Marriott is doing is called *data mining*. This is the science of combing through digitized customer files to detect patterns. Marriott starts with names, mostly of hotel guests. Digging into a trove of motor vehicle records, property records, warranty cards and lists of people who have bought by mail, Acxiom enriches the prospect list. It adds such facts as the customers' ages, children's ages and estimated income, what cars they drive and if they golf. Then Marriott uses a *complex computer program* (neural networks) to figure out who is most likely to respond to a mailed flier.

Using these clues, Marriott is able to cast its net a little more narrowly and catch more fish. Data mining has increased the response rate to Marriott's direct mail time-share pitches to certain hotel guests from 0.75% to 1%. . . . That seems like a slim gain, but it makes a big difference to a company that sent out 3 million glossy solicitations at a cost of up to $1.50 each last year.

agency. Today, however, computerized data archives, electronic data interchange, and the Internet make external data as accessible as internal data. Exhibit 6.7 illustrates some traditional ways and some modern ways of distributing information.

Because secondary data have value, they can be bought and sold in the same way other products are. Just as bottles of perfume or plumbers' wrenches may be distributed in many ways, secondary data also flow through various channels of distribution.[17] Many users, such as the Fortune 500 corporations, purchase government documents and computerized census data directly from the government. Many small companies get census data from a library or another intermediary or vendor of secondary information.

**Libraries**  Traditionally libraries' vast storehouses of information have served as a bridge between users and producers of secondary data. The library staff deals directly with the creators of information, such as the federal government, and intermediate distributors of information, such as abstracting and indexing services. The user needs only to locate the appropriate secondary data on the library shelves. Libraries provide collections of books, journals, newspapers, and so on for reading and reference. They also stock many bibliographies, abstracts, guides, directories, and indexes, as well as offering access to basic databases.

The word *library* typically connotes a public or university facility. However, many major corporations and government agencies also have libraries. A corporate librarian's advice on sources of industry information or the United Nations librarian's help in finding statistics about international markets can be invaluable. Today, libraries, such as the New York Public Library (www.nypl.org), have much of their collections on the Internet.

**The Internet**  The Internet is a more recent source of distribution of much secondary data. Its creation has added an international dimension to the acquisition of secondary data.

In Chapter 2, we discussed how to access and use the Internet. Exhibit 6.8 shows some of the more common Internet addresses where one can find secondary data.

■ **Exhibit 6.7**

**Information as a Product and Its Distribution Channels**

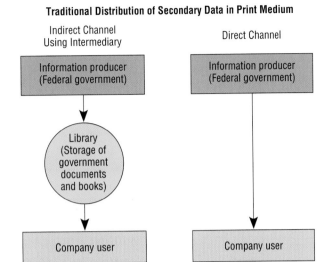

**Traditional Distribution of Secondary Data in Print Medium**

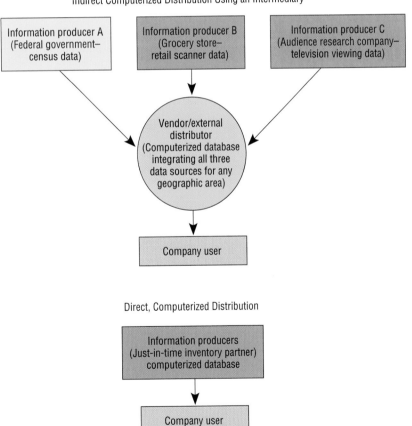

| | Name | Description | Web Address |
|---|---|---|---|
| ■ **Exhibit 6.8** **Popular Internet Addresses** | The New York Public Library Home Page | Library resources and links available on-line | http://www.nypl.org |
| | Yahoo—Maps | Allows users to enter an address and zip code and see a map on the desktop. | http://maps/yahoo.com/yahoo |
| | NAICS—North American Industry Classification System | Describes the new classification system that will replace the old SIC systerm. | http://www.census.gov/epcd/www/naics.html |
| | Inc. Online | *Inc.* Magazine's Resources for Growing a Small Business | http://www.inc.com/ |
| | The Internet World Trade Complex | The Internet World Trade Association's comprehensive "elevator" system for linking to commercial, educational, and governmental resources. | http://www.internetwtc.com |
| | Edgar | The Web source of corporate disclosure filings | http://town.hall.org/edgar/edgar.html |
| | Pathfinder | Time Warner's collection of news and entertainment products | http://www.pathfinder.com |
| | Census Bureau | Demographic information from U.S. Census | http://www.census.gov/ |
| | Statistical Abstract | Highlights from the primary reference book for government statistics | http://www.census.gov/stat_abstract/ |
| | STAT-USA/Internet | A comprehensive source of U.S. government information that focuses on economic, financial, and trade data | http://www.stat-usa.gov/inqsample.html |
| | Advertising Age | *Advertising Age* magazine provides marketing media, advertising, and public relations content | http://www.adage.com |
| | Wall Street Journal Interactive | Provides a continually updated view of business news around the world | http://www.wsj.com |
| | CNN Financial News | Provides business news, information on managing a business, information on managing money, and other business data | http://www.cnnfn.com |

**Vendors**  The information age offers many channels besides libraries through which to access data. Many external producers make secondary data available directly from the organizations that produce the data or through intermediaries (often called *vendors*). In recent years, the growth of on-line vendor services has allowed managers to access external databases via desktop computers with telecommunications capabilities.

**Producers**  Classifying external secondary data by the nature of the producer of information yields five basic sources: books and periodicals, government sources, media sources, trade association sources, and commercial sources. The following sections discuss each of these sources in detail.

**Books and Periodicals**  Books and periodicals found in a library often are considered the quintessential secondary data source. A researcher who finds books on a topic of interest obviously is off to a good start.

Professional journals such as the *Journal of Marketing, Journal of Marketing Research, Journal of the Academy of Marketing Science, Marketing Research: A Magazine of Management and Application,* and *The Public Opinion Quarterly,* as well as commercial business periodicals such as *The Wall Street Journal, Fortune,* and *Business Week,* contain much useful material. Sales and Marketing Management's *Survey of Buying Power* is a particularly useful source for information about markets. Indexing services such as ABI/INFORM, the Business Periodicals Index, and The Wall Street Journal Index are valuable for locating data in periodicals. Guides to data sources, such as *American Statistical Index and Business Information Sources,* are also very useful.

**Government Sources**  Government agencies produce data prolifically. Most of the data published by the federal government can be counted on for accuracy and quality of investigation. Most students are familiar with the U.S. *Census of Population,* which provides a wealth of data.

The *Census of Population* is only one of many resources the government provides. Banks and savings and loans rely heavily on the *Federal Reserve Bulletin* and the *Economic Report of the President* for data relating to research on financial and economic conditions. Builders and contractors use the information in the *Current Housing Report* and *Annual Housing Survey* for their research. The *Statistical Abstract of the United States* is an extremely valuable source of information about the social, political, and economic organization of the United States. It abstracts data available in hundreds of other government publications and serves as a convenient reference to more specific statistical data. **Visit the home page for this book (http://www.dryden.com/mktng/zikmund) for links to many of these important documents.**

The federal government is a leader in making secondary data available on the Internet. STAT-USA/Internet is an authoritative and comprehensive source of U.S. government information that focuses on economic, financial, and trade data. It contains

- More than 18,000 market research reports on individual countries and markets compiled by foreign experts at U.S. embassies
- Economic data series, current and historical, such as gross domestic product, balance of payment, and merchandise trade
- Standard reference works, such as the *Economic Report of the President,* the *Budget of the United States Federal Government,* and the *World Fact Book*
- Worldwide listings of businesses interested in buying U.S. products

The STAT-USA/Internet World Wide Web server address is (http//www.stat-usa.gov/inqsample.html). However, only subscribers who pay a fee have access to this service.

State, county, and local government agencies also can be useful sources of information. Many state governments publish state economic models and forecasts, and many cities have metropolitan planning agencies that provide data about the population, economy, transportation system, and so on. These are similar to the federal government data, but are more current and structured to suit local needs.

Several cities and states publish information on the Internet. Many search engines have directory entries that allow easy navigation to states. A researcher using Yahoo, for example, needs only to click "regional information" to find considerable paths to information about states.[18] The Yahoo address on the World Wide Web is http://www.yahoo.com.

**Media Sources**    Information on a broad range of subjects is available from broadcast and print media. *The Wall Street Journal* and *Business Week* are valuable sources for information on the economy and many industries. Information about special-interest topics also may be available. For example, *Money* magazine commissioned a research study about all aspects of Americans' financial affairs, and the report of this survey is available free to potential advertisers. Data about the readers of magazines and the audiences for broadcast media typically are profiled in media kits and advertisements.

*American Woodworker* magazine reports there are nearly 19.6 million woodworkers: 17.2 million of these are amateurs, while 2.4 million are professionals. *American Woodworker* also provides the demographic characteristics of woodworking households: 84 percent are male, 78 percent are married, the average age is 45, and the average household income is $48,000.[19]

Data such as these are plentiful because the media like to show that their vehicles are viewed or heard by advertisers' target markets. This type of data should be given careful evaluation, however, because often it covers only limited aspects of a topic. Nevertheless, it can be quite valuable for research, and it generally is available free of charge.

**Trade Association Sources**    Trade associations, such as the Food Marketing Institute and the American Petroleum Institute, serve the information needs of particular industries. The trade association collects data on a number of topics of specific interest to firms, especially market size and market trends. Association members have a source of information that is particularly germane to their industry questions. For example, the Newspaper Advertising Bureau (NAB) has cataloged and listed in its computer the specialized sections currently popular in newspapers. The NAB has surveyed all daily, Sunday, and weekend newspapers in the United States and Canada on their editorial content and stored this information, along with data on rates, circulation, and mechanical requirements, in its computer for advertisers' use.

**Commercial Sources**    Numerous firms specialize in selling and/or publishing information. For example, R. L. Polk Company publishes information on the automotive field, such as average car values and new-car purchase rates by zip code. Many of these organizations offer information in published formats and as on-line or CD-ROM databases. The following discussion of several of these firms provides a sampling of the diverse data available.

*Market Share Data*    A number of syndicated services supply either wholesale or retail sales volume data based on product movement. A. C. Nielsen Company, the world's largest marketing research service, performs a wide range of marketing research activities. Although best known for its television rating operations, its National Scan Track and Nielsen Retail Index Service combine to offer a major market-tracking service. Scanner data and in-store audits measure consumer response at the point of sale. Using a carefully selected sample of stores, Nielsen Retail Index Service tracks volume at the retail level in nonscanner stores. Nielsen auditors visit the stores at regular intervals to track sales to customers, retail inventories, brand distribution, out-of-stock conditions, prices, and the like for competing brands as well as the client's own brand.

Information Resources, Inc., surveys a national sample of supermarkets with optical scanning checkouts for its INFOSCAN, a syndicated service that provides on-line or weekly data about product item movement and brand share as well as other aggregate product sales information. Organizations such as this allow researchers to monitor sales data before, during, and after changes in advertising frequency, price, distribution of free samples, and similar marketing tactics. Many primary-data investigations use scanner data to measure the results of experimental manipulations such as altering advertising copy. Systems based on UPC bar code technology have been implemented in factories, warehouses, and transportation companies to research inventory levels, shipments, and the like.

*Demographic and Census Updates*   A number of firms, such as CACI/Instant Demographics and Urban Decision Systems, offer computerized U.S. Census files and updates of these data by small geographic areas, such as zip codes. Impact Resources provides in-depth information on minority customers and other market segments through its MA·RT Consumer Intelligence System.

*Consumer Attitude and Public Opinion Research*   Many research firms offer specialized syndicated services that report findings from attitude research and opinion polls. For example, Yankelovich and Associates provides custom research—research tailored for specific projects—and several syndicated services. Its public opinion research studies, such as the voter and public attitude surveys that appear in *Time,* are a source of secondary data. One of the more interesting of these services is the *Yankelovich Monitor,* a cost-shared annual census of changing social values and how they can affect consumer marketing. The *Monitor* charts the growth and spread of new social values, the types of customers who support the new values and those who continue to support traditional values, and the ways in which people's values affect purchasing behavior.

Louis Harris Company is another public opinion research firm that provides syndicated and custom research for business. One of its services is the ABC News/Harris survey. This survey is released three times per week and monitors the pulse of the American public on topics such as inflation, unemployment, energy, attitudes toward the president, elections, and so on.

*Consumption and Purchase Behavior Data*   The National CREST Report (Consumer Report on Eating Share Trends) is a syndicated source of data about the types of meals people eat and how people consume food. The data, called *diary panel data,* are based on records of meals in diaries kept by a group of households that have agreed to record their consumption behavior over an extended period of time.

National Family Opinion (NFO), Marketing Research Corporation of America (MRCA), and many other syndicated sources sell diary panel data about consumption and purchase behavior. Since the advent of scanner data, purchase panels are more commonly used to record purchases of apparel, hardware, home furnishings, jewelry, and other durable goods than purchases of nondurable consumer packaged goods.

*Advertising Research*   A number of firms supply readership and audience data. W. R. Simmons and Associates measures magazine audiences; Arbitron measures radio audiences; the Nielsen Television Index measures television audiences. By specializing in collecting and selling audience information on a continuing basis, these commercial sources provide a valuable service to their subscribers.

Assistance in measuring advertising effectiveness is another syndicated service. For example, Starch INRA Hooper measures the impact of advertising in magazines. Readership information is obtained for competitors' ads or the client's own ads. Respondents are classified as noted readers, associated readers, or read-most readers.

Burke Marketing Research provides a service that measures the extent to which respondents recall television commercials aired the night before. It provides product category norms, or average DAR (day-after recall) scores, and DAR scores for other products.

An individual advertiser would be unable to monitor every minute of every television program before deciding on the appropriate ones in which to place advertising. However, the Nielson Television Index service is sold to numerous clients, agencies, television networks, and advertisers at relatively inexpensive rates.

### ■ Single-Source Data: Integrated Information

A. C. Nielsen Company offers data from both its television meters and its scanner operations. The integration of these two types of data helps marketers investigate the impact of television advertising on retail sales. Users of data find that merging two or more diverse types of data into a single database offers many other advantages as well. The marketing research industry uses the term **single-source data** for diverse types of data offered by a single company.

**Single-source data**
Diverse types of data offered by a single company; usually integrated by a common variable such as geographic area.

National Decision Systems, Claritas Corporation's PRIZM, Mediamark Research Inc., and many other syndicated databases report product purchase behavior, media usage, demographic characteristics, lifestyle variables, and business activity by small geographic areas such as zip code. These single-source data are often called *geodemographic* because they use geographic areas as the unit of analysis. They cover such a broad range of phenomena that no one name is a good description. Exhibit 6.9 identifies several major marketers of single-source data.

### ■ Sources for Global Research

As business has become more global, so has the secondary data industry. The Japan Management Association Research Institute (JMAR), Japan's largest provider of secondary research data to government and industry, operates an office in San Diego. JMAR's goal is to help U.S. firms access its enormous store of data about Japan to develop and plan their

---

### ■ Exhibit 6.9

**Examples of Single-Source Databases**

| | |
|---|---|
| National Decision Systems<br>http://www.natdecsys.com | Integrates geodemographic data with many syndicated databases to provide data about product purchase behavior, media usage, demographic characteristics, lifestyle variables, and business activity by many geographical breakdowns. |
| PRIZM by Claritas Corporation<br>http://www.claritas.com | PRIZM, which stands for Potential Rating Index for Zip Markets, is based on the birds-of-a-feather assumption that people live near others who are like themselves. PRIZM combines census data, consumer surveys about shopping and lifestyle, and purchase data to identify market segments. Colorful names such as Young Suburbia and Shot Guns and Pickups describe 40 segments that can be identified by zip code. Claritis also has a lifestyle census in the United Kingdom (www.claritas.co.uk). |
| MRI Cable Report—Mediamark<br>    Research Inc.<br>http://www.mediamark.com | Integrates information on cable television viewing, including pay cable channels (HBO, Disney Channel, etc.), with demographic and product usage information. |

business there. The office in San Diego will translate and act as an intermediary between Japanese researchers and U.S. clients.

Secondary data compiled outside the United States have the same limitations domestic secondary data do. However, international researchers should watch for certain pitfalls frequently associated with foreign data and cross-cultural research. First, data may simply be unavailable in certain countries. Second, the accuracy of some data may be questionable. This is especially likely with official statistics that may have been adjusted for the political purposes of foreign governments. Finally, while economic terminology may be standardized, various countries use different definitions and accounting/recording practices for many economic concepts. For example, different countries may measure disposable personal income in radically different ways. International researchers should take extra care to investigate the comparability of data among countries.

The U.S. government and other organizations compile databases that may aid international marketers. For example, *The Arthur Andersen European Community Sourcebook* is a comprehensive reference guide that provides information about suppliers, sources of funding, and laws and regulations, and detailed profiles of each European Union member state. Arthur Andersen also publishes *European Review,* a newsletter that reports on current activity in the European Union.

## ■ INVESTIGATING GLOBAL MARKETS USING SECONDARY DATA: AN EXAMPLE

The U.S. government offers a wealth of data about foreign countries. The *CIA Factbook* and the National Trade Data Bank are especially useful; both can be accessed using the Internet. This section describes the National Trade Data Bank (NTDB), the U.S. government's most comprehensive source of world trade data, to illustrate what is available.

The National Trade Data Bank was established by the Omnibus Trade and Competitiveness Act of 1988.[20] Its purpose was to provide " . . . reasonable public access, including electronic access . . . " to an export promotion data system that was centralized, inexpensive, and easy to use.

The U.S. Department of Commerce is responsible for operating and maintaining the NTDB, and it works with federal agencies that collect and distribute trade information to keep the NTDB up to date. The NTDB has been published monthly on CD-ROM since October 1990. Over 1,000 public and university libraries offer public access to the NTDB through the Federal Depository Library system.

Within the U.S. Department of Commerce, the organization with primary responsibility for the NTDB is the Economics and Statistics Administration (ESA). STAT-USA is the ESA office that coordinates, produces, and fulfills orders for the NTDB on the Internet and CD-ROM.

The National Trade Data Bank consists of 133 separate trade- and business-related programs (databases). It gives small- and medium-size companies immediate access to information that only Fortune 500 companies could afford until now.

Topics on the NTDB include export opportunities by industry, country, and product; foreign companies or importers looking for specific products; how-to market guides; demographic, political, and socioeconomic conditions in hundreds of countries; and much more. The NTDB offers one-stop shopping for trade information from more than 20 federal sources. One no longer needs to know which federal agency produces the information; all one needs to know is that the NTDB exists. Exhibit 6.10 shows some specific information the NTDB offers.

■ **Exhibit 6.10**

**Examples of Information Contained in the NTDB**

Agricultural Commodity Production and Trade
Basic Export Information
Calendars of Trade Fairs and Exhibitions
Capital Markets and Export Financing
Country Reports on Economic and Social Policies and Trade Practices
Energy Production, Supply, and Inventories
Exchange Rates
Export Licensing Information
Guides to Doing Business in Foreign Countries
International Trade Terms Directory
How-to Guides
International Trade Regulations/Agreements
International Trade Agreements
Labor, Employment, and Productivity
Maritime and Shipping Information
Market Research Reports
Overseas Contacts
Overseas and Domestic Industry Information
Price Indexes
Small Business Information
State Exports
State Trade Contacts
Trade Opportunities
U.S. Export Regulations
U.S. Import and Export Statistics by Country and Commodity
U.S. International Transactions
World Fact Book
World Minerals Production

■ **SUMMARY**

Secondary data are data that have been gathered and recorded previously by someone else for purposes other than those of the current researcher. Secondary data usually are historical, are already assembled, and do not require access to respondents or subjects. Primary data are data gathered for the specific purpose of the current researcher.

The chief advantage of secondary data is that they are almost always less expensive to obtain than primary data. Generally they can be obtained rapidly and may include information not otherwise available to the researcher. The disadvantage of secondary data is that they were not intended specifically to meet the researcher's needs. The researcher must examine secondary data for accuracy, bias, and soundness. One way to do this is to cross-check various available sources.

Secondary research designs can address many common marketing problems. There are three general categories of secondary research objectives: fact finding, model building, and *database marketing.* A typical fact-finding study might seek to uncover all available information about consumption patterns for a particular product category or to identify business trends that affect an industry. Model building is more complicated; it involves specifying relationships between two or more variables. Model building need not involve a complicated mathematical process, but it can help marketers estimate market potential, forecast sales, select sites, and accomplish many other objectives. *Databased marketing,* which involves maintaining customer databases with data about individual customers, demographic and financial data, and other relevant data, is increasingly being supported by marketing research efforts.

Managers often get data from internal proprietary sources such as accounting records. Data mining is the use of "massively parallel" computers to dig through volumes of data to discover patterns about an organization's customers and products.

External data are created, recorded, or generated by an entity other than the researcher's organization. The government, newspapers and journals, trade associations, and other organizations create or produce information. Traditionally this information has been distributed in published form, either directly from producer to researcher or indirectly through intermediaries such as public libraries. Modern computerized data archives, electronic data interchange, and the Internet have changed the distribution of external data, making them almost as accessible as internal data.

The marketing of multiple types of related data by single-source suppliers has radically changed the nature of secondary data research.

As business has become more global, so has the secondary data industry. International researchers should watch for certain pitfalls that can be associated with foreign data and cross-cultural research.

## ■ Key Terms and Concepts

| | |
|---|---|
| Secondary data | Index of retail saturation |
| Data conversion | Database marketing |
| Cross-check | Internal and proprietary data |
| Market tracking | Data mining |
| Environmental scanning | External data |
| Model building | Single-source data |
| Site analysis techniques | |

## ■ Questions

1. Secondary data have been called the first line of attack for marketing researchers. Discuss this description.
2. Suppose you wish to learn about the size of the soft-drink market, particularly root beer sales, growth patterns, and market shares. Indicate probable sources for these secondary data.
3. Over the past five years, a manager has noted a steady growth in sales and profits for her division's product line. Does she need to use any secondary data to further evaluate her division's condition?
4. Identify some typical research objectives for secondary data studies.
5. What would be the best source for the following data?
   (a) State population, state income, and state employment for Illinois and Indiana
   (b) Maps of U.S. counties and cities
   (c) Trends in automobile ownership
   (d) Divorce trends in the United States
   (e) Median weekly earnings of full-time, salaried workers for the previous five years
   (f) Annual sales of the top ten fast-food companies
   (g) Brands of beer recently introduced in the United States
   (h) Attendance at professional sports contests

6. Suppose you are a marketing research consultant. A client comes to your office and says, "Within the next 24 hours, I must have the latest information on the supply and demand of Maine potatoes." What will you do?

7. Find the following data in the *Survey of Current Business* for May 1995:
    (a) U.S. gross domestic product for the first quarter of 1995
    (b) Fixed investment for residential structures for the first quarter of 1995
    (c) Exports of goods and services for the first quarter of 1995

8. Use the most recent Sales and Marketing Management *Survey of Buying Power* to find the total population, median age, and total retail sales for (a) your home town (county) and (b) the town (county) in which your school is located.

9. A newspaper reporter reads a study that surveyed children. The reporter writes that a high percentage of children recognize Joe Camel, cigarette *spokestoon,* but fails to report that the study also found that a much higher percentage of children indicated very negative attitudes toward smoking. Is this a proper use of secondary data?

## EXPLORING THE INTERNET

1. Use the Internet to learn what you can about Indonesia.
    (a) Use your Web browser to go to http://www.indonesiatoday.com.
    (b) Visit the *CIA Factbook* at http://www.odci.cia.gov.
    (c) Go to INFOSEEK or Yahoo and use *Indonesia* as a search word. How much information is available?

2. FIND/SVP is a company that provides information about many different industries. Go to the FIND/SVP home page at http://www.findsvp.com and select an industry. What industry information is available?

3. The home page of BRINT Research Initiative: Business Research, Management Research & Information Technology Research is http://www.brint.com. It contains links to hundreds of information base Web sites. Visit this site and report on the interesting sources you can go to.

4. Use the Internet to find information to answer the following questions:
    (a) What is today's weather like in Denver?
    (b) Is there information about Brazil and its population demographics?
    (c) How do you get a passport?

5. Select one of the following locations and report what categories of information are available.
    (a) The New York Public Library Home Page at
        http://web.nypl.org
    (b) Penn Library-Business Resources at
        http://www.library.upenn.edu/resources/business/business.html
    (c) U.S. Department of Commerce Bureaus at
        http://www.doc.gov/bureaus/bureaus.htm
    (d) The Conference Board Home Page at
        http://www.conference-board.org/
    (e) NAICS (North American Industry Classification System) at
        http://www.census.gov/epcd/www/naics.html
    (f) Claritas at
        http://www.claritas.com

## CASE 6.1   Porter and Gentry Advertising, Inc.

Porter and Gentry, Inc., is a medium-size advertising agency known for its creative marketing planning. A client, Joseph S. Yarbrough Brewing Company, has been extremely pleased with its long-standing relationship with the agency.

One Friday, during a business lunch with the client at which the client's product was conscientiously consumed by the agency's principals, Porter, the agency's president, suggested to Yarbrough that the brewery was not advertising to a major market segment. Porter explained that the Asian American market was the fastest-growing minority market in the country and was projected to become a major market segment by 2000. He indicated there were more than 3 million Asian Americans in California alone.

The client seemed more interested in performing quality control on his product than in what Porter was saying.

The agency president wisely allowed the conversation to drift for awhile.

Later Gentry again brought up the subject of the Asian American market. Yarbrough said, "Right now, I've got other priorities. And to be quite honest with you, I think that most Asian Americans are mainstream. They watch network TV. They read the same stuff as the average working person. But I'll tell you something: If you can come up with some hard data to show me that this market really deserves serious consideration, I'll give it a try."

### Questions

1. What secondary sources might Porter and Gentry use to determine the exact size of the Asian American market?
2. What characteristics are peculiar to the Asian American market? List and discuss some of these characteristics.
3. Prepare a research presentation for Yarbrough.

## CASE 6.2   Middlemist Precision Tool Company (A)

Dennis Middlemist was a weekend do-it-yourselfer. A hobby he particularly enjoyed was custom building furniture for his own home. After many years of frustration with trial-and-error adjustment of his radial arm saw using a T square and trial cuts, Middlemist decided he needed to invent an alignment device.

Before long, Middlemist had designed a solution. A custom prototype was built at a local engineering job shop. When Middlemist tested the device, it seemed to work perfectly for his needs. The proud inventor sought out an attorney to patent the device, and it looked as if a patent would be available. At this point, Middlemist started to dream about the possibility of Middlemist Precision Tool Company and the vast empire he would leave to his children. In reality, however, he knew little about marketing and wondered what market information he would need,

such as what the market potential would be, before getting serious about manufacturing the device. He thought the best place to start would be to determine the number of radial arm saws in the United States and the number of prospective customers for his invention.

### Questions

1. If you were a research consultant called in to help Dennis Middlemist define his marketing problem, what information do you think would be most important to him?
2. Middlemist has decided to see what information about the radial arm saw market can be found in secondary data sources. Go to your library and find what you can about radial arm saws and/or any related information that might be of value to Middlemist.

## ■ Endnotes

[1] John F. Rooney Jr., "American Sports Regions." Excerpted from a presentation at the American Demographics Consumer Outlook Conference.

[2] The idea for Exhibit 6.1 came from Robert W. Joselyn, *Designing the Marketing Research Project* (New York: Petrocelli/Charter, 1977).

[3] "Rising Stars in Frozen Pizza," *Milling & Baking News,* November 26, 1996, p. 30.

[4] Lee Fleming, "Digital Delivery: Pushing Content to the Desktop," Digital Information Group, January 31, 1997.

[5]"How Smart Agents Will Change Selling," *Forbes ASAP,* August 28, 1995, p. 95.

[6]"How Smart Agents Will Change Selling," *Forbes ASAP,* August 28, 1995, p. 95.

[7]"Datawatch," *Advertising Age,* January 18, 1993, p. I-12.

[8]"The Lodging Industry Today," *USA Today,* October 28, 1997, p. 12B.

[9]This section is based on Michael Levy and Barton Weitz, *Retail Management* (Homewood, Ill.: Richard D. Irwin, 1992), pp. 357–358.

[10]For an excellent source of information about *database marketing*, see David Shepard and Associates, *The New Direct Marketing* (Burr Ridge, Ill.: Irwin Professional Publishing, 1995).

[11]Based on material from DataMind's home page at http://www.datamindcorp.com.

[12]Srikumar S. Rao, "Technology: the Hot Zone," *Forbes,* November 18, 1996.

[13]IBM Business Intelligence Data Mining Product Discovery at http://www.ibm.com. See Peter R. Peacock, "Data Mining and Marketing: Part I," *Marketing Management,* Winter 1998, pp. 9–18 for an excellent article on this topic.

[14]Ira Sager, "Big Blue Wants to Mine Your Data," *Business Week,* June 3, 1996.

[15]Based on materials from DataMind's home page at http://www.datamindcorp.com.

[16]Srikumar S. Rao, "Technology: the Hot Zone," *Forbes,* November 18, 1996.

[17]Lorna M. Daniells, *Business Information Sources,* 3d ed. (Berkeley, Cal.: University of California Press, 1993).

[18]Note that the Internet changes daily, and a particular URL or instruction may not apply after the passage of time.

[19]"Going with the Grain," *Advertising Age,* September 11, 1995, p. 3.

[20]The description of the data bank is reprinted from information that can be accessed from the NTDB home page.

# 7

# SURVEY RESEARCH

To understand the advantages of using surveys.

To discuss the type of information that may be gathered in a survey.

To recognize that few surveys are error free.

To distinguish between random sampling error and systematic error.

To classify the various types of systematic error and give examples of each type.

To discuss how response error may be an unconscious misrepresentation and/or deliberate falsification.

To describe the classification of surveys according to method of communication.

To distinquish between cross-sectional surveys and longitudinal surveys.

Frito Lay International, a division of PepsiCo, Inc. and marketer of the number one potato chip in the United States, is unifying its current market-leading potato chip brands—such as Walkers Crisps in the United Kingdom, Papas Sabritas in Mexico, and Matutano chips in Spain—with the Lay's name. A new, global package design is highlighted by a bold red-and-yellow color scheme centered on a new icon called the Banner Sun. The company strategy involved introducing Lay's potato chips to more than 20 new markets around the world.

This initiative follows the most comprehensive marketing research program in food products history. More than 100,000 consumers were interviewed in over 30 countries to describe, understand, and develop the worldwide potato chip market. From its global research program, PepsiCo learned that potato chips are "the cola of snacks." The survey research showed that in country after country, potato chips are consumers' favorite snack, ranked ahead of chocolate bars, ice cream, candy, and all other salty snacks. The company's new, worldwide marketing approach enables Lay's to communicate and enhance the concept of potato chips as a timeless, simple pleasure to consumers around the world.[1]

The purpose of survey research is to collect primary data—data gathered and assembled specifically for the project at hand. This chapter focuses on survey research. It describes various advantages of the survey method and explains many potential errors researchers must be careful to avoid. Finally, the chapter classifies the various survey research methods.

# ■ THE NATURE OF SURVEYS

**Respondent**
The person who verbally answers an interviewer's questions or provides answers to written questions.

**Survey**
A method of primary data collection in which information is gathered by communicating with a representative sample of people.

Surveys require asking a representative sample of people, called **respondents,** for information using either verbal or written questioning. Questionnaires or interviews collect data face to face, over the telephone, by mail, or through other means of communication. Thus, a **survey** is a method of primary data collection based on communication with a representative sample of individuals.

Surveys provide a quick, inexpensive, efficient, and accurate means of assessing information about a population. Surveys are quite flexible and, when properly conducted, extremely valuable to the manager.

As we discussed in Chapter 1, marketing research has proliferated since the general adoption of the marketing concept. The growth of survey research is related to the simple idea that to find out what consumers think, one should *ask* them.

Properly conducted surveys can be quite accurate. However, many surveys conducted today are a waste of time and money because they are poorly designed or improperly implemented. As one writer describes,

> Samples are biased; questions are poorly phrased; interviewers are not properly instructed and supervised; and results are misinterpreted. Such surveys are worse than none at all because the sponsor may be misled into a costly area. Even well-planned and neatly executed surveys may be useless if, as often happens, the results come too late to be of value or converted into a bulky report which no one has time to read.[2]

The disadvantages of surveys are best described in specific sections for each form of data collection (personal interview, telephone, mail, and other self-administered formats). However, errors are common to all forms of surveys, so it is appropriate to describe them generally.

■ Marketing managers at Marriott Corporation know that people want a hotel room to feel residential because hotel guests see a hotel room as a home away from home. Customers prefer a clearly marked place to sit down, straight furniture legs, light walls, big bathrooms, spacious desk areas, and a long telephone cord.

How did Marriott Corporation, the largest operator of hotels in the country, learn about its customers' preferences? Simple! Marketing researchers have built an assortment of fake hotel rooms modeled on the competition and conducted surveys to test consumers' reactions. Customers walk through and rate the rooms.

# ■ ERRORS IN SURVEY RESEARCH

A manager who is evaluating the quality of a survey must estimate its accuracy. Exhibit 7.1 outlines the various forms of survey error. The two major sources of survey error are random sampling error and systematic error.

## ■ Random Sampling Error

**Random sampling error**
A statistical fluctuation that occurs because of chance variations in the elements selected for a sample.

Most surveys try to portray a representative cross-section of a particular target population. Even with appropriate probability samples, however, statistical errors will occur because of chance variation. Without increasing sample size, these statistical problems are unavoidable. However, **random sampling errors** can be estimated; *Chapter 13* will discuss these in greater detail.

## ■ Systematic Error

**Systematic error**
Error resulting from some imperfect aspect of the research design or from a mistake in the execution of the research.

**Systematic error** results from some imperfect aspect of the research design or from a mistake in the execution of the research. Because all sources of error other than those

---

■ **Exhibit 7.1**             **Categories of Survey Errors**

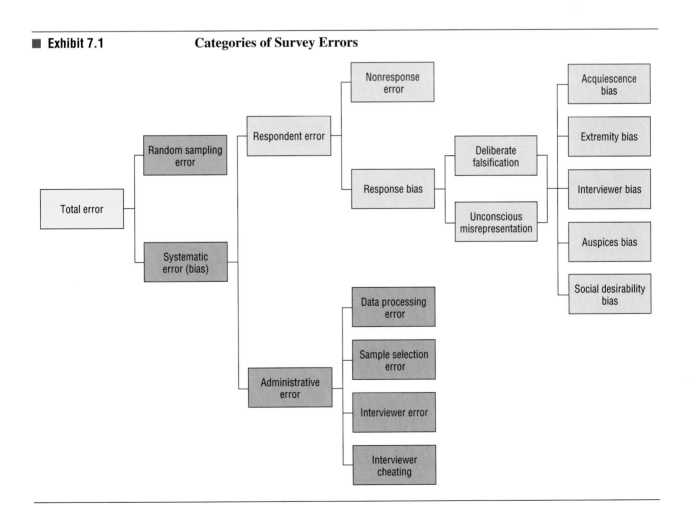

## WHAT WENT WRONG?

### Obstacles to Consumer Research

Many managers view consumer research as a necessary precursor to product introduction. Unfortunately, innovative products that lack much in common with existing products often prove this attitude wrong. Hairstyling mousse is now a massive hit, yet its initial U.S. market tests flopped. People said it was "goopy and gunky," and they did not like its feel when it "mooshed" through their hair. Similarly, when the telephone answering machine was consumer tested, it faced an almost universally negative reaction since most individuals felt that using a mechanical device to answer a phone was rude and disrespectful. Today, of course, many people regard their answering machines as indispensable and would dread scheduling daily activities without them. In the same vein, the computer mouse flunked its initial testing. Surveys indicated that potential customers found it awkward and unnecessary.

Surveys about new food products face terrible problems. For one, a person's desire for food is powerfully influenced by the ambience of the meal, dining companions, and what foods were eaten recently, all of which confound the results of survey research. Even more erratic results come from studies of children's food, such as a new cereal or snack. The responses of kids are strongly swayed by how well they like the people doing the test and the playthings available. Worse, kids quickly change their minds. In a taste test of several foods, a child can judge one food the best but an hour later proclaim the same food as "icky."

Marketing researchers must be aware of the potential problems when deciding exactly which research design will best solve their research problems.

---

**Sample bias**
A persistent tendency for the results of a sample to deviate in one direction from the true value of the population parameter.

introduced by the random sampling procedure are included, these errors or biases are also called *nonsampling errors*. A **sample bias** exists when the results of a sample show a persistent tendency to deviate in one direction from the true value of the population parameter. The many sources of error that in some way systematically influence answers can be divided into two general categories: respondent error and administrative error. These are discussed in the following sections.

---

## ■ RESPONDENT ERROR

**Respondent error**
A classification of sample biases resulting from some respondent action or inaction such as nonresponse or response bias.

**Nonresponse error**
The statistical differences between a survey that includes only those who responded and a perfect survey that would also include those who failed to respond.

**Nonrespondent**
A person who is not contacted or who refuses to cooperate in the research.

**Not-at-home**
A person who is not at home on the first or second contact.

Surveys ask people for answers. If people cooperate and give truthful answers, the survey will likely accomplish its goal. If these conditions are not met, nonresponse error or response bias, the two major categories of **respondent error,** may cause a sample bias.

### ■ Nonresponse Error

Few surveys have 100 percent response rates. A researcher who obtains an 11 percent response to a five-page questionnaire concerning various brands of spark plugs may face a serious problem. To be able to use the results, the researcher must be sure that those who did respond to the questionnaire were representative of those who did not.

The statistical differences between a survey that includes only those who responded and a survey that also includes those who failed to respond are referred to as a **nonresponse error.** This problem is especially acute in mail surveys, but it also threatens telephone and face-to-face interviews.

People who are not contacted or who refuse to cooperate are called **nonrespondents.** A nonresponse occurs if someone is not at home and a subsequent callback also finds the subject not at home. (The number of **not-at-homes** is increasing with the proportion of

**Refusal**
A person who is unwilling to participate in the research.

**Self-selection bias**
A bias that occurs because people who feel strongly about a subject are more likely to respond than people who feel indifferent about it.

married women in the labor force, now over 60 percent.) A parent who must juggle the telephone and a half- diapered child and refuses to participate in the survey because he or she is too busy is also a nonrespondent. **Refusals** occur when people are unwilling to participate in the research. Not-at-homes and refusals can seriously bias survey data.

**Self-selection bias** is a problem that frequently plagues self-administered questionnaires. In a restaurant, for example, a customer on whom a server spilled soup, a person who was treated to a surprise dinner, or others who feel strongly about the service are more likely to respond to self-administered questionnaires left at the table than individuals who are indifferent about the restaurant. Self-selection biases distort surveys because they over-represent extreme positions while underrepresenting responses from those who are indifferent.

After a refusal, an interviewer can do nothing other than be polite. The respondent who is not at home when called or visited should be scheduled for contact at a different time of day or on a different day of the week.

In a mail survey, the researcher never really knows whether a nonrespondent has refused to participate or is simply indifferent. Researchers know those who are most involved in an issue are more likely to respond to a mail survey. Later we will discuss several techniques for encouraging respondents to reply to mail surveys.

## ■ Response Bias

**Response bias**
A bias that occurs when respondents tend to answer questions with a certain slant that consciously or unconsciously misrepresents the truth.

A **response bias** occurs when respondents tend to answer questions with a certain slant. People may consciously or unconsciously misrepresent the truth. If a distortion of measurement occurs because respondents' answers are falsified or misrepresented, either intentionally or inadvertently because they have forgotten the exact details, the resulting answers have a response bias.

Response bias can arise from the question format, the question content, or some other stimulus. For example, bias can be introduced by the situation in which the survey is administered. The results of two in-flight surveys concerning aircraft preference illustrate this point. Passengers flying on B-747s preferred B-747s to L-1011s (74 percent versus 19 percent), while passengers flying on L-1011s preferred L-1011s to B-747s (56 percent versus 38 percent). The reversal in preference between the B-747 and the L-1011 appears to

■ Nonresponse error can be high when conducting international marketing research. Many cultures do not share the same values about providing information. In Mexico, citizens are reluctant to provide information over the phone to strangers. In many Middle Eastern countries, many women would refuse to be interviewed by a male interviewer.

■ The National Restaurant Association research shows that when it comes to diet, considerable response bias exists. In response to survey questions, Americans say they intend to be virtuous in their eating (fresh fruit and bran muffins), but what they actually eat (many hamburgers) is quite different.

have been largely a function of the aircraft the respondent was flying on when the survey was conducted, although sample differences may have been a factor. A likely influence was the respondent's satisfaction with the plane on which he or she was flying when surveyed. In other words, in the absence of any strong preference, the respondent may simply have been trying to identify the aircraft traveled on and indicated that as his or her preference.[3] Occasionally people deliberately give false answers. Deliberate falsification may occur when people misrepresent answers to appear intelligent, conceal personal information, avoid embarrassment, and so on.

**Types of Response Bias**    There are five specific categories of response bias: acquiescence bias, extremity bias, interviewer bias, auspices bias, and social desirability bias. These categories overlap and are not mutually exclusive. A single biased answer may be distorted for many complex reasons; some misrepresentations may be deliberate and some unconscious.

**Acquiescence bias**
A category of response bias that results because some individuals tend to agree with all questions or to concur with a particular position.

*Acquiescence Bias*    Some respondents are very agreeable; these yea-sayers accept all statements they are asked about. This tendency to agree with all or most questions is particularly prominent in new-product research. Questions about a new product idea generally elicit some **acquiescence bias** because respondents give positive connotations to most new ideas. For example, Spaulding, Rawlings, and Mizuno found that consumers responded

■ Asian values about survey research differ from those in American culture. Asians have less patience with the abstract and rational question wording commonly used in the United States. Researchers must be alert for culture-bound sources of response bias in international marketing research. For example, the Japanese do not wish to contradict others, leading to a bias toward acquiescence and yea-saying.

favorably when asked about pump baseball gloves (which have a mechanism similar to those on pump basketball shoes). However, when these expensive gloves hit the market, they sat on the shelves. When conducting new-product research, researchers should recognize the high likelihood of acquiescence bias.

*Extremity Bias*   Some individuals tend to use extremes when responding to questions; others always avoid extreme positions and tend to respond more neutrally. Response styles vary from person to person, and they may cause an **extremity bias** in the data.

*Interviewer Bias*   Response bias may arise from interplay between interviewer and respondent. If the interviewer's presence influences respondents to give untrue or modified answers, the survey will have **interviewer bias.** Many homemakers and retired people welcome the interviewer's visit as a break in routine activities. Respondents may give answers they believe will please the interviewer rather than the truthful responses. Respondents may wish to appear intelligent and wealthy; of course, they read *Scientific American* rather than *Spin.*

Quite often respondents give socially acceptable rather than truthful responses to save face in the presence of an interviewer. The interviewer's age, sex, style of dress, tone of voice, facial expressions, or other nonverbal characteristics may have some influence on a respondent's answer. If an interviewer smiles and makes a positive statement after a respondent's answer, the respondent will be more likely to give similar responses. In a research study on sexual harassment against saleswomen, male interviewers may generate less candid responses than female interviewers would.

Many interviewers, contrary to instructions, will shorten or rephrase a question to suit their needs. This potential source of influenced responses can be avoided to some extent if interviewers receive training and supervision that emphasize the necessity for them to appear neutral.

*Auspices Bias*   Suppose the National Rifle Association is conducting a study on gun control. The answers to the survey may be deliberately or subconsciously misrepresented because respondents are influenced by the organization conducting the study. If a national committee on gun control conducted the same study, respondents' answers might vary. This result would constitute an **auspices bias.**

*Social Desirability Bias*   A **social desirability bias** may affect a response either consciously or unconsciously because the respondent wishes to create a favorable impression. Answering that one's income is only $30,000 a year might be difficult for someone whose self-concept is that of an upper-middle-class person "about to make it big." Incomes may be inflated, education overstated, or perceived respectable answers given to gain prestige. In contrast, answers to questions that seek factual information or matters of public knowledge (zip code, number of children, and so on) usually are quite accurate. An interviewer's presence may increase a respondent's tendency to give an inaccurate answer to sensitive questions such as "Did you vote in the last election?"; "Do you have termites or roaches in your home?"; or "Do you have dandruff?"

**Extremity bias**
A category of response bias that results because response styles vary from person to person; some individuals tend to use extremes when responding to questions.

**Interviewer bias**
A response bias that occurs because the presence of the interviewer influences answers.

**Auspices bias**
Response bias that results because respondents are influenced by the organization conducting the study.

**Social desirability bias**
Bias in responses caused by respondents' desire, either conscious or unconscious, to gain prestige or appear in a different social role.

# ■ ADMINISTRATIVE ERROR

**Administrative error**
An error caused by the improper administration or flawed execution of a research task.

The results of improper administration or execution of the research task are **administrative errors.** They are inadvertently (or recklessly) caused by confusion, neglect, omission, or some other blunder. Four types of administrative errors are data- processing error, sample selection error, interviewer error, and interviewer cheating.

■ When Pampers introduced Luvs for Girls and Luvs for Boys, a competitor's survey research showed that gender-specific diapers were not important to consumers. However, this research suffered from response bias. When asked in surveys, parents gave a socially desirable answer when they said they did not want to stereotype their children in male or female roles. However, the American cultural value—blue for boys and pink for girls—in fact could not be overcome. Analysis of sales and subsequent research shows parents will not put pink diapers on boys.[4]

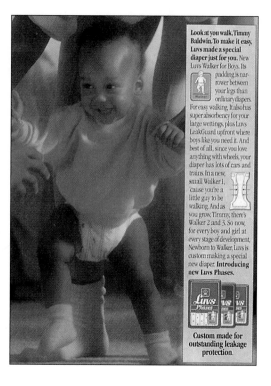

### ■ Data-Processing Error

Data processed by computer, as with any arithmetic or procedural process, are subject to error because they must be edited, coded, and entered into the computer by people. The accuracy of data processed by computer depends on correct data entry and programming. **Data-processing errors** can be minimized by establishing careful procedures for verifying each step in the data-processing stage.

**Data-processing error**
A category of administrative error that occurs because of incorrect data entry, computer programming, or other procedural errors during the data-processing stage.

### ■ Sample Selection Error

**Sample selection error** is systematic error that results in an unrepresentative sample because of an error in either the sample design or the execution of the sampling procedure. Executing a sampling plan free of procedural error is difficult. A firm that selects its sample from the phone book will encounter some systematic error, because unlisted numbers are not included. Stopping female respondents during daytime hours in shopping centers excludes working women who shop by mail or telephone. In other cases, the wrong person may be interviewed. Consider a political pollster who randomly selects telephone numbers for a sample rather than basing the sample on a list of registered voters. Unregistered 17-year-olds may be willing to give their opinions, but they are the wrong people to ask because they cannot vote.

**Sample selection error**
An administrative error caused by improper sample design or sampling procedure execution.

### ■ Interviewer Error

Interviewers' abilities vary considerably. When interviewers record answers, they may check the wrong responses or may be unable to write fast enough to record answers verbatim. Selective perception may cause **interviewer error** by influencing the way interviewers record data that do not support their own attitudes and opinions.

**Interviewer error**
Mistakes made by interviewers when performing their tasks.

### ■ Interviewer Cheating

**Interviewer cheating**
The practice by interviewers of filling in fake answers or falsifying questionnaires.

**Interviewer cheating** occurs when an interviewer falsifies entire questionnaires or fills in answers to questions that have been intentionally skipped. Some interviewers cheat to finish an interview as quickly as possible or to avoid questions about sensitive topics.

If interviewers are suspected of faking questionnaires, they should be told that a small percentage of respondents will be called back to confirm whether the initial interview was actually conducted. This will discourage interviewers from cheating.

Now that we have examined the sources of error in surveys, you may have lost some of your optimism about survey research. Don't be discouraged! The discussion emphasized the bad news because it is important for marketing managers to realize that surveys are not a panacea. There are, however, ways to handle and reduce survey errors. Much of the remainder of this book discusses various techniques for reducing bias in marketing research. The good news lies ahead!

## ■ CLASSIFYING SURVEY RESEARCH BY METHOD OF COMMUNICATION

Now that we have discussed the various advantages and disadvantages of surveys in general, we will classify surveys according to the method of communication used.

Survey data are obtained when individuals respond to questions asked by interviewers (interviews) or to questions they have read (questionnaires). Interviewers may communicate with respondents face-to-face or over the telephone. In a sample survey using a self-administered questionnaire, distribution by mail is the most common way to obtain a representative sample, but there are other means of distribution are growing in popularity. Each technique for conducting surveys has its merits and shortcomings.

## ■ USING INTERVIEWS TO COMMUNICATE WITH RESPONDENTS

Interviews can be categorized based on the medium through which the researcher communicates with individuals and records data. For example, interviews may be conducted door-to-door, in shopping malls, or on the telephone. Traditionally interview results have been recorded using paper and pencil, but computers are increasingly supporting survey research.

We begin our discussion of interviewing by examining the general characteristics of personal interviews, which are conducted face-to-face. Then we look at the unique characteristics of door-to-door personal interviews and personal interviews conducted in shopping malls. In the next section, we investigate telephone interviewing.

## ■ PERSONAL INTERVIEWS

**Personal interview**
An interview that gathers information through face-to-face contact with individuals.

**Personal interviews** are direct communications between businesses and consumers in which interviewers ask respondents questions face-to-face. This versatile and flexible method is a two-way conversation between interviewer and a respondent.

### ■ Advantages of Personal Interviews

Marketing researchers find that personal interviews offer many unique advantages. One of the most important is the opportunity for feedback.

**The Opportunity for Feedback**    Personal interviews provide an opportunity to give feedback to the respondent. For example, in a personal interview a consumer who is reluctant to provide sensitive information may be reassured that his or her answers will be strictly confidential. Personal interviews offer the lowest chance of misinterpretation of questions because the interviewer can clarify any difficulties respondents have with the instructions or questions. After the interview has been terminated, circumstances may dictate that the respondent be given additional information concerning the purpose of the study. This is easily accomplished with the personal interview.

**Probing Complex Answers**    An important characteristic of personal interviews is the opportunity to probe. If a respondent's answer is too brief or unclear, the researcher may probe for a more comprehensive or clearer explanation. In **probing,** the interviewer asks for clarification or expansion of answers to standardized questions, such as "Can you tell me more about what you had in mind?"

Although interviewers are expected to ask questions exactly as they appear on the questionnaire, probing allows them some flexibility. Depending on the research purpose, personal interviews vary in the degree to which questions are structured and in the amount of probing required. The personal interview is especially useful for obtaining unstructured information. Skilled interviewers can handle complex questions that cannot easily be asked in telephone or mail surveys.

**Probing**
The verbal prompts made by an interviewer when the respondent must be motivated to communicate his or her answer more fully; used to get respondents to enlarge on, clarify, or explain answers.

**Length of Interview**    If the research objective requires an extremely lengthy questionnaire, personal interviews may be the only alternative. Generally telephone interviews last less than 10 minutes, whereas a personal interview can be much longer, perhaps three to four hours. A general rule of thumb for mail surveys is that they not exceed six pages.

**Completeness of Questionnaires**    The social interaction between a well-trained interviewer and a respondent in a personal interview increases the likelihood that the respondent will answer all the items on the questionnaire. The respondent who grows bored with a telephone interview may terminate the interview at his or her discretion simply by hanging up. Self-administration of a mail questionnaire, on the other hand, requires more effort by the respondent. Rather than write lengthy responses, however, the respondent may fail to complete some of the questions. **Item nonresponse,** failure to provide an answer to a question, is less likely to occur when an experienced interviewer asks questions directly.

**Item nonresponse**
Failure by a respondent to answer a question on a questionnaire.

**Props and Visual Aids**    Interviewing respondents face to face allows the investigator to show them new-product samples, sketches of proposed advertising, movie clips, or other visual aids. In a survey to determine whether a super-lightweight chain saw should be manufactured, visual props were necessary because the concept of weight is difficult to imagine. Two small chain saws currently on the market and a third, wooden prototype disguised and weighted to look and feel like the proposed model were put in the back of a station wagon. Respondents were asked to go to the car, pick up each chain saw, and compare them. This research could not have been done in a telephone interview or mail survey.

**High Participation**    The presence of an interviewer generally increases the percentage of people willing to complete the interview. Respondents typically are required to do no reading or writing; all they have to do is talk. People enjoy sharing information and insights with friendly and sympathetic interviewers.

## ■ Disadvantages of Personal Interviews

Personal interviews also have some disadvantages. Respondents are not anonymous and therefore may be reluctant to provide confidential information to another person. Suppose a survey asked top executives, "Do you see any major internal instabilities or threats (people, money, material, etc.) to the achievement of your marketing objectives?" Many managers may be reluctant to answer this sensitive question honestly in a personal interview in which their identities are known.

**Interviewer Influence**   Some evidence suggests that demographic characteristics of the interviewer influence respondents' answers. For example, one research study revealed that male interviewers produced larger amounts of interviewer variance than females in a survey in which 85 percent of the respondents were female. Older interviewers who interviewed older respondents produced more variance than other age combinations, while younger interviewers who interviewed younger respondents produced the least variance.[5]

Differential interviewer techniques may be a source of bias. The rephrasing of a question, the interviewer's tone of voice, and the interviewer's appearance may influence the respondent's answer. Consider the interviewer who had conducted 100 personal interviews. During the next one, he or she may selectively perceive or anticipate the respondent's answer. The interpretation of the response may differ somewhat from the intended response. Our image of the person who does marketing research typically is that of the dedicated scientist. Unfortunately, some interviewers do not fit that ideal. Considerable interviewer variability exists. Cheating is possible; interviewers may cut corners to save time and energy, faking parts of their reports by dummying up part or all of the questionnaire. Control over interviewers is important to ensure that difficult, embarrassing, or time-consuming questions are handled in the proper manner.

**Anonymity of Respondent**   In a personal interview, the respondent is not anonymous and may be reluctant to provide confidential information to another person. Researchers often spend considerable time and effort to phrase sensitive questions to avoid social desirability bias. For example, the interviewer may show the respondent a card that lists possible answers and ask the respondent to read a category number rather than verbalize a sensitive answer.

**Cost**   Personal interviews are expensive, generally more so than mail or telephone interviews. The geographic proximity of respondents, the length and complexity of the questionnaire, and the number of people who are nonrespondents because they could not be contacted (not-at-homes) will all influence the cost of the personal interview.

## ■ Door-to-Door Interviews and Shopping Mall Intercepts

Personal interviews may be conducted at the respondents' homes or offices, or in many other places. Increasingly personal interviews are being conducted in shopping malls. The locale for the interview generally influences the participation rate and thus the degree to which the sample represents the general population.

**Door-to-Door Interviews**   The presence of an interviewer at one's door generally increases the likelihood that one will be willing to complete the interview. Because **door-to-door interviews** increase the participation rate, they provide a more representative sample of the population than mail questionnaires do. People who do not have telephones, have unlisted telephone numbers, or are otherwise difficult to contact may be reached using door-to-door

**Door-to-door interview**
A personal interview conducted at the respondent's home or place of business.

interviews. Such interviews can help solve the problem of nonresponse; however, they may underrepresent some groups and overrepresent others.

Door-to-door interviews may exclude individuals who live in multiple-dwelling units with security systems, such as high-rise apartment dwellers or executives who are too busy to grant personal interviews during business hours. Telephoning an individual in one of these subgroups to make an appointment may make the total sample more representative; however, obtaining a representative sample of this security-conscious subgroup based on a listing in the telephone directory may be difficult.

People who are at home and willing to participate, especially if interviewing is conducted in the daytime, are somewhat more likely to be over 65 years of age, homemakers, and/or retired people. These and other variables related to respondents' tendencies to stay at home may affect participation.

**Callback**
An attempt to recontact an individual selected for the sample.

**Callbacks**   When a person selected to be in the sample cannot be contacted on the first visit, a systematic procedure normally is initiated to call back at another time. **Callbacks,** or attempts to recontact individuals selected for the sample, are the major means of reducing nonresponse error. The cost per interview of an interviewer calling back on a sampling unit is higher because subjects who initially were not at home generally are more widely dispersed geographically than the original sample units. Callbacks in door-to-door interviews are important because not-at-home individuals (e.g., working parents) may systematically vary from those who are at home (nonworking parents, retired people, and the like).

**Mall intercept interview**
A personal interview conducted in a shopping mall or other high-traffic area.

**Mall Intercept Interviews**   Personal interviews conducted in shopping malls are referred to as **mall intercept interviews,** or *shopping center sampling.* Interviewers typically intercept shoppers at a central point within or at an entrance to the mall and then ask respondents to come to a permanent research facility to taste new food items or view advertisements. The main reason mall intercept interviews are conducted is their lower costs. No travel is required to the respondent's home; instead, the respondent comes to the interviewer, and many interviews thus can be conducted quickly.

The mall intercept interview allows the researcher to show large, heavy, or immobile visual materials, such as a television commercial, or give an individual a product to take home and use, to be recontacted later by telephone. Mall intercept interviews are also valuable when the cooking and tasting of products must be closely coordinated and timed to follow each other. They may also be appropriate when a consumer durable product must be demonstrated.

A major problem with mall intercept interviews is that individuals usually are in a hurry to shop, so the incidence of refusal is high—an average of 54 to 56 percent.[6] Nevertheless, the commercial marketing research industry conducts more personal interviews in shopping malls than it conducts door to door.

In such an interview, the researcher must recognize that she or he should not be looking for a representative sample of the total population. Each mall will have its own target market's characteristics, and there is likely to be a larger bias than with careful household probability sampling. However, personal interviews in shopping malls are appropriate when the target group is similar to shoppers at the malls where the interviews take place.

## ■ Global Considerations

Willingness to participate in a personal interview varies dramatically around the world. For example, in many Middle Eastern countries, women would never consent to be interviewed by a man. Also in many countries, the idea of discussing grooming behavior and personal care products with a stranger would be highly offensive. Few people would consent to be interviewed on such topics.

The norms for appropriate business conduct also influence businesspeople's willingness to provide information to interviewers. For example, conducting business-to-business interviews in Japan during business hours is difficult because managers, who are deeply loyal to their employers, believe they owe absolute commitment to their employees while on the job. In some cultures, when a businessperson is reluctant to be interviewed, it may be possible to get a reputable third party to intervene so that an interview may take place.

## ■ TELEPHONE INTERVIEWS

**Telephone interview**
An interview that gathers information through telephone contact with individuals.

**Telephone interviews** have several distinctive characteristics that set them apart from other survey techniques. First, we will consider the advantages and disadvantages of these characteristics.

### ■ Characteristics of Telephone Interviews

**Speed**    One advantage of telephone interviewing is the speed of data collection. Rather than taking several weeks for data collection by mail or personal interviews, hundreds of telephone interviews can be conducted literally overnight. When the interviewer enters the respondents' answers directly into a computerized system, the data processing speeds up even more.

**Cost**    As the cost of personal interviews continues to increase, telephone interviews are becoming relatively inexpensive. It is estimated that telephone interviews cost less than 25 percent of the cost of door-to-door personal interviews.[7] Travel time and costs of travel are eliminated.

**Absence of Face-to-Face Contact**    Telephone interviews are more impersonal than face-to-face interviews. Respondents may answer embarrassing or confidential questions more willingly in a telephone interview than in a personal interview. However, a mail survey, although not perfect, is a far better medium for gathering extremely sensitive information because it is anonymous.

Although telephone calls may be less threatening because no interviewer is present, the absence of face-to-face contact can also be a liability. The respondent cannot see that the interviewer is still writing down the previous comment and may continue to elaborate on an answer. If the respondent pauses to think about an answer, the interviewer may not realize this and go on to the next question. Hence, there is a greater tendency to record no answers and incomplete answers in telephone interviewing than in personal interviewing.

**Cooperation**    In some neighborhoods, people are reluctant to allow a stranger to come inside the house or even stop on the doorstep. The same individuals, however, may be perfectly willing to cooperate with a telephone survey request. Likewise, interviewers may be somewhat reluctant to conduct face-to-face interviews in certain neighborhoods, especially during the evening hours. Some individuals will refuse to participate, and the researcher should be aware of potential nonresponse bias.

Ownership of telephone answering machines and caller Id systems is growing.[8] Although their effect has not been studied extensively, it appears unlikely that many individuals would return a call to help someone conduct a survey. However, if enough callbacks are made at different times and on different days, most respondents are reachable.[9]

Refusal to cooperate with interviews is directly related to interview length. A good rule of thumb is to keep telephone interviews approximately 10 to 15 minutes long.

**Representative Samples**   Practical difficulties complicate obtaining representative samples based on listings in the telephone book. Approximately 95 percent of households in the United States have telephones. People without phones are more likely to be poor, aged, or residents of rural areas. They may be a minor segment of the market, but unlisted phone numbers and numbers too recent to be printed in the directory are a greater problem. Individuals with unlisted numbers differ slightly from those with published numbers. The unlisted group tends to be younger; has larger families; has fewer professionals and managers and more sales, craft, and service workers; has more low-income households; and has more people in the early stages of the family cycle.[10] Researchers conducting surveys in areas where the proportion of unlisted phone numbers is high, such as in California (Sacramento, 64.7 percent; Los Angeles/Long Beach, 64.6 percent; and Oakland, 64.4 percent), would have to pay special attention to making accurate estimates of these numbers.[11]

**Random digit dialing**
A method of obtaining a representative sample in a telephone interview by using random numbers to generate telephone numbers.

The problem with unlisted phone numbers can be partially resolved through the use of random digit dialing. **Random digit dialing** eliminates the counting of names in a list (for example, calling every 50th name in a column) and subjectively determining whether a directory listing is a business, an institution, or a legitimate household. In its simplest form, random digit dialing begins with telephone exchanges (prefixes) for the geographic areas in the sample. Using a table of random numbers, the last four digits to complete the telephone number are selected. Telephone directories can be ignored entirely or used in combination with the assignment of one or several random digits. Random digit dialing also helps overcome the problem of new listings and absence of recent changes in numbers from directories.

**Callbacks**   An unanswered call, a busy signal, or a not-at-home respondent requires a callback. Telephone callbacks are much easier to make than callbacks in personal interviews. However, as mentioned earlier, ownership of telephone answering machines is growing, and their effects on callbacks need to be studied.

**Limited Duration**   Respondents who run out of patience with the interview can merely hang up. To encourage participation, interviews should be relatively short. The length of the telephone interview is definitely limited.

**Lack of Visual Medium**   Because visual aids cannot be used in telephone interviews, packaging research, television and print advertising copy testing, and concept tests that require visual materials cannot be conducted by phone.

### ■ Central Location Interviewing

**Central location interviewing**
Telephone interviews conducted from a central location; allows more effective supervision and control of the quality of interviewing.

A research agency or an interviewing service typically conducts all telephone interviews from a central location. These organizations contract for WATS (Wide-Area Telecommunications Service) lines from AT&T, MCI Communications, or other long-distance telephone services at fixed charges so that they can make unlimited telephone calls throughout the entire country or within specific geographic areas. Such **central location interviewing** allows firms to hire a staff of professional interviewers and to supervise and control the quality of interviewing more effectively. When telephone interviews are centralized and computerized, additional cost economies are realized.

## ■ Computer-Assisted Telephone Interviewing

**Computer-assisted telephone interview (CATI)**
A type of telephone interview in which the interviewer reads questions from a computer screen and enters the respondent's answers directly into the computer.

Advances in computer technology allow telephone interviews to be directly entered into the computer through the on-line **computer-assisted telephone interviewing (CATI)** process. Telephone interviewers are seated at computer terminals. Monitors, similar to television screens, display the questionnaires, one question at a time, along with precoded possible responses to the question. The terminal includes a keyboard for entering the response directly into the computer. The interviewer reads each question as it appears on the screen. When the respondent answers, the interviewer enters the response into the computer, and it is automatically transcribed into the computer's memory. The computer then displays the next question on the screen. This type of computer-assisted telephone interviewing requires that answers to the questionnaire be highly structured. If a respondent gives an unacceptable answer—that is, one not precoded and programmed—the computer will reject it.

Computer-assisted telephone interviewing systems include telephone management systems to handle phone number selection and perform automatic dialing and other labor-saving functions. These systems can automatically control sample selection by randomly generating names or fulfilling a sample quota. A computer can generate an automatic callback schedule. A typical call management system might schedule recontact attempts to recall no answers after 2 hours, recall busy numbers after 10 minutes, and allow the interviewer to enter a more favorable time slot (day and hour) when a respondent indicates that he or she is too busy to be interviewed. Software systems also allow researchers to request daily status reports on the number of completed interviews relative to quotas.

Technological advances have combined computerized telephone dialing and voice-activated computer messages to allow researchers to conduct telephone interviews without human interviewers. To date, however, researchers have employed computerized voice-activated telephone interviewing only for very short, simple questionnaires. One system includes a voice-synthesized module controlled by a microprocessor. This allows the sponsor to register a caller's single response, such as "true/false," "yes/no," "like/dislike," or "for/against." This type of system has been used by television and radio stations to register callers' response to certain issues.

## ■ Global Considerations

Different cultures often have different norms for proper telephone behavior. For example, Latin American business-to-business researchers have learned that businesspeople will not open up to strangers on the telephone. Hence, survey respondents usually find personal interviews more suitable than telephone surveys. In Japan, because the language does not lend itself to long telephone interviews, respondents consider interviews that go beyond 20 minutes to be ill mannered.[12]

## ■ SELF-ADMINISTERED QUESTIONNAIRES

Many surveys do not require an interviewer's presence. Marketing researchers distribute questionnaires to consumers through the mail and in many other ways. They may insert questionnaires in packages and magazines. They may locate questionnaires at the points of purchase or in high-traffic locations. They may even fax questionnaires to individuals. Questionnaires are usually printed on paper, but they may be programmed into computers

**Self-administered
questionnaire**
A questionnaire, such as a mail
questionnaire, that is read and
filled in by the respondent
rather than by the interviewer.

and placed on the Internet. No matter how **self-administered questionnaires** are distributed to the members of the sample, they differ from interviews because the respondent takes responsibility for reading and answering the questions.

Self-administered questionnaires present a challenge to the marketing researcher because they rely on the efficiency of the written word rather than the skills of the interviewer. The nature of self-administered questionnaires is best illustrated by mail questionnaires.

## ■ Mail Questionnaires

**Mail survey**
A self-administered
questionnaire sent to
respondents through the mail.

A **mail survey** is a self-administered questionnaire sent to respondents through the mail. This paper-and-pencil method has several advantages and disadvantages.

**Geographic Flexibility**   Mail questionnaires can reach a geographically dispersed sample simultaneously because they do not require interviewers. Respondents who are located in isolated areas (e.g., farmers) or are otherwise difficult to reach (e.g., executives) can easily be contacted by mail. For example, a pharmaceutical firm may find that doctors are inaccessible to personal or telephone interviews. A mail survey can reach both rural and urban doctors who practice in widely dispersed geographic areas.

**Cost**   Mail questionnaires are relatively low in cost compared with personal interviews and telephone surveys, though they are not cheap. Most include follow-up mailings, which require additional postage and printing costs. Questionnaires photocopied on poor-grade paper are more likely to end up in the wastebasket than more expensive, high-quality printing jobs.

**Respondent Convenience**   Mail and other self-administered questionnaires can be filled out when the respondent has time; thus, there is a better chance that respondents will take time to think about their replies. In some situations, particularly in business-to-business marketing research, mail questionnaires allow respondents to collect facts, such as sales statistics, that they may not recall accurately. Checking information by verifying records or, in household surveys, by consulting with other family members should provide more valid, factual information than either personal or telephone interviews would. A catalog retailer may use mail surveys to estimate sales volume for catalog items by sending a mock catalog as part of the questionnaire. Respondents are asked to indicate how likely they would be to order selected items. Using the mail allows respondents to consult other family members and make their decisions within normal time spans. Many hard-to-reach respondents are best contacted by mail because they place a high value on their own convenience.

**Anonymity of Respondent**   In the cover letter that accompanies a mail or self-administered questionnaire, marketing researchers almost always state that the respondents' answers will be confidential. Respondents are more likely to provide sensitive or embarrassing information when they can remain anonymous.

For example, the question "Have you borrowed money at a regular bank?" was asked in a personal interview and a mail survey conducted simultaneously. The results: a 17 percent response in personal interviews and a 42 percent response in mail surveys.[13] Although random sampling error may have accounted for part of this difference, the results suggest that for personal and sensitive financial issues, mail surveys are more confidential than personal interviews.

Anonymity can also reduce social desirability bias. People are more likely to agree with controversial issues, such as extreme political candidates, when given self-administered ballots than when speaking to interviewers on the phone or at their doorsteps.

**Absence of Interviewer**   Although the absence of an interviewer can induce respondents to reveal sensitive or socially undesirable information, it can also be a disadvantage. Once the respondent receives the questionnaire, the questioning process is beyond the researcher's control. Although the printed stimulus is the same, each respondent will attach a different personal meaning to each question. Selective perception operates in research as well as in advertising. The respondent does not have the opportunity to question the interviewer. Problems that might be clarified in a personal or telephone interview remain misunderstandings in a mail survey. There is no interviewer to probe for additional information or clarification of an answer, and the recorded answers may be assumed to be complete.

Respondents have the opportunity to read the entire questionnaire before they answer individual questions. Often the text of a later question will provide information that affects responses to earlier questions.

**Standardized Questions**   Mail questionnaires typically are highly standardized, and the questions are quite structured. Questions and instructions must be clear-cut and straightforward; if they are difficult to comprehend, respondents must use their own interpretations, which may be wrong. Interviewing allows for feedback from the interviewer regarding the respondent's comprehension of the questionnaire. An interviewer who notices that the first 50 respondents are having some difficulty understanding a question can report this to the research analyst so revisions can be made. With a mail survey, however, once the questionnaires are mailed, it is difficult to change the format or the questions.

**Time Is Money**   If time is a factor in mangement's interest in the research results or if attitudes are rapidly changing (for example, toward a political event), mail surveys may not be the best communication medium. A minimum of two to three weeks is necessary to receive the majority of the responses. Follow-up mailings, which usually are sent when the returns begin to trickle in, require an additional two to three weeks. The lapsed time between the first mailing and the cutoff date (when questionnaires will no longer be accepted) normally is six to eight weeks. In a regional or local study, personal interviews can be conducted more quickly. However, conducting a national study by mail may be substantially faster than conducting personal interviews across the nation.

**Length of Mail Questionnaire**   Mail questionnaires vary considerably in length, ranging from extremely short, postcard questionnaires to lengthy, multipage booklets that require respondents to fill in thousands of answers. A general rule of thumb is that a mail questionnaire should not exceed six pages in length. When a questionnaire requires a respondent to expend a great deal of effort, an incentive is generally required to induce the respondent to return the questionnaire. The following sections discuss several ways to obtain high response rates even when questionnaires are longer than average.

### ■ Response Rates

Surveys that are boring, unclear, or too complex get thrown in the wastebasket. A poorly designed survey may be returned by only 15 percent of those sampled; thus, it will have a

**Response rate**
The number of questionnaires returned or completed divided by the total number of eligible people who were contacted or requested to participate in the survey.

15 percent **response rate.** The basic calculation for obtaining a response rate is to count the number of questionnaires returned or completed, then divide the total by the number of eligible people who were contacted or requested to participate in the survey. Typically, the number in the denominator will be adjusted for faulty addresses and similar problems that reduce the number of eligible participants.[14]

The major limitations of mail questionnaires relate to response problems. Respondents who complete the questionnaire may not be typical of all people in the sample. Individuals with a special interest in the topic are more likely to respond to a mail survey than those who are indifferent.

A researcher has no assurance that the intended subject will be the person who fills out the questionnaire. The wrong person answering the questions may be a problem when surveying corporate executives, physicians, and other professionals, who may pass questionnaires on to subordinates to complete.

Mail survey respondents tend to be better educated than nonrespondents. Poorly educated respondents who cannot read and write well may skip open-ended questions (to which they are required to write out their answers), if they return the questionnaire at all. Rarely will a mail survey have an 80 to 90 percent response rate that can be achieved with personal interviews. However, the use of follow-up mailings and other techniques may increase the response rate to an acceptable percentage.

## ■ Increasing Response Rates for Mail Surveys

Nonresponse error is always a potential problem with mail surveys. Individuals who are interested in the general subject of the survey are more likely to respond than those with less interest or experience. Thus, people who hold extreme positions on an issue are more likely to respond than individuals who are largely indifferent to the topic. To minimize this bias, researchers have developed a number of techniques to increase the response rate among sampling units.[15] For example, almost all surveys include prepaid-postage return envelopes. Forcing respondents to pay their own postage can substantially reduce the response rate. Designing and formatting attractive questionnaires and wording questions so they are easy to understand also help ensure a good response rate. However, special efforts may be required even with a sound questionnaire. Several of these are discussed in the following subsections.

**Cover letter**
The letter that accompanies the questionnaire in a mail survey; generally is intended to induce the reader to complete and return the questionnaire.

**Cover Letter**  The **cover letter** that accompanies the questionnaire or is printed on the first page of the questionnaire booklet is an important means of inducing the reader to complete and return the questionnaire. Exhibit 7.2 illustrates a cover letter and some of the points a marketing research professional considers important to gain respondents' attention and cooperation. The first paragraph of the letter explains why the study is important. The basic appeal is one of social usefulness. Two other frequently used appeals are to ask the respondent to help the sponsor—"Will you do us a favor?"—and the egotistical appeal—"Your opinions are important! It's important for you to express your opinions so retailers will know the types of products and shopping facilities you would like to have available." Cover letters ensure confidentiality, indicate a postpaid reply envelope, describe the incentive as a reward for participation, explain that answering the questionnaire will not be difficult and will take only a short time, and describe how the person was scientifically selected for participation.

**Monetary Inducements**  The respondent's motivation for returning a questionnaire may be increased by offering monetary incentives or premiums. Although pens, frequent flyer miles, lottery tickets, and a variety of premiums have been tried, monetary incen-

■ **Exhibit 7.2**

**Example of
Cover Letter for
Household Survey**

| | |
|---|---|
| *Official letterhead* | WASHINGTON STATE UNIVERSITY<br>PULLMAN, WASHINGTON 99968<br>DEPARTMENT OF RURAL SOCIOLOGY<br>ROOM 23, Wilman Hall |
| *Date mailed* | April 19, 19XX |
| *Inside address in matching type* | Oliver Jones<br>2190 Fontane Road<br>Spokane, Washington 99467 |
| *What study is about; its social usefulness* | Bills have been introduced in Congress and our State Legislature to encourage the growth of rural and small town areas and slow down that of large cities. These bills could greatly affect the quality of life provided in both rural and urban places. However, no one really knows in what kinds of communities people like you want to live or what is thought about these proposed programs. |
| *Why recipient is important (and, if needed, who should complete the questionnaire)* | Your household is one of a small number in which people are being asked to give their opinion on these matters. It was drawn in a random sample of the entire state. In order that the results will truly represent the thinking of the people of Washington, it is important that each questionnaire be completed an returned. It is also important that we have about the same number of men and women participating in this study. Thus, we would like the questionnaire for your household to be completed by an adult female. If none is present, then it should be completed by an adult male. |
| *Promise of confidentiality; explanation of identification number* | You may be assured of complete confidentiality. The questionnaire has an identification number for mailing purposes only. This is so that we may check your name off of the mailing list when your questionnaire is returned. Your name will never be placed on the questionnaire. |
| *Usefulness of study*<br><br>*"Token" reward for participation* | The results of this research will be made available to officials and representatives in our state's government, members of Congress, and all interested citizens. You may receive a summary of results by writing "copy of results requested" on the back of the returns envelope, and printing your name and address below it. Please do not put this information on your questionnaire itself. |
| *What to do if questions arise* | I would be most happy to answer any questions you might have. Please write or call. The telephone number is (509) 335-8623. |
| *Appreciation* | Thank you for your assistance. |
| | Sincerely, |
| *Pressed blue ballpoint signature*<br><br>*Title* | Don A. Dillman<br>Project Director |

tives appear to be the most effective and least biasing incentive. Although money may be useful to all respondents, its primary advantage may be as a way to attract attention. It is perhaps for this reason that monetary incentives work for all income categories. Often cover letters try to boost response rates with messages such as "We know that the attached dollar [or coin] cannot compensate you for your time. It is just a token of our appreciation."

**Interesting Questions**    The topic of the research cannot be manipulated without changing the definition of the marketing problem. However, certain interesting questions can be added to the questionnaire, perhaps at the beginning, to stimulate respondents' interest and induce cooperation. Questions of little concern to the researchers but of great interest to the respondents may give respondents who are indifferent to the major portion of the questionnaire a reason to respond.[16]

**Follow-up**
A letter or postcard reminder requesting that the respondent return the questionnaire.

**Follow-ups**   The response rates for most mail surveys start off relatively high for the first two weeks after questionnaires begin to be returned, then gradually taper off. After responses from the first wave of mailings begin to trickle in, most studies use **follow-ups**—letter or postcard reminders. The follow-up letter generally requests that respondents return the questionnaire because a 100 percent response rate is important for the survey's purposes. A follow-up may include a second questionnaire or merely serve as a reminder to respondents to fill out the questionnaire that was initially mailed.

**Advance Notification**   Advance notification, by either letter or telephone, has been successful in some situations. Advance notices that go out closer to the questionnaire mailing time produce better results than those sent too far in advance. The optimal lead time for advance notification is approximately three days before the mail survey is to arrive.[17]

**Survey Sponsorship**   Auspices bias may result from the sponsorship of a survey. One industrial marketer wished to conduct a survey of its wholesalers to learn their stock-

■ Samsonite inserts this product registration questionnaire into all luggage and business case products. The chance to win a "sweepstakes" prize encourages consumers to respond to the questionnaire. The results of the questionnaire become a key element of Samsonite's consumer database and its direct marketing programs.

1. ☐ Mr.   2. ☐ Mrs.   3. ☐ Ms.   4. ☐ Miss   U4E01-01
First Name   Initial   Last Name
Street   Apt. No.
City   State   ZIP Code

❷ Date of purchase: ____ / ____ / ____  Month Day Year   ❸ Home Telephone Number: ____ ____ (area code)

❹ What price did you pay for this piece of luggage? (exclude tax)  $ ____ .00

❺ Store where purchased: ____

❻ What were the most important factors and features that influenced your purchase of this Samsonite product? Please choose up to two (2) factors from Column A and up to three (3) features from Column B.

**A. Factors (2)**
1. ☐ Brand Reputation
2. ☐ Prior Experience with Samsonite Brand
3. ☐ Value for the Price
4. ☐ Quality/Durability
5. ☐ Meets Travel Needs
6. ☐ Warranty
7. ☐ Advertising
8. ☐ Other

**B. Features (3)**
1. ☐ Style/Appearance
2. ☐ Color
3. ☐ Shape
4. ☐ Carry Handle
5. ☐ Wheels
6. ☐ Other Features
7. ☐ Information on Case
8. ☐ Ease of Operation

❼ What member(s) of your household decided to purchase this product?
1. ☐ Received as Gift
2. ☐ Both Male and Female Heads of Household
3. ☐ Male Head of Household
4. ☐ Female Head of Household
5. ☐ Other Female
6. ☐ Other Male

❽ What is your primary intended use for this product in a normal 12-month period? (Check all that apply)
1. ☐ Business/Convention
2. ☐ Business or Convention and Pleasure Combined
3. ☐ Visit Friends/Relatives
4. ☐ Resort Vacation
5. ☐ Sightseeing Vacation
6. ☐ Foreign Vacation
7. ☐ Outdoor (e.g., Camping, Fishing, Hiking, Skiing)
8. ☐ Cruise
9. ☐ Other (Specify) ____

❾ Who will be the primary user of this product?
|  | Male | Female |
|---|---|---|
| Under 12 yrs. | ☐ 1. | ☐ |
| 12 - 17 yrs. | ☐ 2. | ☐ |
| 18 - 24 yrs. | ☐ 3. | ☐ |
| 25 - 34 yrs. | ☐ 4. | ☐ |
| 35 - 44 yrs | ☐ 5. | ☐ |
| 45 - 54 yrs | ☐ 6. | ☐ |
| 55 and over | ☐ 7. | ☐ |

❿ Where did you purchase this product?
1. ☐ Received as a Gift
2. ☐ Department Store
3. ☐ Luggage/Specialty Store
4. ☐ Sears, J.C. Penney or Wards Retail Store
5. ☐ Catalog (e.g., Sears, J.C. Penney, Spiegel)
6. ☐ Discount Store
7. ☐ Catalog Showroom
8. ☐ Factory Outlet
9. ☐ Warehouse Club
10. ☐ Drug Store
11. ☐ Through the Mail
12. ☐ Military PX
13. ☐ Other

⓫ Please indicate how many and what type of trips you take in a normal 12-month period. (Please choose one from each column as applicable).

| | Business | | Personal/Pleasure | |
|---|---|---|---|---|
| | You | Spouse | You | Spouse |
| 1 to 3 trips | ☐ 1. | ☐ | ☐ 1. | ☐ |
| 4 to 9 trips | ☐ 2. | ☐ | ☐ 2. | ☐ |
| 10+ trips | ☐ 3. | ☐ | ☐ 3. | ☐ |

⓬ Model Number: ____

⓭ Date of birth of person whose name appears above: ____ / 1 9 ____  Month Year

⓮ Excluding yourself, what is the SEX and AGE (in years) of children and other adults living in your household?
1. ☐ No one else in household

| Male | Female | Age | | Male | Female | Age | |
|---|---|---|---|---|---|---|---|
| 1. ☐ | 2. ☐ | ____ years | | 1. ☐ | 2. ☐ | ____ years |
| 1. ☐ | 2. ☐ | ____ years | | 1. ☐ | 2. ☐ | ____ years |

⓯ Marital Status:
1. ☐ Married   3. ☐ Widowed
2. ☐ Divorced/Separated   4. ☐ Never Married (Single)

⓰ Occupation:
| | You | Spouse |
|---|---|---|
| Homemaker | ☐ 1. | ☐ |
| Professional/Technical | ☐ 2. | ☐ |
| Upper Management/Executive | ☐ 3. | ☐ |
| Middle Management | ☐ 4. | ☐ |
| Sales/Marketing | ☐ 5. | ☐ |
| Clerical or Service Worker | ☐ 6. | ☐ |
| Tradesman/Machine Oper./Laborer | ☐ 7. | ☐ |
| Retired | ☐ 8. | ☐ |
| Student | ☐ 9. | ☐ |
| Self Employed/Business Owner | ☐ 10. | ☐ |

⓱ Which group describes your annual family income?
1. ☐ Under $15,000
2. ☐ $15,000-$19,999
3. ☐ $20,000-$24,999
4. ☐ $25,000-$29,999
5. ☐ $30,000-$34,999
6. ☐ $35,000-$39,999
7. ☐ $40,000-$44,999
8. ☐ $45,000-$49,999
9. ☐ $50,000-$59,999
10. ☐ $60,000-$74,999
11. ☐ $75,000-$99,999
12. ☐ $100,000 & over

⓲ Education: (please check those which apply)
| | You | Spouse |
|---|---|---|
| Some High School or Less | ☐ 1. | ☐ |
| Completed High School | ☐ 2. | ☐ |
| Vocational/Technical School | ☐ 3. | ☐ |
| Some College | ☐ 4. | ☐ |
| Completed College | ☐ 5. | ☐ |
| Some Graduate School | ☐ 6. | ☐ |
| Completed Graduate School | ☐ 7. | ☐ |

*(PLEASE CONTINUE ON BACK!)* 🖙 🖙 🖙

Samsonite SILHOUETTE® 4 GREY ULTRAVALET™ CARRY-ON WITH WHEELS (See bottom of product tag)

ing policies and attitudes concerning competing manufacturers. A mail questionnaire sent under the corporate letterhead very likely would have received a much lower response rate than the questionnaire actually sent, which used a commercial marketing research firm's letterhead. The sponsorship of well-known and prestigious organizations such as universities or government agencies may also significantly influence response rates.

### ■ Keying Mail Questionnaires with Codes

A marketing researcher planning a follow-up should not disturb respondents who already have returned the questionnaires. The expense of mailing questionnaires to those who already have responded is usually avoidable. One device for eliminating those who have already responded from the mailing list for follow-up mailings is to mark the questionnaires so that they may be keyed to identify members of the sample with code numbers as respondents or nonrespondents. Blind keying of questionnaires on a return envelope (systematically varying the job number or room number of the marketing research department, for example) or use of visible code numbers on the questionnaire has been used for this purpose. Visible keying is indicated with statements such as "The sole purpose of the number on the last pages is to avoid sending a second questionnaire to people who complete and return the first one." Ethical researchers key questionnaires strictly to increase response rates, thereby preserving respondents' anonymity.

### ■ Global Considerations

Researchers conducting surveys in more than one country must recognize that postal services and cultural circumstances differ around the world. For example, Backer Spielvogel & Bates Worldwide advertising agency conducts its Global Scan survey in 18 countries. In the United States, the questionnaire is mailed to individuals selected for the sample, but mail is not used in several other countries. In certain countries, the questionnaire may be personally delivered to respondents because of a fear of letter bombs, unreliable delivery service, or low literacy rates.[18]

### ■ Printed, Self-Administered Questionnaires That Use Other Forms of Distribution

Many forms of self-administered questionnaires are very similar to mail questionnaires. Airlines frequently pass out questionnaires to passengers during flights. Restaurants, hotels, and other service establishments often print short questionnaires on cards so that customers can evaluate the service.[19] *Wired, Tennis Magazine, Advertising Age,* and many other publications have inserted questionnaires to inexpensively survey current readers and, often, to provide the source for a magazine article. Many manufacturers use their warranty or owner registration cards to collect demographic information and data about where and why products were purchased.

Using owner registration cards is an extremely economical technique for tracing trends in consumer habits. Again, problems may arise because people who fill out self-administered questionnaires differ from those who do not.

Questionnaires also can be distributed via fax machines. These fax surveys replace the sender's printing and postage costs and are delivered and/or returned faster than traditional mail surveys. Of course, most households do not have fax machines. However, when the sample consists of organizations that are likely to have fax machines, the sample coverage may be adequate.

### WHAT WENT WRONG?

## Old Joe and the Fax Survey

A few years ago, a FaxTrack opinion poll in an issue of *Advertising Age* asked the marketing community how it felt about health officials' recent criticism of the Camel spokescartoon. Earlier fax polls on other subjects had received up to 300 responses over 5 days. The Old Joe poll got close to 1,400 in less than 2 days, crippling *Advertising Age*'s fax machines and offering insight into the swiftness and strength of the tobacco industry.

Several memos and notes not meant for the researchers' eyes were inadvertently faxed to the *Advertising Age* office. After seeing the fax questionnaire in *Advertising Age,* R. J. Reynolds Tobacco Co. and several ad agencies, outdoor media companies, and cigarette industry suppliers started letting the trade publication know where they stood.

RJR VP–Purchasing Kimberly J. Keiser faxed around a memo and copy of the FaxTrack. The note asked people to complete the survey and send it to *Advertising Age*'s Chicago office.

"We were getting so many calls from our suppliers and ad agencies, who wanted us to send them the form because they hadn't seen it yet," said Peggy Carter, RJR Manager–Media Relations.

From Tuesday morning until *Advertising Age* turned off the machines at 5:00 P.M. (CT) Wednesday, they received hundreds upon hundreds of pro–Old Joe responses.

The letter in no way indicated how the recipients should respond. "Gentlemen—Please consider responding to this poll with your opinion," Mr. Keiser's letter read. "But before faxing, please cut along the 'the dotted lines' of the FaxTrack form and submit only the clipped form."

Oops. Someone at a North Carolina company faxed *Advertising Age* the letter.

Transportation Displays Inc., New York, one of the largest transit display agencies in the United States, had the same problem. VP–Marketing Jodi Yegelwel issued a note to all marketing managers telling them to fill out and return the fax, but someone accidentally sent the memo to *Advertising Age.*

Several companies with ties to the cigarette industry photocopied the survey and distributed it to every employee. P. H. Glatfelter Co.'s Ecusta Division of Pisgah Forest, N.C., which supplies cigarette paper to RJR and other tobacco marketers, was among those companies—and it has 1,700 workers.

Some faxes came back with notes on top, like the one from "B," who wrote, "Would you mind responding to this? Thanks!" on top of several forms. And a company called Southchem faxed *Advertising Age* a note requesting more FaxTrack forms.

*Advertising Age* believes there's nothing wrong with what companies like RJR and TDI did—in fact, *Advertising Age* anticipated that the antismoking lobby might do the same thing (to the best of our knowledge, it did not).

But the volume of pro–Old Joe responses—often the same form sent over and over and over again—makes it nearly impossible to get an accurate reading on how *Advertising Age* readers in general feel. Fax polls have a high likelihood of self-selection error.

**Drop-off method**
A method of distributing self-administered questionnaires whereby an interviewer drops off the questionnaire and picks it up at a later time.

**Computer-interactive survey**
A survey in which the respondent completes a self-administered questionnaire displayed on a computer monitor of a computer. Respondents interact directly with a computer programmed to ask questions in a sequence determined by respondents' previous answers.

Extremely long questionnaires may be dropped off by an interviewer and then picked up at a later time. The **drop-off method** sacrifices some cost savings since it requires travel to each respondent's location.

### ■ Computerized Self-Administered Questionnaires

**Computer-interactive surveys** are programmed in much the same way as computer-assisted telephone interviewing surveys. However, the respondent interacts directly with an on-site computer at a trade show or other event location. In other words, the respondent self-administers a computer program that asks questions in a sequence determined by his or her previous answers. The questions appear on the computer screen, and answers are recorded by simply pressing a key, thus immediately entering the data into the computer's memory.

One major advantage of computer-assisted surveys is the computer's ability to personalize question wording and sequence questions based on previous responses. The computer can be programmed to skip from question 6 to question 9 if the answer to question 6 is *no*. Further, responses to previous questions can lead to questions that can be personalized for individual respondents (for example, "When you cannot buy your favorite brand, Revlon, what brand of lipstick do you prefer?"). However, the questionnaire is designed for the research problem, and computerization should not compromise this.[20] In many cases, a fieldworker must be at the on-site location to explain how to use the computer system.

A major disadvantage of computer-interactive surveys is that open-ended response questions require that respondents have both the skill and the willingness to type lengthy answers into the computer.

### ■ E-Mail, Internet, and Other Interactive Surveys

Questionnaires are beginning to be distributed electronically via e-mail, or electronic mail. E-mail is a relatively new method of communication, and many individuals cannot be accessed by it. However, certain circumstances lend themselves to **e-mail surveys,** such as internal surveys of employees or surveys of retail buyers who regularly deal with the organization via e-mail. The benefits of this method include lower distribution and processing fees, faster turnaround time, more flexibility, and less paper chasing.[21] It has been argued that many respondents feel they can be more candid on e-mail than on personal or telephone surveys for the same reasons they are candid on other self-administered questionnaires. Researchers at Socratic Technologies and American Research claim that when people are contacted to take part in electronic research, they are more likely to participate than in identical investigations using written materials.[22] E-mail questionnaires are believed to be successful for two reasons: They arouse curiosity because they are novel, and they reach respondents when they are opening their e-mail, a time when they are prepared to interact.

Surveys conducted on the Internet, at interactive kiosks, or on disks sent by mail share many features with e-mail surveys. Many of these interactive surveys can utilize color,

**E-mail survey**
A self-administered questionnaire sent to respondents via e-mail.

■ Lifescapes is an overnight survey of life in America conducted on-line by American Dialogue on American Online. Self- selected respondents e-mail responses to the Lifescape address on America Online (lifescape@aol.com). Typically, for each completed questionnaire, one dollar is donated to charity.[23]

sound, and animation, which help to increase participants' cooperation and willingness to spend more time answering the questionnaires.

**Internet survey**
A self-administered questionnaire placed on an Internet Web site. The respondent reads the questions on a personal computer and answers are directly entered into the researchers computer.

The main advantages of **Internet surveys** are speed and low cost. You can post a questionnaire on a Web site and people will begin to respond almost at once.[24] Further, as soon as a questionnaire is completed, most Internet survey software instantly prepares a preliminary running tabulation. As with other self-administered questionnaires there is no need to hire, train, or supervise interviewers. There are no printing or postage costs.

The disadvantages of Internet surveys involve problems about the nature of the samples. Internet users tend to be younger, better educated, and more technology-oriented than the public at large. Results should not be extrapolated beyond Internet users. However, there are no other problems because all responses are voluntary and filled out by respondents at their leisure. Thus, self-selection error is likely. Finally, many Internet programs cannot detect if a respondent filled our more than one questionnaire.

As the number of Internet users grow, their profile is expected to become more similar to that of the average American.[25] For now, Internet surveys are most appropriate when the research subject relates specific questions about use of the Internet, satisfaction with Web sites, and products of interest to Internet users. Many marketers ask first-time visitors to a Web site to register, which means the first time someone visits a site, the organization surveys visitors about such matters as their interest, demographic background, postal address, and e-mail address.

## ■ SELECTING THE APPROPRIATE SURVEY RESEARCH DESIGN

Earlier discussions of research design and problem definition emphasized that many research tasks may lead to similar decision-making information. There is no best form of survey; each has advantages and disadvantages. A researcher who must ask highly confidential questions may use a mail survey, thus sacrificing speed of data collection to avoid interviewer bias. If a researcher must have considerable control over question phrasing, central location telephone interviewing may be appropriate.

To determine the appropriate technique, the researcher must ask several questions: Is the assistance of an interviewer necessary? Are respondents interested in the issues being investigated? Will cooperation be easily attained? How quickly is the information needed? Will the study require a long and complex questionnaire? How large is the budget? The criteria—cost, speed, anonymity, and so forth—may differ for each project.

Exhibit 7.3 summarizes the major advantages and disadvantages of typical mail, telephone, mall intercept, and personal interview surveys. Note that it emphasizes the "typical." For example, a creative researcher might be able to design highly versatile and flexible questionnaires, but most researchers use standardized questions. An elaborate mail survey may be far more expensive than a short personal interview, but generally this is not the case.

## ■ CROSS-SECTIONAL AND LONGITUDINAL SURVEYS

Most surveys are individual projects conducted only once over a short time period, but some projects require multiple surveys over a long period. Thus, some surveys are cross-sectional, whereas others are longitudinal.

### ■ Cross-Sectional Studies

A nationwide survey was taken to examine the different attitudes of cross-sections of the American public toward the arts. One aspect of the survey dealt with museums. In general,

■ **Exhibit 7.3**                    **Typical Advantages and Disadvantages of the Traditional Survey Methods**

| | Door-to-Door Personal Interview | Mail Intercept Personal Interview | Telephone | Mail |
|---|---|---|---|---|
| Speed of Data Collection | Moderate to fast | Fast | Very fast | Researcher has no control over return of questionnaire; slow |
| Geographic Flexibility | Limited to moderate | Confined, urban bias | High | High |
| Respondent Cooperation | Excellent | Moderate to low | Good | Moderate—poorly designed questionnaire will have low response rate |
| Versatility of Questioning | Quite versatile | Extremely versatile | Moderate | Highly standardized format |
| Questionnaire Length | Long | Moderate to long | Moderate | Varies depending on incentive |
| Item Nonresponse | Low | Medium | Medium | High |
| Possibility for Respondent Misunderstanding | Lowest | Lowest | Average | Highest—no interviewer present for clarification |
| Degree of Interviewer Influence of Answers | High | High | Moderate | None—interviewer absent |
| Supervision of Interviewers | Moderate | Moderate to high | High, especially with central location WATS interviewing | Not applicable |
| Anonymity of Respondent | Low | Low | Moderate | High |
| Ease of Callback or Follow-up | Difficult | Difficult | Easy | Easy, but takes time |
| Cost | Highest | Moderate to high | Low to moderate | Lowest |
| Special Features | Visual materials may be shown or demonstrated; extended probing possible | Taste tests, viewing of TV commercials possible | Fieldwork and supervision of data collection are simplified; quite adaptable to computer technology | Respondent may answer questions at own convenience; has time to reflect on answers |

Note: The emphasis is on *typical* surveys. For example, an elaborate mail survey may be far more expensive than a short personal interview, but this generally is not the case.

**Cross-sectional study**
A study that samples various segments of a population and collects data at a single moment in time.

the public's attitudes toward museums were very positive. Museum preferences varied by demographics or cross-sections of the population: People in towns and rural areas showed greater interest in historical museums, whereas city and suburban residents leaned more heavily toward art museums. Young people (16-to-20-year-olds) were more interested than others in art museums and less interested in historical museums.[26] Such a study is a **cross-sectional study** because it collected the data at a single point in time. Such a study samples various segments of the population to investigate differences in the appropriate subgroups. Most marketing research surveys fall into this category, particularly those that deal with market segmentation.

# ■ Longitudinal Studies

**Longitudinal study**
A survey of respondents conducted at different times, thus allowing analysis of changes over time.

In a **longitudinal study,** respondents are questioned at two or more different times. The purpose of longitudinal surveys is to examine continuity of responses and observe changes that occur over time. Many syndicated polling services, such as Yankelovich Partners and Market Development, are conducted on a regular basis. The Yankelovich survey of Hispanic consumers periodically asks whether weekday television viewers watch Spanish television programs. The longitudinal results reveal that the percentage of Hispanic Americans who watch Spanish television programs grew from 74 percent in 1988 to 81 percent in 1990 to 86 percent in 1992.[27] This illustrates a longitudinal study with successive samples because researchers surveyed several different samples (of Hispanics) at different times.

**Tracking study**
A type of longitudinal study that uses successive samples to compare trends and identify changes in variables such as consumer satisfaction, brand image, or advertising awareness.

Longitudinal studies that use successive samples often are referred to as **tracking studies** because successive waves are designed to compare trends and identify changes in variables such as consumer satisfaction, brand image, or advertising awareness. These studies are useful for assessing aggregate trends but do not allow for tracking changes in individuals over time.

**Total quality management**
A business philosophy that emphasizes market-driven quality as a top organizational priority.

A **total quality management** strategy expresses the conviction that to improve quality, an organization must regularly conduct surveys to evaluate customer satisfaction and quality improvement. Thus, total quality management is one of the most common applications of longitudinal survey research. A firm must routinely ask customers to rate its quality against its competitors'. It must periodically measure employee knowledge, attitudes, and

■ Consumer panels provide longitudinal data. NFO Research, Inc. has the largest consumer panel in the world, with more than 550,000 households representing over 1.3 million people.

**NFO RESEARCH, INC.** 1996-1997 Household Sample and Services Overview

the NFO Panel helps you…

understand your consumers…

make the *right choices*

…and turn *strategies* into results

expectations. It must monitor company performance against benchmark standards. It must determine whether customers found any delightful surprises or major disappointments.

**Consumer Panel**    A longitudinal study that gathers data from the same sample of individuals or households over time is called a **consumer panel.** Consider the packaged-goods marketer that wishes to learn about brand-switching behavior. A consumer panel that consists of a group of people who record their purchasing habits in a diary over time will provide the manager with a continuous stream of information about the brand and product class. Diary data that are recorded regularly over an extended period enable the investigator to track repeat-purchase behavior and changes in purchasing habits, along with changes in price, special promotions, or other aspects of marketing strategy.

**Consumer panel**
A longitudinal survey of the same sample of individuals or households to record (in a diary) their attitudes, behavior, or purchasing habits over time.

---

## ■ SUMMARY

Survey research is a common tool for asking respondents questions. Surveys can provide quick, inexpensive, and accurate information about awareness, product knowledge, brand usage behavior, opinions, and so on.

Two major forms of error are common in survey research. The first, random sampling error, is caused by chance variation and results in a sample that is not absolutely representative of the target population. The second, systematic error, falls into two general categories. Nonresponse error, the first category, results from people who are sampled but do not respond and from those whose answers differ from those of respondents in some significant way. Response bias occurs when a response to a questionnaire is deliberately falsified or inadvertently misrepresented. Five specific categories of response bias exist: acquiescence bias, extremity bias, interviewer bias, auspices bias, and social desirability bias. The second category of systematic error includes administrative problems such as inconsistencies in interviewers' abilities, cheating, data-processing mistakes, and so forth.

Surveys may be classified according to method of communication. Interviews and self-administered questionnaires are used to collect survey data. Interviews may be conducted door to door, in shopping malls, or on the telephone. Traditionally interviews have been recorded manually, but survey researchers are increasingly using computers for this purpose.

Personal interviews are a flexible method that offer both advantages and shortcomings. Door-to-door personal interviews get high response rates, but they are also more costly to administer than other types of surveys. The presence of an interviewer may also influence subjects' responses. When a sample need not represent the national population, mall intercept interviews may reduce costs.

Telephone interviewing has the advantage of speed in data collection and lower costs per interview. However, not all households have telephones, and not all telephone numbers are listed in directories. This causes problems in obtaining a representative sampling frame. Absence of face-to-face contact and inability to use visual materials also limit telephone interviewing. However, computer-assisted telephone interviewing from central locations is improving the quality of telephone surveys.

Traditionally self-administered questionnaires have been delivered via the mail. Today self-administered questionnaires may be dropped off, administered at central locations, or administered via computer interactive means, such as the Internet. Mail questionnaires generally are less expensive than telephone or personal interviews, but they also introduce a much larger chance of nonresponse error; however, several methods can be used to increase response rates.

Surveys may consider the population at a given moment or follow trends over a period of time. The first approach, the cross-sectional study, usually is intended to separate the population into meaningful subgroups. The second type of study, the longitudinal study, can reveal important population changes over time. Longitudinal studies may involve contacting different sets of respondents or the same ones repeatedly (consumer panels).

## ■ Key Terms and Concepts

| | |
|---|---|
| Respondent | Item nonresponse |
| Survey | Door-to-door interview |
| Random sampling error | Callback |
| Systematic error | Mall intercept interview |
| Sample bias | Telephone interview |
| Respondent error | Random digit dialing |
| Nonresponse error | Central location interviewing |
| Nonrespondent | Computer-assisted telephone interview (CATI) |
| Not-at-home | |
| Refusal | Self-administered questionnaire |
| Self-selection bias | Mail survey |
| Response bias | Response rate |
| Acquiescence bias | Cover letter |
| Extremity bias | Follow-up |
| Interviewer bias | Drop-off method |
| Auspices bias | Computer-interactive survey |
| Social desirability bias | E-mail survey |
| Administrative error | Internet survey |
| Data-processing error | Cross-sectional study |
| Sample selection error | Longitudinal study |
| Interviewer error | Tracking study |
| Interviewer cheating | Total quality management |
| Personal interview | Consumer panel |
| Probing | |

## ■ Questions

1. Give an example of each type of survey error listed in Exhibit 7.1.
2. A survey indicated that chief executive officers (CEOs) would prefer to relocate their businesses in Atlanta (first choice), San Diego, Tampa, Los Angeles, or Boston. The CEOs who said they were going to build the required office space in the following year were asked where they were going to build. They indicated they were going to build in New York, Los Angeles, San Francisco, or Chicago. Explain this discrepancy.
3. What potential sources of error might be associated with the following situations?
   (a) In a survey of frequent flyers age 50 and older, researchers concluded that price does not play a significant role in airline travel because only 25 percent of the respondents checked off price as the most important determinant of where and how they traveled, while 35 percent rated price as unimportant.
   (b) A survey of voters finds that most respondents do not like negative political ads, that is, advertising by one political candidate that criticizes or exposes secrets about the opponent's "dirty laundry."

    (c) Researchers who must conduct a 45-minute personal interview decide to offer $10 to each respondent because they believe people who will sell their opinions are more typical than people who will talk to a stranger for 45 minutes.

    (d) A company's sales representatives are asked what percentage of time they spend making presentations to prospects, traveling, talking on the telephone, participating in meetings, working on the computer, and engaging in other on-the-job activities. What potential sources of error might such a question generate?

4. What topics about consumer behavior might be extremely sensitive issues about which to directly question respondents?

5. A survey conducted by the National Endowment for the Arts asked, "Have you read a book within the last year?" What response bias might be possible with this question?

6. What type of survey (classified by communications medium) would you use in the following situations? Why?

    (a) Survey of the buying motives of industrial engineers

    (b) Survey of the satisfaction levels of rental-car users

    (c) Survey of television commercial advertising awareness

    (d) Survey of top corporate executives

7. Evaluate the following survey designs:

    (a) A researcher suggests mailing a small safe (a metal file box with a built-in lock) without the lock combination to respondents with a note explaining that respondents will be called in a few days for a telephone interview. During the telephone interview, the combination is given and the safe may be opened.

    (b) A shopping center that wishes to evaluate its image places packets including a questionnaire, cover letter, and stamped return envelope in the mall where customers can pick them up if they wish.

    (c) A questionnaire is programmed on a 3-inch floppy disk and then mailed to individuals who own computers. Respondents stick the disk into their computers, answer the questions, and mail the disk back to the research company in a special mailer. Each respondent is guaranteed a monetary incentive, but has the option to increase it by playing a slot machine–type game programmed onto the floppy disk.

    (d) A mall intercept interviewing service is located in a regional shopping center. The facility contains a small room for television and movie presentations. Shoppers are used as sampling units. However, mall intercept interviewers recruit additional subjects for television commercial experiments by offering them several complimentary tickets for special sneak previews. Individuals contacted at the mall are allowed to bring up to five guests. In some cases, the complimentary tickets are offered through ads in a local newspaper.

    (e) Time selects a mail survey rather than a telephone survey for a study conducted to determine the demographic characteristics and purchasing behavior of its subscribers.

8. What types of research studies lend themselves to the use of e-mail as a method of survey research? What are the advantages and disadvantages of survey communication using e-mail?

9. Give an example of a political situation in which longitudinal research might be useful. Identify some common objectives for a longitudinal study in a business situation.

10. Page through your local newspaper to find some stories derived from survey research results. Was the study's methodology appropriate for this news item? Could the research have been termed advocacy research?

11. Suppose you are the marketing research director for your state's tourism bureau. Assess the state's information needs, and identify the information you will collect in a survey of tourists who visit your state.

## EXPLORING THE INTERNET

1. Go to the Los Angeles Times poll's page (http://www.latimes.com/HOME/NEWS/POLLS). Select a poll (survey) topic. Then navigate to the answer poll option. Participate in the survey. What was the first question on the survey?

2. Go to ASI Research's Web site (http://www.asiresearch.com) to learn what types of survey research services the firm offers. What hot links about other surveys and survey research services can be accessed through ASI's Web site?

3. Go to NPD Group's Web site (http://www.npd.com) and click on the company overview. What types of custom and syndicated survey research services does it offer? Search "What's New" and report any information you find about the company's PC-Meter service.

4. Use a search engine, such as Yahoo, Lycos, or Infoseek, to see what you find if you enter "telephone survey" as key words.

---

## CASE 7.1   Royal Bee Electric Fishing Reel[28]

Royal Barton started thinking about an electric fishing reel some 14 years earlier when his father had a stroke and lost the use of an arm. To see that happen to his dad, who had taught him the joys of fishing and hunting, made Barton realize what a chunk a physical handicap could take out of a sports enthusiast's life. Being able to cast and retrieve a lure or experience the thrill of a big bass trying to take your rig away from you were among the joys of life that would be denied Barton's father forever.

Barton was determined to do something about it—if not for his father, then at least for others who had suffered a similar fate. So, after tremendous personal expense and years of research and development, Barton has perfected what is sure to be the standard bearer for all future freshwater electric reels. Forget those saltwater jobs, which Barton refers to as "winches." He has developed something that is small, compact, and has incredible applications.

He calls it the Royal Bee. The first word, obviously, is his first name. The second word refers to the low buzzing sound the reel makes when in use.

The Royal Bee system looks simple enough and probably is if you understand the mechanical workings of a reel. A system of gears ties into the gears of the existing spool, and a motor switch in the back drives the gears attached to the triggering system.

All gearing of the electrical system is disengaged so that you can cast normally. But when you push the button for "retrieve," it engages two gears. After the gears are engaged, the trigger travels far enough to touch the switch that tightens the drive belt, and there is no slipping. You

cannot hit the switch until the gears are properly engaged. This means you cast manually, just as you would normally fish, then you reengage the reel for the levelwind to work. And you can do all that with one hand!

The system works on a 6-volt battery that you can attach to your belt or hang around your neck if you are wade fishing. If you have a boat with a 6-volt battery system, the reel can actually work off of it. There is a small connector that plugs into the reel, so you could easily use more than one of the reels off the same battery. For instance, if you have two or three outfits equipped with different lures, you just switch the connector from reel to reel as you use it. A reel with the Royal Bee system can be used in a conventional manner. You do not have to use it as an electric reel unless you choose to do so.

Barton believes the Royal Bee may not be just for handicapped fishermen. Ken Cook, one of the leading professional anglers in the country, is sold on the Royal Bee. After he suffered a broken arm, he had to withdraw from some tournaments because fishing with one hand was difficult. By the time his arm healed, he was hooked on the Royal Bee because it increased bassing efficiency. As Cook explains, "The electric reel has increased my efficiency in two ways. One is for flipping, where I use it all the time. The other is for fishing topwater when I have to make a long cast. When I'm flipping, the electric reel gives me instant control over slack line. I can keep both hands on the rod. I never have to remove them to take up slack. I flip, engage the reel, and then all I have to do is push the lever with my thumb to take up slack instantly."

Cook's reel (a Ryobi 4000) is one of several that can be converted to the electric retrieve. For flipping, he loads his reel with 20-pound test line. He uses a similar reel with lighter line when fishing a surface lure. "What you can do with the electric reel is eliminate unproductive reeling time," Cook says.

A few extra seconds may not mean much if you are out on a neighborhood pond just fishing on the weekend. But it can mean a bunch if you are in tournament competition where one extra cast might make the difference in going home with $50,000 tucked in your pocket. "Look at it this way," Cook explains. "Let's suppose we're in clear water and it's necessary to make a long cast to the cover we want to fish with a topwater lure. There's a whole lot of unproductive water between us and the cover. With the electric reel, I make my long cast and fish the cover. Then, when I'm ready to reel in, I just press the retrieve lever so the battery engages the necessary gears, and I've got my lure back ready to make another cast while you're still cranking."

When Royal Barton retired from his veterinary supply business, he began enjoying his favorite pastimes: hunting, fishing, and developing the Royal Bee system. He realized he needed help in marketing his product, so he sought professional assistance to learn how to reach the broadest possible market for the Royal Bee system.

**Questions**

1. What is the marketing problem? What are Barton's information needs? Outline some survey research objectives for a research project on the Royal Bee system.
2. What type of survey—personal interview, telephone interview, or mail survey—should Barton select?
3. What sources of survey error are most likely to occur in a study of this type?
4. What means should be used to obtain a high response rate?

---

 **VIDEO CASE 7.2**    Walker Marketing Research

Walker Marketing Research is one of the 15 largest marketing research firms in the United States. It is based in Indianapolis and has client service offices in New York, Cincinnati, and San Francisco. The company was founded in 1939 as a field interviewing service by Tommie Walker, mother of Frank Walker, the current chairperson and chief executive officer of the organization.

In the 1920s, Tommie Walker's late husband worked for a bank that was considering sponsoring an Indianapolis radio show featuring classical music. The bank wanted to know who was listening to this show. Tommie was hired to do the interviewing, and she threw herself into the work. After that, referrals brought her more interviewing work for surveys. During an interview with a woman whose husband was a district sales manager for the A&P grocery chain, she learned that A&P was looking for a surveyor in the Midwest. A&P's sales manger liked Tommie but wouldn't hire anyone without a formal company, a field staff, and insurance. Tommie founded Walker Marketing Research on October 20, 1939, and her business with A&P lasted 17 years.

Today the company's domestic operation is organized into three strategic business units for marketing research. Research and Analysis performs custom ad hoc survey research projects for client organizations. Data-source offers data collection, tabulation, database management, and computer services. This business unit maintains several offices, each with central telephone interviewing facilities. It has more than 240 telephone interviewing stations. It also conducts personal interviews in shopping malls. Walker's Customer Satisfaction Measurement unit is a quality improvement consulting organization that specializes in design and administration of surveys to measure customer satisfaction. In 1995, Walker's research revenues were approximately $39 million. Walker's Customer Satisfaction Measurement unit has grown approximately 25 percent annually.

The company anticipates further growth in foreign markets. In 1991 this operation went global when Walker CSM Worldwide, Inc., was launched. The company saw increased demand for customer satisfaction research from multinational corporations that wanted to break into or expand in Canada, Europe, and the Pacific Rim countries. The research is being conducted by an eight-firm network. Each research firm is essentially a franchise that uses Walker's standard research formula but retains local autonomy to select the most efficient process available for each project.

**Questions**

1. What types of custom survey research projects might a research supplier such as Walker Marketing Research conduct for its clients?

2. What stages are involved in conducting a survey? For which stages might a client company hire a research supplier such as Walker Marketing Research?

3. What ethical considerations does a research supplier such as Walker Marketing Research face?

4. What special considerations will arise when Walker conducts customer satisfaction research in Canada, Europe, and Asia?

5. What measures, other than findings from surveys, might Walker researchers use to evaluate the effectiveness of a total quality management program?

## ■ Endnotes

[1] Based on the press release "PepsiCo Foods International to Introduce Lay's Potato Chips to Consumers Worldwide," PRNewswire, November 30, 1995.

[2] Paul B. Sheatsley, "Survey Design," in *Handbook of Marketing Research,* ed. Robert Ferber (New York: McGraw-Hill, 1974), pp. 2–66.

[3] Douglas Aircraft, Consumer Research, p. 13.

[4] Jennifer Lawrence, "Gender-Specific Works for Diapers—Almost Too Well," *Advertising Age,* February 8, 1993, pp. S-1–S-11.

[5] John Frieman and Edgar Butler, "Some Sources of Interviewer Variance in Surveys," *Public Opinion Quarterly,* Spring 1976, pp. 79–81.

[6] "Your Opinion Counts, *1986 Refusal Rate Study* (Indianapolis: Walker Marketing Research, 1986).

[7] Estimate calculated from information in Vincent P. Barabba, "The Marketing Encyclopedia," *Harvard Business Review,* January–February 1990.

[8] Peter Tuckel and Harry W. O'Neill, "Screened Out," *Marketing Research,* Fall 1996, pp. 34–42.

[9] P. S. Tuckel and B. M. Feinberg, "The Answering Machine Poses Many Questions for Telephone Survey Research," *Public Opinion Quarterly,* Summer 1991.

[10] These differences were found in a major investigation of Pacific Telephone subscribers. See Clyde L. Rich, "Is Random Digit Dialing Really Necessary?" *Journal of Marketing Research,* August 1977, pp. 300–305.

[11] "Top 20 Unlisted Markets," *The Frame,* March 1994, p. 1.

[12] "Some Things We've Learned about Global Research," advertisement from Research International, New York, NY.

[13] William F. O'Dell, "Personal Interviews for Mail Panels," *Journal of Marketing,* October 1962, pp. 34–39.

[14] For various response rate calculations, see Frederick Wiseman and Maryann Billington, "Comment on a Standard Definition of Response Rates," *Journal of Marketing Research,* August 1984, pp. 336–338. Also, the researcher may wish to take into account the possibility of respondents registering opinions twice. See Thomas J. Steele, Warren L. Schwendig, and Nina M. Ray, "Do Multi-Wave Mailings Lead to Multi-Response in Mail Surveys?" *Applied Marketing Research,* Spring 1989, pp. 15–20; Thomas J. Steele, W. Lee Schwendig, and John A. Kilpatrick, "Duplicate Responses to Multiple Survey Mailings: A Problem," *Journal of Advertising Research,* March 1992.

[15] For excellent reviews of this topic, see Leslie Kanuk and Conrad Berenson, "Mail Surveys and Response Rates: A Literature Review," *Journal of Marketing Research,* November 1975, pp. 440–453; Richard T. Hise and Paul J. Solomon, "Improving Response Rates in Mail Surveys" (Paper presented to the Southwest Marketing Association, 1975); Julie Yu and Harris Cooper, "A Quantitative Review of Research Design Effects on Response Rates to Questionnaires," *Journal of Marketing Research,* February 1983, pp. 36–44; Michael J. Houston and John R. Nevin, "The Effects of Source and Appeal on Mail Survey Response Patterns," *Journal of Marketing Research*, August 1977, pp. 374–378. See also Bruce J. Walker, Wayne Kirchmann, and Jeffrey S. Conant, "A Method to Improve Response to Industrial Surveys," *Industrial Marketing Management* 16 (1987), pp. 305–314; L. L. Neidel and P. K. Sugrue, "Addressing Procedures as a Mail Survey Response Inducement Technique," *Journal of the Academy of Marketing Sciences,* Fall 1983, pp. 455–460; Gary L. Clark and Peter F. Kaminski, "How to Get More for Your Money in Mail Surveys," *Journal of Consumer Marketing,* Summer 1989, pp. 45–51.

[16] For an interesting article dealing with this issue, see Michael Geurts and David Whitlark, "A Little Inducement Goes a Long Way," *Marketing Research*, Summer 1994, pp. 13–15.

[17] For an empirical research study that deals with this issue, see Ronald D. Taylor, John Beisel, and Vicki Blakney, "The Effect of Advanced Notification by Mail of a Forthcoming Mail Survey on Response Rates, Item Omission Rates and Response to Speed" (Paper presented at the 1984 Southern Marketing Association Convention, New Orleans, LA).

[18] Lewis C. Winters, "International Psychographics," *Marketing Research,* September 1992, p. 48.

[19]For a complete discussion of fax surveys, see the excellent article by John P. Dickson and Douglas L. Maclachlan, "Fax Surveys: Return Patterns and Comparison with Mail Surveys," *Journal of Marketing Research,* February 1996, pp. 108–113.

[20]James D. Larson, "Considerations for the Design of Computer Aided Interviewing Systems" (Paper presented at the American Marketing Association Educators' Conference, 1985); Kieran Mathieson, "Forms-Based Software," *Marketing Research,* Winter 1993, p. 46.

[21]Aileen Crowley, "E-mail Surveys Elicit Fast Response, Cut Costs," *PC Week*, January 30, 1995.

[22]Bill MacElroy and Bill Geissler, "Interactive Surveys Can Be More Fun Than Traditional," *Marketing News,* October 24, 1994, pp. 4–5.

[23]Bernice Kanner, "Lifescapers Don't Feel Mired in Media's Output," *Advertising Age,* April 10, 1995, p. 26.

[24]Bill Eaton, "Internet Surveys: Does WWW stand for 'Why Waste the Work?'" Quirks Review, June–July 1997, downloaded November 22, 1997.

[25]Brad Edmondson, "The Wired Bunch: On-line Surveys and Focus Groups Might Solve the Toughest Problems in Market Research. But Can Internet Users Really Speak for Everyone?" *American Demographics,* June 1997, p. 10.

[26]Americans and the Arts: Highlights from a Survey of Public Opinion, Research Center of the Arts, p. 14.

[27]"Ethnic Marketing: Surveys Point to Group Differences," *Brandweek,* July 18, 1994, p. 32.

[28]Based on material that originally appeared in C. C. Risenhoover, "A Bee and His Reel," *Bassmaster Magazine;* Bob Bledsoe, "Inventor's Latest Line Hooks Some Converts," *Tulsa Tribune* (September 20, 1984) p. 6C; and Stan Fagerstrom, "A Reel with a Motor," *Pro Bass* (April 1985) p. 61.

# *8* OBSERVATION

O̲ne day, Sherlock Holmes asked Dr. Watson how many steps led up to the Baker Street apartment. Watson responded that he did not know. Holmes replied, "Ah, Watson, you see but you do not *observe*."

Although we, like Dr. Watson, constantly look around us in our daily lives, we often do not observe in a scientific sense. Holmes, however, trained himself to see what others overlook by systematically observing the environment. This chapter discusses the observation method of data gathering in marketing research.

## ■ WHEN IS OBSERVATION SCIENTIFIC?

Observation becomes a tool for scientific inquiry when it is systematically planned to achieve a formulated research purpose. Scientific observation systematically records data and relates them to well-formulated hypotheses rather than simply reflecting a set of interesting curiosities.[1]

**Observation**
The systematic process of recording the behavioral patterns of people, objects, and occurrences without questioning or otherwise communicating with them.

In marketing research, **observation** is the systematic process of recording the behavioral patterns of people, objects, and occurrences without questioning or otherwise communicating with them. The researcher who uses the observation method of data collection witnesses and records information as events occur or compiles evidence from records of past events.

## ■ WHAT CAN BE OBSERVED?

One can observe a wide variety of information about the behavior of people and objects. Seven kinds of observable content exist: **physical actions,** such as shopping patterns or television viewing; **verbal behavior,** such as sales conversations; **expressive behavior,** such as tone of voice or facial expressions; **spatial relations and locations,** such as traffic counts; **temporal patterns,** such as amount of time spent shopping or driving; **physical objects,** such as the amount of newspapers recycled; and **verbal and pictorial records,** such as the content of advertisements.

The observation method may be used to describe a wide variety of behavior, but cognitive phenomena such as attitudes, motivations, and preferences cannot be observed. Thus, observation research cannot provide an explanation of why a behavior occurred or what actions were intended. Another limitation is that the observed behavior generally is of short duration. Behavior patterns that occur over a period of several days or weeks generally are either too costly or impossible to observe.

■ In Japan, senior marketing executives take pride in doing observation research. Executives recognize the importance of watching actual shopping and consumption behavior as it takes place.

# ■ THE NATURE OF OBSERVATION STUDIES

Marketing researchers can observe people, objects, events, or other phenomena using either human observers or machines designed for specific observation tasks. Human observation best suits a situation or behavior that is not easily predictable in advance of the research. Mechanical observation, as performed by supermarket scanners or traffic counters, can very accurately record situations or types of behavior that are routine, repetitive, or programmatic.

Human or mechanical observation may be unobtrusive; that is, it may not require communication with a respondent.[2] For example, rather than asking customers how much time they spend shopping in his or her store, a supermarket manager might observe and record the intervals between when shoppers enter and leave the store. The unobtrusive or nonreactive nature of the observation method often generates data without a subject's knowledge. Situations in which an observer's presence is known to the subject involve **visible observation;** situations in which a subject is unaware that observation is taking place involve **hidden observation.** Hidden, unobtrusive observation minimizes respondent error. Asking subjects to participate in the research is not required when they are unaware that they are being observed.

The major advantage of observation studies over surveys, which obtain self-reported data from respondents, is that the data do not have distortions, inaccuracies, or other response biases due to memory error, social desirability bias, and so on. The data are recorded when the actual behavior takes place.

**Visible observation**
A situation in which the observer's presence is known to the subject.

**Hidden observation**
A situation in which the subject is unaware that observation is taking place.

# ■ OBSERVATION OF HUMAN BEHAVIOR

Surveys emphasize verbal responses, while observation studies emphasize and allow for the systematic recording of nonverbal behavior. Toy manufacturers such as Fisher Price use the observation technique because children often cannot express their reactions to products. By observing children at play with a proposed toy, doll, or game, marketing researchers can identify the elements of a potentially successful product. Toy marketing researchers might observe play to answer the following questions: How long does the child's attention stay with the product? Does the child put it down after 2 minutes or 20 minutes? Are the child's peers equally interested in the toy?

Behavioral scientists have recognized that nonverbal behavior can be a communication process by which meanings are exchanged among individuals. Head nods, smiles, raised eyebrows, and other facial expressions or body movements have been recognized as communication symbols. Observation of nonverbal communication may hold considerable promise for the marketing researcher. For example, in customer-salesperson interactions, it has been hypothesized that in low-importance transactions wherein potential customers are plentiful and easily replaced (for example, a shoe store), the salesperson may show definite nonverbal signs of higher status than the customer. When customers are scarce, as in big-ticket purchase situations (for example, real estate sales), the opposite should hold: The salesperson may emit many nonverbal indicators of deference. An observation study using the nonverbal communication measures shown in Exhibit 8.1 could test this hypothesis.

## ■ Complementary Evidence

The results of observation studies may amplify the results of other forms of research by providing complementary evidence concerning individuals' true feelings. Focus group interviews often are conducted behind one-way mirrors from which marketing executives

### ■ Exhibit 8.1                              Nonverbal Communication: Status and Power Gestures

| Behavior | Between Status Equals | | Between Status Nonequals | | Between Men and Women | |
|---|---|---|---|---|---|---|
| | Intimate | Nonintimate | Used by Superior | Used by Subordinate | Used by Men | Used by Women |
| Posture | Relaxed | Tense (less relaxed) | Relaxed | Tense | Relaxed | Tense |
| Personal space | Closeness | Distance | Closeness (optional) | Distance | Closeness | Distance |
| Touching | Touch | Don't touch | Touch (optional) | Don't touch | Touch | Don't touch |
| Eye gaze | Establish | Avoid | Stare, ignore | Avert eyes, watch | Stare, ignore | Avert eyes |
| Demeanor | Informal | Circumspect | Informal | Circumspect | Informal | Circumspect |
| Emotional expression | Show | Hide | Hide | Show | Hide | Show |
| Facial expression | Smile[a] | Don't smile[a] | Don't smile | Smile | Don't smile | Smile |

observe as well as listen to what is occurring. This allows for interpretation of nonverbal behavior, such as facial expressions or head nods, to supplement information from interviews.

One focus group session concerning hand lotion recorded that all the women's hands were above the table while they were casually waiting for the session to begin. Seconds after the women were told the topic was to be hand lotion, "all hands had been placed under the table or out of sight and the women's faces became tense."[3] This observation, along with the group discussion, revealed the women's anger, guilt, and shame about the condition of their hands. Although they felt they were expected to have soft, pretty hands, their housework obligations required them to wash dishes, clean floors, and do other chores detrimental to their hands.

When focus group behavior is videotaped, observation of the nonverbal communication symbols can add even more to marketers' knowledge of the situation.

■ When Steelcase, an office furniture manufacturer, decided there was an opportunity for a new product specifically designed for work teams, researchers believed observation was the best research method. Steelcase placed video cameras at various companies so its staff could observe firsthand how teams operate. After the recording period ended, the researchers exhaustively analyzed the tapes, looking for the patterns of behavior and motion that workers themselves don't even notice. The main observation was that people in teams function best if they can do some work collaboratively and some privately. These findings were utilized to design the Personal Harbor brand of modular office units. The units are similar in shape and size to a phone booth and can be arranged around a common space where a team works, fostering synergy but also allowing a person to work alone when necessary.[4] Of course, verbal behavior is not ignored; indeed, in certain observation studies, it is very important.

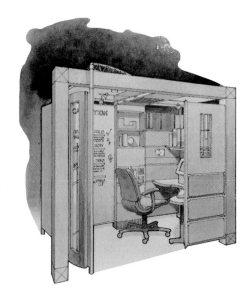

# ■ DIRECT OBSERVATION

**Direct observation**
A straightforward attempt to observe and record what naturally occurs; the investigator does not create an artificial situation.

**Direct observation** can produce a detailed record of events that occur or what people actually do. The observer plays a passive role; that is, there is no attempt to control or manipulate a situation—the observer merely records what occurs. Many types of data can be obtained more accurately through direct observation than by questioning. For example, recording traffic counts and/or observing the direction of traffic flows within a supermarket can help managers design store layouts that will maximize the exposure of departments that sell impulse goods. A manufacturer can determine the number of facings, shelf locations, display maintenance, and other factors regarding store conditions. If directly questioned in a survey, most shoppers would be unable to accurately portray the time they spent in each department. The observation method, however, could accomplish this task without difficulty.

In the direct observation method, the data consist of records of events made as they occur. An observation form often helps keep the observations consistent and ensures that all relevant information is recorded. A respondent is not required to recall—perhaps inaccurately—an event after it has occurred; instead, the observation is instantaneous.

In many cases, direct observation is the only or the most straightforward form of data collection. The produce manager at a Jewel grocery store may periodically gather competitive price information at the Safeway and IGA stores in the neighborhood. In other situations, observation is the most economical technique. In a common observation study, a shopping center manager may observe the license plate (tag) numbers on cars in the parking lot. These data, along with automobile registration information, provide an inexpensive means of determining where customers live.

Certain data may be more quickly or easily obtained using direct observation than by other methods. Sex, race, and other respondent characteristics often are simply observed. Researchers investigating a diet product may use observation when selecting respondents in a shopping mall. Overweight people may be prescreened by observing pedestrians, thus eliminating a number of screening interviews.

**Response latency**
The amount of time necessary to make a choice between two alternatives; used as a measure of the strength of preference.

Recording the decision time necessary to make a choice between two alternatives is a relatively simple, unobtrusive task that can be done through direct observation. **Response latency** refers to the recording of choice time as a measure of the strength of the preference between alternatives.[5] It is hypothesized that the longer a decision maker takes to choose between two alternatives, the closer the two alternatives are in terms of preference.

■ Focus groups observed behind one-way mirrors are often videotaped. The ability to replay video records allows researchers to perform detailed analyses of physical actions.

# WHAT WENT RIGHT?

## Envirosell

Paco Underhill runs Envirosell, a New York consumer research company that conducts observation research. He became interested in using cameras to analyze the flow of human traffic through public places after hearing a lecture by urban geographer William Whyte. Envirosell's clients now include companies like Quaker Foods, Revlon, Hallmark Cards, and Bloomingdale's. The following is one reporter's account of what he learned about the value of observation research.

Underhill's research in retail settings led him to develop a body of observations he calls *aisle theory*. Among his seminal findings is something we'll call the derriere-brush factor, although he calls it by another name. At his offices in New York, he showed me a film clip shot with a time-lapse camera aimed at a tie display in a narrow, heavily traveled aisle of the Bloomingdale's department store in Manhattan. Such aisles, meant to carry shoppers from store entrances onward into the store, are known in the retail industry as "driveways" or "power aisles."

Shoppers entered and dispersed; most zipped right by a tie display. Underhill stopped the projector.

"Stand up," he commanded.

I stood.

"OK, you are standing at a counter. You are looking at ties. One of the most sensitive parts of your anatomy is your tail."

He began brushing my tail with his hand. Derriere-brush factor, he told me, "is simply the idea that the more likely you are to be brushed from the rear while you shop, the less likely you'll be converted from browser to buyer." In retail-speak the "conversion ratio" of that display or counter will be low.

Underhill's stop-action film showed how few people stopped to examine the ties in the rack. Traffic swept past the few browsers in disconcerting volume.

When Bloomingdale's chairman saw the video, he called the clerk in charge of that department and had him move the tie rack out of the driveway. Later, a Bloomingdale's vice president called Underhill and told him the chairman had personally had the sales tracked from that lone tie rack and discovered that within 6 weeks the increase had paid for Underhill's services. "That told me two things," Underhill said. "One, I wasn't charging enough, and two, the markup on ties was even more obscene than I thought."

"He picks up commonsense things," said Judith Owens, vice president, marketing, of the National Retail Federation in New York, who periodically invites Underhill to show his stop-action films to the federation's many members. She watched one film of an audio store that drew mostly teenage clientele, yet placed its racks of CDs so high the kids couldn't reach them. "You watch that happen, then you hear Paco say if you drop your display by 18 inches you'll increase your productivity. Everybody says, my God, I never thought of that."

He showed AT&T that almost 20 percent of the people who came into its Phone Center stores were under 10 years old, and how salespeople spent a lot of their time simply protecting expensive phone systems displayed too close to the ground. His films showed how most people who entered a Revco drugstore failed to pick up a shopping basket and thus were automatically limited to buying only what they could carry.

Early in 1991 the Woolworth Corporation asked Underhill to study several of its Champs Sports stores to help figure out which layouts and designs worked best. Woolworth was planning a huge national expansion of the chain. It knew that sales from the rear section of each store—the hard goods section displaying such items as weights and basketballs—lagged far behind sales from other sections, but it didn't know why.

John Shanley, director of research for Woolworth, remembers how Underhill's stop-action film instantly solved the mystery. During peak sales periods a line of customers would form from the cash register to the opposite wall of the store. "It literally prevented people from going from the front to the back," Shanley recalls. "They walked up to this line, turned and walked away." As a result, all of Champs' 500 stores now feature a checkout area (known in the industry as the "cash-wrap") designed so that lines form along an axis from front to back. "All of a sudden the sales in the back of the store picked up," Shanley recalled.

But, I asked, shouldn't that barrier effect have been obvious without Underhill's help? "The obvious," Shanley answered, "isn't always that apparent."

However, a quick decision is assumed to indicate that the psychological distance between alternatives is considerable. The response latency measure is gaining popularity now that computer-assisted data collection methods are becoming more common, because the computer can record decision times.

### ■ Errors Associated with Direct Observation

Although no interaction with the respondent occurs in direct observation, the method is not error free; the observer may record events subjectively. The same visual cues that influence the interplay between interviewer and respondent (e.g., the subject's age or sex) may come into play in some types of direct observation settings. For example, the observer may subjectively attribute a particular economic status or education background to the subject. A distortion of measurement resulting from the cognitive behavior or actions of the witnessing observer is called **observer bias.** A research project using observers to evaluate whether sales clerks are rude or courteous illustrates how fieldworkers may be required to rely on their own interpretations of people or situations during the observation process.

**Observer bias**
A distortion of measurement resulting from the cognitive behavior or actions of the witnessing observer.

If the observer does not record every detail that describes the persons, objects, and events in a given situation, accuracy may suffer. As a general guideline, the observer should record as much detail as possible. However, the pace of events, the observer's memory, the observer's writing speed, and other factors will limit the amount of detail that can be recorded.

Interpretation of observation data is another major problem. Facial expressions and other nonverbal communication may have several meanings. Does a smile always mean happiness? Does a person who is seated next to the company president necessarily enjoy high status?

### ■ Scientifically Contrived Observation

Most observation takes place in a natural setting. Intervention by the investigator to create an artificial environment to test a hypothesis is called **contrived observation.** This increases the frequency of occurrence of certain behavior patterns. For example, an airline passenger complaining about a meal or service from the flight attendant may actually be a researcher recording that person's reactions. If the situation were not contrived, the research time spent waiting and observing situations would expand considerably. A number of retailers use observers called *mystery shoppers* to come into a store and pretend to be interested in a particular product or service; after leaving the store, the "shopper" evaluates the salesperson's performance.

**Contrived observation**
Observation in which the investigator creates an artificial environment to test a hypothesis.

## ■ ETHICAL ISSUES IN THE OBSERVATION OF HUMANS

Observation methods introduce a number of ethical issues. Hidden observation raises the issue of the respondent's right to privacy. For example, a firm interested in acquiring information about how women put on their brassieres might persuade some retailers to place one-way mirrors in dressing rooms so that this behavior may be observed unobtrusively. Obviously, such a situation raises a moral question. Other observation methods, especially contrived observation, raise the possibility of deception of subjects.

Some people may see contrived observation as entrapment. To *entrap* means to deceive or trick into difficulty, which clearly is an abusive action. The difficulty is one of balancing values. If the researcher obtains permission, the subject may not act in a typical manner. Thus, the researcher must determine his or her own view of the ethics involved and decide whether the usefulness of the information is worth telling a "white lie."

## WHAT WENT WRONG?

### Doctors Should Examine Their Watches

When questioned in a survey, doctors answered that they spent about nine times more time informing patients than they actually did. The physicians who were directly questioned answered that they spent about 12 minutes giving information to the average patient, but videotapes of the doctor/patient encounters indicated the doctors spent only 1.3 minutes giving information. Further, the doctors underestimated how much the patients wanted to know about their illnesses. When doctors' answers were compared with patients' answers about how much patients wanted to know, doctors underestimated the amount of information two out of three times.

## ■ OBSERVATION OF PHYSICAL OBJECTS

**Physical-trace evidence**
A visible mark of some past occurrence.

Physical phenomena may be the subject of an observation study. **Physical-trace evidence** is a visible mark of some past occurrence. For example, the wear on a library book indirectly indicates which books are actually read (handled most often) when checked out. A classic example of physical-trace evidence in a nonprofit setting investigates erosion traces:

> The floor tiles around the hatching-chick exhibit at Chicago's Museum of Science and Industry must be replaced every six weeks. Tiles in other parts of the museum need not be replaced for years. The selective erosion of tiles, indexed by the replacement rate, is a measure of the relative popularity of exhibits.[6]

This research design indicates that a creative marketing researcher has many options available for determining the solution to a problem.

Physical-trace evidence is the focus of a scientific project at the University of Arizona in which aspiring archaeologists sift through modern garbage; they examine soggy cigarette butts, empty milk cartons, and half-eaten Big Macs. Investigation of Arizona household garbage has revealed many interesting findings. For example, in Hispanic households the most popular baby food is squash.[7] It accounts for 38 percent of the strained vegetables Hispanic babies consume. In contrast, in Anglo households peas account for 29 percent of all baby vegetables; squash ranks only above spinach, which is last. (Squash has been a dietary staple in Mexico and Central America for more than 9,000 years.)

Sorting through fast-food restaurants' garbage reveals that wasted food from chicken restaurants (not counting bones) accounts for 35 percent of all food bought. This is substantially greater than the 7 percent of wasted food at fast-food hamburger restaurants.

What is most interesting about the garbage project is the comparison between the results of surveys about food consumption and the contents of respondents' garbage; garbage does not lie.[8] The University of Arizona project indicates that people consistently underreport the quantity of junk food they eat and overreport the amount of fruit and diet soda they consume. Most dramatically, however, studies show that 40 to 60 percent underreport alcohol consumption.

Counting and recording physical inventories by retail or wholesale audits allows researchers to investigate brand sales on regional and national levels, market shares, seasonal purchasing patterns, and so on. Marketing research suppliers offer audit data at both the retail and wholesale levels.

An observer can record physical-trace data to discover things a respondent could not recall accurately. For example, actually measuring the number of ounces of a liquid bleach used during a test provides a precise physical-trace answer without relying on the respondent's memory. The accuracy of respondents' memories is not a problem for the firm that conducts a pantry audit. The *pantry audit* requires an inventory of the brands, quantities, and package sizes in a consumer's home rather than responses from individuals. The problem of untruthfulness or some other form of response bias is avoided. For example, the pantry audit prevents the possible problem of respondents erroneously claiming to have prestige brands in their cabinets. However, gaining permission to physically check consumers' pantries is not easy, and the fieldwork is expensive. Further, the brand in the pantry may not reflect the brand purchased most often if it was substituted because of a cents-off coupon, an out-of-stock condition, or another reason.

## ■ CONTENT ANALYSIS

**Content analysis**
The systematic observation and quantitative description of the manifest content of communication.

**Content analysis** obtains data by observing and analyzing the contents or messages of advertisements, newspaper articles, television programs, Web sites, and the like. It involves analysis as well as observation, systematically analyzing people's communications to identify the specific information contents and other characteristics of their messages. Content analysis studies the message itself; it involves the design of a systematic observation and recording procedure for quantitative description of the manifest content of communication. This technique measures the extent of emphasis on or omission of a given analytical category. For example, the content of advertisements might be investigated to evaluate their use of words, themes, characters, or space and time relationships. The frequency of appearance of African Americans, women, or other minorities in mass media has been a topic of content analysis.

A content analysis may ask questions such as whether some advertisers use certain types of themes, appeals, claims, or deceptive practices more than others or whether recent consumer-oriented actions by the Federal Trade Commission have influenced the contents of advertising. A cable television programmer might do a content analysis of network programming to evaluate its competition. For example, every year researchers analyze the Super Bowl to see how much of the visual material is live-action play and how much is replay or how many shots focus on the cheerleaders and how many on spectators. The information content of television commercials directed at children can be investigated, as can company images portrayed in advertising and numerous other topics.[9]

Study of the content of communications is more sophisticated than simply counting the items; it requires a system of analysis to secure relevant data.

## ■ MECHANICAL OBSERVATION

In many situations, the primary—and sometimes only—means of observation is mechanical rather than human. Video cameras, traffic counters, and other machines help observe and record behavior. Some unusual observation studies have used motion picture cameras and time-lapse photography. An early application of this observation technique photographed train passengers and determined their levels of comfort by observing how they sat and moved in their seats. Another time-lapse study filmed traffic flows in an urban square and resulted in a redesign of the streets. Similar techniques may help managers design store layouts and resolve problems dealing with people or objects moving through spaces over time.

### ■ Television Monitoring

Perhaps the best-known marketing research project involving mechanical observation and computerized data collection is the A. C. Nielsen Television Index (NTI), the system for

**Television monitoring**
Computerized mechanical observation used to obtain television ratings.

estimating national television audiences, or **television monitoring.** The NTI uses a consumer panel and mechanical observation to obtain ratings for television programs. More than 4,000 households, scientifically selected to be representative of the U.S. population, have agreed to become members of the panel and have meters placed in their homes. For years A. C. Nielsen Company was criticized because its audimeter passively recorded only which shows were playing on TV sets. Because it indicated only whether a set was on a particular channel or turned off, advertisers did not know whether the entire family or just one individual (or perhaps no one) was watching. The diary system, in which family members logged in their viewing habits, was used to supplement the passive meter. However, the diary system had problems too. It worked well during the network-only television era, but recording viewing activity in a diary became increasingly complex in an age of cable television systems with dozens of channels.

Many experts also believe diaries exhibit a so-called *halo bias.* When viewers fill out diaries two or three days after watching television, they tend to remember only their favorite shows and forget others. As a result, top-rated programs such as *Star Trek: Voyager* could receive disproportionately high audience estimates.

Nielsen set out to make improvements. After spending years developing and testing, Nielsen developed a system that promised to be an improvement because information about who was watching which programs would be built into the measuring system.

The People Meter, a microwave-based, computerized television rating system, was designed to use state-of-the-art electronic measuring to replace passive meters and the 30-year-old diary system. When the panel household's television set is turned on, a question mark appears on the screen to remind viewers to indicate who is watching. The viewer then uses a hand-held electronic device that resembles a television remote control to record who is watching. A device attached to the television automatically sends the viewer's age and sex and the programs being watched over telephone lines to Nielsen's computers. People Meters measure a show's ratings and provide demographic profiles overnight.

Critics of the People Meter argue that subjects in Nielsen's panel grow bored over time and do not always record when they begin or stop watching television. Nielsen Media Research is now working on a unique technology that will allow its People Meters to scan the room, recognize each family member by his or her facial characteristics, and record when the person enters or leaves the room.

## ■ Internet Monitoring

PC-Meter LP is a marketing research company that tracks which sites on the World Wide Web are most popular. The company installs a special tracking program on the personal computers of a sample of computer users who volunteer to participate in the research effort. Many organizations with Web sites consisting of multiple pages track how many users visit each page on the Web site. They also use "cookies" (see Chapter 2) to track the paths visitors follow.

## ■ Scanner-Based Research

Lasers performing optical character recognition and bar code technology such as the Universal Product Code (UPC) have accelerated the use of mechanical observation in marketing research. Several syndicated services offer secondary data about product category movement generated from retail stores using scanner technology.

**Scanner-based consumer panel**
A type of consumer panel in which the participants' purchasing habits are recorded with a laser scanner rather than a purchase diary.

This technology now allows researchers to investigate more demographically or promotionally specific questions. For example, scanner research has investigated the different ways consumers respond to price promotions and how those differences affect a promotion's profitability. One primary means of implementing this type of research is through the establishment of a **scanner-based consumer panel** to replace consumer purchase diaries.

In a typical scanner panel, each household is assigned a bar-coded card that members present to the clerk at the register. The household's code number is coupled with the purchase information recorded by the scanner. Further, as with other consumer panels, background information about the household obtained through answers to a battery of demographic and psychographic survey questions also can be coupled with the household code number.

Aggregate data, such as actual store movement as measured by scanners, will also be available. These data parallel the results of a standard mail diary panel, with some important improvements:

1. The data measure observed (actual) purchase behavior versus reported behavior (recorded later in a diary).
2. Substituting mechanical for human recordkeeping improves accuracy.
3. Measures are unobtrusive, eliminating interviewing and possible respondent (social desirability) bias as in a mail diary.
4. More extensive purchase data can be collected because all UPC categories are measured. In a mail diary, respondents could not reliably record all items purchased. Because all UPC-coded items are measured in the panel, users can investigate many product categories to determine loyalty, switching rates, and so on for their own brands as well as for other companies' products and to locate product categories for possible market entry.
5. The data collected from computerized checkout scanners can be combined with data about advertising, price changes, and sales promotions. Researchers can scrutinize them with powerful analytical software available from the scanner data providers.

Scanner data can show a marketer week by week how a product is doing, even in a single store, and track sales against local ads or promotions. Further, several organizations, such as Information Resources Inc.'s Behavior Scan System, have developed scanner panels and expanded them into electronic test market systems. These are discussed in greater detail in *Chapter 9*.

**At-home scanning system**
A system whereby consumer panelists after taking home the products perform their own scanning using hand-held wands that read UPC symbols.

Advances in bar code technology have led to **at-home scanning systems** that use hand-held wands to read UPC symbols. Consumer panelists perform their own scanning after they have taken home the products. This advance makes it possible to investigate purchases made at hardware stores, department stores, and other retailers that do not have in-store scanning equipment.

## ■ Measuring Physiological Reactions

Marketing researchers have used a number of other mechanical devices to evaluate consumers' physical and physiological reactions to advertising copy, packaging, and other stimuli. Researchers use such means when they believe consumers are unaware of their actual reactions to stimuli such as advertising or consumers will not provide honest responses. Four major categories of mechanical devices are used to measure physiological reactions: (1) eye-tracking monitors, (2) pupilometers, (3) psychogalvanometers, and (4) voice pitch analyzers.

A magazine or newspaper advertiser may wish to grab readers' attention with a visual scene and then direct it to a package or coupon. Eye-tracking equipment records how the subject reads the ad or views a TV commercial and how much time is spent looking at various parts of the stimulus.

**Eye-tracking monitor**
A mechanical device used to observe eye movements. Some eye monitors use infrared light beams to measure unconscious eye movements.

In physiological terms, the gaze movements of a viewer's eye are measured with an **eye-tracking monitor,** which measures unconscious eye movements. Originally developed to measure astronauts' eye fatigue, this device tracks eye movements through invisible infrared light beams that lock into the subject's eyes. The light reflects off the eye, and eye movement data are recorded while another tiny video camera monitors which magazine page is being perused. The data are analyzed by computer to determine which components in an ad (or other stimuli) were seen and which were overlooked.

■ The eye-tracking system from Perception Research Services, the leader in eye-tracking equipment, projects 35mm slides and pinpoints where the individual is looking. The ad shown here illustrates how the eye-tracking system monitors how individuals react to a magazine advertisement. The time the viewer spends on the communications elements in an ad that are directly product related is important information to the advertiser.

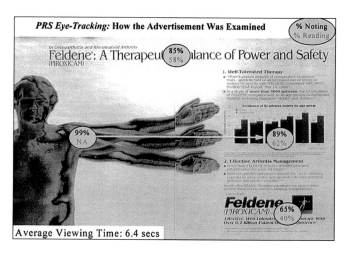

**PRS Eye-Tracking: How the Advertisement Was Examined**

**% Noting**
**% Reading**

Average Viewing Time: 6.4 secs

Modern eye-tracking systems need not keep a viewer's head in a stationary position. Measuring rough television commercials, especially animations, with the eye-tracking system helps advertisers emphasize selling points.

The remaining physiological observation techniques are based on a common principle:

Physiological research depends on the fact that adrenalin is produced when the body is aroused. When adrenalin goes to work, the heart beats faster and more strongly, and even enlarges. Blood flows to the extremities and increases capillary dilation at the fingertips and earlobes. Skin temperature increases, hair follicles stand up, skin pores emit perspiration, and the electrical conductivity of skin surfaces is affected. Eye pupils dilate, electrical waves in the brain increase in frequency, breathing is faster and deeper, and the chemical composition of expired air is altered. This process offers a choice of about 50 different measures—the question of which measure to use is to some extent irrelevant since they are all measuring arousal.[10]

**Pupilometer**
A mechanical device used to observe and record changes in the diameter of a subject's pupils.

The **pupilometer** observes and records changes in the diameter of a subject's pupils. A subject is instructed to look at a screen on which an advertisement or other stimulus is projected. Holding constant the brightness and distance of the stimulus from the subject's eyes, changes in pupil size may be interpreted as changes in cognitive activity that result from the stimulus rather than eye dilation and constriction from light intensity, distance from the object, or other physiological reactions to the conditions of observation. This method of research is based on the assumption that increased pupil size reflects a strong attitude toward the product or interest in advertisements.

**Psychogalvanometer**
A device that measures galvanic skin response, a measure of involuntary changes in the electrical resistance of the skin.

The **psychogalvanometer** measures galvanic skin response (GSR), a measure of involuntary changes in the electrical resistance of the skin. This device uses the assumption that physiological changes, such as increased perspiration, accompany emotional reactions to advertisements, packages, and slogans. Excitement increases the body's perspiration rate, which increases the electrical resistance of the skin. The test is an indicator of emotional arousal or tension.

**Voice pitch analysis**
A physiological measurement technique that records abnormal frequencies in the voice that supposedly reflect emotional reactions to various stimuli.

**Voice pitch analysis** is a relatively new physiological measurement technique. Emotional reactions are measured through physiological changes in a person's voice. Abnormal frequencies in the voice, caused by changes in the autonomic nervous system, are measured with sophisticated, audio-adapted computer equipment. Computerized analysis compares the respondent's voice pitch during warm-up conversations (normal range) with verbal response to questions about his or her evaluative reaction to television commercials or other stimuli. This technique, unlike other physiological devices, does not require the researcher to surround subjects with mazes of wires or equipment.

All of these devices assume physiological reactions are associated with persuasiveness or predict some cognitive response. This has not yet been clearly demonstrated, however. No strong theoretical evidence supports the argument that a physiological change is a valid measure of future sales, attitude change, or emotional response. Another major problem with physiological research involves the *calibration,* or sensitivity, of measuring devices. Identifying arousal is one thing, but precisely measuring *levels* of arousal is another. In addition, most of these devices are expensive. However, as a prominent researcher points out, physiological measurement is coincidental: "Physiological measurement isn't an exit interview. It's not dependent on what was remembered later on. It's a live blood, sweat, and tears, moment-by-moment response, synchronous with the stimulus."[11]

Each of these mechanical devices has another limitation in that the subjects are usually placed in artificial settings (watching television in the laboratory rather than at home) and know they are being observed.[12]

## ■ SUMMARY

Observation is a powerful tool for the marketing researcher. Scientific observation is the systematic process of recording the behavioral patterns of people, objects, and occurrences without questioning or otherwise communicating with them. A wide variety of information about the behavior of people and objects can be observed. Seven kinds of content are observable: physical actions, verbal behavior, expressive behavior, spatial relations and locations, temporal patterns, physical objects, and verbal and pictorial records. Thus, both verbal and nonverbal messages may be observed.

A major disadvantage of the observation technique is that cognitive phenomena such as attitudes, motivations, expectations, intentions, and preferences are not observable. Further, only overt behavior of short duration can be observed. Nevertheless, many types of data can be obtained more accurately through direct observation than by questioning respondents. Observation is the most direct, and sometimes the only, method for collecting certain data.

Marketing researchers employ both human observers and machines designed for specific observation tasks. Human observation is commonly used when the situation or behavior to be recorded is not easily predictable in advance of the research. Mechanical observation can be used when the situation or behavior to be recorded is routine, repetitive, or programmatic. Human or mechanical observation may be unobtrusive. Human observation carries the possibility of subjective error even though the observer does not interact with the respondent.

Observation sometimes can be contrived by creating the situations to be observed. This can reduce the time and expense of obtaining reactions to certain circumstances. Contrived observation, hidden observation, and other observation research designs that might use deception often raise ethical concerns about subjects' right to privacy and right to be informed.

Physical-trace evidence serves as a visible record of past events. Content analysis obtains data by observing and analyzing the contents of messages in written and/or spoken communications. Content analysis can determine the information content of phenomena. Mechanical observation uses a variety of devices to record behavior directly. Mechanical observation takes many forms. National television audience ratings are based on mechanical observation and computerized data collection. Scanner-based research is growing in popularity because of increased use of laser scanners in retail stores. Many syndicated services offer secondary data collected through scanner systems. Physiological reactions, such as arousal or eye movement patterns, may be observed using a number of mechanical devices.

## ■ Key Terms and Concepts

| | |
|---|---|
| Observation | Content analysis |
| Visible observation | Television monitoring |
| Hidden observation | Scanner-based consumer panel |
| Direct observation | At-home scanning system |
| Response latency | Eye-tracking monitor |
| Observer bias | Pupilometer |
| Contrived observation | Psychogalvanometer |
| Physical-trace evidence | Voice pitch analysis |

## ■ Questions

1. Yogi Berra, former New York Yankee catcher, said, "You can observe a lot just by watching." How does this statement fit in with the definition of scientific observation?
2. What are the advantages and disadvantages of observation studies relative to surveys?
3. Under what conditions are observation studies most appropriate?
4. Suggest some new uses for observation studies. Be creative!
5. A multinational fast-food corporation plans to locate a restaurant in La Paz, Bolivia. Secondary data for this city are outdated. How might you determine the location using observation?
6. Discuss how an observation study might be combined with a personal interview.

7. The lost-letter technique has been used to predict voting behavior. Letters addressed to various political groups are spread throughout a city. The "respondent" finds an envelope, reads the address of a group supporting (or opposing) a candidate, and mails back (or throws away) the envelope. It is assumed that the respondent's action indicates a favorable (or unfavorable) attitude toward the organization. Would this technique be appropriate in marketing research?
8. Outline a research design using observation for each of the following situations:
   (a) A bank wishes to collect data on the number of customer services and the frequency of customer use of these services.
   (b) A state government wishes to determine the driving public's use of seat belts.
   (c) A researcher wishes to know how many women have been featured on *Time* covers over the years.
   (d) A fast-food franchise wishes to determine how long a customer entering a store has to wait for his or her order.
   (e) A magazine publisher wishes to determine exactly what people see and what they pass over while reading one of its magazines.
   (f) A food manufacturer wishes to determine how people use snack foods in their homes.
   (g) An overnight package delivery service wishes to observe delivery workers beginning at the point where they stop the truck, continuing to the point where they deliver the package, and finally at the point where they return to the truck.
9. Watch the nightly news on a major network for one week. Observe how much time reporters spend on national news, commercials, and other activity. (Hint: Think carefully about how you will record the contents of the programs.)
10. Comment on the ethics of the following situations:
    (a) During the course of telephone calls to investors, a stockbroker records their voices when they are answering sensitive investment questions and then conducts a voice pitch analysis. The respondents do not know their voices are being recorded.

(b) A researcher plans to invite consumers to be test users in a simulated kitchen located in a shopping mall and to videotape their reactions to a new microwave dinner from behind a one-way mirror.

(c) A marketing researcher arranges to purchase trash from the headquarters of a major competitor. The purpose is to sift through discarded documents to determine the company's strategic plans.

## EXPLORING THE INTERNET

The University of Arizona Department of Anthropology houses the Bureau of Applied Research in Anthropology (BARA). The garbage project described in the chapter is one of the bureau's research activities. Go to the University of Arizona's home page at http://www.arizona.edu and then go to the anthropology department in the College of Social and Behavioral Sciences. Then navigate to the BARA's garbage project. What information is available?

---

## CASE 8.1    Pretesting Company[13]

Basically it looks like a desk lamp with a chunky smoked-glass body. In fact, it is Lee Weinblatt's People Reader, a device designed to surreptitiously monitor the way people react to magazine advertising. Behind the smoked glass are two tiny, remote-controlled video cameras, one that tracks eye movements and another that monitors which page is being perused. In a nearby office, technicians measure each dismissive glance and longing gaze.

Will a high school senior unconsciously dwell on an Air Force recruitment ad featuring computer screens that look like video games? Will a middle-aged man linger over an automobile ad featuring leggy female models? The People Reader was intended to answer questions like these for companies that spend millions of dollars on advertising and, in the past, have had to depend on the accuracy of a test subject's memory.

Mr. Weinblatt is founder of the Pretesting Company in Englewood, N.J., that has become the leader in sleight-of-hand advertising research. He has developed an extensive bag of tricks, some of them incorporating technology originally developed for espionage. The People Reader is one; another is a mock car radio that plays prerecorded material and measures the speed with which a driver silences a commercial. There is also a television system that measures the tendency of viewers armed with remote-control devices to "zap" a particular commercial and a computer-simulated supermarket to measure the allure of a new package. Mr. Weinblatt has hidden video cameras in a fake bar of Ivory soap, a box of cereal ("old hat," he says now), and in a ceiling sprinkler.

The unifying theme of Mr. Weinblatt's technology is eliciting responses consumers may not be aware of. Typically, people being tested are given only a limited idea—and often the wrong one—about what is actually being measured.

Since starting his company in 1985, Mr. Weinblatt has acquired an impressive list of clients, including Ralston Purina, RJR Nabisco's Planter's peanuts, S. C. Johnson's Raid insecticide, *Sports Illustrated,* and *The New Yorker.* Although Pretesting remains small, with revenues of $5.5 million, clients say Mr. Weinblatt offers them insights unlike those generated by any other advertising researchers. "I've recommended his tests many times," said Sue Le Barron, a project manager for pet food marketing research at Ralston Purina.

Traditionally, advertising research has been based on fairly overt approaches. To test a proposed television ad, for example, companies arrange to transmit the commercials to television sets of test subjects during normal programming and then interview them the next day on their ability to remember the ad and on their reactions. Similarly, the traditional method of pretesting a new package or design is to expose it to a "focus group" of consumers who examine and react to it. Mr. Weinblatt argues that such techniques provide at best a murky picture, often failing to measure the impact of subliminal messages or, in the case of focus groups, prompting judgments in situations that don't mirror real life.

"Diagnostical research can be very useful for understanding what the problem is with a product, but it can never tell you what people are going to do in the real world," said Mr. Weinblatt. "Do people read *Newsweek* from the front or the back? How do you time the sequence of television ads? How does print stack up against TV? The questions have been piling up."

Mr. Weinblatt has been tinkering with attention-measuring devices since 1971. Armed with a master's degree in industrial psychology (and, later, in photography), he started out with the research subsidiary of the Interpublic Group of Companies Inc., which owns several major advertising agencies.

At the time, many advertising researchers were experimenting with "pupilmetrics," the measurement of pupil dilation, by filming people who were strapped into chairs and whose heads were anchored into wax molds. Mr. Weinblatt designed equipment that was less intrusive. His first assignment came from Philip Morris, which he said wanted to find the least noticeable place to mount warning labels required by the Surgeon General on a pack of cigarettes. "We found that it didn't make any difference," said Mr. Weinblatt. "Smokers don't want to see."

In 1976, Mr. Weinblatt started Telcom Research, a manufacturer of portable eye movement recorders, which he sold in 1982, just before it was about to go bankrupt. But he continued inventing increasingly unobtrusive measurement devices, and founded the Pretesting Company in 1985. Today he holds 28 patents.

To measure the chances that consumers will be attracted to a new package on crowded supermarket shelves, Mr. Weinblatt developed a computer-simulated shopping spree. Researchers evaluating a new line of dog food, for example, begin by recreating a supermarket rack in the dog food section that contains the new package. They then photograph the shelf as a whole and take close-ups of each quadrant of the shelf. This material is mixed in with similar sequences depicting the store entrance and several other supermarket sections.

People being tested are then told to "walk" through the store by reviewing slides of these images on a screen. Pressing buttons on a controller, they can move forward or backward between shelves and move in for closeups. At each section they are asked to pick out what, if anything, they would like to buy. Their answers, however, constitute only a small part of the test. The key measurements, according to Mr. Weinblatt, are based on the way they move through the slides. Unknown to the customers, a computer linked to the controller logs the amount of time spent at each picture and provides an instant tabulation of how long a person lingered at the dog food rack and at a particular part of it containing the new product. That data, in turn, can be compared with data for the rest of the supermarket and for competing products.

Mr. Weinblatt concedes there have been instances in which he incorrectly predicted that a commercial would fail. Nevertheless, he argues, his measurements offer crucial information in a world of cluttered store shelves, where nine out of ten new products fail. "The typical person spends 22 minutes shopping in a supermarket that contains 18,000 products," said Mr. Weinblatt. "What we're saying is, before you bet all that money on a new product, let's do the ideal and see if people are even going to notice it."

### Question

1. Evaluate each observation technique used by the Pretesting Company. What possible applications might each technique have?

### ■ Endnotes

[1] Claire Selltiz, Lawrence S. Wrightsman, and Stuart W. Cook, *Research Methods in Social Relations* (New York: Holt, Rinehart and Winston, 1976), p. 251.

[2] E. J. Webb, Donald T. Campbell, Richard D. Schwartz, and Lee Sechrest, *Unobtrusive Measures: Nonreactive Research in the Social Sciences* (Chicago: Rand McNally, 1971).

[3] Glen L. Urban and John R. Hauser, *Design and Marketing of New Products* (Englewood Cliffs, N.J.: Prentice-Hall, 1980), p. 129.

[4] Justin Martin, "Ignore Your Customer," *Fortune,* May 1, 1995, p. 126.

[5] Tyzoon T. Tyebjee, "Response Latency: A New Measure for Scaling Behavior and Preferences," *Journal of Marketing Research,* February 1979, pp. 96–101.

[6] Webb et al., *Unobtrusive Measures.*

[7] William Rathje and Cullen Murphy, "Garbage Demographics," *American Demographics,* May 1992, pp. 50–53.

[8] Witold Rybczynski, "We Are What We Throw Away," *New York Times Book Review,* July 5, 1992, pp. 5–6.

[9] For an excellent discussion of the inherent problems of content analysis, see Camille P. Schuster, "Content Analysis, Interactive Data, and Reliability" (Paper presented at the American Marketing Association Conference on Research Methods and Causal Modeling, February 27–March 2, 1983).

[10] "Live, Simultaneous Study of Stimulus, Response Is Physiological Measurement's Great Virtue," *Marketing News,* May 15, 1981, pp. 1, 20.

[11]Herbert B. Krugman's statement as quoted in "Live, Simultaneous Study of Stimulus," p. 1.

[12]For an expanded discussion of the physiological research, see James A. Muncy, "Physiological Responses of Consumer Emotions: Theory, Methods, and Implications for Consumer Research" (Paper presented at the American Marketing Association Marketing Educators' Conference, 1987).

[13]Edmund L. Andrews, "Delving into the Consumer Unconscious," *New York Times,* July 22, 1990, p. F-9. Copyright © 1990 by The New York Times Company.

# CHAPTER

## 9

# EXPERIMENTAL RESEARCH

**WHAT YOU WILL LEARN IN THIS CHAPTER:**

To define *experimentation* and discuss the requirements necessary to make a true experiment.

To understand the terminology of experimentation.

To discuss the factors that influence the choice and manipulation of the independent variables.

To evaluate the factors that influence the selection and measurement of the dependent variables.

To understand how to select and assign test units.

To compare and contrast the two basic types of experimental error.

To give examples of demand characteristics.

To discuss how to control extraneous variables in experimental situations.

To discuss some ethical issues in experimentation.

To compare and contrast field and laboratory experiments.

To distinguish between internal and external validity.

To list the six major factors that threaten internal validity and provide examples of each.

To outline the various quasi-experimental designs and alternative, better experimental designs.

To understand that test marketing provides an opportunity to experiment with new marketing strategies under realistic market conditions.

To identify what factors to consider in test market selection.

**D**oes the size of a package influence a person to increase or decrease consumption? A series of tightly controlled laboratory experiments found evidence that larger packages encourage consumers to increase the amount of the product they use. The hypothesis for one experiment was that the larger a package's size, the more of it one will use on a given occasion.[1] The experiment required altering package size while holding the total supply of the product constant. The procedure went as follows.

The researchers recruited 98 adult women through local Parent-Teacher Associations (PTAs), and six dollars were donated to the respective organization for each participant. Two different products—Crisco Oil and Creamette Spaghetti—in two different sizes were selected for the study. In both cases, the larger package held twice as much of the product as the smaller package. The supply for each brand was held constant by leaving the smaller package full and using only half of the larger package. The volume of each product was determined by the package sizes in which it was sold.

Each subject was randomly assigned to use either a relatively small or a relatively large package, each holding identical volumes of the product. Two products were used for generalizability, and the pattern of results was expected to be similar for both products.

In individual meetings, each subject was told that researchers were collecting some basic "home economics–related" information about two different types of products. The subject was then led to one of four isolated cubicles containing either a large or a small package of one of the two products. The research assistant assigned to each cubicle did not know the purpose of the study. When the subject arrived, the research assistant read a scenario involving the use of the product (for Crisco Oil, "You are frying a chicken dinner for yourself and another adult," and for Creamette Spaghetti, "You are making spaghetti for yourself and another adult"). The subject was asked to show how much of the product she would use in this situation and how much money that use of the product would entail. After the subject left the cubicle, a researcher measured the amount the subject intended to use. The procedure was repeated for all subjects.

The dependent measure was the volume of the product each subject indicated she would use. Subjects indicated their use of oil by pouring it into a frying pan; they indicated their use of spaghetti by placing it in a large (dry) pot. The volume of oil they used was measured by pouring the liquid into a narrow beaker. The volume of spaghetti was measured by holding the strands together and measuring the circumference with a finely graduated tape measure; this was later translated to an approximation of an individual count.

As was hypothesized, manipulating the package size while holding the supply of each product constant indicated that increases in a package's size were associated with increases in product usage.

Related experiments also show that consumers will use more from a full container than from a half-empty one. Even when a package recommends an amount to use, as household cleaners do, research shows consumers ignore such instructions 70 percent of the time.[2]

This chapter explores the use of experimentation in marketing.

## ■ THE NATURE OF EXPERIMENTS

Most students are familiar with the concept of experimentation in the physical sciences. When the term *experiment* is mentioned, we typically think of a chemist surrounded by bubbling test tubes and Bunsen burners. Behavioral and physical scientists have been far ahead of marketing researchers in the use of experimentation. Nevertheless, the purpose of experimental research is the same.

Experimental research allows the investigator to control the research situation so that causal relationships among variables may be evaluated. The standard marketing experimenter manipulates a single variable in an investigation and holds constant all other relevant, extraneous variables. Events may be controlled in an experiment to a degree not possible in a survey.

The researcher's goal in conducting an experiment is to determine whether the experimental treatment is the cause of the effect being measured. If a new marketing strategy (for example, new advertising) is used in a test market and sales subsequently increase in that market but not in markets where the new strategy is not employed, the experimenter can feel confident that the new strategy caused the increase in sales.

Experiments differ from other research methods in the degree of control over the research situation. In an **experiment,** one variable (the *independent variable*) is manipulated and its effect on another variable (the *dependent variable*) is measured while all other variables that may confound the relationship are eliminated or controlled. The experimenter either creates an artificial situation or deliberately manipulates the given situation.

One famous marketing experiment investigated the influence of brand name identification on consumers' taste perceptions. The experimenter manipulated whether consumers

**Experiment**
A research investigation in which conditions are controlled so that an independent variable(s) can be manipulated to test a hypothesis about a dependent variable. Allows evaluation of causal relationships among variables while all other variables are eliminated or controlled.

tasted beer in labeled or unlabeled bottles. One week respondents were given a six-pack containing bottles labeled with tags bearing only letters. The following week, respondents received another six-pack with brand labels. Thus, respondents never made an actual purchase from a store but drank the beer at home at their leisure. The experimenter measured reactions to the beers after each tasting. The beer itself was the same in each case, so differences in taste perception were attributed to label (brand) influence. This example illustrates that once an experimenter manipulates the independent variable, changes in the dependent variable are measured. The essence of an experiment is to do something to an individual and observe the reaction under conditions that allow his or her performance to be measured against a known baseline.

## ■ BASIC ISSUES IN EXPERIMENTAL DESIGN

Decisions must be made about several basic elements of an experiment. These issues are (1) manipulation of the independent variable, (2) selection and measurement of the dependent variable, (3) selection and assignment of subjects, and (4) control over extraneous variables.

### ■ Manipulation of the Independent Variable

**Independent variable**
In an experimental design, the variable that can be manipulated, or altered, independently of any other variable.

**Experimental treatments**
Alternative manipulations of the independent variable being investigated.

The experimenter has some degree of control over the **independent variable.** The variable is independent because the experimenter can manipulate, or alter, its value to whatever he or she wishes it to be independently of any other variable. The independent variable is hypothesized to be the causal influence.

**Experimental treatments** are the alternative manipulations of the independent variable being investigated. For example, prices of $1.29, $1.69, and $1.99 might be the treatments in a pricing experiment. Price changes, advertising strategy changes, taste formulation, and so on are typical treatments.

In marketing research, the independent variable often is a categorical or classificatory variable that represents some classifiable or qualitative aspect of marketing strategy. To determine the effects of point-of-purchase displays, the experimental treatments that represent the independent variable are themselves the varying displays. Alternative advertising copy is another example of a categorical or classificatory variable. In other situations, the independent variable is a continuous variable. The researcher must select the appropriate levels of that variable as experimental treatments. For example, the number of dollars that can be spent on advertising may be any number of different values.

**Experimental group**
The group of subjects exposed to the experimental treatment.

**Control group**
The group of subjects exposed to the control condition, that is, not exposed to the experimental treatment.

**Experimental and Control Groups**  In the simplest type of experiment, only two values of the independent variable are manipulated. Consider an experiment measuring the influence of advertising on sales. In the experimental condition (treatment administered to the **experimental group**), the advertising budget may be at $200,000. In the control condition (treatment administered to the **control group**), advertising may remain at zero or without change. By holding conditions constant in the control group, the researcher controls for potential sources of error in the experiment. Sales (the dependent variable) in the two treatment groups are compared at the end of the experiment to determine whether the level of advertising (the independent variable) had any effect.

**Several Experimental Treatment Levels**  The advertising/sales experiment using one experimental and one control group may not tell the advertiser everything he or she wishes to know about the advertising-sales relationship. If the advertiser wished to understand the functional nature of the relationship between sales and advertising at several treatment levels, additional experimental groups with advertising expenditures of $200,000, $500,000, and $1 million might be studied. This type of design would allow the experimenter to get a better idea of an optimal advertising budget.

**More Than One Independent Variable**    It is possible to assess the effects of more than one independent variable. In basic experimental designs, a single independent variable is manipulated to observe its effect on another single dependent variable. However, we know that complex marketing-dependent variables such as sales, product usage, and brand preference are influenced by several factors. The simultaneous change in independent variables such as price and advertising may have a greater influence on sales than either variable changed alone. *Factorial experimental designs* are more sophisticated than basic experimental designs; they allow for an investigation of the interaction of two or more independent variables. Whether the experiment is basic or factorial, the purpose of marketing research experimentation is to measure and compare the effects of experimental treatments on the dependent variable.

### ■ Selection and Measurement of the Dependent Variable

**Dependent variable**
The criterion by which the results of an experiment are judged; a variable expected to be dependent on the experimenter's manipulation.

The **dependent variable** is so called because its value is expected to be dependent on the experimenter's manipulation; it is the criterion, or standard, by which the results are judged. Changes in the dependent variable are presumed to be a consequence of changes in the independent variable.

Selection of the dependent variable is a crucial decision in the design of an experiment. If we introduce a new pink grapefruit tea mix in a test market experiment, sales volume is most likely to be the dependent variable. However, if we are experimenting with different forms of advertising copy appeals, defining the dependent variable may be more difficult. For example, measures of advertising awareness, recall, changes in brand preference, or sales might be used as the dependent variable depending on the purposes of the ads. In the package size experiment dealing with Crisco Oil, the dependent variable was the volume of oil that would be used. However, the dependent variable might have been the consumer's estimate of the total cost of the meal or attitude toward using a given amount of oil (a cognitive variable). Often the dependent-variable selection process, like the problem definition process, is considered less carefully than it should be. The experimenter's choice of a dependent variable determines what type of answer is given to the research question.

In a test market, the time period needed for the effects to become evident should be considered in choosing the dependent variable. Sales may be measured several months after the experiment to determine if any carryover effects occurred. Changes that are relatively permanent or longer lasting than changes generated only during the period of the experiment should be considered; repeat purchase behavior may be important.

Consumers may try a "loser" once, but they may not rebuy. The introduction of the original Crystal Pepsi illustrates the need to think beyond consumers' initial reactions. When Crystal Pepsi was introduced, it received high initial trial but experienced difficulty in repeat purchases. The brand never achieved high repeat sales within a sufficiently large market segment. Brand awareness, trial purchase, and repeat purchase are all possible dependent variables in an experiment. The dependent variable therefore should be considered carefully. Thorough problem definition will help the researcher select the most important dependent variable(s).

### ■ Selection and Assignment of Test Units

**Test unit**
An entity whose responses to experimental treatments are being observed or measured.

**Test units** are the subjects, or entities, whose responses to the experimental treatment are measured or observed. Individuals, organizational units, sales territories, or other entities may be the test units. People are the most common test units in most marketing and consumer behavior experiments. In our unit pricing example, supermarkets were the test units.

**Sample Selection and Random Sampling Errors** As in other forms of marketing research, random sampling errors and sample selection errors may occur in experimentation. For example, experiments sometimes go awry even when a geographic area is specially chosen for a particular investigation. A case in point was the experimental testing of a new lubricant for outboard motors by Dow Chemical Company. The lubricant was tested in Florida and Michigan. Florida was chosen because researchers thought a warm-weather state, in which the product would have to stand up under continuous use, would prove the most demanding test. In Florida, the lubricant was a success. In Michigan, however, the story was quite different. Although the lubricant sold well and worked well during the summer, the following spring Dow discovered that in the colder northern climate it had congealed, allowing the outboard motors, idle all winter, to rust. The rusting problem never came to light in Florida, where the motors were in year-round use. Thus, some sample selection error may result from the procedure used to assign subjects or test units to either the experimental or the control group.

**Random sampling error**
An error that occurs because of chance; statistical fluctuations in which repetitions of the basic experiment sometimes favor one experimental condition and sometimes the other.

**Random sampling error** may occur if repetitions of the basic experiment sometimes favor one experimental condition and sometimes the other on a chance basis. An experiment dealing with charcoal briquets may require that the people in both the experimental and control groups be identical with regard to incidence of product usage and barbecuing habits. However, if subjects are randomly assigned to conditions without knowledge of their product usage, errors resulting from differences in that usage will be random sampling errors.

Suppose a potato chip manufacturer wishes to experiment with new advertising appeals and wants to have the groups identical with respect to advertising awareness, media exposure, and so on. The experimenter must decide how to place subjects in each treatment group and which group should receive treatment. Researchers generally agree that the random assignment of participants to groups and experimental treatments to groups is the best procedure.

**Randomization**
A procedure in which the assignment of subjects and treatments to groups is based on chance.

**Randomization** **Randomization,** the random assignment of subjects and treatments to groups, is one device for equally distributing or scattering the effects of extraneous variables to all conditions. Thus, the chance of unknown nuisance effects piling up in particular experimental groups can be identified. The effects of the nuisance variables will not be eliminated, but they will be controlled. Randomization assures the researcher that overall repetitions of the experiment under the same conditions will show the true effects, if those effects exist. Random assignment of conditions provides "control by chance."[3] Random assignment of subjects allows the researcher to assume the groups are identical with respect to all variables except the experimental treatment.

**Matching**
A procedure for the assignment of subjects to groups that ensures each group of respondents is matched on the basis of pertinent characteristics.

**Matching** Random assignment of subjects to the various experimental groups is the most common technique used to prevent test units from differing from one another on key variables. However, if the experimenter believes certain extraneous variables may affect the dependent variable, he or she can make sure the subjects in each group are matched on these characteristics. **Matching** the respondents on the basis of pertinent background information is another technique for controlling assignment errors. For example, in a taste test experiment for a dog food, it might be important to match the dogs into various experimental groups on the basis of age or breed. Similarly, if age is expected to influence savings behavior, a savings and loan conducting an experiment may have greater assurance that there are no differences among subjects if subjects in all experimental conditions are matched according to age.

Although matching assures the researcher that the subjects in each group are similar on the matched characteristics, the researcher cannot be certain that subjects have been matched on all characteristics potentially important to the experiment.

**Repeated Measures**   In some experiments, the same subjects are exposed to all experimental treatments. This eliminates any problems due to subject differences, but it causes some other problems that we will discuss later. When this occurs, the experiment is said to have **repeated measures.**

**Repeated measures**
A situation that occurs when the same subjects are exposed to all experimental treatments to eliminate any problems due to subject differences.

## ■ Control over Extraneous Variables

The fourth decision about the basic elements of an experiment concerns control over extraneous variables. To understand this issue, we will examine the various types of experimental error.

In Chapter 7, we classified total survey error into two basic categories: random sampling error and systematic error. The same dichotomy applies to all research designs, but the terms *random (sampling) error* and *constant (systematic) error* are more frequently used when discussing experiments.

**Constant error**
An error that occurs in the same experimental condition every time the basic experiment is repeated; a systematic bias.

**Constant Experimental Error from Extraneous Variables**   We already discussed random error in the context of experimental selection and assignment of test units. **Constant error** (bias) occurs when the extraneous variables or the conditions of administering the experiment are allowed to influence the dependent variables every time the experiment is repeated. When this occurs, the results will be confounded because the extraneous variables will not have been controlled or eliminated.

For example, if subjects in an experimental group are always administered the treatment in the morning and subjects in the control group always receive it in the afternoon, a constant, systematic error will occur. In such a situation, the time of day—an uncontrolled extraneous variable—is a cause of constant error. In a training experiment, the sources of constant error might be the persons who do the training (operations personnel or external specialists) or whether the training is on the employees' own time or on company time. These and other characteristics of the training may have an impact on the dependent variable and will have to be taken into account.

A number of extraneous variables may affect the dependent variable, thereby distorting the experiment. The following example shows how extraneous variables may affect results.[4] Suppose a television commercial for brand Z gasoline shows two automobiles on a highway. The announcer states that one car has used brand Z without the special additive and the other has used it with the additive. The car without the special additive comes to a stop first, and the car with it comes to a stop 10 to 15 yards farther down the road. (We will assume both cars used the same quantity of gasoline.) The implication of this commercial is that the special additive (the independent variable) results in extra mileage (the dependent variable). As experimenters who are concerned with extraneous variables that could affect the result, we can raise the following questions:

1. Were the engines of the same size and type? Were the conditions of the engines the same (tuning, etc.)?
2. Were the cars of the same condition (gear ratios, fuel injector settings, weight, wear and tear, etc.)?
3. Were the drivers different? Were there differences in acceleration? Were there differences in the drivers' weights?

Because an experimenter does not want extraneous variables to affect the results, she or he must control or eliminate such variables.

**Demand characteristics**
Experimental design procedures or situational aspects of an experiment that provide unintentional hints about the experimenter's hypothesis to subjects.

**Demand Characteristics** **Demand characteristics** refer to experimental design procedures that unintentionally hint to subjects about the experimenter's hypothesis. Demand characteristics are situational aspects of the experiment that demand that participants respond in a particular way; hence, they are a source of constant error. If participants recognize the experimenter's expectation or demand, they are likely to act in a manner consistent with the experimental treatment; even slight nonverbal cues, such as a smile, may influence their reactions.

In most experiments, the most prominent demand characteristic is the person who actually administers the experimental procedures. If an experimenter's presence, actions, or comments influence subjects' behavior or sway subjects to slant their answers to cooperate with the experimenter, the experiment has **experimenter bias.** When subjects slant their answers to cooperate with the experimenter, they in effect are acting as guinea pigs and tend to exhibit behaviors that might not represent their behavior in the marketplace. For example, if subjects in an advertising experiment understand that the experimenter is interested in whether they changed their attitudes in accord with a given advertisement, they may answer in the desired direction to please him or her. This attitude change reflects a **guinea pig effect** rather than a true experimental treatment effect.

**Experimenter bias**
An effect on the subjects' behavior caused by an experimenter's presence, actions, or comments.

**Guinea pig effect**
An effect on the results of an experiment caused by subjects changing their normal behavior or attitudes to cooperate with an experimenter.

**Blinding**
A technique used to control subjects' knowledge of whether or not they have been given a particular experimental treatment.

To reduce demand characteristics, the researcher typically takes steps to make it difficult for subjects to know what he or she is trying to find out. **Blinding** is used to control subjects' knowledge of whether or not they have been given a particular experimental treatment. In a cola taste test, one group of subjects might be exposed to the new formulation and the other exposed to the regular cola. If the subjects were blinded, all may have been told they had not been given the new formulation (or all may have been told they had received the new formulation). This technique frequently is used in medical research when subjects are given chemically inert pills (placebos) rather than medication.

## ■ Establishing Control of Extraneous Variables

The major difference between experimental research and other research is an experimenter's ability to hold conditions constant and manipulate the treatment. To conclude that A causes B, a brewery experimenting with a new, dark lager beer's influence on beer drinkers' taste perceptions must determine the possible extraneous variables other than the treatment that may affect the results and attempt to eliminate or control them. We know brand image and packaging are important factors in beer drinkers' reactions, so the experimenter may wish to eliminate the effects associated with them. He or she may eliminate these two extraneous variables by packaging the test beers in plain packages without brand identification. When extraneous variables cannot be eliminated, experimenters may strive for **constancy of conditions,** that is, expose all subjects in each experimental group to situations that are exactly alike except for the differing conditions of the independent variable. For example, experiments to measure consumers' evaluations of tissue paper softness have indicated that variation in humidity influences reactions. In this situation, holding extraneous variables constant might require that all experimental sessions be conducted in the same room at the same time of day.

**Constancy of conditions**
A situation in which subjects in experimental groups and control groups are exposed to situations identical except for differing conditions of the independent variable.

If the experimental method requires that the same subjects be exposed to two or more experimental treatments, an error may occur due to the *order of presentation.* If a soft-drink company plans to test consumers' comparison of a high-caffeine, extra-sugar version of its cola versus its regular cola, one of the drinks must be tasted before the other. Consumers may tend to prefer the first drink tasted if they cannot tell any difference between

**Counterbalancing**
A technique requiring that half the subjects be exposed to treatment A first and then to treatment B while the other half receive treatment B and then treatment A. This is an attempt to eliminate the confounding effects of order of presentation.

the drinks. Another example is a video games manufacturer that has subjects perform an experimental task requiring some skill (that is, playing a game). Subjects may perform better on the second task simply because they have had some experience with the first task. **Counterbalancing** attempts to eliminate the confounding effects of order of presentation by requiring that half the subjects be exposed to treatment A first and then to treatment B while the other half receive treatment B first and then treatment A.

The random assignment of subjects and experimental treatments to groups is an attempt to control extraneous variations that result from chance. If certain extraneous variations cannot be controlled, the researcher must assume the confounding effects will be present in all experimental conditions with approximately the same influence. (This assumption may not hold true if the assignments were not made on a random basis.) In many experiments, especially laboratory experiments, interpersonal contact between members of the various experimental groups and/or the control group must be eliminated or minimized. After the subjects have been assigned to groups, the various individuals should be kept separated so that discussion about what occurs in a given treatment situation will not become an extraneous variable that contaminates the experiment.

## ■ ETHICAL ISSUES IN EXPERIMENTATION

Experimental researchers concern themselves with problems associated with privacy, confidentiality, deception, accuracy of reporting, and other ethical issues common to other research methods. The issues related to subjects' right to be informed, however, tend to be very prominent in experimentation. Research codes of conduct often suggest the experimental subject should be fully informed and receive accurate information. Yet experimental researchers who know demand characteristics can invalidate an experiment may not give subjects complete information about the nature and purpose of the study. Simply put, experimenters often intentionally hide the true purposes of their experiments from the subjects, perhaps by remaining silent. They then frequently debrief the subjects after the experiment. **Debriefing** is the process of providing subjects with all the pertinent facts about the nature and purpose of the experiment after the experiment has been completed.

**Debriefing**
The process of providing subjects with all pertinent facts about the nature and purpose of the experiment after its completion.

Debriefing experimental subjects may relieve stress that results from deception or other questionable procedures. Communicating the purpose of the experiment and the researcher's hypotheses about the nature of consumer behavior is expected to counteract negative effects of deception and/or stress and to provide the educational experience for the subject. It has been suggested that

> Proper debriefing allows the subject to save face by uncovering the truth for himself. The experimenter should begin by asking the subject if he has any questions or if he found any part of the experiment odd, confusing, or disturbing. This question provides a check on the subject's suspiciousness and effectiveness of manipulations. The experimenter continues to provide the subject cues to the deception until the subject states that he believes there was more to the experiment than met the eye. At this time the purpose and procedure of the experiment [are] revealed.[5]

When there is clear-cut deception or when the researcher perceives that psychological harm may result from participating in an experiment (a rarity in marketing research), debriefing is often performed. However, if the researcher does not foresee potentially harmful consequences in participation, she or he may omit debriefing due to time and cost considerations.[6]

Another issue that may—but typically does not—arise in marketing experiments is the subject's right to safety from physical and mental harm. Most researchers believe that if the subject's experience may be stressful or cause physical harm, the subject should receive adequate information about this aspect of the experiment before agreeing to participate.

---

# ■ FIELD AND LABORATORY EXPERIMENTS

**Laboratory experiment**
An experiment conducted in a laboratory or other artificial setting to obtain almost complete control over the research setting.

A marketing experiment can be conducted in a natural setting (a field experiment) or in an artificial setting—one contrived for a specific purpose (a laboratory experiment). In a **laboratory experiment,** the researcher has almost complete control over the research setting. For example, subjects are recruited and brought to an advertising agency's office, a research agency's office, or perhaps a mobile unit designed for research purposes. They are exposed to a television commercial within the context of a program that includes competitors' ads, and they are not interrupted as they view the commercials. They are then allowed to make a purchase—the advertised product or one of several competing products—in a simulated store environment. Trial purchase measures are thus obtained. A few weeks later, subjects are contacted again to measure their satisfaction and determine repeat purchasing intention. This typical laboratory experiment simulates the shopping experience and gives the consumer an opportunity to "buy" and "invest." Within a short time span, the marketer gets the chance to collect information on decision making.

Another variation of a simulated shopping experiment involves using a representative panel of homemakers who receive a weekly visit at home from a salesperson in a mobile shopping van. This allows the researcher to measure trial, repeat purchase, and buying rates. The visit is preceded by a mailed sales catalog and an order form that features the products being tested along with all the leading brands and any promotional support that is either current or being tested.

**Tachistoscope**
A device that controls the amount of time a visual image is exposed to a subject.

Other laboratory experiments may be more controlled or artificial. The **tachistoscope** allows the researcher to experiment with the visual impact of advertising, packaging, and so on by controlling the amount of time a visual image is exposed to a subject. Each stimulus (for example, package design) is projected from slides to the tachistoscope at varying exposure lengths ($\frac{1}{10}$ of a second, $\frac{3}{10}$, and so). It simulates the split-second duration of a customer's attention in the same way a package might in a mass display.

**Field experiment**
An experiment conducted in a natural setting, where complete control of extraneous variables is not possible.

In the **field experiment,** the researcher manipulates some variables but cannot control all the extraneous ones in the marketplace. Field experiments generally are used to fine-tune marketing strategies and to determine sales volume. For example, Betty Crocker's Squeezit (a 10 percent fruit juice drink in a squeeze-and-drink bottle) could not keep up with demand in test marketing. The research showed the product's national introduction needed to be postponed until production capacity could be increased.

McDonald's conducted a field experiment to test market Triple Ripple, a three-flavored ice cream product. The product was dropped because the experiment revealed distribution problems combined with limited customer acceptance. In the distribution system the product would freeze, defrost, and refreeze. Solving the problem would have required each McDonald's city to have a local ice cream plant with special equipment to roll the three flavors into one. A naturalistic setting for the experiment helped McDonald's executives realize the product was impractical.

These examples illustrate that experiments vary in their degree of artificiality. Exhibit 9.1 shows that as experiments increase in naturalism, they begin to approach the pure field experiment and as they become more artificial, they approach the laboratory type. The *degree of artificiality* in experiments refers to the amount of manipulation and control of the situation the experimenter uses to ensure that subjects will be exposed to the exact conditions desired.

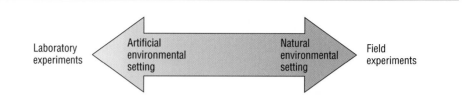

Laboratory
experiments

Artificial
environmental
setting

Natural
environmental
setting

Field
experiments

## ■ ISSUES OF EXPERIMENTAL VALIDITY[7]

### ■ Internal Validity

**Internal validity**
The ability of an experiment to answer the question of whether an experimental treatment was the sole cause of changes in a dependent variable or whether the experimental manipulation did what it was supposed to do.

Managers must address two fundamental problems when choosing or evaluating experimental research designs: internal validity and external validity. The first has to do with the interpretation of the cause-and-effect relationship in the experiment. **Internal validity** refers to the question of whether the experimental treatment was the sole cause of observed changes in the dependent variable. If the observed results were influenced or confounded by the extraneous factors previously discussed, the researcher will have problems making valid conclusions about the relationship between the experimental treatment and the dependent variable. If the observed results can be unhesitatingly attributed to the experimental treatment, the experiment will be internally valid.

It is helpful to classify several types of extraneous variables that may jeopardize internal validity. The six major ones are history, maturation, testing, instrumentation, selection, and mortality.

**History effect**
The loss of internal validity caused by specific events in the external environment occurring between the first and second measurements that are beyond the experimenter's control.

**Cohort effect**
A change in the dependent variable that occurs because members of one experimental group experienced different historical situations than members of other experimental groups.

**History** Suppose a before-and-after experiment is being conducted to test a new packaging strategy for an imported Chinese toy. If the Chinese engage in an anti-American political action that gets considerable media coverage, this action may jeopardize the validity of the experiment because many Americans may boycott this brand of toy. This is an example of a **history effect,** specific events in the external environment between the first and second measurements that are beyond the experimenter's control. A common history effect occurs when competitors change their marketing strategies during a test marketing experiment.

A special case of the history effect sometimes occurs. The **cohort effect** refers to a change in the dependent variable that occurs because members of one experimental group experienced different historical situations than members of other experimental groups. For example, two groups of managers used as subjects may be in different cohorts because one group experienced the turmoil of a corporate takeover while the other, hired after the takeover, experienced a different history and therefore may behave differently in a workplace experiment.

**Maturation effect**
An effect on the results of an experiment caused by experimental subjects maturing or changing over time.

**Maturation** People change over time; that is, they undergo a process of maturation. During the course of an experiment, subjects may mature or change in some way that will affect the results. **Maturation effects** are changes within the respondents that operate as a function of time rather than of a specific event. During a daylong experiment, subjects may grow hungry, tired, or bored. In an experiment over a longer time span, their maturation may influence internal validity because they grow older or more experienced or change in other ways that may influence the results. For example, suppose an experiment was designed to test the impact of a new compensation program on sales productivity. If this

## WHAT WENT RIGHT?

### The Monkey Attacks the Elephant

The strategy used for Formula 409 liquid cleaner to interrupt Procter & Gamble's test market and subsequent national introduction of Cinch is rather unique. Although it occurred several years ago, it dramatically illustrates how a small company can influence the actions of a giant one by manipulating a test market. Formula 409 was a family effort and the company's only product. When the company's president learned that Procter & Gamble would be test marketing Cinch in Denver, he did not increase advertising or lower prices for Formula 409. Indeed, he did just the opposite: he unobtrusively withdrew distribution in the Denver area. Salespeople were discouraged from restocking shelves. Thus, Procter & Gamble's test market success was overwhelming.

But wait: The marketers of Formula 409 had decided on a strategy that would discourage Procter & Gamble and other marketers in the long run. As Cinch was regionally rolling out, Formula 409's president decided to load up spray cleaner users with about a six-month supply of the product; a giant-size bottle was attached to the regular-size one at a reduced price. Since most 409 users were thus stocked up when Cinch was introduced, they did not need to buy the new product. Hence, initial sales for the giant packaged-goods marketer were disastrous. Thinking that the volume of Formula 409 was extremely small and that Denver test market results were abnormal, Procter & Gamble pulled out of the market. The president of Formula 409 had bet that Procter & Gamble was too big to notice the subtle moves of small Formula 409. It was an elephant grown so large that the monkey (Formula 409) had heard it coming and darted out of the way.

---

program were tested over a year's time, some of the salespeople probably would have matured due to increased selling experience or perhaps increased knowledge.

**Testing effect**
The effect of pretesting in a before-and-after study, which may sensitize respondents or subjects when taking a test for the second time, thus affecting internal validity.

**Testing**    **Testing effects** are also called **pretesting effects** because the initial measurement or test alerts respondents to the nature of the experiment and respondents may act differently than they would if no pretest measures were taken. In a before-and-after study, taking a pretest before the independent variable is manipulated may sensitize respondents when they are taking the test the second time. For example, students taking standardized achievement and intelligence tests for the second time usually do better than those taking the tests for the first time.[8] The effect of testing may increase awareness of socially approved answers, increase attention to experimental conditions (that is, the subject may watch closely), or make the subject more conscious than usual of the dimensions of a problem.

**Instrumentation**    Measuring the dependent variable in an experiment requires the use of a questionnaire or other form of measuring instrument. If the identical instrument is used more than once, a testing effect may occur. To avoid the effects of testing, an alternative form of the measuring instrument (for example, a questionnaire or test) may be given during the postmeasurement. Although this may reduce the effect of testing because of a change in the measuring instrument, it may also result in an **instrumentation effect.**

**Instrumentation effect**
An effect on the results of an experiment caused by a change in the wording of questions, interviewers, or other procedures used to measure the dependent variable.

A change in the wording of questions, in interviewers, or in other procedures used to measure the dependent variable cause an instrumentation effect, which may jeopardize internal validity. For example, if the same interviewers are used to ask questions for both before and after measurement, some problems may arise. With practice, interviewers may acquire increased skill in interviewing, or interviewer boredom may cause the instrument to be reworded in the interviewer's own terms. To avoid this problem, new interviewers are hired, but different individuals are a source of extraneous variation due to instrumentation variation. Numerous sources of instrument decay or variation are possible.

**Selection**    The **selection effect** is a sample bias that results from differential selection of respondents for the comparison groups. We already addressed this topic.

**Mortality**    If the experiment is conducted over a period of a few weeks or more, some sample bias may occur due to **mortality,** or **sample attrition.** Sample attrition occurs when some subjects withdraw from the experiment before it is completed. Mortality effects may occur if many subjects drop from one experimental treatment group and not from other treatment or control groups. Consider a sales training experiment investigating the effects of close supervision (high pressure) versus low supervision (low pressure). The high-pressure condition may misleadingly appear superior if those subjects who completed the experiment did very well. However, suppose the high-pressure condition caused more subjects to drop out than other conditions did. This apparent superiority may be due to a self-selection bias if only very determined and/or talented salespeople remain throughout the training period.

## ■ External Validity

The second validity problem concerns the researcher's ability to generalize the results from the experiment to the marketplace or external environment. **External validity** is the ability of an experiment to generalize beyond the experiment data to other subjects or groups in the population under study. In essence, it is a sampling question: To what extent can the results of a simulated shopping experiment be transferred to real-world supermarket shopping? Will a test market in Fort Wayne, Indiana, be representative of a nationwide introduction of the product under study? Can one extrapolate the results of a tachistoscope to an in-store shopping situation? Problems of external validity generally are related to the threat that a specific but limited set of experimental conditions will not deal with the interactions of untested variables in the real world. In other words, the experimental situation may be artificial and fail to represent the true setting and conditions in which the investigated behavior took place. If the study lacks external validity, the researcher will have difficulty repeating the experiment with different subjects, settings, or time intervals.

If subjects in a shopping mall view a videotape that simulates an actual television program with a test commercial inserted along with other commercials, will the subjects view the commercial just as they would if it were being shown on a regular program? Some contamination probably will occur, but the experiment may still be externally valid if the researcher knows how to adjust results from an artificial setting to the marketplace. Comparative norms may be established based on similar, previous studies so that the results can be projected beyond the experiment. If an experiment lacks internal validity, projecting its result is not possible. Thus, the same threats to internal validity may jeopardize external validity.

## ■ Trade-Offs between Internal and External Validity

Naturalistic field experiments tend to have greater external validity than artificial laboratory experiments. One problem the marketing researcher faces is that internal validity generally is traded off for external validity because a laboratory experiment provides more control. A researcher who wishes to test advertising effectiveness via a split cable experiment has the assurance that the advertisement will be viewed in an externally valid situation, that is, in the respondent's home. However, the researcher has no assurance that some interruption (for example, a telephone call) will not have some influence that will reduce

---

**Selection effect**
A sampling bias that results from differential selection of respondents for the comparison groups.

**Mortality (sample attrition) effect**
A sample bias that results from the withdrawal of some subjects from the experiment before it is completed.

**External validity**
The ability of an experiment to generalize beyond the experiment data to other subjects or groups in the population under study.

the internal validity of the experiment. Laboratory experiments with many controlled factors usually are high in internal validity, while field experiments generally have less internal validity but greater external validity.

# ■ CLASSIFICATION OF EXPERIMENTAL DESIGNS

The design of an experiment may be compared to an architect's plans for a structure, whether a giant skyscraper or a modest home. The basic requirements for the structure are given to the architect by the prospective owner. It is the architect's task to fill these basic requirements; yet the architect has ample room for exercising his or her ingenuity. Several different plans may be drawn up to meet all the basic requirements. Some may be more costly than others; given two plans having the same cost, one may offer potential advantages that the second does not.[9]

**Basic experimental design**
An experimental design in which a single independent variable is manipulated to measure its effect on another single dependent variable.

There are various types of experimental designs. If only one variable is manipulated, the experiment is a **basic experimental design.** If the experimenter wishes to investigate several levels of the independent variables (for example, four price levels) or to investigate the interaction effects of two or more independent variables, the experiment requires a *complex,* or *statistical,* experimental design.

## ■ Symbolism for Diagramming Experimental Designs

The work of Campbell and Stanley has helped many students master the subject of basic experimental designs.[10] The following symbolism facilitates the description of the various experimental designs:

$X$ = exposure of a group to an experimental treatment
$O$ = observation or measurement of the dependent variable; if more than one observation or measurement is taken, subscripts ($O_1$, $O_2$, etc.) indicate temporal order[11]
$\boxed{R}$ = random assignment of test units; $\boxed{R}$ symbolizes that individuals selected as subjects for the experiment will be randomly assigned to the experimental groups

As we diagram the experimental designs using these symbols, the reader should assume a time flow from left to right. Our first example will make this clearer.

## ■ Three Examples of Quasi-Experimental Designs

**Quasi-experimental design**
A research design that cannot be classified as a true experiment because it lacks adequate control of extraneous variables.

**Quasi-experimental designs** do not quality as true experimental designs because they do not adequately control for the problems associated with loss of external or internal validity.

**One-shot design**
An after-only design in which a single measure is recorded after the treatment is administered.

**One-Shot Design**   The **one-shot design,** or *after-only design,* is diagrammed as follows:

$$X \qquad O_1$$

Suppose that after a very cold winter, an automobile dealer finds herself with a large inventory of cars. She decides to experiment with a promotional scheme offering a free trip to New Orleans with every car sold. She experiments with the promotion ($X$ = experimental treatment) and measures sales ($O_1$ = measurement of sales after the treatment is administered). The dealer is not really conducting a formal experiment; she is just "trying something out."

This one-shot design is a case study of a research project fraught with problems. Subjects or test units participate because of voluntary self-selection or arbitrary assignment, not because of random assignment. The study lacks any kind of comparison or any means of controlling extraneous influences. We need a measure of what will happen when the test units have not been exposed to $X$ to compare with the measures that result when subjects have been exposed to $X$. Nevertheless, under certain circumstances, even though this design lacks internal validity, it is the only viable choice.

The nature of taste tests or product usage tests may dictate the use of this design. In a taste test experiment, consumers sampled Borden ice cream from boxes and cartons. When asked which was "creamier," they invariably chose the premium-shaped carton.

**One-Group Pretest–Posttest Design**   Suppose a real estate franchisor wishes to provide a training program for its franchisees. If it measures subjects' knowledge of real estate selling before ($O_1$) being exposed to the experimental treatment *(X)* and then measures real estate selling knowledge after ($O_2$) being exposed to the treatment, the design will be as follows:

$$O_1 \qquad X \qquad O_2$$

**One-group pretest–posttest design**
A quasi-experimental design in which the subjects in the experimental group are measured before and after the treatment is administered, but there is no control group.

In this example, the trainer is likely to conclude that the difference between $O_2$ and $O_1$ ($O_2 - O_1$) is the measure of the influence of the experimental treatment. This **one-group pretest–posttest design** offers a comparison of the same individuals before and after training. Although this is an improvement over the one-shot design, this research still has several weaknesses that may jeopardize internal validity. For example, if the time lapse between $O_1$ and $O_2$ was a period of several months, the trainees may have matured due to experience on the job (maturation effect). History effects also may influence this design. Perhaps some subjects dropped out of the training program (mortality effect). The effect of testing also may have confounded the experiment. For example, taking a test on real estate selling may have made subjects more aware of their lack of specific knowledge; either during the training sessions or on their own, they may have sought to learn subject material on which they realized they were ignorant.

If the second observation or measure ($O_2$) of salespersons' knowledge was not an identical test, the research may have the influence of instrument variation. If it gave an identical test but had different graders for the before and after measurements, the data may not be directly comparable.

Although this design has a number of weaknesses, it is used frequently in marketing research. Remember, the cost of the research is a consideration in most business situations. While there will be some problems of internal validity, the researcher must always take into account questions of time and cost.

**Static group design**
An after-only design in which subjects in the experimental group are measured after being exposed to the experimental treatment and the control group is measured without having been exposed to the experimental treatment; no premeasure is taken.

**Static Group Design**   In the **static group design,** each subject is identified as a member of either an experimental group or a control group (for example, exposed or not exposed to a commercial). The experimental group is measured after being exposed to the experimental treatment, and the control group is measured without having been exposed to the experimental treatment.

Experimental group: $X \qquad O_1$
Control group: $\qquad\qquad O_2$

The results of the static group design are computed by subtracting the observed results in the control group from those in the experimental group ($O_1 - O_2$).

A major weakness of this design is its lack of assurance that the groups were equal on variables of interest before the experimental group received the treatment. If the groups were selected arbitrarily by the investigator, or if entry into either group was voluntary, systematic differences between the groups could invalidate the conclusions about the effect of the treatment. For example, suppose a company that manufactures trash compactors wishes to compare the attitudes of subjects who have used a trash compactor for the first time with those who have not. If selection into the groups is voluntary, we might find that the group that receives the use of a trash compactor might have had some reason for choosing that option (for example, atypical amounts of garbage or incompetent garbage collectors). Sample attrition of experimental group members who do not like trash compactors might also be a source of error.

Random assignment of subjects may minimize problems with group differences. If groups can be determined by the experimenter rather than existing as a function of some other causation, the static group design is referred to as an *after-only design with control group.*

On many occasions, after-only designs are the only possible options. This is particularly true when conducting use tests for new products or brands. Cautious interpretation and recognition of the design's shortcomings may make this necessary evil quite valuable. For example, Airwick Industries Inc. conducted in-use tests with Carpet Fresh, a rug cleaner and room deodorizer. Experiments with Carpet Fresh, which originally was conceived as a granular product to be sprinkled on the floor before vacuuming, indicated that people were afraid the granules would lodge under furniture. This research led to changing the product to have a powdery texture.

### ■ Three Better Experimental Designs

In a formal, scientific sense, the three designs just discussed are not true experimental designs. Subjects for the experiments were not selected from a common pool of subjects and randomly assigned to one or another group. The three basic experimental designs discussed next have the symbol $\boxed{R}$ to the left of the diagram to indicate that the first step in a true experimental design is the randomization of subject assignment.

**Pretest–posttest control group design**
A true experimental design in which the experimental group is tested before and after exposure to the treatment and the control group is tested at the same two times without being exposed to the experimental treatment.

**Pretest–Posttest Control Group Design (Before–After with Control)** The **pretest–posttest control group design,** or *before–after with control group design,* is the classic experimental design:

$$\text{Experimental group:} \quad \boxed{R} \quad O_1 \quad X \quad O_2$$
$$\text{Control group:} \quad \boxed{R} \quad O_3 \quad \quad O_4$$

As the diagram indicates, the experimental group is tested before and after exposing these subjects to the treatment. The control group is tested at the same two times as the experimental group, but subjects are not exposed to the experimental treatment. This design has the advantages of the before–after design with the additional advantages gained by its having a control group. The effect of the experimental treatment equals

$$(O_2 - O_1) - (O_4 - O_3)$$

If there is brand awareness among 20 percent of the subjects ($O_1 = 20$ percent, $O_3 = 20$ percent) before an advertising treatment, 35 percent awareness after in the experimental group ($O_2 = 35$ percent), and 22 percent awareness in the control group ($O_4 = 22$ percent), the treatment effect equals 13 percent:

$$(0.35 - 0.20) - (0.22 - 0.20)$$
$$(0.15) - (0.02) = 0.13 \text{ or } 13\%$$

The effect of all extraneous variables is assumed to be the same on both the experimental and the control groups. For instance, since both groups receive the pretest, no difference between them is expected for the pretest effect. This assumption is also made for effects of other events between the before-and-after measurement (history), changes within the subjects that occur with the passage of time (maturation), testing effects, instrument decay, and regression effects. In reality there will be some differences in the sources of extraneous variation. Nevertheless, in most cases, assuming the effect is approximately equal for both groups is a sound premise.

However, a *testing effect* is possible when subjects are sensitized to the subject of the research. This is analogous to what occurs when people learn a new vocabulary word. Soon they discover that they notice it much more frequently in their reading. In an experiment, the combination of being interviewed on a subject and receiving the experimental treatment might be a potential source of error. For example, a subject exposed to a certain advertising message in a split cable experiment might say, "Ah, there is an ad about the product I was interviewed about yesterday!" The respondent may pay more attention than normal to the advertisement and be more prone to change his or her attitude than in a situation with no testing effects. This weakness in the before–after with control group design can be corrected (see the next two designs).

Testing the effectiveness of television commercials in movie theaters provides an example of the before–after with control group design. Subjects are selected for the experiments by being told they are going to preview several new television show pilots. When they enter the theater, they learn that a drawing for several types of products will be held, and they are asked to complete a product preference questionnaire (see Exhibit 9.2); then a first drawing is held. Next, the television commercials are shown. Finally, the emcee might indicate there are some additional prizes and a second drawing will be held; then the same questionnaire about prizes is filled out. The information from the first questionnaire is the before measurement, and that from the second questionnaire is the after measurement. The control group will receive similar treatment except that on the day they view the pilot television films, different (or no) television commercials will be substituted for the experimental commercials.

---

■ **Exhibit 9.2**           **Product Preference Measure in an Experiment**

We are going to give away a series of prizes. If you are selected as one of the winners, which brand from each of the groups listed below would you truly want to win?

Special arrangements will be made for any product for which bulk, or one-time, delivery is not appropriate.

Indicate your answers by *filling* in the box like this: ■
*Do not "X," check, or circle the boxes please.*

| Cookies | | | Allergy Relief Products | | |
|---|---|---|---|---|---|
| (A 3-months' supply, pick *ONE*.) | | | (A year's supply, pick *ONE*.) | | |
| NABISCO OREO | ☐ | (1) | ALLEREST | ☐ | (1) |
| NABISCO OREO DOUBLE STUFF | ☐ | (2) | BENADRYL | ☐ | (2) |
| NABISCO NUTTER BUTTER | ☐ | (3) | CONTAC | ☐ | (3) |
| NABISCO VANILLA CREMES | ☐ | (4) | CORICIDIN | ☐ | (4) |
| HYDROX CHOCOLATE | ☐ | (5) | DRISTAN | ☐ | (5) |
| HYDROX DOUBLES | ☐ | (6) | SUDAFED | ☐ | (6) |
| NABISCO COOKIE BREAK | ☐ | (7) | TAVIST-D | ☐ | (7) |
| NABISCO CHIPS AHOY | ☐ | (8) | OTHER (Please specify) | ☐ | (8) |
| KEEBLER E.L. FUDGE | ☐ | (9) | | | |
| KEEBLER FUDGE CREMES | ☐ | (10) | | | |
| KEEBLER FRENCH VANILLA CREMES | ☐ | (11) | | | |

**Posttest-only control group design**
An after-only design in which the experimental group is tested after exposure to the treatment and the control group is tested at the same time without having been exposed to the treatment: no premeasure is taken. Random assignment of subjects and treatment occurs.

**Posttest-Only Control Group Design (After-Only with Control)**    In some situations pretest measurements are impossible. In others selection error is not anticipated to be a problem because the groups are known to be equal. The **posttest-only control group design,** or *after-only with control group design,* is diagrammed as follows:

$$\text{Experimental group:} \quad \boxed{R} \quad X \quad O_1$$
$$\text{Control group:} \quad \quad \boxed{R} \quad \quad O_2$$

The effect of the experimental treatment is equal to $O_1 - O_2$.

Suppose the manufacture of an athlete's foot remedy wishes to demonstrate by experimentation that its product is better than the leading brand. No pretest measure about the effectiveness of the remedy is possible. The design is to randomly select subjects, perhaps students, who have contracted athlete's foot and randomly assign them to the experimental or control group. With only the posttest measurement, the effects of testing and instrument variation are eliminated. Further, all of the same assumptions about extraneous variables are made: that is, they operate equally on both groups, as in the before–after with control group design.

**Solomon four-group design**
A true experimental design that combines the pretest–posttest with control group and the posttest-only with control group designs, thereby providing a means for controlling the interactive testing effect and other sources of extraneous variation.

**Solomon Four-Group Design**    By combining the pretest–posttest (before–after) with control group and the posttest-only (after-only) with control group designs, the **Solomon four-group design** provides a means for controlling the testing effect as well as other sources of extraneous variation. In the following diagram, the two $X$'s symbolize the same experimental treatment given to each experimental group:

$$\text{Experimental group 1} \quad \boxed{R} \quad O_1 \quad X \quad O_2$$
$$\text{Control group 1} \quad \quad \boxed{R} \quad O_3 \quad \quad O_4$$
$$\text{Experimental group 2} \quad \boxed{R} \quad \quad X \quad O_5$$
$$\text{Control group 2} \quad \quad \boxed{R} \quad \quad \quad O_6$$

Although we will not go through the calculations, it is possible to isolate the effects of the experimental treatment and testing in this design. Although this design allows for the isolation of the various effects, it is rarely used in marketing research because of the effort, time, and cost of implementing it. However, it points out that there are ways to isolate or control most sources of variation.

---

# ■ TEST MARKETING

**Test marketing**
An experimental procedure that provides an opportunity to measure sales or profit potential for a new product or to test a new marketing plan under realistic marketing conditions.

**Test marketing** is an experimental procedure that provides an opportunity to test a new product or new marketing plan under realistic market conditions to measure sales or profit potential. Cities such Eau Claire (Wisconsin) or other small marketing areas where a new product is distributed and marketed usually provide a marketplace setting for field experiments.

The major advantage of test marketing is that no other form of research can beat the real world when it comes to testing actual purchasing behavior and consumer acceptance of a product. For example, Benefit, an innovative cereal that General Mills claimed would reduce cholesterol, was a health-oriented product that stirred up controversy and angered some consumer activists when it was test marketed. Although Benefit contained psyllium, a soluble fiber scientifically shown to reduce cholesterol, Procter & Gamble asked the Food and Drug Administration to prevent General Mills from making health claims for Benefit and to rule that psyllium is a drug and not a food. In addition, General Mills learned that Benefit, which didn't taste all that good, appealed to a much narrower market segment than what the marketing strategist had envisioned.

## ■ Functions of Test Marketing

Test marketing provides two useful functions for management. First, it offers the opportunity to estimate the outcomes of alternative courses of action. Estimates can be made about the optimal advertising expenditures, the need for product sampling, or how advertising and product sampling will interact. Researchers may be able to predict the sales effects of specific marketing variables, such as package design, price, or couponing and select the best alternative action. Test marketing permits evaluation of the proposed national marketing mix.

A marketing manager for Beech-Nut Life-Savers vividly portrays this function of experimentation in the marketplace:

> A market test may be likened to an orchestra rehearsal. The violinists have adjusted their strings, the trumpeters have tested their keys, the drummer has tightened his drums. Everything is ready to go. But all these instruments have not worked in unison. So a test market is like an orchestra rehearsal where you can practice with everything together before the big public performance.[12]

A researcher may not only evaluate the outcome by investigating the product's sales volume; he or she can also investigate the new product's impact on other items within the firm's product line. Test marketing allows a firm to determine whether a new product will cannibalize sales from already profitable company lines. For example, Nabisco's cracker business is mature. The company has many brands, and it may use test marketing to make sure it is hitting the right consumer segment. A new cracker positioned at saltine users may be a tremendous sales success, but a test market may show that the people who are actually buying it are snack cracker users, and the new brand may take sales away from existing brands. Similarly, H. J. Heinz Company was concerned that the introduction of Heinz Salsa ketchup would take sales away from Heinz regular ketchup. Test marketing provided the necessary information, and Heinz no longer markets salsa ketchup in the United States. Test marketing is the best way to establish these market share relationships and to understand the problem of cannibalization.

The second useful function of test market experimentation is that it allows management to identify and correct any weaknesses in either the product or its marketing plan before making the commitment to a national sales launch, by which time it normally will be too late to incorporate product modifications and improvements. Thus, if test market results fall short of management's expectations, advertising weights, package sizes, and so on may be adjusted.

For example, McDonald's test marketed pizza for years. It learned competitors' reactions and the problems associated with small, individual-portion pizzas in its first test market experiment. The product strategy was repositioned, and the product testing shifted to marketing a 14-inch pizza that was not available until late afternoon. The research then focused on how consumers reacted to these pizzas sold in experimental restaurants remodeled to include "Pizza Shoppes," in which employees assemble ingredients on ready-made dough. Ultimately, McDonald's decided pizza should not be on its menu.

## ■ Factors to Consider in Test Market Selection

Obtaining a representative test market requires considering many factors that may not be obvious to the inexperienced researcher. A vice president of ITT Continental Banking says,

> When I started in the business, I thought people picked cities like Columbus, Ohio, because their populations were typical. But I found the main reasons were that they were isolated media mar-

■ Shortly after Coca-Cola launched Urge in Norway, it test marketed a renamed version, Surge, in the United States. The test market purpose was to determine the effectiveness of positioning the product against PepsiCo's Mountain Dew.

kets and the distribution patterns were such that they didn't have to worry about the chain warehouse shipping outside of Columbus. It's difficult to translate information from a city which represents 0.1 percent of the United States and multiply that to get 99.9 percent. I think it is much more important to get control of the distribution and the advertising message.[13]

As with all decisions, the objectives of the decision makers will influence the choice of alternative.

The following factors should be considered in the selection of a test market.

**Population Size**   The population should be large enough to provide reliable, projectable results, yet small enough to ensure that costs will not be prohibitive. New York City is not a popular test market; its size makes it unacceptable.

**Demographic Composite and Lifestyle Considerations**   Ethnic backgrounds, incomes, age distributions, lifestyles, and other characteristics of the market should be representative of the nation or other target market. For example, test marketing on the West Coast may not be representative because people there tend to be quick to accept innovations that might not be adopted elsewhere.

**Competitive Situation**   Competitive market shares, competitive advertising, and distribution patterns should be typical so that test markets will represent other geographic regions. If they are not representative, projectability will be difficult.

Consider the firm that test markets in one of its strongest markets. Its sales force has an easy time getting trade acceptance but may have difficulty in a market in which the firm is weak. That will influence the acceptance level, the cost of the sell-in (obtaining initial distribution), and the ultimate results of the test market. Hence, projecting the results of the test market into weaker markets becomes difficult.

Selecting an area with an unrepresentative market potential may cause innumerable problems. Firms probably should not test orange juice products in Florida, dairy products in Wisconsin, or antihistamines in Arizona.

**Media Coverage and Efficiency**   Local media (television spots, newspapers) will never exactly replicate national media. However, duplicating the national media plan or one similar to it is important. Newspapers' Sunday supplements used as a substitute for magazine advertising do not duplicate the national plan, but they may provide a rough estimate of the plan's impact. Ideally, a market should be represented by the major television networks, typical cable television programming, and newspaper coverage. Some magazines have regional editions or advertising inserts.

**Media Isolation**   Advertising from outside communities may contaminate the test market. Further, advertising money is wasted when it reaches consumers who cannot buy the advertised product because they live outside the test area. Markets such as Tulsa (Oklahoma) and Green Bay (Wisconsin) are highly desirable because advertising does not spill over into other areas.

**Self-Contained Trading Area**   Distributors should sell primarily or exclusively in the test market area. *Spill-outs* or *shipments* out of markets from chain warehouses yield confusing shipping figures. Similarly, spill-ins sales are made to shoppers from outside the territory.

**Overused Test Markets**   If consumers or retailers become aware of the tests, they will react in a manner different from their norm. Thus, one great test market should not be established. Tucson is one area now used less frequently than in the past because it has displayed an atypical reaction to new-product introductions. There always seemed to be a new display in the stores, and the public's reaction ceased to be average.

■ Some companies test market outside the United States. Carewell Industries of Fairfield, N.J., tested its Dentax toothbrush in Singapore. While Singapore may not represent America's demographic profile, it offers extreme secrecy. It also offers a low-cost environment for launching a new product.

**Loss of Secrecy**    If a firm delays national introduction by test marketing, a competitor may find out about the experiment and "read" the results of the test market. The firm therefore runs the risk of exposing a new product or its plans to competitors. If the competitor finds the product easy to imitate, it may beat the originating company to the national marketplace. While Clorox Super Detergent with Bleach remained in the test market stage, Procter & Gamble (P&G) introduced Tide with Bleach nationally. Fab 1 Shot, a pouch laundry from Colgate-Palmolive, preempted Cheer Power Pouches by Procter & Gamble, but P&G wasn't sorry: Fab 1 Shot failed to be a commercial success. Although customers tried the new product, they stayed with the more traditional means of doing laundry over the long run.

Marketing research companies often select test market locations because the experiment will have a low chance of being detected by the competition. The **control method of test marketing** uses a "minimarket test" in a small city, using control store distribution, or forced distribution. A marketing research company that specializes in test marketing performs the entire test marketing task, including the initial sale to retailers (referred to as *sell-in*), warehousing, distribution, and shelving of the test product. The research company pays retailers for shelf space and therefore can guarantee distribution to stores that represent a predetermined percentage of the market's all-commodity volume (the total dollar sales for that product in a defined market). Thus, the firm is guaranteed distribution in stores that represent a predetermined percentage of the market. The control method increases the chances that the test market will be undetected.

**Control method of test marketing**
A "minimarket test" using forced distribution in a small city. Retailers are paid for shelf space so that the test marketer can be guaranteed distribution.

---

## ■ SUMMARY

Experimental research allows the investigator to control the research situation to evaluate causal relationships among variables. In a basic experiment, one variable (the independent variable) is manipulated to determine its effect on another (the dependent variable). The alternative manipulations of the independent variable are referred to as *experimental treatments*.

The choice of dependent variable is crucial because this determines the kind of answer given to the research problem. In some situations, deciding on an appropriate operational measure of the dependent variable is difficult.

For experiments, random sampling error is especially associated with selection of subjects and their assignment to the treatments. The best way to overcome this problem is by random assignment of subjects to groups and of groups to treatments.

Other errors may arise from using nonrepresentative populations (for example, college students) as sources of samples or from sample mortality, or attrition, in which subjects withdraw from the experiment before it is completed. In addition, marketing experiments often involve extraneous variables that may affect dependent variables and obscure the effects of independent variables. Experiments also may be affected by demand characteristics when experimenters inadvertently give cues to the desired responses. Also, the guinea pig effect occurs when subjects modify their behavior because they wish to cooperate with an experiment.

Extraneous variables can be controlled by eliminating them or by holding them constant for all treatments. Some extraneous error may arise from the order of presentation; this can be controlled by counterbalancing the order. Random assignment is an attempt to control extraneous variables by chance.

Two main types of marketing experiments are field experiments (such as test markets) conducted in natural environments and laboratory experiments conducted in artificial settings contrived for specific purposes.

Experiments are judged by two measures of validity. One is internal validity, the question of whether the independent variable was the sole cause of the change in the dependent variable. Six types of extraneous variables may jeopardize internal validity: history, maturation, testing, instrumentation, selection, and mortality. The second measure of validity is external validity, the extent to which the results can be generalized to the real world. Field experiments are lower than laboratory experiments in internal validity but higher on external validity. There are many different types of experimental designs. Among the better experimental designs are pretest–posttest control group design, pretest only control group design, and the Solomon four-group design.

Test marketing is an experimental procedure that provides an opportunity to test a new product or marketing plan under realistic conditions to obtain a measure of sales or profit potential. Its major advantage as a research tool is that it closely approximates reality. Test marketing provides the opportunity to estimate the outcomes of alternative courses of action.

## Key Terms and Concepts

| | |
|---|---|
| Experiment | Field experiment |
| Independent variable | Internal validity |
| Experimental treatments | History effect |
| Experimental group | Cohort effect |
| Control group | Maturation effect |
| Dependent variable | Testing effect |
| Test unit | Instrumentation effect |
| Random sampling error | Selection effect |
| Randomization | Mortality (sample attrition) effect |
| Matching | External validity |
| Repeated measures | Basic experimental design |
| Constant error | Quasi-experimental design |
| Demand characteristics | One-shot design |
| Experimenter bias | One-group pretest–posttest design |
| Guinea pig effect | Static group design |
| Blinding | Pretest–posttest control group design |
| Constancy of conditions | Posttest-only control group design |
| Counterbalancing | Solomon four-group design |
| Debriefing | Test marketing |
| Laboratory experiment | Control method of test marketing |
| Tachistoscope | |

## ■ Questions

1. Name some independent and dependent variables frequently studied in marketing.
2. A tissue manufacturer that has the fourth-largest market share plans to experiment with a 50-cents-off coupon during November. It plans to measure sales volume for November using store scanners to determine effectiveness. What is the independent variable? The dependent variable? Do you see any problems with the dependent variable?
3. What purpose does the random assignment of subjects serve?
4. In a test of a new coffee, three styrofoam cups labeled A, B, and C are placed before subjects. The subjects are instructed to taste the coffee from each cup. What problems might arise in this situation?
5. What are demand characteristics? Give some examples.
6. Do you think the guinea pig effect is a common occurrence in experiments? Why or why not?

7. How may an experimenter control for extraneous variation?

8. In the following situations, name the type of experiment described and evaluate the strengths and weaknesses of each design.

    (a) A major petroleum corporation is considering phasing out its premium unleaded gasoline. It selects Nashville, Tennessee, as an experimental market in which the product might be eliminated and decides to watch product line sales results.

    (b) A soft-drink manufacturer puts the same brand of orange drink into two different containers with different designs. Two groups are given a package and asked about the drink's taste. A third group is given the orange drink in an unlabeled package and asked the same question.

    (c) An advertising agency pretested a television commercial with a portable television set, simulating an actual television program with the test commercial inserted along with other commercials. This program was shown to a focus group, and group discussion followed.

    (d) A manufacturer of a new brand of cat food tested product sampling with a trial-size package versus no sampling and three price levels simultaneously to determine the best market penetration strategy.

9. Provide an example for each of the six major factors that influence internal validity.

10. Consider the following research project conducted by a company to investigate a self-contained heating and lighting source designed for use during power failures. The product was given to the experimental subjects, who were asked to wait until dark, then turn off their heat and lights and test the product. A few days later, they were telephoned and interviewed about their opinions of the product. Discuss the external and internal validity of this experiment.

 11. Evaluate the ethical and research design implications of the following study:

    Sixty-six willing Australian drinkers helped a Federal Court judge decide that Tooheys didn't engage in misleading or deceptive advertising for its 2.2 beer.

    The volunteers were invited to a marathon drinking session after the Aboriginal Legal Service claimed Tooheys advertising implied beer drinkers could imbibe as much 2.2 as desired without becoming legally intoxicated. Drunken driving laws prohibit anyone with a blood-alcohol level above 0.05 from getting behind the wheel. The beer contains 2.2 percent alcohol, compared with 6 percent for other beers.

    But the task wasn't easy; nor was it all fun. Some couldn't manage to drink in 1 hour the required 10 "middies," an Aussie term for a beer glass of 10 fluid ounces.

    Thirty-six participants could manage only nine glasses. Four threw up and were excluded; another two couldn't manage the "minimum" nine glasses and had to be replaced.

    Justice J. Beaumont observed that consuming enough 2.2 in an hour to reach the 0.05 level was "uncomfortable and therefore an unlikely process." Because none of the ads mentioned such extreme quantities, he ruled they couldn't be found misleading or deceptive.[14]

 12. A nighttime cough relief formula contains alcohol. An alternative formulation contains no alcohol. During the experiment, the subjects are asked to try the product in their homes. Alternative formulations are randomly assigned to subjects. No mention of alcohol is given in the instructions to subjects.

13. What are the benefits of test marketing? When is test marketing likely? When is it unlikely?

 **EXPLORING THE INTERNET**

Using the Yahoo search engine, click on the Business and Economy option and continue clicking so that you follow this string: Marketing/Marketing Research/Companies. Find a company that conducts experimental research. Discuss the nature of its service.

**CASE 9.1**    The I.G.A. Grocery Store

Dan Kessler, the manager of an I.G.A. grocery store, had a brother-in-law who supervised a large number of keyboard operators at a public utility company. At a family gathering, Kessler's brother-in-law mentioned that his company recently had begun programming background music into the keyboard operators' room. As a result, productivity had increased and the number of errors had decreased.

Kessler thought music within a grocery store might have an impact on customers. Specifically, he thought customers might stay in the store longer if slow, easy-to-listen-to music were played. After some serious thought,

he considered whether he should hire a marketing researcher to design an experiment to test the influence of music tempo on shopper behavior.

**Questions**
1. Operationalize the independent variable.
2. What dependent variables do you think might be important in this study?
3. Develop a hypothesis for each of your dependent variables.

 **CASE 9.2**    Sandra Brown, D.D.S.

Dentists recommend twice-yearly checkups. Although the benefits of preventive health care have been promoted for several decades, some people visit dental services only when in pain.

One dentist, Sandra Brown, had read that sending out a recall card might increase participation in the six-month dental checkup. She thought that having patients address a standard reminder card (see Case Exhibit 9.2-1) in their own handwriting would be more effective than

the standard reminder card alone. She also thought a promotional message appealing to an individual's aesthetic concerns might be more appropriate than a reminder message.

She designed the following experiment for her dental clinic, located on the fringe of the downtown area. The clinic patients were primarily African Americans and Mexican Americans, and most were from blue-collar households. All patients were considered subjects for the experiment.

■ **Case Exhibit 9.2-1**

**Standard Recall Card and One Experimental Version**

> Dear Patient,
>     This is to remind you that it is time for a preventive dental examination.
>     Please call so that we may arrange a time that is convenient for you.
>
>                                   Sandra Brown, D.D.S.

> Dear Patient,
>     Preventive dental examinations keep you looking your best. Your teeth are part of your good looks.
>     Please call so that we may arrange a time that is convenient for you.
>     Let's keep your smile looking its best.
>
>                                   Sandra Brown, D.D.S.

There were four experimental groups: (1) Patients who visited the dentist in May were given the standard recall card (to return in October) and asked to fill it out in their own handwriting; (2) patients who visited the dentist in June were given a promotional recall card (to return in November) and asked to fill it out in their own handwriting; (3) patients who visited the dentist in July received the standard recall card, which was typed out (to return in December); (4) patients who visited the dentist in August received the promotional recall card, which was typed out (to return in January).

**Questions**

1. Evaluate this experimental design.
2. What type of experimental design is this?
3. What improvements would you suggest for the experiment?

## ■ Endnotes

[1] Brian Wansink, "How and Why a Package's Size Influences Usage Volume".

[2] Anne G. Perkins, "Package Size: When Bigger Is Better," *Harvard Business Review,* March–April 1995, p. 14.

[3] Barry F. Anderson, *The Psychological Experiment: An Introduction to the Scientific Method* (Belmont, Cal.: Brooks-Cole, 1971), p. 28.

[4] M. Venkatesan and Robert J. Holloway, *An Introduction to Marketing Experimentation: Methods, Applications and Problems* (New York: The Free Press, 1971), p. 14.

[5] Alice M. Tybout and Gerald Zaltman, "Ethics in Marketing Research: Their Practical Relevance," *Journal of Marketing Research,* November 1974, pp. 357–368.

[6] Daniel Toy, Jerry Olsen, and Lauren Wright, "Effects of Debriefing in Marketing Research Involving 'Mild' Deceptions," *Psychology and Marketing,* Spring 1989, pp. 65–85.

[7] This section is based on Donald T. Campbell and Julian C. Stanley, *Experimental and Quasi-Experimental Designs for Research* (Chicago: Rand McNally, 1963), pp. 5–9.

[8] Ibid., p. 9.

[9] B. J. Winer, *Statistical Principles in Experimental Design* (New York: McGraw-Hill, 1979), p. 1.

[10] Campbell and Stanley, *Experimental and Quasi-Experimental Designs,* pp. 13–25.

[11] The term *observation* is used in the most general sense. Although most marketing experiments will use some form of measurement other than direct observation of some dependent variable, the terminology used by Campbell and Stanley is used here because of its traditional nature.

[12] *Market Testing Consumer Products* (New York: National Industrial Conference Board, 1967), p. 13.

[13] Sally Scanlon, "The True Test," *Sales and Marketing Management* (March 1979), p. 57.

[14] Geoffrey Lee Martin, "Drinkers Get Court Call" *Advertising Age,* May 20, 1991.

# PART

# *III* MEASUREMENT

# 10 MEASUREMENT AND ATTITUDE SCALING

**WHAT YOU WILL LEARN IN THIS CHAPTER:**

To explain how a researcher might answer the question "What is to be measured?"

To define *operational definition.*

To distinguish among nominal, ordinal, interval, and ratio scales.

To understand the need for index or composite measures.

To define the three criteria for good measurement.

To understand that an attitude is a hypothetical construct.

To explain the attitude-measuring process.

To discuss the differences among ranking, rating, sorting, and making choices to measure attitudes and preferences.

To explain Likert scales, semantic differentials, and many other types of attitude scales.

To understand how to measure behavioral intentions.

**B**BDO, an advertising agency, has developed a measuring system to evaluate consumers' emotional responses to advertising. Its Emotional Measurement System is a proprietary device that uses photographs of actors' faces to help consumers choose their reactions to commercials. Researchers at BBDO believe that the process virtually eliminates the inherent bias in traditional copy testing. With the conventional system, consumers often underestimate their emotional responses because they feel silly putting them into words, and words are subject to varying interpretations. Thus, traditional copy tests have tended to measure thoughts rather than feelings and therefore have failed to adequately measure emotional responses.

Rather than ask consumers to choose from a simple list or write in their own words, the agency has devised a deck of 53 photos—narrowed down from 1,800—representing what BBDO calls the "universe of emotions." Each features one of six actors with different expressions ranging from happy/playful to disgusted/revolted. A total of 26 categories of emotions are expressed.

Here's how the system works. As with most copy testing, participants are shown a single commercial or group of spots and then are given a questionnaire to test whether they remembered

215

brand names and copy points. At any point during this process, the researchers hand out the photos. Each person is asked not to write or speak about the spot but to quickly sort through the photos, setting aside any or all that reflect how he or she feels after viewing the commercial.[1]

Innovative techniques such as the Emotional Measurement System have improved the measurement of marketing phenomena. This chapter discusses the basic measurement issues in marketing research and attitude measurement.

## ■ WHAT IS TO BE MEASURED?

An object, such as the edge of your textbook, can be measured with either side of a ruler (see Exhibit 10.1). Note that one side has inches and the other has centimeters. However, the scale of measurement will vary depending on whether the metric side or the standard side is used. Many measurement problems in marketing research are similar to this ruler with its alternative scales of measurement. Unfortunately, unlike the two-sided ruler, many measurement scales used in marketing research are not directly comparable.

The first question the researcher must answer is "What is to be measured?" This question is not as simple as it sounds. The definition of the problem, based on exploratory research or managerial judgment, indicates the concept to be investigated (for example, sales performance). However, a precise definition of the concept may require a description of how it will be measured, and frequently there is more than one way to measure a particular concept. For example, if we are conducting research to determine which factors influence a sales representative's performance, we might use a number of measures to indicate a salesperson's success, such as dollar or unit sales volume or share of accounts lost. Further, true measurement of concepts requires a process of precisely assigning scores or numbers to the attributes of people or objects.[2] The purpose of assigning numbers is to convey information about the variable being measured. Hence, the key question becomes "On what basis will numbers or scores be assigned to the concept?"

Suppose the task is to measure the height of a boy named Michael. We can proceed as follows:

1. We can create five categories:
    (1) Quite tall for his age
    (2) Moderately tall for his age
    (3) About average for his age

## ■ Exhibit 10.1     A Two-Sided Ruler That Offers Alternative Scales of Measurement

cm  1  2  3  4  5  6  7  8  9  10  11  12  13  14  15

*For Good Measure*   from the   **National Bureau of Standards**
Washington, D.C. 20234

Inches  1  2  3  4  5  6

(4)  Moderately short for his age

(5)  Quite short for his age

Then we can measure Michael by saying that because he is moderately tall for his age, his height measurement is 2.

2.  We can compare Michael to 10 other neighborhood children. We give the tallest child the rank of 1 and the shortest the rank of 11; Michael's height measurement using this procedure is 4 if he is fourth tallest among the 11 neighborhood children.

3.  We can use some conventional measuring unit such as centimeters and, measuring to the nearest centimeter, designate Michael's height as 137.

4.  We can define two categories of height:

(1)  A nice height

(2)  A not-so-nice height

By our personal standard, Michael's height is a nice height, so his height measurement is 1.[3]

In each measuring situation, we have assigned a score for Michael's height: 2, 4, 137, and 1. In scientific marketing, research precision is the goal. The researcher must determine the best way to measure what is to be investigated.

On college campuses, girl or boy watching constitutes a measurement activity: What might be a 7 to one person may be a 9 to another. Precise measurement in marketing research requires a careful conceptual definition, an operational definition, and a system of consistent rules for assigning numbers or scores.

## ■ Concepts

**Concept**
A generalized idea about a class of objects, attributes, occurrences, or processes.

Before beginning the measurement process, a marketing researcher must identify the concepts relevant to the problem. A **concept** (or *construct*) is a generalized idea about a class of objects, attributes, occurrences, or processes. Concepts such as age, gender, and number of children are relatively concrete properties, and they present few problems in definition or measurement. Other characteristics of individuals or properties of objects may be more abstract. Concepts such as brand loyalty, personality, channel power, and so on present greater problems in definition and measurement. For example, brand loyalty has been measured using the percentage of a person's purchases going to one brand in a given period of time, sequences of brand purchases, number of different brands purchased, amount of brand deliberation, and various cognitive measures, such as attitude toward a brand.

## ■ Operational Definitions

**Operational definition**
An explanation that gives meaning to a concept by specifying the activities or operations necessary to measure it.

To be measurable, concepts must be made operational. An **operational definition** gives meaning to a concept by specifying the activities or operations necessary to measure it.[4] For example, the concept of nutrition consciousness might be indicated when a shopper reads the nutritional information on a cereal package. Inspecting a nutritional label is not the same as nutrition consciousness, but it is a clue that a person may be nutrition conscious.

The operational definition specifies what the researcher must do to measure the concept under investigation. If we wish to measure consumer interest in a specific advertisement, we may operationally define *interest* as a degree of increase in pupil dilation. Another operational definition of interest might rely on direct responses: what people say they are interested in. Each operational definition has advantages and disadvantages.

An operational definition is like a manual of instructions or a recipe: Even the truth of a statement such as "Gaston Gourmet likes key lime pie" depends on the recipe. Different instructions lead us to different results.[5]

---

■ **Exhibit 10.2**                    **Media Skepticism: An Operational Definition**

| Concept | Conceptual Definition | Operational Definition |
|---|---|---|
| Media skepticism | Media skepticism is the degree to which individuals are skeptical toward the reality presented in the mass media. Media skepticism varies across individuals, from those who are mildly skeptical and accept most of what they see and hear in the media to those who completely discount and disbelieve the facts, values, and portrayal of reality in the media. | Please tell me how true each statement is about the media. Is it very true, not very true, or not at all true?<br><br>1. The program was not very accurate in its portrayal of the problem.<br>2. Most of the story was staged for entertainment purposes.<br>3. The presentation was slanted and unfair.<br>4. I think the story was fair and unbiased.<br>5. I think important facts were purposely left out of the story.<br><br>Individual items were scored on a 4-point scale with values from 1 to 4; higher scores represented greater skepticism. Media skepticism is defined as the sum of these five scores. |

---

**Conceptual definition**
A verbal explanation of the meaning of a concept; defines what the concept is and what it is not.

An operational definition tells the investigator, "Do such-and-such in so-and-so manner."[6] Exhibit 10.2 presents a **conceptual definition** and an operational definition from a study on media skepticism.

## ■ RULES OF MEASUREMENT

**Rule**
A guide that instructs the investigator about what to do.

A **rule** is a guide that instructs us about what to do.[7] An example of a measurement rule might be: Assign the numerals 1 through 7 to individuals according to how brand loyal they are. If the individual is extremely brand loyal, assign a 7. If the individual is a total brand switcher with no brand loyalty, assign a 1.

Operational definitions help the researcher specify the rules for assigning numbers. If the purpose of an advertising experiment is to increase the amount of time shoppers spend in a department store, for example, *shopping time* must be operationally defined. Once shopping time is defined as the interval between entering the door and receiving the receipt from the clerk, assignment of numbers via a stopwatch is facilitated. If a study on gasohol, a blend of ethyl alcohol and gasoline, is not concerned with a person's depth of experience but defines people as users or nonusers, it could assign a 1 for *experience with gasohol* and a 0 for *no experience with gasohol*.

The values assigned in the measuring process can be manipulated according to certain mathematical rules. The properties of the scale of numbers may allow the researcher to add, subtract, or multiply answers. In other cases, there may be problems with the simple addition of the numbers or other mathematical manipulations because the procedure is not permissible within the mathematical system.

## ■ TYPES OF SCALES

A **scale** is a quantifying measure or combination of items that is progressively arranged according to value or magnitude. In other words, a scale is a continuous spectrum or series

**Scale**
A quantifying measure or combination of items that is progressively arranged according to value or magnitude.

of categories. The purpose of scaling is to represent, usually quantitatively, an item's, person's, or event's place in the spectrum.

Marketing researchers use many scales or number systems. It is traditional to classify scales of measurement on the basis of the mathematical comparisons they allow. The four types of scale are the nominal, ordinal, interval, and ratio scales.

### ■ Nominal Scale

**Nominal scale**
A scale in which the numbers or letters assigned to the object serve as labels for identification or classification.

Number 16 on the Los Angeles Dodgers is Hideo Nomo. Larry Walker is number 33 on the Colorado Rockies. These numbers nominally identify these superstars. A **nominal scale** is the simplest type of scale. The numbers or letters assigned to objects serve as labels for identification or classification. These are scales in name only. Tulsa's census tract 25 and census tract 87 are merely labels. The number 87 does not imply that this area has more people or higher incomes than number 25. An example of a typical nominal scale in marketing research would be the coding of males as 1 and females as 2. As another example, the first drawing in Exhibit 10.3 depicts the number 7 on a horse's colors. This is merely a label for the bettors and racing enthusiasts.

### ■ Ordinal Scale

We know that when our horse comes in the "show" position at the racetrack, it has come in third behind the win and the place horses (see the second drawing in Exhibit 10.3). An

---

### ■ Exhibit 10.3

**Nominal, Ordinal, Interval, and Ratio Scales Provide Different Information**

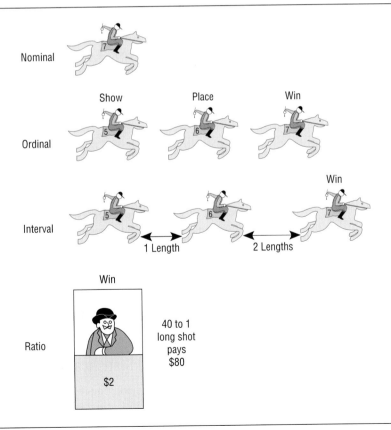

**Ordinal scale**
A scale that arranges objects or alternatives according to their magnitude in an ordered relationship.

**ordinal scale** arranges objects or alternatives according to their magnitude in an ordered relationship. When respondents are asked to *rank order* their shopping center preferences, ordinal values are assigned. In our racehorse example, if we assign 1 to the win position, 2 to the place position, and 3 to the show position, we can say that 1 was before 2 and 2 was before 3. However, we cannot say anything about the degree of distance or the interval between the win and show horses or the show and place horses.

A typical ordinal scale in marketing asks respondents to rate brands, companies, and so on as excellent, good, fair, or poor. We know excellent is higher than good, but we do not know by how much.

### ■ Interval Scale

The third drawing in Exhibit 10.3 depicts a horse race in which the win horse was two lengths ahead of the place horse, which was one length ahead of the show horse. Not only is the order of finish known, but the distance between the horses is known. **Interval scales** not only indicate order, but they also measure order (or distance) in units of equal intervals.[8]

**Interval scale**
A scale that both arranges objects according to their magnitudes and distinguishes the ordered arrangement in units of equal intervals.

The location of the zero point is arbitrary. In the consumer price index, if the base year is 1993, the price level during 1993 will be set at 100. Although this is an equal-interval measurement scale, the zero point is arbitrary. The classic example of an interval scale is the Fahrenheit temperature scale. If the temperature is 80°, it cannot be said that it is twice as hot as a 40° temperature, because 0° represents not a lack of temperature but a relative point on the Fahrenheit scale. Due to the lack of an absolute zero point, the interval scale does not allow the conclusion that the number 36 is three times as great as the number 12; it allows us to conclude only that the distance is three times as great. Likewise, when an interval scale is used to measure psychological attributes, the researcher can comment about the magnitude of differences or compare the average differences on the attributes that were measured, but cannot determine the actual strength of the attitude toward an object. However, the changes in concepts over time can be compared if the researcher continues to use the same scale in longitudinal research.

### ■ Ratio Scale

**Ratio scale**
A scale that has absolute rather than relative quantities and an absolute zero where a given attribute is absent.

To be able to say that winning tickets pay 40 to 1 for win bets or that racehorse number 7 is twice as heavy as racehorse number 5, we need a ratio scale (see the fourth drawing in Exhibit 10.3). **Ratio scales** assign absolute rather than relative quantities. For example, both money and weight are ratio scales because they possess absolute zeros and interval properties. The absolute zero represents a point on the scale where a given attribute is absent. When one states that a person has zero ounces of gold, we understand the natural zero value for weight. In the measurement of temperature, the Kelvin scale (a ratio scale) begins at absolute zero, a point that corresponds to –273.16° on the Celsius scale (an interval scale). In distribution or logistical research, it may be appropriate to think of physical attributes such as weight or distance as ratio scales in which the ratio of scale values are meaningful. For most behavioral marketing research, however, interval scales typically are the appropriate measurements.

### ■ Mathematical and Statistical Analysis of Scales

The type of scale used in marketing research will determine the form of the statistical analysis. For example, a number of operations, such as calculation of a mean (mathematical average), can be conducted only if the scale is of an interval or a ratio nature; they are not permissible with nominal or ordinal scales. Chapter 14, "Basic Data Analysis," further explores how the type of scale influences the choice of the appropriate statistical technique.

# ■ INDEX MEASURES

So far we have focused on measuring a concept with a single question or observation. Measuring brand awareness, for example, might involve one question such as "Are you aware of _____?" However, measuring more complex concepts may require more than one question because the concept has several attributes. An **attribute** is a single characteristic or fundamental feature that pertains to an object, a person, a situation, or an issue.

Multi-item instruments for measuring a single concept with several attributes are called **index measures,** or **composite measures.** One index of social class is based on three weighted variables: residence, occupation, and education. Measures of cognitive phenomena often are composite indexes of sets of variables or scales. Items are combined into composite measures. For example, a salesperson's morale may be measured by combining questions such as "How satisfied are you with your job? How satisfied are you with your territory? How satisfied are you in your personal life?" Measuring the same underlying concept using a variety of techniques is one method for increasing accuracy. Asking different questions to measure the same concept provides a more accurate cumulative measure than does a single-item estimate.

**Attribute**
A single characteristic or fundamental feature that pertains to an object, a person, a situation, or an issue.

**Index (composite) measure**
A multi-item instrument that uses several variables to measure a single concept.

# ■ THREE CRITERIA FOR GOOD MEASUREMENT

The three major criteria for evaluating measurements are reliability, validity, and sensitivity.

## ■ Reliability

A tailor measuring fabric with a tape measure obtains a "true" value of the fabric length. If the tailor repeatedly measures the fabric and each time estimates the same length, it is assumed the tape measure is reliable. When the outcome of the measuring process is reproducible—that is, when similar results are obtained over time and across situations—the measuring instrument is reliable. Broadly defined, **reliability** is the degree to which a measure is free from random error and therefore yields consistent results. For example, ordinal-level measures are reliable if they consistently rank order subjects in the same manner; reliable interval-level measures consistently rank order and maintain the distance between subjects. Imperfections in the measuring process that affect the assignment of scores or numbers in different ways each time a measure is taken, such as a respondent misunderstanding a question, cause low reliability. The actual choice among plausible responses may be governed by such transitory factors as mood, whim, or the context set by surrounding questions; measures are not always error free and stable over time.

**Reliability**
The degree to which a measure is free from random error and therefore yields consistent results.

## ■ Validity

The purpose of measurement is to measure what we intend to measure. Achieving this obvious goal is not, however, as simple as it sounds. Consider the student who takes a test (measurement) in a statistics class and receives a poor grade. The student may say, "I really understood that material because I studied hard. The test measured my ability to do

■ Airline travelers put "space," especially the distance between seat backs and leg room, high on their list. Space becomes extremely important if a flight is several hours long. Plog Travel Research found that when TWA gave people more leg room, they rated the meals higher, even though the meals did not change. In fact, a halo effect influenced the ratings of most other characteristics, not just the food.[9] Were the measures of food quality and airline characteristics other than leg room valid?

arithmetic and to memorize formulas rather than measuring my understanding of statistics." The student's complaint is that the test did not measure *understanding* of statistics, which was what the professor had intended to measure; it measured something else.

One technique for measuring the intention to buy is the gift method. Respondents are told a drawing will be held at some future period for a year's supply of a certain product. Respondents report which of several brands they would prefer to receive if they won. Do the respondents' reports of the brands they would prefer to win necessarily constitute a valid measure of the brands they will actually purchase in the marketplace if they do not win the contest? Could there be a systematic bias to identify brands they wish they could afford rather than the brands they would usually purchase? This is a question of **validity,** the ability of an instrument (for example, an attitude measure in marketing) to measure what it is intended to measure. If it does not, problems will result.

Students should be able to empathize with the following validity problem. Consider the ongoing controversy about highway patrol officers using radar guns to clock speeders. A driver is clocked at 75 mph in a 55 mph zone, but the same radar gun aimed at a house registers 28 mph. The error occurred because the radar gun had picked up impulses from the electrical system of the squad car's idling engine. The house was not moving, and the test was not valid.

**Validity**
The ability of an instrument to measure what it is intended to measure.

### ■ Reliability versus Validity

Let's compare the concepts of reliability and validity. A tailor using a ruler may obtain a reliable measurement of length over time with a bent ruler. A bent ruler cannot provide perfect accuracy, however, and it is not a valid measure. Thus, reliability, although necessary for validity, is not in itself sufficient. In marketing, a measure of a subject's physiological reaction to a package (for example, pupil dilation) may be highly reliable, but it will not necessarily constitute a valid measure of purchase intention.

The differences between reliability and validity can be illustrated using the rifle targets in Exhibit 10.4. An expert sharpshooter fires an equal number of rounds with a century-old rifle and a modern rifle.[10] The shots from the older gun are considerably scattered, but those from the new gun are closely clustered. The variability of the old rifle compared with that of the new one indicates it is less reliable. Target C illustrates the concept of a systematic bias influencing validity. The new rifle is reliable (little variance), but the sharpshooter's vision is hampered by glare from the sun; although consistent, the sharpshooter is unable to hit the bull's-eye.

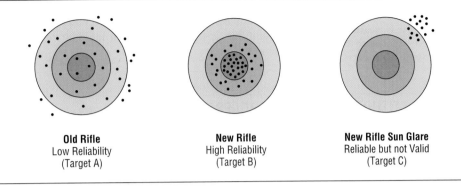

**■ Exhibit 10.4**

**Reliability and Validity on Target**

**Old Rifle**
Low Reliability
(Target A)

**New Rifle**
High Reliability
(Target B)

**New Rifle Sun Glare**
Reliable but not Valid
(Target C)

## ■ Sensitivity

**Sensitivity**
An instrument's ability to accurately measure variability in stimuli or responses.

The sensitivity of a scale is an important measurement concept, particularly when changes in attitudes or other hypothetical constructs are under investigation. **Sensitivity** refers to an instrument's ability to accurately measure variability in stimuli or responses. A dichotomous response category, such as "agree or disagree," does not reflect subtle attitude changes. A more sensitive measure with numerous categories on the scale may be needed. For example, adding "strongly agree," "mildly agree," "neither agree nor disagree," "mildly disagree," and "strongly disagree" will increase the scale's sensitivity.

The sensitivity of a scale based on a single question or item also can be increased by adding questions or items. In other words, because index measures allow for a greater range of possible scores, they are more sensitive than single-item scales.

## ■ ATTITUDES: DEFINITION AND COMPONENTS

**Attitude**
An enduring disposition to consistently respond in a given manner to various aspects of the world; composed of affective, cognitive, and behavioral components.

There are many definitions of *attitude*. **Attitude** usually is viewed as an enduring disposition to consistently respond in a given manner to various aspects of the world, including people, events, and objects. One conception of attitude is reflected in this brief statement: "Sally loves shopping at Sam's. She believes it's clean, conveniently located, and has the lowest prices. She intends to shop there every Thursday." This short description has identified three components of attitudes: affective, cognitive, and behavioral.

The *affective* component reflects an individual's general feelings or emotions toward an object. Statements such as "I love my Chevrolet Corvette," "I liked that book *A Corporate Bestiary,*" or "I hate cranberry juice" reflect the emotional character of attitudes. The way one feels about a product, advertisement, or other object is usually tied to one's beliefs or cognitions. The *cognitive* component represents one's awareness of and knowledge about an object. One person might feel happy about the purchase of an automobile because she believes "it gets great gas mileage" or knows the dealer is "the best in New Jersey." The *behavioral* component reflects buying intentions and behavioral expectations. It reflects a predisposition to action.

### ■ Attitudes as Hypothetical Constructs

Many variables marketing researchers wish to investigate are psychological variables that cannot be directly observed. For example, someone may have an attitude toward a particular brand of shaving cream, but we cannot observe this attitude. To measure an attitude, we

**Hypothetical construct**
A variable that is not directly observable but is measured by an indirect means, such as verbal expression or overt behavior.

must infer from the way an individual responds (by a verbal expression or overt behavior) to some stimulus. The term **hypothetical construct** describes a variable that is not directly observable but is measurable by an indirect means such as verbal expression or overt behavior.

# ■ THE ATTITUDE-MEASURING PROCESS

**Ranking**
A measurement task that requires respondents to rank order a small number of stores, brands, or objects in overall preference or on the basis of some characteristic of the stimulus.

**Rating**
A measurement task that requires respondents to estimate the magnitude of a characteristic or quality that a brand, store, or object possesses.

**Sorting**
A measurement task that presents respondents with several objects or with information typed on cards and requires them to arrange the objects or cards into a number of piles or otherwise classify the product concepts.

A remarkable variety of techniques have been devised to measure attitudes. This stems in part from a lack of consensus about the exact definition of the concept. Further, the affective, cognitive, and behavioral components of an attitude may be measured by different means. For example, sympathetic nervous system responses may be recorded using physiological measures to quantify affect, but they are not good measures of behavioral intentions. Direct verbal statements concerning affect, belief, or behavior are used to measure behavioral intent. However, attitudes also may be measured indirectly using the qualitative exploratory techniques discussed in Chapter 5. Obtaining verbal statements from respondents generally requires that the respondents perform a task such as ranking, rating, sorting, or making choices.

A **ranking** task requires the respondent to rank order a small number of stores, brands, or objects in overall preference or on the basis of some characteristic of the stimulus. A **rating** task asks the respondent to estimate the magnitude of a characteristic or quality that an object possesses. A quantitative score, which lies along a continuum that has been supplied to the respondent, is used to estimate the strength of the attitude or belief; in other words, the respondent indicates the position on one or more scales at which he or she would rate the object. A **sorting** task might present the respondent with several product concepts printed on cards and require the respondent to arrange the cards into a number of piles or otherwise classify the product concepts. **Choice** between two or more alternatives is another type of attitude measurement. If a respondent chooses one object over another, the researcher can assume the chosen object is preferred over the other. The following sections describe the most popular techniques for measuring attitudes.

# ■ PHYSIOLOGICAL MEASURES OF ATTITUDES

**Choice**
A measurement task that identifies preferences by requiring respondents to choose between two or more alternatives.

Galvanic skin response, measures of blood pressure, pupil dilation, and other physiological measures may be used to assess the affective components of attitudes. These measures provide a means of measuring attitudes without verbally questioning the respondent. In general, these measures can provide a gross measure of like or dislike, but they are not extremely sensitive measures for identifying the different gradients of an attitude. Each of these measures is discussed elsewhere in the text.

# ■ ATTITUDE RATING SCALES

Using rating scales to measure attitudes is perhaps the most common practice in marketing research. This section discusses many rating scales designed to enable respondents to report the intensity of their attitudes.

## ■ Simple Attitude Scaling

In its most basic form, attitude scaling requires that an individual agree with a statement or respond to a single question. For example, respondents in a political poll may be asked whether they agree or disagree with the statement "The president should run for reelection." An individual may indicate whether he or she likes or dislikes jalapeño bean dip. This type of self-rating scale merely classifies respondents into one of two categories; thus, it has only the properties of a nominal scale and limits the type of mathematical analysis that may be used with the simplified or basic scale.

Despite its disadvantages, simple attitude scaling may be used when questionnaires are extremely long, when respondents have little education, or for other specific reasons. A number of simplified scales are merely checklists: A respondent indicates past experience, preference, and the like merely by checking an item. In many cases, the items are adjectives that describe a particular object.

Most attitude theorists believe attitudes vary along a continuum. Early attitude researchers pioneered the view that the task of attitude scaling is to measure the distance between "good to bad," "low to high," "like to dislike," and so on. Thus, the purpose of an attitude scale is to find an individual's position on the continuum. If this is the case, these simple scales do not allow for fine distinctions among attitudes. Several other scales have been developed to make these more precise measurements.

### ■ Category Scales

The example just given is a rating scale that contains only two response categories: agree/disagree. Expanding the response categories gives the respondent more flexibility in the rating task. Even more information is provided if the categories are ordered according to a particular descriptive or evaluative dimension. Consider the following question:

**How often do you disagree with your spouse about how much to spend on various things?**

☐ **Never**        ☐ **Rarely**        ☐ **Sometimes**        ☐ **Often**        ☐ **Very often**

**Category scale**
A rating scale that consists of several response categories, often providing respondents with alternatives to indicate positions on a continuum.

This **category scale** is a more sensitive measure than a scale that has only two response categories; it provides more information.

Question wording is an extremely important factor in the usefulness of these scales. Exhibit 10.5 shows some common wordings for category scales. Question wording is discussed in Chapter 11.

### ■ Method of Summated Ratings: The Likert Scale

Marketing researchers' adaptation of the method of summated ratings developed by Likert is an extremely popular means for measuring attitudes because it is simple to administer. With the **Likert scale,** respondents indicate their attitudes by checking how strongly they agree or disagree with carefully constructed statements ranging from very positive to very negative attitudes toward some object. Individuals generally choose from approximately five response alternatives: *strongly agree, agree, uncertain, disagree,* and *strongly disagree.* The number of alternatives typically ranges from three to nine.

**Likert scale**
A measure of attitudes in which respondents rate how strongly they agree or disagree with carefully constructed statements; several scale items ranging from very positive to very negative attitudes toward an object may be used to form a summated index.

Consider the following example from a study of food shopping behavior:

**In buying food for my family, price is no object.**

| Strongly agree (5) | Agree (4) | Uncertain (3) | Disagree (2) | Strongly disagree (1) |
|---|---|---|---|---|

To measure the attitude, researchers assign scores or weights to the alternative responses. In this example, weights of 5, 4, 3, 2, and 1 are assigned. (The weights, shown in parentheses, would not be printed on the questionnaire.) Strong agreement indicates the most favorable attitudes on the statement, and a weight of 5 is assigned to this response.

■ **Exhibit 10.5**

**Selected Category Sales**

| Quality | | | | |
|---|---|---|---|---|
| Excellent | Good | Fair | Poor | |
| Very good | Fairly good | Neither good nor bad | Not very good | Not good at all |

| Importance | | | | |
|---|---|---|---|---|
| Very important | Fairly important | Neutral | Not so important | Not at all important |

| Interest | | | | |
|---|---|---|---|---|
| Very interested | | Somewhat interested | | Not very interested |

| Satisfaction | | | | |
|---|---|---|---|---|
| Completely satisfied | Somewhat satisfied | Neither satisfied nor dissatisfied | Somewhat dissatisfied | Completely dissatisfied |
| Very Satisfied | Quite satisfied | | Somewhat satisfied | Not at all satisfied |

| Frequency | | | | |
|---|---|---|---|---|
| All of the time | Very often | Often | Sometimes | Hardly ever |
| Very often | Often | Sometimes | Rarely | Never |
| All of the time | Most of the time | | Some of the time | Just now and then |

| Truth | | | | |
|---|---|---|---|---|
| Very true | Somewhat true | | Not very true | Not at all true |
| Definitely yes | Probably yes | | Probably no | Definitely no |

| Uniqueness | | | | |
|---|---|---|---|---|
| Very different | Somewhat different | | Slightly different | Not at all different |
| Extremely unique | Very unique | Somewhat unique | Slightly unique | Not at all unique |

The statement used as an example is positive toward the attitude. If a negative statement toward the object (such as "I carefully budget my food expenditures") were given, the weights would be reversed, and "strongly disagree" would be assigned a weight of 5. A single scale item on a summated scale is an ordinal scale.

A Likert scale may include several scale items to form an index. Each statement is assumed to represent an aspect of a common attitudinal domain. For example, Exhibit 10.6 shows the items in a Likert scale for measuring attitudes toward patients' interaction with a physician's service staff. The total score is the summation of the weights assigned to an individual's total responses. Here the maximum possible score for the index would be 20 if a 5 were assigned to "strongly agree" responses for each of the positively worded statements and a 5 to "strongly disagree" responses for the negative statement. (Item 3 is negatively worded and therefore is reverse coded.)

■ **Exhibit 10.6**

**Likert Scale Items for Measuring Attitudes toward Patients' Interaction with a Physician's Service Staff**

1. My doctor's office staff takes a warm and personal interest in me.
2. My doctor's office staff is friendly and courteous.
3. My doctor's office staff is more interested in serving the doctor's needs than in serving my needs.
4. My doctor's office staff always acts in a professional manner.

In Likert's original procedure, a large number of statements are generated and an item analysis is performed. The item analysis ensures that final items evoke a wide response and discriminate among those with positive and negative attitudes. Items that are poor because they lack clarity or elicit mixed response patterns are eliminated from the final statement list. However, many marketing researchers do not follow the exact procedure Likert prescribed. Hence, a disadvantage of the Likert-type summated rating method is that it is difficult to know what a single summated score means. Many patterns of response to the various statements can produce the same total score. Thus, identical total scores may reflect different attitudes because of different combinations of statements endorsed.

## ■ Semantic Differential

**Semantic differential**
A measure of attitudes that consists of a series of 7-point rating scales that use bipolar adjectives to anchor the beginning and end of each scale.

The **semantic differential** is actually a series of attitude scales. This popular attitude measurement technique consists of the identification of a product, brand, store, or other concept followed by a series of 7-point bipolar rating scales. Bipolar adjectives, such as *good* and *bad, modern* and *old-fashioned,* or *clean* and *dirty,* anchor the beginning and the end (or poles) of the scale. The subject makes repeated judgments about the concept under investigation on each scale. Exhibit 10.7 shows a series of scales to measure attitudes toward jazz saxophone recordings.

The scoring of the semantic differential can be illustrated using the scale bounded by the anchors "modern" and "old-fashioned." Respondents are instructed to check the place that indicates the nearest appropriate adjective. From left to right, the scale intervals are interpreted as "extremely modern," "very modern," "slightly modern," "both modern and old-fashioned," "slightly old-fashioned," and "extremely old-fashioned":

Modern__:__:__:__:__:__:__Old-fashioned

The semantic differential technique originally was developed as a method for measuring the meanings of objects or the "semantic space" of interpersonal experience. Marketing researchers have found the semantic differential versatile and have modified its

■ **Exhibit 10.7**

**Semantic Differential Scales for Measuring Attitude toward Jazz Saxophone Recordings**

Fast__:__:__:__:__:__Slow
Intellectual__:__:__:__:__:__Emotional
Contemporary__:__:__:__:__:__Traditional
Composed__:__:__:__:__:__Improvised
Flat__:__:__:__:__:__Sharp
Busy__:__:__:__:__:__Lazy
New__:__:__:__:__:__Old
Progressive__:__:__:__:__:__Regressive

use for business applications. Replacing the bipolar adjectives with descriptive phrases is a frequent adaptation in image studies. The phrases "aged a long time," "not aged a long time," "not watery looking," and "watery looking" were used in a beer brand image study.

A savings and loan might use the phrases "low interest on savings" and "favorable interest on savings." These phrases are not polar opposites. Consumer researchers have found that respondents often are unwilling to use the extreme negative side of a scale. Research with industrial salespeople, for example, found that in rating their own performances, salespeople would not use the negative side of the scale. Hence it was eliminated, and the anchor opposite the positive anchor showed "satisfactory" rather than "extremely poor" performance.

A weight is assigned to each position on the rating scale. Traditionally scores are 7, 6, 5, 4, 3, 2, 1, or +3, +2, +1, 0, –1, –2, –3. Many marketing researchers find it desirable to assume the semantic differential provides interval data. This assumption, although widely accepted, has its critics, who argue that the data have only ordinal properties because the weights are arbitrary.

Exhibit 10.8 illustrates a typical **image profile** based on semantic differential data. Depending on whether the data are assumed to be interval or ordinal, the arithmetic mean or the median will be used to compare the profile of one product, brand, or store with that of a competing product, brand, or store.

**Image profile**
A graphic representation of semantic differential data for competing brands, products, or stores to highlight comparisons.

**Numerical scale**
An attitude rating scale that is similar to a semantic differential except that it uses numbers as response options instead of verbal descriptions to identify response positions.

## ■ Numerical Scales

**Numerical scales** have numbers as response options, rather than semantic space or verbal descriptions, to identify categories (response positions). For example, if the scale items

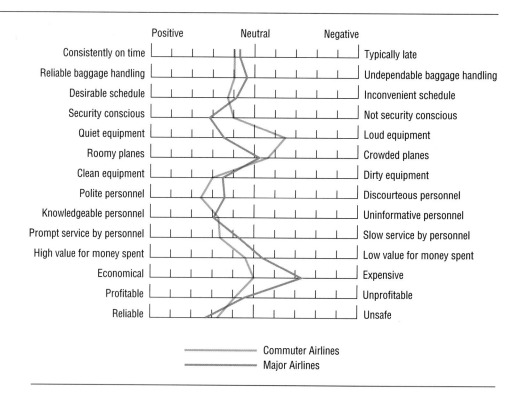

■ **Exhibit 10.8**

**Image Profile of Commuter Airlines versus Major Airlines**

have five response positions, the scale is called a *5-point numerical scale;* a scale with seven response positions is called a *7-point numerical scale;* and so on.

Consider the following numerical scale:

**Now that you've had your automobile for about 1 year, please tell us how satisfied you are with your Ford Taurus.**

**Extremely satisfied    7    6    5    4    3    2    1    Extremely dissatisfied**

This numerical scale uses bipolar adjectives in the same manner as the semantic differential. In practice, researchers have found that educated populations provide numerical labels for intermediate points on the scale that constitute as effective a measure as the true semantic differential.

## ■ Stapel Scale

**Stapel scale**
A measure of attitudes that consists of a single adjective in the center of an even-numbered range of numerical values.

The **Stapel scale** originally was developed in the 1950s to measure simultaneously the direction and intensity of an attitude. Modern versions of the scale use a single adjective as a substitute for the semantic differential when it is difficult to create pairs of bipolar adjectives. The modified Stapel scale places a single adjective in the center of an even number of numerical values (ranging, perhaps, from +3 to –3).[11] It measures how close to or distant from the adjective a given stimulus is perceived to be. Exhibit 10.9 illustrates a Stapel scale item used in a measurement of a retailer's store image.

The advantages and disadvantages of the Stapel scale are very similar to those for the semantic differential. However, the Stapel scale is easier to administer, especially over the telephone.[12] Because the Stapel scale does not call for the construction of bipolar adjectives as the semantic differential does, it is easier to construct. Research comparing the semantic differential with the Stapel scale indicates that results from the two techniques are largely the same.[13]

## ■ Constant-Sum Scale

Suppose United Parcel Service (UPS) wishes to determine the importance of the attributes of accurate invoicing, delivery as promised, and price to organizations that use its service

---

■ **Exhibit 10.9**

**A Stapel Scale for Measuring a Store's Image**

Bloomingdale's
_____

+3
+2
+1

Wide Selection

–1
–2
–3

Select a plus number for words that you think describe the store accurately. The more accurately you think the word describes the store, the larger the plus number you should choose. Select a *minus* number for words you think do not describe the store accurately. The less accurately you think the word describes the store, the larger the minus number you should choose; therefore, you can select any number from +3 for words that you think are very accurate all the way to –3 for words that you think are very inaccurate.

in business-to-business marketing. Respondents might be asked to divide a constant sum to indicate the relative importance of the attributes. For example:

**Divide 100 points among the following characteristics of a delivery service according to how important each characteristic is to you when selecting a delivery company.**

**Accurate invoicing** _____

**Delivery as promised** _____

**Lower price** _____

**Constant-sum scale**
A measure of attitudes in which respondents are asked to divide a constant sum to indicate the relative importance of attributes.

This **constant-sum scale** works best with respondents who have higher educational levels. If respondents follow the instructions correctly, the results will approximate interval measures. As the number of stimuli increases, this technique becomes increasingly complex.

Brand preference may be measured using this technique in a manner similar to the paired-comparison method (discussed later), as follows:

**Divide 100 points among each of the following brands according to your preference for the brand:**

**Brand A** _____

**Brand B** _____

**Brand C** _____

The constant-sum scale as described here is a rating technique. However, with minor modifications it can be classified as a sorting technique.

## ■ Graphic Rating Scales

**Graphic rating scale**
A measure of attitude that allows respondents to rate an object by choosing any point along a graphic continuum.

A **graphic rating scale** presents respondents with a graphic continuum. The respondents are allowed to choose any point on the continuum to indicate their attitude. The scale illustrated in Exhibit 10.10 shows a traditional graphic scale ranging from one extreme position to the opposite position. Typically a respondent's score is determined by measuring the length (in millimeters) from one end of the graphic continuum to the point marked by the respondent. Many researchers believe that scoring in this manner strengthens the assumption that graphic rating scales of this type are interval scales. Alternatively, the researcher may divide the line into predetermined scoring categories (lengths) and record respondents' marks accordingly. In other words, the graphic rating scale has the advantage of allowing the researcher to choose any interval desired for scoring purposes. The disadvantage of the graphic rating scale is that it provides no standard answers.

The pictorial scale is a special form of the graphic rating scale. It utilizes picture response options or other type of visual communication to portray a graphic continuum (see Exhibit 10.11). Its purpose is to enhance communication with respondents who are not highly literate, such as children.

Exhibit 10.12 summarizes the attitude-rating techniques discussed in this section.

---

**■ Exhibit 10.10**
**Graphic Rating Scale**

Please evaluate each attribute in terms of how important it is to you by placing an *X* at the position on the horizontal line that most reflects your feelings.

| | | |
|---|---|---|
| **Seating comfort** | Not important _____ | Very important |
| **In-flight meals** | Not important _____ | Very important |
| **Airfare** | Not important _____ | Very important |

**■ Exhibit 10.11**

**Scales with Picture Response Categories Stress Visual Communication**

**Happy Face Scale**

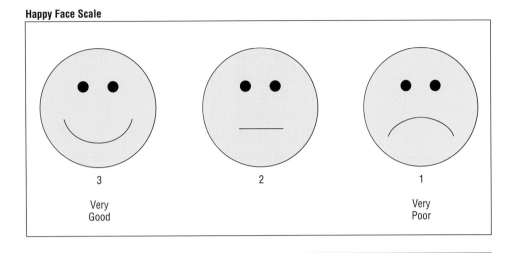

|  |  |  |
|---|---|---|
| 3 | 2 | 1 |
| Very Good |  | Very Poor |

**■ Exhibit 10.12**

**Summary of Advantages and Disadvantages of Rating Scales**

| Rating Measure | Subject Must: | Advantages | Disadvantages |
|---|---|---|---|
| Category scale | Indicate a response category | Flexible, easy to respond | Items may be ambiguous; with few categories, only gross distinctions can be made |
| Likert scale | Evaluate statements on a 5-point scale | Easiest scale to construct | Hard to judge what a single score means |
| Semantic differential and numerical scales | Choose points between bipolar adjectives on relevant dimensions | Easy to construct; norms exist for comparison, such as image profile analysis | Bipolar adjectives must be found; data may be ordinal, not interval |
| Constant-sum scale | Divide a constant sum among response alternatives | Scale approximates an interval measure | Difficult for respondents with low education levels |
| Stapel scale | Choose points on a scale with a single adjective in the center | Easier to construct than semantic differential, easy to administer | Endpoints are numerical, not verbal, labels |
| Graphic scale | Choose a point on a continuum | Visual impact, unlimited scale points | No standard answers |
| Graphic scale— picture response | Choose a visual picture | Visual impact, easy for poor readers | Hard to attach a verbal explanation to a response |

## ■ MEASURING BEHAVIORAL INTENTION

The behavioral component of an attitude involves the behavioral expectations of an individual toward an attitudinal object. Typically this represents a buying intention, a tendency to seek additional information, or plans to visit a showroom. Category scales for measuring the behavioral component of an attitude ask about a respondent's likelihood of purchase or intention to perform some future action, such as:

**How likely is it that you will purchase a DVD player?**

☐ **I definitely will buy**

☐ **I probably will buy**

☐ **I might buy**

☐ **I probably will not buy**

☐ **I definitely will not buy**

**I would write a letter to my representative in Congress or other government official in support of this company if it were in a dispute with government.**

☐ **Extremely likely**

☐ **Very likely**

☐ **Somewhat likely**

☐ **Likely, about a 50–50 chance**

☐ **Somewhat unlikely**

☐ **Very unlikely**

☐ **Extremely unlikely**

The wording of statements used in these scales often includes phrases such as "I would recommend," "I would write," or "I would buy" to indicate action tendencies.

A scale of subjective probabilities, ranging from 100 for "absolutely certain" to 0 for "absolutely no chance," may be used to measure expectations. Researchers have used the following subjective probability scale to estimate the chance that a job candidate will accept a sales position:

_____ **100% (Absolutely certain) I will accept**

_____   **90% (Almost sure) I will accept**

_____   **80% (Very big chance) I will accept**

_____   **70% (Big chance) I will accept**

_____   **60% (Not so big a chance) I will accept**

_____   **50% (About even) I will accept**

_____   **40% (Smaller chance) I will accept**

_____   **30% (Small chance) I will accept**

_____   **20% (Very small chance) I will accept**

_____   **10% (Almost certainly not) I will accept**

_____     **0  (Certainly not) I will accept**

## ■ Behavioral Differential

**Behavioral differential**
A rating scale instrument, similar to a semantic differential, developed to measure the behavioral intentions of subjects toward future actions.

A general instrument, the **behavioral differential,** has been developed to measure the behavioral intentions of subjects toward any object or category of objects. As in the semantic differential, a description of the object to be judged is placed on the top of a sheet and the subjects indicate their behavioral intentions toward this object on a series of scales. For example, one item might be:

**A 25-year-old female sales representative**

**Would__:__:__:__:__:__:__:__:__:Would not**

**Ask this person for advice.**

---

# ■ RANKING

Consumers often rank order their preferences. An ordinal scale may be developed by asking respondents to rank order (from most preferred to least preferred) a set of objects or attributes. Respondents easily understand the task of rank ordering the importance of product attributes or arranging a set of brand names according to preference.

## ■ Paired Comparisons

**Paired comparison**
A measurement technique that consists of presenting respondents with two objects and asking them to pick the preferred object. Two or more objects may be presented, but comparisons are made in pairs.

Some time ago, a chain saw manufacturer learned that a major competitor had introduced a new, lightweight (6 ½-pound) chain saw. The manufacturer's lightest chain saw weighed 9 ½ pounds. Executives wondered if they needed to introduce a 6-pound chain saw into the product line. The research design chosen was a **paired comparison.** A 6-pound chain saw was designed and a prototype built. To control for color preferences, the competitor's chain saw was painted the same color as the 9 ½- and 6-pound models. Respondents were presented with two chain saws at a time, then asked to pick the one they preferred. Three pairs of comparisons were required to determine the most preferred chain saw.

The following question illustrates the typical format for asking about paired comparisons:[14]

**I would like to know your overall opinion of two brands of adhesive bandages. They are Curad and Band-Aid. Overall, which of these two brands—Curad or Band-Aid—do you think is the better one? Or are both the same?**

**Curad is better _____**

**Band-Aid is better _____**

**They are the same _____**

If researchers wish to compare four brands of pens on the basis of attractiveness or writing quality, six comparisons $[(n)(n-1)/2]$ will be necessary.

Ranking objects with respect to one attribute is not difficult if only a few products or advertisements are compared. As the number of items increases, the number of comparisons increases geometrically. If the number of comparisons is too large, respondents may fatigue and no longer carefully discriminate among them.

---

# ■ SORTING

Sorting tasks require that respondents indicate their attitudes or beliefs by arranging items on the basis of perceived similarity or some other attribute. Researchers at the BBDO advertising agency have consumers sort photographs of people to measure their perceptions of a brand's typical user. R. H. Bruskin Associates has used a sorting technique called AIM (Association-Identification-Measurement), which consists of cards from a deck of 52. Each card reflects an element from advertising for the brand name being measured. This omnibus service measures how closely customers associate and identify these elements with a particular product, company, or advertising campaign.[15] The following condensed interviewer instructions illustrate how sorting is used in the AIM survey:

**Thoroughly shuffle deck.**

**Hand respondent deck.**

**Ask respondent to sort cards into two piles:**

*Definitely Not Seen or Heard.*

*Definitely or Possibly Seen or Heard.*

**Set aside Definitely Not Seen or Heard pile.**

**Hand respondent the Definitely or Possibly Seen or Heard pile.**

**Have respondent identify the item on each card in Definitely or Possibly Seen or Heard pile.**

**Record on questionnaire.**

A variant of the constant-sum technique uses physical counters (for example, poker chips or coins) to be divided among the items being tested. In an airline study of customer preferences, the following sorting technique could be used:

**Here is a sheet that lists several airlines. Next to the name of each airline is a pocket. Here are 10 cards. I would like you to put these cards in the pockets next to the airlines you would prefer to fly on your next trip. Assume that all of the airlines fly to wherever you would choose to travel. You can put as many cards as you want in front of an airline, or you can put no cards in front of an airline.**

|                      | Cards  |
| -------------------- | ------ |
| **American Airlines**   | _____ |
| **Delta Airlines**      | _____ |
| **United Airlines**     | _____ |
| **Southwest Airlines**  | _____ |
| **Continental Airlines**| _____ |

## ■ SUMMARY

Many marketing research problems require the choice of an appropriate measuring system. The concept to be measured must be given an operational definition that specifies how it will be measured. There are four types of measuring scales. Nominal scales assign numbers or letters to objects only for identification or classification. Ordinal scales arrange objects or alternatives according to their magnitudes in an ordered relationship. Interval scales measure order (or distance) in units of equal intervals. Ratio scales are absolute scales, starting with absolute zeros at which the attribute is totally absent. The type of scale determines the form of statistical analysis to use.

Index or composite measures often are used to measure complex concepts with several attributes. Asking several questions may yield a more accurate measure than basing measurement on a single question.

Measuring instruments are evaluated based on reliability, validity, and sensitivity. Reliability is the measuring instrument's ability to provide consistent results in repeated uses. Validity is the degree to which the instrument measures the concept the researcher wants to measure. Sensitivity is the instrument's ability to accurately measure variability in stimuli or responses.

Attitude measurement is particularly important in marketing research. Attitudes are enduring dispositions to consistently respond in a given manner to various aspects of the world, including persons, events, and objects. Attitudes contain three components: the affective, or the emotions or feelings involved; the cognitive, or awareness or knowledge; and the behavioral, or the predisposition to action. Attitudes are hypothetical constructs; that is, they are variables that are not directly observable but are measurable indirectly. Many methods for measuring attitudes have been developed, such as ranking, rating, sorting, and choice techniques.

One class of rating scales, category scales, provides several response categories to allow respondents to indicate the intensity of their attitudes. The simplest is a "yes/no" or "agree/disagree" response to a single question. The Likert scale uses a series of statements for which subjects indicate agreement or disagreement. The responses are assigned weights that are summed to indicate the respondents' attitudes.

The semantic differential uses a series of attitude scales anchored by bipolar adjectives. The respondent indicates where his or her attitude falls between the polar attitudes. Variations on this method, such as numerical scales and the Stapel scale, are also used. The Stapel scale puts a single adjective in the center of a range of numerical values from +3 to –3.

Constant-sum scales require the respondent to divide a constant sum into parts, indicating the weights to be given to various attributes of the item being studied. Graphic rating scales use a continuum by which respondents indicate their attitudes.

Several scales, such as the behavioral differential, have been developed to measure the behavioral component of attitude.

People often rank order their preferences. Thus, ordinal scales that ask respondents to rank order a set of objects or attributes may be developed. In the paired-comparison technique, two alternatives are paired and respondents are asked to pick the preferred one. Sorting requires respondents to indicate their attitudes by arranging items into piles or categories.

## ■ Key Terms and Concepts

| | |
|---|---|
| Concept | Hypothetical construct |
| Operational definition | Ranking |
| Conceptual definition | Rating |
| Rule | Sorting |
| Scale | Choice |
| Nominal scale | Category scale |
| Ordinal scale | Likert scale |
| Interval scale | Semantic differential |
| Ratio scale | Image profile |
| Attribute | Numerical scale |
| Index (composite) measure | Stapel scale |
| Reliability | Constant-sum scale |
| Validity | Graphic rating scale |
| Sensitivity | Behavioral differential |
| Attitude | Paired comparison |

## ■ Questions

1. What is the difference between a conceptual definition and an operational definition?
2. What descriptive statistics are allowable with nominal, ordinal, and interval scales?
3. Discuss the differences between validity and reliability.
4. Why might a researcher wish to use more than one question to measure satisfaction with a particular aspect of retail shopping?
5. Comment on the validity and reliability of the following:
   (a) A respondent's report of an intention to subscribe to *Consumer Reports* is highly reliable. A researcher believes this constitutes a valid measurement of dissatisfaction with the economic system and alienation from big business.

(b) A general-interest magazine advertised that the magazine was a better advertising medium than television programs with similar content. Research had indicated that for a soft drink and other test products, recall scores were higher for the magazine ads than for 30-second commercials.

(c) A respondent's report of frequency of magazine reading consistently indicates that she regularly reads *Good Housekeeping* and *Gourmet* and never reads *Cosmopolitan.*

6. Indicate whether the following measures are nominal, ordinal, interval, or ratio scales:
   (a) Prices on the stock market
   (b) Marital status, classified as "married" or "never married"
   (c) Whether a respondent has ever been unemployed
   (d) Professorial rank: assistant professor, associate professor, or professor
   (e) Grades: A, B, C, D, or F  Ordinal

7. Go to the library and find out how *Sales and Marketing Management* magazine constructs its buying-power index.

8. Define the following concepts, then operationally define each one:
   (a) A good bowler
   (b) A television audience for *The Tonight Show*
   (c) Purchasing intention for a new stereo
   (d) Consumer involvement with cars
   (e) A workaholic
   (f) A fast-food restaurant
   (g) The American Dream

9. What is an attitude? Is there a consensus concerning its definition?

10. Distinguish between rating and ranking. Which is a better attitude measurement technique? Why?

11. What advantages do numerical scales have over semantic differential scales?

12. Name some situations in which a semantic differential might be useful.

13. Should a Likert scale ever be treated as though it had ordinal properties?

14. For each of the following situations, indicate the type of scale and evaluate its use:
   (a) A U.S. representative's questionnaire to constituents:

   **Do you favor or oppose a constitutional amendment to balance the budget?**

   **Favor □     Oppose □     Don't know □**

   (b) In an academic study on consumer behavior:

   **Most people who are important to me think I**

   | **–3** | | **+3** |
   |---|---|---|
   | **Definitely should not buy** | | **Definitely should buy** |

   **[test brand] sometime during the next week.**

   (c) For a psychographic statement:

   **I shop a lot for specials.**

   | **Strongly agree** | **Moderately agree** | **Neutral** | **Moderately disagree** | **Strongly disagree** |
   |---|---|---|---|---|
   | 5 | 4 | 3 | 2 | 1 |

15. If a Likert summated scale has 10 scale items, do all 10 items have to be phrased as either positive or negative statements, or can positive and negative statements be mixed?

16. If a semantic differential has 10 scale items, should all the positive adjectives be on the right and all the negative adjectives on the left?

17. A researcher wishes to compare two hotels on the following attributes: (1) convenience of location, (2) friendly personnel, and (3) value for money.
    (a) Design a Likert scale to accomplish this task.
    (b) Design a semantic differential scale to accomplish this task.
    (c) Design a graphic rating scale to accomplish this task.

18. Education often is used as an indicator of a person's socioeconomic status. Historically, the number of years of schooling completed has been recorded in the *Census of Population* as a measure of education. Critics say this measure is no longer accurate as a measure of education. Comment.

19. A researcher thinks many respondents will answer "don't know" or "can't say" if these options are printed along with agreement categories on the attitude scale. The researcher omits both options on the questionnaire because the resulting data will be less complicated to analyze and report. Is this proper?

## EXPLORING THE INTERNET

1. SRI International investigates American consumers by asking questions about their attitudes and values. It has a Web site at which people on the Internet can VALS-type themselves. To find out your VALS-type, go to http://future.sri.com.

2. The Office of Scale Research (OSR) is located within the Department of Marketing at Southern Illinois University at Carbondale. The OSR Internet site provides a number of "technical reports" that deal with a wide variety of scaling issues. Go to http://www.siu.edu/departments/coba/mktg/osr/ and select an article from the reading list. What types of scales are listed?

## CASE 10.1    Ha-Pah-Shu-Tse

Raymond RedCorn is an Osage Indian. The Ha-Pah-Shu-Tse (Osage for "red corn") restaurant in Pawhuska, Oklahoma, is the only authentic Native American restaurant in the state and one of the few in the country.

The Ha-Pah-Shu-Tse restaurant opened in 1972 with a seating capacity of 8; today, after expansion, crowds of up to 90 keep RedCorn and his wife busy. They are currently marketing an Indian fry bread mix, and they are planning on increased sales for their only packaged good. Indian fry bread mix has long been a staple of the Native American diet. The bread is sweet and contains basic ingredients such as flour, shortening, and sugar.

**The Restaurant**

Waltina RedCorn married into the Osage tribe 47 years ago and learned how to cook from two women named Grandma Baconrind and Grandma Lookout. They must have taught her well because customers of the Ha-Pah-

Shu-Tse are not content just to eat there; they often have the RedCorns mail them fry bread mix. Raymond RedCorn finds that people who eat the unusual native dish usually request the recipe. He says, "I have not found anyone who does not like the bread." Customers aren't limited to local fans of Indian food. Because the fry bread is sold or served in restaurants and stores in Oklahoma as well as at one museum, people from as far away as Europe have tried it.

According to RedCorn, "About once a week, someone from England comes in." He serves these British customers fry bread or the restaurant's "best sellers, Indian Meat Pie or Navaho Taco," and tells them the story of fry bread and how it got him an invitation to the Buckingham Palace. When he was 18 years old, he was in London for a Boy Scout Jamboree. One evening he was frying the Indian bread when the British Boy Scout organizer approached with two young men. Only after everyone had tasted RedCorn's culinary effort was the Prince of Wales introduced. "The Indian delegation from Oklahoma was invited to set up their tents on the ground at the palace and spend the weekend being entertained by the young royalty," RedCorn tells.

### The Product

The product as it is today took several years to perfect. The RedCorns wanted a mix that would need only the addition of water. Each batch was sent to relatives and friends for judgment on the taste until everyone was convinced it was the best it could be.

The mix, consisting of Indian flour, is already distributed in Tulsa, Bartlesville, and surrounding towns under the Ha-Pah-Shu-Tse brand name. It is packaged in 2- and 5-pound silver bags with Raymond RedCorn pictured in Osage tribal costume. Directions for making the fry bread are listed on the back of the package.

### The Research Problem

When planning the marketing for the Indian fry bread mix, student consultants working with the Small Business Administration suggested some attitude research. They believed successful marketing of the Ha-Pah-Shu-Tse product depended on knowing what consumer reactions to Indian foods would be. They believed that if the image of Indian foods and consumers' awareness of it were measured, RedCorn would have a better chance to market his product. In addition, the student consultants thought the name Ha-Pah-Shu-Tse violated many of the requirements for selecting a good brand name; it was not short, simple, or easy to recall and was difficult to pronounce and spell.

### Questions

1. What marketing questions must be answered as Ha-Pah-Shu-Tse plans for expansion? How can marketing research help answer those questions?
2. What type of attitude scale would you recommend? How would you generate a set of items (attributes) to be measured?
3. Does an image profile seem appropriate in this case?

### ■ Endnotes

[1]Gary Levin, "Emotion Guides BBDO's Ad Tests."

[2]Jum C. Nunnally, *Psychometric Theory* (New York: McGraw-Hill, 1967), p. 2.

[3]Sarah M. Dinham, *Exploring Statistics: An Introduction for Psychology and Education* (Monterey, Cal.: Brooks/Cole, 1976), p. 3.

[4]This definition is adapted from Fred N. Kerlinger, *Foundations of Behavioral Research* (New York: Holt, Rinehart and Winston, 1973), p. 31.

[5]Barry F. Anderson, *The Psychology Experiment* (Monterey, Cal.: Brooks/Cole, 1971), p. 26.

[6]Fred N. Kerlinger, *Behavioral Research: A Conceptual Approach* (New York: Holt, Rinehart and Winston, 1979), p. 41.

[7]Ibid., p. 428.

[8]This example assumes a standard measure for the term *length*.

[9]Cathy Lynn Grossman, "Passenger-Jet Designers Ponder Pie-in-the- Sky Idea," *USA Today,* April 18, 1995, p. 3D.

[10]Fred N. Kerlinger, *Foundations of Behavioral Research,* 3d ed. (Fort Worth: Holt, Rinehart and Winston, 1986).

[11]Irving Crespi, "Use of a Scaling Technique in Surveys," *Journal of Marketing,* July 1961, pp. 69–72.

[12]Del I. Hawkins, Gerald Albaum, and Roger Best, "Stapel Scale or Semantic Differential in Marketing Research?" *Journal of Marketing Research,* August 1974, pp. 318–322.

[13]Dennis Menezes and Nobert F. Elbert, "Alternative Semantic Scaling Formats for Measuring Store Image: An Evaluation," *Journal of Marketing Research,* February 1979, pp. 80–87.

[14]Yoram Wind, Joseph Denny, and Arthur Cunningham, "A Comparison of Three Brand Evaluation Procedures," *Public Opinion Quarterly,* Summer 1979, p. 263.

[15]R. H. Bruskin Associates, 303 George Street, New Brunswick, N.J.

# QUESTIONNAIRE DESIGN

**WHAT YOU WILL LEARN IN THIS CHAPTER:**

To recognize that questionnaire design is not a simple task and that proper wording of relevant questions can immensely improve the accuracy of a survey.

To understand that the type of information needed to answer a manager's questions will substantially influence the structure and content of a questionnaire.

To recognize that decisions about the data collection methods (mail, telephone, or personal interviews) will influence question format and questionnaire layout.

To describe the difference between open-ended response and fixed-alternative questions.

To understand the guidelines that help prevent the most common mistakes in questionnaire design.

To discuss how the proper sequence of questions may improve the questionnaire.

To understand how to plan and design a questionnaire layout.

To recognize the importance of pretesting and revising a questionnaire.

To understand how global markets may require a special effort.

**A**n early Gallup Poll illustrates that the answer to a question frequently is a function of the question's wording: "People were asked if they owned any stock. A surprisingly high degree of stock ownership turned up in interviews in the Southwest where respondents were naturally thinking of livestock. The question had to be reworded to make reference to 'securities listed on any stock exchange.'"[1]

Many experts in survey research generally believe that improving the wording of questions can contribute far more to accuracy than can improvements in sampling. Experiments have shown that the range of error due to vague questions or use of ambiguous words may be as high as 20 or 30 percentage points. Consider the following illustration of the critical consideration of selecting the word with the right meaning. The questions differ only in the use of the words *should, could,* and *might:*

Do you think anything *should* be done to make it easier for people to pay doctor or hospital bills?

Do you think anything *could* be done to make it easier for people to pay doctor or hospital bills?

Do you think anything *might* be done to make it easier for people to pay doctor or hospital bills?[2]

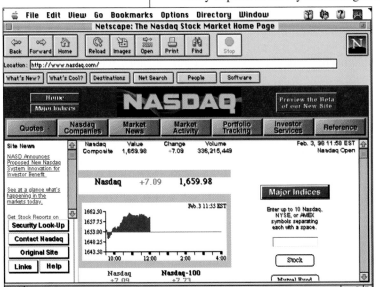

The results from the matched examples: 82 percent replied that something *should* be done, 77 percent that something *could* be done, and 63 percent that something *might* be done. A 19-percentage-point difference separated the two extremes *should* and *might*. Ironically, this is the same percentage point error as that in the *Literary Digest* poll, a frequently cited example of error associated with sampling.

This chapter outlines a procedure for questionnaire design and illustrates that a little bit of research knowledge can be a dangerous thing.

## ■ A SURVEY IS ONLY AS GOOD AS THE QUESTIONS IT ASKS

Each stage is important in the interdependent marketing research process. However, a marketing research survey is only as good as the questions it asks. The importance of question wording is easily overlooked, but questionnaire design is one of the most critical stages in the survey research process.

"A good questionnaire appears as easy to compose as does a good poem. The end product should look as if effortlessly written by an inspired child—but it is usually the result of long, painstaking work."[3] Businesspeople who are inexperienced in marketing research frequently believe that constructing a questionnaire is a simple task. Amateur researchers find it quite easy to write short questionnaires in a matter of hours. Unfortunately, newcomers who naively believe common sense and good grammar are all one needs to construct a questionnaire generally learn that their hasty efforts are inadequate.

While common sense and good grammar are important in question writing, the art of questionnaire design requires far more. To assume people will understand the questions is a common error. Respondents simply may not know what is being asked. They may be unaware of the product or topic of interest. They may confuse the subject with something else. The question may not mean the same thing to everyone interviewed. Finally, respondents may refuse to answer personal questions. Most of these problems can be minimized, however, if a skilled researcher composes the questionnaire.

## ■ QUESTIONNAIRE DESIGN: AN OVERVIEW OF THE MAJOR DECISIONS

*Relevance* and *accuracy* are the two basic criteria to meet if a questionnaire is to fulfill a researcher's purposes.[4] To achieve these ends, a researcher who is systematically planning to design a questionnaire will be required to make several decisions, typically, but not necessarily, in the following order:

1. What should be asked?
2. How should questions be phrased?
3. In what sequence should the questions be arranged?
4. What questionnaire layout will best serve the research objectives?
5. How should the questionnaire be pretested? Does the questionnaire need to be revised?

## ■ WHAT SHOULD BE ASKED?

Certain decisions made during the early stages of the research process will influence the questionnaire design. The preceding chapters stressed the need to have a good problem definition and clear objectives for the study. The problem definition will indicate the type of information that must be collected to answer the manager's questions; different types of questions may obtain certain types of information more successfully than others. Further, the communication medium of data collection—telephone interview, personal interview, or self-administered questionnaire—will have been determined. This decision is another forward linkage that influences the structure and content of the questionnaire. The specific questions to be asked will be a function of the previous decisions.

The latter stages of the research process will have an important impact on questionnaire wording. The questions to be asked will, of course, take the form of data analysis into account. When designing the questionnaire, the researcher should consider the types of statistical analysis that will be conducted.

## ■ HOW SHOULD QUESTIONS BE PHRASED?

There are many ways to phrase questions, and many standard question formats have been developed in previous research studies. This section presents a classification of question types and provides some helpful guidelines for writing questions.

### ■ Open-Ended Response versus Fixed-Alternative Questions

Two basic types of questions can be identified based on the amount of freedom respondents have in answering.

**Open-ended response questions** pose some problem or topic and ask respondents to answer in their own words. If the question is asked in a personal interview, the interviewer may probe for more information. For example:

**Open-ended response question**
A question that poses some problem and asks the respondent to answer in his or her own words.

**What names of local banks can you think of offhand?**

**What comes to mind when you look at this advertisement?**

**In what way, if any, could this product be changed or improved? I'd like you to tell me anything you can think of, no matter how minor it seems.**

**What things do you like most about Federal Express's service?**

**Why do you buy more of your clothing at Nordstrom than at other stores?**

**How can our stores better serve your needs?**

**Please tell me anything at all that you remember about the BMW commercial you saw last night.**

Open-ended response questions are free-answer questions. They may be contrasted with fixed-alternative questions—sometimes called *closed* questions—which give respondents specific limited alternative responses and ask them to choose the one closest to their own viewpoints. For example:

**Did you use any commercial feed or supplement for livestock or poultry in 1997?**

□ **Yes**
□ **No**

**Compared with 10 years ago, would you say that the quality of most products made in Japan is higher, about the same, or not as good?**

□ **Higher**
□ **About the same**
□ **Not as good**

**Do you think the Americans with Disabilities Act has affected your business?**

☐ **Yes, for the better**

☐ **Yes, for the worse**

☐ **Not especially**

**In which type of store is it easier for you to shop—a regular department store or a discount department store?**

☐ **Regular department store**

☐ **Discount department store**

**How much of your shopping for clothes and household items do you do in wholesale club stores?**

☐ **All of it**

☐ **Most of it**

☐ **About one-half of it**

☐ **About one-quarter of it**

☐ **Less than one-quarter of it**

Open-ended response questions are most beneficial when the researcher is conducting exploratory research, especially when the range of responses is not known. Such questions can be used to learn which words and phrases people spontaneously give to the free-response question. Respondents are free to answer with whatever is uppermost in their minds. By obtaining free and uninhibited responses, the researcher may find some unanticipated reaction toward the product. Such responses will reflect the flavor of the language that people use in talking about products or services and thus may provide a source of new ideas for advertising copywriting. Also, open-ended response questions are valuable at the beginning of an interview because they allow respondents to warm up to the questioning process.

The cost of administering open-ended response questions is substantially higher than that for fixed-alternative questions because the job of editing, coding, and analyzing the data is quite extensive. As each respondent's answer is somewhat unique, there is some difficulty in categorizing and summarizing the answers. This process requires that an editor go over a sample of questions to classify the responses into a given scheme; then all the answers must be reviewed and coded according to the classification scheme.

Another potential disadvantage of the open-ended response question is the possibility that interviewer bias will influence the answer. While most interviewer instructions state that answers are to be recorded verbatim, rarely does even the best interviewer get every word spoken by the respondent. Thus, an interviewer tends to take shortcuts in recording the answers. But even a few words different from the respondent's may substantially influence the results; the final answer thus may combine the respondent's and interviewer's ideas rather than the respondent's ideas alone. Also, when using open-ended response questions, articulate individuals tend to give longer answers. Such respondents often are better educated and from higher income groups and therefore may not be representative of the entire population.

In contrast, **fixed-alternative questions** require less interviewer skill, take less time, and are easier for the respondent to answer. This is because answers to closed questions must be classified into standardized groupings prior to data collection. Standardizing alternative responses to a question provides comparability of answers, which facilitates coding and tabulating, and ultimately interpreting the data.

**Fixed-alternative question** A question in which the respondent is given specific, limited-alternative responses and asked to choose the one closest to his or her own viewpoint.

## What a Difference Words Make

Does advertising lower or raise prices? The wording of the question influences the answer.

Consumer Attitude toward Distribution
*The consumer must pay more for goods because of advertising.*

| | |
|---|---|
| No | 33 |
| Yes | 39 |
| Doubtful | 17 |
| No answer | 11 |

Consumer Attitude toward Distribution
*Advertising may cause the consumer to pay less for a product than if it were not advertised because it increases sales and makes it possible to cut the cot of production and marketing.*

| | |
|---|---|
| Yes | 52 |
| No | 18 |
| Doubtful | 20 |
| No answer | 10 |

**Types of Fixed-Alternative Questions** Earlier we saw a variety of fixed-alternative questions. We will now identify and categorize the various types.

**Simple-dichotomy (dichotomous-alternative) question**
A fixed-alternative question that requires the respondent to choose one or two dichotomous alternatives.

The **simple-dichotomy,** or **dichotomous-alternative, question** requires the respondent to choose one of two alternatives. The answer can be a simple "yes" or "no" or a choice between "this" and "that." For example:

**Did you make any long-distance calls last week?**

☐ **Yes**          ☐ **No**

Several types of questions provide the respondent with *multiple-choice alternatives.* The **determinant-choice question** requires the respondent to choose one, and only one, response from among several possible alternatives. For example:

**Determinant-choice question**
A fixed-alternative question that requires a respondent to choose one, and only one, response from among multiple alternatives.

**Please give us some information about your flight. In which section of the aircraft did you sit?**

☐ **First class**

☐ **Business class**

☐ **Coach class**

**Frequency-determination question**
A fixed-alternative question about the general frequency of occurrence.

The **frequency-determination question** is a determinant-choice question that asks about the general frequency of occurrence. For example:

**How frequently do you watch MTV television channel?**

☐ **Every day**

☐ **5–6 times a week**

☐ **2–4 times a week**

☐ **Once a week**

☐ **Less than once a week**

☐ **Never**

*Attitude rating scales,* such as the Likert scale, semantic differential. Staple scale, and so on, are also fixed-alternative questions. These were discussed in Chapter 10.

The **checklist question** allows the respondent to provide multiple answers to a single question. The respondent indicates past experience, preference, and the like merely by checking off items. In many cases, the choices are adjectives that describe a particular object. A typical checklist question might ask:

**Checklist question**
A fixed-alternative question that allows the respondent to provide multiple answers to a single question by checking off items.

**Please check which of the following sources of information about investments you regularly use, if any.**

&#9633; **Personal advice of your broker(s)**

&#9633; **Brokerage newsletters**

&#9633; **Brokerage research reports**

&#9633; **Investment advisory service(s)**

&#9633; **Conversations with other investors**

&#9633; **Your own study and intuition**

&#9633; **None of these**

&#9633; **Other (please specify)** _____

A major problem in developing dichotomous or multiple-choice alternatives is the framing of the response alternatives. There should be no overlap among categories. Each alternative should be *mutually exclusive;* that is, only one dimension of an issue should be related to that alternative. The following listing of income groups illustrates a common error:

&#9633; **Under $15,000**

&#9633; **$15,000–$30,000**

&#9633; **$30,000–$55,000**

&#9633; **$55,000–$70,000**

&#9633; **Over $70,000**

How many people with incomes of $30,000 will be in the second group, and how many will be in the third group? We would not know the answer. Alternatives grouped without forethought or analysis may diminish accuracy.

Few people relish being in the lowest category. Including a category lower than the lowest expected answers often helps to negate the potential bias caused by respondents avoiding an extreme category.

When the researcher is unaware of the potential response to a question, fixed-alternative questions obviously cannot be used. If the researcher assumes what the responses might be but is in fact wrong, he or she will have no way of knowing the extent to which the assumption was incorrect.

Unanticipated alternatives emerge when respondents feel that closed answers do not adequately reflect their feelings. They may make comments to the interviewer or write additional answers on the printed questionnaire indicating that the exploratory research did not yield a complete array of responses. After the fact, little can be done to correct a closed question with some alternatives missing: therefore, the research may benefit from time spent conducting exploratory research with open-ended response questions to identify the most likely alternatives before writing a descriptive questionnaire. The researcher should strive to ensure sufficient response choices to include almost all possible answers.

Respondents may check off obvious alternatives, such as price or durability, if they do not see their individual choices among the answers. Thus, a fixed-alternative question may tempt respondents to check an answer that is untrue, but perhaps more prestigious or socially acceptable. Rather than stating that they do not know why they choose a given product, they may select an alternative among those presented, or, as a matter of convenience, they may select a given alternative rather than think of the most correct response.

Most questionnaires mix open-ended and closed questions. As we have discussed, each form has unique benefits. In addition, a change of pace can eliminate respondent boredom and fatigue.

### ■ Phrasing Questions for Mail, Telephone, and Personal Interview Surveys

The means of data collection (telephone, personal interviews, mail, or computer) will influence the question format and question phrasing. In general, mail and telephone questions must be less complex than those used in personal interviews. Questionnaires for telephone and personal interviews should be written in a conversational style. Exhibit 11.1 illustrates how a question may be revised for a different medium.

Consider the following question from a personal interview:

**Recently there has been a lot of discussion about the potential health to nonsmokers from tobacco smoke in public buildings, restaurants, and business offices. How serious a health threat to you personally is the inhaling of this second-hand smoke, often called** *passive smoking:* **Is it a very serious health threat, somewhat serious, not too serious, or not serious at all?**

### ■ Exhibit 11.1

**Reducing Complexity by Providing Fewer Responses**

---

Mail Form:

**How satisfied are you with your community?**

1 Very satisfied
2 Quite satisfied
3 Somewhat satisfied
4 Slightly satisfied
5 Neither satisfied nor dissatisfied
6 Slightly dissatisfied
7 Somewhat dissatisfied
8 Quite dissatisfied
9 Very dissatisfied

Revised for Telephone:

**How satisfied are you with your community? Would you say you are very satisfied, somewhat satisfied, neither satisfied nor dissatisfied, somewhat dissatisfied, or very dissatisfied?**

| | |
|---|---|
| Very satisfied | 1 |
| Somewhat satisfied | 2 |
| Neither satisfied nor dissatisfied | 3 |
| Somewhat dissatisfied | 4 |
| Very dissatisfied | 5 |

1. **Very serious**
2. **Somewhat serious**
3. **Not too serious**
4. **Not serious at all**
5. **(Don't know)**

You probably noticed that the last portion of the question is a listing of the four alternatives that serve as answers. This listing at the end is often used in interviews to serve as a reminder of the alternatives to the respondent who has no visual material to portray the choices. The fifth alternative, "Don't know," is in parentheses because, although it is known to the interviewer as an acceptable answer, it is not read because the researcher would prefer to "force" the respondent to choose from among the four listed alternatives.

The data collection technique also influences the layout of the questionnaire. This will be discussed later in the chapter.

## ■ THE ART OF ASKING QUESTIONS[5]

No hard-and-fast rules determine how to develop a questionnaire. Fortunately, research experience has yielded some guidelines that help prevent the most common mistakes.

### ■ Avoid Complexity: Use Simple, Conversational Language

Words used in questionnaires should be readily understandable to all respondents. The researcher usually has the difficult task of using the conversational language of people from lower education levels without talking down to the better-educated respondents. Remember, not all people have the vocabulary of a college student; a substantial number of Americans have never gone beyond high school.

Respondents may be able to tell an interviewer whether they are married, single, divorced, separated, or widowed, but providing their *marital status* may present a problem. The technical jargon of top corporate executives should be avoided when surveying retailers or industrial users. Brand image, positioning, marginal analysis, and other corporate staff language will not have the same meaning for or be understood by the owner-operator in a retail survey. The vocabulary used in the following question from an attitude survey on social problems probably would confuse many respondents:

**When effluents from a paper mill can be drunk and exhaust from factory smokestacks can be breathed, then man will have done a good job in saving the environment. . . . What we want is zero toxicity; no effluents?**

Besides being too long, this questions tends to be leading.

### ■ Avoid Leading and Loaded Questions

Asking leading and loaded questions is a major source of bias in question wording. **Leading questions** suggest or imply certain answers. A study of the dry cleaning industry asked this question:

**Many people are using dry cleaning less because of improved wash-and-wear clothes. How do you feel wash-and-wear clothes have affected your use of dry cleaning facilities in the past 4 years?**

□ **Use less**        □ **No change**        □ **Use more**

**Leading question**
A question that suggests or implies certain answers.

## WHAT WENT WRONG?

### Too Good a Name!

The Arm & Hammer brand name has been used for a number of product line extensions, for example, heavy-duty laundry detergent, oven cleaner, and liquid detergent. Unfortunately, when the markers of Arm & Hammer baking soda launched Arm & Hammer underarm spray deodorant and Arm & Hammer spray disinfectant, they did not fare well, even though marketing research studies indicated that consumers had expressed positive feelings about both products. What went wrong?

Researchers who investigated the product failures found that the Arm & Hammer name had such strong consumer franchise that whenever it was associated with a new product or concept, consumer acceptance and buying intentions were always artificially high. When question wording included the socially desirable Arm & Hammer name, consumers were reluctant to reject it. The company had failed to realize how much response bias its name caused.

The potential "bandwagon effect" implied in this question threatens the study's validity. *Partial mention of alternatives* is a variation of this phenomenon:

**Do small imported cars, such as Toyotas, get better gas mileage than small U.S. cars? How do you generally spend your free time, watching television or what?**

Merely mentioning an alternative may have a dramatic effect. The following question was asked in a research study for a court case (*Universal City v. Nintendo,* 1984).[6]

**To the best of your knowledge, was "Donkey Kong" made with the approval or under the authority of the people who produced the *King Kong* movies?**

Eighteen percent of the respondents answered "yes." In contrast, 0 percent correctly answered the question "As far as you know, who makes 'Donkey Kong'?"

**Loaded question**
A question that suggests socially desirable answers or is emotionally charged

**Loaded questions** suggest social desirability or are emotionally charged. Consider the following:

**In light of today's savings-and-loan crisis, it would be in the public's best interest to offer interest-free loans to farmers.**

☐ **Strongly agree**    ☐ **Agree**    ☐ **Disagree**    ☐ **Strongly disagree**

A different answer might be given if the loaded portion of the statement, *savings-and-loan crisis,* were worded to suggest a problem of less magnitude than a crisis.

A television station produced a 10-second spot to ask the following question:

**We are happy when you like programs on Channel 7. We are sad when you dislike programs on Channel 7. Write us and let us know what you think of our programming.**

Few people wish to make others sad. This question invites only positive comments.

Answers to certain questions are more socially desirable than others. For example, a truthful answer to the following classification question might be painful:

**Where did you rank academically in your high school graduating class?**

☐ **Top quarter**

☐ **2nd quarter**

☐ **3rd quarter**

☐ **4th quarter**

When taking personality or pyschographic tests, respondents frequently can interpret which answers are most socially acceptable even if the answers do not portray the respondents' true feelings. For example, which are the socially desirable answers for the following questions on a self-confidence scale?

**I feel capable of handling myself in most social situations.**

☐ **Agree**        ☐ **Disagree**

**I seldom fear my actions will cause others to have low opinions of me.**

☐ **Agree**        ☐ **Disagree**

Invoking the status quo is a form of loading that results in bias because most people tend to resist change.[7]

An experiment conducted in the early days of polling illustrates the unpopularity of change.[8] Comparable samples of respondents were simultaneously asked two questions about the presidential succession. One sample was asked: **"Would you favor or oppose adding a law to the Constitution preventing a president from succeeding himself more than once?"** The other sample was asked: **"Would you favor or oppose changing the Constitution in order to prevent a president from succeeding himself more than once?"** To the first question, 50 percent of the respondents answered in the negative; to the second question, 65 percent answered in the negative. Thus, the public would rather have added to than changed the Constitution.

Asking respondents "how often" they use a product or visit a store leads them to generalize about their habits because their behavior usually exhibits some variance. In generalizing, one is likely to portray one's *ideal* behavior rather than one's *average* behavior. For instance, brushing one's teeth after each meal may be ideal, but busy people may skip a brushing or two. An introductory **counterbiasing statement** or preamble to a question that reassures respondents that their "embarrassing" behavior is not abnormal may yield truthful responses:

**Counterbiasing statement**
An introductory statement or preamble to a potentially embarrassing question that reduces a respondent's reluctance to answer by suggesting that certain behavior is not unusual.

**Some people have the time to brush three times daily; others do not. How often did you brush your teeth yesterday?**

If a question embarrasses the respondent, it may elicit no answer or a biased response. This is particularly true with personal or classification data such as income or education. This problem may be mitigated by introducing the section of the questionnaire with a statement such as

**To help classify your answers, we'd like to ask you a few questions. Again, your answers will be kept in strict confidence.**

A question statement may be leading because it is phrased to reflect either the negative or the positive aspects of the issue. To control for this bias, the wording of attitudinal questions may be reversed for 50 percent of the sample. This **split-ballot technique** is used with the expectation that two alternative phrasings of the same question will yield a more accurate total response than will a single phrasing. For example, in a study on small-car buying behavior, one-half of the sample of imported-car purchasers received a questionnaire in which the statement read: **"Small U.S. cars are cheaper to maintain than small imported cars."** The other half of the import-car owners received a questionnaire in which the statement read: **"Small imported cars are cheaper to maintain than small U.S. cars."**

**Split-ballot technique**
Using two alternative phrasings of the same question for respective halves of the sample to yield a more accurate total response than a single phrasing would.

### ■ Avoid Ambiguity: Be as Specific as Possible

Items on questionnaires often are ambiguous because they are too general. Consider such indefinite words as *often, occasionally, regularly, frequently, many, good, fair,* and *poor.* Each of these words has many different meanings. For one person, *frequent* reading of *For-*

*tune* magazine may be six or seven issues a year; for another, twice a year. A great variety of meanings are attributed to *fair*. The same is true for many other indefinite words.

Questions such as that used in a study of consumers to measure the reaction to a television boycott should be interpreted with care:

**Please indicate the statement that best describes your family's television viewing during the boycott of Channel 7**

- ☐ **We did *not* watch any television programs on Channel 7.**
- ☐ **We watched *hardly any* television programs on Channel 7.**
- ☐ **We *occasionally* watched television programs on Channel 7.**
- ☐ **We *frequently* watched television programs on Channel 7.**

Some marketing scholars have suggested that the rate of diffusion of an innovation is related to the perception of the product attributes, such as *divisibility,*[9] which refers to the extent to which an innovation may be tried or tested on a limited scale. An empirical attempt to test this theory using semantic differentials was a disaster. Pretesting found that the bipolar adjectives *divisible–not divisible* were impossible for consumers to understand because they did not have the theory in mind as a frame of reference. A revision of the scale used these bipolar adjectives:

| *Testable*<br>(sample use<br>possible) | ——:——:——:——:——:——:—— | *Not testable*<br>(sample use not<br>possible) |
|---|---|---|

However, the question remained ambiguous because the meaning was still unclear.

A brewing industry study on point-of-purchase advertising (store displays) asked:

**What degree of durability do you prefer in your point-of-purchase advertising?**

- ☐ **Permanent (lasting more than 6 months)**
- ☐ **Semipermanent (lasting from 1 to 6 months)**
- ☐ **Temporary (lasting less than one month)**

Here the researchers clarified the terms *permanent, semipermanent,* and *temporary* by defining them for the respondent. However, the question remained somewhat ambiguous. Beer marketers often use a variety of point-of-purchase devices to serve different purposes—but in this case, what purpose? Further, a disadvantage in analysis existed because mere preference was given rather than a rating of the *degree* of preference. Thus, the meaning of a question may not be clear because it gives an inadequate frame of reference for interpreting the context of the question.

A student research group asked this question:

**What media do you rely on most?**

- ☐ **Television**
- ☐ **AM radio**
- ☐ **FM radio**
- ☐ **Newspapers**

This question is ambiguous because it does not ask about the content of the media. "Rely on most" for what—news, sports, entertainment?

## ■ Avoid Double-Barreled Items

**Double-barreled question**
A question that may induce bias because it covers two issues at once.

A question covering several issues at once is referred to as a **double-barreled question** and should always be avoided. Making the mistake of asking two questions rather than one is easy, for example, **"Please indicate your degree of agreement with the following statement: 'Wholesalers and retailers are responsible for the high cost of meat.'"** Which intermediaries are responsible, the wholesalers or the retailers? When multiple questions are asked in one question, the results may be exceedingly difficult to interpret. For example, consider the following question from a survey entitled "How Do You Feel about Being a Woman?"

**Between you and your husband, who does the housework (cleaning, cooking, dishwashing, laundry) over and above that done by any hired help?**

| | |
|---|---|
| ☐ **I do all of it.** | **47.0%** |
| ☐ **I do almost all of it.** | **35.6%** |
| ☐ **I do over half of it.** | **12.1%** |
| ☐ **We split the work fifty-fifty.** | **4.7%** |
| ☐ **My husband does over half of it.** | **0.6%** |

The answers to this question do not tell us if the wife cooks and the husband washes the dishes.

Another survey by a consumer-oriented library asked:

**Are you satisfied with the percent system of handling "closed-reserve" and "open-reserve" readings? (Are enough copies available? Are the required materials ordered promptly? Are the borrowing regulations adequate for students' use of materials?)**

☐ **Yes**

☐ **No**

A respondent may feel torn between a "yes" to one part of the question and a "no" to another part. The answer to this question does not tell the researcher which problem or combination of problems concerns the library user.

Consider this comment about double-barreled questions:

> Generally speaking, it is hard enough to get answers to one idea at a time without complicating the problem by asking what amounts to two questions at once. If two ideas are to be explored, they deserve at least two questions. Since question marks are not rationed, there is little excuse for the needless confusion that results [from] the double-barreled question.[10]

### ■ Avoid Making Assumptions

Consider the following question:

**Should Macy's continue its excellent gift-wrapping program?**

☐ **Yes**

☐ **No**

This question has a built-in assumption: that people believe the gift-wrapping program is excellent. By answering "yes," the respondent implies that things are fine just as they are; by answering "no," he or she implies that the store should discontinue the gift wrapping. The researchers should not place the respondent in that sort of bind by including an implicit assumption in the question.

Another frequent mistake is assuming the respondent had previously thought about an issue. For example, the following question appeared in a survey concerning Jack-in-the-Box: **"Do you think Jack-in-the-Box restaurants should consider changing their** name?" It is not at all likely that the respondent had thought about this question before being asked it. Nevertheless, most respondents answered the question even though they had no prior opinion concerning the name change. Research that induces people to express attitudes on subjects they do not ordinarily think about is meaningless.

### ■ Avoid Burdensome Questions That May Tax the Respondent's Memory

A simple fact of human life is that people forget. Researchers writing questions about past behavior or events should recognize that certain questions may make serious demands on the respondent's memory. Writing questions about prior events requires a conscientious attempt to minimize the problems associated with forgetting.

In many situations, respondents cannot recall the answer to a question. For example, a telephone survey conducted during the 24-hour period following the airing of the Super Bowl may establish whether the respondent watched the Super Bowl and then ask: **"Do you recall any commercials on that program?"** If the answer is positive, the interviewer might ask: **"What brands were advertised?"** These two questions measure *unaided recall,* because they give the respondent no clue as to the brand of interest.

If the researcher suspects the respondent may have forgotten the answer to a question, he or she may rewrite the question in an *aided-recall* format, that is, provide a clue to help jog the respondent's memory. For instance, the question about an advertised beer in an aided-recall format might be: **Do you recall whether there was a brand of beer advertised on that program?"** or **"I am going to read you a list of beer names. Can you pick out the name of beer that was advertised on the program?"** While aided recall is not as strong a test of attention or memory as unaided recall, it is less taxing to the respondent's memory.

### ■ WHAT IS THE BEST QUESTION SEQUENCE?

The order of questions, or the question sequence, may serve several functions for the researcher. If the opening questions are interesting, simple to comprehend, and easy to answer, respondents' cooperation and involvement can be maintained throughout the questionnaire. Asking easy-to-answer questions teaches respondents their role and allows them to build confidence; they know this is a professional researcher and not another salesperson posing as one. If respondents' curiosity is not aroused at the outset, they can become disinterested and terminate their interviews.

A mail research expert reports that a mail survey among department store buyers drew an extremely poor return rate.[11] A substantial improvement in response rate occurred, however, when some introductory questions seeking opinions on pending legislation of great importance to these buyers were added. Respondents completed all the questions, not only those in the opening section.

In their attempt to "warm up" respondents toward the questionnaire, student researchers frequently ask demographic or classificatory questions at the beginning. This generally is not advisable because asking for personal information such as income level or education may be embarrassing or threatening to respondents. It usually is better to ask potentially embarrassing questions at the middle or end of the questionnaire, after a rapport has been established between respondent and interviewer.

**Order bias**
Bias caused by the influence of earlier questions in a questionnaire or by an answer's position in a set of answers.

### ■ Order Bias

**Order bias** results from an answer alternative's position in a set of answers or from the sequencing of questions. In political elections in which candidates lack high visibility, such as county commissioner and judgeship elections, the first name listed on the ballot often receives the highest percentage of votes. For this reason, many election boards print several ballots so that each candidate's name appears in every possible position on the ballot.

Order bias can also distort survey results. For example, a questionnaire's purpose is to measure level of awareness of several charitable organizations: Big Brothers and Big Sisters is always mentioned first, Red Cross second, and the American Cancer Association third. Big Brothers and Big Sisters may receive an artificially higher awareness rating because respondents were more prone to yea-saying (by indicating awareness) for the first item in the list.

As another example, if questions about a specific clothing store are asked prior to those concerning the criteria for selecting a clothing store, respondents who state that they shop at a store where parking needs to be improved may also state that parking is less important a factor than they really believe it is to avoid appearing inconsistent. Specific questions may thus influence the more general ones. Therefore, it is advisable to ask general questions before specific questions to obtain the freest of open-ended responses. This procedure, known as the **funnel technique,** allows the researcher to understand the respondent's frame of reference before asking more specific questions about the respondent's particular level of information and intensity of opinions.

Consider the possibility that later answers will be biased by previous questions in this questionnaire on environmental pollution:

**Circle the number on the following table that best expresses your feelings about the severity of each environment problem:**

| Problem | Not a Problem | | | | Very Severe Problem |
|---|---|---|---|---|---|
| Air pollution from automobile exhausts | 1 | 2 | 3 | 4 | 5 |
| Air pollution from open burning | 1 | 2 | 3 | 4 | 5 |
| Air pollution from industrial smoke | 1 | 2 | 3 | 4 | 5 |
| Air pollution from foul odors | 1 | 2 | 3 | 4 | 5 |
| Noise pollution from airplanes | 1 | 2 | 3 | 4 | 5 |
| Noise pollution from cars, trucks, motorcycles | 1 | 2 | 3 | 4 | 5 |
| Noise pollution from industry | 1 | 2 | 3 | 4 | 5 |

Not surprisingly, researchers found that the responses to each air pollution question were highly correlated—in fact, almost identical.

When using attitude scales, an *anchoring effect* also may occur. The first concept measured tends to become a comparison point from which subsequent evaluations are made. Randomization of these items on a questionnaire of this type helps minimize order bias.

A related problem concerns the order of alternatives on closed questions. To avoid this problem, the order of these choices should be rotated if alternative forms of the questionnaire are possible. However, marketing researchers rarely print alternative questionnaires to eliminate problems resulting from order bias. A more common practice is to pencil in *X*s or check marks on printed questionnaires to indicate that the interviewer should start a series of repetitive questions at a certain point. For example, the capitalized phrases in the following question provide instructions to the interviewer to "rotate" brands:

**I would like to determine how likely you would be to buy certain brands of candy in the future. Let's start with (X'ED BRAND). (RECORD BELOW UNDER THE**

**Funnel technique**
A procedure whereby general questions are asked before specific questions to obtain unbiased responses.

**APPROPRIATE BRAND. REPEAT QUESTIONS FOR ALL OF THE REMAIN-
ING BRANDS.)**

| START HERE: | ( )<br>Mounds | (x)<br>Almond Joy | ( )<br>Snickers |
|---|---|---|---|
| Definitely would buy | –1 | –1 | –1 |
| Probably would buy | –2 | –2 | –2 |
| Might or might not buy | –3 | –3 | –3 |
| Probably would not buy | –4 | –4 | –4 |
| Definitely would not buy | –5 | –5 | –5 |

**Filter question**
A question that screens out respondents who are not qualified to answer a second question.

Asking a question that does not apply to the respondent or that the respondent is not qualified to answer may be irritating or cause a biased response because the respondent wishes to please the interviewer or avoid embarrassment. Including a **filter question** minimizes asking questions that may be inapplicable. Asking, **"Where do you generally have check-cashing problems in Springfield?"** may elicit a response even though the respondent has had no check-cashing problems; he or she may wish to please the interviewer with an answer. A filter question such as **"Do you ever have a problem cashing a check in Springfield? ____ Yes ____ No"** would screen out the people who are not qualified to answer.

**Pivot question**
A filter question used to determine which version of a second question will be asked.

Another form of filter question, the **pivot question,** is used to obtain income information and other data respondents may be reluctant to provide. For example:

**"Is your total family income over or under $50,000?" If under, ask, "Is it over or under $25,000?" If over, ask. "Is it over or under $75,000?"**

| | |
|---|---|
| **Under $25,000** | **$50,001–$75,000** |
| **$25,001–$50,000** | **Over $75,000** |

Exhibit 11.2 gives an example of a flowchart plan for a questionnaire. Structuring the order of the questions so that they are logical is another technique for ensuring the respondent's cooperation and eliminates any confusion or indecision. The researcher ensures maintaining legitimacy when the respondent can comprehend the relationship between a given question (or section of the questionnaire) and the overall purpose of the study. Further, a logical order may also aid the individual's memory. Traditional comments to explain the logic of the questionnaire may ensure the respondent's continuation. Here are two examples:

**We have been talking so far about general shopping habits in this city. Now I'd like you to compare two types of grocery stores—regular supermarkets and grocery departments in wholesale club stores.**

**So that I can combine your answers with other farmers who are similar to you, I need some personal information about you. Your answers to these questions—as all of the others you've answered—are confidential, and you will never be identified to anyone without your permission. Thanks for your help so far. If you'll answer the remaining questions, it will help me analyze all your answers.**

### ■ What Is the Best Layout?

The layout and physical attractiveness of the questionnaire are crucial in self-administered mail questionnaires. For different reasons it is also important to have a good layout in questionnaires designed for personal and telephone interviews. Exhibit 11.3 illustrates a warranty card that serves a dual purpose as a questionnaire. The layout is neat, attractive, and easy to follow.

■ **Exhibit 11.2**        **Flow of Questions to Illustrate the Level of Prompting Required to Stimulate Recall**

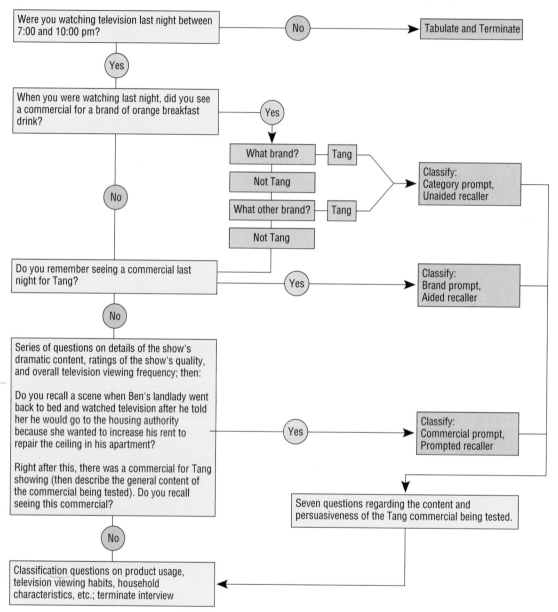

Often the rate of return can be improved by adding the money that might have been spent on an incentive to improve the attractiveness and quality of the questionnaire. An expert in mail surveys suggests that questionnaires should never be overcrowded, space should be provided to ensure decent margins, white space should be used to separate solidly printed blocks, and the unavoidable columns of multiple boxes should be kept to a minimum.[12]

Questionnaires should be designed to appear as short as possible. Sometimes it is advisable to use a booklet form of questionnaire rather than stapling a large number of pages

**■ Exhibit 11.3**

**A Dual-Purpose Warranty Registration Form**

How did you acquire your Hartmann?

_____ Individual purchase (purchased for myself)

_____ Joint purchase

_____ Received as gift

What influenced your choice of Hartmann?

_____ Style          _____ Unique features

_____ Guarantee     _____ Previous ownership

_____ Durability    _____ Hand craftsmanship

_____ Light weight  _____ Quality reputation

_____ Other: _____

Your Hartmann will be used primarily for:

_____ Business travel     _____ Leisure travel

How did you become interested in Hartmann?

_____ Advertising

_____ Displayed in store

_____ Recommended by salesperson

_____ Recommended by friend/relative

_____ Other: _____

_____ Received as gift

Age:

_____ Under 18     _____ 45-54

_____ 18-24        _____ 55-64

_____ 25-34        _____ 65 and over

_____ 35-44

Annual Household Income:

_____ Under $25,000       _____ $50,000-$69,999

_____ $25,000-$34,999     _____ $70,000-$89,999

_____ $35,000-$49,999     _____ $90,000 +

Occupation: _____

□ full-time  □ part-time  □ retired

Comments about item purchased: _____

Other comments: _____

If you'd like more information about Hartmann products, please contact our Customer Service Department toll-free at 1-800-331-0613.

please moisten to seal

---

**Multiple-grid question**
Several similar questions arranged in a grid format.

together. In situations where it is necessary to conserve space on the questionnaire or to facilitate data entry or tabulation of the data, a multiple-grid layout may be used. The **multiple-grid question** asks several questions and instructs the respondent to answer the categories as they appear in a grid format. For example:

**Airlines often offer special fare promotions. On a vacation trip would you take a connecting flight instead of a nonstop flight if the connecting flight were longer?**

|                      | Yes | No | Not sure |
|----------------------|-----|-----|----------|
| **One hour longer?**   | □   | □  | □        |
| **Two hours longer?**  | □   | □  | □        |
| **Three hours longer?**| □   | □  | □        |

Experienced researchers have found that it pays to carefully phrase the title of the questionnaire. In mail and other self-administered questionnaires, a carefully constructed title may capture the respondent's interest, underline the importance of the research ("Nationwide Study of Blood Donors"), emphasize the interesting nature of the study ("Study of the Internet Usage"), appeal to the respondent's ego ("Survey among Top Executives"), or emphasize the confidential nature of the study ("A Confidential Survey among . . ."). To avoid any negative influence from the wording of the title, the researcher should take steps to ensure that the title will not bias the respondent in the same way a leading question may.

The researcher can design the questionnaire to facilitate the interviewer's job of following interconnected questions by using several forms, special instructions, and other tricks of the trade. Exhibits 11.4 and 11.5 illustrate portions of telephone and personal interview questionnaires. Note how the layout and easy-to-follow instructions for interviewers in questions 1, 2, and 3 of Exhibit 11.4 help the interviewer follow the question sequence. Note that questions 3 and 6 in Exhibit 11.5 instruct the interviewer to hand the respondent a card bearing a list of alternatives. Cards may help respondents grasp the intended meaning of the question and remember all the brand names or other items. Also, questions 2, 3, and 6 in Exhibit 11.5 instruct the interviewer that ratings of the banks will start with the bank that has been checked in red pencil on the printed questionnaire. The name of the red-checked bank is not the same on every questionnaire. By rotating the order of the check marks, the researchers attempted to reduce order bias caused by respondents reacting more favorably to the first set of questions. To facilitate coding, question responses should be precoded when possible, as in Exhibit 11.4.

---

■ **Exhibit 11.4**

**Telephone Questionnaire**

1. Did you take the car you had checked to the Standard Auto Repair Center for repairs?
   -1 Yes     (Skip to Q. 3)              -2 No
2. (If no, ask:) Did you have the repair work done?
   -1 Yes                                 -2 No
       ↓                                    ↓
   1. Where was the repair work          1. Why didn't you have the car
      done? _____                 repaired? _____
      _____

   2. Why didn't you have the repair       _____
      work done at the Standard Auto       _____
      Repair Center? _____       _____
      _____
      _____
      _____

3. (If yes to Q. 1, ask:) How satisfied were you with the repair work? Were you . . .
   -1 Very satisfied
   -2 Somewhat satisfied
   -3 Somewhat dissatisfied
   -4 Very dissatisfied
   (If somewhat or very dissatisfied:) In what way were you dissatisfied?
   _____
   _____

4. (Ask everyone:) Do you ever buy gas at the 95th Street Standard Center?
   -1 Yes                                 -2 No (Skip to Q. 6)
5. (If yes, ask:)   How often do you buy gas there?
   -1 Always
   -2 Almost always
   -3 Most of the time
   -4 Part of the time
   -5 Hardly ever
6. Have you ever had your car washed there?      -1 Yes   -2 No
7. Have you ever had an oil change or lubrication done there?      -1 Yes   -2 No

■ **Exhibit 11.5**           **Personal Interview Questionnaire**

"Hello, my name is _____. I'm a Public Opinion Interviewer with Research Services, Inc. We're making an opinion survey about Banks and Banking, and I'd like to ask you . . ."

1. What are the names of local banks you can think of offhand? (INTERVIEWER: List names in order mentioned.)
   a. _____
   b. _____
   c. _____
   d. _____
   e. _____
   f. _____
   g. _____

2. Thinking now about the experiences you have had with the different Banks here in Boulder . . . have you ever talked to or done business with . . . (INTERVIEWER: Insert name of bank name red-checked below.)
   a. Are you personally acquainted with any of the employees or officers at _____?
   b. (If YES) Who is that?
   c. How long has it been since you have been inside _____?
      (INTERVIEWER: Now go back and repeat 2–2c for all other banks listed.)

| | (2)<br>Talked | | (2a and 2b)<br>Know Employee<br>Or Officer | | (2c)<br>Been in Bank in: | | | | |
|---|---|---|---|---|---|---|---|---|---|
| | Yes | No | No | Name | Last<br>Year | 1–5 | 5-Plus | No | DK |
| Arapahoe National Bank | 1 | 2 | 1 | _____ | 1 | 2 | 3 | 4 | 5 |
| First National Bank | 1 | 2 | 1 | _____ | 1 | 2 | 3 | 4 | 5 |
| Boulder National Bank | 1 | 2 | 1 | _____ | 1 | 2 | 3 | 4 | 5 |
| Security Bank | 1 | 2 | 1 | _____ | 1 | 2 | 3 | 4 | 5 |
| United Bank of Boulder | 1 | 2 | 1 | _____ | 1 | 2 | 3 | 4 | 5 |
| National State Bank | 1 | 2 | 1 | _____ | 1 | 2 | 3 | 4 | 5 |

3. (HAND BANK RATING CARD) On this card there are a number of contrasting phrases or statements, for example, "Large" and "Small." We'd like to know how you rate (NAME OF BANK RED-CHECKED BELOW) in terms of these statements or phrases. Just for example: let's use the terms "fast service" and "slow service." If you were to rate Bank #1 on this scale it would mean you find their service "very fast." On the other hand, a 7 rating would indicate you feel their service is "very slow," whereas a 4 rating means you don't think of them as being either "very fast" or "very slow." Are you ready to go ahead? Good! Tell me then how you would rate (NAME OF BANK RED-CHECKED) in terms of each of the phrases or statements on that card.
   How about (READ NEXT BANK NAME)? . . . Continue on until Respondent has evaluated all six banks.

| | | Arapahoe<br>National | First<br>National | Boulder<br>National | Security<br>Bank | United<br>Bank | National<br>State |
|---|---|---|---|---|---|---|---|
| a. | Service | _____ | _____ | _____ | _____ | _____ | _____ |
| b. | Size | _____ | _____ | _____ | _____ | _____ | _____ |
| c. | Business vs. Family | _____ | _____ | _____ | _____ | _____ | _____ |
| d. | Friendliness | _____ | _____ | _____ | _____ | _____ | _____ |
| e. | Big/Small Business | _____ | _____ | _____ | _____ | _____ | _____ |
| f. | Rate of Growth | _____ | _____ | _____ | _____ | _____ | _____ |
| g. | Modernness | _____ | _____ | _____ | _____ | _____ | _____ |
| h. | Leadership | _____ | _____ | _____ | _____ | _____ | _____ |
| i. | Loan Ease | _____ | _____ | _____ | _____ | _____ | _____ |
| j. | Location | _____ | _____ | _____ | _____ | _____ | _____ |
| k. | Hours | _____ | _____ | _____ | _____ | _____ | _____ |
| l. | Ownership | _____ | _____ | _____ | _____ | _____ | _____ |
| m. | Community Involvement | _____ | _____ | _____ | _____ | _____ | _____ |

*continued*

■ **Exhibit 11.5**          *continued*

| | | |
|---|---|---|
| 4. Suppose a friend of yours who has just moved to Boulder asked you to recommend a bank. Which local bank would you recommend? Why would you recommend that particular bank? | Arapahoe National | 1 |
| | First National | 2 |
| | Boulder National | 3 |
| | Security Bank | 4 |
| | United Bank of Boulder | 5 |
| | National State Bank | 6 |
| | Other (Specify)_____ | |
| | DK/Wouldn't | 9 |

5. Which of the local banks do you think of as: (INTERVIEWER: Read red-checked item first, then read each of the other five.)
the newcomer's bank? _____
the student's bank? _____
the Personal Banker bank? _____
the bank where most C.U. faculty and staff bank? _____
the bank most interested in this community? _____
the most progressive bank? _____

| | | |
|---|---|---|
| 6. Which of these financial institutions, if any, (HAND CARD 2) are you or any member of your immediate family who lives here in this home doing business with now? | Bank | 1 |
| | Credit Union | 2 |
| | Finance Company | 3 |
| | Savings and Loan | 4 |
| | Industrial Bank | 5 |
| (IF NONE, Skip to 19.) | None of these | 6 |
| | DK/Not sure | 7 |

| | | |
|---|---|---|
| 7. If a friend asked you to recommend a place where he or she could get a loan with which to buy a home, which financial institution would you probably recommend? (INTERVIEWER: Probe for specific name.) Why would you recommend (INSTITUTION NAMED IN 7)? | Would Recommend: _____ | |
| | Wouldn't | 0 |
| | DK/Not Sure | 9 |

Layout is extremely important when questionnaires are long or require the respondent to fill in a large amount of information. In many circumstances, headings or subtitles can indicate groups of questions to help the respondent grasp the scope or nature of the questions to be asked. Thus, at a glance, the respondent can follow the logic of the questionnaire.

# ■ HOW MUCH PRETESTING AND REVISING ARE NECESSARY?

After the questionnaires have been completed or returned, an investigator who is surveying 3,000 consumers does not want to find that most respondents misunderstood a particular question, skipped a series of questions, or misinterpreted the instructions for filling out the questionnaire. To avoid problems such as these, screening procedures, or *pretests,* are often used. **Pretesting** involves a trial run with a group of respondents in the target population to iron out fundamental problems in the questionnaire survey design. Here the researcher looks for such things as the point at which respondent fatigue sets in, whether there are any particular places in the questionnaire where respondents tend to terminate, and other considerations. Unfortunately, this stage of research may be eliminated due to costs or time pressures.

**Pretesting**
Administering a questionnaire to a small group of respondents to detect ambiguity or bias in the questions or to iron out fundamental problems in the instructions or administrative procedures.

Broadly speaking, there are three basic ways to pretest. The first two involve screening the questionnaire with other research professionals, and the third—the one most often called *pretesting*—is a trial run with a group of respondents. When screening the questionnaire with other research professionals, the investigator asks them to look for such things as difficulties with question wording, problems with leading questions, and bias due to question order. An alternative screening process might involve a client or the manager who ordered the research. Often managers ask for information but, when they see the questionnaire, find it does not really meet their needs. Only by checking with the individual who has requested the questionnaire does the researcher know for sure that the information needed will be provided.

Once the researcher has decided on the final questionnaire, data should be collected with a small number of respondents (say, 100) to determine whether the questionnaire needs further refinement. Usually the questionnaire is tried out on a group selected on a convenience basis and similar in makeup to the one that ultimately will be sampled. Pretesting does not require a statistical sample; however, the researcher should not select a group too divergent from the target market (for example, selecting business students as surrogates for businesspeople). The pretesting process allows the researcher to determine whether respondents have any difficulty understanding the questionnaire or if there are any ambiguous or biased questions. This process is exceedingly beneficial. Making a mistake with 25 or 50 subjects can save the potential disaster of administering an invalid questionnaire to several hundred individuals.

Counting the number of responses to each question and other means of tabulating the results of a pretest help determine whether the questionnaire will meet the objectives of the

---

## WHAT WENT WRONG?

### Burger Favorites: A Failure to Communicate

Sometimes it is just a matter of how you ask the question. When Burger King sent a survey company into the field to query fast-food fanciers on whether they preferred flame-broiled or fried hamburgers, they found a three-to-one preference for the open flame, or flame-broiled method—Burger King's own. The company and its agency immediately incorporated that finding into a comparative advertising campaign.

But when Leo Shapiro, president of a marketing research company, conducted his own survey, he rephrased the question and came up with distinctly different answers. "If you have two methods of cooking and it's a verbal survey, the choice of words could influence the outcome," Shapiro said in explaining why he decided to conduct his own survey of 308 fast-food customers. An interviewer asked: "Do you prefer a hamburger that is grilled on a hot stainless-steel grill or cooked by passing the raw meat through an open gas flame?" Shapiro's researchers found that 53 percent preferred their burgers from a stainless-steel grill. This means they opted for McDonald's fried over Burger King's open flame. The interviewer then added another dimension: "The chain that grills on a hot stainless-steel griddle serves its cooked hamburgers at the proper temperature without having to use a microwave oven. And the chain that uses the flame puts the hamburgers after they are cooked into a microwave oven before serving them. Just knowing this, from which of these two chains would you prefer to buy a hamburger?"

McDonald's hot stainless-steel griddles and microwaveless restaurants won again. This time they pulled in a 5½-to-1 margin over Burger King. The Burger King hamburgers do come off one at a time, so in rush periods the microwave is used to preserve the serving temperature and to melt the cheese. Burger King refuses to provide details on its survey beyond saying it was national, done by a nationally known public opinion company, that the question asked was "Do you prefer your hamburgers flame-broiled or fried?", and that they are completely satisfied with the survey.

"We found the word 'fried' was unappetizing," Shapiro said. "You don't eat fried foods. The word 'cooked' is neutral, and 'open-gas' is more precise but less appetizing [than Burger King's 'flame-broiled' description]." Shapiro stated that the most significant finding of this survey is how important the methods of cooking and serving were to the hamburger consumer.

**Preliminary tabulation**
A tabulation of the results of a pretest to help determine whether the questionnaire will meet the objectives of the research.

research. A **preliminary tabulation** often illustrates that while a question is easily comprehended and answered by the respondent, it is inappropriate because it does not provide relevant information to help solve the marketing problem.

Many novelists write, rewrite, revise, and rewrite again certain chapters, paragraphs, or even sentences. The researcher works similarly. Rarely does he or she write only a first draft of a questionnaire. The exact number of revisions depends on the researcher's and client's judgment. The revision process usually ends when both agree that the desired information is being collected in an unbiased manner.

## ■ DESIGNING QUESTIONNAIRES FOR GLOBAL MARKETS

Now that marketing research is being conducted around the globe, researchers must take cultural factors into account when designing questionnaires. The most common problem involves translation into another language. A questionnaire developed in one country may be difficult to translate because equivalent language concepts do not exist or because of differences in idiom and vernacular. For example, the concepts of uncles and aunts are not the same in the United States as in India. In India the words for *uncle* and *aunt* are different for the maternal and paternal sides of the family.[13] Although Spanish is spoken in both Mexico and Venezuela, one researcher found the Spanish translation of the English term *retail outlet* works in Mexico but not in Venezuela. Venezuelans interpreted the translation to refer to an electrical outlet, an outlet of a river into an ocean, and the passageway into a patio.

**Back translation**
The process of translating a questionnaire into another language and then having a second, independent translator translate it back to the original language.

International marketing researchers often have questionnaires back translated. **Back translation** is the process of translating the questionnaire from one language to another and then translating it back again by a second, independent translator. The back translator is often a person whose native tongue is the language that will be used for the questionnaire. This can reveal inconsistency between the English version and the translation, for correction if necessary. For example, when a soft-drink company translated its slogan "Baby, it's cold inside" into Cantonese for research in Hong Kong, the result read "Small Mosquito, on the inside, it is very cold." In Hong Kong, *small mosquito* is a colloquial expression for a small child. Obviously the intended meaning of the advertising message had been lost in the translated questionnaire.[14] In another international marketing research project, "out of sight, out of mind" was back translated as "invisible things are insane."[15]

As indicated in Chapter 7, literacy influences the designs of self-administered questionnaires and interviews. Knowledge of the literacy rates in foreign countries, especially those that are just developing modern economies, is vital.

## ■ SUMMARY

Good questionnaire design is a key to obtaining accurate survey results. The specific questions to be asked will be a function of the type of information needed to answer the manager's questions and the communication medium of data collection. Relevance and accuracy are the basic criteria for judging questionnaire results. *Relevance* means no unnecessary information is collected and the information needed to solve the marketing problem is obtained. *Accuracy* means the information is reliable and valid.

Knowing how each question should be phrased requires some knowledge about the different types of questions available. Open-ended response questions pose some topic or problem and ask the respondent to answer in his or her own words. Fixed-alternative questions require less interviewer skill, take less time, and are easier to answer. Standardized responses are easier to code, tabulate, and interpret. Care must be taken to formulate the responses so they do not overlap. Respondents whose answers do not fit any of the fixed alternatives may be forced to select alternatives that do not communicate what they really mean.

Open-ended response questions are especially useful in exploratory research or at the beginning of a questionnaire. They are more costly than fixed-alternative questions because of the uniqueness of the answers. Also, interviewer bias can influence the responses to such questions.

In fixed-alternative questions, the respondent is given specific limited alternative responses and asked to choose the one closest to his or her own viewpoint.

Some guidelines for questionnaire construction have emerged from research experience. The language should be simple to allow for variations in education level. Leading or loaded questions suggest answers to the respondents. Other questions induce them to give socially desirable answers. Respondents have a bias against questions that suggest changes in the status quo. Their reluctance to answer personal questions can be reduced by explaining the need for them and by assuring the respondents of the confidentiality of their replies. The researcher should carefully avoid ambiguity in questions. Another common problem is the double-barreled question, which asks two questions at once.

Question sequence can be very important to the success of a survey. The opening questions should be designed to capture respondents' interest and keep them involved. Personal questions should be postponed to the middle or end of the questionnaire. General questions should precede specific ones. In a series of attitude scales, the first response may be used as an anchor for comparison with the other responses. The order of alternatives on closed questions also can affect the results. Filter questions are useful for avoiding asking unnecessary questions that do not apply to a particular respondent. Such questions may be put into a flowchart for personal or telephone interviewing.

The layout of a mail or self-administered questionnaire can affect its response rate. An attractive questionnaire encourages a response, as does a carefully phrased title. Finally, pretesting helps reveal errors while they can still be corrected easily.

International marketing researchers must take cultural factors into account when designing questionnaires. The most widespread problem involves translation into another language. International questionnaires are often back translated.

## ■ Key Terms and Concepts

Open-ended response question

Fixed-alternative question

Simple-dichotomy (dichotomous-alternative) question

Determinant-choice question

Frequency-determination question

Checklist question

Leading question

Loaded question

Counterbiasing statement

Split-ballot technique

Double-barreled question

Order bias

Funnel technique

Filter question

Pivot question

Multiple-grid question

Pretesting

Preliminary tabulation

Back translation

## ■ Questions

1. Evaluate and comment on the following questions taken from several questionnaires:
   (a) A university computer center survey on SPSS usage:

How often do you use SPSS statistical software? Please check one.

_____ Infrequently (once a semester)
_____ Occasionally (once a month)
_____ Frequently (once a week)
_____ All the time (daily)

(b) A survey of advertising agencies:

**Do you understand and like the Federal Trade Commission's new corrective advertising policy?**

_____ Yes
_____ No

*Double barreled Question*

(c) A survey on a new, small electric car:

**Assuming 90 percent of your driving is in town, would you buy this type of car?**

_____ Yes
_____ No

**If this type of *electric* car had the same initial cost as a current "Big 3" full-size, fully equipped car, but operated at one-half the cost over a 5-year period, would you buy one?**

_____ Yes
_____ No

(d) A student survey:

**Since the beginning of this semester, approximately what percentage of the time do you get to campus using each of the forms of transportation available to you per week?**

**Walk _____ Bicycle _____**
**Public transportation _____ Motor vehicle _____**

(e) A survey of motorcycle dealers:

**Should the company continue its generous cooperative advertising program?**

(f) A survey of farmer media behavior:

**Thinking about *yesterday*, put an *X* in the box below for *each* quarter-hour time period during which, so far as you can recall, you *personally* listened to *radio*. Do the same for *television*.**

**If you did not watch TV any time yesterday. *X* here** ☐
**If you did not listen to radio any time yesterday, *X* here** ☐

| 6:00 to 10:00 a.m. by quarter-hours | 6:00–6:15 | 6:15–6:30 | 6:30–6:45 | 6:45–7:00 | 7:00–7:15 | 7:15–7:30 | 7:30–7:45 | 7:45–8:00 | 8:00–8:15 | 8:15–8:30 | 8:30–8:45 | 8:45–9:00 | 9:00–9:15 | 9:15–9:30 | 9:30–9:45 | 9:45–10:00 |
|---|---|---|---|---|---|---|---|---|---|---|---|---|---|---|---|---|
| Radio → | | | | | | | | | | | | | | | | |
| TV → | | | | | | | | | | | | | | | | |

(g) A government survey of gasoline retailers:

**Suppose the full-service pump selling price for unleaded premium gasoline is 132.8 cents per gallon on the first day of the month. Suppose on the 10th of the month the price is raised to 134.9 cents per gallon, and on the 25th of the month it is reduced to 130.9 cents per gallon. In order to provide the required data, you should list the accumulator reading on the full-service unleaded premium gasoline pump when the station opens on the 1st day, the 10th day, and the 25th day of the month and when the station closes on the last day of the month.**

(h) An antigun control group's survey:

**Do you believe that private citizens have the rights to own firearms to defend themselves, their families, and their property from violent criminal attack?**

_____**Yes**

_____**No**

(i) A survey of the general public:

**In the next year, after accounting for inflation, do you think your real personal income will go up or down?**

1. **Up**
2. **(Stay the same)**
3. **Down**
4. **(Don't know)**

(j) A survey of the general public:

**Some people say that companies should be required by law to label all chemicals and substances that the government states are potentially harmful. The label would tell what the chemical or substance is, what dangers it might pose, and what safety procedures should be used in handling the substance. Other people say that such laws would be too strict. They say the law should require labels on only those chemicals and substances that the companies themselves decide are potentially harmful. Such a law, they say, would be less costly for the companies and would permit them to exclude those chemicals and substances they consider to be trade secrets. Which of these views is closest to your own?**

1. **Require labels on all chemicals and substances that the government states are potentially harmful.**
2. **(Don't know)**
3. **Require labels on only those chemicals and substances that companies decide are potentially harmful.**

(k) A survey of voters:

**Since agriculture is vital to our state's economy, how do you feel about the administration's farm policies?**

**Strongly favor**

**Somewhat favor**

**Somewhat oppose**

**Strongly oppose**

**Unsure**

2. When the Agency for Consumer Advocacy was under consideration, there was considerable debate regarding the validity of the poll. The Consumer Federation of America charged that the following question was loaded:

**Those in favor of setting up an additional federal consumer protection agency on top of the other agencies say that current agencies are not getting the job done themselves. Those who oppose setting up the additional agency say we already have plenty of government agencies to protect consumers, and it's just a matter of making them work better. How do you feel?**

The researchers felt otherwise. How do you feel about this disputed question?

3. How might the wording of a question about income influence respondents' answers?

4. What is the difference between a leading and a loaded question?

5. Design an open-ended response question(s) to measure reactions to a magazine ad for a Xerox photocopier.

6. Design a question(s) to measure how a person who has just been shown a television commercial might describe the commercial.

7. It has been said that surveys show that consumers hate advertising but like specific ads. Comment.

8. Design a complete questionnaire to evaluate a new fast-food fried chicken restaurant.

9. Design a short but complete questionnaire to measure consumer satisfaction with an airline.

10. Develop a checklist of things to consider in questionnaire construction.

11. Design a complete personal interview questionnaire for a zoo that wishes to determine who visits the zoo and how they evaluate it.

12. Design a complete self-administered questionnaire for a bank to give to customers immediately after they open new accounts.

13. Design a questionnaire for your local Big Brothers and Big Sisters organization to investigate awareness and willingness to volunteer time to this organization.

14. Design a questionnaire for a bank located in a college town to investigate the potential for college students as checking account customers.

15. The Apple Assistance Center is a hotline to solve problems for users of Macintosh computers and other Apple products. Design a short, postcard consumer satisfaction/ service quality questionnaire for the Apple Assistance Center.

16. A client tells a researcher that she wants a questionnaire that evaluates the importance of 30 product characteristics and rates her brand and 10 competing brands on these characteristics. The researcher believes this questionnaire will induce respondent fatigue because it will be far too long. Should the researcher do exactly what the client says or risk losing the business by suggesting a different approach?

17. A lobbying organization designs a short questionnaire about its political position. It also includes a membership solicitation with the questionnaire. Is this right?

18. A public figure who supports cost cutting in government asks the following question in a survey: **"Do you support a presidential line item veto to eliminate waste in government?"** Is this ethical?

## EXPLORING THE INTERNET

1. Visit The Internet Survey Experts at http://www.customersat.com/samplequestions.htm.

Click on "Customer Satisfaction and Loyalty." What you find will depend on when you visit the site. However, you should find numerous survey questions to measure customer satisfaction. Pick three questions and evaluate the questions in the poll.

2. Visit HotBot at http://www.hotbot.com and search for the key phrase *questionnaire design*. How many Web sites contain this phrase? Find an interesting Web site and report on your findings.

---

## CASE 11.1    Canterbury Travels

Hometown was located in the east-north-central United States and had a population of about 50,000. There were two travel agencies in Hometown before Canterbury Travels opened its doors.

Canterbury Travels was in its second month of operations. Owner Roxanne Freeman had expected to have more business than she actually had. She decided that she needed to conduct a survey to determine how much business Hometown offered. She also wanted to learn whether people were aware of Canterbury Travels. She thought this survey would determine the effectiveness of her advertising.

The questionnaire Roxanne Freeman designed is shown in Case Exhibit 11.1-1.

**Questions**

1. Critically evaluate the questionnaire.
2. Will Canterbury Travels gain the information it needs from this survey?

---

■ **Case Exhibit 11.1-1**
**Travel Questionnaire**

The following questionnaire pertains to a project being conducted by a local travel agency. The intent of the study is to better understand the needs and attitudes of Hometown residents toward travel agencies. The questionnaire will take only 10 to 15 minutes to fill out at your convenience. Your name will in no way be connected with the questionnaire.

1. Have you traveled out of state?          _____ Yes    _____ No
2. If yes, do you travel for:
   Business    Both
   Pleasure
3. How often do you travel for the above?

   0–1 times per month          0–1 times per year
   2–3 times per month          2–3 times per year
   4–5 times per month          4–5 times per year
   6 or more times per month    6 or more times per year

4. How do you make your travel arrangements?
   Airline    Travel agency
   Other (please specify) _____
5. Did you know that travel agencies do not charge the customer for their services?
   _____ Yes    _____ No
6. Please rate the following qualities that would be most important to you in the selection of a travel agency:

|  | Good |  |  |  | Bad |
|---|---|---|---|---|---|
| Free services (reservations, advice, and delivery of tickets and literature) | ____ | ____ | ____ | ____ | ____ |
| Convenient location | ____ | ____ | ____ | ____ | ____ |
| Knowledgeable personnel | ____ | ____ | ____ | ____ | ____ |
| Friendly personnel | ____ | ____ | ____ | ____ | ____ |
| Casual atmosphere | ____ | ____ | ____ | ____ | ____ |
| Revolving charge account | ____ | ____ | ____ | ____ | ____ |
| Reputation | ____ | ____ | ____ | ____ | ____ |
| Personal sales calls | ____ | ____ | ____ | ____ | ____ |

*continued*

**■ Case Exhibit 11.1-1**

*continued*

7. Are you satisfied with your present travel agency?

| | Very Satisfied | | | | Very dissatisfied |
|---|---|---|---|---|---|
| Holiday Travel | ____ | ____ | ____ | ____ | ____ |
| Leisure Tours | ____ | ____ | ____ | ____ | ____ |
| Canterbury Travel | ____ | ____ | ____ | ____ | ____ |
| Other _____ | ____ | ____ | ____ | ____ | ____ |

8. If not, what are you dissatisfied with about your travel agency?

| | Good | | | Bad |
|---|---|---|---|---|
| Free services<br>(reservations, advice, and delivery of tickets<br>and literature) | ____ | ____ | ____ | ____ |
| Convenient location | ____ | ____ | ____ | ____ |
| Knowledgeable personnel | ____ | ____ | ____ | ____ |
| Friendly personnel | ____ | ____ | ____ | ____ |
| Casual atmosphere | ____ | ____ | ____ | ____ |
| Revolving charge account | ____ | ____ | ____ | ____ |
| Reputation | ____ | ____ | ____ | ____ |
| Personal sales calls | ____ | ____ | ____ | ____ |

9. Did you know that there is a new travel agency in Hometown?

_____ Yes    _____ No

10. Can you list the travel agencies in Hometown and their locations?

_____
_____
_____

11. Do you use the same travel agency repeatedly?

| | 0–1 times per month | 2–3 times per month | 4–5 times per month | 6 or more times per month | 0–1 times per year | 2–3 times per year | 4–5 times per year | 6 or more times per year |
|---|---|---|---|---|---|---|---|---|
| Holiday Travel | | | | | | | | |
| Leisure Tours | | | | | | | | |
| Canterbury Travel | | | | | | | | |
| Other (please specify) | | | | | | | | |

12. Have you visited the new travel agency in Hometown?

_____ Yes    _____ No

13. If yes, what is its name? _____

14. How do you pay for your travel expenses?

| | |
|---|---|
| Cash | Company charge |
| Check | Personal charge |
| Credit card | Other _____ |

15. Which of these have you seen advertising for?

Holiday Travel
Canterbury Travel
Other _____

16. If yes, where have you seen or heard this advertisement?

17. Would you consider changing travel agencies?

_____ Yes    _____ No

The following are some personal questions about you that will be used for statistical purposes only. Your answers will be held in the strictest confidence.

18. What is your age?

| | |
|---|---|
| 19–25 | 46–55 |
| 26–35 | 56–65 |
| 36–45 | Over 65 |

19. What is your sex?

| | |
|---|---|
| Male | Female |

*continued*

■ **Case Exhibit 11.1-1**

*continued*

20. What is your marital status?
    Single          Divorced
    Married         Widowed

21. How long have you lived in Hometown?
    0–6 months      5–10 years
    7–12 months     11–15 years
    1–4 years       Over 15 years

22. What is your present occupation?
    Business and professional        Laborer
    Salaried and semiprofessional    Student
    Skilled worker

23. What is the highest level of education you have completed?
    Elementary school          1–2 years of college
    Junior high school         3–4 years of college
    Senior high school         More than 4 years of college
    Trade or vocational school

24. What is your yearly household income?
    $0–$5,000            $25,001–$40,000
    $5,001–$10,000       $40,001–$60,000
    $10,001–$15,000      $60,000 and above
    $15,001–$25,000

## CASE 11.2    GTE Airfone

The questionnaire in Case Exhibit 11.2-1 was sent to a sample of frequent airline fliers.

**Question**

Evaluate the questionnaire.

■ **Case Exhibit 11.2-1**    **Airfone Questionnaire**

If you have used the Airfone service please indicate your level of satisfaction with the Airfone service by circling the appropriate number below.

|  |  | Excellent 5 | Good 4 | Average 3 | Fair 2 | Poor 1 |
|---|---|---|---|---|---|---|
| **GTE Airfone service** | | | | | | |
| A1 | Considering your Airfone usage, how would you rate your overall experience | 5 | 4 | 3 | 2 | 1 |
| A2 | Availability of Airfone on flights on which you've traveled | 5 | 4 | 3 | 2 | 1 |
| A3 | Availability of operating instructions | 5 | 4 | 3 | 2 | 1 |
| A4 | Understandability of operating instructions | 5 | 4 | 3 | 2 | 1 |
| A5 | Length of time to obtain dial tone | 5 | 4 | 3 | 2 | 1 |
| A6 | Ability to complete a call on the first attempt | 5 | 4 | 3 | 2 | 1 |
| A7 | Transmission quality (static) | 5 | 4 | 3 | 2 | 1 |
| A8 | Level of telephone background noise | 5 | 4 | 3 | 2 | 1 |
| A9 | Calls fading | 5 | 4 | 3 | 2 | 1 |
| A10 | Hearing the called party clearly | 5 | 4 | 3 | 2 | 1 |
| A11 | Called party hearing you clearly | 5 | 4 | 3 | 2 | 1 |
| A12 | Frequency of calls disconnected | 5 | 4 | 3 | 2 | 1 |
| A13 | Convenience of computer voice messages | 5 | 4 | 3 | 2 | 1 |
| A14 | Current price structure | 5 | 4 | 3 | 2 | 1 |
| A15 | Flight attendant helpfulness, assistance, and knowledge of the Airfone service | 5 | 4 | 3 | 2 | 1 |

*continued*

■ **Case Exhibit 11.2-1**    *continued*

Billing

| | | | | | | |
|---|---|---|---|---|---|---|
| B1 | Accuracy of monthly charges | 5 | 4 | 3 | 2 | 1 |
| B2 | Ease of understanding charges | 5 | 4 | 3 | 2 | 1 |

The following questions concern your Airfone usage, airline travel, preferred charge method, and a comparison of the Airfone to cellular phones. Please answer as completely as possible.

1.  In the past *year,* how often have you used the Airfone service?

                                                                          *(Enter # Times)*

2.  Have you used our Seatfone product?
    *(Circle one answer)*                                                 Yes                        1
                                                                          No                         2

3.  Did you use the Airfone service to make urgent business calls, nonurgent
    business calls, or personal calls?                                    Urgent business calls      1
    *(Circle all that apply)*                                             Nonurgent business calls   2
                                                                          Personal calls             3

4.  Approximately how many airline round trips do you make annually?

                                                                          *(Enter # Times)*

5.  Which airline do you most frequently travel on?

                                                                          *(Enter Name of Airline)*

6.  Has the Airfone service made your travel time productive and more beneficial to your    Yes     1
    completing business while in flight?                                                    No      2
    *(Circle one answer)*
    If yes, please explain how _____

7.  Considering the value of the Airfone service, do you feel the cost of a call is comparable to    Yes    1
    the quality of service you've experienced?                                                        No     2
    *(Circle one answer)*
    If no, please explain why _____

8.  Given a choice of flights with the same schedule, destination, and cost, one with the Airfone
    service, the other without, which flight would you choose to travel on? *(Circle one answer)*    With Airfone       1
                                                                                                     Without Airfone    2

9.  Which credit cards do you own? *(Circle all that apply)*
    1.  American Express          4.  Discover          7.  UATP
    2.  Carte Blanche             5.  Enroute           8.  Visa
    3.  Diners Club               6.  MasterCard         9.  AT&T

10. Which credit card have you used in the past to pay for the Airfone service? *(Circle all that apply)*
    1.  American Express          4.  Discover          7.  UATP
    2.  Carte Blanche             5.  Enroute           8.  Visa
    3.  Diners Club               6.  MasterCard         9.  AT&T

11. Have you experienced problems activating the Airfone Service with your card(s)?    Yes    1
    *(Circle one answer)*                                                               No     2

12. Which card would you prefer to use to pay for the Airfone service?
    *(Circle all that apply)*
    1.  American Express          4.  Discover          7.  UATP
    2.  Carte Blanche             5.  Enroute           8.  Visa
    3.  Diners Club               6.  MasterCard         9.  AT&T

13. Do you own a cellular phone or use a company-paid cellular phone?    Yes    1
    *(Circle one answer)*                                                No     2
    If yes, how does the quality of the GTE Airfone compare to that of the cellular phone?
    *(Circle one answer)*                       Airfone is much higher quality than cellular        1
                                                Airfone is somewhat higher quality than cellular    2
                                                Airfone is about the same quality as cellular        3
                                                Airfone is somewhat lower quality than cellular      4
                                                Airfone is much lower than cellular                  5

*continued*

■ **Case Exhibit 11.2-1**        *continued*

| | | |
|---|---|---|
| 14. Have you ever seen any advertising for GTE Airfone? | Yes | 1 |
| If yes, what did the advertising tell you about GTE Airfone? | No | 2 |

| | |
|---|---|
| If yes, where have you seen GTE Airfone advertising? *(Circle all that apply)* | |
| In-flight airline magazines | 1 |
| Posters or billboards | 2 |
| TV at airport | 3 |
| Newspapers | 4 |
| Business publications | 5 |
| Card located in the seatback pocket | 6 |
| Other | 7 |

| | | |
|---|---|---|
| 15. Are you aware of our Service Guarantee that provides credit when you are not satisfied with the quality of an Airfone call? | Yes | 1 |
| | No | 2 |
| If yes, how did you first become aware of it? *(Circle one only)* | | |
| In-flight airline magazines | | 1 |
| Posters or billboards | | 2 |
| TV at airport | | 3 |
| Newspapers | | 4 |
| Business publications | | 5 |
| Card located in the seatback pocket | | 6 |
| Flight attendant | | 7 |
| Other | | 8 |

These next few questions are for classification purposes only.

| | | |
|---|---|---|
| 16. What is your job classification? *(Circle one answer)* | Professional | 1 |
| | Executive | 2 |
| | Managerial | 3 |
| | Administrative | 4 |
| | Technical | 5 |
| | Other | 6 |
| 17. What is your age? *(Circle one answer)* | 18–24 | 1 |
| | 25–34 | 2 |
| | 35–44 | 3 |
| | 45–54 | 4 |
| | 55–64 | 5 |
| | 65 or over | 6 |
| 18. What is your sex? *(Circle one answer)* | Male | 1 |
| | Female | 2 |
| 19. What is your annual *individual* income? *(Circle one answer)* | Under $20,000 | 1 |
| | $20,000–$39,999 | 2 |
| | $40,000–$59,999 | 3 |
| | $60,000–$79,999 | 4 |
| | $80,000–$99,999 | 5 |
| | $100,000–$149,999 | 6 |
| | $150,000+ | 7 |
| 20. What is your level of education? *(Circle one answer)* | Attended high school | 1 |
| | High school graduate | 2 |
| | Some college | 3 |
| | College graduate | 4 |
| | Postgraduate degree | 5 |

*continued*

■ **Case Exhibit 11.2-1**    *continued*

21.   Finally, what changes/improvements would you like to see in our service?

_____

_____

_____

_____

Thanks again for your assistance! Please return this completed survey in the enclosed preaddressed, postage-paid envelope.

---

## CASE 11.3    Middlemist Precision Tool Company (B)

Middlemist Precision Tool Company was conducting research for its radial arm saw adjustment device (see Case 6.2). The company decided it had two major markets for its product: professional woodworkers, such as carpenters, and do-it-yourself homeowners. It decided to concentrate on the do-it-yourself market and thought a survey would be appropriate.

**Questions**

1. What were Middlemist's primary information needs?
2. What type of survey should have been used in this study?
3. Design a questionnaire to satisfy Middlemist's information needs.

---

## CASE 11.4    McDonald's Spanish-Language Questionnaire

The following questions about a visit to McDonald's originally appeared in Spanish and were translated into English.

---

**AQUI ➜ SE EMPIEZA**

**1. En general, ¿qué tan satisfecho/a quedó con su visita a este McDonald's hoy?**

☹ NADA SATISFECHO/A .......... [1] [2]     [3]     [4]     MUY SATISFECHO/A ☺ [5]

**2. Su visita fue.......** Adentro (**A**) o en el Drive-thru (**DT**)     [A] Adentro     [DT] Drive-thru

**3. Su visita fue.......** Durante el Desayuno (**D**), Almuerzo (**A**), Cena (**C**)     [D] Desayuno     [A] Almuerzo     [A] Cena

**4. Su visita fue.......** Entre semana (**E**) o Fin de semana (**F**)     [E] Entre semana     [F] Fin de semana

**COMIDA**

**5.** ¿Quedó satisfecho/a con la comida que recibio hoy?     [S] Si     [N] No ⌐
Si NO, ¿cuál fue el problema?     Sandwich / platillo frío     ◀
Favor de rellenar el(los) círculo(s)     Apariencia desagradable     ☐
apropiado(s).     Mal sabor de la comida     ☐
Pocas papas en la bolsa / caja     ☐
Papas / tortitas de papa frías     ☐
Papas no bien saladas     ☐
Bebida aguada / de mal sabor     ☐

---

**Questions**

1. What is the typical process for developing questionnaires for markets in which a different language is spoken?

2. Find someone who speaks Spanish and have them back translate the questions that appear in the case. Are these Spanish-language questions adequate?

## ■ Endnotes

[1]Charles W. Roll Jr. and Albert H. Cantril, *Polls, Their Use and Misuse in Politics* (New York: Basic Books, 1972), p. 106.

[2]Stanley L. Payne, *The Art of Asking Questions* (Princeton, N.J.: Princeton University Press, 1951), pp. 8–9. The reader who wants a more detailed account of question wording is referred to this classic book on that topic.

[3]Paul L. Erdos, *Professional Mail Surveys* (New York: McGraw-Hill, 1970), p. 37.

[4]Donald P. Warwick and Charles A. Lininger, *The Sample Survey: Theory and Practice* (New York: McGraw-Hill, 1975), p. 127.

[5]This heading is borrowed from Payne, *The Art of Asking Questions.*

[6]Fred W. Morgan, "Judicial Standards for Survey Research: An Update and Guidelines," *Journal of Marketing* (January 1990), pp. 59–70.

[7]Payne, *The Art of Asking Questions,* p. 185.

[8]Roll and Cantril, *Polls: Use and Misuse,* pp. 106–107.

[9]The others are *relative advantage, compatibility, complexity,* and *communicability.* See Thomas S. Robertson, *Innovative Behavior and Communication* (New York: Holt, Rinehart and Winston, 1971), pp. 46–47.

[10]Payne, *The Art of Asking Questions,* pp. 102–103.

[11]Erdos, *Professional Mail Surveys,* p. 59.

[12]This section relies heavily on Erdos, *Professional Mail Surveys.*

[13]Philip R. Cateora, *International Marketing* (Homewood, Ill., Richard D. Irwin, 1990), pp. 387–389.

[14]Cateora, *International Marketing,* pp. 387–389.

[15]Subhash C. Jain, *International Marketing* (Boston: PWS Kent, 1990), p. 338.

**PART**

*IV*  SAMPLING AND STATISTICAL THEORY

# SAMPLING DESIGNS AND SAMPLING PROCEDURES

**WHAT YOU WILL LEARN IN THIS CHAPTER:**

To define *sample, population, population element,* and *census.*

To explain why a sample rather than a complete census may be taken.

To discuss the issues concerning the identification of the target population and the selection of a sampling frame.

To describe common forms of sampling frames and sampling frame error.

To distinguish between random sampling and systematic (nonsampling) errors.

To explain the various types of systematic (nonsampling) errors that result from sample selection.

To discuss the advantages and disadvantages of the various types of probability and nonprobability samples.

To understand how to choose an appropriate sample design.

**W**e know that making a good first impression is important because after a sample exposure to us, people make judgments about the types of people we are. Unless you are a member of the Polar Bear swimming club, you will test the early March waters of Lake Michigan with a toe before diving in. Stand in a bookstore and observe the process of sampling. Customers generally pick up a book, look at the cover, and then sample a few pages to get a feeling for the writing style and the content before deciding whether to buy. The high school student who visits a college classroom to listen to a professor's lecture is employing a sampling technique. Selecting a university on the basis of one classroom visit may not be a scientific sample, but in a personal situation it may be a practical sampling experience. These examples illustrate the intuitive nature of sampling in everyday uses when it is impossible, inconvenient, or too expensive to measure every item in the population.

Although sampling is commonplace in daily activities, most of these familiar samples are not scientific. The concept of sampling may seem simple and intuitive, but the actual process of sampling can be quite complex. Sampling is a central aspect of marketing research, and it requires in-depth examination.

This chapter explains the nature of sampling and how to determine the appropriate sample design.

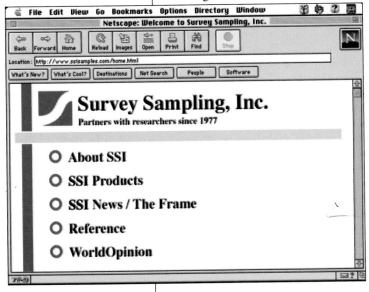

# ■ SAMPLING TERMINOLOGY

**Sample**
A subset or some part of a larger population.

**Population (universe)**
Any complete group of entities that share some common set of characteristics.

**Population element**
An individual member of a population.

The process of sampling involves using a small number of items or parts of the population to make conclusions about the whole population. A **sample** is a subset or some part of a larger population. The purpose of sampling is to enable one to estimate some unknown characteristic of the population.

We have defined sampling in terms of the population to be studied. A **population,** or **universe,** is any complete group—for example, of people, sales territories, stores, or college students—that share some common set of characteristics. **Population element** refers to an individual member of the population. A **census** is an investigation of all the individual elements that make up the population, that is, a total enumeration rather than a sample.

# ■ WHY SAMPLE?

**Census**
An investigation of all the individual elements that make up a population.

At a wine-tasting party, all guests recognize the impossibility of anything but sampling. However, in a scientific study whose objective is to estimate an unknown population value, why should a sample rather than a complete census be taken?

A researcher who wants to investigate a population with an extremely small number of population elements may elect to conduct a census rather than a sample because the cost, labor, and time drawbacks would be relatively insignificant. Thus, a company concerned about salespeople's satisfaction with its computer networking system may have no pragmatic reason to avoid in-house circulation of a questionnaire to all 25 of its employees. In most situations, however, there are many practical reasons to sample. Sampling cuts costs, reduces labor requirements, and gathers vital information quickly.[1]

Another major reason to sample is that most properly selected samples give sufficiently accurate results. If the elements of a population are quite similar, only a small sample is necessary to accurately portray the characteristic of interest. Most of us have had blood samples taken from the finger, the arm, or another part of the body. The assumption is that the blood is sufficiently similar throughout the body to determine its characteristics on the basis of a sample. When the population elements are largely homogeneous, samples are highly representative of the population. Under these circumstances, almost any sample is as good as another. Even when populations have considerable heterogeneity, large samples provide sufficiently precise data to make most decisions. Of course, samples are accurate only when researchers have taken care to properly draw representative samples. We will say more about this later in the chapter.

# ■ PRACTICAL SAMPLING CONCEPTS

Researchers must make several decisions before taking a sample. Exhibit 12.1 overviews these decisions as a series of sequential stages even though the order of the decisions does not always follow this sequence. These decisions are highly interrelated.

## ■ Defining the Target Population

Once the decision to sample has been made, the first question concerns identifying the target population. What is the relevant population? In many cases, this is not a difficult question. Registered voters may be clearly identifiable. Likewise, if a company's 106-person sales force is the population of concern, few definitional problems exist. In other cases, the

■ **Exhibit 12.1**

**Stages in the Selection of
a Sample**

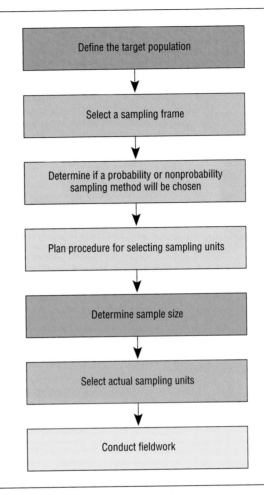

decision may be difficult. One survey concerning organizational buyer behavior incorrectly defined the population as purchasing agents whom sales representatives regularly contacted. After the survey, investigators discovered that industrial engineers within the customer companies had substantially affected buying decisions, but they rarely talked with the salespeople. Frequently the appropriate population element is the household rather than the individual member of the household. This presents some problems if household lists are not available.

At the outset of the sampling process, it is vital to carefully define the target population to be able to identify the proper sources from which the data are to be collected. Answering questions about the crucial characteristics of the population is the usual technique for defining the target population. Does the term *comic book reader* include children under six years of age who do not actually read the words? Does *all persons west of the Mississippi* include people in east bank towns that border the river, such as East St. Louis, Illinois? The question "Whom do we want to talk to?" must be answered. It may be users, nonusers, recent adopters, or brand switchers. To implement the sample in the field, tangible characteristics should be used to define the population. A baby food manufacturer might define the population as all women still capable of bearing children. However, a more specific *operational definition* would be women between ages 12 and 50. While this definition by age

## How Private Are Mailing Lists?

The direct marketing and survey research industries require mailing lists to reach carefully targeted market segments. Survey research companies generally purchase mailing lists that they can use for sampling purposes, or they hire the mailing list company to stuff envelopes and post surveys. Mailing list companies may use credit reports, driver's license information, and voter registration records as well as other databases to compile these lists. For example, TRW Target Marketing Services, a company that originated as a service to approve individuals as creditworthy, sells mailing lists based on an individual's available credit or ownership of bank credit cards with nonzero balances.

Most credit agreements indicate that the consumer's name may be used for other purposes, and it has long been accepted practice to use credit information for purposes beyond establishing an individual's creditworthiness.

The Direct Marketing Association's Mail Preference Service allows consumers to write to have their names taken off mailing lists. However, many consumers are unaware of this service. This raises the ethical question of how to balance the right of privacy against marketing researchers' need to know.

may exclude a few women who are capable of childbearing and include some who are not, it is still more explicit and provides a manageable basis for the sample design.

## ◼ The Sampling Frame

**Sampling frame**
A list of elements from which a sample may be drawn; also called *working population.*

In practice, the sample will be drawn from a list of population elements that often differs somewhat from the defined target population. A **sampling frame** is a list of elements from which the sample may be drawn. A simple example of a sampling frame would be a list of all members of the American Medical Association. Generally it is not feasible to compile a list that does not exclude some members of the population. For example, if the student telephone directory is assumed to be a sampling frame of your university's student population, it may exclude those students who registered late, those without phones, or those who have their telephones listed only under their roommates' or pets' names. The sampling frame is also called the *working population* because it provides the list for operational work. If a complete list of population elements is not accessible, materials such as maps or aerial photographs may be used as a sampling frame. The discrepancy between the definition of the population and a sampling frame is the first potential source of error associated with sample selection. We will discuss such errors later in the chapter.

**Mailing Lists**    Some firms, called *list brokers,* specialize in providing mailing lists that give the names, addresses, and phone numbers of specific populations. Exhibit 12.2 shows a page from a mailing list company's offerings. Companies such as this offer lists based on subscriptions to professional journals, ownership of credit cards, and a variety of other sources. One mailing list company obtained its listing of households with children from an ice cream retailer that gave children free ice cream cones on their birthdays. (The children filled out cards with their names, addresses, and birthdays, which the retailer then sold to the mailing list company.)

**Sampling frame error**
An error that occurs when certain sample elements are excluded from or overrepresented in the sampling frame.

**Sampling Frame Error**    A **sampling frame error** occurs when certain population elements are excluded from or overrepresented in the sampling frame—in other words, when the entire population is not accurately represented in the sampling frame. One city's manager for community development, in preparation for an upcoming bond issue election, used randomly generated telephone numbers as the basis for a sample survey to gauge

■ **Exhibit 12.2**         **Mailing List Directory Page**

# *Lists Available* - *Alphabetical*

| S.I.C. Code | List Title | United States Total Count | United States State Count Page | Canadian Count |
|---|---|---|---|---|
| | **A** | | | |
| 5122-02 | Abdominal Supports | 201 | ‡ | 28 |
| 8399-03 | Abortion Alternatives Organizations` | 946 | ‡ | * |
| 8093-04 | Abortion Information & Services | 551 | ‡ | 277 |
| 5085-23 | Abrasives | 1811 | ‡ | * |
| 5169-04 | Absorbents | 145 | ‡ | * |
| 6541-03 | Abstracters | 4057 | 58 | * |
| 6411-06 | Accident & Health Insurance | 2113 | ‡ | 9 |
| 8748-52 | Accident Reconstruction Service | 125 | ‡ | * |
| 8721-01 | Accountants | 127392 | 64 | 6933 |
| 8721-02 | Accounting & Bookkeeping General Svc | 27996 | 64 | 2072 |
| 5044-08 | Accounting & Bookkeeping Machines/Supls | 889 | ‡ | 50 |
| 5044-01 | Accounting & Bookkeeping Systems | 624 | ‡ | 1230 |
| 8711-02 | Acoustical Consultants | 381 | ‡ | 91 |
| 1742-02 | Acoustical Contractors | 3063 | 47 | 433 |
| 1742-01 | Acoustical Materials | 878 | ‡ | 210 |
| 8999-10 | Actuaries | 1185 | ‡ | * |
| 8049-13 | Acupuncture (Acupuncturists) | 2921 | 62 | 493 |
| 5044-02 | Adding & Calculating Machines/Supplies | 5524 | 49 | 648 |
| 5044-09 | Addressing Machines & Supplies | 345 | ‡ | 29 |
| 5169-12 | Adhesives & Glues | 1187 | ‡ | 4 |
| 3579-02 | Adhesives & Gluing Equipment | 170 | ‡ | 204 |
| 6411-02 | Adjusters | 6164 | 57 | 8357 |
| 6411-01 | Adjusters-Public | 161 | ‡ | * |
| 8322-01 | Adoption Agencies | 1621 | ‡ | 32 |
| 8059-03 | Adult Care Facilities | 596 | ‡ | * |
| 8361-08 | Adult Congregate Living Facilities | 170 | ‡ | * |
| 7319-03 | Advertising-Aerial | 337 | ‡ | 26 |
| 7311-01 | Advertising-Agencies & Counselors | 27753 | 59 | 2552 |
| 7336-05 | Advertising-Art Layout & Production Svc | 457 | ‡ | 101 |
| 7331-05 | Advertising-Direct Mail | 6347 | 59 | 540 |
| 7311-03 | Advertising-Directory & Guide | 2465 | ‡ | 124 |
| 7319-01 | Advertising-Displays | 3441 | 59 | 571 |
| 7319-11 | Advertising-Indoor | 209 | ‡ | 63 |
| 7311-05 | Advertising-Motion Picture | 143 | ‡ | 11 |
| 7311-06 | Advertising-Newspaper | 4274 | 59 | 404 |
| 7312-01 | Advertising-Outdoor | 3052 | 59 | 297 |
| 7311-08 | Advertising-Periodical | 817 | ‡ | 78 |

| S.I.C. Code | List Title | United States Total Count | United States State Count Page | Canadian Count |
|---|---|---|---|---|
| 7313-03 | Advertising-Radio | 2866 | 59 | 247 |
| 7311-07 | Advertising-Shoppers' Guides | 392 | ‡ | 4 |
| 5199-17 | Advertising-Specialties | 12827 | 52 | 1648 |
| 7389-12 | Advertising-Telephone | 120 | ‡ | * |
| 7313-05 | Advertising-Television | 1746 | ‡ | 102 |
| 7319-02 | Advertising-Transit & Transportation | 179 | ‡ | 38 |
| 0721-03 | Aerial Applicators (Service) | 1479 | ‡ | 61 |
| 3999-01 | Aerosols | 158 | ‡ | * |
| 3812-01 | Aerospace Industries | 426 | ‡ | * |
| | Affluent Americans | | 73 | |
| 5191-04 | Agricultural Chemicals | 549 | ‡ | 210 |
| 8748-20 | Agricultural Consultants | 1047 | ‡ | 474 |
| 9999-32 | Air Balancing | 353 | ‡ | * |
| 5084-64 | Air Brushes | 219 | ‡ | * |
| 4512-02 | Air Cargo Service | 6005 | 48 | * |
| 5075-01 | Air Cleaning & Purifying Equipment | 2055 | ‡ | 342 |
| 5084-02 | Air Compressors | 4358 | 50 | 717 |
| | (See Compressors Air & Gas) | | | |
| 1711-17 | Air Conditioning Contractors & Systems | 50951 | 47 | 2667 |
| | ***Available By Brands Sold*** | | | |
| | Airtemp (A) | 187 | | |
| | Amana (B) | 1450 | | |
| | Arco Aire (2) | 673 | | |
| | Armstrong/Magic Chef (C) | 395 | | |
| | Arvin (4) | 106 | | |
| | Bryant (D) | 2223 | | |
| | Carrier (E) | 5927 | | |
| | Coleman (5) | 1176 | | |
| | Comfortmaker/Singer (O) | 989 | | |
| | Day & Night (Z) | 749 | | |
| | Fedders (H) | 318 | | |
| | Heli/Quaker (3) | 1977 | | |
| | Janitrol (7) | 587 | | |
| | Kero-Sun (W) | 2 | | |
| | Lennox (K) | 4390 | | |
| | Luxaire (L) | 510 | | |
| | Payne (M) | 553 | | |

attitudes toward capital improvements. When the bond issue failed, consultants pointed out that the appropriate sampling frame would have been a list of registered voters, not any adult with a phone (since some might not have voted in this type of election). By including respondents who should not have been listed as members of the population, a sampling frame error occurred.

**Sampling Frames for International Marketing Research**   The availability of sampling frames around the globe varies dramatically. Not every country's government conducts a census of population, telephone directories are often incomplete, no voter registration lists exist, and accurate maps of urban areas are unobtainable.[2] However, in Taiwan, Japan, and other Asian countries, a researcher can build a sampling frame relatively easily because those governments release some census information about individuals. If a family changes households, the change, along with updated census information, must be reported to a centralized government agency before communal services (water, gas, electricity, education, etc.) are made available.[3] This information is then easily accessible in the local *Inhabitants' Register.*

■ In countries with less well-developed economies, such as Sri Lanka, fewer than 5 percent of households may have telephones. Telephone directories cannot serve as sampling frames in such countries.

### ■ Sampling Units

**Sampling unit**
A single element or group of elements selected for the sample.

During the actual sampling process, the elements of the population must be selected according to a certain procedure. The **sampling unit** is a single element or group of elements selected for the sample. For example, if an airline wishes to sample passengers, it may take every 25th name on a complete list of passengers. In this case, the sampling unit would be the same as the population element. Alternatively, the airline could first select certain flights as the sampling unit, then select certain passengers on each flight. In this instance, the sampling unit contains many elements.

**Primary sampling unit (PSU)**
A unit selected in the first stage of sampling.

**Secondary sampling unit**
A unit selected in the second stage of sampling.

**Tertiary sampling unit**
A unit selected in the third stage of sampling.

If the target population has first been divided into units, such as airline flights, additional terminology must be used. The term **primary sampling unit (PSU)** designates a unit selected in the first stage of sampling. Units selected in successive stages of sampling (if necessary) are called **secondary sampling units, tertiary sampling units,** and so on. When there is no list of population elements, the sampling unit generally is something other than the population element. In a random digit dialing study, for example, the sampling unit will be telephone numbers.

---

## ■ RANDOM SAMPLING AND NONSAMPLING ERRORS

**Random sampling error**
The difference between the result of a sample and the result of a census conducted using identical procedures; a statistical fluctuation due to chance variations in the elements selected for a sample.

An estimation from a sample may not be exactly the same as a census count because of random sampling errors or systematic (nonsampling) errors.

**Random sampling error** is the difference between the sample result and the result of a census conducted using identical procedures. Of course, the result of a census is unknown unless one is taken, which is rarely done. Random sampling error results from chance variation in the scientific selection of sampling units. The sampling units, even if properly selected according to sampling theory, may not perfectly represent the population, but generally they are reliable estimates. Our discussion of the process of randomization (a procedure designed to give everyone in the population an equal chance of being selected as a sample member) will show that because random sampling errors follow chance variations, they tend to cancel one another out when averaged. This means that properly selected samples generally are good approximations of the population. There is almost always a slight difference between the true population value and the sample value, hence a small random sampling error. Thus, every once in awhile an unusual sample is selected because too many atypical people were included in the sample and a large random sampling error occurred. The theory behind this concept of sample reliability and other basic statistical concepts is reviewed in detail in Chapter 13. At this point, simply recognize that *random sampling error* is a technical term that refers only to statistical fluctuations due to chance variations in the elements selected for the sample.

Random sampling error is a function of sample size. As sample size increases, random sampling error decreases. Of course, the resources available will influence how large a sample may be taken. It is possible to estimate the random sampling error that may be expected with various sample sizes. Suppose a survey of approximately 1,000 people has been taken in Portland to determine the feasibility of a new soccer franchise. Assume 30 percent of the respondents favor the idea of a new professional sport in town. The researcher will know, based on the laws of probability, that 95 percent of the time a survey of slightly fewer than 900 people will produce results with an error of approximately plus or minus 3 percent. Had the survey been collected with only 325 people, the margin of error would increase to approximately plus or minus 5 percentage points. This example illustrates random sampling errors.

**Systematic (nonsampling) errors** that lead to unrepresentative samples result primarily from the nature of a study's design and the imperfections in execution. Such errors are *not* due to chance fluctuations. For example, highly educated respondents are more likely to cooperate with mail surveys than poorly educated ones, for whom filling out forms is a more difficult and intimidating task.[4] Systematic errors or biases such as these account for a large portion of errors in marketing research.

**Systematic (nonsampling) error**
Error resulting from factors not due to chance fluctuations, such as the nature of a study's design and imperfections in execution.

### ■ Less Than Perfectly Representative Samples

Random sampling errors and systematic errors associated with the sampling process may combine to yield a sample that is less than perfectly representative of the population. Exhibit 12.3 illustrates two nonsampling errors (sampling frame error and nonresponse error) related to sample design. The total population is represented by the area of the

### ■ Exhibit 12.3    Errors Associated with Sampling

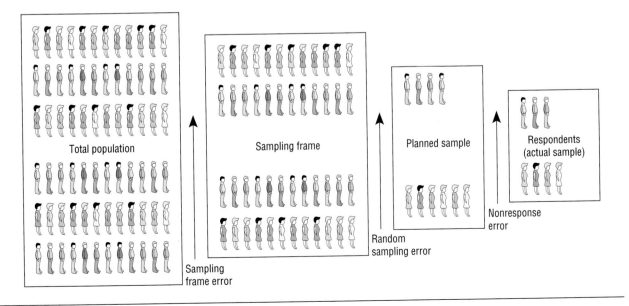

## WHAT WENT WRONG?

### Random Sequences That Don't Look Random

Every basketball player and fan knows that players have hot and cold streaks. Players who have hot hands can't seem to miss, while those who have cold ones can't find the center of the hoop. When psychologists interviewed team members of the Philadelphia 76ers, the players estimated they were about 25 percent more likely to make a shot after they had just made one than after a miss. Nine in ten basketball fans surveyed concurred that a player "has a better chance of making a shot after having just made his last two or three shots than he does after having just missed his last two or three shots." Believing in shooting streaks, players will feed a teammate who has just made two or three shots in a row, and many coaches will bench the player who misses three in a row. When you're hot you're hot.

The only trouble is, it isn't true. When the psychologists studied detailed individual shooting records, they found that the 76ers—and the Boston Celtics, the New Jersey Nets, the New York Knicks, and Cornell University's men's and women's basketball players—were equally likely to score after a miss as after a basket. Fifty percent shooters average 50 percent after just missing three shots, and 50 percent after just making three shots.

Why, then, do players and fans alike believe that players are more likely to score after scoring and miss after missing? In any series of 20 shots by a 50 percent shooter (or 20 flips of a coin), there is a 50-50 chance of four baskets (or heads) in a row, and it is quite possible that one person out of five will have a streak of five or six. Players and fans notice these random streaks and so form the myth that when you're hot, you're hot.

The same type of thing happens with investors who believe that a fund is more likely to perform well after a string of good years than after a string of bad years. Past performances of mutual funds do not predict their future performances. When funds have streaks of several good or bad years, we may nevertheless be fooled into thinking that past success predicts future success.

The moral: Whether watching basketball, choosing stocks, flipping coins, or drawing a sample, remember the statistical principle that random sequences often don't look random. Even when the next outcome cannot be predicted from the preceding ones, streaks are to be expected.

**Nonresponse error**
The statistical differences between a survey that includes only those who responded and a perfect survey that would also include those who failed to respond.

largest square. Sampling frame errors eliminate some potential respondents. Random sampling error (due exclusively to random, chance fluctuation) may cause an imbalance in the representativeness of the group. Additional errors will occur if individuals refuse to be interviewed or cannot be contacted. Such **nonresponse error** also may cause the sample to be less than perfectly representative. Thus, the actual sample is drawn from a population different (or smaller) than the ideal.

## ■ PROBABILITY VERSUS NONPROBABILITY SAMPLING

**Probability sampling**
A sampling technique in which every member of the population has a known, nonzero probability of selection.

There are several ways to take a sample. The main alternative sampling plans may be grouped into two categories: probability techniques and nonprobability techniques.

In **probability sampling,** every element in the population has a *known, nonzero probability* of selection. The simple random sample, in which each member of the population has an equal probability of being selected, is the best-known probability sample.

In **nonprobability sampling,** the probability of any particular member of the population being chosen is unknown. The selection of sampling units in nonprobability sampling is quite arbitrary, as researchers rely heavily on personal judgment. *There are no appropriate statistical techniques for measuring random sampling error from a nonprobability*

**Nonprobability sampling**
A sampling technique in which units of the sample are selected on the basis of personal judgment or convenience; the probability of any particular member of the population being chosen is unknown.

*sample. Thus, projecting the data beyond the sample is statistically inappropriate.* Nevertheless, on certain occasions, nonprobability samples are best suited for the researcher's purpose.

We will now explore the various types of nonprobability and probability sampling. Although probability sampling is preferred, we will discuss nonprobability sampling first to illustrate some potential sources of error and other weaknesses in sampling.

# ■ NONPROBABILITY SAMPLING

## ■ Convenience Sampling

**Convenience sampling**
The sampling procedure of obtaining those people or units that are most conveniently available.

**Convenience sampling** (also called *haphazard* or *accidental sampling*) refers to obtaining the people or units that are most conveniently available. It may be convenient and economical to set up an interviewing booth from which to intercept consumers at a shopping center. During election times, television stations often present person-on-the-street interviews that are presumed to reflect public opinion. (Of course, the television station often warns that the survey was "unscientific and random" [sic].) The college professor who uses his or her students has a captive sample—convenient but perhaps unwilling and unrepresentative.

Researchers generally use convenience samples to obtain a large number of completed questionnaires quickly and economically. The user of research based on a convenience sample should remember that projecting the results beyond the specific sample is inappropriate. Convenience samples are best used for exploratory research when additional research will subsequently be conducted with a probability sample.

## ■ Judgment Sampling

**Judgment (purposive) sampling**
A nonprobability sampling technique in which an experienced researcher selects the sample based on personal judgment about some appropriate characteristic of the sample members.

**Judgment,** or **purposive, sampling** is a nonprobability sampling technique in which an experienced individual selects the sample based on his or her judgment about some appropriate characteristics required of the sample member. Researchers select samples to satisfy their specific purposes, even if the resulting samples are not fully representative. The consumer price index (CPI) is based on a judgment sample of market basket items, housing costs, and other selected goods and services expected to reflect a representative sample of items consumed by most Americans. Test market cities often are selected because they are viewed as typical cities whose demographic profiles closely match the national profile. A fashion manufacturer regularly selects a sample of key accounts that it believes are capable of providing the information it needs to predict what will sell in the fall; the judgment sample is selected to achieve a specific objective.

## ■ Quota Sampling

**Quota sampling**
A nonprobability sampling procedure that ensures that various subgroups of a population will be represented on pertinent characteristics to the exact extent the investigator desires.

Suppose a firm wishes to investigate consumers who currently own digital versatile disc (DVD) players. The researchers may wish to ensure that each brand of DVD player/recorder is proportionately included in the sample. Strict probability sampling procedures would likely underrepresent certain brands and overrepresent others. If the selection process were left strictly to chance, some variation would be expected. The purpose of **quota sampling** is to ensure that the various subgroups in a population are represented on pertinent sample characteristics to the exact extent the investigators desire. Stratified sampling, a probability sampling procedure, also has this objective, but it should not be confused with quota sampling. In quota sampling, the interviewer has a quota to achieve. For example, an interviewer in a particular city may be assigned 100 interviews, 35 with

■ Judgment sampling often is used in attempts to forecast election results. People frequently wonder how a television network can predict the results of an election with only 2 percent of the votes reported. Political and sampling experts judge which small voting districts approximate overall state returns from previous election years; then these bellwether precincts are selected as the sampling units. Of course, the assumption is that the past voting records of these districts are still representative of the state's political behavior.

owners of Sony DVD players, 30 with owners of Samsung DVD players, 18 with owners of Toshiba DVD players, and the rest with owners of other brands. The interviewer is responsible for finding enough people to meet the quota. Aggregating the various interview quotas yields a sample that represents the desired proportion of each subgroup.

**Possible Sources of Bias**   The logic of classifying the population by pertinent subgroups is essentially sound. However, because respondents are selected according to a convenience sampling procedure rather than on a probability basis as in stratified sampling, the haphazard selection of subjects may introduce bias. For example, a college professor hired some of his students to conduct a quota sample based on age. When analyzing the data, the professor discovered that almost all the people in the "under 25 years" category were college educated. Interviewers, being human, tend to prefer to interview people who are similar to themselves. Quota samples tend to include people who are easily found, willing to be interviewed, and middle class. Fieldworkers are given considerable leeway to exercise their judgment concerning selection of actual respondents. Interviewers often concentrate their interviewing in areas with heavy pedestrian traffic such as downtowns, shopping malls, and college campuses. Those who interview door-to-door learn quickly that quota requirements are difficult to meet by interviewing whoever happens to appear at the door; this tends to overrepresent less active people who are likely to stay at home. One interviewer related a story about working in an upper-middle-class neighborhood. After a few blocks, it changed into a neighborhood of mansions. Believing most of the would-be subjects were above his station, the interviewer skipped those houses because he felt uncomfortable knocking on doors that would be answered by servants.

**Advantages of Quota Sampling**   Speed of data collection, lower costs, and convenience are the major advantages of quota sampling over probability sampling. Although this method has many problems, careful supervision of the data collection may provide a representative sample for analyzing the various subgroups within a population. Quota sampling may be appropriate when the researcher knows a certain demographic group is more likely to refuse to cooperate with a survey. For instance, if older men are more likely to refuse, a higher quota can be set for this group so that the proportions of each demographic category will be similar to the proportions in the population. A number of laboratory experiments also rely on quota sampling because it is difficult to find a sample of the general population who are willing to visit a laboratory to participate in an experiment.

## ■ Snowball Sampling

**Snowball sampling**
A sampling procedure in which initial respondents are selected by probability methods and additional respondents are obtained from information provided by the initial respondents.

**Snowball sampling** refers to a variety of procedures in which initial respondents are selected by probability methods and additional respondents are obtained from information provided by the initial respondents.[5] This technique is used to locate members of rare populations by referrals. Suppose a manufacturer of sports equipment is considering marketing a mahogany croquet set for serious adult players. This market is certainly small. An extremely large sample would be necessary to find 100 serious adult croquet players. It would be much more economical to survey, say, 300 people, find 15 croquet players, and ask them for the names of other players. Reduced sample sizes and costs are a clear-cut advantage of snowball sampling. However, bias is likely to enter into the study because a person who is known to another member of the sample has a higher probability of being similar to the first person. If there are major differences between those who are widely known by others and those who are not, this technique may present some serious problems. However, snowball sampling may be used to locate and recruit heavy users, such as consumers who buy more than 50 compact discs per year, for focus groups. Since the focus group is not expected to be a generalized sample, snowball sampling may be very appropriate.

## ■ PROBABILITY SAMPLING

All probability sampling techniques are based on chance selection procedures. This eliminates the bias inherent in nonprobability sampling procedures, because the probability sampling process is random. Note that *random* refers to the procedure for selecting the sample; it does not describe the data in the sample. *Randomness* refers to a procedure whose outcome cannot be predicted because it depends on chance. It should not be thought of as unplanned or unscientific; it is the basis of all probability sampling techniques. In this section, we examine the various probability sampling methods.

### ■ Simple Random Sampling

**Simple random sampling**
A sampling procedure that assures each element in the population of an equal chance of being included in the sample.

**Simple random sampling** ensures that each element in the population will have an equal chance of being included in the sample. Drawing names from a hat or selecting the winning raffle ticket from a large drum is a typical example of simple random sampling. If the names or raffle tickets are thoroughly stirred, each person or ticket should have an equal chance of being selected. This process is simple because it requires only one stage of sample selection in contrast to other, more complex probability samples.

Although drawing names or numbers out of a fishbowl, using a spinner, rolling dice, or turning a roulette wheel may be used to draw a sample from small populations, when populations consist of large numbers of elements, tables of random numbers (see *Table A.1 in the Appendix*) or computer-generated random numbers are used for sample selection.

**Selecting a Simple Random Sample**   Suppose a researcher is interested in selecting a simple random sample of all the Honda dealers in California, New Mexico, Arizona, and Nevada. Each dealer's name is assigned a number from 1 to 105; then each number is written on a separate piece of paper, and all the slips are placed in a large drum. After the slips of paper have been thoroughly mixed, one is selected for each sampling unit. Thus, if the sample size is 35, the selection procedure must be repeated 34 times after the first slip has been selected. Mixing the slips after each selection will ensure that those at the bottom of the bowl will continue to have an equal chance of being selected in the sample.

To use a table of random numbers, a serial number is assigned to each element of the population. Assuming a population of 99,999 or less, five-digit numbers are selected from the table of random numbers merely by reading the numbers in any column or row, by moving upward, downward, left, or right. A random starting point should be selected at the outset. For convenience, we will assume we have randomly selected the first five digits in columns 1 through 5, row 1, of *Table A.1 in the Appendix* as our starting point. The first number in our sample would be 37751; moving downward, the following numbers would be 50915, 99142, and so on.

The random digit dialing technique of sample selection requires that the researcher identify the exchange or exchanges of interest (the first three numbers) and then use a table of numbers to select the next four numbers.

## ■ Systematic Sampling

**Systematic sampling**
A sampling procedure in which a starting point is selected by a random process and then every *n*th number on the list is selected.

To illustrate **systematic sampling,** suppose we wish to take a sample of 1,000 from a list of 200,000 names. Using systematic selection, we will draw every 200th name from the list.

The procedure is extremely simple. A starting point is selected by a random process; then every *n*th number on the list is selected. In a sample from a rural telephone directory that does not separate business from residential listings, every 23rd name might be selected as the sampling interval. In this sample of consumers, it is possible that Mike's Restaurant will be selected. This unit is inappropriate because it is a business listing rather than a consumer listing, so the next eligible name is selected as the sampling unit and the systematic process continues.

**Periodicity**
A problem that occurs in systematic sampling when the original list has a systematic pattern.

While this procedure is not actually a random selection procedure, it does yield random results if the arrangement of the items in the list is random in character. The problem of **periodicity** occurs if a list has a systematic pattern, that is, is not random in character. Collecting retail sales information every seventh day would result in a distorted sample because there would be a systematic pattern of selecting sampling units. Sales for only one day of the week, perhaps Monday's sales, would be sampled. Another possible periodicity bias might occur in a list of contributors to a charity in which the first 50 are extremely large donors. If the sampling interval is every 200th name, a problem could result. Periodicity is rarely a problem for most sampling in marketing research, but researchers should be aware of the possibility.

## ■ Stratified Sampling

The usefulness of dividing the population into subgroups, or strata, that are more or less equal with respect to some characteristic was illustrated in our discussion of quota sampling. The first step of choosing strata on the basis of existing information, such as classifying retail outlets based on annual sales volume, is the same for both stratified and quota sampling. However, the process of selecting sampling units within the strata differs sub-

**Stratified sampling**
A probability sampling procedure in which simple random subsamples are drawn from within each stratum that are more or less equal on some characteristic.

stantially. In **stratified sampling,** a subsample is drawn using a simple random sample within each stratum. This is not true with quota sampling.

The reason for taking a stratified sample is to obtain a more efficient sample than would be possible with simple random sampling. Suppose urban and rural groups have widely different attitudes toward energy conservation, but members within each group hold very similar attitudes. Random sampling error will be reduced because the groups are internally homogeneous but comparatively different between them. More technically, a smaller standard error may result from this stratified sample because the groups will be adequately represented when strata are combined.

Another reason to conduct a stratified sample is to ensure that the sample will accurately reflect the population on the basis of the criterion or criteria used for stratification. This is a concern because occasionally a simple random sample yields a disproportionate number of one group or another and the representativeness of the sample could be improved.

A researcher can select a stratified sample as follows. First, a variable (sometimes several variables) is identified as an efficient basis for stratification. A stratification variable must be a characteristic of the population elements known to be related to the dependent variable or other variables of interest. The variable chosen should increase homogeneity within each stratum and increase heterogeneity between strata. The stratification variable usually is a categorical variable or one easily converted into categories, that is, subgroups.

For example, a pharmaceutical company interested in measuring how often physicians prescribe a certain drug might choose physicians' training as a basis for stratification. In this example, the mutually exclusive strata are M.D.'s (medical doctors) and O.D.'s (osteopathic doctors).

Next, for each separate subgroup or stratum, a list of population elements must be obtained. If a complete listing is not available, a true stratified probability sample cannot be selected. Using a table of random numbers or some other device, a separate simple random sample is then taken within each stratum. If stratified lists are not available, they can be costly to prepare. Of course, the researcher must determine how large a sample to draw for each stratum.

## ■ Cluster Sampling

**Cluster sampling**
An economically efficient sampling technique in which the primary sampling unit is not the individual element in the population but a large cluster of elements; clusters are selected randomly.

The purpose of **cluster sampling** is to sample economically while retaining the characteristics of a probability sample. Consider the researcher who must conduct 500 interviews with consumers scattered throughout the United States. Travel costs are likely to be enormous because the amount of time spent traveling will be substantially greater than the time spent in the interviewing process. If an aspirin marketer can assume the product will work as well in Phoenix as it does in Baltimore, or if a frozen pizza manufacturer assumes its product will taste the same in Texas as it does in Oregon, cluster sampling may be used. In a cluster sample, the primary sampling unit is no longer the individual element in the population (for example, grocery stores) but a larger cluster of elements located in proximity to one another (for example, cities). The *area sample* is the most popular type of cluster sample. A grocery store researcher, for example, may randomly choose several geographic areas as primary sampling units and then interview all or a sample of grocery stores within the geographic clusters. Interviews are confined to these clusters only. No interviews occur in other clusters. Cluster sampling is classified as a probability sampling technique because of either the random selection of clusters or the random selection of elements within each cluster.

Cluster samples frequently are used when lists of the sample population are not available. For example, in a downtown revitalization project to investigate employees and

■ **Exhibit 12.4**

**Examples of Clusters**

| Population Element | Possible Clusters in the United States |
|---|---|
| U.S. adult population | States |
| | Counties |
| | Metropolitan Statistical Areas |
| | Census tracts |
| | Blocks |
| | Households |
| College seniors | Colleges |
| Manufacturing firms | Counties |
| | Metropolitan Statistical Areas |
| | Localities |
| | Plants |
| Airline travelers | Airports |
| | Planes |
| Sports fans | Football stadia |
| | Basketball arenas |
| | Baseball parks |

self-employed workers, a comprehensive list of these people was not available. A cluster sample was taken by selecting organizations (business and government) as the clusters. A sample of firms within the central business district was developed using a stratified probability sample to identify clusters. Next, individual workers within the firms (clusters) were randomly selected and interviewed concerning the central business district. Some examples of clusters appear in Exhibit 12.4.

Ideally a cluster should be as heterogeneous as the population itself—indeed, a mirror image of the population. A problem may arise with cluster sampling if the characteristics and attitudes of the elements within the cluster are too similar. For example, geographic neighborhoods tend to have residents of the same socioeconomic status. To an extent, this problem may be mitigated by constructing clusters composed of diverse elements and selecting a large number of sampled clusters.

## ■ Multistage Area Sampling

**Multistage area sampling**
Sampling that involves using a combination of two or more probability sampling techniques.

So far we have described two-stage cluster sampling. **Multistage area sampling** involves two or more steps that combine some of the probability techniques already described. Typically geographic areas are randomly selected in progressively smaller (lower-population) units. For example, a political pollster investigating an election in Arizona may first choose counties within the state to ensure that the different areas are represented in the sample. In the second step, precincts within the selected counties may be chosen. As a final step, the pollster may select blocks (or households) within the precincts, then interview all the blocks (or households) within the geographic area. Researchers may take as many steps as necessary to achieve a representative sample. Exhibit 12.5 graphically portrays a multistage area sampling process frequently used by a major academic research center. Progressively smaller geographic areas are chosen until a single housing unit is selected for interviewing.

The Bureau of the Census provides maps, population information, demographic characteristics for population statistics, and so on by several small geographical areas that may be useful in sampling. Census classifications of small geographic areas vary depending on the extent of urbanization within Metropolitan Statistical Areas (MSAs) or counties.

■ **Exhibit 12.5**          **An Illustration of Multistage Area Sampling**

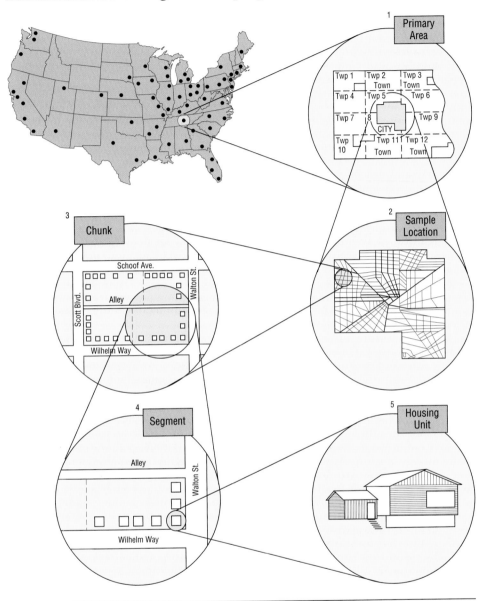

## ■ WHAT IS THE APPROPRIATE SAMPLE DESIGN?

### ■ Degree of Accuracy

Selecting a representative sample is important to all researchers. However, the degree of accuracy required or the researcher's tolerance for sampling and nonsampling error may vary from project to project, especially when cost savings or another consideration may be a trade-off for a reduction in accuracy.

For example, when the sample is being selected for an exploratory research project, accuracy may not have a high priority because a highly representative sample is unnecessary.

For other, more conclusive projects, the sample result must precisely represent a population's characteristics, and the researcher must be willing to spend the time and money needed to achieve accuracy.

### ■ Resources

The cost associated with the different sampling techniques varies tremendously. If the researcher's financial and human resources are restricted, certain options will have to be eliminated. For a graduate student working on a master's thesis, conducting a national survey is almost always out of the question because of limited resources. Managers concerned with the cost of the research versus the value of the information often will opt for cost savings from a certain nonprobability sampling design rather than make the decision to conduct no research at all.

### ■ Time

A researcher who needs to meet a deadline or complete a project quickly will be more likely to select a simple, less time-consuming sample design. A telephone survey using a sample based on random digit dialing takes considerably less time than a survey that uses an elaborate disproportional stratified sample.

### ■ Advance Knowledge of the Population

Advance knowledge of population characteristics, such as the availability of lists of population members, is an important criterion. In many cases, however, no list of population elements will be available to the researcher. This is especially true when the population element is defined by ownership of a particular product or brand, by experience in performing a specific job task, or on a qualitative dimension. A lack of adequate lists may automatically rule out systematic sampling, stratified sampling, or other sampling designs, or it may dictate that a preliminary study, such as a short telephone survey using random digit dialing, be conducted to generate information to build a sampling frame for the primary study. In many developing countries adequate sampling frames are the exception rather than the rule; thus, researchers planning sample designs will have to work around this limitation.

### ■ National versus Local Project

Geographic proximity of population elements will influence sample design. When population elements are unequally distributed geographically, a cluster sample may become much more attractive.

### ■ Need for Statistical Analysis

The need for statistical projections based on the sample often is a criterion. Nonprobability sampling techniques do not allow researchers to use statistical analysis to project data beyond their samples.

---

### ■ SUMMARY

Sampling is a procedure that uses a small number of units of a given population as a basis for conclusions about the whole population. Sampling often is necessary because it would be practically impossible to conduct a census to measure characteristics of all units of a population. Samples also are needed in cases where measurement involves destruction of the measured unit.

The first problem in sampling is to define the target population. An incorrect or vague definition of this population is likely to produce misleading results. A sampling frame is a list of elements, or individual members, of the overall population from which the sample is drawn. A sampling unit is a single element or group of elements subject to selection in the sample.

There are two sources of discrepancy between the sample results and the population parameters. The first, random sampling error, arises from chance variations of the sample from the population. The second, systematic (or nonsampling) error comes from sources such as sampling frame error, mistakes in recording responses, or nonresponses from persons who were not contacted or refused to participate.

The two major classes of sampling methods are probability and nonprobability techniques. Nonprobability techniques include convenience sampling, quota sampling, and snowball sampling. They are convenient to use, but no statistical techniques are available to measure their random sampling error. Probability samples are based on chance selection procedures. These include simple random sampling, systematic sampling, stratified sampling, and cluster sampling. With these techniques, random sampling error can be accurately predicted.

A researcher who must determine the most appropriate sampling design for a specific project will identify a number of sampling criteria and evaluate the relative importance of each criterion before selecting a design. The most common criteria concern accuracy requirements, available resources, time constraints, knowledge availability, and analytical requirements.

## ■ Key Terms and Concepts

| | |
|---|---|
| Sample | Probability sampling |
| Population (universe) | Nonprobability sampling |
| Population element | Convenience sampling |
| Census | Judgment (purposive) sampling |
| Sampling frame | Quota sampling |
| Sampling frame error | Snowball sampling |
| Sampling unit | Simple random sampling |
| Primary sampling unit (PSU) | Systematic sampling |
| Secondary sampling unit | Periodicity |
| Tertiary sampling unit | Stratified sampling |
| Random sampling error | Cluster sampling |
| Systematic (nonsampling) error | Multistage area sampling |
| Nonresponse error | |

## ■ Questions

1. If we judge whether we want to see a new movie or television program on the basis of the "coming attractions" or television commercial previews, are we using a sampling technique? A scientific sampling technique?
2. Name some possible sampling frames for the following:
   (a) Electrical contractors
   (b) Tennis players
   (c) Dog owners
   (d) Foreign-car owners
   (e) Wig and hair goods retailers
   (f) Minority-owned businesses
   (g) Men over 6 feet tall

3. Describe the difference between a probability sample and a nonprobability sample.
4. In what types of situations is conducting a census more appropriate than sampling? When is sampling more appropriate than taking a census?
5. Comment on the following sampling designs:
   (a) A citizen's group interested in generating public and financial support for a new university basketball arena prints a questionnaire in area newspapers. Readers return the questionnaires by mail.
   (b) A department store that wishes to examine whether it is losing or gaining customers draws a sample from its list of credit card holders by selecting every 10th name.
   (c) A motorcycle manufacturer decides to research consumer characteristics by sending 100 questionnaires to each of its dealers. The dealers will then use their sales records to track down buyers of this brand of motorcycle and distribute the questionnaires.
   (d) An advertising executive suggests that advertising effectiveness be tested in the real world. A one-page ad will be taken out in a magazine. One-half of the space will be used for a half-page ad. On the other half, a short questionnaire will request that readers comment on the ad. An incentive will be given for the first 1,000 responses.
   (e) In selecting its sample for a focus group, a research company obtains a sample through organized groups such as church groups, clubs, and schools. The organizations are paid to secure respondents; no individual is directly compensated.
   (f) A researcher suggests replacing a consumer diary panel with a sample of customers who regularly shop at a supermarket that uses optical scanning equipment. The burden of recording purchases by humans will be replaced by computerized longitudinal data.
6. When would a researcher use a judgment, or purposive, sample?
7. A telephone interviewer asks, "I would like to ask you about race. Are you Native American, Hispanic, African American, Asian, or white?" After the respondent replies, the interviewer says, "We have conducted a large number of surveys with people of your background, and we do not need to question you further. Thank you for your cooperation." What type of sampling was used?
8. If researchers know that consumers in various geographic regions respond quite differently to a product category such as tomato sauce, is area sampling appropriate? Why or why not?
9. What are the benefits of stratified sampling?
10. What geographic units within a metropolitan area are useful for sampling?
11. Marketers often are particularly interested in the subset of a market that contributes most to sales (for example, heavy beer drinkers or large-volume retailers). What type of sampling might be best in this type of situation? Why?
12. Outline the step-by-step procedure you would use to select the following:
    (a) A simple random sample of 150 students at your university
    (b) A quota sample of 50 light users and 50 heavy users of beer in a shopping mall intercept sample
    (c) A stratified sample of 50 mechanical engineers, 40 electrical engineers, and 40 civil engineers from the subscriber list of an engineering journal
13. Selection for jury duty is supposed to be a totally random process. Comment on the following computer selection procedures, and determine if they are indeed random processes.
    (a) A program instructed the computer to scan the list of names and pluck names that were next to those from the last scan.
    (b) Three-digit numbers were randomly generated to select jurors from a list of licensed drivers. If the weight information listed on the license matched the random number, the person was selected.
    (c) The juror source list was obtained by merging a list of registered voters with a list of licensed drivers.

14. A company gathers focus group members from a list of articulate participants. It does not conduct a random sample but selects its sample from this group to ensure a good session. The client did not inquire about sample selection when it accepted the proposal.

## EXPLORING THE INTERNET

1. NYNEX Interactive Yellow Pages lists 16.5 million businesses. Go to http://www.niyp.com and select the Business Type option. Then *select a state and bicycle.* How many bicycle dealers are located in the state you chose? Select a systematic sample from this list.

2. Go to the United States Census Bureau's home page at:

   http://www.census.gov

   To view a complete list of metropolitan areas (MSAs), select the population and housing option and then select the Metropolitan Areas option.

3. The Institute of Museum Services' (IMS) 1992 National Needs Assessment survey of museums may be found at http://palimpsest.stanford.edu/byorg/ims/survey. (You may also go to Conservation On-Line at http://palimpsest.stanford.edu and click on "Survey Results." This allows you to navigate to this and other studies.) This location describes the methodology and results of a study of U.S. museums. Visit this site to view the sampling methodology.

4. Use Lycos to search for ski resorts. At what URL can you find a sampling frame of U.S. ski resorts?

5. Survey Sampling Incorporated's Web page is located at http://www.ssisamples.com. Click on "About SSI" and learn what services the company provides. Then navigate to their newsletter, *The Frame,* and read an article about sampling.

## CASE 12.1   ACTION FEDERAL SAVINGS AND LOAN CORPORATION

Steve Miles made his big move six months ago. He quit his job as director of retail marketing at the largest bank in the state to become marketing manager for Action Federal Savings and Loan. He received his bachelor's degree in marketing at the largest university in the state only 3 years ago, but he was bright, personable, and ambitious. Now, after several months of orientation at Action Federal (Steve called it "Mickey Mouse"), he was beginning his own marketing operations and hired Roberta Nimoy from City University as his marketing research assistant.

Steve wanted to do an image study of each of the 13 branches of Action Federal located throughout the state. The main branch and three others were located in the capital city and nearby suburbs; these were housed in tall office buildings in downtown locations. The other branches were located in rural areas, and their architecture was designed around the surroundings. One was located in a restored colonial home. Another, the Old Mill branch, located next to a park with a historic windmill, was designed to be compatible with the nearby river and mill.

Steve asked Roberta to develop the sampling plan for the study. After some investigation, she learned that all the accounts were alphabetically listed in the main branch's computer. She thought a list of names and addresses could be generated by taking a sample of 1,300. The computer would be programmed to randomly select every nth name. Since the savings and loan had approximately 112,000 customers, every 86th name would be selected.

**Questions**
1. Evaluate Action Federal's sampling plan.
2. What alternative sampling plans might Action Federal use?

**CASE 12.2**    The Internal Revenue Service

The Internal Revenue Service wishes to conduct a survey on income tax cheating. The objectives for this survey are

1. To identify the extent to which taxpayers cheat on their returns, their reasons for doing so, and approaches the IRS can take to deter this kind of behavior
2. To determine taxpayers' experience and satisfaction with various IRS services
3. To determine what services taxpayers need
4. To develop an accurate profile of taxpayers' behavior as they prepare their income tax returns
5. To assess taxpayers' knowledge and opinions about various tax laws and procedures

The federal government always wishes to be extremely accurate in its survey research. A survey of approximately 5,000 individuals located throughout the country will provide the database for this study. The sample will be selected on a probability basis from all households in the continental United States.

Eligible respondents will be adults over age 18. Within each household, an effort will be made to interview the individual who is most familiar with completing federal tax forms. For households with more than one taxpayer, a random process will be used to select the member to be interviewed.

### Question
Suppose you are a consultant hired to design the sample for a personal, in-home interview. Design a sample for the Internal Revenue Service survey.

■ **Endnotes**

[1]Morris James Slonim, *Sampling in a Nutshell* (New York: Simon and Schuster, 1960), p. 3.

[2]Philip R. Cateora, *International Marketing* (Homewood, Ill.: Irwin, 1990), pp. 384–385.

[3]Sabra E. Brock, "Marketing Research in Asia: Problems, Opportunities, and Lessons," *Marketing Research,* September 1989, p. 47.

[4]Seymour Sudman, *Applied Sampling* (New York: Academic Press, 1976), p. 17.

[5]Ibid., pp. 210–222.

# 13

# DETERMINATION OF SAMPLE SIZE: A REVIEW OF STATISTICAL THEORY

The determination of the appropriate sample size is a crucial element of marketing research. To formally identify the proper sample size, statistical theory is necessary. Unfortunately, statistics has a bad image among students.

The fear of statistics is one of college students' most universal phobias. "Stat is too difficult—I'll never pass" is a lament often heard on campus. Students postpone their statistics classes until their last semester. Statistics students are frequently subject to mental blocks; they feel like Saint George trying to tame the raging statistical dragon, as the cartoon

**Taming the Statistical Beast**

here illustrates. There is no need, however, for students to have this dread. Statistics can be easily mastered if one learns the tricks of the trade.

Why are there so many myths about statistics? Statisticians, much like lawyers, medical doctors, and computer scientists, have developed their own jargon. Laypeople do not understand professionals' technical terms. Cynics suspect this terminology is a ploy to impress others and, possibly, to justify charging higher fees. How many fishermen have you heard say, "Hand me the reticulated lattice joined at the interstices," when they simply want a *net*? Then again, when compared with professionals who use complex terminology, fishermen do not make much money.[1]

The point is simple: If you do not understand the basics of the language, you will have problems in conversation. Statistics is the language of the marketing researcher. If administrators and marketing researchers do not speak the same language, communication will fail.

This chapter explains how to determine sample size and reviews some of the basic terminology of statistical analysis.

## ■ REVIEWING SOME BASIC TERMINOLOGY

The first five sections of this chapter summarize several key statistical concepts necessary for understanding the theory that underlies the derivation of sample size. These sections are intended for students who need to review many basic aspects of statistics theory. Many students, even those who received good grades in their elementary statistics classes, probably will benefit from a quick review of the basic statistical concepts. Some students will prefer to just skim this material and proceed to page 315, where the discussion of the actual determination of sample size begins. Others should study these sections carefully to acquire an understanding of statistics.

### ■ Descriptive and Inferential Statistics

The *Statistical Abstract of the United States* presents table after table of figures associated with the number of births, number of employees in each county of the United States, and other data that the average person calls "statistics." These are *descriptive* statistics. Another type of statistics, *inferential* statistics, is used to make inferences about a whole population from a sample. For example, when a firm test markets a new product in Sacramento and Birmingham, it wishes to make an inference from these sample markets to predict what will happen throughout the United States. Thus, there are two applications of statistics: (1) to describe characteristics of the population or sample and (2) to generalize from the sample to the population.

### ■ Sample Statistics and Population Parameters

The primary purpose of inferential statistics is to make a judgment about the population or the collection of all elements about which one seeks information. The sample is a subset or relatively small fraction of the total number of elements in the population. It is useful to distinguish between the data computed in the sample and the data or variables in the population. The term **sample statistics** designates variables in the sample or measures computed from the sample data. The term **population parameters** designates the variables or measured characteristics of the population. Sample statistics are used to make inferences about population parameters.[2] In our notation, we will generally use Greek lowercase letters, for example $\mu$ or $\sigma$, to denote population parameters and English letters to denote sample statistics, such as $\overline{X}$ or $S$.

**Sample statistics**
Variables in a sample or measures computed from sample data.

**Population parameters**
The variables in a population or measured characteristics of the population.

## ■ MAKING DATA USABLE

### ■ Frequency Distributions

**Frequency distribution**
Organizing a set of data by summarizing the number of times a particular value of a variable occurs.

Suppose a telephone survey has been conducted for a savings and loan association. The data have been recorded on a large number of questionnaires. To make the data usable, this information must be organized and summarized. Constructing a *frequency table* or **frequency distribution** is one of the most common means of summarizing a set of data. The process begins by recording the number of times a particular value of a variable occurs. This is the frequency of that value. In our survey example, Table 13.1 represents a frequency distribution of respondents' answers to a question that asked how much customers had deposited in the savings and loan.

**Percentage distribution**
The organization of a frequency distribution into a table (or graph) that summarizes percentage values associated with particular values of a variable.

Constructing a distribution of relative frequency, or a **percentage distribution,** is also quite simple. In Table 13.2, the frequency of each value in Table 13.1 has been divided by the total number of observations. Multiplying the relative class frequencies by 100 converts them to percentages to give a frequency distribution of percentages.

**Probability**
The long-run relative frequency with which an event will occur.

**Probability** is the long-run relative frequency with which an event will occur. Inferential statistics uses the concept of a probability distribution, which is conceptually the same as percentage distribution except that the data are converted into probabilities (see Table 13.3).

**Proportion**
The percentage of elements that meet some criterion.

### ■ Proportions

When a frequency distribution portrays only a single characteristic as a percentage of the total, it defines the *proportion* of occurrence. A **proportion,** such as the proportion of

### ■ Table 13.1

**Frequency Distribution of Deposits**

| Amount | Frequency (Number of People Who Hold Deposits in Each Range) |
|---|---|
| Under $3,000 | 499 |
| $3,000–$4,999 | 530 |
| $5,000–$9,999 | 562 |
| $10,000–$14,999 | 718 |
| $15,000 or more | 811 |
| | 3,120 |

### ■ Table 13.2

**Percentage Distribution of Deposits**

| Amount | Percent (Percentage of People Who Hold Deposits in Each Range) |
|---|---|
| Under $3,000 | 16 |
| $3,000–$4,999 | 17 |
| $5,000–$9,999 | 18 |
| $10,000–$14,999 | 23 |
| $15,000 or more | 26 |
| | 100 |

■ **Table 13.3**

**Probability Distribution
of Deposits**

| Amount | Probability |
|---|---|
| Under $3,000 | .16 |
| $3,000–$4,999 | .17 |
| $5,000–$9,999 | .18 |
| $10,000–$14,999 | .23 |
| $15,000 or more | .26 |
| | 1.00 |

tenured professors at a university, indicates the percentage of population elements that successfully meet some standard concerning the particular characteristic. It may be expressed as a percentage, a fraction, or a decimal value.

## ■ Central Tendency

On a typical day, the sales manager counts the number of sales calls each sales representative makes. He or she wishes to inspect the data to see the center, or middle area, of the frequency distribution. Central tendency can be measured in three ways—the mean, median, or mode—each of which has a different meaning.

**Mean**
A measure of central tendency;
the arithmetic average.

**The Mean**   We all have been exposed to the average known as the *mean*. The **mean** is simply the arithmetic average, and it is a common measure of central tendency. At this point it is appropriate to introduce the summation symbol, the capital Greek letter *sigma* ($\Sigma$). A typical use might look like this:

$$\sum_{i=1}^{n} X_i$$

This is a shorthand way to write the sum:

$$X_1 + X_2 + X_3 + X_4 + X_5 + \ldots + X_n$$

Suppose a sales manager supervises the eight salespeople listed in Table 13.4. Below the $\Sigma$ is the initial value of an index, usually, $i$, $j$, or $k$, and above it is the final value; in this case $n$, the number of observations. The shorthand expression says to replace $i$ in the formula with the values from 1 to 8 and total the observations obtained. The initial and final

■ **Table 13.4**

**Number of Sales Calls
per Day by Salespeople**

| Salesperson | Number of Sales Calls |
|---|---|
| Mike | 4 |
| Patty | 3 |
| Billie | 2 |
| Bob | 5 |
| John | 3 |
| Frank | 3 |
| Chuck | 1 |
| Samantha | 5 |
| Total | 26 |

index values may be replaced by other values to indicate different starting or stopping points without changing the basic formula.

To express the sum of the salespeople's calls in $\Sigma$ notation, we just number the salespeople (this is the index number) and associate subscripted variables with their number of calls:

| Index | | Salesperson | Variable | | Number of Sales Calls |
|---|---|---|---|---|---|
| 1 | = | Mike | $X_1$ | = | 4 |
| 2 | = | Patty | $X_2$ | = | 3 |
| 3 | = | Billie | $X_3$ | = | 2 |
| 4 | = | Bob | $X_4$ | = | 5 |
| 5 | = | John | $X_5$ | = | 3 |
| 6 | = | Frank | $X_6$ | = | 3 |
| 7 | = | Chuck | $X_7$ | = | 1 |
| 8 | = | Samantha | $X_8$ | = | 5 |

We then write an appropriate $\Sigma$ formula and evaluate it:

$$\sum_{i=1}^{8} X_i = X_1 + X_2 + X_3 + X_4 + X_6 + X_7 + X_8$$

$$= 4 + 3 + 2 + 5 + 3 + 3 + 1 + 5$$

$$= 26$$

The formula for the arithmetic mean is:

$$\text{Mean} = \frac{\sum_{i=1}^{n} X}{n} = \frac{26}{8} = 3.25$$

The sum $\sum_{i=1}^{n} X$ tells us to add all the $X$s whose subscripts are between 1 and $n$ inclusive, where $n$ equals the number of observations. The mean number of sales calls in this example is 3.25.

Researchers generally wish to know the population mean, $\mu$ (lowercase Greek letter *mu*), which is calculated as follows:

$$\mu = \frac{\sum_{i=1}^{n} X}{N}$$

where

$N$ = number of all observations in the population

Often we will not have enough data to calculate the population mean $\mu$, so we will calculate a sample mean, $\overline{X}$ (read as "$X$ bar") with the following formula:

$$\overline{X} = \frac{\sum_{i=1}^{n} X}{n}$$

where

$n$ = number of observations made in the sample

More likely than not, you already know how to calculate a mean. However, knowing how to distinguish among the symbols $\Sigma$, $\mu$, and $\overline{X}$ is necessary to understand statistics. In our introductory discussion of the summation sign ($\Sigma$), we have used very detailed notation that included the subscript for the initial index value ($i$) and final index value ($n$). However, from this point on, references to $\Sigma$ will not use the subscript for the initial index value ($i$) and final index value ($n$) unless there is a unique reason to highlight these index values.

**Median**

A measure of central tendency that is the midpoint, the value below which half the values in a distribution fall.

**The Median**   The next measure of central tendency, the **median,** is the midpoint of the distribution, or the 50th percentile. In other words, the median is the value below which half the values in the samples fall. In the sales manager example, 3 is the median because half the observations are greater than 3 and half are less than 3.

**Mode**

A measure of central tendency; the value that occurs most often.

**The Mode**   In apparel, *mode* refers to the most popular fashion. In statistics, the **mode** is the measure of central tendency that identifies the value that occurs most often. In our example Patty, John, and Frank make three sales calls per day. The value 3 occurs most often, and thus 3 is the mode. This is determined by listing each possible value and noting the number of times each value occurs.

EXPLORING RESEARCH ISSUES

## The Well-Chosen Average

When you read an announcement by a corporation executive or a business proprietor that the average pay of the people who work in his or her establishment is so much, the figure may mean something and it may not. If the average is a median, you can learn something significant from it: Half the employees make more than that: half make less. But if it is a mean (and believe me, it may be that if its nature is unspecified), you may be getting nothing more revealing than the average of one $252,000 income—the proprietor's—and the salaries of a crew of underpaid workers. "Average annual pay of $28,500" may conceal both the $10,000 salaries and the owner's profits taken in the form of a whopping salary.

Let's take a longer look at that one. This table shows how many people get how much. The boss might like to express the situation as "average wage $28,500," using that deceptive mean. The mode, however, is more revealing: The most common rate of pay in this business is $10,000 a year. As usual, the median tells more about the situation than any other single figure does; half the people get more than $15,000 and half gets less.

| Number of People | Title | Salary |
|---|---|---|
| 1 | Proprietor | $225,000 |
| 1 | President | 75,000 |
| 2 | Vice presidents | 50,000 |
| 1 | Controller | 28,500 ← **Arithmetical average** |
| 3 | Directors | 25,000 |
| 4 | Managers | 18,500   (the one in the middle; |
| 1 | Foreman | 15,000 ← **Median**   12 above, 12 below ) |
| 12 | Workers | 10,000 ← **Mode (occurs most frequently)** |

## ■ Measures of Dispersion

The mean, median, and mode summarize the central tendency of frequency distributions. Knowing the tendency of observations to depart from the central tendency is also important. Calculating the dispersion of the data, or how the observations vary from the mean, is another way to summarize the data. Consider the 12-month sales patterns of the two products shown in Table 13.5. Both have mean monthly sales volumes of 200 units, but the dispersion of observations for product B is much greater than that for product A. There are several measures of dispersion.

**The Range**    The *range* is the simplest measure of dispersion. It is the distance between the smallest and the largest values of a frequency distribution. Thus, for product A the range is between 196 units and 202 units (6 units), whereas for product B the range is between 150 units and 261 units (111 units). The range does not take into account all the observations; it merely tells us about the extreme values of the distribution.

Just as people may be fat or skinny, distributions may be fat or skinny. For example, for product A the observations are close together and reasonably close to the mean. While we do not expect all observations to be exactly like the mean, in a skinny distribution they will lie a short distance from the mean, while in a fat distribution they will be spread out. Exhibit 13.1 illustrates this concept graphically with two frequency distributions that have identical modes, medians, and means but different degrees of dispersion.

The *interquartile range* is the range that encompasses the middle 50 percent of the observations—in other words, the range between the bottom quartile (lowest 25 percent) and the top quartile (highest 25 percent).

**Deviation Scores**    A method of calculating how far any observation is from the mean is to calculate individual deviation scores. To calculate a deviation from the mean, use the following formula:

$$d_i = (X_i - \overline{X})$$

If the value of 150 units for product B represents the month of January, we calculate its deviation score to be −50, that is, $150 - 200 = -50$. If the deviation scores are large, we will have a fat distribution because the distribution exhibits a broad spread.

| ■ Table 13.5 | | Units Product A | Units Product B |
|---|---|---|---|
| **Sales Levels for Products A and B (Both Average 200 Units)** | January | 196 | 150 |
| | February | 198 | 160 |
| | March | 199 | 176 |
| | April | 200 | 181 |
| | May | 200 | 192 |
| | June | 200 | 200 |
| | July | 200 | 201 |
| | August | 201 | 202 |
| | September | 201 | 213 |
| | October | 201 | 224 |
| | November | 202 | 240 |
| | December | 202 | 261 |

■ **Exhibit 13.1**

**Low Dispersion versus High Dispersion**

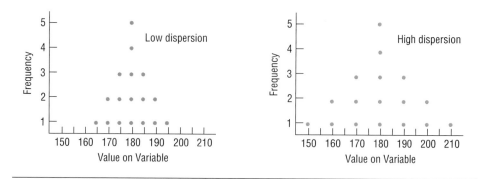

**Why Use the Standard Deviation?**   Statisticians have derived several quantitative indexes to reflect a distribution's spread or variability. The *standard deviation* is perhaps the most valuable index of spread or dispersion. Students often have difficulty understanding this concept. Learning about the standard deviation will be easier if we present several other measures of dispersion that may be used. Each of these measures has certain limitations that the standard deviation does not.

The first measure is the average deviation. We compute the average deviation by calculating the deviation score of each observation value—that is, its difference from the mean—and summing up each score, then dividing by the simple size (*n*):

$$\text{Average deviation} = \frac{\Sigma(X_i - \overline{X})}{n}$$

While this measure of spread seems interesting, it is never used. The positive deviation scores are always canceled out by the negative scores, leaving an average deviation value of zero. Hence, the average deviation is useless as a measure of spread.

One might correct for the disadvantage of the average deviation by computing the absolute values of the deviations. In other words, we would ignore all the positive and negative signs and use only the absolute values of each deviation. The formula for the mean absolute deviation is

$$\text{Mean absolute deviation} = \frac{\Sigma|X_i - \overline{X}|}{n}$$

While this procedure eliminates the problem of always having a zero score for the deviation measure, there are some technical mathematical problems that make it less valuable than some other measures: it is mathematically intractable.[3]

*Variance*   Another means of eliminating the sign problem caused by the negative deviations canceling out the positive deviations is to square the deviation scores. The following formula gives the mean squared deviation:

$$\text{Mean squared deviation} = \frac{\Sigma(X_i - \overline{X})^2}{n}$$

**Variance**
A measure of dispersion; the sum of squared deviation scores divided by sample size minus 1.

This measure is useful to describe the sample variability. However, we typically wish to make an inference about a population from the sample. The divisor $n - 1$ is used rather than $n$ in most pragmatic marketing research problems.[4] This new measure of spread, called the **variance,** has the formula

$$\text{Variance, } S^2 = \frac{\Sigma(X_i - \overline{X})^2}{n - 1}$$

The variance is a very good index of the degree of dispersion. The variance, $S^2$, will equal zero if, and only if, each and every observation in the distribution is the same as the mean. The variance will grow larger as the observations tend to differ increasingly from one another and from the mean.

*Standard Deviation*   While the variance is frequently used in statistics, it has one major drawback: The variance reflects a unit of measurement that has been squared. For instance, if measures of sales in a territory are made in dollars, the mean number will be reflected in dollars, but the variance will be in squared dollars. Because of this, statisticians have taken the square root of the variance. The square root of the variance for a distribution, called the **standard deviation,** eliminates the drawback of having the measure of dispersion in squared units rather than in the original measurement units. The formula for the standard deviation is[5]

**Standard deviation**
A quantitative index of a distribution's spread or variability; the square root of the variance for distribution.

$$S = \sqrt{S^2} = \sqrt{\frac{\Sigma(X_i - \overline{X})^2}{n - 1}}$$

Table 13.6 illustrates that the calculation of a standard deviation requires the researcher to first calculate the sample mean. In the example with eight salespeople's sales calls (Table 13.4), we calculated the sample mean as 3.25. Table 13.6 illustrates how to calculate the standard deviation for these data.

At this point, you should think about the original purpose for measures of dispersion. We wanted to summarize the data from survey research and other forms of marketing research. Indexes of central tendencies, such as the mean, help us interpret the data. In addition, we wish to calculate a measure of variability that will give us a quantitative index of the dispersion of the distribution. We have looked at several measures of dispersion to arrive at two very adequate means of measuring dispersion: the variance and the standard deviation. The formula given is for the sample standard deviation, $S$.

The formula for the population standard deviation, $\sigma$, which is conceptually very similar, has not been given. Nevertheless, the reader should understand that $\sigma$ measures the dispersion

■ **Table 13.6**

**Calculating a Standard Deviation: Number of Sales Calls per Day by Salespersons**

$n = 8$   $\overline{X} = 3.25$

| $X$ | $(X - \overline{X})$ | $(X - \overline{X})^2$ |
|---|---|---|
| 4 | $(4 - 3.25) = 0.75$ | 0.5625 |
| 3 | $(3 - 3.25) = -0.25$ | 0.0625 |
| 2 | $(2 - 3.25) = -1.25$ | 1.5625 |
| 5 | $(5 - 3.25) = 1.75$ | 3.0625 |
| 3 | $(3 - 3.25) = -0.25$ | 0.0625 |
| 3 | $(3 - 3.25) = -0.25$ | 0.0625 |
| 1 | $(1 - 3.25) = -2.25$ | 5.0625 |
| 5 | $(5 - 3.25) = 1.75$ | 3.0625 |
| $\Sigma$ a | a | 13.5000 |

$$s = \sqrt{\frac{\Sigma(X - \overline{X})^2}{n - 1}} = \sqrt{\frac{13.5}{8 - 1}} = \sqrt{\frac{13.5}{7}} = \sqrt{1.9286} = 1.3887$$

aThe summation of this column is not used in the calculation of the standard deviation.

in the population, and *S* measures the dispersion in the sample. These concepts are crucial to understanding statistics. Remember, the student of statistics must learn the language to use it in a research project. If you do not understand the concept at this point, review this material now.

## ■ THE NORMAL DISTRIBUTION

**Normal distribution**
A symmetrical, bell-shaped distribution that describes the expected probability distribution of many chance occurrences.

One of the most useful probability distributions in statistics is the **normal distribution,** also called the *normal curve.* This mathematical and theoretical distribution describes the expected distribution of sample means and many other chance occurrences. The normal curve is bell shaped, and almost all (99 percent) of its values are within ±3 standard deviations from its mean. An example of a normal curve, the distribution of IQ scores, appears in Exhibit 13.2. In our example, a standard deviation for IQ equals 15. We can identify the proportion of the curve by measuring a score's distance (in this case, standard deviation) from the mean (100).

**Standardized normal distribution**
A purely theoretical probability distribution that reflects a specific normal curve for the standardized value, *Z.*

The **standardized normal distribution** is a specific normal curve that has several characteristics: (1) It is symmetrical about its mean; (2) the mean of the normal curve identifies its highest point (the mode) and the vertical line about which this normal curve is symmetrical; (3) the normal curve has an infinite number of cases (it is a continuous distribution), and the area under the curve has a probability density equal to 1.0; (4) the standardized normal distribution has a mean of 0 and a standard deviation of 1. Exhibit 13.3 illustrates these properties. Table 13.7 is a summary version of the typical standardized normal table found at the end of most statistics textbooks. A more complex table of areas under the standardized normal distribution appears in Table A.2 in the appendix.

The standardized normal distribution is a purely theoretical probability distribution, but it is the most useful distribution in inferential statistics. Statisticians have spent a great deal of time and effort making it convenient for researchers to find the probability of any portion of the area under the standardized normal distribution. All we must do is transform or convert the data from other observed normal distributions to the standardized normal curve. In other words, the standardized normal distribution is extremely valuable because we can translate or transform any normal variable, *X,* into the standardized value, *Z.*

## ■ Exhibit 13.2

**The Normal Distribution: An Example of the Distribution of Intelligence Quotient (IQ) Scores**

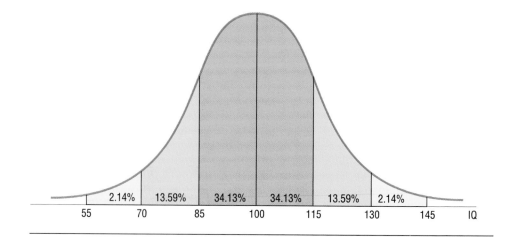

**■ Exhibit 13.3**

**The Standardized
Normal Distribution**

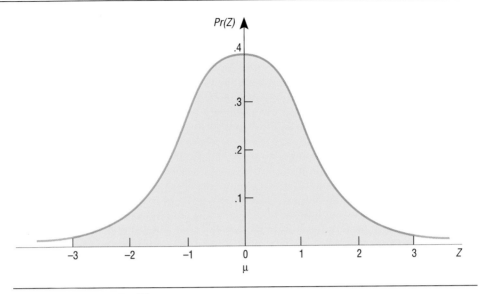

The term Pr(Z) is read "the probability of Z."

**■ Table 13.7**

**The Standardized
Normal Table**

| $Z$ Standard Deviation from the Mean (Units) | Z—Standard Deviations from the Mean (Tenths of Units) | | | | | | | | | |
|---|---|---|---|---|---|---|---|---|---|---|
| | 0.0 | 0.1 | 0.2 | 0.3 | 0.4 | 0.5 | 0.6 | 0.7 | 0.8 | 0.9 |
| | Area under One-Half of the Normal Curve[a] | | | | | | | | | |
| 0.0 | .000 | .040 | .080 | .118 | .155 | .192 | .226 | .258 | .288 | .316 |
| 1.0 | .341 | .364 | .385 | .403 | .419 | .433 | .445 | .455 | .464 | .471 |
| 2.0 | .477 | .482 | .486 | .489 | .492 | .494 | .495 | .496 | .497 | .498 |
| 3.0 | .499 | .499 | .499 | .499 | .499 | .499 | .499 | .499 | .499 | .499 |

[a]Area under the normal curve over the segment measured in one direction from the mean to the distance indicated in each row-column combination. For example, the table shows that about 68 percent of normally distributed events can be expected to fall within 1.0 standard deviations on either side of the mean (0.341 times 2). An interval of almost 2.0 standard deviations around the mean will include 95 percent of all cases.

Exhibit 13.4 illustrates how to convert either a *skinny* distribution or a *fat* distribution into the standardized normal distribution. This has many pragmatic implications for the marketing researcher. The standardized normal table in the back of most statistics and marketing research books allows us to evaluate the probability of the occurrence of certain events without any difficulty.

The computation of the standardized value, Z, of any measurement expressed in original units is simple. It can be done by subtracting the mean from the value to be transformed and dividing by the standard deviation (all expressed in original units). The formula for this procedure and its verbal statement follows. In the formula note that σ, the population standard deviation, is used for the calculation:[6]

$$Z = \frac{X - \mu}{\sigma}$$

■ **Exhibit 13.4**

**Linear Transformation of Any Normal Variable into a Standardized Normal Variable**

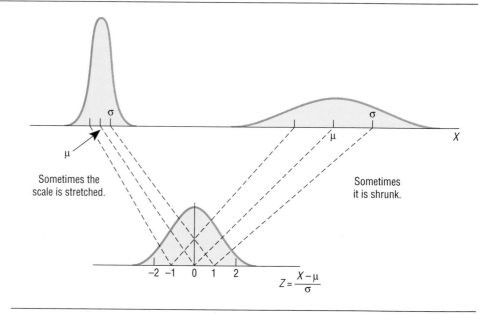

where

$$\mu = \text{the hypothesized or expected value of the mean}$$

$$\text{Standardized value} = \frac{\text{Value to be transformed} - \text{Mean}}{\text{Standard deviation}}$$

Suppose that in the past a toy manufacturer has experienced mean sales, $\mu$, of 9,000 units and a standard deviation, $\sigma$, of 500 units during September. The production manager wishes to know if wholesalers will demand between 7,500 and 9,625 units during September in the upcoming year. Because no tables in the back of the textbook show the distribution for a mean of 9,000 and a standard deviation of 500, we must transform our distribution of toy sales, $X$, into the standardized form using our simple formula. The following computation shows that the probability ($Pr$) of obtaining sales in this range is equal to .893:

$$Z = \frac{X - \mu}{\sigma} = \frac{7,500 - 9,000}{500} = -3.00$$

$$= \frac{9,625 - 9,000}{500} = 1.25$$

Using Table 13.7 (or Table A.2 in the appendix),

When $Z = 3.00$ or $-3.00$ the area under the curve (probability) equals .499.

When $Z = 1.25$, the area under the curve (probability) equals .394.

Thus the total area under the curve is .499 + .394 = .893. The area under the curve that portrays this computation is the shaded area in Exhibit 13.5. The sales manager therefore knows there is a .893 probability that sales will be between 7,500 and 9,625.

At this point, it is appropriate to repeat that to understand statistics, one must understand the language statisticians use. Each concept discussed thus far is relatively simple, but a clear-cut command of these terminologies is essential for understanding what we will discuss later on.

■ **Exhibit 13.5**

**Standardized
Distribution Curve**

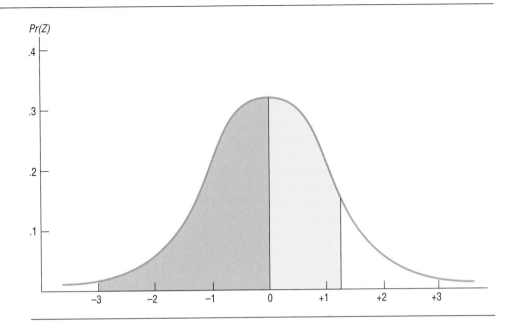

Now that we have covered certain basic terminology, we will outline the technique of statistical inference. However, before we do so, three additional types of distributions must be defined: population distribution, sample distribution, and sampling distribution.

## ■ POPULATION DISTRIBUTION, SAMPLE DISTRIBUTION, AND SAMPLING DISTRIBUTION

When conducting a research project or survey, the researcher's purpose is not to describe the sample of respondents but to make an inference about the population. As defined previously, a *population* or *universe* is the total set or collection of potential units for observation. The *sample* is a smaller subset of this population.

**Population distribution**
A frequency distribution of the elements of a population.

**Sample distribution**
A frequency distribution of a sample.

A frequency distribution of the population elements is called a **population distribution.** The mean and standard deviation of the population distribution are represented by the Greek letters μ and σ, respectively. A frequency distribution of a sample is called a **sample distribution.** The sample mean is designated $\overline{X}$, and the sample standard deviation is designated $S$. The concepts of population distribution and sample distribution are relatively simple. However, we must now introduce another distribution: the *sampling distribution of the sample mean.*

Understanding the sampling distribution is the crux of understanding statistics. The sampling distribution is a theoretical probability distribution that in actual practice would never be calculated. Hence, practical, business-oriented students have difficulty understanding why the notion of the sampling distribution is important. Statisticians, with their mathematical curiosity, have asked themselves, "What would happen if we were to draw a large number of samples (say, 50,000), each having $n$ elements, from a specified population?" Assuming the samples are randomly selected, the sample means, $\overline{X}$s, could be arranged in a frequency distribution. Because different people or sample units will be selected in the different samples, the sample means will not be exactly equal. The shape of the sampling distribution is of considerable importance to statisticians. If the sample size is sufficiently large and if the samples were randomly drawn, we know from the central-limit theorem (discussed shortly) that the sampling distribution of the mean will be approximately normally distributed.

A formal definition of the sampling distribution is as follows:

**Sampling distribution**
A theoretical probability distribution of sample means for all possible samples of a certain size drawn from a particular population.

A **sampling distribution** is a theoretical probability distribution that shows the functional relation between the possible values of some summary characteristic of $n$ cases drawn at random and the probability (density) associated with each value over all possible samples of size $n$ from a particular population.[7]

**Standard error of the mean**
The standard deviation of the sampling distribution.

The sampling distribution's mean is called the *expected value* of the statistic. The expected value of the mean of the sampling distribution is equal to $\mu$. The standard deviation of the sampling distribution of $\overline{X}$ is called the **standard error of the mean** ($S_{\overline{X}}$) and is approximately equal to

$$S_{\overline{X}} = \frac{\sigma}{\sqrt{n}}$$

To review, there are three important distributions we must know about to make an inference about a population from a sample: the population distribution, the sample distribution, and the sampling distribution. They have the following characteristics:

| Distribution | Mean | Standard Deviation |
|---|---|---|
| Population | $\mu$ | $\sigma$ |
| Sample | $\overline{X}$ | $S$ |
| Sampling | $\mu_{\overline{X}} = \mu$ | $S_{\overline{X}}$ |

We now have much of the information we need to understand the concept of statistical inference. To clarify why the sampling distribution has the characteristic just described, we will elaborate on two concepts: the standard error of the mean and the central-limit theorem. The reader may be wondering why the standard error of the mean, $S_{\overline{X}}$, is defined as $S_{\overline{X}} = \sigma/\sqrt{n}$. The reason is based on the notion that the variance or dispersion within the sampling distribution of the mean will be less if we have a larger sample size for independent samples. Most students will know intuitively that a larger sample size allows the researcher to be more confident that the sample mean is closer to the population mean. In actual practice, the standard error of the mean is estimated using the sample's standard deviation. Thus, $S_{\overline{X}}$ is estimated using $S/\sqrt{n}$.

Exhibit 13.6 shows the relationship among a population distribution, the sample distribution, and three sampling distributions for varying sample sizes. In part (a), the population distribution is not a normal distribution. In part (b), the sample distribution resembles the distribution of the population; however, there may be some differences. In part (c), each sampling distribution is normally distributed and the mean of each is the same. Note that as sample size increases, the spread of the sample means around $\mu$ decreases. Thus, with a larger sample size, we will have a skinnier sampling distribution.

# ■ CENTRAL-LIMIT THEOREM

Finding that the means of random samples of a sufficiently large size will be approximately normal in form and that the mean of the sampling distribution will approach the

■ **Exhibit 13.6**

**Schematic of the Three Fundamental Types of Distributions**

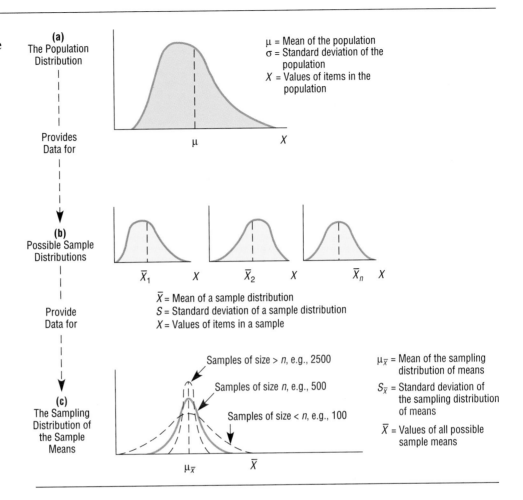

**(a)** The Population Distribution

$\mu$ = Mean of the population
$\sigma$ = Standard deviation of the population
$X$ = Values of items in the population

Provides Data for

**(b)** Possible Sample Distributions

$\bar{X}$ = Mean of a sample distribution
$S$ = Standard deviation of a sample distribution
$X$ = Values of items in a sample

Provide Data for

Samples of size > $n$, e.g., 2500
Samples of size $n$, e.g., 500
Samples of size < $n$, e.g., 100

**(c)** The Sampling Distribution of the Sample Means

$\mu_{\bar{x}}$ = Mean of the sampling distribution of means
$S_{\bar{x}}$ = Standard deviation of the sampling distribution of means
$\bar{X}$ = Values of all possible sample means

**Central-limit theorem**
A theory that states that as a sample size increases, the distribution of sample means of size $n$, randomly selected, approaches a normal distribution.

population mean is very useful. Mathematically, this is the assertion of the **central-limit theorem,** which states: As the sample size, $n$, increases, the distribution of the mean, $\bar{X}$, of a random sample taken from practically any population approaches a normal distribution (with a mean, $\mu$, and a standard deviation; $\sigma/\sqrt{n}$).[8] The central-limit theorem works regardless of the shape of the original population distribution (see Exhibit 13.7).

A simple example will demonstrate the nature of the central-limit theorem. Assume a consumer researcher is interested in the number of dollars children spend on toys each month. Assume further that the population the consumer researcher is investigating consists of eight-year-old children in a certain school. In this example, the population consists of only six individuals. (This is a simple example and perhaps somewhat unrealistic: nevertheless, assume the population size consists of only six elements.) Table 13.8 shows the frequency distribution of the six individuals. Alice, a relatively deprived child, has only $1 per month, whereas fat Freddy, the rich kid, has $6 to spend. The average expenditure on toys each month is $3.50, so the population mean, $\mu$, equals 3.5 (see Table 13.9). Now assume we do not know everything about the population and we wish to take a sample size of two, to be drawn randomly from the population of the six individuals. How many possible samples are there? The answer is 15, as follows:

1, 2
1, 3   2, 3
1, 4   2, 4   3, 4
1, 5   2, 5   3, 5   4, 5
1, 6   2, 6   3, 6   4, 6   5, 6

■ **Exhibit 13.7**

**Distribution of Sample Means for Samples of Various Sizes and Population Distributions**

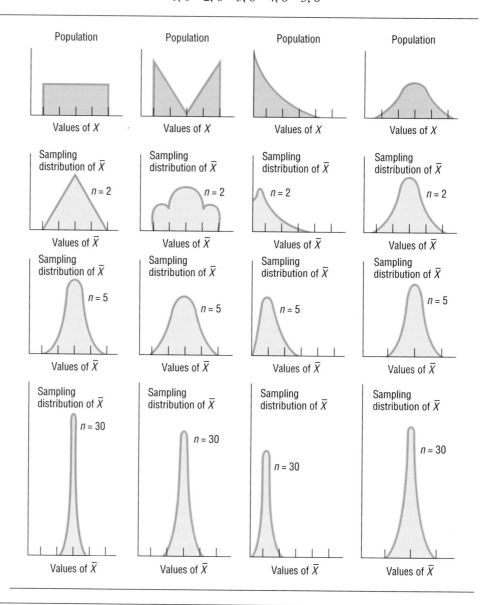

■ **Table 13.8**

**Hypothetical Population Distribution of Toy Expenditures**

| Child | Expenditures |
| --- | --- |
| Alice | $1.00 |
| Becky | 2.00 |
| Noah | 3.00 |
| Tobin | 4.00 |
| George | 5.00 |
| Freddy | 6.00 |

■ **Table 13.9**

**Calculation of Population Mean**

| $X$ |
| --- |
| $ 1.00 |
| 2.00 |
| 3.00 |
| 4.00 |
| 5.00 |
| 6.00 |
| Σ $21.00 |

Calculations:

$$\mu = \frac{\Sigma X}{N} = \frac{21}{6} = 3.5 = \mu$$

■ **Table 13.10**

**Arithmetic Mean of Samples and Frequency Distribution of Sample Means**

Sample Means

| Sample | $\Sigma X$ | $\overline{X}$ | Probability |
| --- | --- | --- | --- |
| $1, $2 | $ 3.00 | $1.50 | 1/15 |
| 1, 3 | 4.00 | 2.00 | 1/15 |
| 1, 4 | 5.00 | 2.50 | 1/15 |
| 1, 5 | 6.00 | 3.00 | 1/15 |
| 1, 6 | 7.00 | 3.50 | 1/15 |
| 2, 3 | 5.00 | 2.50 | 1/15 |
| 2, 4 | 6.00 | 3.00 | 1/15 |
| 2, 5 | 7.00 | 3.50 | 1/15 |
| 2, 6 | 8.00 | 4.00 | 1/15 |
| 3, 4 | 7.00 | 3.50 | 1/15 |
| 3, 5 | 8.00 | 4.00 | 1/15 |
| 3, 6 | 9.00 | 4.50 | 1/15 |
| 4, 5 | 9.00 | 4.50 | 1/15 |
| 4, 6 | 10.00 | 5.00 | 1/15 |
| 5, 6 | 11.00 | 5.50 | 1/15 |

Frequency Distribution

| Sample Mean | Frequency | Probability |
| --- | --- | --- |
| $1.50 | 1 | 1/15 |
| 2.00 | 1 | 1/15 |
| 2.50 | 2 | 2/15 |
| 3.00 | 2 | 2/15 |
| 3.50 | 3 | 3/15 |
| 4.00 | 2 | 2/15 |
| 4.50 | 2 | 2/15 |
| 5.00 | 1 | 1/15 |
| 5.50 | 1 | 1/15 |

Table 13.10 lists the sample mean of each of the possible 15 samples and the frequency distribution of these sample means with their appropriate probabilities. These sample means comprise a sampling distribution of the mean, and the distribution is *approximately* normal. If we increased the sample size to 3, 4, or more, the distribution of sample means would more closely approximate a normal distribution. While this simple example is not a proof of the central-limit theorem, it should give you a better understanding of the nature of the sampling distribution of the mean.

This theoretical knowledge about distributions can be used to solve two practical marketing research problems: estimating parameters and determining sample size.

---

# ■ ESTIMATION OF PARAMETERS

A catalog retailer, such as Horchow, may rely on sampling and statistical estimation to prepare for Christmas orders. The company can expect that 28 days after mailing a catalog, it will have received $X$ percent of the orders it will get. With this information, Horchow can tell within 5 percent how many ties it will sell by Christmas. Making a proper inference about population parameters is highly practical for a marketer that must have the inventory appropriate for a short selling season.

Suppose you are a product manager for Beatrice Foods and you recently conducted a taste test to measure intention to buy a reformulated Swiss Miss Lite Cocoa Mix. The results of the research indicate that when the product was placed in 800 homes and a callback was made two weeks later, 80 percent of the respondents said they would buy: 76 percent of those who did not previously use low-calorie cocoa and 84 percent of those who did. How can you be sure there were no statistical errors in your estimate? How confident can you be in these figures?

Students often wonder whether statistics are used in the business world. The two situations just described provide contemporary examples of the need for statistical estimation of parameters and the value of statistical techniques as managerial tools.

Our goal in using statistics is to make an estimate about the population parameters. The population mean, $\mu$, and standard deviation, $\sigma$, are constants, but in most instances of marketing research they are unknown. To estimate the population values, we are required to sample. As we have discussed, $\overline{X}$ and $S$ are random variables that will vary from sample to sample with a certain probability (sampling) distribution. A specific example of statistical inference would be a prospective racquetball entrepreneur who wishes to estimate the average number of days players participate in this sport each week. Our previous example was somewhat unrealistic, because the population had only six individuals. When statistical inference is needed, the population mean, $\mu$, is a constant but unknown parameter. To estimate the average number of playing days, we may take a sample of 300 racquetball players throughout the area where our entrepreneur is thinking of building club facilities. If the sample mean, $\overline{X}$, equals 2.6 days per week, we may use this figure as a **point estimate.** This single value, 2.6, is the best estimate of the population mean. However, we would be extremely lucky if the sample estimate were exactly the same as the population value. A less risky alternative would be to calculate a confidence interval.

**Point estimate**
An estimate of the population mean using a single value, usually the sample mean.

## ■ Confidence Interval

If we specify a range of numbers or an interval within which the population mean should lie, we may be more confident that our inference is correct. A **confidence interval estimate** is based on the knowledge that the confidence interval for $\mu = \overline{X} \pm$ a small sampling error. After calculating an interval estimate, we will be able to determine how probable it is that the population mean will fall within a range of statistical values. In the racquetball project the researcher, after setting up a confidence interval, would be able to make a statement such as "With 95 percent confidence, I think that the average number of days played per week is between 2.3 and 2.9." This information can be used to estimate market demand, because the researcher has a certain confidence that the interval contains the value of the true population mean.

**Confidence interval estimate**
A specified range of numbers within which a population mean should lie; an estimate of the population mean based on the knowledge that it will equate the sample mean plus or minus a small sampling error.

The crux of the problem for the researcher is to determine how much random sampling error to tolerate. In other words, what should the *confidence interval* be? How much of a

**Confidence level**
A percentage or decimal value that tells how confident a researcher can be about being correct. It states the long-run percentage of confidence intervals that will include the true population mean.

gamble should be taken that $\mu$ will be included in the range: 80 percent, 90 percent, 99 percent? The **confidence level** is a percentage that indicates the long-run probability that the results will be correct. Traditionally, researchers have used the 95 percent confidence level. While there is nothing magical about the 95 percent confidence level, it is useful to select this confidence level in our examples.

**Calculating a Confidence Interval**   As already mentioned, the point estimate gives no information about the possible magnitude of random sampling error. The confidence interval gives an estimate plus or minus the estimated value of the population parameter. We may express the idea of the confidence interval as follows:

$$\mu = \overline{X} \pm \text{a small sampling error}$$

More formally, assuming the researchers select a large sample (more than 30 observations), the small sampling error is equal to

$$\text{Small sampling error} = Z_{c.l.}S_{\overline{X}}$$

where

$\overline{X}$ = sample mean

$Z_{c.l.}$ = value of $Z$, or standardized normal variable, at a specified confidence level $(c.l.)$

$S_{\overline{X}}$ = standard error of the mean

The precision of our estimate is indicated by the value of $Z_{c.l.}S_{\overline{X}}$. It is useful to define the range of possible error, $E$, as follows:

$$E = Z_{c.l.}S_{\overline{X}}$$

where

$E$ = range of random sampling error

Thus,

$$\mu = \overline{X} \pm E$$

or

$$\mu = \overline{X} \pm Z_{c.l.}S_{\overline{X}}$$

The confidence interval ($\pm E$) is always stated as one-half of the total interval.

The following step-by-step procedure allows researchers to calculate confidence intervals:

1. Calculating $\overline{X}$ from the sample.
2. Assuming $\sigma$ is unknown, estimate the population standard deviation by finding $S$, the sample standard deviation.
3. Estimate the standard error of the mean using the following formula: $S_{\overline{X}} = S/\sqrt{n}$.
4. Determine the $Z$-values associated with the desired confidence level. The confidence level should be divided by 2 to determine what percentage of the area under the curve to include on each side of the mean.
5. Calculate the confidence interval.

The following example shows how calculation of a confidence interval can be used in a demographic profile, a useful tool for market segmentation. Suppose you plan to open a sporting goods store to cater to working women who golf. In a survey of your market area, you find that the mean age ($\overline{X}$) of 100 women is 37.5 years, with a standard deviation ($S$) of 12.0 years. Knowing it would be extremely coincidental if the point estimate from the sample were exactly the same as the population mean age ($\mu$), you decide to construct a confidence interval around the sample mean using the steps just given:

1. $\overline{X} = 37.5$ years.
2. $S = 12.0$ years.
3. $S_{\overline{X}} = 12/\sqrt{100} = 1.2$.
4. Suppose you wish to be 95 percent confident, that is, assured that 95 times out of 100, the estimates from your sample will include the population parameter. Including 95 percent of the area requires that 47.5 percent (one-half of 95 percent) of the distribution on each side be included. From the $Z$-table (Table A.2 in the Appendix), you will find that .475 corresponds to the $Z$-value 1.96.
5. Substitute the values for $Z_{c.l.}$ and $S_{\overline{X}}$ into the confidence interval formula:

$$\mu = 37.5 \pm (1.96)(1.2)$$
$$= 37.5 \pm 2.352.$$

You can thus expect that $\mu$ is contained in the range from 35.148 to 39.852 years. Intervals constructed in this manner will contain the true value of $\mu$ 95 percent of the time.

Step 3 can be eliminated by entering $S$ and $n$ directly in the confidence interval formula:

$$\mu = \overline{X} \pm Z_{c.l.} \frac{S}{\sqrt{n}}$$

Remember that $S/\sqrt{n}$ represents the standard error of the mean, $S_{\overline{X}}$. Its use is based on the central-limit theorem.

If the researcher wants to increase the probability that the population mean will lie within the confidence interval, he or she can use the 99 percent confidence level with a $Z$-value of 2.57. The reader may want to calculate the 99 percent confidence interval for the above example. The answer will be in the range between 34.416 and 40.584 years.

We have now examined the basic concepts of inferential statistics. You should understand the notion that the sample statistics, such as the sample means, $\overline{X}$s, can provide good estimates of population parameters such as $\mu$. You should also realize there is a certain probability of being in error when you make an estimate of the population parameter from sample statistics. In other words, there will be a random sampling error, which is the difference between the survey results and the results of surveying the entire population. If you have a firm understanding of these basic terms and ideas, the remaining statistics concept will be relatively simple for you. The concepts already discussed are the essence of statistics. Several ramifications of the simple ideas presented so far will permit better decisions about populations based on surveys or experiments.

# ■ SAMPLE SIZE

## ■ Random Error and Sample Size

When asked to evaluate a marketing research project, most people, even those with little marketing research training, begin by asking. "How big was the sample?" Intuitively we know the larger the sample, the more accurate the research. This is in fact a statistical truth; random sampling error varies with samples of different sizes. In statistical terms, increasing the sample size decreases the width of the confidence interval at a given confidence level. When the standard deviation of the population is unknown, a confidence interval is calculated using the following formula:

$$\bar{X} \pm Z \frac{S}{\sqrt{n}}$$

Observe that the equation for the plus-or-minus error factor in the confidence interval includes *n*, the sample size:

$$E = Z \frac{S}{\sqrt{n}}$$

If *n* increases, *E* is reduced, Exhibit 13.8 illustrates that the confidence interval (or magnitude of error) decreases as the sample size, *n*, increases.

We already noted that it is not necessary to take a census of all elements of the population to conduct an accurate study. The laws of probability give investigators sufficient confidence regarding the accuracy of collecting data from a sample. Knowledge of the theory concerning the sampling distribution helps researchers make reasonably precise estimates.

Students familiar with the law of diminishing returns in economics will easily grasp the concept that increases in sample size reduce sampling error at a *decreasing rate*. For example, doubling a sample of 1,000 will reduce random sampling error by 1 percentage point but doubling the sample from 2,000 to 4,000 will reduce random sampling error by only another ½ percentage point. More technically, random sampling error is inversely proportional to the square root of *n*. (Exhibit 13.8 gives an approximation of the relationship between sample size and error.) Thus, the main issue becomes one of determining the optimal sample size.

# DETERMINING SAMPLE SIZE

## Questions That Involve Means

Three factors are required to specify sample size: (1) the variance, or heterogeneity, of the population; (2) the magnitude of acceptable error; and (3) the confidence level. Suppose a researcher wishes to find out whether nine-year-old boys are taller than four-year-old boys. Even with a very small sample size, the correct information probably will be obtained. Intuitively we know this is logical based on the fact that the determination of sample size depends on the research question and the variability within the sample.

The *variance,* or *heterogeneity;* of the population is the first necessary bit of information. In statistical terms, this refers to the *standard deviation* of the population. Only a

■ **Exhibit 13.8**

**Relationship between Sample Size and Error**

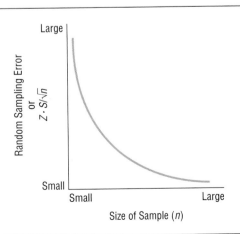

small sample is required if the population is homogeneous. For example, predicting the average age of college students requires a smaller sample than predicting the average age of people who visit the zoo on a given Sunday afternoon. To test the effectiveness of an acne medicine, the sample must be large enough to cover the range of skin types because as *heterogeneity* increases, so must sample size.

The *magnitude of error*, or the precision level from the confidence interval, is the second necessary bit of information. Defined in statistical terms as $E$, the magnitude of error indicates how precise the estimate must be. From a managerial perspective, the importance of the decision in terms of profitability will influence the researcher's specifications of the range of error. If, for example, favorable results of a test market sample will result in the construction of a new plant and unfavorable results will dictate not to market the product, the acceptable range of error probably will be small; the cost of an error would be too great to allow much room for random sampling errors. In other cases, the estimate need not be extremely precise. Allowing an error of ±$1,000 in total family income instead of $E = ±\$50$ may be acceptable in most market segmentation studies.

The third factor of concern is the *confidence level*. In our examples, we will typically use the 95 percent confidence level. This, however, is an arbitrary decision based on convention; there is nothing sacred about the .05 chance level (that is, the probability of the true population parameter being incorrectly estimated).[9] Exhibit 13.9 summarizes the information required about these factors to determine sample size.

## ■ Estimating the Sample Size

Once the preceding concepts are understood, determining the actual size for a simple random sample is quite easy. The researcher

1. Estimates the standard deviation of the population
2. Makes a judgment about the allowable magnitude of error
3. Determines a confidence level

The only problem is estimating the standard deviation of the population. Ideally, similar studies conducted in the past will give a basis for judging the standard deviation. In practice, researchers who lack prior information conduct a pilot study to estimate the population parameters so that another, larger sample, with the appropriate sample size, may be drawn. This procedure is called a *sequential sampling* because researchers take an initial look at the pilot study results before deciding on a larger sample to provide more precise information.

A rule of thumb for estimating the value of the standard deviation is to expect it to be one-sixth of the range. If a study on television purchases expected the price paid to range from $100 to $700, a rule-of-thumb estimate for the standard deviation would be $100.

For the moment, assume the standard deviation has been estimated in some preliminary work. If our concern is to estimate the mean of a particular population, the formula for sample size is

$$n = \left(\frac{ZS}{E}\right)^2$$

---

■ **Exhibit 13.9**

**Statistical Information Needed to Determine Sample Size for Questions That Involve Means**

| Variable | Symbol | Typical Source of Information |
|---|---|---|
| Standard deviation | $S$ | Pilot study or rule of thumb |
| Magnitude of error | $E$ | Managerial judgment or calculation ($ZS_{\bar{X}}$) |
| Confidence level | $Z_{c.l.}$ | Managerial judgment |

where

$Z$ = standardized value that corresponds to the confidence level

$S$ = sample standard deviation or estimate of the population standard deviation

$E$ = acceptable magnitude of error, plus-or-minus error factor (range is one-half of the total confidence interval)[10]

Suppose a survey researcher studying annual expenditures on lipstick wishes to have a 95 percent confidence level ($Z$ = 1.96) and a range of error $(E)$ of less than \$2. The estimate of the standard deviation is \$29.

$$n = \left(\frac{ZS}{E}\right)^2 = \left[\frac{(1.96)(29)}{2}\right]^2 = \left(\frac{56.84}{2}\right)^2 = 28.42^2 = 808$$

If the range of error $(E)$ is acceptable at \$4, sample size is reduced:

$$n = \left(\frac{ZS}{E}\right)^2 = \left[\frac{(1.96)(29)}{4}\right]^2 = \left(\frac{56.84}{4}\right)^2 = 14.21^2 = 202$$

Thus, doubling the range of acceptable error reduces sample size to approximately one-quarter of its original size—or, stated conversely in a general sense, doubling sample size will reduce error by only approximately one-quarter.

## ■ Proportions: Sample Size Determination Requires Knowledge about Confidence Intervals

Researchers frequently are concerned with determining sample size for problems that involve estimating population proportions or percentages. When the sample size question involves the estimation of a proportion, the researcher requires some knowledge of the logic for determining a confidence interval around a sample proportion estimation $(p)$ of the population proportion $(\pi)$. For a confidence interval to be constructed around the sample proportion $(p)$, an estimate of the standard error of the proportion $(S_p)$ must be calculated and a confidence level specified.

The precision of our estimate is indicated by the value $Z_{c.l.}S_p$. Thus, our *plus-or-minus* estimate of the population proportion is

$$\text{Confidence interval} = p \pm Z_{c.l.}S_p$$

If the researcher selects a 95 percent probability for the confidence interval, $Z_{c.l.}$ will equal 1.96 (see Table A.2 in the appendix).

The formula for $S_p$ is

$$S_p = \sqrt{\frac{pq}{n}} \qquad \text{or} \qquad \sqrt{\frac{p(1-p)}{n}}$$

where

$S_p$ = estimate of the standard error of the proportion

$p$ = proportion of successes

$q = (1 - p)$, or proportion of failures

Suppose that 20 percent of a sample of 1,200 recall seeing an advertisement. The proportion of success $(p)$ equals .2, and the proportion of failures $(q)$ equals .8. To estimate the 95 percent confidence interval,

$$\text{Confidence interval} = p \pm Z_{c.l}S_p$$
$$= .2 \pm 1.96 \, S_p$$
$$= .2 \pm 1.96 \, \sqrt{\frac{p(1-p)}{n}}$$
$$= .2 \pm 1.96 \, \sqrt{\frac{(.2)(.8)}{1,200}}$$
$$= .2 \pm 1.96 \, (.0115)$$
$$= .2 \pm .022$$

Thus, the population proportion who see an advertisement is estimated to be included in the interval between .178 and .222, or roughly between 18 and 22 percent, with a 95 percent confidence coefficient.

To determine *sample size* for a proportion, the researcher must make a judgment about confidence level and the maximum allowance for random sampling error. Further, the size of the proportion influences random sampling error; thus, an estimate of the expected proportion of successes must be made based on intuition or prior information. The formula is

$$n = \frac{Z_{c.l}^2 \, pq}{E^2}$$

where

$n$ = number of items in sample

$Z_{c.l}^2$ = square of the confidence level in standard error units

$p$ = estimated proportion of successes

$q = (1 - p)$, or estimated proportion of failures

$E^2$ = square of the maximum allowance for error between the true proportion and sample proportion, or $Z_{c.l}S_p$ squared

To make this calculation, suppose a researcher believes that a simple random sample will show that 60 percent of the population ($p$) will recognize the name of an automobile dealership. The researcher wishes to estimate with 95 percent confidence ($Z_{c.l} = 1.96$) that the allowance for sampling error will not be greater than 3.5 percentage points ($E$). Substituting these values into the formula,

$$n = \frac{(1.96)^2(.6)(.4)}{.035^2}$$
$$= \frac{(3.8416)(.24)}{.001225}$$
$$= \frac{.922}{.001225}$$
$$= 753$$

### ■ Actual Calculation of Sample Size for a Sample Proportion

In practice a number of tables have been constructed for determining sample size. Table 13.11 illustrates a sample size table for problems that involve sample proportions ($p$).

The theoretical principles for calculation of sample sizes of proportions are similar to the concepts discussed in this chapter. Suppose researchers wish to take samples in two large cities. New Orleans and Miami. They wish no more than 2 percentage points of error, and

■ **Table 13.11**

**Selected Tables for Determining Sample Size When the Characteristic of Interest Is a Proportion**

Parameter in Population Assumed to Be over 70 Percent or under 30 Percent and for 95 Percent Confidence Level

| Size of Population | Sample Size for Reliabilities of | | | |
|---|---|---|---|---|
| | ±1% Point | ±2% Points | ±3% Points | ±5% Points |
| 1,000 | a | a | 473 | 244 |
| 2,000 | a | a | 619 | 278 |
| 3,000 | a | 1,206 | 690 | 291 |
| 4,000 | a | 1,341 | 732 | 299 |
| 5,000 | a | 1,437 | 760 | 303 |
| 10,000 | 4,465 | 1,678 | 823 | 313 |
| 20,000 | 5,749 | 1,832 | 858 | 318 |
| 50,000 | 6,946 | 1,939 | 881 | 321 |
| 100,000 | 7,465 | 1,977 | 888 | 321 |
| 500,000 to ∞ | 7,939 | 2,009 | 895 | 322 |

Parameter in Population Assumed to Be over 85 Percent or under 15 Percent and for 95 Percent Confidence Level

| Size of Population | Sample Size for Reliabilities of | | | |
|---|---|---|---|---|
| | ±1% Point | ±2% Points | ±3% Points | ±5% Points |
| 1,000 | a | a | 353 | 235 |
| 2,000 | a | 760 | 428 | 266 |
| 3,000 | a | 890 | 461 | 278 |
| 4,000 | a | 938 | 479 | 284 |
| 5,000 | a | 984 | 491 | 289 |
| 10,000 | 3,288 | 1,091 | 516 | 297 |
| 20,000 | 3,935 | 1,154 | 530 | 302 |
| 50,000 | 4,461 | 1,195 | 538 | 304 |
| 100,000 | 4,669 | 1,210 | 541 | 305 |
| 500,000 to ∞ | 4,850 | 1,222 | 544 | 306 |

[a]In these cases, more than 50 percent of the population is required in the sample. Since the normal approximation of the hypergeometric distribution is a poor approximation in such instances, no sample value is given.

they would be satisfied with a 95 percent confidence level (see Table 13.11). If we assume all other things are equal, in the New Orleans market, where 15 percent of the consumers favor our product and 85 percent prefer competitors' brands, we need a sample of 1,222 to get results with only 2 percentage points of error. In the Miami market, however, where 30 percent of the consumers favor our brand and 70 percent prefer other brands (a less heterogeneous market), we need a sample size of 2,009 to get the same sample reliability.

Table 13.12 shows a sampling error table typical of those that accompany research proposals or reports. Most studies will estimate more than one parameter. Thus, in a survey of 100 people in which 50 percent agree with one statement and 10 percent agree with another, the sampling error is expected to be 10 and 6 percentage points of error, respectively.

## ■ Determining Sample Size on the Basis of Judgment

Just as it is easy to select sample units to suit the convenience or judgment of the researcher, sample size may also be determined on the basis of managerial judgments.

■ **Table 13.12**

**Allowance for Random Sampling Error (Plus and Minus Percentage Points) at 95 Percent Confidence Level**

| Response | Sample Size | | | | | | |
|---|---|---|---|---|---|---|---|
| | 2,500 | 1,500 | 1,000 | 500 | 250 | 100 | 50 |
| 10(90) | 1.2 | 1.5 | 2.0 | 3.0 | 4.0 | 6.0 | 8.0 |
| 20(80) | 1.6 | 2.0 | 2.5 | 4.0 | 5.0 | 8.0 | 11.0 |
| 30(70) | 1.8 | 2.5 | 3.0 | 4.0 | 6.0 | 9.0 | 13.0 |
| 40(60) | 2.0 | 2.5 | 3.0 | 4.0 | 6.0 | 10.0 | 14.0 |
| 50(50) | 2.0 | 2.5 | 3.0 | 4.0 | 6.0 | 10.0 | 14.0 |

Using a sample size similar to those used in previous studies provides the inexperienced researcher with a comparison of other researchers' judgments.[11]

Another judgmental factor that affects the determination of sample size concerns the selection of the appropriate item, question, or characteristic to be used for the sample size calculations. Several characteristics affect most studies and the desired degree of precision may vary for these items. The researcher must exercise some judgment to determine which item will be used. Often the item that will produce the largest sample size will be used to determine the ultimate sample size. However, the cost of data collection becomes a major consideration, and judgment must be exercised regarding the importance of such information.

Another sampling consideration stems from most researchers' need to analyze various subgroups within the sample. For example, suppose an analyst wishes to look at differences in retailers' attitudes by geographic region. The analyst will want to make sure to sample an adequate number of retailers in the New England, Mid-Atlantic, and South Atlantic regions to ensure that subgroup comparisons are reliable. There is a judgmental rule of thumb for selecting minimum subgroup sample size: Each subgroup to be separately analyzed should have a minimum of 100 or more units in each category of the major breakdowns.[12] According to this procedure, the total sample size is computed by totaling the sample sizes necessary for these subgroups.

## ■ Determining Sample Size for Stratified and Other Probability Samples

Stratified sampling involves drawing separate probability samples within the subgroups to make the sample more efficient. With a stratified sample, the sample variances are expected to differ by strata. This makes the determination of sample size more complex. Increased complexity may also characterize the determination of cluster sampling and other probability sampling methods. These formulas are beyond the scope of this book. Students interested in these advanced sampling techniques should investigate advanced sampling textbooks.

## ■ A REMINDER ABOUT STATISTICS

The terms and symbols defined in this chapter provide the basics of the language of statisticians and researchers. To learn more about the pragmatic use of statistics in marketing research, one cannot forget these concepts. The speller who forgets that *i* comes before *e* except after *c* will have trouble every time he or she must tackle the spelling of a word with the *ie* or *ei* combination. The same is true for the student who forgets the basics of the "foreign language" of statistics.

# ■ SUMMARY

Determination of sample size requires a knowledge of statistics. Statistics is the language of the researcher, and this chapter introduced its vocabulary. Descriptive statistics describe characteristics of a population or sample. Inferential statistics investigate samples to draw conclusions about entire populations.

A frequency distribution summarizes data by showing how frequently each response or classification occurs. A proportion indicates the percentage of a group that have a particular characteristic.

Three measures of central tendency are commonly used: the mean, or arithmetic average; the median, or halfway value; and the mode, or most frequently observed value. Each of these values may differ, and care must be taken to understand distortions that may arise from using the wrong measure of central tendency.

Measures of dispersion along with measures of central tendency can describe a distribution. The range is the difference between the largest and smallest values observed. The variance and standard deviation are the most useful measures of dispersion.

The normal distribution fits many observed distributions. It is symmetrical about its mean, with equal mean, median, and mode. Almost the entire area of the normal distribution lies within ±3 standard deviations of the mean. Any normal distribution can easily be compared with the standardized normal, or Z, distribution, whose mean is 0 and standard deviation is 1. This allows easy evaluation of the probabilities of many occurrences.

The techniques of statistical inference are based on the relationship among the population distribution, the sample distribution, and the sampling distribution. This relationship is expressed in the central-limit theorem.

Estimating a population mean with a single value give a point estimate. A range of numbers within which the researcher is confident that the population mean will lie is a confidence interval estimate. The confidence level is a percentage that indicates the long-run probability that the confidence interval estimate will be correct.

The statistical determination of sample size requires knowledge of (1) the variance of the population, (2) the magnitude of acceptable error, and (3) the confidence level. Several computational formulas are available for determining sample size. The main reason a large sample size is desirable is that sample size is related to random sampling error. A smaller sample makes a larger error in estimates more likely.

Many research problems involve the estimation of proportions. Statistical techniques may be used to determine a confidence interval around a sample proportion. Calculation of sample size for a sample proportion is not difficult. In fact, however, most researchers use easy-to-use tables that indicate predetermined sample sizes.

## ■ Key Terms and Concepts

| | |
|---|---|
| Sample statistics | Normal distribution |
| Population parameters | Standardized normal distribution |
| Frequency distribution | Population distribution |
| Percentage distribution | Sample distribution |
| Probability | Sampling distribution |
| Proportion | Standard error of the mean |
| Mean | Central-limit theorem |
| Median | Point estimate |
| Mode | Confidence interval estimate |
| Variance | Confidence level |
| Standard deviation | |

## ■ Questions

1. What is the difference between descriptive and inferential statistics?
2. The speed limits in 13 countries are as follows:

| Country | Highway Miles per Hour |
| --- | --- |
| Italy | 87 |
| France | 81 |
| Hungary | 75 |
| Belgium | 75 |
| Portugal | 75 |
| Britain | 70 |
| Spain | 62 |
| Denmark | 62 |
| Netherlands | 62 |
| Greece | 62 |
| Japan | 62 |
| Norway | 56 |
| Turkey | 56 |

Calculate the mean, median, and mode for these data.
3. Prepare a frequency distribution for the data in question 2.
4. Why is the standard deviation rather than the average deviation typically used?
5. Calculate the standard deviation for the data in question 2.
6. Draw three distributions that have the same mean value but different standard deviation values. Draw three distributions that have the same standard deviation value but different mean values.
7. A manufacturer of compact disc players surveyed 100 retail stores in each of the firm's sales regions. An analyst noticed that in the South Atlantic region, the average retail price was $165 (mean) and the standard deviation $30. However, in the Mid-Atlantic region, the mean price was $170, with a standard deviation of $15. What do these statistics tell us about these two sales regions?
8. What is the sampling distribution? How does it differ from the same distribution?
9. What would happen to the sampling distribution of the mean if we increased sample size from 5 to 25?
10. Suppose a fast-food restaurant wishes to estimate average sales volume for a new menu item. The restaurant has analyzed the sales of the item at a similar outlet and observed the following results:

$$\bar{X} = 500 \text{ (mean daily sales)}$$
$$S = 100 \text{ (standard deviation of sample)}$$
$$n = 25 \text{ (sample size)}$$

The restaurant manager wants to know into what range the mean daily sales should fall 95 percent of the time. Perform this calculation.
11. In our example of research on lipstick, where $E = \$2$ and $S = \$29$, what sample size would we require if we desired a 99 percent confidence level?
12. Suppose you are planning a sample of cat owners to determine the monthly average number of cans of cat food they purchase. The following standards have been set: a confidence level of 99 percent and an error of less than 5 units. Past research has indicated that the standard deviation should be 6 units. What would be the required sample size?
13. In a survey of 500 people, 60 percent responded positively to an attitude question. Calculate a confidence interval at 95 percent to get an interval estimate for a proportion.

14. In a nationwide survey, a researcher expects that 30 percent of the population will agree with an attitude statement. She wishes to have less than 2 percentage points of error and to be 95 percent confident. What sample size does she need?

15. To understand how sample size is conceptually related to random sampling error, costs, and nonsampling errors, graph these relationships.

16. Suppose you are a political analyst and wish to be highly confident that you can predict the outcome of an extremely close primary election. What should the sample size be for your poll? Are there any problems involved in determining the sample size for this election?

17. A researcher expects the population proportion of Cubs fans in Chicago to be 80 percent. The researcher wishes to have an error of less than 5 percent and to be 95 percent confident of an estimate to be made from a mail survey. What sample size is required?

18. An automobile dealership plans to conduct a survey to determine what proportion of new-car buyers continue to have their cars serviced at the dealership after the warranty period ends. It estimates that 30 percent of customers do so. It wants the results of its survey to be accurate within 5 percent, and it wants to be 95 percent confident of the results. What sample size is necessary?

19. City Opera, a local opera company, wishes to take a sample of its subscribers to learn the average number of years people have been subscribing. The researchers expects the average number of years to be 12 and believes the standard deviation would be about 2 years (approximately one-sixth of the range). He wishes to be 95 percent confident in his estimate. What is the appropriate sample size?

20. Using the formula discussed in this chapter, a researcher determines that at the 95 percent confidence level, a sample of 2,500 is required to satisfy a client's requirements. The sample the researcher actually uses is 1,200 because the client has specified a budget cap for the survey. What are the ethical considerations in this situation?

## EXPLORING THE INTERNET

1. Go to http://www.dartmouth.edu/~chance to visit the CHANCE database. The CHANCE course is an innovative program to creatively teach introductory materials about probability and statistics. It is designed to enhance quantitative literacy.

2. Go to Lycos at http://www.lycos.com. Enter "population sampling" into the query box, and then hit the search icon. How extensive is the list of sources?

3. The IMS's 1992 National Needs Assessment survey of museums may be found at:

   http://palimpsest.stanford.edu/byorg/ims/survey

   Visit this site to view population estimates in a stratified sample. The results include the best and most recent estimates, for a number of U.S. museums and numerous other statistics on museums' demographics, activities, funding, and desired assistance.

4. The 1995 National Household Survey on drug abuse discusses sampling error and statistical significance in the context of its study. To investigate these estimates of sampling error from the survey data, visit http://www.health.org/survey.htm and navigate to the report of The National Household Survey.

5. The University of Oregon Biology Software Lab "Sampling" is a software tool designed to help biology students learn some of the fundamental concepts related to population estimation and experimental design. Visit this site at:

   http://biology.uoregon.edu/Biology_www/bsl/Sampling.html

## CASE 13.1 Coastal Star Sales Corporation (A)

Coastal Star Sales Corporation is a West Coast wholesaler that markets leisure products from several manufacturers. Coastal Star has an 80-person sales force that sells to wholesalers in a 6-state area divided into 2 sales regions. Case Exhibit 13.1-1 on page 325 shows the names from a sample of 11 salespeople. Some descriptive information about each person, and sales performance of each for the last 2 years.

### Questions

1. Calculate a mean and a standard deviation for each variable.

2. Set a 95 percent confidence interval around the mean for each variable.
3. Calculate the median, mode, and range for each variable.
4. Organize the data for the current sales variable into a frequency distribution with classes (a) under $500,000, (b) $500,001 to $999,999, and (c) $1,000,000 and over.
5. Organize the data for years of selling experience into a frequency distribution with two classes, one less than five years and the other five or more years.
6. Convert the frequency distributions from question 5 to percentage distributions.

## CASE 13.2 The *New York Times*/CBS News Poll[13]

The *New York Times*/CBS News Poll of American business executives conducted telephone interviews with 499 senior executives at companies throughout the United States. The survey asked questions about their attitudes toward the political environment and its impact on business.

The sample of companies and executives was provided by Dun and Bradstreet Information Services and was randomly drawn from those listed in its nationwide database of private and publicly owned companies.

Companies with $5 million or more in annual revenues were eligible for the survey. Within each company one senior executive was interviewed. Titles eligible for the poll included owner, partner, chief executive, chairman, president, executive vice president, and senior vice president, with the first opportunity for an interview given to the most senior official.

The completed sample included 245 interviews in companies with $5 million to $99 million in annual revenue, 120 interviews in companies with $100 million to $499 million, and 134 interviews in companies with

$500 million or more. The completed sample was then weighted by revenue size to reflect the actual distribution of all listed companies in the country because small companies predominate.

In theory in 19 cases out of 20, results based on such samples will differ by no more than 6 percentage points in either direction from what would have been obtained by seeking out senior executives at all listed companies in the country with annual revenues of $5 million or more.

The potential sampling error for smaller subgroups is larger. For example, for the biggest companies, those with $500 million or more in annual revenue, it is plus or minus 9 percentage points.

### Questions

1. What type of sampling method was utilized? What are the strengths and weaknesses of this procedure?
2. What confidence level was used to determine sample size?
3. Explain how to evaluate the random sampling error in the study.

*Sampling Distribution*
*9/M*

■ **Case Exhibit 13.1-1**        **Coastal Star Sales Corporation: Salesperson Data**

| Region | Salesperson | Age | Years of Experience | Sales | |
|---|---|---|---|---|---|
| | | | | Previous Year | Current Year |
| Northern | Jackson | 40 | 7 | $ 412,744 | $ 411,007 |
| Northern | Gentry | 60 | 12 | 1,491,024 | 1,726,630 |
| Northern | La Forge | 26 | 2 | 301,421 | 700,112 |
| Northern | Miller | 39 | 1 | 401,241 | 471,001 |
| Northern | Mowen | 64 | 5 | 448,160 | 449,261 |
| Southern | Young | 51 | 2 | 518,897 | 519,412 |
| Southern | Fisk | 34 | 1 | 846,222 | 713,333 |
| Southern | Kincaid | 62 | 10 | 1,527,124 | 2,009,041 |
| Southern | Krieger | 42 | 3 | 921,174 | 1,030,000 |
| Southern | Manzer | 64 | 5 | 463,399 | 422,798 |
| Southern | Weiner | 27 | 2 | 548,011 | 422,001 |

## ■ Endnotes

[1] Morris James Slonim, *Sampling in a Nutshell* (New York: Simon and Schuster, 1960), pp. 1–2.

[2] Most of the statistical material in this book assumes that the population parameters are unknown, which is the typical situation in most applied research projects.

[3] For a discussion of this problem, see Thomas H. Wonnacott and Ronald J. Wonnacott, *Introductory Statistics* (New York: Wiley, 1969), pp. 6–7.

[4] The reasons for this are related to the concept of degrees of freedom, which will be explained later. At this point, disregard the intuitive notion of division by $n$, because it produces a biased estimate of the population variance.

[5] There is an alternative version of this formula that is easier to use in computation:

$$S = \sqrt{\frac{\sum\limits_{j=1}^{n} X_i^2 - \frac{\left(\sum\limits_{j=1}^{n} X_i\right)^2}{n}}{n-1}}$$

Rather than computing each individual deviation and summing, we can find the sum and sum of squares of the observations, substitute them into the formula, and evaluate. Many pocket calculators have features that make it easy to accumulate $\sum\limits_{j=1}^{n} X_i$ and $\sum\limits_{j=1}^{n} X_i^2$ at the same time.

[6] In practice, most survey researchers will not use this exact formula. A modification of the formula, $Z = \dfrac{(X - \mu)}{S}$, using the sample standard deviation in an adjusted form, is frequently used.

[7] William L. Hayes, *Statistics* (New York: Holt, Rinehart and Winston, 1963), p. 193.

[8] Thomas H. Wonnacott and Ronald J. Wonnacott, *Introductory Statistics,* 2d ed. (New York: Wiley, 1972), p. 125.

[9] See, for example, James K. Skipper, Anthony Guenther, and Gilbert Mass, "the Sacredness of .05 Levels of Significance in Social Science." *American Sociologist* 2 (1967), pp. 16–18.

[10] Note that the derivation of this formula is

$$(1)\ E = ZS_{\overline{X}}\,;\ (2)\ E = \frac{ZS}{\sqrt{n}}\,;\ (3)\ \sqrt{n} = \frac{ZS}{E}\,;\ (4)\ n = \left(\frac{ZS}{E}\right)^2$$

[11] Seymour Sudman, *Applied Sampling* (New York: Academic Press, 1976), pp. 86–87.

[12] Ibid., p. 30.

[13] "How the Poll was Conducted," *New York Times,* December 13, 1992, p. y-19. Copyright © 1992 by The New York Times Company.

# PART

# V  ANALYSIS AND REPORTING

# CHAPTER

## *14* BASIC DATA ANALYSIS

**WHAT YOU WILL LEARN IN THIS CHAPTER:**

To understand that analysis consists of summarizing, rearranging, ordering, or manipulating data.

To define *descriptive analysis.*

To outline which types of descriptive analysis are permissible with nominal, ordinal, interval, and ratio scales.

To compute and explain the purposes of simple tabulations and cross-tabulations.

To discuss how percentages help the researcher understand the natures of relationships.

To discuss the relationship between two variables with cross-tabulation procedures.

To elaborate and refine basic cross-tabulations.

To define and explain spurious relationships.

To discuss the nature of data transformations.

To explain how to summarize rank-order data.

To describe some computer software designed for descriptive analysis.

To explain how computer mapping aids descriptive analysis.

To define *hypothesis, null hypothesis, alternative hypothesis,* and *significance level.*

To discuss the steps in the hypothesis-testing procedure.

To describe the factors that influence the choice of statistical method to use for analysis.

For most Americans (59 percent), dinner away from home means a full-service restaurant. The only exception is for adults under age 30; a slight majority (52 percent) of this group say their last dinner out was at a fast-food place. Elderly, affluent, and college-educated adults are most likely to choose a full-service restaurant.

For 51 percent of Americans, the most recent decision to eat out was made at the last minute. Young adults were the most likely to decide to eat out on the spur of the moment (64 percent), while those aged 60 and older were the most likely to plan (52 percent). Planning increases with income. Only 35 percent of adults with household incomes of less than $15,000 planned their last dinner outing, compared with 49 percent of those with incomes of $50,000 or more. Higher-income adults may plan because they are more likely than others to eat at full-service restaurants that require reservations. Fifty-eight percent of dinners at full-service restaurants are planned, compared with just 25 percent of trips to fast-food places.

What really draws so many Americans away from their cozy kitchens? It's not necessarily that they don't want to cook, didn't have time, or couldn't get home for dinner. The most frequently given reason for eating dinner at a restaurant is that the respondent "just felt like going out." Forty-two percent of Roper respondents gave this answer. The next most popular reason, "socializing with friends," received only a 14 percent share.

Americans enjoy giving in to their food impulses. This fact boosts sales of candy bars at the checkout counter, and it also supports fancy restaurants.[1]

These findings illustrate the results of a typical descriptive analysis. This chapter explains how to perform basic data analysis and univariate statistical tests.

## ■ THE NATURE OF DESCRIPTIVE ANALYSIS

Within the context of marketing research, providing a simple definition of *analysis* is difficult because the term refers to a variety of activities and processes. One form of analysis consists of summarizing large quantities of raw data so that the results can be interpreted. Categorizing, or separating out the components or relevant parts of the whole data set, is also a form of analysis for comprehending patterns in the data. Rearranging, ordering, or manipulating data may provide descriptive information that will answer questions posed in the problem definition. All forms of analysis attempt to portray data so that the results may be studied and interpreted in concise and meaningful ways.

**Descriptive analysis**

The transformation of raw data into a form that will make them easy to understand and interpret; rearranging, ordering, and manipulating data to generate descriptive information.

**Descriptive analysis** refers to the transformation of raw data into a form that will make them easy to understand and interpret. Describing responses or observations typically is the first stage of analysis. Calculation of averages, frequency distributions, and percentage distributions are the most common ways to summarize data.

As the analysis progresses beyond the descriptive stage, researchers generally apply the tools of inferential statistics. When the research focuses on one variable at a time, researchers use univariate statistical analysis. Their goal is to assess the statistical significance of various hypotheses about a single variable.

## ■ TABULATION

*Tabulation* refers to the orderly arrangement of data in a table or other summary format. Counting the number of responses to a question and arranging them in a frequency distribution is a simple tabulation, or *marginal tabulation*. Simple tabulation of the responses or observations on a question-by-question or item-by-item basis provides the most basic—and, in many cases, the most useful—form of information for the researcher. It tells the researcher how frequently each response occurs. This starting point for analysis requires the researcher to count responses or observations for each category or code assigned to a variable. Exhibit 14.1 illustrates a **frequency table.** When done by hand, this tabulation process is called *tallying*. Large sample sizes generally require computer tabulation of the data.

**Frequency table**

The arrangement of statistical data in a row-and-column format that exhibits the count of responses or observations for each category assigned to a variable.

### ■ Percentages

Whether the data are tabulated by computer or by hand, percentages, cumulative percentages, and frequency distributions are useful. For example, most people find part b of

■ **Exhibit 14.1**

**A Frequency Table for a Simple Tabulation**

| Do you shop at IGA | |
| --- | --- |
| Response | Frequency |
| Yes | 330 |
| No | 120 |
| Total | 450 |

Exhibit 14.2 on page 332 easier to interpret than part a because the percentages in part b are useful for comparing data for various time periods.

When a frequency distribution portrays only a single characteristic as a percentage of the total, the proportion of occurrence is defined. It may be expressed as a percentage, a fraction, or a decimal value.

When discussing percentages, researchers must use precise language. For example, the difference between 40 percent and 60 percent is not 20 percent but 20 percentage points, or an increase of 50 percent.

## ■ MEASURES OF CENTRAL TENDENCY

According to *Bride's Magazine,* the cost of the average wedding is $16,144.[2] This is a measure of *central tendency.* Describing central tendencies of the distribution with the mean, median, or mode is another basic form of descriptive analysis. These measures are most useful when the purpose is to identify typical values of a variable or the most common characteristic of a group. If knowing the average or typical performance will satisfy the information need, the mean, median, or mode should be considered.

## ■ CROSS-TABULATION

Mere tabulation of data may answer many research questions; in fact, many studies do not go beyond examining simple tabulations of question-by-question responses to a survey. Although frequency counts, percentage distributions, or averages summarize considerable information, stopping with simple tabulation may not yield the full value of the research. Most data can be further organized in a variety of ways. For example, in a survey that samples both men and women, the data commonly are analyzed by separating them into groups or categories based on sex. Analyzing results by groups, categories, or classes is the technique of **cross-tabulation.** The purpose of categorization and cross-tabulation is to allow the inspections and comparisons of differences among groups. This form of analysis also helps determine the type of relationship among variables. Because market segmentation is a major component of marketing strategy for many organizations, cross-tabulating the results of marketing research helps clarify the research findings as they pertain to market segments.

**Cross-tabulation**
A technique for organizing data by groups, categories, or classes, thus facilitating comparisons; a joint frequency distribution of observations on two or more sets of variables.

Exhibit 14.3 summarizes several cross-tabulations from American citizens' responses to a questionnaire on ethical behavior in the United States. A researcher interested in the relative ethical perspectives of business executives and the general public can inspect this table and easily compare the two groups. The percentage table illustrates the added value of calculating percentages.

■ **Exhibit 14.2**

**Percentages Aid the Interpretation of Frequency Distributions and Cross-Tabulations**

**(a) Number of People in Projected Population, 1990 to 2020[a]**

| | Population at End of Period | Population Change |
|---|---|---|
| **1990 to 2000** | | |
| UNITED STATES ......... | 276,241 | 28,819 |
| Northeast ............... | 51,885 | 1,035 |
| Midwest ............... | 63,837 | 4,050 |
| South ................. | 97,241 | 11,497 |
| West .................. | 63,277 | 10,238 |
| **2000 to 2010** | | |
| UNITED STATES ......... | 300,431 | 24,118 |
| Northeast ............... | 53,301 | 1,409 |
| Midwest ............... | 66,332 | 2,476 |
| South ................. | 107,385 | 10,114 |
| West .................. | 73,412 | 10,120 |
| **2010 to 2020** | | |
| UNITED STATES ......... | 325,942 | 25,535 |
| Northeast ............... | 53,352 | 2,057 |
| Midwest ............... | 68,984 | 2,657 |
| South ................. | 117,498 | 10,116 |
| West .................. | 84,109 | 10,703 |

**(b) Number and Percentage of People in Projected Population, 1990 to 2020[a]**

| | Population Number | Percent of Population | Population Change | Percent Increase |
|---|---|---|---|---|
| **1990 to 2000** | | | | |
| UNITED STATES ......... | 276,241 | 100.0 | 28,819 | 10.4 |
| Northeast ............... | 51,885 | 18.8 | 1,035 | 2.0 |
| Midwest ............... | 63,837 | 23.1 | 4,050 | 6.3 |
| South ................. | 97,241 | 35.2 | 11,497 | 11.8 |
| West .................. | 63,277 | 22.9 | 10,238 | 16.2 |
| **2000 to 2010** | | | | |
| UNITED STATES ......... | 300,431 | 100.0 | 24,118 | 8.0 |
| Northeast ............... | 53,301 | 17.7 | 1,409 | 2.6 |
| Midwest ............... | 66,332 | 22.1 | 2,476 | 3.7 |
| South ................. | 107,385 | 35.8 | 10,114 | 9.4 |
| West .................. | 73,412 | 22.4 | 10,120 | 13.8 |
| **2010 to 2020** | | | | |
| UNITED STATES ......... | 325,942 | 100.0 | 25,535 | 7.8 |
| Northeast ............... | 53,352 | 16.4 | 2,057 | 3.9 |
| Midwest ............... | 68,984 | 21.7 | 2,657 | 3.9 |
| South ................. | 117,498 | 36.1 | 10,116 | 8.6 |
| West .................. | 84,109 | 25.8 | 10,703 | 12.7 |

[a]Population in thousands

■ **Exhibit 14.3**                **Cross-Tabulation Tables from a Survey on Ethics in America**

(a) Reported Behavior by General Public (Percentage Who Have Ever Done Each Activity)

| | General Public | | | | | |
|---|---|---|---|---|---|---|
| | Age | | Gender | | Education | |
| Activity | Under 50 Years Old | Over 50 Years Old | Men | Women | College Graduate | High School Graduate |
| Taken home work supplies | 50 | 26 | 47 | 33 | 58 | 21 |
| Called in sick to work when not ill | 40 | 18 | Not reported | | 36 | 21 |

(b) Reported Behavior (Percentage Who Have Ever Done Each Activity)

| Activity | Business Executives | General Public |
|---|---|---|
| Taken home work supplies | 74 | 40 |
| Called in sick to work when not ill | 14 | 31 |
| Used company telephone for personal long-distance calls | 78 | 15 |
| Overstated deductions somewhat on tax forms | 35 | 13 |
| Driven while drunk | 80 | 33 |
| Saw a fellow employee steal something at work and did not report it | 7 | 26 |

■ **Exhibit 14.4**

**Frequency Counts in a Contingency Table**

Cross-Tabulation of Question "Do you shop at IGA?" by Sex of Respondent

| | Yes | No | Total |
|---|---|---|---|
| Men | 150 | 75 | 225 |
| Women | 180 | 48 | 225 |
| Total | 330 | 120 | 450 |

## ■ Contingency Table

**Contingency table**
The results of a cross-tabulation of two variables, such as survey questions.

Exhibit 14.4 shows how the cross-tabulation of two survey questions (or variables) results in a **contingency table,** or data matrix. The frequency counts for the question "Do you shop at IGA?" are presented as column totals. The total number of men and women in the sample are presented as row totals. These row and column totals often are called *marginals,* because they appear in the table's margin. Each of the four cells represents a specific combination of the two variables. The cell that represents women who said they do not shop at IGA has a frequency count of 48.

The contingency table in Exhibit 14.4 is referred to as a $2 \times 2$ *table* because it has two rows and two columns. Any cross-tabulation table may be classified according to the number of rows by the number of columns (*R* by *C*). Thus, a $3 \times 4$ table has three rows and four columns.

## ■ Percentage Cross-Tabulation

**Base**
The number of respondents or observations (in a row or column) used as a basis for computing percentages.

When cross-tabulating data from a survey, percentages help the researcher understand the nature of the relationship by allowing relative comparisons. The total number of respondents or observations may be used as a **base** for computing the percentage in each cell.

**(a) Percentage Cross-Tabulation of Question "Do you shop at IGA?" by Sex of Respondent, Row Percentage**

|  | Yes | No | Total (Base) |
|---|---|---|---|
| Men | 66.7% | 33.3% | 100% (225) |
| Women | 80.0% | 20.0% | 100% (225) |

**(b) Percentage Cross-Tabulation of Question "Do you shop at IGA?" by Sex of Respondent, Column Percentage**

|  | Yes | No |
|---|---|---|
| Men | 45.5% | 62.5% |
| Women | 54.5% | 37.5% |
| Total (base) | 100% (330) | 100% (120) |

When the objective of the research is to identify a relationship between the two questions (or variables), one of the questions is commonly chosen as a base for determining percentages. Exhibit 14.5 shows the possible percentage cross-tabulations from the data in Exhibit 14.4. For example, compare part a with part b. Selecting either the row percentages or the column percentages will emphasize a particular comparison or distribution. The nature of the problem the researcher wishes to answer will determine which marginal total will serve as a base for computing percentages. Fortunately, a conventional rule determines the direction of percentages if the researcher has identified which variable is the independent variable and which is the dependent variable: The percentages should be computed *in the direction of the independent variable;* that is, the margin total of the independent variable should be used as the base for computing the percentages. Although survey research does not identify cause-and-effect relationships, one might argue that it is logical to assume a variable such as gender might predict shopping behavior. Therefore, independent and dependent variables may be established to present the most useful information.

## ■ Elaboration and Refinement

The *Oxford Universal Dictionary* defines *analysis* as "the resolution of anything complex into its simplest elements." This suggests that once the researcher has examined the basic relationship between two variables, he or she may wish to investigate this relationship under a variety of conditions. Typically a third variable is introduced into the analysis to elaborate and refine the researcher's understanding by specifying the conditions under which the relationship is strongest and weakest.[3] In other words, a more elaborate analysis asks, "Will interpretation of the relationship be modified if other variables are simultaneously considered?"

Performing the basic cross-tabulation within various subgroups of the sample is a common form of **elaboration analysis.** The researcher breaks down the analysis for each level of another variable. For example, if the researcher has cross-tabulated shopping behavior by sex (see Exhibit 14.6) and wishes to investigate another variable (say, marital status) that may modify the original relationship, she or he may conduct a more elaborate analysis. Exhibit 14.6 breaks down the responses to the question "Do you shop at IGA?" by sex

**Elaboration analysis**
An analysis of the basic cross-tabulation for each level of another variable, such as subgroups of the sample.

| | Married | | Single | |
|---|---|---|---|---|
| | Men | Women | Men | Women |
| "Do you shop at IGA?" | | | | |
| Yes | 55% | 80% | 86% | 80% |
| No | 45% | 20% | 14% | 20% |

■ **Exhibit 14.6**

**Cross-Tabulation of Marital Status, Sex, and Responses to the Question "Do You Shop at IGA?"**

and marital status. The data show that marital status does not change the original cross-tabulation relationship among women, but it does change that relationship among men. The analysis suggests that we retain the original conclusion about the relationship between sex and shopping behavior for women; the data confirm our original interpretation. However, our refinements in analysis have pointed out a relationship among men that was not immediately discernible in the two-variable case: A higher percentage of single men shop at IGA than married men. The researcher can then conclude that marital status modifies the original relationship among men; that is, an interaction effect occurs. In this situation, marital status is a **moderator variable,** a third variable that, when introduced into the analysis, alters or has a contingent effect on the relationship between an independent variable and a dependent variable.

In other situations, the addition of a third variable to the analysis may lead us to reject the original conclusion about the relationship. When this occurs, the elaboration analysis will have indicated a **spurious relationship**; that is, the relationship between the original two variables was not authentic. Our earlier example of high ice cream cone sales and drownings at the beach (Chapter 3) illustrated a spurious relationship.

**Moderator variable**
A third variable that, when introduced into an analysis, alters or has a contingent effect on the relationship between an independent variable and a dependent variable.

**Spurious relationship**
An apparent relationship between two variables that is not authentic.

## ■ How Many Cross-Tabulations?

Surveys may ask dozens of questions. Computer-assisted marketing researchers often indulge in "fishing expeditions," cross-tabulating every question on a survey with every other question. Thus, every possible response becomes a possible explanatory variable. All too often this activity provides reams of extra computer output but no additional insight to management. The number of cross-tabulations should be determined early, when research objectives are stated.

## ■ DATA TRANSFORMATION

**Data transformation (data conversion)**
The process of changing the original form of the data to a format suitable to achieve the research objective.

**Data transformation** (also called **data conversion**) is the process of changing the original form of the data to a format suitable for performing a data analysis that will achieve research objectives. Researchers often modify the values of scalar data or create new variables. For example, many researchers believe less response bias will result if the interviewer asks respondents for their years of birth rather than their ages even though the objective of the data analysis is to investigate respondents' ages in years. This presents no problem for the research analyst because a simple data transformation is possible. The raw data coded as birth year can easily be transformed to age by subtracting the birth year from the current year.

Creating new variables by respecifying the data with numeric or logical transformations is a common form of data transformation. For example, the Likert summated scales reflect combinations of scores (raw data) from each attitude statement. The summative score for an attitude scale with three statements is calculated as follows:

$$\text{Summative score} = \text{Variable 1} + \text{Variable 2} + \text{Variable 3}$$

This can be accomplished with simple arithmetic or by programming a computer with a data transformation equation that creates a new variable for the summative score.

## ■ CALCULATING RANK ORDER

Respondents often rank order their brand preferences or other variables of interest to researchers. To summarize these data for all respondents, the analyst performs a data transformation by multiplying the frequency by the rank (score) to develop a new scale that represents the summarized rank orders.

For example, suppose a manager of a frequent-flyer program had 10 executives rank their preferences for dream destinations that would be prizes in a sales promotion contest. Exhibit 14.7 shows how the executives ranked each of four locations; Hawaii, Greece, Paris, and Hong Kong. Exhibit 14.8 tabulates the frequencies of these rankings. To calculate a summary rank ordering, the destination with the first (highest) preference was given the lowest number (1) and the least preferred destination was assigned the highest number (4). The summarized rank orderings were obtained with the following calculation:

| Hawaii: | $(3 \times 1) + (4 \times 2) + (2 \times 3) + (1 \times 4) = 21$ |
|---|---|
| Paris: | $(3 \times 1) + (1 \times 2) + (3 \times 3) + (3 \times 4) = 26$ |
| Greece: | $(2 \times 1) + (2 \times 2) + (4 \times 3) + (2 \times 4) = 26$ |
| Hong Kong: | $(2 \times 1) + (2 \times 2) + (2 \times 3) + (4 \times 4) = 28$ |

■ **Exhibit 14.7**

**Individual Rankings of Dream Destinations**

| Executive | Hawaii | Paris | Greece | Hong Kong |
|---|---|---|---|---|
| 1 | 1 | 2 | 4 | 3 |
| 2 | 1 | 3 | 4 | 2 |
| 3 | 2 | 1 | 3 | 4 |
| 4 | 3 | 4 | 3 | 1 |
| 5 | 2 | 1 | 3 | 4 |
| 6 | 3 | 4 | 1 | 2 |
| 7 | 2 | 3 | 1 | 4 |
| 8 | 1 | 4 | 2 | 3 |
| 9 | 4 | 3 | 2 | 1 |
| 10 | 2 | 1 | 3 | 4 |

■ **Exhibit 14.8**

**Frequency Table of Dream Destinations Rankings**

| Destination | Preference Rankings | | | |
|---|---|---|---|---|
| | 1st | 2nd | 3rd | 4th |
| Hawaii | 3 | 4 | 2 | 1 |
| Paris | 3 | 1 | 3 | 3 |
| Greece | 2 | 2 | 4 | 2 |
| Hong Kong | 2 | 2 | 2 | 4 |

The lowest total score indicates the first (highest) preference ranking. The results show the following rank ordering: (1) Hawaii, (2) Paris, (3) Greece, and (4) Hong Kong.

# ■ TABULAR AND GRAPHIC METHODS OF DISPLAYING DATA

The person who first said, "A picture is worth a thousand words" probably had graphic aids in mind. When used properly, graphic aids can clarify complex points or emphasize a message. When used improperly or sloppily, however, they can distract or even mislead. The key to effective use of graphic aids is to make them an integral part of the text. The graphics should always be interpreted in the text. This does not mean the writer should exhaustively explain an obvious chart or table, but it does mean the key points should be pointed out and related to the discussion in progress.

Tabular and graphic representations of the data may take a number of forms, ranging from a direct computer printout to an elaborate pictograph.

## ■ Tables

Tables are most useful for presenting numerical information, especially when several pieces of information have been gathered about each item discussed. The purpose of each table, however, is to facilitate the summarization and communication of the data's meaning. For example, Exhibit 14.9 illustrates the relationships among education, income, and regional airline usage expenditures for vacation/pleasure trips. The shaded area emphasizes a key conclusion about market share. (Summarizing the information in the shaded box, 32 percent of the population makes 78 percent of the expenditures.) This form of presentation simplifies interpretation.

**■ Exhibit 14.9**

**Regional Airline Usage for Vacation/Pleasure by Income and Education Class**

| | Total | Under $20,000 | $20,000–$39,000 | $40,000–$59,000 | $60,000 and Over |
|---|---|---|---|---|---|
| All consumers | | | | | |
| Expenditures (%) | 100 | 10 | 7 | 16 | 67 |
| Consumer units (%) | 100 | 42 | 19 | 16 | 23 |
| Index | 100 | 26 | 36 | 100 | 291 |
| Non–high school graduate | | | | | |
| Expenditures (%) | 8 | 1 | 2 | 1 | 4 |
| Consumer units (%) | 35 | 21 | 6 | 4 | 4 |
| Index | 21 | 5 | 33 | 25 | 100 |
| High school graduate | | | | | |
| Expenditures (%) | 29 | 4 | 2 | 8 | 15 |
| Consumer units (%) | 30 | 11 | 6 | 6 | 7 |
| Index | 96 | 36 | 33 | 133 | 214 |
| Attended/graduated college | | | | | |
| Expenditures (%) | 63 | 5 | 3 | 7 | 48 |
| Consumer units (%) | 35 | 10 | 6 | 6 | 13 |
| Index | 180 | 50 | 50 | 116 | 369 |

Percentage population   Percentage expenditures

32   =   78

## ■ Bannerheads and Stubheads for Tables

Suppose an airline asks a question about customers' satisfaction with its baggage-handling service. In addition to a table showing the simple frequency for each category, most research analysts would cross-tabulate answers to the baggage-handling questions with several demographic variables such as gender, income, education, and age. Presenting multiple cross-tabulations individually in a separate table requires considerable space. Thus, many research reports use a space-saving format with either *stubheads* for rows or *bannerheads* for columns to allow the reader to view several cross-tabulations at the same time.

Exhibit 14.10 presents several cross-tabulations in a single table with stubheads.

## ■ Charts and Graphs

Charts translate numerical information into visual form so that relationships may be easily grasped. Although a number of standardized forms exist for presenting data in charts or graphs, the researcher may use his or her creativity to increase the effectiveness of a particular presentation. Bar charts, pie charts, line charts, and other graphic forms of presentation create strong visual impressions. Exhibit 14.11 shows simple versions of a pie chart, horizontal bar graph, vertical bar graph, and line graph.

---

**■ Exhibit 14.10**

**A Stubhead Format Allowing Several Cross-Tabulations to Be Included in a Single Table**

**Confidence in Church/Organized Religion**

Question: I am going to read you a list of institutions in American society. Would you tell me how much confidence you, yourself, have in each one—a great deal, quite a lot, some, or very little?

The Church or Organized Religion

|  | Great Deal | Quite a Lot | Some | Very Little | None | No Opinion | Number of Interviews |
|---|---|---|---|---|---|---|---|
| National | 42% | 24% | 21% | 11% | 1% | 1% | 1,528 |
| *Sex* | | | | | | | |
| Men | 36 | 27 | 22 | 13 | 1 | 1 | 755 |
| Women | 48 | 21 | 20 | 9 | 1 | 1 | 773 |
| *Age* | | | | | | | |
| Total under 30 | 39 | 26 | 24 | 10 | 1 | * | 320 |
| 18–24 years | 38 | 28 | 24 | 9 | 1 | * | 138 |
| 25–29 years | 40 | 23 | 23 | 13 | 1 | * | 182 |
| 30–49 years | 38 | 25 | 23 | 12 | 1 | 1 | 593 |
| Total 50 & older | 50 | 21 | 18 | 10 | * | 1 | 608 |
| 50–64 years | 48 | 23 | 18 | 10 | * | 1 | 302 |
| 65 & older | 52 | 18 | 18 | 10 | 1 | 1 | 306 |
| *Region* | | | | | | | |
| East | 33 | 24 | 28 | 13 | 1 | 1 | 388 |
| Midwest | 44 | 26 | 20 | 9 | * | 1 | 398 |
| South | 51 | 24 | 14 | 9 | 1 | 1 | 444 |
| West | 39 | 20 | 25 | 15 | 1 | * | 298 |
| *Race* | | | | | | | |
| Whites | 42 | 23 | 22 | 11 | 1 | 1 | 1,334 |
| Nonwhites | 45 | 27 | 18 | 8 | 1 | 1 | 184 |
| Blacks | 47 | 26 | 18 | 7 | * | 2 | 151 |
| Hispanics | 42 | 25 | 21 | 10 | 1 | 1 | 104 |

*Less than 1 percent.

## WHAT WENT RIGHT?

### Florence Nightingale: Inventor of the Pie Chart

Florence Nightingale is remembered as a pioneering nurse and hospital reformer. Less well known is her equally pioneering use of statistics to persuade people. In advocating medical reform, Nightingale also promoted statistical description; she developed a uniform procedure for hospitals to report statistical information. She invented the pie chart, in which proportions are represented as wedges of a circular diagram, and she struggled to get the study of statistics introduced into higher education.

One of Nightingale's analyses compared the peacetime death rates among British soldiers and civilians. She discovered and showed that the soldiers, who lived in barracks under unhealthy conditions, were twice as likely to die as civilians of the same age and sex. She then used the soldiers' 2 percent death rate to persuade the queen and the prime minister to establish a Royal Commission on the Health of the Army. It is just as criminal, she wrote, for the army to have a mortality of 20 per 1,000 "as it would be to take 1,100 men per annum out upon Salisbury Plain and shoot them."

**Pie Charts**   One of the most useful kinds of charts is the *pie chart,* which shows the composition of some total quantity at a particular time. As Exhibit 14.11 shows, each angle, or "slice," is proportioned to its percentage of the whole and should be labeled with its description and percentage. The writer should not try to include too many small slices; about six slices is a typical maximum. Companies commonly use pie charts to show how their revenues were used or the composition of their sales.

**Line Graphs**   *Line graphs* are useful for showing the relationship of one variable to another. The dependent variable generally is shown on the vertical axis and the independent variable on the horizontal axis. The most common independent variable for such

■ **Exhibit 14.11**

**The Basic Forms of Graphic Presentation**

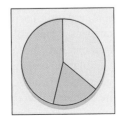

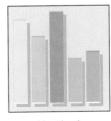
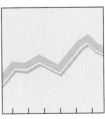

| Pie Chart | Horizontal Bar Graph | Vertical Bar Graph | Line Graph |

■ **Exhibit 14.12**

**Line Graphs to Highlight Comparisons over Time**

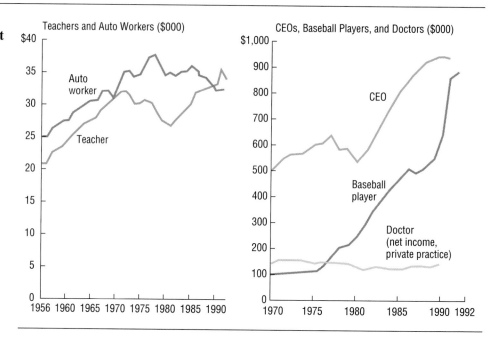

charts is time, but it is by no means the only one. Exhibit 14.12 depicts a multiple line graph. It shows how line graphs can display comparisons among groups over time. The lines for each dependent variable need to be in contrasting colors or patterns and should be clearly labeled. The researcher should not try to squeeze in too many variables; this can quickly lead to confusion rather than clarification.

**Bar Charts** *Bar charts* show changes in the dependent variable (again, on the vertical axis) at discrete intervals of the independent variable (on the horizontal axis). A *simple bar chart* often presents the frequency of response to various questions. The *multiple bar chart* (Exhibit 14.13) shows how multiple variables are related to the primary variable. In each case, each bar needs to be clearly identified with a different color or pattern. The researcher should not use too many divisions or dependent variables. Too much detail obscures the essential advantage of charts, which is to make relationships easy to grasp.

## ■ COMPUTER PROGRAMS FOR ANALYSIS

The proliferation of computer technology within businesses and universities has greatly facilitated tabulation and statistical analysis. Many collections, or packages, of programs for mainframe computers and workstations have been designed to tabulate and analyze numerous types of data. Such widely available computer program packages and statistical analysis systems as Statistical Package for the Social Sciences (SPSS), SAS, SYSTAT, and EDUSTAT eliminate the need to write a program every time you want to analyze data on the computer. There is also a wide variety of spreadsheet software for applications in marketing research. Microsoft Excel and Lotus 1-2-3 are examples.

Exhibit 14.14 shows an SAS computer printout of descriptive statistics for two variables: EMP (number of employees working in an MSA, or Metropolitan Statistical Area)

■ **Exhibit 14.13**

**Multiple Bar Chart**

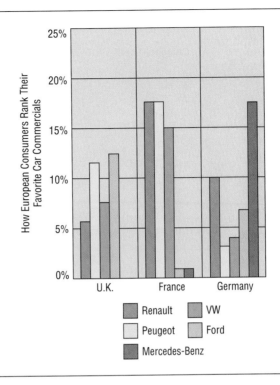

■ **Exhibit 14.14**   **SAS Output of Descriptive Statistics**

| State = NY Variable | N | Mean | Standard Deviation | Minimum Value | Maximum Value | Std Error of Mean | Sum | Variance | C.V. |
|---|---|---|---|---|---|---|---|---|---|
| EMP | 10 | 142.930000 | 232.66490 | 12.8000000 | 788.80000 | 73.575100 | 1429.30000 | 54133.0 | 162.782 |
| SALES | 10 | 5807.800000 | 11905.12701 | 307.0000000 | 39401.00000 | 3764.731718 | 58078.00000 | 141732049.1 | 204.985N |

Key:   EMP = number of employees (000)
    SALES = Sales (000)

and SALES (sales volume in dollars in an MSA) for 10 MSAs. The number of data elements ($N$), mean, standard deviation, and other descriptive statistics are calculated.

Exhibit 14.15 presents output from the SPSS package that shows the results of a question on a survey about national problems in a frequency table. This SPSS output shows the absolute frequency of observations, the relative frequency as a percentage of all observations, and the adjusted frequency as a percentage of the number of respondents who provided a recorded answer rather than answering "don't know" or leaving the question blank.

A histogram is similar to a bar chart. Exhibit 14.16 shows an SPSS histogram plot of purchase price data from a survey. Each bar indicates the number of purchases.

Exhibit 14.17 shows an SPSS cross-tabulation of two variables, education (EDLEVEL) and job category (JOBCAT), with the row total used as a basis for percentages. (Note: The program identifies the number of respondents for whom data were not provided for both variables as missing observations.)

■ **Exhibit 14.15**

**SPSS Computer Output Showing Frequencies**

**National Problems Mentioned**

| Category Label | Code | Count | Pct. of Responses | Pct. of Cases |
|---|---|---|---|---|
| Recession | 1 | 119 | 12.0 | 26.5 |
| Inflation | 2 | 144 | 14.6 | 32.1 |
| Lack of Religion | 3 | 150 | 15.2 | 33.4 |
| Political Corruption | 4 | 129 | 13.1 | 28.7 |
| Racial Conflict | 5 | 92 | 9.3 | 20.5 |
| Unions Too Strong | 6 | 9 | 0.9 | 2.0 |
| Big Business | 7 | 141 | 14.3 | 31.4 |
| Middle East Aggression | 8 | 138 | 14.0 | 30.7 |
| Weather | 9 | 66 | 6.7 | 14.7 |
| Total Responses | | 988 | 100.0 | 220.0 |

16 Missing Cases    449 Valid Cases

■ **Exhibit 14.16**

**SPSS Histogram Output**

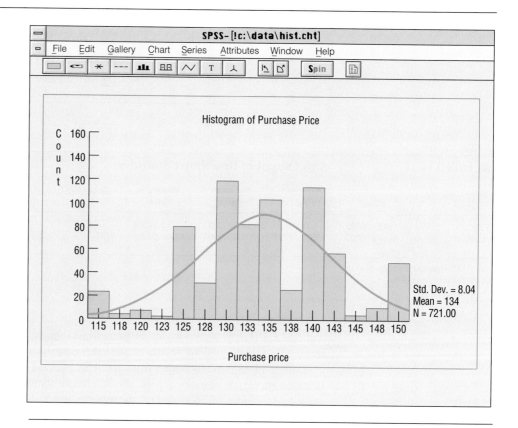

## ■ COMPUTER GRAPHICS AND COMPUTER MAPPING

Graphic aids prepared by computers are rapidly replacing graphic aids drawn by artists. They are extremely useful for descriptive analysis. Computer-generated graphics and charts may be created inexpensively and quickly with easy-to-use computer software pro-

**Computer map**
The portrayal of demographic, sales, or other data on a two- or three-dimensional map generated by a computer.

grams such as Microsoft Excel and Harvard Graphics. These software programs are both user friendly and versatile, allowing researchers to explore many alternative ways to communicate findings visually.

As we mentioned in Chapter 2, decision support systems can generate **computer maps** to portray data about sales, demographics, lifestyles, retail stores, and other features on two- or three-dimensional maps generated by computer. Exhibit 14.18 shows a computer

---

■ **Exhibit 14.17**

**SPSS Cross-Tabulation**

CROSS-TABULATION WITH ROW PERCENTS

SPSS/PC Release 1.0

Cross-tabulation:  JOBCAT  Employment Category
By EDLEVEL  Education

| JOBCAT | Count Row Pct. | Some High School 1 | High School Diploma 2 | Some College 3 | College Degree 4 | Advanced Degree 5 | Row Total |
|---|---|---|---|---|---|---|---|
| **Clerical** | 1 | 115 | 160 | 20 | 5 | | 300 |
| | | 38.3 | 53.3 | 6.7 | 1.7 | | 71.4 |
| **White Collar** | 2 | | | 70 | 25 | 15 | 110 |
| | | | | 63.6 | 22.7 | 13.6 | 26.2 |
| **Management** | 3 | | | | 5 | 5 | 10 |
| | | | | | 50.0 | 50.0 | 2.4 |
| | Column Total | 115 | 160 | 90 | 35 | 20 | 420 |
| | | 27.4 | 38.1 | 21.4 | 8.3 | 4.8 | 100.0 |

Number of Missing Observations = 80

---

■ **Exhibit 14.18**

**Market Area Map to Display Data for Site Location and Performance Evaluation**

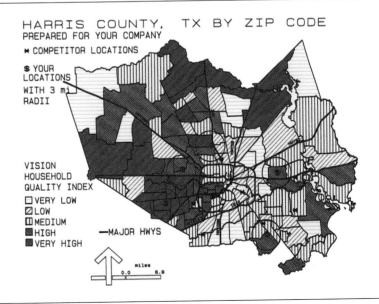

HARRIS COUNTY, TX BY ZIP CODE
PREPARED FOR YOUR COMPANY
＊ COMPETITOR LOCATIONS
$ YOUR LOCATIONS WITH 3 mi RADII

VISION HOUSEHOLD QUALITY INDEX
☐ VERY LOW
▨ LOW
▥ MEDIUM
▩ HIGH
▦ VERY HIGH

—MAJOR HWYS

miles
0.0   6.0

customer segmentation map from National Decision Systems' Vision software. It shows a company's locations in specific counties relative to where high-quality customer segments are located. Competitors' locations, as well as major highways, are overlaid for additional quick and easy visual reference. Scales that show miles, population densities, and other characteristics can be highlighted in color, with shading, and with symbols.

# ■ STATING A HYPOTHESIS

Often researchers will wish to go beyond the simple tabulation of frequency distributions and the calculation of averages. In these cases, they may conduct hypotheses tests.

## ■ What Is a Hypothesis?

**Hypothesis**
An unproven proposition or supposition that tentatively explains certain facts or phenomena; a proposition that is empirically testable.

In marketing theory, a **hypothesis** is an unproven proposition or supposition that tentatively explains certain facts or phenomena; it is a statement of assumption about the nature of the world. In its simplest form, a hypothesis is a guess. A sales manager may hypothesize that salespeople who are highest in product knowledge will be the most productive. An advertising manager may hypothesize that if consumers' attitudes toward a product change in a positive direction, consumption of the product will increase. Statistical techniques allow us to decide whether or not empirical evidence confirms our theoretical hypothesis.

## ■ Null and Alternative Hypotheses

**Null hypothesis**
A statement about a status quo asserting that any change from what has been thought to be true will be due entirely to random error.

**Alternative hypothesis**
A statement that indicates the opposite of the null hypothesis.

Because scientists should be bold in conjecturing but extremely cautious in testing, statistical hypotheses generally are stated in a null form. A **null hypothesis** is a statement about a status quo. It is a conservative statement that communicates the notion that any change from what has been thought to be true or observed in the past will be due entirely to random error. In fact, the true purpose of setting up the null hypothesis is to provide an opportunity to nullify it. For example, the academic researcher may expect that highly dogmatic (that is, closed-minded) consumers will be less likely to try a new product than will less dogmatic consumers. The researcher generally would formulate a conservative null hypothesis. The null hypothesis in this case would be that high dogmatics and low dogmatics do not differ in their willingness to try an innovation. The **alternative hypothesis** is that there *is* a difference between high dogmatics and low dogmatics. It states the opposite of the null hypothesis.

# ■ HYPOTHESIS TESTING

Generally we assign the symbol $H_0$ to the null hypothesis and the symbol $H_1$ to the alternative hypothesis. The purpose of hypothesis testing is to determine which of the two hypotheses is correct. The process of hypothesis testing is slightly more complicated than that of estimating parameters because the decision maker must choose between the two hypotheses. However, the student need not worry, because the mathematical calculations are no more difficult than those we have already made.

## ■ The Hypothesis-Testing Procedure

The process of hypothesis testing goes as follows. First, we determine a statistical hypothesis. Then we imagine what the sampling distribution of the mean would be if this hypothesis were a true statement of the nature of the population. Next, we take an actual sample and calculate the sample mean (or appropriate statistic, if we are not concerned about the mean). We know from our previous discussions of the sampling distribution of the mean that obtaining a sample value that is exactly the same as the population parameter would be highly unlikely; we expect some small difference (although it may be large) between the sample mean and the population mean. Then we must determine if the deviation between the obtained value of the sample mean and its expected value (based on the statistical hypothesis) would have occurred by chance alone—say, 5 times out of 100—if in fact the statistical hypothesis had been true. In other words, we ask this question: "Has the sample mean deviated from the mean of the hypothesized sampling distribution by a value large enough for us to conclude that this large a deviation would be somewhat rare if the statistical hypothesis were true?" Suppose we observe that the sample value differs from the expected value. Before we can conclude that these results are improbable (or even probable), we must have some standard, or decision rule, for determining if in fact we should reject the null hypothesis and accept the alternative hypothesis. Statisticians define this decision criterion as the *significance level.*

**Significance level**
The critical probability in choosing between the null and alternative hypotheses; the probability level that is too low to warrant support of the null hypothesis.

The **significance level** is a critical probability in choosing between the null hypothesis and the alternative hypothesis. The level of significance determines the probability level— say, .05 or .01—that is to be considered too low to warrant support of the null hypothesis. Assuming the hypothesis being tested is true, if the probability of occurrence of the observed data is smaller than the significance level, the data suggest that the null hypothesis should be rejected. In other words, there has been evidence to support contradiction of the null hypothesis, which is equivalent to supporting the alternative hypothesis.

The terminology used in discussing confidence intervals identifies what we call the *confidence level,* or a *confidence coefficient.* The *confidence interval* may be regarded as the set of acceptable hypotheses or the level of probability associated with an interval estimate. However, when discussing hypothesis testing, statisticians change their terminology and call this the *significance level,* $\alpha$ (the Greek letter *alpha*).

## ■ AN EXAMPLE OF TESTING A HYPOTHESIS ABOUT A MEAN

An example should clarify the nature of hypothesis testing. Suppose the Red Lion restaurant is concerned about its store image, one aspect being the friendliness of the service. In a personal interview, customers are asked to indicate their perceptions of services on a 5-point scale, where 1 indicates "very unfriendly" service and 5 indicates "very friendly" service. The scale is assumed to be an interval scale, and experience has shown that previous distribution of this attitudinal measurement assessing the service dimensions was approximately normal.

Now suppose the researcher entertains the hypothesis that customers believe the restaurant has neither friendly nor unfriendly service. The researcher formulates the null hypothesis that the mean is equal to 3.0:

$$H_0 : \mu = 3.0$$

The alternative hypothesis is that the mean does not equal 3.0:

$$H_1 : \mu \neq 3.0$$

Next, the researcher must decide on a region of rejection. Exhibit 14.19 shows a sampling distribution of the mean assuming the null hypothesis, that is, assuming $\mu = 3.0$. The shaded area shows the region of rejection when $\alpha = .025$ in each tail of the curve. In other words, the *region of rejection* shows those values that are very unlikely to occur if the null hypothesis is true but relatively probable if the alternative hypothesis is true. The values

■ **Exhibit 14.19**

**A Sampling Distribution of the Mean Assuming $\mu = 3.0$**

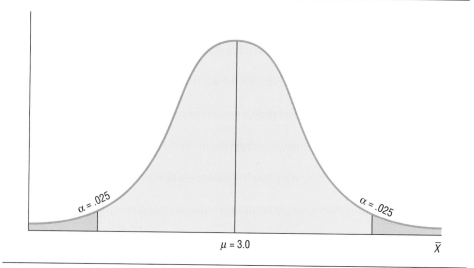

$\alpha = .025$      $\alpha = .025$

$\mu = 3.0$      $\bar{X}$

within the unshaded area are called acceptable at the 95 percent confidence level (or 5 percent significance level, or .05 alpha level), and if we find our sample mean lies within this region of acceptance, we conclude that the null hypothesis is true. More precisely, we fail to reject the null hypothesis. In other words, the range of acceptance (1) identifies those acceptable values that show a difference between the hypothesized mean in the null hypothesis and (2) shows difference in any sample values in this range to be so minuscule that we would conclude this difference was due to random sampling error rather than to a false null hypothesis.

In our example, the Red Lion restaurant hired research consultants who collected a sample of 225 interviews. The mean score on the 5-point scale equaled 3.78. If $\sigma$ is known, it is used in the analysis; however, this is rarely true and was not true in this case. The sample standard deviation was $S = 1.5$. Now we have enough information to test the hypothesis.

The researcher has decided that the decision rule will be to set the significance level at the .05 level. This means that in the long run, the probability of making an erroneous decision when $H_0$ is true will be fewer than 5 times in 100 (.05). From the table of the standardized normal distribution, the researcher finds that the Z score of 1.96 represents a probability of .025 that a sample mean will lie above 1.96 standard errors from $\mu$. Likewise, the tables show that about .025 of all sample means will fall below $-1.96$ standard errors from $\alpha$.

**Critical values**
The values that lie exactly on the boundary of the region of rejection.

The values that lie exactly on the boundary of the region of rejection are called the **critical values** of $\mu$. Theoretically, the critical values are $Z = -1.96$ and $+1.96$. Now we must transform these critical Z-values to the sampling distribution of the mean for this image study. The critical values are:

$$\text{Critical value—lower limit} = \mu - ZS_{\bar{X}} \text{ or } \mu - Z\frac{S}{\sqrt{n}}$$

$$= 3.0 - 1.96 \left( \frac{1.5}{\sqrt{225}} \right)$$

$$= 3.0 - 1.96(.1)$$

$$= 3.0 - .196$$

$$= 2.804$$

■ **Exhibit 14.20**

**A Hypothesis Test
Using the Sampling
Distribution of $\overline{X}$ under
the Hypothesis $\mu = 3.0$**

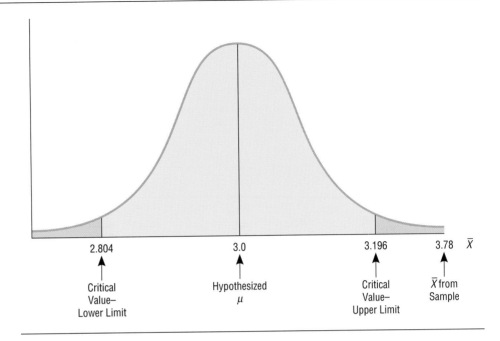

Critical value—upper limit $= \mu + ZS_{\overline{X}}$ or $\mu + Z\dfrac{S}{\sqrt{n}}$

$$= 3.0 + 1.96\left(\frac{1.5}{\sqrt{225}}\right)$$

$$= 3.0 + 1.96(.1)$$

$$= 3.0 + .196$$

$$= 3.196$$

Based on the survey, $\overline{X} = 3.78$. In this case, the sample mean is contained in the region of rejection (see Exhibit 14.20). Thus, since the sample mean is greater than the critical value, 3.196, the researcher says that the sample result is statistically significant beyond the .05 level. In other words, fewer than 5 of each 100 samples will show results that deviate this widely from the hypothesized null hypothesis, when in fact the $H_0$ is actually true.

What does this mean to the management of the Red Lion? The results indicate that customers believe the service is friendly. It is unlikely (less than 5 in 100) that this result would occur because of random sampling error. It means the restaurant should worry about factors other than the friendliness of the service personnel.

An alternative way to test the hypothesis is to formulate the decision rule in terms of the Z-statistic. Using the following formula, we can calculate the observed value of the Z-statistic given a certain sample mean, $\overline{X}$:

$$Z_{\text{obs}} = \frac{\overline{X} - \mu}{S_{\overline{X}}}$$

$$= \frac{3.78 - \mu}{S_{\overline{X}}}$$

$$= \frac{3.78 - 3.0}{.1}$$

$$= \frac{.78}{.1} = 7.8$$

In this case, the Z-value is 7.8 and we find we have met the criterion of statistical significance at the .05 level. As a matter of fact, this is statistically significant at the .000001 level.

# AN EXAMPLE OF TESTING A HYPOTHESIS ABOUT A DISTRIBUTION

**Chi-square ($\chi^2$) test**
A hypothesis test that allows for investigation of statistical significance in the analysis of a frequency distribution.

The **chi-square ($\chi^2$) test** allows us to test for significance in the analysis of frequency distributions. Thus, categorical data on variables such as sex, education, or dichotomous answers may be statistically analyzed. Suppose we wish to test the null hypothesis that the number of consumers aware of a certain tire brand equals the number unaware of the brand. The logic inherent in the $\chi^2$ test allows us to compare the observed frequencies ($O_i$) with the expected frequencies ($E_i$) based on our theoretical ideas about the population distribution or our presupposed proportions. In other words, the technique tests whether the data come from a certain probability distribution. It tests the "goodness of fit" of the observed distribution with the expected distribution.

## Calculation of the Univariate $\chi^2$

Calculation of the chi-square statistic allows us to determine whether the difference between the observed frequency distribution and the expected frequency distribution can be attributed to sampling variation. The steps in this process are as follows:

1. Formulate the null hypothesis, and determine the expected frequency of each answer.
2. Determine the appropriate significance level.
3. Calculate the $\chi^2$ value using the observed frequencies from the sample and the expected frequencies.
4. Make the statistical decision by comparing the calculated $\chi^2$ value with the critical $\chi^2$ value. (We will soon see how to find this value in Table A.4 in the Appendix.)

To analyze the brand awareness data in Exhibit 14.21, we start with a null hypothesis that suggests that the number of respondents aware of the brand will equal the number of respondents unaware of it. Thus, the expected probability of each answer (aware or unaware) is .5; in a sample of 100, 50 people would be expected to respond *yes,* or aware, and 50 would be expected to respond *no,* or unaware. After we have determined that the chi-square test is appropriate at the .05 level of significance (or some other probability level), we may calculate the chi-square statistic.

---

■ **Exhibit 14.21**

**One-Way Frequency Table for Brand Awareness**

| Awareness of Tire Manufacturer's Brand | Frequency |
|---|---|
| Aware | 60 |
| Unaware | 40 |
| | 100 |

To calculate the chi-square statistic, we use the following formula:

$$\chi^2 = \Sigma \frac{(O_i - E_i)^2}{E_i}$$

where

$\chi^2$ = chi-square statistic
$O_i$ = observed frequency in the $i$th cell
$E_i$ = expected frequency in the $i$th cell

Then we sum the squared differences:

$$\chi^2 = \frac{(O_1 - E_1)^2}{E_1} + \frac{(O_2 - E_2)^2}{E_2}$$

Thus, we determine that the chi-square value equals 4:

$$\chi^2 = \frac{(60 - 50)^2}{50} + \frac{(40 - 50)^2}{50}$$
$$= 4$$

Exhibit 14.22 shows the detailed calculation for this problem.

Like many other probability distributions, the $\chi^2$ distribution is not a single probability curve but a family of curves. These curves, although similar, vary according to the number of degrees of freedom (k − 1). Thus, we must calculate the number of degrees of freedom. (*Degrees of freedom* refers to the number of observations that can be varied without changing the constraints or assumptions associated with a numerical system.)[4] We do this as follows:

$$d.f. = k - 1,$$

where

$k$ = number of cells associated with column or row data.[5]

In the brand awareness problem, there are only two categorical responses. Thus, its degrees of freedom equal 1 ($d.f. = 2 - 1 = 1$).

Now the computed chi-square value needs to be compared with the critical chi-square values associated with the .05 probability level with 1 degree of freedom. In Table A.4 of the Appendix, the critical chi-square value is 3.84. Thus, the calculated chi-square is larger than the tabular chi-square, and the null hypothesis—that the observed values are comparable to the expected values—is rejected.[6]

| ■ **Exhibit 14.22** **Calculating the Chi-Square Statistic** | Brand Awareness | Observed Frequency ($O_i$) | Expected Probability | Expected Frequency ($E_i$) | ($O_i - E_i$) | $\frac{(O_i - E_i)^2}{E_i}$ |
|---|---|---|---|---|---|---|
| | Aware | 60 | .5 | 50 | 10 | $\frac{100}{50} = 2.0$ |
| | Unaware | 40 | .5 | 50 | −10 | $\frac{100}{50} = 2.0$ |
| | Total | 100 | 1.0 | 100 | 0 | $x^2 = 4.0$ |

We discuss the chi-square test further in Chapter 15, because it is also frequently used to analyze contingency tables.

# CHOOSING THE APPROPRIATE TECHNIQUE FOR DESCRIPTIVE AND STATISTICAL ANALYSIS

Now that we have looked at two statistical techniques for hypothesis testing, we will identify a number of descriptive and statistical techniques to assist the researcher in interpreting data. The choice of the method of analysis depends on (1) the number of variables, (2) the scale of measurement, and (3) the type of question to be answered.

## Number of Variables

The number of variables to be simultaneously investigated is a primary consideration in the choice of statistical technique. A researcher who is interested only in the average number of times a prospective home buyer visits financial institutions to shop for interest rates concentrates on investigating only one variable at a time. The researcher conducts *univariate statistical analysis* when attempting to generalize from a sample about one variable at a time. Statistically describing the relationship between two variables at one time, such as the relationship between advertising expenditures and sales volume, requires *bivariate statistical analysis*. Tests of group differences and measuring the relationship (association) among variables are the subjects of Chapter 15.

## Scale of Measurement

The scale of measurement on which the data are based or the type of measurement reflected in the data determines the permissible statistical techniques and appropriate empirical operations to perform. As we discussed earlier, testing a hypothesis about a

---

**Exhibit 14.23**

**Descriptive Statistics Permissible with Different Types of Measurement**

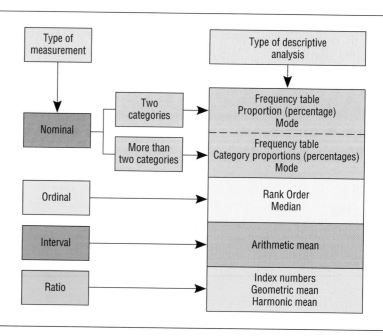

mean requires interval-scaled or ratio-scaled data. We have also seen that the chi-square test can be used when the researcher employs a nominal scale to measure awareness versus unawareness.

Exhibit 14.23 shows the appropriate descriptive statistics for each type of scale. It is important to remember that all statistics appropriate for lower-order scales (*nominal is the lowest*) are suitable for higher-order scales (*ratio is the highest*).

The most sophisticated form of statistical analysis for nominal-scale data is counting. Because numbers are merely labels for classification purposes, they have no quantitative meaning. The researcher tallies the frequency in each category and identifies which category contains the highest number of observations (individuals, objects, etc.). An ordinal scale provides data that may be rank ordered from lowest to highest. For example, the ranking of brand preferences generally employs an ordinal scale. Observations may be associated with percentile ranks. With ordinal data, the median may be used as the average. Because all statistical analyses appropriate for lower-order scales are suitable for higher-order scales, an interval scale may be used as a nominal scale to uniquely classify or as an ordinal scale to preserve order. In addition, an interval scale's property of equal intervals allows researchers to compare differences among scale values and perform arithmetic operations such as addition and subtraction. Numbers may be changed, but the numerical operations must preserve order and relative magnitudes of differences. The mean and standard deviation may be calculated from true interval-scale data. A ratio scale has all the properties of nominal, ordinal, and interval scales. In addition, it allows researchers to compare absolute magnitudes because the scale has an absolute zero point. Using the actual quantities for arithmetic operations is permissible. Thus, the ratios of scale values are meaningful.

| ■ **Exhibit 14.24**<br><br>**Examples of Selecting the Appropriate Univariate Statistical Method** | Sample Marketing Problem | Statistical Question to Be Asked | Possible Test of Statistical Significance |
|---|---|---|---|
| | **Interval or Ratio Scales** | | |
| | Compare actual vs. hypothetical values of average salary | Is the sample mean significantly different from the hypothesized population mean? | $Z$-test (if sample is large)<br>$t$-test (If sample is small) |
| | **Ordinal Scales** | | |
| | Compare actual evaluations and expected evaluations | Does the distribution of scores for a scale with the categories excellent, good, fair, and poor differ from the expected distribution? | Chi-square test |
| | Determine ordered preferences for all brands in a product class | Does a set of rank orderings in a sample differ from an expected or hypothetical rank ordering? | Kolmogorov-Smirnov test |
| | **Nominal Scales** | | |
| | Identify sex of key executives | Is the number of female executives equal to the number of male executives? | Chi-square test |
| | Indicate percentage of key executives who are male | Is the proportion of male executives the same as the hypothesized proportion? | $t$-test of a proportion |

### ■ Type of Question to Be Answered

The type of question the researcher is attempting to answer is a consideration in the choice of statistical technique. For example, we already illustrated a hypothesis test for a researcher who wants to determine whether the calculated mean value of a variable differs from the expected value. Marketing researchers frequently question whether a mean, a proportion, or a distribution differs from what was expected.

Two other frequently asked questions are: (1) Are there differences between two (or more) groups and (2) is there a relationship between two or more variables? These topics are discussed in the following chapter.

Exhibit 14.24 provides guidelines for selecting the appropriate statistical method. Although you may be unfamiliar with most of them, the exhibit illustrates that a variety of statistical techniques exist and the proper one maybe selected based on the research situation. A complete discussion of all the relevant techniques is beyond the scope of our discussion thus far. The important point is that the researcher should anticipate the method of statistical analysis before selecting the research design and before determining the type of data to collect. Once the data are collected, the research design will reflect the initial approach to analysis of the problem.

## SUMMARY

*Descriptive analysis* refers to the transformation of raw data into an understandable form. Descriptive information is obtained by summarizing, categorizing, rearranging, and other forms of analysis. *Tabulation* refers to the orderly arrangement of data in a table or other summary format. Percentages, cumulative percentages, and frequency distributions are useful. The data may be described by measures of central tendency, such as the mean, median, or mode. Cross-tabulation shows how one variable relates to another to reveal differences between groups. Such cross-tabulations should be limited to categories related to the research problem and purpose. Putting the results into percentage form facilitates intergroup comparisons.

Performing the basic cross-tabulation within various subgroups of the sample is a common form of elaboration analysis. Elaboration analysis often identifies moderator variables or spurious relationships. A moderator variable is a third variable that, when introduced into the analysis, alters or has a contingent effect on the relationship between an independent variable and a dependent variable. A spurious relationship exists when adding a third variable to the analysis indicates that the relationship between the original two variables was not authentic.

Data transformation is the process of changing data's original form to a format that is more suitable for performing a data analysis. To summarize rank-order data, a data transformation is performed. Rank scores are multiplied by their frequency of occurrence to develop a new scale that represents summarized rank orderings.

Tables and graphs help to simplify and clarify the research data. Computer software greatly facilitates descriptive analysis. Many programs that enhance the construction of graphs and charts are available.

Computer mapping portrays demographic, sales, and other data on two- or three-dimensional maps that facilitate interpretation of descriptive data.

A hypothesis is a statement of assumption about the nature of the world. A null hypothesis is a statement about the status quo. An alternative hypothesis is a statement that indicates the opposite of the null hypothesis.

In hypothesis testing, a researcher states a null hypothesis about a population mean and then attempts to disprove it. The Z-test defines a region of rejection based on a significance level of the standardized normal distribution beyond which it is unlikely that the null hypothesis is true. If a sample mean is contained in the region of rejection, the null hypothesis is rejected.

The chi-square test allows testing of statistical significance in the analysis of frequency distributions: An observed distribution of categorical data from a sample may be compared with an expected distribution for goodness of fit.

A number of appropriate statistical techniques are available to assist the researcher in interpreting data. The choice of statistical analysis method depends on (1) the number of variables, (2) the scale of measurement, and (3) the type of question to be answered.

## ■ Key Terms and Concepts

| | |
|---|---|
| Descriptive analysis | Data transformation (data conversion) |
| Frequency table | Computer map |
| Cross-tabulation | Hypothesis |
| Contingency table | Null hypothesis |
| Base | Alternative hypothesis |
| Elaboration analysis | Significance level |
| Moderator variable | Critical values |
| Spurious relationship | Chi-square ($\chi^2$) test |

## ■ Questions

1. A survey asked respondents to respond to the statement "My work is interesting." Interpret the frequency distribution in the following SPSS output:

My work is interesting.

| Category Label | Code | Abs. Freq. | Rel. Freq. (Pct.) | Adj. Freq. (Pct.) | Cum. Freq. (Pct.) |
|---|---|---|---|---|---|
| Very true | 1. | 650 | 23.9 | 62.4 | 62.4 |
| Somewhat true | 2. | 303 | 11.2 | 29.1 | 91.5 |
| Not very true | 3. | 61 | 2.2 | 5.9 | 97.3 |
| Not at all true | 4. | 28 | 1.0 | 2.7 | 100.0 |
| | 0. | 1,673 | 61.6 | Missing | |
| | Total | 2,715 | 100.0 | 100.0 | 100.0 |
| Valid cases    1,042 | Missing cases | 1,673 | | | |

2. Using the data in the following table, perform the tasks listed below:

| Individual | Gender | Age | Cola Preference | Weekly Unit Purchases |
|---|---|---|---|---|
| John | M | 19 | Coke | 2 |
| Al | M | 17 | Pepsi | 5 |
| Bill | M | 20 | Pepsi | 7 |
| Mary | F | 20 | Coke | 2 |
| Jim | M | 18 | Coke | 4 |
| Karen | F | 16 | Coke | 4 |
| Tom | M | 17 | Pepsi | 8 |
| Dawn | F | 19 | Pepsi | 1 |

(a) Prepare a frequency distribution of the respondents' ages.

(b) Cross-tabulate the respondents' genders with cola preference.

3. The following computer output shows a cross-tabulation of frequencies and provides frequency number (N) and row (R), column (C), and total (T) percentages. Interpret this output.

|  | ACROSS–E2<br>DOWN–G28 | –HAVE HIGH SCHOOL DIPLOMA?<br>–HAVE YOU READ A BOOK IN PAST 3 MOS? | | | |
|---|---|---|---|---|---|
| N;R,C,T% | Yes<br>1. | :NO<br>2. | | TOTAL | |
| 1. | 489<br>73.8<br>50.8<br>32.3 | 174<br>26.2<br>31.5<br>11.5 | :<br>:<br>:<br>: | 663<br><br><br>43.8 | YES |
| 2. | 473<br>55.6<br>49.2<br>31.2 | 378<br>44.4<br>68.5<br>25.0 | :<br>:<br>:<br>: | 851<br><br><br>56.2 | NO |
|  | ...... | ...... | | ...... | |
| TOTAL | 962<br>63.5 | 552<br>36.5 | :<br>: | 1514 | |

4. Interpret the following table:

Estimate of percentage of net undercount of the population by sex, race, and selected broad age groups

| Age | All Races | | White | | Black | |
|---|---|---|---|---|---|---|
|  | Male | Female | Male | Female | Male | Female |
| All ages | 3.3 | 1.8 | 2.5 | 1.4 | 9.9 | 5.5 |
| 20–24 years | 3.3 | 1.4 | 2.5 | 1.1 | 12.1 | 5.2 |
| 25–34 years | 5.7 | 2.8 | 4.3 | 2.4 | 18.5 | 6.7 |
| 35–44 years | 5.3 | 0.9 | 3.6 | 0.5 | 17.7 | 4.0 |

5. Visit your local computer center and see if it has SPSS, SAS, SYSTAT, or MINITAB computer packages.
6. What type of scalar data (that is, nominal, ordinal, interval, and ratio) typically are used in cross-tabulation analysis?
7. It has been argued that the analysis and interpretation of data is a managerial art. Comment.
8. The data in the following tables show some of the results of an Internal Revenue Service survey of taxpayers. Analyze and interpret the data.

The last year you filed an income tax return, did you get any suggestions or information that was especially helpful to you in filing?

|  | Absolute<br>Frequency | Rel.<br>Freq.<br>(Pct.) | Adj.<br>Freq.<br>(Pct.) |
|---|---|---|---|
| Yes | 156 | 29.5 | 29.8 |
| No | 368 | 69.7 | 70.2 |
| Don't know | 1 | 0.2 | Missing |
| Not ascertained | 1 | 0.2 | Missing |
| Blank | 2 | 0.4 | Missing |
|  | 528 | 100.0 | 100.0 |

What kind of information was it?

| | Absolute Frequency | Rel. Freq. (Pct.) | Adj. Freq. (Pct.) |
|---|---|---|---|
| Learned about energy credit | 8 | 1.5 | 5.4 |
| Learned about another deduction | 46 | 8.7 | 31.3 |
| Obtained info. about forms to use | 9 | 1.7 | 6.1 |
| Received pamphlets/forms | 40 | 7.6 | 27.2 |
| Other | 44 | 8.3 | 29.9 |
| Don't know | 6 | 1.1 | Missing |
| Not ascertained | 2 | 0.4 | Missing |
| Blank | 373 | 70.6 | Missing |
| | 528 | 100.0 | 100.0 |

9. What is the purpose of a statistical hypothesis?
10. What is the significance level? How does a researcher choose a significance level?
11. List the steps in the hypothesis-testing procedure.
12. After a bumper crop, a mushroom grower hypothesizes that mushrooms will remain at the wholesale average price of *$1 per pound.* State the null hypotheses and the alternative hypothesis.
13. Assume you have the following data: $H_0$: $\mu = 200$, $S = 30$, $n = 64$, and $\overline{X} = 218$. Conduct a two-tailed hypothesis test at the .05 significance level.
14. Assume you have the following data: $H_0$: $\mu = 2{,}450$, $S = 400$, $n = 100$, and $\overline{X} = 2{,}300$. Conduct a hypothesis test at the .01 significance level.
15. The answers to a researcher's question will be nominally scaled. What statistical test is appropriate to compare the sample data with the hypothesized population data?
16. What factors determine the choice of the appropriate statistical technique?
17. A researcher plans to ask employees whether they favor, oppose, or are indifferent about a change in the company retirement program. Formulate a null hypothesis for a chi-square test, and determine the expected frequencies for each answer.

18. A data-processing analyst for a research supplier finds that preliminary computer runs of survey results show that consumers love a client's new product. The employee buys a large block of the client's stock. Is this ethical?
19. A researcher finds that in a survey of 100 people, 15 respondents answer "don't know" to a question that has "yes" and "no" as alternatives. The researcher uses 85 as a base for calculating the percentage of respondents who answer "yes" or "no." Is this the correct choice?

## EXPLORING THE INTERNET

1. Go to http://www.spss.com to learn about the statistical software programs SPSS offers.
2. Go to http://www.sas.com to learn about the statistical software programs the SAS Institute offers.
3. The IMS's 1992 National Needs Assessment survey of museums may be found at:

   http://palimpsest.stanford.edu/byorg/ims/survey

   Visit this site to review how descriptive statistics can be reported.
4. The Federal Reserve Bank of St. Louis maintains a database called FRED (Federal Reserve Economic Data). Use a search engine to navigate to the FRED database. Then

select the U.S. Employment in Retail Trade option. Calculate a mean for the last five-year period. Then set up a hypothesis for the next five-year period.

5. To see a report on smokeless tobacco go to the Federal Trade Commission's Bureau of Consumer Protection at http://www.ftc.gov.bcp/reports/smokeless97.htm.

## CASE 14.1   Quality Motors

Quality Motors is an automobile dealership that regularly advertises in its local market area. It has claimed that a certain make and model of car averages 30 miles to a gallon of gas and mentions that this figure may vary with driving conditions. A local consumer group wishes to verify the advertising claim. To do so, it selects a sample of recent purchasers of this make and model of automobile. It asks them to drive their cars until two tanks of gasoline are used up and to record the mileage. The group then calculates

and records the miles per gallon for each year. The data in Case Exhibit 14.1-1 portray the results of the tests.

**Questions**

1. Formulate a statistical hypothesis to test the consumer group's purpose.
2. Calculate the mean average miles per gallon. Compute the sample variance and sample standard deviation.
3. According to your hypothesis, construct the appropriate statistical test using a .05 significance level.

### ■ CASE EXHIBIT 14.1-1

**Miles per Gallon Information**

| Purchaser | Miles per Gallon | Purchaser | Miles per Gallon |
|-----------|------------------|-----------|------------------|
| 1 | 30.9 | 13 | 24.2 |
| 2 | 24.5 | 14 | 27.0 |
| 3 | 31.2 | 15 | 26.7 |
| 4 | 28.7 | 16 | 31.0 |
| 5 | 35.1 | 17 | 23.5 |
| 6 | 29.0 | 18 | 29.4 |
| 7 | 28.8 | 19 | 26.3 |
| 8 | 23.1 | 20 | 27.5 |
| 9 | 31.0 | 21 | 28.2 |
| 10 | 30.2 | 22 | 28.4 |
| 11 | 28.4 | 23 | 29.1 |
| 12 | 29.3 | 24 | 21.9 |
|   |   | 25 | 30.9 |

## CASE 14.2   Coastal Star Sales Corporation (B)

See Coastal Star Sales Corporation (A), Case 13.1, for a description of the data.

**Questions**

1. Develop a hypothesis concerning the average age of the sales force at Coastal Star, and test the hypothesis.
2. Calculate the mean for the previous year's sales, and use this as the basis to form a hypothesis concerning the current year's sales. Test the hypothesis concerning the current year's sales.

# CASE 14.3    Downy-Q Quilt[7]

The research for Downy-Q is an example of a commercial test that was conducted when an advertising campaign for an established brand had run its course. The revised campaign, "Fighting the Cold," emphasized that Downy was an "extra-warm quilt"; previous research had demonstrated this to be an important and deliverable product quality. The commercial test was requested to measure the campaign's ability to generate purchase interest.

The marketing department had recommended this revised advertising campaign and was now anxious to know how effectively this commercial would perform. The test concluded that "Fighting the Cold" was a persuasive commercial. It also demonstrated that the new campaign would have greater appeal to specific market segments.

## Method

Brand choices for the same individuals were obtained before and after viewing the commercial. The commercial was tested in 30-second, color-moving, storyboard form in a theater test. Invited viewers were shown programming with commercial inserts. Qualified respondents were women who had bought quilts in outlets that carried Downy-Q. The results are shown in Case Tables 14.3-1 through 14.3-4.

## Question

1. Interpret the data in these tables. What recommendations and conclusions would you offer to Downy-Q management?

■ **Case Table 14.3-1**

**Shifts in Choice of Downy-Q Quilt before and after Showing of Commercial**

| Brand Choice after Commercial | Brand Choice before Commercial | |
| --- | --- | --- |
| | Downy-Q ($n = 23$) | Other Brand ($n = 237$) |
| Downy-Q | 78 | 19 |
| Other brand | 22 | 81 |

Question: We are going to give away a series of prizes. If you are selected as one of the winners, which of the following would you truly want to win?

■ **Case Table 14.3-2**

**Prepost Increment in Choice of Downy-Q**

| Demographic Group | "Fighting the Cold" | | Norm: All Quilt Comercials | |
| --- | --- | --- | --- | --- |
| | Base | Score | Average | Range |
| Total audience | (260) | +15 | +10 | 6–19 |
| By marital status | | | | |
| Married | (130) | +17 | | |
| Not married | (130) | +12 | | |
| By age | | | | |
| Under 35 | (130) | +14 | | |
| 35 and over | (130) | +15 | | |
| By employment status | | | | |
| Not employed | (180) | +13 | | |
| Employed | (170) | +18 | | |

Question: We are going to give away a series of prizes. If you are selected as one of the winners, which of the following would you truly want to win? (Check list.)

■ **Case Table 14.3-3**

**Adjective Checklist for Downy-Q Quilt Commercial**

| Adjective | "Fighting the Cold" (%) | Norm: All Quilt Commercials (%) |
|---|---|---|
| Positive | | |
| Appealing | 18 | 24 |
| Clever | 11 | 40 |
| Convincing | 20 | 14 |
| Effective | 19 | 23 |
| Entertaining | 5 | 24 |
| Fast moving | 12 | 21 |
| Genuine | 7 | 4 |
| Imaginative | 7 | 21 |
| Informative | 24 | 18 |
| Interesting | 13 | 17 |
| Original | 7 | 20 |
| Realistic | 8 | 3 |
| Unusual | 3 | 8 |
| Negative | | |
| Amateurish | 9 | 11 |
| Dull | 33 | 20 |
| Bad Taste | 4 | 4 |
| Repetitious | 17 | 16 |
| Silly | 8 | 19 |
| Slow | 8 | 7 |
| Unbelievable | 3 | 5 |
| Unclear | 3 | 2 |
| Unimportant | 14 | 14 |
| Uninteresting | 32 | 19 |

Question: Which of these words do you feel come closest to describing the commercial you've just seen? (Check list.)

■ **Case Table 14.3-4**

**Product Attribute Checklist for Downy-Q**

| Attributes | "Fighting the Cold" (%) |
|---|---|
| Extra warm | 56 |
| Lightweight | 48 |
| Pretty designs | 45 |
| Durable fabrics | 28 |
| Nice fabrics | 27 |
| Good construction | 27 |

Question: Which of the following statements do you feel apply to Downy-Q? (Mark as many or as few as you feel apply.)

## CASE 14.4   American Pharmaceutical Industries

American Pharmaceutical Industries is a relatively well-established firm whose major source of revenue is derived from physician-prescribed drugs. Until recently most of its significant marketing research activities were contracted out with agencies that specialized in this type of research. However, a major decision has been made to establish its own marketing research department under the direction of Franklin Link. Link is responsible directly to the vice president for marketing, who holds a Ph.D. in marketing. Link himself has several years of research experience with a major manufacturer of hospital and medical office supplies.

Virtually all the research American Pharmaceutical Industries has conducted in the past, and most of that expected in the future, closely relates to very specific questions. However, at Link's suggestion, senior corporate management has approved a relatively extensive study on physician decision making with regard to the selection of drugs. Part of the data-gathering process involves personal as well as telephone interviews in which the interviewer represents himself or herself as an employee of a fictitious marketing research agency. Since some of the questions involve having physicians make evaluative statements about specific brands or drug companies, it is believed that a response bias might be introduced if American Pharmaceutical Industries were identified. Moreover, the interviewers were instructed to tell physicians that the research agency was conducting the research for its own general purposes and not for a specific client. This procedure was not discussed with George Hempel, vice president for marketing.

Physician cooperation was relatively good, and Link felt the data to be of high quality and considerable practical value. The project was completed at the end of Link's seventh month with American Pharmaceutical Industries, and he was anxious to make an extensive report to senior management. Link felt that they would share his feeling about the merits of the study. Link asked Hempel if a meeting with senior management could be arranged. Hempel asked for a written report first and was provided with an extensive document. To the vice president's dismay, the report contained considerable information that directly and indirectly seriously challenged the wisdom of much of American Pharmaceutical Industries' marketing strategy for introducing new products while supporting the general strategy for well-established products. Hempel directed Link to write up a brief summary of the research results pertaining to well-established products and to make only passing reference to the implications of the research for new product marketing. This report was to serve as a substitute for the meeting Link had requested.

**Question**

1. What ethical questions about data collection and reporting of results face American Pharmaceutical?

## ■ Endnotes

[1]Judith Waldrop, "Most Restaurant Meals Are Bought on Impulse," *American Demographics,* February 1, 1994, p. 16.

[2]*Bride's Magazine* survey, as reported in Jo-Ann Johnson, "The Cost of I-Do," *Tulsa World,* February 21, 1993, p. G–5.

[3]Herman J. Loether and Donald G. McTavish, *Descriptive Statistics for Sociologists: An Introduction* (Boston: Allyn & Bacon, 1974), pp. 265–266.

[4]The number of degrees of freedom (*d.f.*) is equal to the number of observations minus the number of constraints or assumptions needed to calculate a statistical term. Another way to look at degrees of freedom is to think of adding four numbers together when you know their sum, for example,

$$
\begin{array}{r}
4 \\
2 \\
1 \\
\underline{X} \\
10
\end{array}
$$

The value of the fourth number has to be 3. In other words, there is a freedom of choice for the first three digits, but the fourth value is not free to vary. In this example there are three degrees of freedom.

[5]The reader with an extensive statistics background will recognize that in a few rare cases, the degrees of freedom do not equal $k - 1$. However, readers of this level of book will rarely encounter these cases, and to present them would only confuse the discussion here.

[6]An example of how to use the chi-square table is given in Table A.4 of the appendix.

[7]Melvin Prince, *Consumer Research for Management Decisions* (New York: John Wiley and Sons, 1982), pp. 163–166.

# *15*

# DIFFERENCES BETWEEN GROUPS AND RELATIONSHIPS AMONG VARIABLES

**WHAT YOU WILL LEARN IN THIS CHAPTER:**

To discuss reasons to conduct test of differences.

To understand how the type of measurement scale influences the test of difference.

To calculate a chi-square test for a contingency table.

To understand that analysis of variance (ANOVA) tests for differences among three or more groups.

To give examples of marketing questions that may be answered by analyzing the associations among variables.

To discuss the concept of the simple correlation coefficient.

To understand that correlation does not mean causation.

To explain the concept of bivariate linear regression.

To discuss why multivariate regression is an important tool for analysis.

**D**DB Needham Worldwide, an international advertising agency, conducts an annual Life Style Study to track the psychographic character of the American public. After it ran an abridged version of the lifestyle questionnaire in its in-house magazine, it decided to include an article with the title, "I Have Met the Customer and He Ain't Me," for a subsequent issue. Comparisons between the group of people who worked at the advertising agency and the average Americans who participated in the survey were dramatic and statistically significant. For example, only 52 percent of the advertising agency staff members responded that job security was more important than money versus 75 percent of the general public.[1]

Some of the findings are especially surprising. For example, 46 percent of agency respondents said they had gone bowling in the previous year, versus 30 percent of the public. And 75 percent of agency respondents said they had bought a lottery ticket in the previous year, versus 61 percent of the public.

Other striking differences:

- I want to look different from others—Agency 82 percent, public 62 percent.
- There's too much sex on prime-time TV—Agency 50 percent, public 78 percent.
- TV is my primary form of entertainment—Agency 28 percent, public 53 percent.

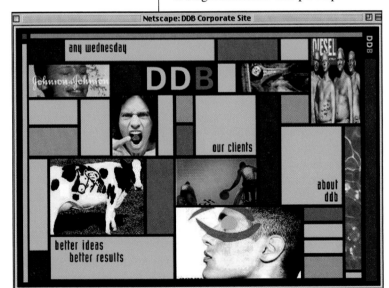

- I went to a bar or tavern in the past year—Agency 91 percent, public 50 percent.
- I like the feeling of speed—Agency 66 percent, public 35 percent.
- There should be a gun in every home—Agency 9 percent, public 32 percent.
- I hate to lose even friendly competition—Agency 58 percent, public 44 percent.
- My favorite music is classic rock—Agency 64 percent, public 35 percent.
- My favorite music is easy listening—Agency 27 percent, public 51 percent.
- Couples should live together before getting married—Agency 50 percent, public 33 percent.
- My greatest achievements are still ahead of me—Agency 89 percent, public 65 percent.

The upshot for ad people is clear. Agency personnel who assume that the target customers are themselves just may end up with advertising that talks to no one—other than themselves.

Making comparisons such as this involves analysis of differences between groups, a major topic of this chapter. The chapter also investigates relationships between variables.

The purpose of descriptive analysis is to summarize data. After accomplishing this, the researcher may wish to measure the associations between variables or test the differences between groups of objects. This chapter goes beyond univariate statistical analysis, which focuses on one variable at a time, and into the realm of **bivariate statistical analysis,** in which the researcher is concerned with scores on two variables.

The chapter also includes a brief discussion of multiple regression, a form of multivariate analysis.

**Bivariate statistical analysis**
Data analysis and hypothesis testing when the investigation concerns simultaneous investigation of two variables.

# ■ DIFFERENCES BETWEEN GROUPS

One of the most frequently tested hypotheses states that two groups differ with respect to some behavior, characteristic, or attitude. For example, in the classical experimental design, the researcher tests differences between subjects assigned to the experimental group and subjects assigned to the control group. Or a researcher may be interested in whether male and female consumers purchase a product with equal frequency. These are bivariate **tests of differences.**

Often researchers are interested in testing differences in mean scores between groups or in comparing how two groups' scores are distributed across possible response categories. We will focus on these issues.

**Test of differences**
An investigation of a hypothesis that states that two (or more) groups differ with respect to measures on a variable.

## ■ Contingency Tables

Construction of contingency tables for chi-square analysis provides a procedure for comparing the distribution of one group with that of another group. This is a good starting point from which to discuss testing of differences.

One of the simplest techniques for describing sets of relationships is the cross-tabulation. A **cross-tabulation,** or **contingency table,** is a joint frequency distribution of observations on two or more sets of variables. This generally means tabulation of subgroups will be conducted for purposes of comparison. The chi-square distribution provides a means for testing the statistical significance of contingency tables. This allows us to test for differences in two groups' distributions across categories.

As mentioned in Chapter 14, the statistical logic involved in the chi-square test for a contingency table is that of comparing the observed frequencies ($O_i$) with the expected frequencies ($E_i$). It tests the goodness of fit of the observed distribution with the expected distribution.

**Cross-tabulation (contingency table)**
A joint frequency distribution of observations on two or more sets of variables.

Exhibit 15.1 reproduces Exhibit 14.21. This one-dimensional table suggests that the majority of the population (60 percent) is aware of the brand. However, if we analyze the data by subgroups based on gender of respondents, as in Exhibit 15.2, we can see the logic of cross-classification procedures. Inspection of Exhibit 15.2 suggests that most men are aware of the brand of tires, but most women are not. Thus, in our simple analysis, we conclude that there is a difference in brand awareness between men and women. (We might also state that brand awareness may be associated with gender of respondent.)

So far we have discussed the notion of statistical significance. Is the observed difference between men and women the result of chance variation due to random sampling? Is the discrepancy more than sampling variation? The chi-square test allows us to conduct tests for significance in the analysis of the $R \times C$ contingency table (where $R$ = row and $C$ = column). The formula for the chi-square statistic is the same as that for one-way frequency tables (see Chapter 14):

$$\chi^2 = \sum \frac{(O_i - E_i)^2}{E_i}$$

where

$\chi^2$ = chi-square statistic
$O_i$ = observed frequency in the $i$th cell
$E_i$ = expected frequency in the $i$th cell

Again, as in the univariate chi-square test, a frequency count of data that nominally identify or categorically rank groups is acceptable for the chi-square test for a contingency table. Both variables in the contingency table will be categorical variables rather than interval- or ratio-scaled continuous variables.

As in all hypothesis-testing procedures, we begin by formulating the null hypothesis and selecting the level of statistical significance for the particular problem. Suppose we wish to test the null hypothesis that an equal number of men and women are aware of the brand in the preceding example and the hypothesis test will be made at the .05 level of statistical significance. In managerial terms, the researcher asks whether men and women have different levels of brand awareness, and the problem is translated into a statistical question: "Is brand awareness independent of the respondent's gender?" Exhibit 15.2 is a $2 \times 2$ ($R \times C$) contingency table that cross-classifies answers to the awareness question (rows) and the respondent's gender (columns).

---

■ **Exhibit 15.1**

**One-Way Frequency Table for Brand Awareness**

| Awareness of Tire Manufacturer's Brand | Frequency |
|---|---|
| Aware | 60 |
| Unaware | 40 |
| Total | 100 |

---

■ **Exhibit 15.2**

**Contingency Table (Cross-Tabulation) for Brand Awareness by Gender**

| Awareness of Tire Manufacturer's Brand | Men | Women | Total |
|---|---|---|---|
| Aware | 50 | 10 | 60 |
| Unaware | 15 | 25 | 40 |
|  | 65 | 35 | 100 |

To compute the chi-square value for the $2 \times 2$ contingency table (Exhibit 15.2), the researcher must first identify an expected distribution for that table. Under the null hypothesis that men and women would be equally aware of the tire brand, the same proportion of positive answers (60 percent) should come from both groups. In other words, the proportion of men aware of the brand would be the same as the proportion of women aware of it. Likewise, the proportion of men unaware of the brand would equal the proportion of women unaware.

There is an easy way to calculate the expected frequencies for the cells in a cross-tabulation. To compute an expected number for each cell, we use the following formula:

$$E_{ij} = \frac{R_i C_j}{n}$$

where

$R_i$ = total observed frequency in the $i$th row
$C_j$ = total observed frequency in the $j$th column
$n$ = sample size

A calculation of the expected values does not utilize the actual observed numbers of respondents in each individual cell; only the total column and total row values are used in this calculation. The expected cell frequencies are calculated as shown in Exhibit 15.3.

To compute a chi-square statistic, we use the same formula as before, but calculate degrees of freedom as the number of rows minus 1 $(R - 1)$ times the number of columns minus 1 $(C - 1)$:

$$\chi^2 = \sum \frac{(O_i - E_i)^2}{E_i}$$

with $(R - 1)(C - 1)$ degrees of freedom.

Exhibit 15.3 shows the observed versus the expected frequencies for the brand awareness question. Using the data in Exhibit 15.3, the chi-square statistic is calculated as follows:

$$\chi^2 = \frac{(50 - 39)^2}{39} + \frac{(10 - 21)^2}{21} + \frac{(15 - 26)^2}{26} + \frac{(25 - 14)^2}{14}$$
$$= 3.102 + 5.762 + 4.654 + 8.643$$
$$= 22.161$$

■ **Exhibit 15.3**

**Calculation of Observed versus Expected Frequencies for Brand Awareness Problem**

| Awareness of Tire Manufacturer's Brand | Men | Women | Total |
|---|---|---|---|
| Aware | 50(39)* | 10(21) | 60 |
| Unaware | 15(26) | 25(14) | 40 |
| | 65 | 35 | 100 |

*Expected frequencies are in parentheses. They were calculated as follows:

$E_{11} = \dfrac{(60)(65)}{100} = 39$

$E_{12} = \dfrac{(60)(35)}{100} = 21$

$E_{21} = \dfrac{(40)(65)}{100} = 26$

$E_{22} = \dfrac{(40)(35)}{100} = 14$

The number of degrees of freedom equals 1:

$$(R - 1)(C - 1) 5 (2 - 1)(2 - 1) = 1$$

From Table A.4 in the Appendix, we see that the critical value at the .05 probability level with 1 d.f. is 3.84. Thus, the null hypothesis is rejected. Brand awareness does not appear to be independent of the respondent's gender; in fact, the tabular $\chi^2$ value for the .001 level is 10.8, and the calculated $\chi^2$ value of 22.1 far exceeds this tabular value.

Proper use of the chi-square test requires that each expected cell frequency ($E_{ij}$) have a value of at least 5. If this sample size requirement is not met, the researcher may take a larger sample or combine (collapse) response categories.

## ■ Difference between Two Groups When Comparing Means

Researchers often wish to test a hypothesis stating that the mean scores on some interval- or ratio-scaled variable will be significantly different for two independent samples or groups.

The null hypothesis about differences between groups is normally stated as follows:

$$\mu_1 = \mu_2 \text{ or } \mu_1 - \mu_2 = 0$$

The question is whether the observed differences have occurred by chance alone. In most cases, comparisons are between two sample means ($\overline{X}_1 - \overline{X}_2$). The formula utilized to test whether the differences are statistically significant depends on the knowledge of the value of the population standard deviation and the number of observations (sample size) in the groups. If either group is small (fewer than 30) and the population standard deviation is unknown, the researcher uses a $t$-test for difference of means. If the number of observations is large, the researcher uses a Z-test for difference of means to test the hypothesis.

## ■ Difference between Two Groups When Comparing Proportions

What type of statistical comparison can be made when the observed statistics are proportions? Suppose a researcher wishes to test a hypothesis that wholesalers in the northern and southern United States differ in the proportion of sales they make to discount retailers. Testing the null hypothesis that the population proportion for group 1 ($\pi_1$) equals the population proportion for group 2 ($\pi_2$) is conceptually the same as the $t$- test or Z-test of two means. Again, sample size is the appropriate criterion for selecting either a $t$-test (small sample) or a Z-test (large sample.)

The hypothesis, which is

$$H_0: \pi_1 = \pi_2$$

may be restated as

$$H_0: \pi_1 - \pi_2 = 0$$

The comparison between the observed sample proportions, $p_1$ and $p_2$, allows the researcher to ask whether the differences between two groups from random samples occurred due to chance alone.

**Analysis of variance (ANOVA)**
Analysis involving the investigation of the effects of one treatment variable on an interval-scaled dependent variable; a hypothesis-testing technique to determine whether statistically significant differences on means occur among three or more groups.

## ■ Difference among Three or More Groups When Comparing Means

When the means of more than two groups or populations are to be compared, one-way **analysis of variance (ANOVA)** is the appropriate statistical tool. Most ANOVA problems have a nominal variable as the independent variable and an interval- or ratio-scaled variable as the dependent variable. An example of an ANOVA problem would be to compare women who work full time outside the home, those who work part time outside the home,

**WHAT WENT RIGHT?**

### The Super Bowl and the Stock Market

If you found a variable that forecast the following year's direction of the stock market with an accuracy of better than 93 percent, would you be interested in its prediction? If so, watch the Super Bowl. In the 31 Super Bowls from 1967 to 1997, 28 out of 31 times the market rose by year's end when a team from the original NFL won the championship or fell by year's end when a team from the old American Football League (now the NFL's American Football Conference) won. The value of stock market indexes is associated with the football league winning the Super Bowl. Most likely this is mere coincidence, but many investors still root for teams from the original NFL.

and those who work full time inside the home on the number of hours they spend shopping in grocery stores each week. Here there is one independent variable: working status. This variable is said to have three levels: full-time employment, part-time employment, and work only within the home. Because there are three groups (levels), we cannot use a $t$-test or a $Z$-test to test for statistical significance.

If we have three groups or levels of the independent variable, the null hypothesis is stated as follows:

$$\mu_1 = \mu_2 = \mu_3$$

The null hypothesis is that all the means are equal. In the grocery shopping example, we are concerned with the average number of hours of three different groups of women.

As the term *analysis of variance* suggests, the problem requires comparing variances to make inferences about the means. The logic of this technique goes as follows: The variance among the means of the three groups will be large if these groups significantly differ from one another in terms of number of hours spent shopping. By calculating the variance within the groups and the variance among the groups, we can determine if the means are significantly different.

## ■ RELATIONSHIPS AMONG VARIABLES

Many marketing questions deal with the association between two (or more) variables. Questions such as "Is sales productivity associated with pay incentives?", "Is socioeconomic status associated with the likelihood of purchasing a recreational vehicle?", or "Does work status relate to attitudes toward the role of women in society?" can be answered by statistically investigating the relationships between the two variables in question. In this section, we investigate how to analyze questions such as these.

In marketing, sales is often the dependent variable we wish to predict. The independent variables we may find to be associated with the dependent variable *sales* may be aspects of the marketing mix, such as price, number of salespeople, or amount of advertising, and/or uncontrollable variables, such as population or gross domestic product. For example, most managers would not be surprised that the sale of baby buggies is associated with the number of babies born a few months prior to the sales period. In this case, the dependent variable is the sales volume of baby buggies and the independent variable is the number of

**Measure of association**
A general term that refers to a number of bivariate statistical techniques used to measure the strength of a relationship between two variables.

babies born. The mathematical symbol $X$ is commonly used for the independent variable, and $Y$ typically denotes the dependent variable. It is appropriate to label dependent and independent variables only when we assume the independent variable caused the dependent variable.

Statisticians have developed several **measures of association.** In this chapter, we discuss simple correlation—*Pearson's product-moment correlation coefficient (r)*—and bivariate linear regression. Both techniques require interval-scaled or ratio-scaled data.

# ■ CORRELATION ANALYSIS

**Correlation coefficient**
A statistical measure of the covariation or association between two variables.

The most popular technique for indicating the relationship of one variable to another is simple correlation analysis. The **correlation coefficient** is a statistical measure of the covariation or association between two variables. The correlation coefficient ($r$) ranges from +1.0 to −1.0. If the value of $r$ equals +1.0, there is a perfect positive linear (straight-line) relationship. If the value of $r$ equals −1.0, a perfect negative linear relationship, or a perfect inverse relationship, is indicated. No correlation is indicated if $r$ equals 0. A correlation coefficient indicates both the magnitude of the linear relationship and the direction of that relationship. For example, if we find that $r = -.92$, we know we have a relatively strong inverse relationship; that is, the greater the value measured by variable $X$, the lower the value measured by variable $Y$.

The formula for calculating the correlation coefficient for two variables, $X$ and $Y$, is as follows:

$$r_{xy} = r_{yx} = \frac{\Sigma(X_i - \overline{X})(Y_i - \overline{Y})}{\sqrt{\Sigma(X_i - \overline{X})^2 \Sigma(Y_i - \overline{Y})^2}}$$

where the symbols $\overline{X}$ and $\overline{Y}$ represent the sample averages of $X$ and $Y$, respectively.

An alternative way to express the correlation formula is:

$$r_{xy} = r_{yx} = \frac{\sigma_{xy}}{\sqrt{\sigma_x^2 \sigma_y^2}},$$

where

$$\sigma_x^2 = \text{variance of } X$$
$$\sigma_y^2 = \text{variance of } Y$$
$$\sigma_{xy} = \text{covariance of } X \text{ and } Y$$

with

$$\sigma_{xy} = \frac{\Sigma(X_i - \overline{X})(Y_i - \overline{Y})}{N}$$

If the associated values of $X_i$ and $Y_i$ differ from their means in the same direction, their covariance will be positive. The covariance will be negative if the values of $X_i$ and $Y_i$ tend to deviate in opposite directions.

The simple correlation coefficient actually is a standardized measure of covariance. In the formula, the numerator represents covariance and the denominator is the square root of the product of the sample variances. Researchers find the correlation coefficient useful because they can compare two correlations without regard for the amount of variance each variable exhibits separately.

## ■ Correlation and Causation

It is important to remember that correlation does not mean causation. No matter how highly correlated the rooster's crow is to the rising of the sun, the rooster does not *cause* the sun to rise. Similarly, a high correlation exists between teachers' salaries and the consumption of liquor over a period of years. The approximate correlation coefficient is $r = 9$. This high correlation does not indicate how much teachers drink, nor does it indicate that the sale of liquor increases teachers' salaries. It is more likely that teachers' salaries and liquor sales covary because both are influenced by a third variable, such as long-run growth in national income and/or population.

## ■ Coefficient of Determination

**Coefficient of determination ($r^2$)**
A measure obtained by squaring the correlation coefficient; that proportion of the total variance of a variable that is accounted for by knowing the value of another variable.

If we wish to know the proportion of variance in $Y$ that is explained by $X$ (or vice versa), we can calculate the **coefficient of determination** by squaring the correlation coefficient ($r^2$):

$$r^2 = \frac{\text{Explained variance}}{\text{Total variance}}$$

The coefficient of determination, $r^2$, measures that part of the total variance of $Y$ that is accounted for by knowing the value of $X$. For example, in a study that investigated whether the average number of hours worked in manufacturing was related to unemployment, $r = -.635$; therefore, $r^2 = .403$. About 40 percent of the variance in unemployment can be explained by the variance in hours worked, and vice versa.

## ■ Correlation Matrix

**Correlation matrix**
The standard format for reporting correlational results.

The **correlation matrix** is the standard format for reporting correlational results. It may be compared to a between-city mileage table, except that the research variables are substituted for cities and a coefficient of correlation is substituted for mileage. Exhibit 15.4 shows a correlation matrix that includes some measures of sales force performance and job satisfaction as they relate to characteristics of the sales force, job attitudes from the Role Orientation Index, and territory workload.[2] The student will encounter this type of matrix on many occasions. Note that the main diagonal consists of correlations of 1.00. This will always be the case when a variable is correlated with itself. The data in this example are

■ **Exhibit 15.4**     **Pearson Product-Moment Correlation Matrix for Salesperson Example[a]**

| | Variables | S | JS | GE | SE | OD | VI | JT | RA | TP | WL |
|---|---|---|---|---|---|---|---|---|---|---|---|
| S | Performance | 1.00 | | | | | | | | | |
| JS | Job satisfaction | .45[b] | 1.00 | | | | | | | | |
| GE | Generalized self-esteem | .31[b] | .10 | 1.00 | | | | | | | |
| SE | Specific self-esteem | .61[b] | .28[b] | .36[b] | 1.00 | | | | | | |
| OD | Other-directedness | .05 | −.03 | −.44[b] | −.24[c] | 1.00 | | | | | |
| VI | Verbal intelligence | −.36[b] | −.13 | −.14 | −.11 | −.18[d] | 1.00 | | | | |
| JT | Job-related tension | −.48[b] | −.56[b] | −.32[b] | −.34[b] | .26[b] | −.02 | 1.00 | | | |
| RA | Role ambiguity | −.26[c] | −.24[c] | −.32[b] | −.39[b] | .38[b] | −.05 | .44[b] | 1.00 | | |
| TP | Territory potential | .49[b] | .31[b] | .04 | .29[b] | .09 | −.09 | −.38[b] | −.26[b] | 1.00 | |
| WL | Work load | .45[b] | .11 | .29[c] | .29[c] | −.04 | −.12 | −.27[c] | −.22[d] | .49[b] | 1.00 |

[a]Numbers below the diagonal are for the sample; those above the diagonal are omitted.
[b]$p < .001$.
[c]$p < .01$.
[d]$p < .05$.

from a survey of industrial salespeople selling steel and plastic strapping and seals used in shipping. Performance ($S$) was measured by identifying the salesperson's actual annual sales volume in dollars. Notice that the performance variable has a .45 correlation with the workload variable, which was measured by recording the number of accounts in the sales territory. Notice also that the salesperson's perception of job-related tension ($JT$) as measured on an attitude scale has a –.48 correlation with performance ($S$). Thus, when perceived job tension is high, performance is low. Of course, the correlation coefficients in these examples are moderate.

## ■ BIVARIATE LINEAR REGRESSION

**Bivariate linear regression**
A measure of linear association that investigates a straight-line relationship of the type $Y = a + \beta X$, where $X$ is the independent variable and $a$ and $\beta$ are two constants to be estimated.

**Bivariate linear regression** investigates a *straight-line relationship* of the type $Y = a + \beta$, where $Y$ is the dependent variable, $X$ is the independent variable, and $a$ and $\beta$ are two constants to be estimated. The symbol $a$ represents the $Y$ intercept, and $\beta$ is the slope coefficient. The slope $\beta$ is the change in $Y$ due to a corresponding change in one unit of $X$.

The slope also may be thought of as *rise over run* (the rise in units on the $Y$-axis divided by the run in units along the $X$- axis).

Suppose a researcher is interested in forecasting sales for a construction distributor (wholesaler) in Florida. Further, the distributor believes a reasonable association exists between sales and building permits issued by counties. Using bivariate linear regression on the data in Exhibit 15.5, the researcher will be able to estimate sales potential ($Y$) in various counties based on the number of building permits ($X$). To better illustrate the data in Exhibit 15.5, we have plotted them on a scatter diagram (Exhibit 15.6). In the diagram the vertical axis indicates the value of the dependent variable, $Y$, and the horizontal axis indicates the value of the independent variable, $X$. Each single point in the diagram represents an observation of $X$ and $Y$ at a given point in time, that is, a paired value of $X$ and $Y$. The relationship between $X$ and $Y$ could be "eyeballed"; that is, a straight line could be drawn through the points in the figure. However, this procedure is subject to human error: Two researchers might draw different lines to describe the same data.

## ■ Exhibit 15.5

**Relationship of Sales Potential to Building Permits Issued**

| Dealer | $Y$ Dealer's Sales Volume (thousands) | $X$ Building Permits |
|---|---|---|
| 1 | 77 | 86 |
| 2 | 79 | 93 |
| 3 | 80 | 95 |
| 4 | 83 | 104 |
| 5 | 101 | 139 |
| 6 | 117 | 180 |
| 7 | 129 | 165 |
| 8 | 120 | 147 |
| 9 | 97 | 119 |
| 10 | 106 | 132 |
| 11 | 99 | 126 |
| 12 | 121 | 156 |
| 13 | 103 | 129 |
| 14 | 86 | 96 |
| 15 | 99 | 108 |

■ **Exhibit 15.6**

**Least-Squares Method of Regression Analysis**

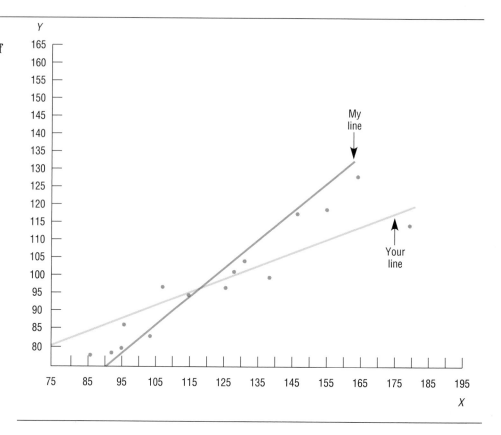

The task of the researcher is to find the best means for fitting a straight line to the data. The *least-squares method* is a relatively simple mathematical technique that ensures that the straight line will most closely represent the relationship between $X$ and $Y$. The logic behind the least-squares technique goes as follows: No straight line can completely represent every dot in the scatter diagram; a discrepancy will occur between most of the actual scores (each dot) and the predicted score based on the regression line. Simply stated, any straight line drawn will generate errors. The least-squares method uses the criterion of attempting to make the least amount of total error in prediction of $Y$ from $X$.

$\hat{Y}_i$ = estimated value of the dependent variable ("$Y$ hat")
$n$ = number of observations
$i$ = number of the particular observation

The general equation for a straight line is $Y = a + \beta X$, where a more appropriate estimating equation includes an allowance for error:

$$Y = \hat{a} + \hat{\beta}X + e$$

The symbols $\hat{a}$ and $\hat{\beta}$ are used when the equation is a regression estimate of the line. Thus, to compute the estimated values of $a$ and $\beta$, we use the following formulas:

$$\hat{\beta} = \frac{n(\Sigma XY) - (\Sigma X)(\Sigma Y)}{(\Sigma X^2) - (\Sigma X)^2}$$

and

$$\hat{a} = \overline{Y} - \hat{\beta}\overline{X}$$

where

$\hat{\beta}$ = estimated slope of the line (the regression coefficient)
$\hat{a}$ = estimated intercept of the $Y$-axis
$Y$ = dependent variable
$\overline{Y}$ = mean of the dependent variable
$X$ = independent variable
$\overline{X}$ = mean of the independent variable
$n$ = number of observations

We can solve these equations with simple arithmetic (see Exhibit 15.7). To estimate the relationship between the distributor's sales to a dealer and the number of building permits, we perform the following manipulations:

$$\hat{\beta} = \frac{n(\Sigma XY) - (\Sigma X)(\Sigma Y)}{n(\Sigma X^2) - (\Sigma X)^2}$$

$$= \frac{15(193,345) - 2,806,875}{15(245,759) - 3,515,625}$$

$$= \frac{2,900,175 - 2,806,875}{3,686,385 - 3,515,625}$$

$$= \frac{93,300}{170,760} = .54638$$

$$\hat{a} = \overline{Y} - \hat{\beta}\,\overline{X}$$

$$= 99.8 - .54638(125)$$

$$= 99.8 - 68.3$$

$$= 31.5$$

The formula $\hat{Y} = 31.5 + 0.546X$ is the regression equation used for the prediction of the dependent variable. Suppose the wholesaler considers a new dealership in an area

---

**■ Exhibit 15.7**

**Least-Squares Computation**

| | $Y$ | $Y^2$ | $X$ | $X^2$ | $XY$ |
|---|---|---|---|---|---|
| 1 | 77 | 5,929 | 86 | 7,396 | 6.622 |
| 2 | 79 | 6,241 | 93 | 8,649 | 7,347 |
| 3 | 80 | 6,400 | 95 | 9,025 | 7,600 |
| 4 | 83 | 6,889 | 104 | 10,816 | 8,632 |
| 5 | 101 | 10,201 | 139 | 19,321 | 14,039 |
| 6 | 117 | 13,689 | 180 | 32,400 | 21,060 |
| 7 | 129 | 16,641 | 165 | 27,225 | 21,285 |
| 8 | 120 | 14,400 | 147 | 21,609 | 17,640 |
| 9 | 97 | 9,409 | 119 | 14,161 | 11,543 |
| 10 | 106 | 11,236 | 132 | 17,424 | 13,992 |
| 11 | 99 | 9,801 | 126 | 15,876 | 12,474 |
| 12 | 121 | 14,641 | 156 | 24,336 | 18,876 |
| 13 | 103 | 10,609 | 129 | 16,641 | 13,287 |
| 14 | 86 | 7,396 | 96 | 9,216 | 8,256 |
| 15 | 99 | 9,801 | 108 | 11,664 | 10,692 |
| $\Sigma$ | $\Sigma Y = 1,497$ | $\Sigma Y^2 = 153,283$ | $\Sigma X = 1,875$ | $\Sigma X^2 = 245,759$ | $\Sigma XY = 193,345$ |
| | $\overline{Y} = 99.8$ | | $\overline{X} = 125$ | | |

where the number of building permits equals 89. Sales may be forecast in this area as follows:

$$\hat{Y} = 31.5 + .546(X)$$
$$= 31.5 + .546(89)$$
$$= 31.5 + 48.6$$
$$= 80.1$$

Thus, the distributor may expect sales of 80.1 ($80,100) in this new area.

Calculation of the correlation coefficient gives an indication of how accurate the predictions may be. In this example, the correlation coefficient is $r = .9356$ and the coefficient of determination is $r^2 = .8754$.

### ■ Drawing a Regression Line

To draw a regression line on the scatter diagram, we need to plot only two predicted values of $Y$. Using data for dealer 7 and dealer 3, we can draw a straight line connecting the points 121.6 and 83.4. Exhibit 15.8 shows the regression line.

$$\text{Dealer 7 (actual } Y \text{ value} = 129): \hat{Y}_7 = 31.5 + .546(165)$$
$$= 121.6$$
$$\text{Dealer 3 (actual } Y \text{ value} = 80): \hat{Y}_3 = 31.5 + .546(95)$$
$$= 83.4$$

■ **Exhibit 15.8**

**Least-Squares Regression Line**

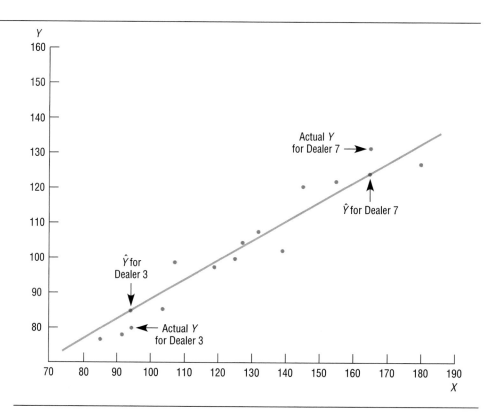

# ■ MULTIPLE REGRESSION ANALYSIS

As we have seen, the investigation of one variable at a time is referred to as *univariate analysis* and the investigation of the relationship between two variables is called *bivariate analysis.* When problems are multidimensional and involve three or more variables, we use *multivariate statistical analysis.* Multivariate statistical methods allow us to consider the effects of more than one variable at the same time. For example, suppose a forecaster wishes to estimate oil consumption for the next five years. While consumption might be predicted by past oil consumption records alone, adding additional variables such as average number of miles driven per year, coal production, and nuclear plants under construction may give greater insight into the determinants of oil consumption. Multivariate analysis will be illustrated in our discussion of multiple regression analysis.

**Multiple regression analysis**
An analysis of association that simultaneously investigates the effect of two or more variables on a single, interval-scaled dependent variable.

**Multiple regression analysis** is an extension of bivariate regression analysis that allows for simultaneous investigation of the effect of two or more independent variables on a single, interval-scaled dependent variable. In the previous section, we illustrated bivariate linear regression analysis with an example concerning a construction dealer's sales volume. In that example, variations in the dependent variable were attributed to changes in a single independent variable. Reality, however, suggests that several factors are likely to affect such a dependent variable. For example, sales volume might be hypothesized to depend not only on the number of building permits but also on price levels, amount of advertising, and income of consumers in the area. Thus, the problem requires identification of a linear relationship with multiple regression analysis. The multiple regression equation is

$$Y = a + \beta_1 X_1 + \beta_2 X_2 + \beta_3 X_3 \ldots + \beta_n X_n$$

Another forecasting example is useful for illustrating multiple regression. Assume a toy manufacturer wishes to forecast sales by sales territory. It is thought that retail sales, the presence or absence of a company salesperson in the territory (a binary variable), and grammar school enrollment are the independent variables that might explain the variation in sales. The data appear in Exhibit 15.9. Exhibit 15.10 shows the statistical results from multiple regression after mathematical computations have been made. The regression equation

$$Y = 102.18 + .387 X_1 + 115.2 X_2 + 6.73 X_3$$

| ■ **Exhibit 15.9** **Data for a Multiple Regression Problem** | $Y$ Sales (000) | $X_1$ Retail Sales (000) | $X_2$ Salesperson (1) or Agent (0) | $X_3$ Grammar School Enrollment (000) |
|---|---|---|---|---|
| | 222 | 106 | 0 | 23 |
| | 304 | 213 | 0 | 18 |
| | 218 | 201 | 0 | 22 |
| | 501 | 378 | 1 | 20 |
| | 542 | 488 | 0 | 21 |
| | 790 | 509 | 1 | 31 |
| | 523 | 644 | 0 | 17 |
| | 667 | 888 | 1 | 25 |
| | 700 | 941 | 1 | 32 |
| | 869 | 1,066 | 1 | 36 |
| | 444 | 307 | 0 | 30 |
| | 479 | 312 | 1 | 22 |

$$Y = 102.18 + .387X_1 + 115.2X_2 + 6.73X_3$$

| | |
|---|---|
| Coefficient of multiple determination ($R^2$) | .845 |
| $F$-value | 14.6 |

indicates that sales are positively related to $X_1$, $X_2$, and $X_3$. The coefficients ($\beta$s) show the effect on the dependent variables of a one-unit increase in any of the independent variables. The value $\beta_2 = 115.2$ indicates that an increase of \$115,200 (000 included) in toy sales is expected with each additional unit of $X_2$. Thus, it appears that adding a company salesperson will have a very positive effect on sales. Grammar school enrollments also may help predict sales. An increase of one unit of enrollment (1,000 students) indicates a sales increase of \$6,730 (000 included). Retail sales volume ($X_1$) in the territory adds little to the predictive power of the equation (\$387).

In multiple regression, the terminology for $\beta_1$, $\beta_2$, and so on changes. These coefficients are now called *coefficients of partial regression.* Each independent variable is usually correlated with the other independent variables. Thus, the correlation between $Y$ and $X_1$ with the correlation that $X_1$ and $X_2$ have in common with $Y$ held constant is the partial correlation. Because the partial correlation between sales and $X_1$ has been adjusted for the effect produced by variation in $X_2$ (and other independent variables), the correlation coefficient obtained from the bivariate regression will not be the same as the partial coefficient in the multiple regression. In other words, the original value of $\beta$ is the simple bivariate regression coefficient. In multiple regression, the coefficient $\beta_1$ is defined as the partial regression coefficient for which the effects of other independent variables are held constant.

The *coefficient of multiple determination,* or *multiple index of determination* ($R^2$), is shown in Exhibit 15.10. As in bivariate regression, the coefficient of multiple determination indicates the percentage of variation in $Y$ explained by the variation in the independent variables. $R^2 = .845$ tells the researcher that the variation in the independent variables accounted for 84.5 percent of the variance in the dependent variable. Typically, introducing additional independent variables into the regression equation explains more of the variation in $Y$ than is possible with fewer variables. In other words, the amount of variation explained by two independent variables in the same equation usually explains more variation in $Y$ than either one explains separately.

■ **SUMMARY**

The chi-square statistic allows the researcher to test whether an observed sample distribution fits some given distribution. It can be used to analyze contingency with cross-tabulation, tables. In this case, the test allows the researcher to determine whether two groups are independent. If they are not, the variables are interrelated.

Either a $Z$-test or $t$-test for two independent samples is used to determine if the means of two independent samples are significantly different. The $t$-test should be chosen over the $Z$-test when the population standard deviation is unknown and if the sample size is small (fewer than 30). Similarly, a $t$-test or $Z$-test for two independent samples may be used to determine if two proportions are significantly different.

One-way analysis of variance (ANOVA) compares the means of samples from more than two populations to determine whether their differences are statistically significant.

Simple correlation is the measure of the relationship of one variable to another. The correlation coefficient ($r$) indicates the strength of the association of two variables and the direction of that association. Correlation does not prove causation, as variables other than those being measured may be involved. The coefficient of determination $(r^2)$ measures the amount of the total variance in the dependent variable that is accounted for by knowing the value of the independent variable. The results of a correlation computation often are presented in a correlation matrix.

Bivariate linear regression investigates a straight-line relationship between one dependent variable and one independent variable. The regression can be done intuitively by plotting a scatter diagram of the $X$ and $Y$ points and drawing a line to fit the observed relationship. The least-squares method mathematically determines the best-fitting regression line for the observed data. The line determined by this method may be used to forecast values of the dependent variable given a value for the independent variable. The goodness of the line's fit may be evaluated by calculating the coefficient of determination.

Multiple regression analysis is an extension of bivariate regression analysis that allows for simultaneous investigation of the effect of two or more independent variables on a single, interval-scaled dependent variable.

## ■ Key Terms and Concepts

| | |
|---|---|
| Bivariate statistical analysis | Correlation coefficient |
| Test of differences | Coefficient of determination $(r^2)$ |
| Cross-tabulation (contingency table) | Correlation matrix |
| Analysis of variance (ANOVA) | Bivariate linear regression |
| Measure of association | Multiple regression analysis |

## ■ Questions

1. What tests of difference are appropriate in the following situations?
   (a) Average campaign contributions of Democrats, Republicans, and independents are to be compared.
   (b) Advertising managers and brand managers respond "yes," "no," or "not sure" to an attitude question. Their answers are to be compared.
   (c) One-half of a sample received an incentive in a mail survey; the other half did not. A comparison of response rates is desired.
   (d) A researcher believes that married men will push the grocery cart when grocery shopping with their wives.
2. What type of analysis should be utilized with the following data?

| a. Regulation Is the Best Way to Ensure Safe Products | Managers | Blue-Collar Workers |
|---|---|---|
| Agree | 58 | 66 |
| Disagree | 34 | 24 |
| No opinion | 8 | 10 |
| Totals | 100 | 100 |

3. A store manager's computer-generated list of all retail sales employees indicates that 70 percent are full-time employees, 20 percent are part-time employees, and 10 percent are furloughed or laid-off employees. A sample of 50 employees from the list indicates that 40 are full-time employees, 6 are part-time employees, and 4 are furlough/laid-off employees. What statistical test should be used to determine whether the sample is representative of the population?

4. A sales force ($n = 67$) received some management-by-objectives training. The mean scores for salespeople's job performance are shown below. What type of data analysis is appropriated?

| Skill | Before | After |
| --- | --- | --- |
| Planning ability | 4.84 | 5.43 |
| Territory coverage | 5.24 | 5.51 |
| Activity reporting | 5.37 | 5.42 |

5. The incomes of owners of trash compactors were compared with those of nonowners. The average income in a sample of 200 was as follows:

| | Owners | Nonowners |
| --- | --- | --- |
| $\overline{X}$ | 4.6 | 3.5 |

Higher values represent higher levels of income. (Actual scaled average: less than $7,500 = 1; $7,500–$15,000 = 2; $15,001–$25,000 = 3; $25,001–$40,000 = 4; $40,001–$60,000 = 5; over $60,000 = 6.) Is a *t*-test appropriate?

6. The discussion in this chapter is limited to linear relationships. Try to diagram some non-linear relationships that show *r* values of zero using the test methods shown in the text.

7. Comment on the following:
   (a) Suppose Abraham Lincoln answered a survey questionnaire and indicated he had not received a grade-school diploma. The researcher found that Lincoln's educational score did not correlate highly with the expected variables. What was wrong?
   (b) An international marketer has said, "When political instability increases, the price of quality increases." Is this a testable hypothesis?
   (c) In 8 out of 11 years, when a race horse won the Triple Crown (Kentucky Derby, Preakness, and Belmont Stakes), the stock market dropped.

8. A manufacturer of disposable washcloths/wipes told a retailer that sales for this product category closely correlated with sales of disposable diapers. The retailer thought he would check this out for his own sales-forecasting pupuses. The researcher says, "Disposable washcloth/wipes sales can be predicted with knowledge of disposable diaper sales." Is this the right thing to say?

 **EXPLORING THE INTERNET**

1. Go to the SPSS home page at http://www.spss.com.

   Navigate to "Statistics Coach" to learn what statistical procedure is best for different types of data.

2. The Federal Reserve Bank of St. Louis (http://www.stls.org) maintains a database called FRED (Federal Reserve Economic Data). Use a search engine to navigate to the FRED database. Randomly select a 5-year period between 1970 and 1995 and then find the correlation between average U.S. employment in retail trade and U.S. employment in wholesale trade. What statistical test is appropriate?

3. Go to the American Statistical Association's home page (http://www.amstat.org).

   Select the careers in statistics option and learn what a career in statistics might have to offer.

---

 **CASE 15.1**    Springfield Electric Company

The Springfield Electric Company manufactured electric pencil sharpeners. The company had always operated in New York and New Jersey and decided to expand beyond that region. The company president thought a new plant needed to be constructed. The president felt no need for contiguous expansion and favored a West Coast plant.

The marketing manager believed that sales were correlated with the number of workers employed in the geographic areas; in fact, she felt that electric pencil sharpener sales were correlated with the number of white-collar workers in an area. However, all she could get were the statistics for total employees. Case Exhibit 15.1-1 shows Springfield's sales of electric pencil sharpeners and the total number of employees in 17 Metropolitan Statistical Areas (MSAs) in New York and New Jersey. Case Exhibit 15.1-2 shows the number of employees in the MSAs in Washington, Oregon, and California. The marketing manager thought she could forecast sales for the western expansion with these data.

**Questions**

1. Calculate and interpret the correlation coefficient data in Case Exhibit 15.1-1.
2. Estimate the regression equation coefficient for the data (assuming sales as the independent variable).
3. Forecast sales in the states of California, Washington, and Oregon based on the data in Case Exhibit 15.1-2.

---

■ **Case Exhibit 15.1-1**

**Data on Total Employees and Springfield Sales in New York and New Jersey MSAs**

| Metropolitan Statistical Area | Number of Employees (thousands) | Sales |
|---|---|---|
| **New York** | | |
| Albany–Schenectady–Troy | 58.3 | 3,749 |
| Binghamton | 37.0 | 2,695 |
| Buffalo | 135.6 | 4,926 |
| Elmira | 12.8 | 2,808 |
| Nassau–Suffolk | 149.0 | 7,423 |
| New York | 788.8 | 43,401 |
| Poughkeepsie | 24.3 | 3,254 |
| Rochester | 139.1 | 8,924 |
| Syracuse | 53.6 | 13,119 |
| Utica–Rome | 30.8 | 3,151 |
| **New Jersey** | | |
| Allentown–Bethlehem–Easton | 110.7 | 6,123 |
| Atlantic City | 8.7 | 2,666 |
| Jersey City | 74.2 | 3,210 |
| Long Branch–Asbury Park | 22.8 | 2,078 |
| New Brunswick–Perth Amboy–Sayreville | 78.9 | 2,894 |
| Newark | 252.1 | 14,989 |
| Paterson–Clifton–Passaic | 60.1 | 3,806 |

■ **Case Exhibit 15.1-2**

**Number of Employees in Selected MSAs**

| Metropolitan Statistical Area | Number of Employees (thousands) |
|---|---|
| **Washington** | |
| Richland–Kennewick | 7.8 |
| Seattle–Everett | 123.6 |
| Spokane | 11.1 |
| Tacoma | 18.7 |
| Yakima | 8.8 |
| **Oregon** | |
| Eugene–Springfield | 18.2 |
| Portland | 90.5 |
| Salem | 12.5 |
| **California** | |
| Anaheim–Santa Ana–Garden Grove | 149.0 |
| Bakersfield | 7.1 |
| Fresno | 20.5 |
| Los Angeles–Long Beach | 750.3 |
| Modesto | 18.7 |
| Oxnard–Simi Valley–Ventura | 14.9 |
| Riverside–San Bernardino–Ontario | 51.8 |
| Sacramento | 20.5 |
| Salinas–Seaside–Monterey | 8.0 |
| San Diego | 71.4 |
| San Francisco–Oakland | 172.7 |
| San Jose | 151.1 |
| Santa Barbara–Santa Maria–Lompoc | 14.0 |
| Santa Cruz | 5.7 |
| Santa Rosa | 8.6 |
| Stockton | 20.0 |
| Vallejo–Fairfield–Napa | 7.4 |

**CASE 15.2**   Center for American Enterprise: A Study of Psychological and Demographic Contributors to Consumerism

A few years ago the Center for American Enterprise commissioned a study to determine the causes of consumerism. This was done in an effort to stem the tide of growing disenchantment with American business and its practices among a wide number of consumers.

The center, located in Dallas, Texas, was a private foundation funded by a large number of corporations to spread the ideal of the free enterprise system. It conducted a number of projects to better understand what Americans knew about business and published numerous brochures that were sent to high schools and elementary schools throughout the United States. The center believed consumerism, that is, consumer discontent, was a major problem facing business and wished to pursue it as an area of study.

Since the center did not have the expertise to properly formulate the research problem and its accompanying theory, it decided to seek outside assistance for this project. Commissioned to do the study were three professors, Thomas, Rogers, and Michaels, at Southern Methodist University, who had done considerable research on the topic. The report they generated follows.

**Report on Psychological and Demographic Correlates of Consumer Discontent**

The study of consumerism and the allied psychological state of consumer discontent has been theoretically and empirically examined within the confines of the economic system. Although these market interfaces provide discrete areas for analyzing consumerism or consumer discontent, they may be only symptomatic of broader psychological states currently existing in society. With the exception of one study relating consumer alienation to marketing activities, little research has actively explored potential relationships between psychological states and discontent with the market system. Identification of those psychological states and demographic characteristics associated with consumer discontent would provide valuable insight into the dynamics of this phenomenon and assist in the development of constructive approaches for dealing with it from a public policy perspective.

## Study Purpose

The purpose of this study is to examine the relationships among selected psychological states, demographic variables, and consumer discontent. Specific objectives of this study are threefold:

1. To determine if consumer discontent with the marketplace is rooted in more basic conceptions of an individual's life-space.
2. To determine the appropriateness of psychological constructs as potential contributors and explanatory states for investigating consumer discontent.

3. To identify demographic correlates of consumer discontent.

## Method

A two-stage area sampling procedure was used to select 228 individuals from the Dallas, Texas, metropolitan area. A subsequent analysis of demographic data indicated that the sample represented a cross section of the area. Individuals were personally contacted in their homes by trained interviewers.

Respondents were given a self-administered questionnaire containing a list of 145 statements designed to measure life satisfaction, powerlessness, anomie, alienation, normlessness, social isolation, aggression, and consumer discontent. All statements were scored on a five-point Likert-type scale except for the six-point Likert-type scale of consumer discontent. Demographic data on the respondents were also collected.

## Results

Results of the study are shown in Case Exhibits 15.2-1 and 15.2-2. Case Exhibit 15.2-1 presents the correlation matrix between the measures of psychological states and

---

■ **Case Exhibit 15.2-1**

**Correlation Matrix of Scale Responses**

| ($N = 228$) | CD | LS | AN | AL | PO | NO | SI | AG |
|---|---|---|---|---|---|---|---|---|
| Consumer discontent (*CD*) | 1.00 | −.11[b] | .37[a] | .42[a] | .37[a] | .28[a] | .34[a] | .21[a] |
| Life satisfaction (*LS*) | | 1.00 | −.44[a] | −.44[a] | −.33[a] | −.25[a] | −.44[a] | −.27[a] |
| Anomie (*AN*) | | | 1.00 | .66[a] | .56[a] | .47[a] | .54[a] | .25[a] |
| Alienation (*AL*) | | | | 1.00 | .80[a] | .77[a] | .79[a] | .31[a] |
| Powerlessness (*PO*) | | | | | 1.00 | .46[a] | .42[a] | .15[b] |
| Normlessness (*NO*) | | | | | | 1.00 | .42[a] | .32[a] |
| Social isolation (*SI*) | | | | | | | 1.00 | .28[a] |
| Aggression (*AG*) | | | | | | | | 1.00 |

[a] $p < .01$.
[b] $p < .05$; Pearson product-moment correlation coefficients.

---

■ **Case Exhibit 15.2-2**

**Correlation of Scale Responses with Demographic Characteristics**

| ($N = 228$) | CD | LS | AN | AL | PO | NO | SI | AG |
|---|---|---|---|---|---|---|---|---|
| Age | .13[b] | .14[b] | .10 | .31[a] | .07 | .29[a] | .37[a] | .13[b] |
| Sex[1] | −.13[b] | −.05 | .02 | −.15[b] | −.11 | −.06 | −.18[b] | .11 |
| Race[2] | −.06 | .08 | .04 | −.15[b] | −.13[b] | −.21[a] | −.03 | −.06 |
| Family Size | .02 | −.16[a] | .21[a] | .24[a] | .11[b] | .17[b] | .27[a] | .09 |
| Income | .31[a] | −.29[a] | .22[a] | .37[a] | .30[a] | .31[a] | .30[a] | .17[b] |
| Occupation[3] | −.26[a] | .08 | −.20[a] | −.26[a] | −.23[a] | −.15[b] | −.23[a] | .01 |
| Education | .15[b] | −.03 | −.11 | .20[a] | .27[a] | .16[b] | .06 | .11 |

[a] $p < .01$.
[b] $p < .05$.
[1] Scored: male = 1, female = 2.
[2] Scored: Caucasian = 1, Black = 2, Mexican American = 3, other = 4.
[3] Scored: professional = 1, skilled worker = 2, unskilled worker = 3, unemployed = 4, retired = 5.

the consumer discontent scale. The correlations indicate that consumer discontent is indeed related to basic psychological states.

Case Exhibit 15.2-2 presents the correlation matrix between demographic variables and the consumer discontent scale. Examination of demographic variables also reveals that discontent is related to certain characteristics of the populace.

Together, the psychological and demographic correlates of consumer discontent provide a profile of the discontented consumer. Consumer discontent may be an outgrowth of more basic psychological states that reflect disassociation with society in general and specifically with the marketplace. One may speculate that dislocation in society will produce consumer discontent. Given the growing complexity of business and society, it appears that this may become an even more pervasive problem in the future and thus warrants further research at this time.

**Questions**

1. Interpret the results of the correlation matrix.
2. Develop a profile of the discontented consumer and the contented consumer.
3. What policy implications would you suggest based on these results?

## ■ Endnotes

[1] Joseph M. Winski, "Study: The Customer Ain't Me." *Advertising Age* (January 20, 1992).

[2] See Richard P. Bagozzi, "Salesforce Performance and Satisfaction as a Function of Individual Difference, Interpersonal and Situational Factors" *Journal of Marketing Research* (November 1978), pp. 517–531.

# 16

# COMMUNICATING RESEARCH RESULTS: RESEARCH REPORT, ORAL PRESENTATION, AND RESEARCH FOLLOW-UP[1]

**WHAT YOU WILL LEARN IN THIS CHAPTER:**

To explain how the research report is the crucial means for communicating the whole research project.

To define *research report*.

To outline the research report format and its parts.

To explain how the oral presentation may be the most efficient means of supplementing the written report.

To understand the importance of research follow-up.

After spending days, weeks, or even months working on a project, the researcher is likely to believe that preparation of the report is just an anticlimactic formality. After all, it seems that all the real work has been done; it just has to be put on paper. This attitude can be disastrous, however. The project may have been well designed, the data carefully collected and analyzed by sophisticated statistical methods, and important conclusions reached, but if the project is not effectively reported, all of the preceding efforts will be wasted. Often the research report is the only part of the project that others will ever see. Users of the report cannot separate the content of the project from the form in which it is presented. If people who need to use the research results have to wade through a disorganized presentation, are detoured by technical jargon they do not understand, or find sloppiness of language or thought, they probably will discount the report and make decisions without it, just as if the project had never been done. Thus, the research report is a crucial means for communicating the whole project—the medium through which the project makes its impact on decisions. This chapter explains how research reports, oral presentations, and follow-up conversations help communicate research results.

# ■ COMMUNICATIONS MODEL INSIGHTS

Once the data have been collected and analyzed, the researcher must become a communicator. The researcher has looked at secondary sources, gathered primary data, used statistical techniques to analyze the data, and reached conclusions. In the writing of the report on the project, all of these elements will affect its contents. The researcher may assume the reader has a lot of background information on the project and produce pages and pages of unexplained tables, assuming the reader will unearth from them the same patterns the researcher observed. The report may contain technical terms such as *parameter, hypothesis test, correlation,* or *regression,* assuming the reader will understand them. Or the researcher may assume the reader lacks any background information and explain everything in sixth-grade terms, perhaps insulting the reader in the process.

When readers receive a report, they typically have not thought much about the project. They may know nothing about statistics and may have many other responsibilities. If they cannot grasp the report quickly, they may put it on the stack of "things to do someday."

For a report to get attention, delivering it to its audience is not sufficient. It needs to be written to hit the common experience of the researcher and the reader. The effort to hit that zone is the writer's responsibility, not the reader's. Unless a report is really crucial, a busy reader will not spend time and effort struggling through an inadequate and difficult document.

# ■ THE REPORT IN CONTEXT

**Research report**
An oral presentation or written statement of research results, strategic recommendations, and/or other conclusions to a specific audience.

A **research report** is an oral presentation and/or written statement whose purpose is to communicate research results, strategic recommendations, and/or other conclusions to management and/or other specific audiences. This chapter deals primarily with the final written report that an extensive research project requires. While one can easily adapt the chapter's suggestions for a shorter, less formal report, the final report may not be the only kind prepared. A small project may require only a short oral or written report on the results. An extensive project may involve many written documents, interim reports, and a final detailed written report containing several oral presentations.

The emphasis on the final report does not mean that other communications, such as progress reports during the course of the project, are any less important to its eventual success.

# ■ THE REPORT FORMAT

**Report format**
The makeup or arrangement of parts that are necessary to a good research report.

Although every research report is custom made for the project it represents, some conventions of **report format** are universal. They represent a consensus about the parts necessary

| WHAT WENT WRONG? |
| :---: |
| **Golden Rule for Report Writing** |
| Never use a long word where a diminutive one will do. |

for a good research report and how they should be ordered. This consensus is not a law, however. Every book on report writing suggests its own unique format, and every report writer has to pick and choose the parts and order that will work best for the project at hand. Many companies and universities also have in-house report formats or writing guides for writers to follow. The format presented in this chapter serves as a starting point from which a writer can shape his or her own appropriate format. This format is as follows:

1. Title page
2. Letter of transmittal
3. Letter of authorization
4. Table of contents (and lists of figures and tables)
5. Summary
    (a) Objectives
    (b) Results
    (c) Conclusions
    (d) Recommendations
6. Body
    (a) Introduction
        (1) Background
        (2) Objectives
    (b) Methodology
    (c) Results
    (d) Limitations
    (e) Conclusions and recommendations
7. Appendix
    (a) Data collection forms
    (b) Detailed calculations
    (c) General tables
    (d) Bibliography
    (e) Other support material

## ■ Tailoring the Format to the Project

The format may need adjustment for two reasons: (1) to obtain the proper level of formality and (2) to decrease the complexity of the report. The format given here is for the most formal type of report, such as that for a large project done within an organization or that from a research agency to a client company. This type of report probably would be bound with a fancy cover and could be hundreds of pages long.

For less formal reports, each part will be shorter and some parts will be omitted. The change may be compared to variations in clothing according to the formality of the occasion. The most formal report is dressed, so to speak, in white tie and tails (or long evening gown).[2] It includes the full assortment of prefatory parts—title page, letters of transmittal, and letter of authorization.

The next level of formality would be like an everyday business suit, dropping parts of the prefatory material that the situation does not call for and reducing the complexity of the report body. In general, as the report goes down through the sport coat, slacks, and blue jeans stages, the prefatory parts are dropped and the complexity and length of the report body are reduced.

How does the researcher decide on the appropriate level of formality? The general rule is to include all the parts needed for effective communication in the particular circumstances—and no more.[3] This factor relates to how far up in management the report is expected to go and on how routine the matter is. A researcher's immediate supervisor does not need a 100-page, "full-dress" report on a routine project. However, the board of directors does not want a one-page, "blue jeans" report on a big project that backs a major expansion program. The "white-tie-and-tails" report to top management may later be stripped of some prefatory parts (and thus reduced in formality) for wider circulation within the company.

## ■ The Parts of the Report

**Title Page**   The *title page* should state the title of the report, for whom the report was prepared, by whom it was prepared, and the date of release or presentation.

**Letter of Transmittal**   The *letter of transmittal* is included in relatively formal to very formal reports. Its purpose is to release or deliver the report to the recipient. It also serves to establish some rapport between reader and writer. This is the one part of the formal report that should convey a personal or even slightly informal tone. The transmittal should not dive into the report findings except in the broadest terms. For example, it might comment generally on findings and matters of interest regarding the research. The closing section should express the writer's personal interest in the project just completed and in doing additional, related work.[4]

**Letter of Authorization**   The *letter of authorization* is a letter to the researcher approving the project, detailing who has responsibility for it, and describing the resources available to support it.

**Table of Contents**   The *table of contents* is essential to any report more than a few pages long. It should list the divisions and subdivisions of the report with page references. The table of contents is based on the final outline of the report, but it should include only the first-level subdivisions. In short reports, inclusion of only the main divisions will be sufficient. If the report contains many figures or tables, a list of these also should be included, immediately following the table of contents.

**Summary**   The *summary* briefly explains why the research project was conducted, what aspects of the problem were considered, what the outcome was, and what should be done. It is a vital part of the report. Studies indicate that nearly all managers read a report's summary while only a minority read the rest of the report. Thus, the writer's only chance to produce an impact may be in the summary.

The summary should be written only after the rest of the report has been completed. It represents the essence of the report. Its length should be one page (or, at most, two), so the writer must carefully sort out what is important enough to include. Several pages of the full report may have to be condensed into one summarizing sentence. Different parts of the report may be condensed more than others; the number of words in the summary need not be in proportion to the length of the section being discussed. The summary should be written to be self-sufficient; in fact, the summary is often detached from the report and circulated by itself.

**Introduction section**
The part of the body of the report that discusses background information and the specific objectives of the research.

**The Body**   The *body* constitutes the bulk of the report. It begins with an **introduction** that sets out the background factors that made the project necessary as well as the objectives of the research. It continues with discussions of the methodology, results, and limitations of the study and finishes with conclusions and recommendations based on the results.

The introduction explains why the project was done and what it aimed to discover. The relevant background comes next. Enough background should be included to explain why the project was worth doing, but unessential historical factors should be omitted. The question of how much is enough should be answered by referring to the needs of the audience. A government report that will be widely circulated requires more background than a company's internal report on customer satisfaction. The last part of the introduction explains exactly what the project tried to discover. It discusses the statement of the problem and research questions in a manner similar to the way they were stated in the research proposal. Each purpose presented here should have a corresponding section on results later in the report.

**Research methodology section**
The part of the body of the report that explains the research design, sampling procedures, and other technical procedures used to collect the data.

The second division of the body explains the **research methodology.** This section is a challenge to write because it must explain technical procedures in a manner appropriate for the audience. The material in this section may be supplemented with more detailed explanations in the appendix or a glossary of technical terms.

**Results section**
The part of the body of the report that presents the findings of the project; includes tables, charts, and an organized narrative.

The presentation of **results** should occupy the bulk of the report. This section presents those findings of the project that bear on the objectives in some logical order. The results should be organized as a continuous narrative, designed to be convincing but not to oversell the project. Summary tables and charts should be used to aid the discussion. (See Chapter 14 for a discussion of this topic.) These may serve as points of reference to the data being discussed and free the prose from excessive facts and figures. Comprehensive or detailed charts, however, should be saved for the appendix.

Because no research is perfect, its limitations should be indicated. If problems arose with nonresponse error or sampling procedures, these should be discussed. However, the discussion of limitations should avoid overemphasizing the weaknesses; its aim should be to provide a realistic basis for assessing the results.

**Conclusions and recommendations section**
The part of the body of the report that provides opinions based on the results and suggestions for action.

The last division of the body presents the **conclusions and recommendations.** As mentioned earlier, conclusions are opinions based on the results and recommendations are suggestions for action. The conclusions and recommendations should be presented here in more detail than in the summary and include justification as needed.

**Appendix**   The *appendix* presents the "too" material. Any material that is too technical or too detailed to go in the body should appear in the appendix. This includes materials of interest only to some readers or subsidiary materials not directly related to the objectives. Some examples of appendix materials are data collection forms, detailed calculations, discussions of highly technical questions, detailed or comprehensive tables of results, and a bibliography (if appropriate).

---

# ■ THE ORAL PRESENTATION

**Oral presentation**
A verbal summary of the major findings, conclusions, and recommendations given to clients or line managers to allow them to clarify any ambiguous issues by asking questions.

The conclusions and recommendations of most research reports will be presented orally as well as in writing. The purpose of an **oral presentation** is to highlight the most important findings and provide clients or line managers with the opportunity to clarify any ambiguous issues by asking questions.

The oral presentation may be as simple as a short conference with a manager at the client organization's location or a formal report to the board of directors. The key to effective presentation in either situation is preparation.

Communication specialists often suggest that a person preparing an oral presentation should begin at the end.[5] In other words, while preparing a presentation, a researcher should think about what he or she wants the client to know when it has been completed.

The researcher should select the three or four most important findings for emphasis and rely on the written report for a full summary. The researcher needs to be ready to defend the results. This is not the same as being defensive; rather, it means being prepared to deal in a confident, competent manner with the questions that will arise. Remember that even the most reliable and valid research project is worthless if the managers who must act on its results are not convinced of its importance.

As with written reports, a key to effective oral presentation is adaptation to the audience. Delivering an hour-long, formal speech when a 10-minute discussion is called for (or vice versa) will reflect poorly on both the presenter and the report.

Many marketing researchers view themselves as technicians who generate numbers using sophisticated research designs and statistical techniques. Unfortunately, some researchers organize their oral presentations around technical details rather than around satisfying the manager's or client's needs.

In Chapter 4, we made a comparison between weather reporters and marketing researchers. The average person watching a TV weather report wants to know whether he or she needs to take an umbrella to work the next day. The weather reporter provides enormous amounts of information: It's snowing in Washington, sunny in San Diego, and raining in Texas. Maps full of lines show fronts, high- and low-pressure areas, and other weather facts. This amounts to extraneous information when the viewer simply wants to avoid getting wet. Fortunately, most weather reporters eventually let us know whether rain is forecast. In a similar vein, if the client wants only an executive summary, the oral presentation should emphasize material that one would expect to find in the summary section of the written report. Managers can always ask for additional details about the methodology or clarification of the data analysis.

The principles of good speech making apply to a research presentation. Lecturing or reading to the audience is sure to impede communication at any level of formality. The presenter should refrain from reading prepared text word for word. By relying on brief notes, familiarity with the subject, and as much rehearsal as the occasion calls for, the presenter will foster better communication. She or he should avoid research jargon and use short, familiar words. The presenter should maintain eye contact with the audience and repeat the main points. Because the audience cannot go back and replay what the speaker has said, the presentation often is organized around a standard format: "tell them what you are going to tell them, tell them, and tell them what you just told them."

Graphic and other visual aids can be as useful in an oral presentation as in a written one. Presenters can choose from a variety of media. Slides, overhead projector acetates, and on-screen computerized presentations are useful for larger audiences. For smaller

**EXPLORING RESEARCH ISSUES**

### Noah's Law of Overhead Transparencies

During many oral research reports, the presenter uses transparencies that viewers in the back row cannot read. In fact, some presenters use transparencies that viewers in the front row cannot read.

All viewers would be much happier if all presenters were to follow Noah's Law of Overhead Transparencies. Noah's Law says: Never, ever, under any circumstances whatsoever, put more than 40 words on a transparency. A number counts as a word. Noah's Law is called Noah's Law because, when God made it rain for 40 days and 40 nights, He flooded the whole world, and no presenter should attempt that with one overhead.

Note that, in Noah's Law, 40 is the absolute upper limit. Twenty is a good average. Seven is even better. If seven words look lonely, presenters can always MAKE THE LETTERS BIGGER.

Advertising legend David Ogilvy was a devout follower of Noah's Law. He thought so highly of it that he invented and enforced Ogilvy's Corollary. Ogilvy's Corollary says: Never put anything on a transparency (or a slide or a chart) that you don't intend to read out loud to your audience word for word. He reasoned that, when one message comes in on the visual channel while another comes in on the auditory channel, the audience will probably neglect one message or the other.

■ Oral presentations can be enhanced with on-screen computerized graphics. Presentation software, such as Microsoft's Power Point, allows the researcher to select background design, color, bullets for highlighting, and other graphic effects that make communication of the message more effective. It is a good idea to use simple, attractive graphics and avoid overwhelming the audience with flashiness.[6]

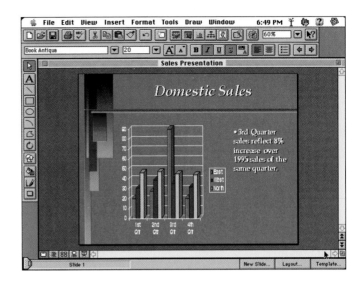

audiences, the researcher may put the visual aids on posters or flip charts. Another possibility is to duplicate copies of the charts for each participant, possibly supplemented with one of the other forms of presentation.

Whatever medium is chosen, each visual aid should be designed to convey a simple, attention-getting message that supports a point on which the audience should focus its thinking. As with written presentations, presenters should interpret the graphics for the audience. The best slides are easy to read and interpret. Large typefaces, multiple colors, bullets that highlight, and other artistic devices can enhance the readability of charts. It is also wise for presenters to allow the audience adequate time to read and familiarize themselves with the variables presented on slides.

The use of gestures during presentations also can help convey the message and make the presentation more interesting.

## ■ THE RESEARCH FOLLOW-UP

**Research follow-up**
Recontacting decision makers and/or clients after they have read the research report to determine whether they need additional information or to have some issues clarified.

Research reports and oral presentations should communicate research findings so that managers can make business decisions. In many cases, the manager who receives the research report is unable to interpret the information and draw conclusions relevant to managerial decisions. For this reason, effective researchers do not treat the report as the end of the research process. They conduct a **research follow-up,** in which they recontact decision makers and/or clients after the latter have had a chance to read over the report. The purpose is to determine whether the researchers need to provide additional information or clarify some issues that may concern management. Just as marketing research may help an organization learn about its customers' satisfaction, the research follow-up can help marketing research staffers ensure the satisfaction of their customers, marketing management.

## SUMMARY

Report preparation is the final stage of the research project. It is an important stage, because the project can guide management decisions only if it is effectively communicated. The research report is the presentation of the research findings directed to a specific audience to accomplish a particular purpose.

The general format for research reports includes certain prefatory sections, the body of the report, and appended parts. The report format should be tailored to the level of formality of the particular situation.

The prefatory parts of a formal report include a title page, letters of transmittal and authorization, a table of contents, and a summary. The summary is the most often read part of a report and should include a brief statement of the objectives, results, conclusions, and recommendations. The report body includes an introduction that gives the background and objectives, a statement of methodology, and a discussion of the results, their limitations, and appropriate conclusions and recommendations. The appendix includes various material that is too specialized to appear in the body of the report.

Most research projects will be reported orally as well as in writing, so the researcher needs to prepare an oral presentation. The presentation should defend the results without being defensive. It must be tailored to the situation and the audience.

The research follow-up involves recontacting decision makers after the report has been submitted to determine whether the researchers need to provide further information or clarify any issues of concern to management.

## ■ Key Terms and Concepts

| | |
|---|---|
| Research report | Results section |
| Report format | Conclusions and recommendations section |
| Introduction section | Oral presentation |
| Research methodology section | Research follow-up |

## ■ Questions

1. Why is the research report important?
2. As a manager, what degree of formality would you want from your research department?
3. Go to your library and find some research reports. How do they meet the standards set forth in this chapter?
4. How does the oral presentation of research differ from the written research report?

## EXPLORING THE INTERNET

1. Georgia Institute of Technology's Graphics, Visualization, and Useability Center (http://www.gvu.gatech.edu) reports results of its WWW surveys. Click on one of its surveys to see an entire research report.

2. For a summary report, see eTRUST Internet Privacy Study. This report prepared by the Boston Consulting Group for the FCC can be found at:
http://www.ftc.gov/bcp/privacy2/comments1/etrust/index.htm.

## ■ Endnotes

[1] This chapter was written by John Bush, Oklahoma State University. It originally appeared in William G. Zikmund, *Business Research Methods* (Hinsdale, Ill.: Dryden Press, 1984), and is adapted with permission.

[2] David M. Robinson, *Writing Reports for Management Decisions* (Columbus, Ohio: Merrill, 1969), p. 294.

[3] Ibid., p. 297.

[4] This discussion is based on Robinson, *Writing Reports,* pp. 300, 338–339, and Jessamon Dawe and William Jackson Lord, Jr., *Functional Business Communication* (Englewood Cliffs, N.J.: Prentice-Hall, 1968), p. 414.

[5] "A Speech Tip," *Communication Briefings,* 14(2), p. 3.

[6] "Present-ability in the real world," *Microsoft Magazine,* Winter 1994, p. 20.

# $1$ ◆ SUNBELT ENERGY CORPORATION

Sunbelt Energy Corporation is a diversified petroleum company engaged in producing and marketing gasoline, motor oil, petrochemicals, and a number of other energy-related activities such as coal mining, uranium extraction, and atomic power generation. Sunbelt markets its petroleum products through its own retail outlets and independent suppliers in a 25-state area within the continental United States. Sunbelt's company-owned service stations feature the latest in station design and automation. Sunbelt's retail marketing strategy emphasizes modern station designs, and the firm continually works to improve the appearance of both its company-owned and independent retail outlets. A research study to investigate consumers' reaction to a new method of payment was conducted in a single town in which the company owns all stations. The company investigated the use of automated payment machines (using the same technology as automated teller machines used by banks) and gasoline credit cards for payment of gasoline services.

The specific objectives of the research were to determine the following:

1. The overall percentage of customers who use the automatic payment machines
2. What machine features people who use the automatic payment machines like
3. What improvements to the machines could be made to assist their current users
4. What improvements to the automatic payment machines could be made to induce nonusers to use the machines
5. The percentage of people who not only purchase gasoline but also purchase something else at the station
6. The percentage of people who pay using cash, a Sunbelt credit card, or a bank credit card

The research was conducted in a southwestern city where the company owns all retail outlets and each station has automatic payment machines. Respondents were interviewed as they filled their cars with gasoline. The personal interview lasted only a few minutes because most people wish to purchase gasoline and then leave as quickly as possible. This time frame restricted the number of questions that could be asked. All questions were short and to the point.

Four stations in the town had automatic teller machines. Fifty interviews were conducted at each station for a total of 200 personal interviews. The stations were

- Station Number 1—Limestone
- Station Number 2—Boulevard
- Station Number 3—Performance Plaza
- Station Number 4—Madison Convenient Store

## ■ SAMPLING

Every automobile that entered the service station in the self-service lanes was considered a member of the sampling frame. After a car arrived, the interviewer waited until the customer got out of his or her car and made a selection at the pump. As the gasoline was being pumped into the tank, interviewers introduced themselves and conducted the interviews. Only one individual refused to grant an interview. The questionnaire is shown in Case Exhibit 1.1.

■ **Case Exhibit 1.1**

**Personal Interview Questionnaire**

"Hello, my name is _____. In cooperation with Sunbelt, I am conducting a survey on how Sunbelt can better serve you. I'd like to ask you a few short questions."

Question 1

To start off, did you know that this station has an automated teller machine?

Yes ___      No ___

Question 2

In addition to a gasoline purchase, are you planning to purchase anything else, such as a soft drink, motor oil, or cigarettes?

Yes ___      No ___

Question 3

For today's purchase, are you planning to pay using the automated teller machine, or are you planning to go inside and pay the station attendant?

Go inside and pay attendant ___          Use the automated teller machine ___
(Skip to Question 9)                      (Proceed to Questions 4, 5, 6, 7, and 8)

Question 4

Have you ever used the automated teller machine to pay for your gasoline purchase?

Yes ___                    No ___
(Proceed to next question)    (Go to question 8)

Question 5

What features of the automated teller machine do you like?

_____
_____
_____
_____
_____

Question 6

What features of the automated teller machine do you dislike?

_____
_____
_____
_____
_____

Question 7

From your viewpoint are there any improvements that could be made to make it easier to use the automated teller machine?

_____
_____
_____
_____
_____

Question 8

Up to today, what features of the automated teller machine have caused you not to use it?

_____
_____
_____
_____

(Skip to the observation section)

Question 9

Will you be paying for your purchase in cash, or will you be using a credit card?

Pay with cash ___              Pay with a credit card ___
(Skip to observation part)     (Proceed to Question 10)

*continued*

**■ Case Exhibit 1.1**

*continued*

Question 10
Will you use a Sunbelt Credit Card, or will you use a Visa or MasterCard for payment?
　　Sunbelt card ___　　　　Use other type ___
　　(Proceed to Question 11)　(Skip to observation section)

Question 11
Have you ever used the automated teller machine for your purchase?
　　Yes ___　　　　　　　No ___
　　(Proceed to Questions 12, 13, and 14)　(Proceed to Question 15)

Question 12
What features of the automated teller machine do you like?

_____
_____
_____
_____
_____

Question 13
What features of the automated teller machine do you dislike?

_____
_____
_____
_____

Question 14
From your viewpoint are there any improvements that could be made to make it easier to use the automated teller machine?

_____
_____
_____
_____
_____

(Skip to observation section)

Question 15
What features of the automated teller machine have caused you not to use it?

_____
_____
_____
_____
_____

(Skip to the observation section)

Observation Section

On behalf of Sunbelt, I thank you for your time and comments.

| | | |
|---|---|---|
| Is the driver of the vehicle male or female? | Male ___ | Female ___ |
| Is the driver under or over 40? | Under ___ | Over ___ |
| Are there any passengers in the vehicle? | Yes ___ | No ___ |
| Does the vehicle have Washington County tags? | Yes ___ | No ___ |

## ■ ADDITIONAL INFORMATION

Several of the questions will require the use of a computerized database. Your instructor will provide information about the floppy disk if this material is part of the case assignment. See Case Exhibit 1.2 for a listing of variable names for the Sunbelt database.

### ■ Questions

1. Evaluate the research objectives.
2. Evaluate the research design in light of the stated research objectives.

■ **Case Exhibit 1.2**

**Variable Names in the Sunbelt Data Set**

| Variable Name | Label |
|---|---|
| ATM | Auto Teller Knowledge |
| ELSE | Purchase Anything Else |
| USE | Use ATM to Pay |
| USEGAS | Use ATM to Pay for Gas |
| CASH | Pay with Cash or Credit Card |
| SUNBELT | Use Sunbelt Credit Card |
| EVER | Ever Use ATM for Purchase |
| SEX | Male or Female |
| AGE | Under or Over 40 |
| PASS | Passengers: Yes or No |
| TAGS | Washington County Tags |

3. Using the computerized database, obtain simple frequencies for the answers to each question (the answers to the open-ended questions are not included in the database).
4. Perform the appropriate cross-tabulations.
5. Perform the appropriate univariate and bivariate statistical tests after you develop hypotheses for these particular tests.

# 2 ◆ EMPLOYEES FEDERAL CREDIT UNION

Employees Federal Credit Union is the credit union for a Fortune 500 firm. Any employee of the organization is eligible for membership in the employees' credit union.

Over the past few years, the Employees Federal Credit Union (EFCU) has accumulated a large amount of surplus cash funds, which have been invested in certificates of deposit. It has also experienced a lower loan/share ratio than other credit unions of similar size. Because of these factors, the credit union's average earnings on its investments have slowly declined and its profit margins are being squeezed. As a result, the EFCU Board of Directors decided that a research project should be conducted to determine why its members are not borrowing money from the credit union. More specifically, the research project was mandated to answer the question of why the members are borrowing money from other alternative sources instead of the credit union.

In addition to the above, the EFCU Board of Directors expressed its desire to determine what the membership's attitudes were toward the overall management and operations of the credit union. It was determined that the following questions should be addressed, as well:

- How informed is the membership about the services provided by the credit union?
- Do any differences in opinion toward borrowing funds and the services provided by the credit union exist between headquarters-based and nonheadquarters-based members?

## ■ RESEARCH OBJECTIVES

To respond to the questions raised by the board, the following objectives were developed. The research design was formulated to address each of the objectives stated below:

- To determine the reasons why people join the credit union
- To determine the reasons why members use other financial institutions when they need to borrow funds
- To measure member attitudes and beliefs about the proficiencies of the credit union employees
- To determine whether there are any perceived differences between headquarters-based and nonheadquarters-based members
- To determine member awareness of the services offered by the credit union
- To measure member attitudes and beliefs about how effectively the credit union is operated

## ■ RESEARCH DESIGN AND DATA COLLECTION METHOD

The research data were collected by a mail questionnaire survey. This technique was determined to be the best method for collecting the research data for the following reasons:

- The wide geographical dispersion of the credit union membership
- The minimization of the cost of conducting the research
- The sensitivity of several of the questions asked in the questionnaire
- The flexibility of being able to wait for the survey results before taking any action

A copy of the questionnaire used to gather the research data is provided in Case Exhibit 2.1. Most of the questions were designed as structured questions because of the variation in the educational backgrounds, job functions, and interests of the members surveyed. However, the respondents were given the flexibility to answer several key questions in an unstructured format. The Likert scale was principally used where attitude measurements were requested.

---

■ **Case Exhibit 2.1**

**EFCU Member Opinion Survey**

1. Are you currently a member of the Employees Federal Credit Union (EFCU)?
   Yes ( )          No ( )
   If no, please have the member of your household who is a member of the EFCU complete the questionnaire. If no one in your household is a member, please return the questionnaire in the enclosed prepaid envelope.

2. Why did you join the credit union? (Check as many answers as are applicable.)
   ___ Convenience
   ___ Higher interest rates on my savings than other financial institutions pay
   ___ More personal than other facilities
   ___ Wanted a readily available source for borrowing money
   ___ Advertisements prompted me to join
   ___ Other—please explain:
   _____

---

Statements 3 through 6 ask for your opinion of the credit union employees. Check the response that best describes your rating of the credit union employees in each category. Please check only one response for each statement.

3. The credit union employees are courteous.

| Strongly disagree | Disagree | Uncertain | Agree | Strongly agree |
|---|---|---|---|---|
| ( ) | ( ) | ( ) | ( ) | ( ) |

4. The credit union employees are helpful.

| Strongly disagree | Disagree | Uncertain | Agree | Strongly agree |
|---|---|---|---|---|
| ( ) | ( ) | ( ) | ( ) | ( ) |

5. The credit union employees are professional.

| Strongly disagree | Disagree | Uncertain | Agree | Strongly agree |
|---|---|---|---|---|
| ( ) | ( ) | ( ) | ( ) | ( ) |

6. The credit union employees are always available.

| Strongly disagree | Disagree | Uncertain | Agree | Strongly agree |
|---|---|---|---|---|
| ( ) | ( ) | ( ) | ( ) | ( ) |

7. What is your opinion about the rates the credit union is paying on its share (members/savings) accounts?
   A. Very high ___          B. High ___          C. Average ___
   D. Low ___               E. Very low ___      F. No opinion ___

8. What is your opinion about the rates the credit union is charging its members to borrow funds?
   A. Very high ___          B. High ___          C. Average ___
   D. Low ___               E. Very low ___      F. No opinion ___

---

*continued*

**■ Case Exhibit 2.1**

*continued*

9. How often do you receive a financial statement of your account activity?

| Too<br>often | Very<br>often | About<br>right | Not often<br>enough | Never |
|:---:|:---:|:---:|:---:|:---:|
| ( ) | ( ) | ( ) | ( ) | ( ) |

10. How would you rate the accuracy of your statements?

| Excellent | Good | Fair | Poor |
|:---:|:---:|:---:|:---:|
| ( ) | ( ) | ( ) | ( ) |

11. Are they easy to understand?
Yes ( )          No ( )

12. Do you feel that the credit union maintains your account information in a confidential manner?
Yes ( )          No ( )

The next set of questions are important in determining how effective the credit union has been in communicating its different services to the members. Please answer each question honestly—remember, there are no right or wrong answers.

Circle the response that best describes your awareness of the services offered by the credit union.

Circle 1—If you were aware of the service and have used it.
Circle 2—If you were aware of the service but have not used it.
Circle 3—If you did not know this service was offered by the credit union.

|  | Aware<br>and<br>Have Used | Aware<br>But Have<br>Not Used | Unaware<br>of<br>Service |
|---|:---:|:---:|:---:|
| 13. Regular share accounts | 1 | 2 | 3 |
| 14. Special subaccounts | 1 | 2 | 3 |
| 15. Christmas club accounts | 1 | 2 | 3 |
| 16. Individual retirement accounts | 1 | 2 | 3 |
| 17. MasterCard credit cards | 1 | 2 | 3 |
| 18. Signature loans | 1 | 2 | 3 |
| 19. New-car loans | 1 | 2 | 3 |
| 20. Late model car loans | 1 | 2 | 3 |
| 21. Older model car loans | 1 | 2 | 3 |
| 22. Household goods/appliance loans | 1 | 2 | 3 |
| 23. Recreational loans | 1 | 2 | 3 |
| 24. Share collateralized loans | 1 | 2 | 3 |
| 25. IRA loans | 1 | 2 | 3 |
| 26. Line of credit loans | 1 | 2 | 3 |

27. Do you currently have a loan with the credit union?
Yes ( )          No ( )

28. During the past year, have you borrowed money from a bank or other lending source other than the credit union?
Yes ( )          No ( )
If no, go to question 30.

29. Why did you go to a source other than the credit union?
____ My loan application at the credit union was not approved.
____ The credit union did not offer this type of credit.
____ I found better loan rates elsewhere.
____ I have an established credit line elsewhere.
____ I prefer to use a local financial institution.
____ Other: _____

For statements 30 through 34, check the response that best describes your feelings about the statements. Check only one response for each statement given.

30. The credit union's loan rates are lower than those offered by other institutions.

| Strongly<br>disagree | Disagree | Uncertain | Agree | Strongly<br>agree |
|:---:|:---:|:---:|:---:|:---:|
| ( ) | ( ) | ( ) | ( ) | ( ) |

*continued*

■ **Case Exhibit 2.1**

*continued*

31. The credit union personnel will keep my personal financial information confidential.

| Strongly disagree | Disagree | Uncertain | Agree | Strongly agree |
|---|---|---|---|---|
| ( ) | ( ) | ( ) | ( ) | ( ) |

32. The credit union is prompt in processing loan applications.

| Strongly disagree | Disagree | Uncertain | Agree | Strongly agree |
|---|---|---|---|---|
| ( ) | ( ) | ( ) | ( ) | ( ) |

33. The current financial services provided by the credit union meet the needs of its members.

| Strongly disagree | Disagree | Uncertain | Agree | Strongly agree |
|---|---|---|---|---|
| ( ) | ( ) | ( ) | ( ) | ( ) |

34. The loan applications used by the credit union are simple and easy to complete.

| Strongly disagree | Disagree | Uncertain | Agree | Strongly agree |
|---|---|---|---|---|
| ( ) | ( ) | ( ) | ( ) | ( ) |

35. Which of the services provided by the credit union do you like best?

36. Which of the services provided by the credit union do you like least?

37. Overall, how do you feel the credit union is being managed and operated?

A. Excellent___      B. Good___      C. Average___

D. Poor___      E. Very poor___      F. No opinion___

38. Do you live in the headquarters area?

Yes ( )      No ( )

If yes, go to question 40.

39. Do you feel the credit union meets your needs as well as those members who live in the headquarters area?

Yes ( )      No ( )

If no, please explain:

_____

_____

40. If you were managing the credit union, what changes would you make and what additional services, if any, would you provide?

_____

_____

_____

_____

_____

I sincerely appreciate the time and effort you made in completing this questionnaire. Thank you for your help.

## ■ SAMPLING PROCEDURES

The population of the EFCU is well-defined; consequently, a simple random sample of the membership was selected. A sample size of 300 was calculated using the estimated population standard deviation based on the responses from 15 members to question 37 of the questionnaire. Question 37 was used because it capsulized the essence of the research project.

The random numbers used in making the selection of the sampling units were generated with the help of a personal computer. The sampling frame used was the January 31, 1992, trial balance listing of the EFCU membership. According to the sampling frame, EFCU had 3,531 members on that date. As a result, the 300 random numbers were generated within the range of 1 to 3,531. The random numbers were matched to a corresponding number in the sampling frame, and those individuals were selected to receive copies of the survey questionnaire.

# ■ FIELDWORK

Most of the fieldwork for the research project, including all of the editing and coding of the survey data, was performed by the Supervisory Committee Chairperson. The following is a list of the (much-appreciated) assistance received during the field procedures:

- Bob Perkins obtained a copy of the most currently available listing of the membership of the EFCU.
- The payroll department prepared mailing labels for all the members in the sample who were having withholding for the credit union made out of their payroll checks.
- The credit union clerks obtained the addresses and prepared mailing labels for all the remaining individuals selected in the sample.
- Administrative assistants helped in copying and collating the survey questionnaires and preparing them for mailing.
- Ron Walker mailed all of the survey questionnaires.

The survey data from the structured questions were coded based on classifications established by the researcher. The codes were input into a series of databases using an IBM personal computer and a statistical software package.

Of the 125 returned questionnaires, two were not included in the survey results. One of the questionnaires was returned without the first two pages attached, and the other questionnaire appeared to be deliberately falsified. Not only were all the responses of the falsified questionnaire at the extremes, but a number of noted contradictions existed, as well.

# ■ ADDITIONAL INFORMATION

Several of the questions will require the use of a computerized database. Each variable name is represented by its question number. Q1 is the variable name for question 1, "Are you a member of the Employees Federal Credit Union?" Q2 is the variable name for question 2, etc. Your instructor will provide information about the floppy disk containing the EFCU's data set if this material is part of the case assignment.

## ■ Questions

1. Evaluate the research objectives.
2. Evaluate the research design in light of the stated research objectives.
3. Using the computerized database, obtain simple frequencies for the answers to each question (the answers to the open-ended questions are not included in the database).
4. Perform the appropriate cross-tabulations.
5. Perform the appropriate univariate and bivariate statistical tests after you develop hypotheses for these particular tests.

# APPENDIX

# *A*  STATISTICAL TABLES

■ **Table A.1**

**Random Digits**

| | | | | | | | | | |
|---|---|---|---|---|---|---|---|---|---|
| 37751 | 04998 | 66038 | 63480 | 98442 | 22245 | 83538 | 62351 | 74514 | 90497 |
| 50915 | 64152 | 82981 | 15796 | 27102 | 71635 | 34470 | 13608 | 26360 | 76285 |
| 99142 | 35021 | 01032 | 57907 | 80545 | 54112 | 15150 | 36856 | 03247 | 40392 |
| 70720 | 10033 | 25191 | 62358 | 03784 | 74377 | 88150 | 25567 | 87457 | 49512 |
| 18460 | 64947 | 32958 | 08752 | 96366 | 89092 | 23597 | 74308 | 00881 | 88976 |
| | | | | | | | | | |
| 65763 | 41133 | 60950 | 35372 | 06782 | 81451 | 78764 | 52645 | 19841 | 50083 |
| 83769 | 52570 | 60133 | 25211 | 87384 | 90182 | 84990 | 26400 | 39128 | 97043 |
| 58900 | 78420 | 98579 | 33665 | 10718 | 39342 | 46346 | 14401 | 13503 | 46525 |
| 54746 | 71115 | 78219 | 64314 | 11227 | 41702 | 54517 | 87676 | 14078 | 45317 |
| 56819 | 27340 | 07200 | 52663 | 57864 | 85159 | 15460 | 97564 | 29637 | 27742 |
| | | | | | | | | | |
| 34990 | 62122 | 38223 | 28526 | 37006 | 22774 | 46026 | 15981 | 87291 | 56946 |
| 02269 | 22795 | 87593 | 81830 | 95383 | 67823 | 20196 | 54850 | 46779 | 64519 |
| 43042 | 53600 | 45738 | 00261 | 31100 | 67239 | 02004 | 70698 | 53597 | 62617 |
| 92565 | 12211 | 06868 | 87786 | 59576 | 61382 | 33972 | 13161 | 47208 | 96604 |
| 67424 | 32620 | 60841 | 86848 | 85000 | 04835 | 48576 | 33884 | 10101 | 84129 |
| | | | | | | | | | |
| 04015 | 77148 | 09535 | 10743 | 97871 | 55919 | 45274 | 38304 | 93125 | 91847 |
| 85226 | 19763 | 46105 | 25289 | 26714 | 73253 | 85922 | 21785 | 42624 | 92741 |
| 03360 | 07457 | 75131 | 41209 | 50451 | 23472 | 07438 | 08375 | 29312 | 62264 |
| 72460 | 99682 | 27970 | 25632 | 34096 | 17656 | 12736 | 27476 | 21938 | 67305 |
| 66960 | 55780 | 71778 | 52629 | 51692 | 71442 | 36130 | 70425 | 39874 | 62035 |
| | | | | | | | | | |
| 14824 | 95631 | 00697 | 65462 | 24815 | 13930 | 02938 | 54619 | 28909 | 53950 |
| 34001 | 05618 | 41900 | 23303 | 19928 | 60755 | 61404 | 56947 | 91441 | 19299 |
| 77718 | 83830 | 29781 | 72917 | 10840 | 74182 | 08293 | 62588 | 99625 | 22088 |
| 60930 | 05091 | 35726 | 07414 | 49211 | 69586 | 20226 | 08274 | 28167 | 65279 |
| 94180 | 62151 | 08112 | 26646 | 07617 | 42954 | 22521 | 09395 | 43561 | 45692 |
| | | | | | | | | | |
| 81073 | 85543 | 47650 | 93830 | 07377 | 87995 | 35084 | 39386 | 93141 | 88309 |
| 18467 | 39689 | 60801 | 46828 | 38670 | 88243 | 89042 | 78452 | 08032 | 72566 |
| 60643 | 59399 | 79740 | 17295 | 50094 | 66436 | 92677 | 68345 | 24025 | 36489 |
| 73372 | 61697 | 85728 | 90779 | 13235 | 83114 | 70728 | 32093 | 74306 | 08325 |
| 18395 | 18482 | 83245 | 54942 | 51905 | 09534 | 70839 | 91073 | 42193 | 81199 |
| | | | | | | | | | |
| 07261 | 28720 | 71244 | 05064 | 84873 | 68020 | 39037 | 68981 | 00670 | 86291 |
| 61679 | 81529 | 83725 | 33269 | 45958 | 74265 | 87460 | 60525 | 42539 | 25605 |
| 11815 | 48679 | 00556 | 96871 | 39835 | 83055 | 84949 | 11681 | 51687 | 55896 |
| 99007 | 35050 | 86440 | 44280 | 20320 | 97527 | 28138 | 01088 | 49037 | 85430 |
| 06446 | 65608 | 79291 | 16624 | 06135 | 30622 | 56133 | 33998 | 32308 | 29434 |

## ■ Table A.2

**Area under the Normal Curve**

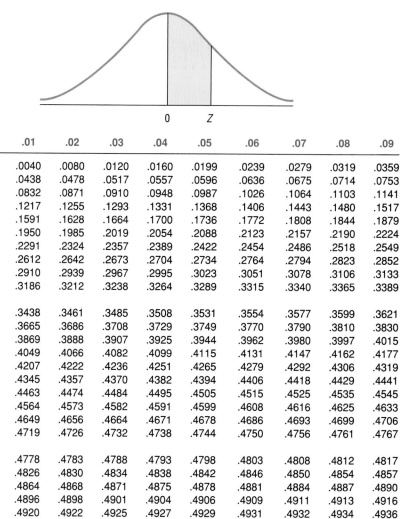

| z | .00 | .01 | .02 | .03 | .04 | .05 | .06 | .07 | .08 | .09 |
|---|-----|-----|-----|-----|-----|-----|-----|-----|-----|-----|
| 0.0 | .0000 | .0040 | .0080 | .0120 | .0160 | .0199 | .0239 | .0279 | .0319 | .0359 |
| 0.1 | .0398 | .0438 | .0478 | .0517 | .0557 | .0596 | .0636 | .0675 | .0714 | .0753 |
| 0.2 | .0793 | .0832 | .0871 | .0910 | .0948 | .0987 | .1026 | .1064 | .1103 | .1141 |
| 0.3 | .1179 | .1217 | .1255 | .1293 | .1331 | .1368 | .1406 | .1443 | .1480 | .1517 |
| 0.4 | .1554 | .1591 | .1628 | .1664 | .1700 | .1736 | .1772 | .1808 | .1844 | .1879 |
| 0.5 | .1915 | .1950 | .1985 | .2019 | .2054 | .2088 | .2123 | .2157 | .2190 | .2224 |
| 0.6 | .2257 | .2291 | .2324 | .2357 | .2389 | .2422 | .2454 | .2486 | .2518 | .2549 |
| 0.7 | .2580 | .2612 | .2642 | .2673 | .2704 | .2734 | .2764 | .2794 | .2823 | .2852 |
| 0.8 | .2881 | .2910 | .2939 | .2967 | .2995 | .3023 | .3051 | .3078 | .3106 | .3133 |
| 0.9 | .3159 | .3186 | .3212 | .3238 | .3264 | .3289 | .3315 | .3340 | .3365 | .3389 |
| 1.0 | .3413 | .3438 | .3461 | .3485 | .3508 | .3531 | .3554 | .3577 | .3599 | .3621 |
| 1.1 | .3643 | .3665 | .3686 | .3708 | .3729 | .3749 | .3770 | .3790 | .3810 | .3830 |
| 1.2 | .3849 | .3869 | .3888 | .3907 | .3925 | .3944 | .3962 | .3980 | .3997 | .4015 |
| 1.3 | .4032 | .4049 | .4066 | .4082 | .4099 | .4115 | .4131 | .4147 | .4162 | .4177 |
| 1.4 | .4192 | .4207 | .4222 | .4236 | .4251 | .4265 | .4279 | .4292 | .4306 | .4319 |
| 1.5 | .4332 | .4345 | .4357 | .4370 | .4382 | .4394 | .4406 | .4418 | .4429 | .4441 |
| 1.6 | .4452 | .4463 | .4474 | .4484 | .4495 | .4505 | .4515 | .4525 | .4535 | .4545 |
| 1.7 | .4554 | .4564 | .4573 | .4582 | .4591 | .4599 | .4608 | .4616 | .4625 | .4633 |
| 1.8 | .4641 | .4649 | .4656 | .4664 | .4671 | .4678 | .4686 | .4693 | .4699 | .4706 |
| 1.9 | .4713 | .4719 | .4726 | .4732 | .4738 | .4744 | .4750 | .4756 | .4761 | .4767 |
| 2.0 | .4772 | .4778 | .4783 | .4788 | .4793 | .4798 | .4803 | .4808 | .4812 | .4817 |
| 2.1 | .4821 | .4826 | .4830 | .4834 | .4838 | .4842 | .4846 | .4850 | .4854 | .4857 |
| 2.2 | .4861 | .4864 | .4868 | .4871 | .4875 | .4878 | .4881 | .4884 | .4887 | .4890 |
| 2.3 | .4893 | .4896 | .4898 | .4901 | .4904 | .4906 | .4909 | .4911 | .4913 | .4916 |
| 2.4 | .4918 | .4920 | .4922 | .4925 | .4927 | .4929 | .4931 | .4932 | .4934 | .4936 |
| 2.5 | .4938 | .4940 | .4941 | .4943 | .4945 | .4946 | .4948 | .4949 | .4951 | .4952 |
| 2.6 | .4953 | .4955 | .4956 | .4957 | .4959 | .4960 | .4961 | .4962 | .4963 | .4964 |
| 2.7 | .4965 | .4966 | .4967 | .4968 | .4969 | .4970 | .4971 | .4972 | .4973 | .4974 |
| 2.8 | .4974 | .4975 | .4976 | .4977 | .4977 | .4978 | .4979 | .4979 | .4980 | .4981 |
| 2.9 | .4981 | .4982 | .4982 | .4983 | .4984 | .4984 | .4985 | .4985 | .4986 | .4986 |
| 3.0 | .49865 | .4987 | .4987 | .4988 | .4988 | .4989 | .4989 | .4989 | .4990 | .4990 |
| 4.0 | .49997 | | | | | | | | | |

■ **Table A.3**

**Distribution of *t* for
Given Probability Levels**

| d.f. | Level of Significance for One-Tailed Test | | | | | |
|---|---|---|---|---|---|---|
| | .10 | .05 | .025 | .01 | .005 | .0005 |
| | Level of Significance for Two-Tailed Test | | | | | |
| | .20 | .10 | .05 | .02 | .01 | .001 |
| 1 | 3.078 | 6.314 | 12.706 | 31.821 | 63.657 | 636.619 |
| 2 | 1.886 | 2.920 | 4.303 | 6.965 | 9.925 | 31.598 |
| 3 | 1.638 | 2.353 | 3.182 | 4.541 | 5.841 | 12.941 |
| 4 | 1.533 | 2.132 | 2.776 | 3.747 | 4.604 | 8.610 |
| 5 | 1.476 | 2.015 | 2.571 | 3.365 | 4.032 | 6.859 |
| 6 | 1.440 | 1.943 | 2.447 | 3.143 | 3.707 | 5.959 |
| 7 | 1.415 | 1.895 | 2.365 | 2.998 | 3.499 | 5.405 |
| 8 | 1.397 | 1.860 | 2.306 | 2.896 | 3.355 | 5.041 |
| 9 | 1.383 | 1.833 | 2.262 | 2.821 | 3.250 | 4.781 |
| 10 | 1.372 | 1.812 | 2.228 | 2.764 | 3.169 | 4.587 |
| 11 | 1.363 | 1.796 | 2.201 | 2.718 | 3.106 | 4.437 |
| 12 | 1.356 | 1.782 | 2.179 | 2.681 | 3.055 | 4.318 |
| 13 | 1.350 | 1.771 | 2.160 | 2.650 | 3.012 | 4.221 |
| 14 | 1.345 | 1.761 | 2.145 | 2.624 | 2.977 | 4.140 |
| 15 | 1.341 | 1.753 | 2.131 | 2.602 | 2.947 | 4.073 |
| 16 | 1.337 | 1.746 | 2.120 | 2.583 | 2.921 | 4.015 |
| 17 | 1.333 | 1.740 | 2.110 | 2.567 | 2.898 | 3.965 |
| 18 | 1.330 | 1.734 | 2.101 | 2.552 | 2.878 | 3.992 |
| 19 | 1.328 | 1.729 | 2.093 | 2.539 | 2.861 | 3.883 |
| 20 | 1.325 | 1.725 | 2.086 | 2.528 | 2.845 | 3.850 |
| 21 | 1.323 | 1.721 | 2.080 | 2.518 | 2.831 | 3.819 |
| 22 | 1.321 | 1.717 | 2.074 | 2.508 | 2.819 | 3.792 |
| 23 | 1.319 | 1.714 | 2.069 | 2.500 | 2.807 | 3.767 |
| 24 | 1.318 | 1.711 | 2.064 | 2.492 | 2.797 | 3.745 |
| 25 | 1.316 | 1.708 | 2.060 | 2.485 | 2.787 | 3.725 |
| 26 | 1.315 | 1.706 | 2.056 | 2.479 | 2.779 | 3.707 |
| 27 | 1.314 | 1.703 | 2.052 | 2.473 | 2.771 | 3.690 |
| 28 | 1.313 | 1.701 | 2.048 | 2.467 | 2.763 | 3.674 |
| 29 | 1.311 | 1.699 | 2.045 | 2.462 | 2.756 | 3.659 |
| 30 | 1.310 | 1.697 | 2.042 | 2.457 | 2.750 | 3.646 |
| 40 | 1.303 | 1.684 | 2.021 | 2.423 | 2.704 | 3.551 |
| 60 | 1.296 | 1.671 | 2.000 | 2.390 | 2.660 | 3.460 |
| 120 | 1.289 | 1.658 | 1.980 | 2.358 | 2.617 | 3.373 |
| ∞ | 1.282 | 1.645 | 1.960 | 2.326 | 2.576 | 3.291 |

■ **Table A.4**

**Chi-Square Distribution**

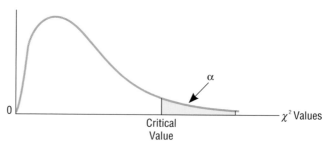

| Degrees of Freedom (d.f.) | Area in Shaded Right Tail ($\alpha$) | | |
|---|---|---|---|
| | .10 | .05 | .01 |
| 1 | 2.706 | 3.841 | 6.635 |
| 2 | 4.605 | 5.991 | 9.210 |
| 3 | 6.251 | 7.815 | 11.345 |
| 4 | 7.779 | 9.488 | 13.277 |
| 5 | 9.236 | 11.070 | 15.086 |
| 6 | 10.645 | 12.592 | 16.812 |
| 7 | 12.017 | 14.067 | 18.475 |
| 8 | 13.362 | 15.507 | 20.090 |
| 9 | 14.684 | 16.919 | 21.666 |
| 10 | 15.987 | 18.307 | 23.209 |
| 11 | 17.275 | 19.675 | 24.725 |
| 12 | 18.549 | 21.026 | 26.217 |
| 13 | 19.812 | 22.362 | 27.688 |
| 14 | 21.064 | 23.685 | 29.141 |
| 15 | 22.307 | 24.996 | 30.578 |
| 16 | 23.542 | 26.296 | 32.000 |
| 17 | 24.769 | 27.587 | 33.409 |
| 18 | 25.989 | 28.869 | 34.805 |
| 19 | 27.204 | 30.144 | 36.191 |
| 20 | 28.412 | 31.410 | 37.566 |
| 21 | 29.615 | 32.671 | 38.932 |
| 22 | 30.813 | 33.924 | 40.289 |
| 23 | 32.007 | 35.172 | 41.638 |
| 24 | 33.196 | 36.415 | 42.980 |
| 25 | 34.382 | 37.652 | 44.314 |
| 26 | 35.563 | 38.885 | 45.642 |
| 27 | 36.741 | 40.113 | 46.963 |
| 28 | 37.916 | 41.337 | 48.278 |
| 29 | 39.087 | 42.557 | 49.588 |
| 30 | 40.256 | 43.773 | 50.892 |

*Example of how to use this table:* In a chi-square distribution with 6 degrees of freedom *(d.f.),* the area to the right of a critical value of 12.592—i.e., the $\alpha$ area—is .05.

■ **Table A.5**  **Critical Values of $F_{\nu_1 \nu_2}$ for $\alpha = .05$**

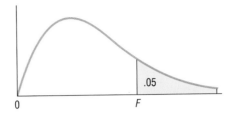

$\nu_1$ = Degrees of Freedom for Numerator

| | 1 | 2 | 3 | 4 | 5 | 6 | 7 | 8 | 9 | 10 | 12 | 15 | 20 | 24 | 30 | 40 | 60 | 120 | ∞ |
|---|---|---|---|---|---|---|---|---|---|---|---|---|---|---|---|---|---|---|---|
| 1 | 161 | 200 | 216 | 225 | 230 | 234 | 237 | 239 | 241 | 242 | 244 | 246 | 248 | 249 | 250 | 251 | 252 | 253 | 254 |
| 2 | 18.5 | 19.0 | 19.2 | 19.2 | 19.3 | 19.3 | 19.4 | 19.4 | 19.4 | 19.4 | 19.4 | 19.4 | 19.5 | 19.5 | 19.5 | 19.5 | 19.5 | 19.5 | 19.5 |
| 3 | 10.1 | 9.55 | 9.28 | 9.12 | 9.01 | 8.94 | 8.89 | 8.85 | 8.81 | 8.79 | 8.74 | 8.70 | 8.66 | 8.64 | 8.62 | 8.59 | 8.57 | 8.55 | 8.53 |
| 4 | 7.71 | 6.94 | 6.59 | 6.39 | 6.26 | 6.16 | 6.09 | 6.04 | 6.00 | 5.96 | 5.91 | 5.86 | 5.80 | 5.77 | 5.75 | 5.72 | 5.69 | 5.66 | 5.63 |
| 5 | 6.61 | 5.79 | 5.41 | 5.19 | 5.05 | 4.95 | 4.88 | 4.82 | 4.77 | 4.74 | 4.68 | 4.62 | 4.56 | 4.53 | 4.50 | 4.46 | 4.43 | 4.40 | 4.37 |
| 6 | 5.99 | 5.14 | 4.76 | 4.53 | 4.39 | 4.28 | 4.21 | 4.15 | 4.10 | 4.06 | 4.00 | 3.94 | 3.87 | 3.84 | 3.81 | 3.77 | 3.74 | 3.70 | 3.67 |
| 7 | 5.59 | 4.74 | 4.35 | 4.12 | 3.97 | 3.87 | 3.79 | 3.73 | 3.68 | 3.64 | 3.57 | 3.51 | 3.44 | 3.41 | 3.38 | 3.34 | 3.30 | 3.27 | 3.23 |
| 8 | 5.32 | 4.46 | 4.07 | 3.84 | 3.69 | 3.58 | 3.50 | 3.44 | 3.39 | 3.35 | 3.28 | 3.22 | 3.15 | 3.12 | 3.08 | 3.04 | 3.01 | 2.97 | 2.93 |
| 9 | 5.12 | 4.26 | 3.86 | 3.63 | 3.48 | 3.37 | 3.29 | 3.23 | 3.18 | 3.14 | 3.07 | 3.01 | 2.94 | 2.90 | 2.86 | 2.83 | 2.79 | 2.75 | 2.71 |
| 10 | 4.96 | 4.10 | 3.71 | 3.48 | 3.33 | 3.22 | 3.14 | 3.07 | 3.02 | 2.98 | 2.91 | 2.85 | 2.77 | 2.74 | 2.70 | 2.66 | 2.62 | 2.58 | 2.54 |
| 11 | 4.84 | 3.98 | 3.59 | 3.36 | 3.20 | 3.09 | 3.01 | 2.95 | 2.90 | 2.85 | 2.79 | 2.72 | 2.65 | 2.61 | 2.57 | 2.53 | 2.49 | 2.45 | 2.40 |
| 12 | 4.75 | 3.89 | 3.49 | 3.26 | 3.11 | 3.00 | 2.91 | 2.85 | 2.80 | 2.75 | 2.69 | 2.62 | 2.54 | 2.51 | 2.47 | 2.43 | 2.38 | 2.34 | 2.30 |
| 13 | 4.67 | 3.81 | 3.41 | 3.18 | 3.03 | 2.92 | 2.83 | 2.77 | 2.71 | 2.67 | 2.60 | 2.53 | 2.46 | 2.42 | 2.38 | 2.34 | 2.30 | 2.25 | 2.21 |
| 14 | 4.60 | 3.74 | 3.34 | 3.11 | 2.96 | 2.85 | 2.76 | 2.70 | 2.65 | 2.60 | 2.53 | 2.46 | 2.39 | 2.35 | 2.31 | 2.27 | 2.22 | 2.18 | 2.13 |
| 15 | 4.54 | 3.68 | 3.29 | 3.06 | 2.90 | 2.79 | 2.71 | 2.64 | 2.59 | 2.54 | 2.48 | 2.40 | 2.33 | 2.29 | 2.25 | 2.20 | 2.16 | 2.11 | 2.07 |
| 16 | 4.49 | 3.63 | 3.24 | 3.01 | 2.85 | 2.74 | 2.66 | 2.59 | 2.54 | 2.49 | 2.42 | 2.35 | 2.28 | 2.24 | 2.19 | 2.15 | 2.11 | 2.06 | 2.01 |
| 17 | 4.45 | 3.59 | 3.20 | 2.96 | 2.81 | 2.70 | 2.61 | 2.55 | 2.49 | 2.45 | 2.38 | 2.31 | 2.23 | 2.19 | 2.15 | 2.10 | 2.06 | 2.01 | 1.96 |
| 18 | 4.41 | 3.55 | 3.16 | 2.93 | 2.77 | 2.66 | 2.58 | 2.51 | 2.46 | 2.41 | 2.34 | 2.27 | 2.19 | 2.15 | 2.11 | 2.06 | 2.02 | 1.97 | 1.92 |
| 19 | 4.38 | 3.52 | 3.13 | 2.90 | 2.74 | 2.63 | 2.54 | 2.48 | 2.42 | 2.38 | 2.31 | 2.23 | 2.16 | 2.11 | 2.07 | 2.03 | 1.98 | 1.93 | 1.88 |
| 20 | 4.35 | 3.49 | 3.10 | 2.87 | 2.71 | 2.60 | 2.51 | 2.45 | 2.39 | 2.35 | 2.28 | 2.20 | 2.12 | 2.08 | 2.04 | 1.99 | 1.95 | 1.90 | 1.84 |
| 21 | 4.32 | 3.47 | 3.07 | 2.84 | 2.68 | 2.57 | 2.49 | 2.42 | 2.37 | 2.32 | 2.25 | 2.18 | 2.10 | 2.05 | 2.01 | 1.96 | 1.92 | 1.87 | 1.81 |
| 22 | 4.30 | 3.44 | 3.05 | 2.82 | 2.66 | 2.55 | 2.46 | 2.40 | 2.34 | 2.30 | 2.23 | 2.15 | 2.07 | 2.03 | 1.98 | 1.94 | 1.89 | 1.84 | 1.78 |
| 23 | 4.28 | 3.42 | 3.03 | 2.80 | 2.64 | 2.53 | 2.44 | 2.37 | 2.32 | 2.27 | 2.20 | 2.13 | 2.05 | 2.01 | 1.96 | 1.91 | 1.86 | 1.81 | 1.76 |
| 24 | 4.26 | 3.40 | 3.01 | 2.78 | 2.62 | 2.51 | 2.42 | 2.36 | 2.30 | 2.25 | 2.18 | 2.11 | 2.03 | 1.98 | 1.94 | 1.89 | 1.84 | 1.79 | 1.73 |
| 25 | 4.24 | 3.39 | 2.99 | 2.76 | 2.60 | 2.49 | 2.40 | 2.34 | 2.28 | 2.24 | 2.16 | 2.09 | 2.01 | 1.96 | 1.92 | 1.87 | 1.82 | 1.77 | 1.71 |
| 30 | 4.17 | 3.32 | 2.92 | 2.69 | 2.53 | 2.42 | 2.33 | 2.27 | 2.21 | 2.16 | 2.09 | 2.01 | 1.93 | 1.89 | 1.84 | 1.79 | 1.74 | 1.68 | 1.62 |
| 40 | 4.08 | 3.23 | 2.84 | 2.61 | 2.45 | 2.34 | 2.25 | 2.18 | 2.12 | 2.08 | 2.00 | 1.92 | 1.84 | 1.79 | 1.74 | 1.69 | 1.64 | 1.58 | 1.51 |
| 60 | 4.00 | 3.15 | 2.76 | 2.53 | 2.37 | 2.25 | 2.17 | 2.10 | 2.04 | 1.99 | 1.92 | 1.84 | 1.75 | 1.70 | 1.65 | 1.59 | 1.53 | 1.47 | 1.39 |
| 120 | 3.92 | 3.07 | 2.68 | 2.45 | 2.29 | 2.18 | 2.09 | 2.02 | 1.96 | 1.91 | 1.83 | 1.75 | 1.66 | 1.61 | 1.55 | 1.50 | 1.43 | 1.35 | 1.25 |
| ∞ | 3.84 | 3.00 | 2.60 | 2.37 | 2.21 | 2.10 | 2.01 | 1.94 | 1.88 | 1.83 | 1.75 | 1.67 | 1.57 | 1.52 | 1.46 | 1.39 | 1.32 | 1.22 | 1.00 |

$\nu_2$ = Degrees of Freedom for Denominator

## ■ Table A.6

### Critical Values of $F_{\nu_1\nu_2}$ for $\alpha = .01$

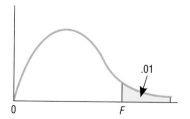

$v_1$ = Degrees of Freedom for Numerator

| $v_2$ | 1 | 2 | 3 | 4 | 5 | 6 | 7 | 8 | 9 | 10 | 12 | 15 | 20 | 24 | 30 | 40 | 60 | 120 | ∞ |
|---|---|---|---|---|---|---|---|---|---|---|---|---|---|---|---|---|---|---|---|
| 1 | 4,052 | 5,000 | 5,403 | 5,625 | 5,764 | 5,859 | 5,928 | 5,982 | 6,023 | 6,056 | 6,106 | 6,157 | 6,209 | 6,235 | 6,261 | 6,287 | 6,313 | 6,339 | 6,366 |
| 2 | 98.5 | 99.0 | 99.2 | 99.2 | 99.3 | 99.3 | 99.4 | 99.4 | 99.4 | 99.4 | 99.4 | 99.4 | 99.4 | 99.5 | 99.5 | 99.5 | 99.5 | 99.5 | 99.5 |
| 3 | 34.1 | 30.8 | 29.5 | 28.7 | 28.2 | 27.9 | 27.7 | 27.5 | 27.3 | 27.2 | 27.1 | 26.9 | 26.7 | 26.6 | 26.5 | 26.4 | 26.3 | 26.2 | 26.1 |
| 4 | 21.2 | 18.0 | 16.7 | 16.0 | 15.5 | 15.2 | 15.0 | 14.8 | 14.7 | 14.5 | 14.4 | 14.2 | 14.0 | 13.9 | 13.8 | 13.7 | 13.7 | 13.6 | 13.5 |
| 5 | 16.3 | 13.3 | 12.1 | 11.4 | 11.0 | 10.7 | 10.5 | 10.3 | 10.2 | 10.1 | 9.89 | 9.72 | 9.55 | 9.47 | 9.38 | 9.29 | 9.20 | 9.11 | 9.02 |
| 6 | 13.7 | 10.9 | 9.78 | 9.15 | 8.75 | 8.47 | 8.26 | 8.10 | 7.98 | 7.87 | 7.72 | 7.56 | 7.40 | 7.31 | 7.23 | 7.14 | 7.06 | 6.97 | 6.88 |
| 7 | 12.2 | 9.55 | 8.45 | 7.85 | 7.46 | 7.19 | 6.99 | 6.84 | 6.72 | 6.62 | 6.47 | 6.31 | 6.16 | 6.07 | 5.99 | 5.91 | 5.82 | 5.74 | 5.65 |
| 8 | 11.3 | 8.65 | 7.59 | 7.01 | 6.63 | 6.37 | 6.18 | 6.03 | 5.91 | 5.81 | 5.67 | 5.52 | 5.36 | 5.28 | 5.20 | 5.12 | 5.03 | 4.95 | 4.86 |
| 9 | 10.6 | 8.02 | 6.99 | 6.42 | 6.06 | 5.80 | 5.61 | 5.47 | 5.35 | 5.26 | 5.11 | 4.96 | 4.81 | 4.73 | 4.65 | 4.57 | 4.48 | 4.40 | 4.31 |
| 10 | 10.0 | 7.56 | 6.55 | 5.99 | 5.64 | 5.39 | 5.20 | 5.06 | 4.94 | 4.85 | 4.71 | 4.56 | 4.41 | 4.33 | 4.25 | 4.17 | 4.08 | 4.00 | 3.91 |
| 11 | 9.65 | 7.21 | 6.22 | 5.67 | 5.32 | 5.07 | 4.89 | 4.74 | 4.63 | 4.54 | 4.40 | 4.25 | 4.10 | 4.02 | 3.94 | 3.86 | 3.78 | 3.69 | 3.60 |
| 12 | 9.33 | 6.93 | 5.95 | 5.41 | 5.06 | 4.82 | 4.64 | 4.50 | 4.39 | 4.30 | 4.16 | 4.01 | 3.86 | 3.78 | 3.70 | 3.62 | 3.54 | 3.45 | 3.36 |
| 13 | 9.07 | 6.70 | 5.74 | 5.21 | 4.86 | 4.62 | 4.44 | 4.30 | 4.19 | 4.10 | 3.96 | 3.82 | 3.66 | 3.59 | 3.51 | 3.43 | 3.34 | 3.25 | 3.17 |
| 14 | 8.86 | 6.51 | 5.56 | 5.04 | 4.70 | 4.46 | 4.28 | 4.14 | 4.03 | 3.94 | 3.80 | 3.66 | 3.51 | 3.43 | 3.35 | 3.27 | 3.18 | 3.09 | 3.00 |
| 15 | 8.68 | 6.36 | 5.42 | 4.89 | 4.56 | 4.32 | 4.14 | 4.00 | 3.89 | 3.80 | 3.67 | 3.52 | 3.37 | 3.29 | 3.21 | 3.13 | 3.05 | 2.96 | 2.87 |
| 16 | 8.53 | 6.23 | 5.29 | 4.77 | 4.44 | 4.20 | 4.03 | 3.89 | 3.78 | 3.69 | 3.55 | 3.41 | 3.26 | 3.18 | 3.10 | 3.02 | 2.93 | 2.84 | 2.75 |
| 17 | 8.40 | 6.11 | 5.19 | 4.67 | 4.34 | 4.10 | 3.93 | 3.79 | 3.68 | 3.59 | 3.46 | 3.31 | 3.16 | 3.08 | 3.00 | 2.92 | 2.83 | 2.75 | 2.65 |
| 18 | 8.29 | 6.01 | 5.09 | 4.58 | 4.25 | 4.01 | 3.84 | 3.71 | 3.60 | 3.51 | 3.37 | 3.23 | 3.08 | 3.00 | 2.92 | 2.84 | 2.75 | 2.66 | 2.57 |
| 19 | 8.19 | 5.93 | 5.01 | 4.50 | 4.17 | 3.94 | 3.77 | 3.63 | 3.52 | 3.43 | 3.30 | 3.15 | 3.00 | 2.92 | 2.84 | 2.76 | 2.67 | 2.58 | 2.49 |
| 20 | 8.10 | 5.85 | 4.94 | 4.43 | 4.10 | 3.87 | 3.70 | 3.56 | 3.46 | 3.37 | 3.23 | 3.09 | 2.94 | 2.86 | 2.78 | 2.69 | 2.61 | 2.52 | 2.42 |
| 21 | 8.02 | 5.78 | 4.87 | 4.37 | 4.04 | 3.81 | 3.64 | 3.51 | 3.40 | 3.31 | 3.17 | 3.03 | 2.88 | 2.80 | 2.72 | 2.64 | 2.55 | 2.46 | 2.36 |
| 22 | 7.96 | 5.72 | 4.82 | 4.31 | 3.99 | 3.76 | 3.59 | 3.45 | 3.35 | 3.26 | 3.12 | 2.98 | 2.83 | 2.75 | 2.67 | 2.58 | 2.50 | 2.40 | 2.31 |
| 23 | 7.88 | 5.66 | 4.76 | 4.26 | 3.94 | 3.71 | 3.54 | 3.41 | 3.30 | 3.21 | 3.07 | 2.93 | 2.78 | 2.70 | 2.62 | 2.54 | 2.45 | 2.35 | 2.26 |
| 24 | 7.82 | 5.61 | 4.72 | 4.22 | 3.90 | 3.67 | 3.50 | 3.36 | 3.26 | 3.17 | 3.03 | 2.89 | 2.74 | 2.66 | 2.58 | 2.49 | 2.40 | 2.31 | 2.21 |
| 25 | 7.77 | 5.57 | 4.68 | 4.18 | 3.86 | 3.63 | 3.46 | 3.32 | 3.22 | 3.13 | 2.99 | 2.85 | 2.70 | 2.62 | 2.53 | 2.45 | 2.36 | 2.27 | 2.17 |
| 30 | 7.58 | 5.39 | 4.51 | 4.02 | 3.70 | 3.47 | 3.30 | 3.17 | 3.07 | 2.98 | 2.84 | 2.70 | 2.55 | 2.47 | 2.39 | 2.30 | 2.21 | 2.11 | 2.01 |
| 40 | 7.31 | 5.18 | 4.31 | 3.83 | 3.51 | 3.29 | 3.12 | 2.99 | 2.89 | 2.80 | 2.66 | 2.52 | 2.37 | 2.29 | 2.20 | 2.11 | 2.02 | 1.92 | 1.80 |
| 60 | 7.08 | 4.98 | 4.13 | 3.65 | 3.34 | 3.12 | 2.95 | 2.82 | 2.72 | 2.63 | 2.50 | 2.35 | 2.20 | 2.12 | 2.03 | 1.94 | 1.84 | 1.73 | 1.60 |
| 120 | 6.85 | 4.79 | 3.95 | 3.48 | 3.17 | 2.96 | 2.79 | 2.66 | 2.56 | 2.47 | 2.34 | 2.19 | 2.03 | 1.95 | 1.86 | 1.76 | 1.66 | 1.53 | 1.38 |
| ∞ | 6.63 | 4.61 | 3.78 | 3.32 | 3.02 | 2.80 | 2.64 | 2.51 | 2.41 | 2.32 | 2.18 | 2.04 | 1.88 | 1.79 | 1.70 | 1.59 | 1.47 | 1.32 | 1.00 |

$v_2$ = Degrees of Freedom for Denominator

*continued*

■ **Table A.7**

**Critical Values of the Pearson Correlation Coefficient**

| | Level of Significance for One-Tailed Test | | | |
|---|---|---|---|---|
| | .05 | .025 | .01 | .005 |
| | Level of Significance for Two-Tailed Test | | | |
| d.f. | .10 | .05 | .02 | .01 |
| 1 | .988 | .997 | .9995 | .9999 |
| 2 | .900 | .950 | .980 | .990 |
| 3 | .805 | .878 | .934 | .959 |
| 4 | .729 | .811 | .882 | .917 |
| 5 | .669 | .754 | .833 | .874 |
| 6 | .622 | .707 | .789 | .834 |
| 7 | .582 | .666 | .750 | .798 |
| 8 | .549 | .632 | .716 | .765 |
| 9 | .521 | .602 | .685 | .735 |
| 10 | .497 | .576 | .658 | .708 |
| 11 | .576 | .553 | .634 | .684 |
| 12 | .458 | .532 | .612 | .661 |
| 13 | .441 | .514 | .592 | .641 |
| 14 | .426 | .497 | .574 | .623 |
| 15 | .412 | .482 | .558 | .606 |
| 16 | .400 | .468 | .542 | .590 |
| 17 | .389 | .456 | .528 | .575 |
| 18 | .378 | .444 | .516 | .561 |
| 19 | .369 | .433 | .503 | .549 |
| 20 | .360 | .423 | .492 | .537 |
| 21 | .352 | .413 | .482 | .526 |
| 22 | .344 | .404 | .472 | .515 |
| 23 | .337 | .396 | .462 | .505 |
| 24 | .330 | .388 | .453 | .496 |
| 25 | .323 | .381 | .445 | .487 |
| 26 | .317 | .374 | .437 | .479 |
| 27 | .311 | .367 | .430 | .471 |
| 28 | .306 | .361 | .423 | .463 |
| 29 | .301 | .355 | .416 | .486 |
| 30 | .296 | .349 | .409 | .449 |
| 35 | .275 | .325 | .381 | .418 |
| 40 | .257 | .304 | .358 | .393 |
| 45 | .243 | .288 | .338 | .372 |
| 50 | .231 | .273 | .322 | .354 |
| 60 | .211 | .250 | .295 | .325 |
| 70 | .195 | .232 | .274 | .303 |
| 80 | .183 | .217 | .256 | .283 |
| 90 | .173 | .205 | .242 | .267 |
| 100 | .164 | .195 | .230 | .254 |

# GLOSSARY OF FREQUENTLY USED SYMBOLS

Greek Letters

| | |
|---|---|
| $\alpha$ (alpha) | level of significance or probability of a Type I error |
| $\beta$ (beta) | probability of a type II error or slope of the regression line |
| $\mu$ (mu) | population mean |
| $\rho$ (rho) | population Pearson correlation coefficient |
| $\Sigma$ (summation) | take the sum of |
| $\pi$ (pi) | population proportion |
| $\sigma$ (sigma) | population standard deviation |
| $\chi^2$ | chi-square statistic |

English Letters

| | |
|---|---|
| $d.f.$ | number of degrees of freedom |
| $F$ | $F$-statistic |
| $n$ | sample size |
| $p$ | sample proportion |
| $\Pr()$ | probability of the outcome in the parentheses |
| $r$ | sample Pearson correlation coefficient |
| $r^2$ | coefficient of determination (squared correlation coefficient) |
| $R^2$ | coefficient of determination (multiple regression) |
| $S$ | sample standard deviation (inferential statistics) |
| $S_{\overline{X}}$ | estimated standard error of the mean |
| $S_p$ | estimated standard error of the proportion |
| $S^2$ | sample variance (inferential statistics) |
| $t$ | $t$-statistic |
| $X$ | variable or any unspecified observation |
| $\overline{X}$ | sample mean |
| $Y$ | any unspecified observation on a second variable, usually the dependent variable |
| $\hat{Y}$ | predicted score |
| $Z$ | standardized score (descriptive statistics) or $Z$-statistic |

# GLOSSARY OF TERMS

**Acquiescence bias** A category of response bias that results because some individuals tend to agree with all questions or to concur with a particular position.

**Administrative error** An error caused by the improper administration or flawed execution of the research task.

**Advocacy research** Research undertaken to support a specific claim in a legal action.

**Alternative hypothesis** A statement that indicates the opposite of the null hypothesis.

**Analysis of variance (ANOVA)** Analysis involving the investigation of the effects of one treatment variable on an interval-scaled dependent variable; a hypothesis-testing technique to determine whether statistically significant differences on means occur among three or more groups.

**Applied research** Research undertaken to answer questions about specific problems or to make decisions about particular courses of action.

**At-home scanning system** A system whereby consumer panelists after taking home the products perform their own scanning using hand-held wands that read UPC symbols.

**Attitude** An enduring disposition to consistently respond in a given manner to various aspects of the world; composed of affective, cognitive, and behavioral components.

**Attribute** A single characteristic or fundamental feature that pertains to an object, a person, a situation, or an issue.

**Auspices bias** Response bias that results because respondents are influenced by the organization conducting the study.

**Back translation** The process of translating a questionnaire into another language and then having a second, independent translator translate it back to the original language.

**Backward linkage** A term implying that the later stages of the research process influence the early stages.

**Base** The number of respondents or observations (in a row or column) used as a basis for computing percentages.

**Basic experimental design** An experimental design in which a single independent variable is manipulated to measure its effect on another single dependent variable.

**Basic (pure) research** Research conducted to expand the boundaries of knowledge itself; undertaken to verify the acceptability of a given theory.

**Behavioral differential** A rating scale instrument, similar to a semantic differential, developed to measure the behavioral intentions of subjects toward future actions.

**Bivariate linear regression** A measure of linear association that investigates a straight-line relationship of the type $Y = a + \beta X$, where $X$ is the independent variable and $a$ and $\beta$ are two constants to be estimated.

**Bivariate statistical analysis** Data analysis and hypothesis testing when the investigation concerns simultaneous investigation of two variables.

**Blinding** A technique used to control subjects' knowledge of whether or not they have been given a particular experimental treatment.

**Callback** An attempt to recontact an individual selected for the sample.

**Case study method** An exploratory research technique that intensively investigates one or a few situations similar to the problem situation.

**Category scale** A rating scale that consists of several response categories, often providing respondents with alternatives to indicate positions on a continuum.

**Causal research** Research conducted to identify cause-and-effect relationships among variables.

**Census** An investigation of all the individual elements that make up a population.

**Central-limit theorem** A theory that states that as a sample size increases, the distribution of sample size increases, the distribution of sample means of size $D$, randomly selected, approaches a normal distribution.

**Central location interviewing** Telephone interviews conducted from a central location; allows more effective supervision and control of the quality of interviewing.

**Checklist question** A fixed-alternative question that allows the respondent to provide multiple answers to a single question by checking off items.

**Chi-square ($\chi^2$) test** A hypothesis test that allows for investigation of statistical significance in the analysis of a frequency distribution.

**Choice** A measurement task that identifies preferences by requiring respondents to choose between two or more alternatives.

**Client** Term often used by the research department to refer to line management for whom it performs services.

**Cluster sampling** An economically efficient sampling technique in which the primary sampling unit is not the individual element in the population but a large cluster of elements; clusters are selected randomly.

**Code of ethics** A set of guidelines that states the standards and operating procedures for ethical practices by researchers.

**Coefficient of determination ($r^2$)** A measure obtained by squaring the correlation coefficient; that proportion of the total variance of a variable that is accounted for by knowing the value of another variable.

**Cohort effect** A change in the dependent variable that occurs because members of one experimental group experienced different historical situations than members of other experimental groups.

**Compromise design** An approximation of an experimental design; may fall short of the requirements of random assignment of subjects or treatments to groups.

**Computer-assisted telephone interview (CATI)** A type of telephone interview

**407**

in which the interviewer reads questions from a computer screen and enters the respondent's answers directly into the computer.

**Computer-interactive survey**  A survey in which the respondent completes a self-administered questionnaire displayed on a computer monitor of a computer. Respondents interact directly with a computer programmed to ask questions in a sequence determined by respondents' previous answers.

**Computer map**  The portrayal of demographic, sales, or other data on a two- or three-dimensional map generated by a computer.

**Concept**  A generalized idea about a class of objects, attributes, occurrences, or processes.

**Concept testing**  Any exploratory research procedure that tests some sort of stimulus as a proxy for an idea about a new, revised, or repositioned product, service, or strategy.

**Conceptual definition**  A verbal explanation of the meaning of a concept; defines what the concept is and what it is not.

**Conclusions and recommendations section**  The part of the body of the report that provides opinions based on the results and suggestions for action.

**Conclusions and report preparation stage**  The stage in which the researcher interprets information and draws conclusions to be communicated to the decision makers.

**Concomitant variation**  The way in which two phenomena or events vary together.

**Confidence interval estimate**  A specified range of numbers within which a population mean should lie; an estimate of the population mean based on the knowledge that it will equate the sample mean plus or minus a small sampling error.

**Confidence level**  A percentage or decimal value that tells how confident a researcher can be about being correct. It states the long-run percentage of confidence intervals that will include the true population mean.

**Constancy of conditions**  A situation in which subjects in experimental groups and control groups are exposed to situa-

tions identical except for differing conditions of the independent variable.

**Constant error**  An error that occurs in the same experimental condition every time the basic experiment is repeated; a systematic bias.

**Constant-sum scale**  A measure of attitudes in which respondents are asked to divide a constant sum to indicate the relative importance of attributes.

**Consumer panel**  A longitudinal survey of the same sample of individuals or households to record (in a diary) their attitudes, behavior, or purchasing habits over time.

**Content analysis**  The systematic observation and quantitative description of the manifest content of communication.

**Contingency table**  The results of a cross-tabulation of two variables, such as survey questions.

**Contrived observation**  Observation in which the investigator creates an artificial environment to test a hypothesis.

**Control group**  The group of subjects exposed to the control condition, that is, not exposed to the experimental treatment.

**Control method of test marketing**  A "minimarket test" using forced distribution in a small city. Retailers are paid for shelf space so that the test marketer can be guaranteed distribution.

**Controlled store test**  A hybrid between a laboratory experiment and a test market; test products are sold in a small number of selected stores to actual customers.

**Convenience sampling**  The sampling procedure of obtaining those people or units that are most conveniently available.

**Correlation coefficient**  A statistical measure of the covariation or association between two variables.

**Correlation matrix**  The standard format for reporting correlational results.

**Counterbalancing**  A technique requiring that half the subjects be exposed to treatment A first and then to treatment B while the other half receive treatment B and then treatment A. This is an attempt to eliminate the confounding effects of order of presentation.

**Counterbiasing statement**  An introductory statement or preamble to a potentially embarrassing question that reduces a respondent's reluctance to answer by suggesting that certain behavior is not unusual.

**Cover letter**  The letter that accompanies the questionnaire in a mail survey; generally is intended to induce the reader to complete and return the questionnaire.

**Critical values**  The values that lie exactly on the boundary of the region of rejection.

**Cross-check**  A comparison of data from one source with data from another source to determine the similarity of independent projects.

**Cross-functional teams**  Teams composed of individuals from various organizational departments, such as engineering, production, finance, and marketing, who share a common purpose.

**Cross-sectional study**  A study that samples various segments of a population and collects data at a single moment in time.

**Cross-tabulation**  A technique for organizing data by groups, categories, or classes, thus facilitating comparisons; a joint frequency distribution of observations on two or more sets of variables. Also called **contingency table.**

**Custom research**  A marketing research study designed for an individual client and tailored to the client's unique needs.

**Data**  Facts or recorded measures of certain phenomena.

**Data conversion**  The process of changing the original form of the data to a format suitable to achieve the research objective. Also called *data transformation.*

**Data-gathering stage**  The stage in which the researcher collects the data.

**Data mining**  The use of powerful computers to dig through volumes of data to discover patterns about an organization's customers and products.

**Data-processing and analysis stage**  The stage in which the researcher performs several interrelated procedures to convert the data into a format that will answer management's questions.

**Data-processing error** A category of administrative error that occurs because of incorrect data entry, computer programming, or other procedural errors during the data-processing stage.

**Data transformation (data conversion)** The process of changing the original form of the data to a format suitable to achieve the research objective.

**Database** A collection of raw data arranged logically and organized in a form that can be stored and processed by a computer.

**Database marketing** The practice of maintaining customer databases with relevant data on individual customers as well as demographic and financial data.

**Debriefing** The process of providing subjects with all pertinent facts about the nature and purpose of the experiment after its completion.

**Decision making** The process used to resolve a problem or to choose from alternative opportunities.

**Decision support system** A computer-based system that helps decision makers confront problems through direct interaction with databases and analytical software programs.

**Degrees of freedom** The number of degrees of freedom is equal to the number of observations minus the number of constraints or assumptions needed to calculate a statistical term.

**Demand characteristics** Experimental design procedures or situational aspects of an experiment that provide unintentional hints about the experimenter's hypothesis to subjects.

**Dependent variable** The criterion by which the results of an experiment are judged; a variable expected to be dependent on the experimenter's manipulation.

**Depth interview** A relatively unstructured, extensive interview in which the interviewer asks many questions and probes for in-depth answers.

**Descriptive analysis** The transformation of raw data into a form that will make them easy to understand and interpret; rearranging, ordering, and manipulating data to generate descriptive information.

**Descriptive research** Research designed to describe characteristics of a population or phenomenon.

**Determinant-choice question** A fixed-alternative question that requires a respondent to choose one, and only one, response from among multiple alternatives.

**Direct observation** A straightforward attempt to observe and record what naturally occurs; the investigator does not create an artificial situation.

**Director of marketing research** The person who provides leadership and integrates staff-level activities by planning, executing, and controlling the marketing research function; sometimes called **director of marketing information systems.**

**Discussion guide** A document prepared by the focus group moderator that contains remarks about the nature of the group and outlines the topics or questions to be addressed.

**Door-to-door interview** A personal interview conducted at the respondent's home or place of business.

**Double-barreled question** A question that may induce bias because it covers two issues at once.

**Double-blind design** A technique in which neither the subjects nor the experimenter knows which are the experimental and which the controlled conditions.

**Drop-off method** A method of distributing self-administered questionnaires whereby an interviewer drops off the questionnaire and picks it up at a later time.

**Elaboration analysis** An analysis of the basic cross-tabulation for each level of another variable, such as subgroups of the sample.

**Electronic data interchange (EDI)** The process of integrating one company's computer system with another company's system.

**Electronic test markets** A system of test marketing that measures results based on Universal Product Code data; often scanner-based consumer panels are combined with high-technology television broadcasting systems to allow experimentation with different advertising

messages via split-cable broadcasts or other technology.

**e-mail** Electronic mail that users send over the Internet to ask questions of experts or communicate in other ways with individuals who share similar interests.

**e-mail survey** A self-administered questionnaire sent to respondents via e-mail.

**Environmental scanning** Information gathering and fact finding designed to detect indications of environmental changes in their initial stages of development.

**Experience survey** An exploratory research technique in which individuals who are knowledgeable about a particular research problem are questioned.

**Experiment** A research investigation in which conditions are controlled so that an independent variable(s) can be manipulated to test a hypothesis about a dependent variable. Allows evaluation of causal relationships among variables while all other variables are eliminated or controlled.

**Experimental group** The group of subjects exposed to the experimental treatment.

**Experimental treatments** Alternative manipulations of the independent variable being investigated.

**Experimenter bias** An effect on the subjects' behavior caused by an experimenter's presence, actions, or comments.

**Exploratory research** Initial research conducted to clarify and define the nature of a problem.

**Expressive behavior** A type of behavior that can be scientifically observed, such as tone of voice or facial expression.

**External data** Data created, recorded, or generated by an entity other than the researcher's organization.

**External validity** The ability of an experiment to generalize beyond the experiment data to other subjects or groups in the population under study.

**Extremity bias** A category of response bias that results because response styles vary from person to person; some individuals tend to use extremes when responding to questions.

**Eye-tracking monitor** A mechanical device used to observe eye movements.

Some eye monitors use infrared light beams to measure unconscious eye movements.

**Field experiment**  An experiment conducted in a natural setting, where complete control of extraneous variables is not possible.

**Filter question**  A question that screens out respondents who are not qualified to answer a second question.

**Fixed-alternative question**  A question in which the respondent is given specific, limited-alternative responses and asked to choose the one closest to his or her own viewpoint.

**Focus group interview**  An unstructured, free-flowing interview with a small group of people.

**Follow-up**  A letter or postcard reminder requesting that the respondent return the questionnaire.

**Forecast analyst**  The person who provides technical assistance such as computer analysis to forecast sales.

**Forward linkage**  A term implying that the early stages of the research process influence the design of the later stages.

**Frequency-determination question**  A fixed-alternative question about the general frequency of occurrence.

**Frequency distribution**  Organizing a set of data by summarizing the number of times a particular value of a variable occurs.

**Frequency table**  The arrangement of statistical data in a row-and-column format that exhibits the count of responses or observations for each category assigned to a variable.

**ftp**  File Transfer Protocol. A software program that allows users to establish an interactive file transfer session with a remote host's computer system so that the user can read and download full-text versions of files from the remote system.

**Funnel technique**  A procedure whereby general questions are asked before specific questions to obtain unbiased responses.

**Global information system**  An organized collection of computer hardware, software, data, and personnel designed to capture, store, update, manipulate, analyze, and immediately display information about worldwide business activity.

**Graphic rating scale**  A measure of attitude that allows respondents to rate an object by choosing any point along a graphic continuum.

**Guinea pig effect**  An effect on the results of an experiment caused by subjects changing their normal behavior or attitudes to cooperate with an experimenter.

**Hawthorne effect**  An unintended effect on the results of a research experiment caused by the subjects knowing that they are participants.

**Hidden observation**  A situation in which the subject is unaware that observation is taking place.

**History effect**  The loss of internal validity caused by specific events in the external environment occurring between the first and second measurements that are beyond the experimenter's control.

**Home page**  A single Web page that serves as the "main entrance" to all of an organization's Internet documents.

**Host**  A computer that one or more people can use directly by logging on to a personal computer connected to it to access network services.

**Hyperlink**  An element in an electronic document that, when a user clicks on it, changes the screen to another document.

**Hypothesis**  An unproven proposition or supposition that tentatively explains certain facts or phenomena; a probable answer to a research question.

**Hypothetical construct**  A variable that is not directly observable but is measured by an indirect means, such as verbal expression or overt behavior.

**Iceberg principle**  The principle indicating that the dangerous part of many marketing problems is neither visible to nor understood by marketing managers.

**Image profile**  A graphic representation of semantic differential data for competing brands, products, or stores to highlight comparisons.

**Independent variable**  In an experimental design, the variable that can be manipulated, or altered, independently of any other variable.

**Index (composite) measure**  A multi-item instrument that uses several variables to measure a single concept.

**Index number**  Score or observation recalibrated to indicate how it relates to a base number.

**Index of retail saturation**  A calculation that describes the relationship between retail demand and supply.

**Information**  Any body of facts in a format suitable for decision making or in a context that defines the relationship between two pieces of data.

**Instrumentation effect**  An effect on the results of an experiment caused by a change in the wording of questions, interviewers, or other procedures used to measure the dependent variable.

**Interactive medium**  A medium a person can use to communicate with and interact with other users, as well as with the Internet.

**Internal and proprietary data**  Secondary data that originate inside the organization.

**Internal validity**  The ability of an experiment to answer the question of whether an experimental treatment was the sole cause of changes in a dependent variable or whether the experimental manipulation did what it was supposed to do.

**Internet**  A worldwide network of computers that allows users access to information and documents from distant sources.

**Internet survey**  A self-administered questionnaire placed on an Internet Web site. The respondent reads the questions on a personal computer and answers are directly entered into the researcher's computer.

**Interpretation**  The process of making pertinent inferences and drawing conclusions concerning the meaning and implications of a research investigation.

**Interval scale**  A scale that both arranges objects according to their magnitudes and distinguishes the ordered arrangement in units of equal intervals.

**Interviewer bias**  A response bias that occurs because the presence of the interviewer influences answers.

**Interviewer cheating**   The practice by interviewers of filling in fake answers or falsifying questionnaires.

**Interviewer error**   Mistakes made by interviewers when performing their tasks.

**Intranet**   A company's private data network that uses Internet standards and technology.

**Introduction section**   The part of the body of the report that discusses background information and the specific objectives of the research.

**Item nonresponse**   Failure by a respondent to answer a question on a questionnaire.

**Judgment (purposive) sampling**   A nonprobability sampling technique in which an experienced researcher selects the sample based on personal judgment about some appropriate characteristic of the sample members.

**Laboratory experiment**   An experiment conducted in a laboratory or other artificial setting to obtain almost complete control over the research setting.

**Leading question**   A question that suggests or implies certain answers.

**Likert scale**   A measure of attitudes in which respondents rate how strongly they agree or disagree with carefully constructed statements; several scale items ranging from very positive to very negative attitudes toward an object may be used to form a summated index.

**Link**   A connection to another screen or document.

**Loaded question**   A question that suggests socially desirable answers or is emotionally charged.

**Longitudinal study**   A survey of respondents conducted at different times, thus allowing analysis of changes over time.

**Mail survey**   A self-administered questionnaire sent to respondents through the mail.

**Mall intercept interview**   A personal interview conducted in a shopping mall or other high-traffic area.

**Manager of customer quality research**   The person who specializes in conducting surveys to measure consumers' satisfaction and perceptions of product quality.

**Manager of decision support systems**   The person who supervises the collection and analysis of sales data and other recurring data.

**Market tracking**   The observation and analysis of industry volume or trends in brand share over time.

**Marketing concept**   The marketing philosophy that stresses consumer orientation, emphasizes long-range profitability, and suggests the integration and coordination of marketing and other organizational functions.

**Marketing research**   The systematic and objective process of generating information to aid in making marketing decisions.

**Matching**   A procedure for the assignment of subjects to groups that ensures each group of respondents is matched on the basis of pertinent characteristics.

**Maturation effect**   An effect on the results of an experiment caused by experimental subjects maturing or changing over time.

**Mean**   A measure of central tendency; the arithmetic average.

**Measure of association**   A general term that refers to a number of bivariate statistical techniques used to measure the strength of a relationship between two variables.

**Median**   A measure of central tendency that is the midpoint, the value below which half the values in a distribution fall.

**Mixed-mode survey**   A survey that combines two different communication modes, such as telephone and mail, to collect data.

**Mode**   A measure of central tendency; the value that occurs most often.

**Model building**   Involves using secondary data to help specify relationships between two or more variables; can include the development of descriptive or predictive equations.

**Moderator**   The person who leads a focus group discussion.

**Moderator variable**   A third variable that, when introduced into an analysis, alters or has a contingent effect on the relationship between an independent variable and a dependent variable.

**Mortality (sample attrition) effect**   A sample bias that results from the withdrawal of some subjects from the experiment before it is completed.

**Multiple-grid question**   Several similar questions arranged in a grid format.

**Multiple regression analysis**   An analysis of association that simultaneously investigates the effect of two or more variables on a single, interval-scaled dependent variable.

**Multistage area sampling**   Sampling that involves using a combination of two or more probability sampling techniques.

**Neural network**   A form of artificial intelligence in which a computer is programmed to mimic the way human brains process information.

**Nominal scale**   A scale in which the numbers or letters assigned to the object serve as labels for identification or classification.

**Nonprobability sampling**   A sampling technique in which units of the sample are selected on the basis of personal judgment or convenience; the probability of any particular member of the population being chosen is unknown.

**Nonrespondent**   A person who is not contacted or who refuses to cooperate in the research.

**Nonresponse error**   The statistical differences between a survey that includes only those who responded and a perfect survey that would also include those who failed to respond.

**Normal distribution**   A symmetrical bell-shaped distribution that describes the expected probability distribution of many chance occurrences.

**Not-at-home**   A person who is not at home on the first or second contact.

**Null hypothesis**   A statement about a status quo asserting that any change from what has been thought to be true will be due entirely to random error.

**Numerical scale**   An attitude rating scale that is similar to a semantic differential except that it uses numbers as response options instead of verbal descriptions to identify response positions.

**Observation** The systematic process of recording the behavioral patterns of people, objects, and occurrences without questioning or otherwise communicating with them.

**Observer bias** A distortion of measurement resulting from the cognitive behavior or actions of the witnessing observer.

**One-group pretest–posttest design** A quasi-experimental design in which the subjects in the experimental group are measured before and after the treatment is administered, but there is no control group.

**One-shot design** An after-only design in which a single measure is recorded after the treatment is administered.

**Open-ended response question** A question that poses some problem and asks the respondent to answer in his or her own words.

**Operational definition** An explanation that gives meaning to a concept by specifying the activities or operations necessary to measure it.

**Oral presentation** A verbal summary of the major findings, conclusions, and recommendations given to clients or line managers to allow them to clarify any ambiguous issues by asking questions.

**Order bias** Bias caused by the influence of earlier questions in a questionnaire or by an answer's position in a set of answers.

**Ordinal scale** A scale that arranges objects or alternatives according to their magnitude in an ordered relationship.

**Paired comparison** A measurement technique that consists of presenting respondents with two objects and asking them to pick the preferred object. Two or more objects may be presented, but comparisons are made in pairs.

**Percentage distribution** The organization of a frequency distribution into a table (or graph) that summarizes percentage values associated with particular values of a variable.

**Performance-monitoring research** Research that regularly, sometimes routinely, provides feedback for evaluation and control of marketing activity.

**Periodicity** A problem that occurs in systematic sampling when the original list has a systematic pattern.

**Personal interview** An interview that gathers information through face-to-face contact with individuals.

**Physical actions** A type of behavior that can be scientifically observed, such as shopping patterns or television viewing.

**Physical-trace evidence** A visible mark of some past occurrence.

**Picture frustration** A version of the TAT that uses a cartoon drawing in which the respondent suggests a possible dialogue between the characters.

**Pilot study** A collective term for any small-scale exploratory research technique that uses sampling but does not apply rigorous standards.

**Pivot question** A filter question used to determine which version of a second question will be asked.

**Point estimate** An estimate of the population mean using a single value, usually the sample mean.

**Population distribution** A frequency distribution of the elements of a population.

**Population element** An individual member of a population.

**Population parameters** The variables in a population or measured characteristics of the population.

**Population (universe)** Any complete group of entities that share some common set of characteristics.

**Posttest-only control group design** An after-only design in which the experimental group is tested after exposure to the treatment and the control group is tested at the same time without having been exposed to the treatment; no premeasure is taken. Random assignment of subjects and treatment occurs.

**Preliminary tabulation** A tabulation of the results of a pretest to help determine whether the questionnaire will meet the objectives of the research.

**Pretest–posttest control group design** A true experimental design in which the experimental group is tested before and after exposure to the treatment and the control group is tested at the same two times without being exposed to the experimental treatment.

**Pretesting** Administering a questionnaire to a small group of respondents to detect ambiguity or bias in the questions or to iron out fundamental problems in the instructions or administrative procedures.

**Primary sampling unit (PSU)** A unit selected in the first stage of sampling.

**Probability** The long-run relative frequency with which an event will occur.

**Probability sampling** A sampling technique in which every member of the population has a known, nonzero probability of selection.

**Probing** The verbal prompts made by an interviewer when the respondent must be motivated to communicate his or her answer more fully; used to get respondents to enlarge on, clarify, or explain answers.

**Problem definition stage** The stage in which management seeks to identify a clear-cut statement of the problem or opportunity.

**Program strategy** The overall plan to conduct a series of marketing research projects; a planning activity that places each marketing project in the context of the company's marketing plan.

**Projective technique** An indirect means of questioning that enables a respondent to project beliefs and feelings onto a third party, onto a inanimate object, or into a task situation.

**Proportion** The percentage of elements that meet some criterion.

**Proprietary marketing research** A data collection system that gathers new data to investigate specific problems.

**Psychogalvanometer** A device that measures galvanic skin response, a measure of involuntary changes in the electrical resistance of the skin.

**Pupilometer** A mechanical device used to observe and record changes in the diameter of a subject's pupils.

**Push technology** An information technology that delivers personalized content to the viewer's desktop, using computer software known as smart agents.

**Quasi-experimental design**   A research design that cannot be classified as a true experiment because it lacks adequate control of extraneous variables.

**Quota sampling**   A nonprobability sampling procedure that ensures that various subgroups of a population will be represented on pertinent characteristics to the exact extent the investigator desires.

**Random digit dialing**   A method of obtaining a representative sample in a telephone interview by using random numbers to generate telephone numbers.

**Random error**   An error that occurs because of chance; statistical fluctuations in which repetitions of the basic experiment sometimes favor one experimental condition and sometimes the other.

**Random sampling error**   The difference between the result of a sample and the result of a census conducted using identical procedures; a statistical fluctuation due to chance variations in the elements selected for a sample.

**Randomization**   A procedure in which the assignment of subjects and treatments to groups is based on chance.

**Ranking**   A measurement task that requires respondents to rank order a small number of stores, brands, or objects in overall preference or on the basis of some characteristic of the stimulus.

**Rating**   A measurement task that requires respondents to estimate the magnitude of a characteristic or quality that a brand, store, or object possesses.

**Ratio scale**   A scale that has absolute rather than relative quantities and an absolute zero where a given attribute is absent.

**Refusal**   A person who is unwilling to participate in the research.

**Reliability**   The degree to which a measure is free from random error and therefore yields consistent results.

**Repeated measures**   A situation that occurs when the same subjects are exposed to all experimental treatments to eliminate any problems due to subject differences.

**Report format**   The makeup or arrangement of parts that are necessary to a good research report.

**Research analyst**   The person responsible for client contact, project design, preparation of proposals, selection of research suppliers, and supervision of data collection, analysis, and reporting activities.

**Research assistant**   The person who provides technical assistance with questionnaire design, analysis of data, and so on.

**Research design**   A master plan that specifies the methods and procedures for collecting and analyzing needed information.

**Research design stage**   The stage in which the researcher determines a framework for the research plan of action by selecting a basic research method.

**Research follow-up**   Recontacting decision makers and/or clients after they have read the research report to determine whether they need additional information or to have some issues clarified.

**Research methodology section**   The part of the body of the report that explains the research design, sampling procedures, and other technical procedures used to collect the data.

**Research objective**   The researcher's version of the marketing problem; it explains the purpose of the research in measurable terms and defines standards for what the research should accomplish.

**Research proposal**   A written statement of the research design that includes a statement explaining the purpose of the study and a detailed, systematic outline of procedures associated with a particular research methodology.

**Research report**   An oral presentation or written statement of research results, strategic recommendations, and/or other conclusions to a specific audience.

**Research sophistication**   A stage in which managers have considerable experience in the proper use of research techniques.

**Research supplier**   A commercial marketing research service that conducts marketing research activity for clients.

**Respondent**   The person who verbally answers an interviewer's questions or provides answers to written questions.

**Respondent error**   A classification of sample biases resulting from some respondent action or inaction such as nonresponse or response bias.

**Response bias**   A bias that occurs when respondents tend to answer questions with a certain slant that consciously or unconsciously misrepresents the truth.

**Response rate**   The number of questionnaires returned or completed divided by the total number of eligible people who were contacted or requested to participate in the survey.

**Response latency**   The amount of time necessary to make a choice between two alternatives; used as a measure of the strength of preference.

**Results section**   The part of the body of the report that presents the findings of the project; includes tables, charts and an organized narrative.

**Role-playing technique**   A projective technique that requires the subject to act out someone else's behavior in a particular setting.

**Rule**   A guide that instructs the investigator about what to do.

**Sample**   A subset or some part of a larger population.

**Sample bias**   A persistent tendency for the results of a sample to deviate in one direction from the true value of the population parameter.

**Sample distribution**   A frequency distribution of a sample.

**Sample selection error**   An administrative error caused by improper sample design or sampling procedure execution.

**Sample statistics**   Variables in a sample or measures computed from sample data.

**Sampling distribution**   A theoretical probability distribution of sample means for all possible samples of a certain size drawn from a particular population.

**Sampling frame**   A list of elements from which a sample may be drawn; also called *working population*.

**Sampling frame error**   An error that occurs when certain sample elements are excluded from or overrepresented in the sampling frame.

**Sampling stage** The stage in which the researcher determines who is to be sampled, how large a sample is needed, and how sampling units will be selected.

**Sampling unit** A single element or group of elements selected for the sample.

**Scale** A quantifying measure or combination of items that is progressively arranged according to value or magnitude.

**Scanner-based consumer panel** A type of consumer panel in which the participants' purchasing habits are recorded with a laser scanner rather than a purchase diary.

**Scientific method** Systematic techniques or procedures used to analyze empirical evidence in an unbiased attempt to confirm or disprove prior conceptions.

**Search engine** A computerized "search and retrieval" system that allows anyone to search the World Wide Web for information in a particular way.

**Secondary data** Data that have been previously collected for a project other than the one at hand.

**Secondary sampling unit** A unit selected in the second stage of sampling.

**Selection effect** A sampling bias that results from differential selection of respondents for the comparison groups.

**Self-administered questionnaire** A questionnaire, such as a mail questionnaire, that is read and filled in by the respondent rather than by the interviewer.

**Self-selection bias** A bias that occurs because people who feel strongly about a subject are more likely to respond than people who feel indifferent about it.

**Semantic differential** A measure of attitudes that consists of a series of 7-point rating scales that use bipolar adjectives to anchor the beginning and end of each scale.

**Sensitivity** An instrument's ability to accurately measure variability in stimuli or responses.

**Sentence completion method** A projective technique in which respondents are required to complete a number of partial sentences with the first word or phrase that comes to mind.

**Server** A computer that provides services on the Internet.

**Significance level** The critical probability in choosing between the null and alternative hypotheses; the probability level that is too low to warrant support of the null hypothesis.

**Simple-dichotomy (dichotomous-alternative) question** A fixed-alternative question that requires the respondent to choose one or two dichotomous alternatives.

**Simple random sampling** A sampling procedure that assures each element in the population of an equal chance of being included in the sample.

**Single-source data** Diverse types of data offered by a single company; usually integrated by a common variable such as geographic area.

**Site analysis techniques** Involve use of secondary data to select the best locations for retail or wholesale operations.

**Smart agent** Software that is capable of learning an Internet user's preferences and automatically searches out information in selected Web sites and then distributes the information.

**Snowball sampling** A sampling procedure in which initial respondents are selected by probability methods and additional respondents are obtained from information provided by the initial respondents.

**Social desirability bias** Bias in responses caused by respondents' desire, either conscious or unconscious, to gain prestige or appear in a different social role.

**Societal norms** Codes of behavior adopted by a group that suggest what a member of a group ought to do under given circumstances.

**Software** Consists of various types of programs that tell computers, printers, and other hardware what to do.

**Solomon four-group design** A true experimental design that combines the pretest–posttest with control group and the posttest-only with control group designs, thereby providing a means for controlling the interactive testing effect and other sources of extraneous variation.

**Sorting** A measurement task that presents respondents with several objects or with information typed on cards and requires them to arrange the objects or cards into a number of piles or otherwise classify the product concepts.

**Spatial relations and locations** Physical distance or other physical patterns studied in scientific observation, such as traffic counts.

**Split-ballot technique** Using two alternative phrasings of the same question for respective halves of the sample to yield a more accurate total response than a single phrasing would.

**Spurious relationship** An apparent relationship between two variables that is not authentic.

**Standard deviation** A quantitative index of a distribution's spread or variability; the square root of the variance for distribution.

**Standard error of the mean** The standard deviation of the sampling distribution.

**Standardized normal distribution** A purely theoretical probability distribution that reflects a specific normal curve for the standardized value, Z.

**Standardized research service** A research organization that has developed a unique methodology for investigating a specialty area, such as advertising effectiveness.

**Stapel scale** A measure of attitudes that consists of a single adjective in the center of an even-numbered range of numerical values.

**Static group design** An after-only design in which subjects in the experimental group are measured after being exposed to the experimental treatment and the control group is measured without having been exposed to the experimental treatment; no premeasure is taken.

**Stratified sampling** A probability sampling procedure in which simple random subsamples are drawn from within each stratum that are more or less equal on some characteristic.

**Survey** A method of primary data collection in which information is gathered by communicating with a representative sample of people.

**Syndicated service** A marketing research supplier that provides standardized information for many clients.

**Systematic (nonsampling) error**   Error resulting from some imperfect aspect of the research design or from a mistake in the execution of the research.

**Systematic sampling**   A sampling procedure in which a starting point is selected by a random process and then every $n$th number on the list is selected.

**Tachistoscope**   A device that controls the amount of time a visual image is exposed to a subject.

**Telephone interview**   An interview that gathers information through telephone contact with individuals.

**Television monitoring**   Computerized mechanical observation used to obtain television ratings.

**Temporal patterns**   In scientific observation, the length of time for an act or event to occur, such as amount of time spent shopping or driving.

**Tertiary sampling unit**   A unit selected in the third stage of sampling.

**Test marketing**   An experimental procedure that provides an opportunity to measure sales or profit potential for a new product or to test a new marketing plan under realistic marketing conditions.

**Test of differences**   An investigation of a hypothesis that states that two (or more) groups differ with respect to measures on a variable.

**Test unit**   An entity whose responses to experimental treatments are being observed or measured.

**Testing effect**   The effect of pretesting in a before-and-after study, which may sensitize respondents or subjects when taking a test for the second time, thus affecting internal validity.

**Thematic apperception test (TAT)**   A projective technique that presents a series of pictures to research subjects and asks them to provide a description of or a story about the pictures.

**Third-person technique**   A projective technique in which the respondent is asked why a third person does what she or he does or thinks about a product. The respondent is expected to transfer his or her attitudes to the third person.

**Time series design**   An experimental design used when experiments are conducted over long periods of time. It allows researchers to distinguish between temporary and permanent changes in dependent variables.

**Total quality management**   A business philosophy that emphasizes market-driven quality as a top organizational priority.

**Tracking study**   A type of longitudinal study that uses successive samples to compare trends and identify changes in variables such as consumer satisfaction, brand image, or advertising awareness.

**Uniform Resource Locater (URL)**   The global address of a Web site on the World Wide Web.

**Validity**   The ability of an instrument to measure what it is intended to measure.

**Variance**   A measure of dispersion; the sum of squared deviation scores divided by sample size minus 1.

**Verbal behavior**   A type of behavior that can be scientifically observed, such as sales conversations.

**Visible observation**   A situation in which the observer's presence is known to the subject.

**Voice pitch analysis**   A physiological measurement technique that records abnormal frequencies in the voice that supposedly reflects emotional reactions to various stimuli.

**Web browser**   A software program that allows a user to locate and display Web pages.

**Word association test**   A projective technique in which the subject is presented with a list of words, one at a time, and asked to respond with the first word that comes to mind.

**World Wide Web**   A portion of the Internet that is a graphical interface system of thousands of interconnected pages, or documents.

# CREDITS

## Chapter One
p. 3 photo: © Harcourt Brace photo/Annette Coolidge. p. 6 photo: Courtesy of Partnership for a Drug Free America. p. 9 Exhibit 1.1: General Electric Company. p. 12 photo: British Airways. p. 16 photo: Courtesy of Colgate-Palmolive Company.

## Chapter Two
p. 21 photo: Courtesy of Texas Instruments. p. 21 Chapter Opening Vignette: Adapted from Angeline Pantages, "TI's Global Window" (*Datamation*, September 1, 1989) p. 49. p. 24 photo: Courtesy of Hewlett-Packard Company. p. 26 photo: Environmental Systems Research Institute. p. 28 *What Went Right?:* From *The Road Ahead* by Bill Gates. Copyright © 1995 by William H. Gates III. Used by permission of Viking Penguin, a division of Penguin Putnam Inc. p. 34 photo: PointCast is a registered trademark and the PointCast logo, PointCast Network and Smart Screen are trademarks of PointCast Incorporated. p. 35 photo: Courtesy of Yahoo! Inc.

## Chapter Three
p. 41 photo: AP/Wideworld Photos. p. 43 photo: © Mary Kate Denny/PhotoEdit. p. 47 *What Went Wrong?:* Reprinted with permission from *Preparing Instructional Objectives*, © 1984. Published by The Center for Effective Performance, 2300 Peachford Road, Suite 2000, Atlanta GA 30338. 1-800-558-4237. p. 48 *What Went Right?:* Patrick Coyne, "ACD Conference on Interactive Media," *Communication Arts* (January/February 1995, Vol. 36, No. 8) p. 140. Reprinted with permission of *Communication Arts*, Copyright 1998, Coyne & Blanchard, Inc. All rights reserved. p. 53 photo: Courtesy of Red Devil, Inc. p. 54 photo: © Columbia Pictures Industries, Inc. Courtesy of The Kobal Collection/photographer Ralph Nelson. p. 55 photo: Permission granted by Lands' End, Inc. p. 60 Exhibit 3.5: Based on *A General Taxpayer Opinion Survey, Office of Planning and Research*, Internal Revenue Service, March 1980.

## Chapter Four
p. 65 photo: © Dennis MacDonald/PhotoEdit. p. 66 Exhibit 4.1: Courtesy of General Foods. p. 71 photo: General Motors Corp. p. 76 *What Went Wrong?:* Cynthia Crossen, *Tainted Truth* (Simon & Schuster, 1994) p. 95. p. 81 Case 4.1: John Harwood and Daniel Pearl, "U.S. Midterm Elections: U.S. Politicians Yell Foul Over Phone Polling Method," *Wall Street Journal Europe* (November 11, 1994). Reprinted by permission of *Wall Street Journal*, © 1994 Dow Jones & Company, Inc. All Rights Reserved.

## Chapter Five
p. 85 photo: © Harcourt Brace photo/Annette Coolidge. p. 85 Chapter Opening Vignette: Copyright © 1994 by The New York Times Co. Reprinted by permission. p. 89 photo: © Joseph Devenney/The Image Bank. p. 92 photo: J. Paul Getty Museum. p. 98 photo: © Tony Freeman/PhotoEdit. p. 99 Exhibit 5.1: Schewe, et al, *Marketing Concepts and Applications* (McGraw-Hill, 1980) p. 115. Reprinted with permission of the McGraw-Hill Companies. p. 103 Case 5.1: Reproduced by permission from William G. Zikmund and William J. Lundstrom, *A Collection of Outstanding Cases in Marketing Management* (St. Paul: West Publishing, 1979). Copyright © 1979 by William G. Zikmund. All

rights reserved. p. 104 Case Exhibit 5.1: Reproduced by permission from William G. Zikmund and William J. Lundstrom, *A Collection of Outstanding Cases in Marketing Management* (St. Paul: West Publishing, 1979). Copyright © 1979 by William G. Zikmund. All rights reserved.

## Chapter Six
p. 109 photo: © Paul Howell/Gamma Liaison. p. 109 Chapter Opening Vignette: Reprinted with permission. © 1992, *American Demographics, Inc.*, Ithaca, New York. p. 114 photo: Provided by H. J. Heinz. p. 115 Exhibit 6.3: Copyright 1997, *USA TODAY*. Reprinted with permission. p. 116 photo: © Greg Stott/Masterfile. p. 119 Exhibit 6.6: Adapted with permission from Urban Decisions Systems, Los Angeles, CA; and from M. Levy and B. Weitz, *Retail Management* (Richard D. Irwin, Inc.: 1992) pp. 357-358.

## Chapter Seven
p. 135 photo: Courtesy of Frito Lay International, a division of PepsiCo, Inc. Steven Watson, photographer. p. 136 photo: Courtesy of Marriott International. © Jeff Zaruba. p. 138 *What Went Wrong?:* Willard I. Zangwill, "Manager's Journal: When Customer Research is a Lousy Idea," *Wall Street Journal* (March 8, 1993) p. A12. Reprinted by permission of *The Wall Street Journal*, © 1993 Dow Jones & Company, Inc. All Rights Reserved. p. 139 photo: © David Hiser/Tony Stone Images. p. 140 photo: © Don Couch Photography p. 140 photo: © Charles Gupton/Tony Stone Images. p. 153 Exhibit 7.2: Don A. Dillman, *Mail and Telephone Surveys: The Total Design Method* (John Wiley and Sons, 1978), p. 209. Reprinted by permission of John Wiley & Sons, Inc. and the author. p. 154 photo: Samsonite. p. 156 *What Went Wrong?:* Reprinted with permission from the March 23, 1992 issue of *Advertising Age*. Copyright, Crain Communications Inc. 1992. p. 157 photo: Reprinted with the permission of America Online, Inc. © 1998 America Online, Inc. All Rights Reserved. p. 160 photo: Courtesy of NFO Research, Inc.

## Chapter Eight
p. 169 photo: SuperStock. p. 170 photo: © Tony Stone Images. p. 172 photo: Illustration of Personal Harbor office systems module courtesy of Steelcase, Inc. p. 174 photo: Iowa Field Research, Des Moines, IA, a Division of Grapentine Company. p. 174 *What Went Wrong?:* Adaptation of Erik Larson, *Attention Shopper's: Don't Look Now But You Are Being Tailed* (1993). Reprinted with permission of Erik Larson, Seattle, WA. p. 180 Courtesy of Perception Research Services, Inc., Fort Lee, NJ. p. 183 Case 8.1: Copyright © 1990 by The New York Times Co. Reprinted by permission.

## Chapter Nine
p. 187 photo: © Harcourt Brace photo/Annette Coolidge. p. 187 Chapter Opening Vignette: Brian Wansink, "Can Package Size Accelerate Usage Volume?," *Journal of Marketing* (July 1996 V. 60 No. 3) pp. 1-14. Reprinted with permission from the *Journal of Marketing*, published by the American Marketing Association and Brian Wansink. p. 205 photo: © Michael Newman/PhotoEdit. p. 206 photo: © Tony Stone Images.

## Chapter Ten

p. 215 photo: BBDO. p. 215 Chapter Opening Vignette: Reprinted with permission from the January 29, 1990 issue of *Advertising Age*. Copyright, Crain Communications Inc. 1990. p. 216 Exhibit 10.1: National Bureau of Standards, Washington, D.C. p. 218 Exhibit 10.2: Modified from materials in Michael D. Cozzens and Noshir S. Contractor, "The Effect of Conflicting Information on Media Skepticism," *Communications Research* (August 1987) pp 437-451. p. 223 Exhibit 10.4: Adapted from Ben M. Enis and Keith K. Cox, *The Marketing Research Process* (Scott, Foresman & Company, 1972) pp. 353-355. p. 227 Exhibit 10.6: Stephen W. Brown and Teresa A. Swarts, "A Gap Analysis of Professional Service Quality," *Journal of Marketing* (April 1989) p. 95. Reprinted with permission. Published by American Marketing Association. p. 227 Exhibit 10.7: Joel Huber and Morris B. Holbrook, "Using Attribute Ratins for Product Positioning: Some Distinctions Among Compositional Approaches," *Journal of Marketing Research* (November 1979) p. 510. Reprinted with permission. Published by American Marketing Association. p. 228 Exhibit 10.8: J. Richard Jones and Sheila I. Cocke, "A Performance Evaluation of Commuter Airlines: The Passengers View," *Proceedings*, Transportation Research Forum, Vol. 22 (1981) p. 254. Reprinted with permission. p. 229 Exhibit 10.9: Dennis Menezes and Norbert F. Elbert, "Alternate Symantic Scaling Formats for Measuring Store Image: An Evaluation," *Journal of Marketing Research* (February 1979) pp. 807-87; Irving Crespi, "Use of Scaling Technique in Surveys," *Journal of Marketing* (July 1961) pp. 69-72. p. 237 Case 10.1: Adapted by permission from Kay Goggin, "Indian Family Sells Food," *Stillwater News Press* (October 17, 1979) p. 24.

## Chapter Eleven

p. 239 photo: © Copyright 1998. The NASDAQ Stock Market, Inc. p. 243 *Exploring Research Issues:* Stephen A. Greyser and Raymond A. Bauer, "What a Difference Words Make," *Americans and Advertising* (Public Opinion Quarterly, Spring 1966) pp. 69-78. p. 245 Exhibit 11.1: Don A. Dillman, *Mail and Telephone Surveys: The Total Design Method* (John Wiley and Sons, 1978) p. 209. Reprinted by permission of John Wiley & Sons, Inc. and the author. p. 247 *What Went Wrong?:* Reprinted with permission from the September 20, 1982 issue of *Advertising Age*. Copyright, Crain Communications Inc. 1982. p. 254 Exhibit 11.2: F. Stewart DeBruicker and Harvey N. Singer, *General Foods Corporation: Tang Instant Breakfast Drink (B)*, © 1978, F. Stewart DeBruicker, The Wharton School, University of Pennsylvania. Reprinted with permission. p. 257 Exhibit 11.5: Courtesy of Research Services Inc., Denver, CO, and the United Bank of Boulder, Boulder, CO. p. 259 *What Went Wrong?:* Reprinted with permission from the March 21, 1983 issue of *Advertising Age*. Copyright, Crain Communications Inc. 1983.

## Chapter Twelve

p. 275 photo: Survey Sampling, Inc. 1998. p. 278 photo: © Hugh Sitton/Tony Stone Images. p. 279 Exhibit 12.2: American Business Information, Inc. ®, Omaha, NE. NASDAQ: AB11A&B, www.salesleadsUSA.com. p. 279 *Exploring Research Issues:* "The Private Debate," *Advertising Age* (October 17, 1988) pp. 12-13; and Diane K. Bowers, "The Privacy Challenger," *Marketing Researcher* (September, 1991) p. 61. p. 281 Exhibit 12.3: Adapted from Keith K. Cox and Ben M. Enis, *The Marketing Research Process* (Pacific Palisades, CA: Goodyear, 1972); and

Danny N. Bellenger and Barnet A. Greenberg, *Marketing Research: A Management Information Approach* (Homewood, IL: Irwin, 1978) pp. 154-155. Adapted with permission of the authors. p. 282 *What Went Wrong?:* Adapted with permission from David G. Myers, *Exploring Psychology* (Worth Publishers, 1990) p. 471. p. 284 photo: © Paul Conklin/PhotoEdit. p. 289 Exhibit 12.5: *Interviewer's Manual* (Institute for Social Research, 1976) p. 36.

## Chapter Thirteen

p. 295 cartoon: From *Exploring Statistics: An Introduction for Psychology and Education* by S.M. Dinham. Copyright © 1976 Brooks/Cole Publishing Company, Pacific Grove, CA 93950, a division of International Thomson Publishing Inc. By permission of the publisher. p. 300 *Exploring Research Issues*: From How To Lie With Statistics by Darrell Huff illustrated by Irving Geis. Copyright 1954 and renewed © 1982 by Darrell Huff and Irving Geis. Reprinted by permission of W.W. Norton & Company, Inc. p. 305 Table 13.7: Donald Warwick and Charles Lininger, *The Sample Survey: Theory and Practice* (McGraw-Hill, 1975) p. 89. p. 306 Exhibit 13.4: Thomas H. Wonnacott and Ronald J. Wonnacott, *Introductory Statistics* (John Wiley and Sons, 1969) p. 70. Reprinted by permission of John Wiley & Sons, Inc. p. 309 Exhibit 13.6: D.H. Sanders, A.F. Murray, and R.J. Eng, *Statistics: A Fresh Approach* (McGraw-Hill, 1980) p. 123. Reprinted with permission of the McGraw-Hill Companies. p. 310 Exhibit 13.7: Ernest Kurnow, Gerald J. Glasser, and Frederick R. Ottman, *Statistics for Business Decisions* (Richard D. Irwin, 1959) pp. 182-183. p. 315 Exhibit 13.8: Figure from *Foundations of Behavioral Research*, Third Edition by Fred N. Kerlinger, copyright © 1986 by Holt, Rinehart and Winston, reproduced by permission of the publisher. p. 319 Table 13.11: Nan Lin, *Foundations of Social Research* (McGraw-Hill, 1976) p. 447. Reprinted with permission of the author. p. 320 Table 13.12: Nan Lin, *Foundations of Social Research* (McGraw-Hill, 1976) p. 447. Reprinted with permission of the author.

## Chapter Fourteen

p. 329 photo: Courtesy of The Olive Garden. p. 329 Chapter Opening Vignette: Reprinted from *American Demographics* magazine with permission. © 1994, American Demographics, Inc., Ithaca, New York. p. 332 Exhibit 14.2: Calculated from Census Bureau, Population Projections for Stats for Age, Sex, Race, and Hispanic Origin: 1993-2020, as reported in "Three Guesses," *American Demographics* (October 1994) p. 41. p. 333 Exhibit 14.3: Based on Roger Ricklefs, "Ethics in America," *The Wall Street Journal* (October 31, 1983, November 1, 1983, November 2, 1983, November 3, 1983) pp. 33, 37. p. 338 Exhibit 14.10: Reprinted from "Confidence in Church/Organized Religion," *The Gallup Report 238*, July 1985, p.4, The Gallup Organization. p. 339 photo: © The Image Bank p. 339 *What Went Right?*: Adapted with permission from David G. Myers, *Exploring Psychology* (Worth Publishers, 1990) p. 464. p. 340 Exhibit 14.12: "Salaries (Constant 1992 Dollars)," *FORBES Magazine*, September 14, 1992, p. 282. Reprinted by permission of *FORBES Magazine*. © Forbes, Inc. 1992. p. 341 Exhibit 14.13: Reprinted with permission from the April 27, 1992 issue of *Advertising Age*. Copyright, Crain Communications Inc. 1992. p. 342 Exhibit 14.15: Courtesy of SPSS, Inc. p. 342 Exhibit 14.16: Courtesy of SPSS, Inc. p. 343 Exhibit 14.17: Courtesy of SPSS, Inc. p. 344 Exhibit 14.18: Courtesy of National Decision Systems, San Diego CA. p. 356

Case 14.2: Melvin Prince, *Consumer Research for Management Decisions* (John Wiley and Sons, 1982) p. 163-166. Reprinted by permission of John Wiley & Sons, Inc. p. 357 Case 14.3: Randall L. Schultz, Gerald Zaltman, and Philip C. Burger, *Cases in Marketing Research* (The Dryden Press, 1975) pp. 229-230.

## Chapter Fifteen

p. 361 photo: Courtesy of DDB Worldwide. p. 378 Case 15.2: Copyright © 1981, Dr. William J. Lundstrom. Reprinted with permission.

## Chapter Sixteen

p. 381 photo: © Index Stock Photography and Matthew Borkoski 1998. p. 387 *Exploring Research Issues:* Adapted from William Wells, "Noah's Law of Overhead Transparencies," *Association for Consumer Research Newsletter* (June 1993) p. 10. Adapted with permission from the author.

## Statistical Tables

Table A.1: Source: *A Million Random Digits with 100,000 Normal Deviates* (New York: Free Press, 1955). Copyright © The Rand Corporation. Table A2: Source: Chaiho Kim, *Statistical Analysis for Induction and Decision.* Copyright © 1973 by The Dryden Press, a division of Holt, Rinehart and Winston, Inc. Reprinted by permission of Holt, Rinehart and Winston. Table A.3: Source: Abridged from Table III of R. A. Fisher and F. Yates, *Statistical Tables for Biological, Agricultural, and Medical Research,* published by Longman Group, Ltd., London (previously published by Oliver & Boyd, Ltd., Edinburgh). Reproduced with the permission of the authors and publishers. Reprinted by permission of Addison Wesley Longmand Ltd. Table A.4: Source: Abridged from Table IV of R. A. Fisher and F. Yates, *Statistical Tables for Biological, Agricultural, and Medical Research,* published by Longman Group, Ltd., London (previously published by Oliver & Boyd, Ltd., Edinburgh). Reproduced with the permission of the authors and publishers. Reprinted by permission of Addison Wesley Longmand Ltd. Table A.5: Source: Maxine Merrington and Catherine M. Thompson, "Tables of the Percentage Points of the Inverted *F*-Distribution," *Biometrica* 33(1943) pp. 73–78. Reprinted with the permission of the Biometrica Trustees. Table A.6: Source: Maxine Merrington and Catherine M. Thompson, "Tables of the Percentage Points of the Inverted *F*-Distribution," *Biometrica* 33(1943): pp. 73–78. Reprinted with the permission of the Biometrica Trustees. Table A.7: Source: Abridged from Table IV of R. A. Fisher and F. Yates, *Statistical Tables for Biological, Agricultural, and Medical Research,* published by Longman Group, Ltd., London (previously published by Oliver & Boyd, Ltd., Edinburgh). Reproduced with the permission of the authors and publishers. Reprinted by permission of Addison Wesley Longmand Ltd. Table A.8: Source: Adapted from Table 2 of Frank Wilcoxon and Roberta A. Wilcox, 1964, *Some Rapid Approximate Statistical Procedures.* New York: American Cyanamid Company, p. 28.

# INDEX